Mordecai Richler

Arts Insights showcases current research in the social
sciences, humanities, and social work.

An initiative of McGill's Faculty of Arts, Arts Insights
brings together research in the Social Sciences,
Humanities, and Social Work. Reflective of the range
of expertise and interests represented by the Faculty
of Arts at McGill, Arts Insights seeks manuscripts
that bring an interdisciplinary perspective to the discussion of ideas, issues, and debates that deepen and
expand our understanding of human interaction,
such as works dealing with society and change, or
languages, literatures, and cultures and the relationships among them. Of particular interest are manuscripts that reflect the work of research collaborations
involving McGill faculty and their colleagues in
universities that are part of McGill's international
affiliation network.

Arts Insights will publish two titles a year in English.
The editors prefer original manuscripts but may
consider the English-language translations of works
that have already appeared in another language.

SERIES EDITORS
Nathalie Cooke, Richard Schultz, Wendy Thomson

Projecting Canada
Government Policy and Documentary Film
at the National Film Board
Zoe Druick

Beyond Wilderness
The Group of Seven, Canadian Identity, and
Contemporary Art
Edited by John O'Brian and Peter White

Mordecai Richler
Leaving St. Urbain
Reinhold Kramer

Women in Power
The Personalities and Leadership Styles of Indira
Gandhi, Gold Meir, and Margaret Thatcher
Blema Steinberg

Mordecai Richler

Leaving St. Urbain

Reinhold Kramer

McGILL-QUEEN'S UNIVERSITY PRESS | Montreal & Kingston • London • Ithaca

© McGill-Queen's University Press 2008

ISBN 978-0-7735-3355-4

Legal deposit second quarter 2008
Bibliothèque nationale du Québec

Printed in Canada on acid-free paper that is 100% ancient forest free
(100% post-consumer recycled), processed chlorine free.

McGill-Queen's University Press acknowledges the support of the Canada
Council for the Arts for our publishing program. We also acknowledge
the financial support of the Government of Canada through the Book
Publishing Industry Development Program (BPIDP) for our publishing
activities.

Library and Archives Canada Cataloguing in Publication

Kramer, Reinhold, 1959–
Mordecai Richler : leaving St. Urbain / Reinhold Kramer.

Includes bibliographical references and index.
ISBN 978-0-7735-3355-4

1. Richler, Mordecai, 1931–2001. 2. Richler, Mordecai,
1931-2001–Criticism and interpretation. 3. Novelists, Canadian
(English)–20th century–Biography. 4. Jewish authors–Canada–
Biography. I. Title.

PS8535.I38Z7 2008   C813'.54   C2007-906828-6

This book was designed and typeset by studio oneonone in Sabon 10/13

To the Jews of Grant Park High School.
No joke.

Contents

Acknowledgments

Although I can no longer thank Mordecai Richler, I want to acknowledge his generosity in allowing me permission to quote from his archival materials and to interview friends and family members. Many thanks to the relatives, friends, and acquaintances of Richler who spoke candidly, among them Avrum Richler, Florence Richler, Noah Richler, Daniel Richler, Lionel Albert, William Weintraub, Jack Rabinovitch, Max Richler, Bernard Richler. Without their participation this would have been an immeasurably poorer book. Myrtle Davidson graciously put my family up in Montreal while some of the interviews were being conducted.

During my months in Calgary I enjoyed the assistance, patience, and good cheer of the librarians at the Calgary University Archives, where the Richler collection is housed: Apollonia L. Steele, Marlys Chevrefils, Judy Loosmore, Lisa Atkinson, Bonnie Woelk, Brooke Montgomery, and Jennifer Willard. The librarians at the John Robbins Library of Brandon University – Alicja Brancewicz, Christine Sadler, Carmen Kazakoff-Lane, Carol Steele – and those at the University of Manitoba's E.K. Williams Law Library – Regena Rumancik and Muriel St. John – were also very accommodating.

Rita Kramer, Tom Mitchell, two anonymous readers, and Claude Lalumière read drafts of the manuscript, correcting errors and offering very helpful suggestions. Ira Robinson did the same for the material on Richler's grandfather, Rabbi Yudel Rosenberg. Special thanks to Kyla Madden and Joan McGilvray, editors at McGill-Queen's, for shepherding this project through to publication. With several Italian articles, I had the kind help of Paola Di Muro. Janice Mahoney typed interview transcripts from tapes that were at times nearly inaudible, Shari Maguire helped with photo rights and endnotes, and many other people supplied information along the road: Rosanne Gasse, Joe Sawchuk, Rachel Major, Meir Serfaty, Bob Thacker,

Paul Voorhis. Robert Florida and Scott Grills, successive Deans at the Faculty of Arts made Brandon University a great place to work and to do research.

Above all, I would like to thank Rita for her constant encouragement, and my children Madeline, Stephanie, and Michelle, who put up not only with those shuffling feet at 6:30 A.M., but with much else besides.

St. Urbain Street, 1930s. (University of Calgary Archives)

Rabbi Yudel Rosenberg Antler Genealogy: the second circle from the left (shaded rust for "female") represents Rosenberg's second youngest child, Leah/Lily, with her two sons, Avrum and Mordecai, listed above her (top circle). The darker circles denote females, and the pale ones males. The senior group – marked Hebrew A (Aleph), i.e., #1 – begins on the left and crosses under the junior group hence reading from left to right along the right-hand side. It is inscribed with the first wife's name, which is hard to decipher, possibly "Chava daughter of?"

The four children of the senior group, with their children, in order from left to right and bottom to top:

1 Daughter Hesil (Glass)
  • Grandson Herschel (Harry)
  • Granddaughter Gittel ("Gussie" Brody)
  • Granddaughter Simah (mother of "Alte" Chaya, widow of the late Rabbi Pinchas Hirschsprung)
  • Grandson Mordecai (Max)
2 Son Aaron Alimelech
  • Grandson Lazar (Louis)
  • Granddaughter Chana (Eva Mintz)
  • Grandson Israel (Irving)
  • Grandson Moshe (Moses "Moe")
  • Granddaughter Braindl (Brenda Kossover)
  • Granddaughter Broche (Bertha Cohen)
3 Son Mair Yehoshua (Rabbi Myer Joshua)
  • Granddaughter Chana (Eva)
  • Grandson Shlomo (Rabbi Israel Solomon Rosenberg) (in Israel as politician Solomon Ben-Mair)
  • Granddaughter Miriam Broche (Rosensweig)
4 Daughter Sureh (Sarah Zucker)
  • Granddaughter Chava (Eva Rosenberg – married a cousin)
  • Granddaughter Miriam (Bennett)
  • Grandson Yitzchak (Isaac, Irving "Zeke")
  • Granddaughter Dvora (Deborah, Dora Maker)
  • Granddaughter Feiga (Fay Leibtag)
  • Grandson Beryl (Dr. Bernard)

The junior group - marked Hebrew B (Beth), i.e., #2 – begins on the right and crosses over the senior group, hence reading from right to left along the left-hand side. It is inscribed with the second wife's name, Sarah Gittel b. (daughter of) Yitzhak (Isaac Greenberg)

The seven children of the second wife with their children, in order from right to left and bottom to top:

5 Son Binyamin (Benjamin) (edged in black as he had died before this chart was prepared.)
  • Granddaughter Raizeh (Rosalie Zinde), wrote under the name Suzanne Rosenberg and was known as Suzanne after ca. 1939
6 Daughter Chana (Annie Hadler)
  • Granddaughter Frimmt (Frances Schwartz, née Hadler)
  • Granddaughter Basha Miriam ("Buhshie," Bessie Pine)
  • Grandson Chaim Yitzhak ("Chum-Itz," Prof. Herbert)
7 Son Israel Mordecai ("Srolke")
  • Granddaughter Rivkah (Rebecca, Betty Perlov)
8 Daughter Broche (Elsie Roher)
  • Grandson Jakov Moshe (Milton)
  • Granddaughter Frimmt ("Florrie" Florence Lesser)
9 Daughter Rivkah (Rebecca, Ruth Albert)
  • Grandson Binyamin (Benjamin, "Benjy")
  • Grandson Leibl (Lionel)
10 Daughter Leah (Lily Richler)
  • Grandson Avrum ("Vrummi")
  • Grandson Mordecai ("Mutti," "Mordy")
11 Son Avrum Yitzhak (Rabbi Abraham Isaac)

Born after the chart was prepared:
  • Grandson Jules
  • Granddaughter Judith (Sklar).

The "leaves" protruding towards the top presumably represent great-grandchildren born before the chart was prepared. (Collection of Lionel Albert)

Rebbitzin Sarah, Rabbi Yudel Rosenberg, and Lily, 1930.
(Collection of Lionel Albert)

Cousin Frances Hadler's sketch
of Mordecai at age 6, 1937.
(Pencil sketch by Frances Hadler,
copyright Mucie Saitowitz)

Rebbitzin Sarah in wheelchair with Lily and Ruth Albert,
ca 1940. (Collection of Lionel Albert)

Shmarya Richler and family, ca 1945. On the far left of the photo are Mordecai (second row), his father Moe (third row), and brother Avrum (fourth row). The photograph was probably taken after the Moe/Lily divorce, since Lily does not appear in the picture. Shmarya's children are tagged only with their names; their spouses are tagged "B"; Shmarya's grandchildren are tagged "C." The children of Shmarya Richler, eldest to youngest, are Moses (Moe), Celia, Harry, Joseph, Sarah, Etta, Anne, Michael, Bernard, Israel, Max, Freda, Lily, and David.

Front row: Libby and Rhoda (daughters of Harry and Goldie), Jerry (son of Sarah and Louie Weiser), Sheila and Benjy (children of Joseph and Sarah), Sarah, Mechel, and Shayna (children of Celia and Shimshon Hershcovich).

Second row: Mordecai (son of Moses), David (son of Sarah and Louie Weiser), Esther (wife of Shmarya), Shmarya, Molly (mother of Esther), Yidel (son of Celia and Shimshon Hershcovich).

Third row: Moses (Moe), Sarah (wife of Louie Weiser), Etta, Sarah (wife of Joseph), Goldie (wife of Harry), Miriam (wife of Bernard), Anne, Lily, Freda, Celia and Shimshon Hershcovich, Shmuel (son of Celia and Shimshon Hershcovich).

Fourth row: Avrum (son of Moses), Harry Cooperman (husband of Etta), Joseph, Harry, Bernard, Israel, Michael, Max, David. (Collection of Sarah Snowbell)

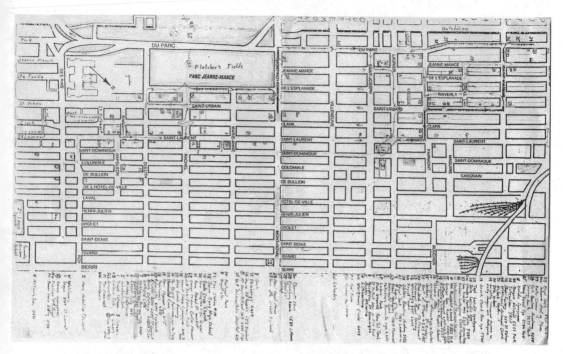

Map of Richler's childhood St. Urbain area. (Richler Fonds, acc. No. 582/50.10)

Avrum, Mordecai, and Lily.
(Photographer unknown)

Mordecai and his father Moe, ca 1953.
(Photographer unknown, University of
Calgary Archives)

Mordecai and Cathy Boudreau at a celebration of their marriage, 1954.
(Collection of Arthur Mackenzie Peers)

Guests at the celebration of Mordecai's marriage to Cathy Boudreau
Front row: (l to r) Marjorie Weiner, Terry McEwen, Cathy, Mordecai, Joyce Weiner,
and on the far right, George Lamming
Crouched to the right of Joyce Weiner, Brian Moore
Second row: far right, Arthur Mackenzie Peers (bearded)
Back row: (l to r) E.M. Forster; David Pitt, Syd Lamb;
in the polka-dot dress, Kate Allan; to her immediate left, Ted Allan
(Collection of Arthur Mackenzie Peers)

Florence, Mordecai, Noah, Daniel, and
Emma on Long Island, 1962.
(Collection of Bill Weintraub)

Ruth Albert, Noah on deck chair, Mordecai; semi-circle in front of Mordecai, counter-clock-
wise: Emma Richler, Vanessa Albert (now Lowry), Joshua Albert, Martha Richler, June Albert
(back to camera), Florence Richler standing, 1966. (Collection of Lionel Albert)

Left to right June Albert, Martha in arms of Daniel, Ruth Albert holding her infant granddaughter Anita Albert (now Beaty), Emma (kissing baby), Noah, Florence, 1966. (Collection of Lionel Albert)

Richler with Bill and Magda Weintraub
at their wedding, 1967.
(Collection of Bill Weintraub)

Richler and Ted Kotcheff on the set of *The Apprenticeship of Duddy Kravitz*, autumn 1973. (Collection of Jean-Yves Bruel)

Faux Richard Holden election poster: image by Aislin, text by Richler (1994).

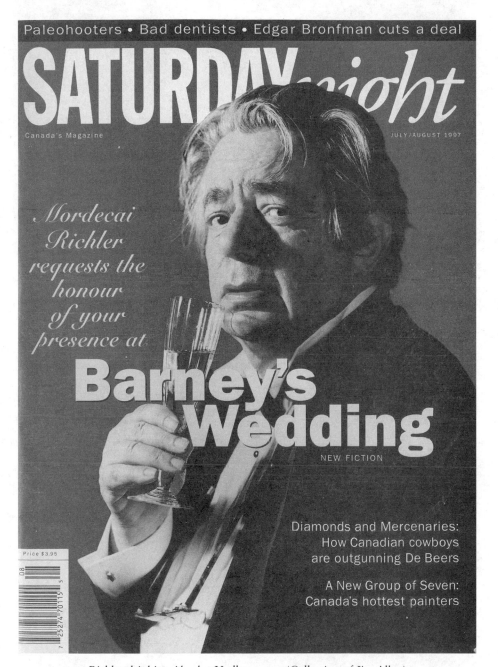

Richler drinking Absolut Vodka, 1997. (Collection of Jim Allen)

Richler and Robert Weaver. (Photographer unknown,
University of Calgary Archives)

Florence and Mordecai. (Photographer unknown, University of Calgary Archives)

Mordecai Richler

But Mordecai bowed not, nor did he do reverence.
   – *Esther* 3:2

If I were contented, I wouldn't be writing.
   – Mordecai Richler

Introduction

MORDECAI RICHLER IS, as demonstrated by his five longest novels, one of the greatest writers this country has produced, an unequaled poet of the colloquial. He had no theory, but a wonderful pudding of detail. He used to say that when scholars want to understand the Russian Revolution they'd turn to Isaac Babel.[1] I'd add: when scholars want to understand Canada at mid-century – from the 1940s to 1970s – or the secularization of Western Jews, they'll turn to Mordecai Richler.

Richler was a crucially important writer in a number of ways. He was the first "ethnic" writer to be read widely in Canada. His second published novel, *Son of a Smaller Hero*, and a number of his later novels dealt intimately with the life of the Orthodox Jewish community in Montreal, so intimately that among many of his English readers, he was considered the *de facto* spokesman for the Jews. The situation was highly ironic because Richler, leading up to and in his first (unpublished) novel and his first published novel had been trying to remake himself as a secular world citizen and to put Jewishness behind him. Ironic, but not unusual: many writers with an "ethnic" label are praised by those outside the ethnic community as accurate interpreters of that community, then criticized from inside the community as unreliable witnesses at best. Richler struggled with his role as simultaneous insider and outsider among the Jews, finally coming to a measure of balance in the later novels. He argued that the community itself changed, broadening enough to include his less than celebratory vision. The account that follows, however, will show that Richler changed too, that he abandoned an early attempt to make himself over as a writer of the Anglo-American avant-garde and moved towards a more inclusive cosmopolitanism.

Beyond Jewishness as an ethnic category, Richler was concerned, antagonistically, with the religious strictures of his Jewish childhood. Richler's

battle with Orthodoxy forms one particularly lucid example of the large sec-
ularizing movements of the twentieth century, apparent in almost all religious traditions. Yet, while this makes broad significance of Richler's case,
more important are the *specific* ways in which the characters in his novels
wrestle with – through parody, burlesque, and even serious imitation – the
narratives of the Hebrew Bible, of Orthodoxy, and of the religious basis for
the nation of Israel. The ultimately secular positions that Richler came to
shifted throughout his life and were sometimes less complex than the positions his characters came to.

Richler was also crucially important as a *Canadian* writer. In large part
he fled Canada because there were no writers here. If that seems a self-serving claim, and if throughout his life he was able repeatedly to make hay out
of a belligerent anti-nationalism, the upshot was to turn him into a spokesman
for Canada in London. One of his characters says, "Canada is no joke ...
Walter Pidgeon was born in this country."[2] Richler's mockery wouldn't have
mattered had he not been a compelling teller of Canadian stories. From the
distance of England, it appeared that no other Canadian measured up to
Richler in literary worth – i.e., sold a lot of books in London. More, in his
novels and his journalism, Canadian politics *mattered*, and over that narrow bridge he arrived at an uneasy truce: he would be allowed to shoot at
the natives, and if he did so with distinction they promised to buy his books.
Yet Richler's original political interest had more to do with the place of socialism in the late twentieth century than with Canada. His great strength
was that he had *felt* the problem of wealth inequity intensely as a young
man and that even when he moved away from socialism and towards liberalism as he grew older, he neither forgot that early sense of injustice, nor allowed his characters to escape it untroubled.

Jews, secularization, Canadians, politics: if that were all, we would be
left with a man of ideas. But, of course, it's Richler's literary achievement that
early books by George Woodcock, Victor Ramraj, and Arnold Davidson attested to. Ramraj's study is particularly significant, showing the ambivalences
– moralist/entertainer, acceptance/rejection of Jewish society, mockery/accom-
modation of human shortcomings, tolerance/censure of rogues such as Duddy
– at the core of Richler's work.[3] The great achievement of Richler is that he
found the fault lines where politics, race, faith, and, above all, language ran
through individual lives. The ability to enter colloquial speech patterns and
find their harsh poetry without being knocked out by Céline's eight ball was-
n't something that Richler was born with. His early writing ranges from a
somewhat romanticized Sholom Aleichem voice, to a clipped version of
Callaghan and Hemingway, to a very showy attempt at avant-garde collo-
quialism. He would be halfway into his writing career before he could mesh

formal literary qualities with a colloquiality rooted in Yiddish inflections and English everyday speech, as in the following example:

> The house Duddy built in Forest Hill, the letter K woven into the aluminum storm door, antique coach lamps riding either side, double garage doors electronically controlled, was sumptuously furnished for Marlene Tyler, the girl of his dreams, pink and white, like a nursery … After the lonely years of struggle and bachelorhood, gulping meals in restaurants and sleeping with *shiksas*, he had yearned for home-cooked meals, an orderly home life, and screwing on demand. "Like on a drippy Saturday afternoons after you come home loaded from a bar mitzvah *kiddush*. Or like on Saturday night after the hockey game and there's only Juliette on TV. I even had a TV set put in the bedroom with remote control, so that we could watch from the bed and get in the mood before they picked the three stars. Foreplay, that's the word I want."[4]

A secularization of language, one might call it. It splashes over from several evolutionary histories – of primates, of technology, of Jews in Canada, of the secularization of motive – and if inklings of this language appear in Henry Roth, it was still entirely Richler's literary invention.

≷

Richler often declared a visceral objection to literary biography. A personality himself, he deplored the cult of "writer as personality."[5] My books are important, he liked to say, but I'm not. Nonsense; literature owes a debt to life. Yet it's easy to see why he would make such claims, since he loathed interviews, the artificiality and showbiz glad-handing, the digging for dirt. He felt that Norman Mailer had been sabotaged by his own larger-than-life ego, turning into "A Personality" rather fulfilling his promise as a writer. Closer to the bone, Richler wasn't always the easiest human being to get along with, and he felt that the naïve reader – meaning just about everybody – was inclined to make simplistic identifications between the characters in his novels and actual people. He had reason to worry. After reading about the main character's mother in *Joshua Then and Now*, Richler's own mother, Lily, said, "Can you imagine, he said I was a *strip-teaser*?" Richler's brother, Avrum, tried to soothe her, "He wasn't talking about you, I mean he's a novelist, he's making up stories." Lily would have none of it, and repeated, "*He said I was a strip-teaser!*"[6]

Richler's mother was onto something. Back in 1935 she had herself published a number of stories in the *Canadian Jewish Review* and knew that one could build stories from wishes, happy exaggerations, imagined disasters – anything that came to hand, really, but what came to hand most often was oneself and one's family. If it is a mistake to make simple equations between characters and real people, it is no less a mistake to think of Richler as simply a fertile imagination. Richler spoke most truly when he characterized writing as "a desire to be known, yes, *but only on your own conditions.*"[7] For this reason biography is essential: to grant some of those conditions, to strip away others. Stories and characters of any worth do not float down out of the ether but come up, mutated, from the mud of the only real world. Richler *ought* to have applauded Lily.

Recent books by Joel Yanofsky (*Mordecai and Me*) and Michael Posner (*The Last Honest Man*) have begun to address Richler's biography. Posner, in particular, while mostly transcribing interviews and attempting no assessment of Richler's novels, has brought out crucial information about Richler's life. In some ways, Posner's title is wide of the mark. Richler's work is full of misdirection and exaggerations, delightful and otherwise – "honesty" is not the best trope. In at least one way, however, the title is apt: Richler's fiction often verges on autobiography. Much of Richler's first, unpublished novel, *The Rotten People*, is autobiographical. *Joshua Then and Now* began life as the unpublished memoir, *Back to Ibiza*. Ryerson Press shied away from *The Incomparable Atuk*, fearing libel suits, and of *St. Urbain's Horseman* Richler's literary agent said, "I had the greatest fun in finding how much of this *roman* was *à clef.*"[8] In the early drafts of a manuscript that probably became *Son of a Smaller Hero*, the characters bore such unrefined names as "*Zeyda* Richler."[9] Diana Athill, his earliest editor, urged him to change some of the names of real streets and organizations so as to ensure that the novel be recognized as fiction, but when his relatives in Montreal read the book, they gave him the cold shoulder for telling too many family secrets. The evidence from the texts, from Richler's life, and from his friends' comments show that, no matter what sophisticated literary structures Richler built on top of his foundations, the foundations were *almost always roman-à-clef.*

A simple defense of *roman-à-clef* readings need only remark that although they may lack in aesthetic complexity, they do identify the historical sources of the writer's mimesis. A more philosophical defense would note that authors take particular stances in favour of certain people and attitudes, against others; and that neither the modernist notion of a hermetically sealed universe of symbol nor the postmodern notion of the artwork as simulacrum can make any sense of the author's preferences. Why should one person or attitude be given gravity while another is dismissed? Only careful attention to personal and public histories can answer such questions, and a *roman-à-clef* reading is above all an historical act. After Mia Farrow saw what Woody

Allen had done with their lives in *Hannah and her Sisters*, she said, "He had taken the ordinary stuff of our lives and lifted them into art. We were honoured and outraged."[10] If *Hannah and her Sisters* and Richler's novels belong among the important relics of contemporary secular culture, nowadays we are allowed to ask where those relics came from, even if the answer involves some demystification.

Real life was not the point, Richler insisted, again and again. Craft was the point. Certainly, craft *was* the point, and one of my intentions is to show how Richler shaped everything he wrote, including the nonfiction. It is that shaping, not his life, that placed him in the forefront of Canadian writing and make him worthy of study. Yet his life was *also* the point, for so much of his best artistry was sawn, still bleeding, from real life. That's not a criticism.

PART I

Tiefste Provinz
1931–1950

"The dominions... are for me *tiefste Provinz*, places which have produced no art and are inhabited by the kind of person with whom I have least in common.
– W.H. Auden

"In the provinces, he had been able to revere London and its offerings with impunity.

Fulminating in Montreal, he could agree with Auden that the dominions were *tiefste Provinz*."
– Richler, *St. Urbain's Horseman*

1

Geyt, yidelech, in der vayter velt[1]

IN THE LATE NINETEENTH and early twentieth century, crowds of anti-
Semitic Russians inadvertently changed the world by attacking the Jews.
These pogroms happened throughout the Pale of Settlement to which some
four million Jews[2] had been officially restricted, including Galicia (now part
of Poland and western Ukraine). The results: the first aliyahs (emigrations)
to Palestine and "a panic flight westwards" to North America, so that within
seventy years large tracts of Eastern Europe were all but emptied of Jews.[3]
It is said that the most adventurous went to Palestine, the most ambitious
to the "*goldeneh medina*" – the "golden land," as North America was called.[4]
The "genteel, Reformist, well-heeled"[5] Jews already there had little idea of
the Yiddish bomb sailing westward.

Among the ambitious fleeing the pogroms were two Galician men – the
intensely Orthodox and wily junk dealer Shmarya (Shmaryahu) Reichler in
1904, followed by the highly educated but just as Orthodox Rabbi Jehudah
(Yudel) Rosenberg in 1912. Mordecai, when he was young, pretended to
have little ambition for material advancement, yet his affluence in North
America and his persona as a secular Jew were made possible by the two
grandfathers who, by the very act of emigrating, both voted for prosperity.
Mordecai would get to know Shmarya well, Shmarya becoming the enemy
against whose Orthodoxy and business ethic Mordecai would rage. As for
Yudel, he died when Mordecai was quite young. But Yudel's influence – an
idealist current that grated on Mordecai – would come to seem just as op-
pressive, arriving through Yudel's daughter (Richler's mother) Lily.

≋

Shmarya Reichler came over first and, a nascent capitalist, found North
America more to his liking than did Yudel Rosenberg. A lazy immigration
officer managed to misplace the *e* in "Reichler" – a fact that Mordecai didn't

know until he saw his father's passport in the 1960s.[6] With a peddler's license and a loan from the philanthropic Baron de Hirsch Institute,[7] Shmarya became "Sam Richler," dealer in scrap metal.[8]

He slaved hard. At home and even in the homes of his adult children, no one challenged his kingship. Children he considered his property. A number of them worked in his scrap-metal business, and one of the sons, Harry Richler, whiled away several years as a guest of the Crown for receiving stolen goods. Every week, a family member, Mr Mandelcorn, visited him in Bordeaux jail with kosher food, so that he wouldn't have to sin against Jewish dietary laws. Rumour, considered false by some of the brothers, had it that Harry took the fall for Shmarya.[9] "Aggressive and astute," Shmarya knew the Torah well and refused to hear any criticism of it. Of the afterlife he was certain, and he loved to conduct synagogue services as cantor.[10] For Mordecai, Shmarya would become a symbol of unthinking orthodoxy. "My fierce, hot-tempered grandfather," Mordecai called him, and added that he was best when playing with babies.[11] Others, requesting anonymity, spoke more bluntly: "He was a son of a bitch ... I hated him."

≶

Mordecai Richler's maternal grandfather, the Rabbi Yudel Rosenberg, cut a very different figure. A Kabbalist, towering, impressively bearded and side-curled, he went about in a shiny, black robe, black shtreimel (the Hasidic Sabbath-hat), and black boots. When a profound insight came to him he would reach for a quill and record the thought in a big golden book, the thoughts eventually solidifying into publications such as *A Brivele fun di Zisse Mame Shabbes Malkese zu Ihre Zihn un Tekhter fun Idishn Folk* (*A Letter from the Sweet Mother Sabbath Queen to Her Sons and Daughters of the Jewish People*). He possessed "a potent humour, penetrating and satirical," but "not bitter."[12]

Although Rosenberg was descended from generations of rabbis and remained devoutly Orthodox his whole life, he read Hebrew works by the maskilim of the Haskalah (scholars of the Jewish enlightenment), popular science, plays, and essays – all of which his parents burned when they discovered the contraband. In order to be recognized by the Russian Government as a rabbi, Rosenberg also had to learn Russian, a compromise that angered non-Russian-speaking rabbis, and when he fell asleep on a bench while reading a Russian book, they took the event as a clear sign from God, who intended to rebuke Rosenberg for selling out.[13]

He was poor, but his students saw no shame in his poverty. On the contrary, one Hasid wrote,

Reb Yidl, my rebbe,

I see you in Lodz,
In the dark room on Polnocna Street,
Lit only by a five-watt bulb
Since it had no windows.
But you did not resent this,
For your home was like a Holy Temple ...[14]

Rosenberg published over twenty works, most notably a seven-volume translation of and commentary on the Zohar from Aramaic into Hebrew, a twenty-year project.[15] Over the protests of more traditional rabbis, he thought that the Zohar – at once venerably ancient and yet also a "new" revelation – could help slow down secularization.[16] Rosenberg considered these literary works to be nothing less than his children. Late in his life, his daughter Lily tried to suggest that it would be his flesh-and-blood children, not his books, that would carry his legacy. He refused to speak to her for two days.[17]

Mordecai, looking back at his grandfather, liked to point at the Zohar translation, at Rosenberg's belief in devils, and at how Rosenberg blamed the Messiah's delay on debauched Jews who failed to observe the Sabbath.[18] But there was much more to him. On the one hand, he claimed that Heaven had revealed to him an amulet that could ease childbirth, while, on the other, he criticized the unhygienic mould that characterized many communal mikva'ot (women's ritual baths) and scolded those who told barren women that they could remedy their condition by eating the foreskin of a circumcised boy.[19] He also wrote fiction, though he took care not to call it that: a story of the how the Maharal (Rabbi Yehudah Loewe, 1525–1609) created a golem, another that shamelessly plagiarized Arthur Conan Doyle's mystery "The Jew's Breastplate" (1899) – exit Anglo detective, enter the Maharal. Rosenberg grasped that young people would be much more interested in mysterious thefts and magical Jewish champions than in the arcane legalities of the Talmud. His grandson would go much further. Finding something very congenial in Rosenberg's style of Judaized narrative, Richler would reveal that Ephraim Gursky, previously unknown to history, had been on the Franklin expedition.[20] "Be in no hurry to suspect that – God forbid – I forged this by myself," Rosenberg protested about one of the legends he published. The evidence suggests otherwise. He claims to have borrowed old manuscripts from a mystery man named Hayyim Sharfstein, of whom there is no trace. Rosenberg's writing reflected honour upon his family and congregations, but had they known that he was *making the stories up*, they would have felt betrayed.[21]

For all his learning and fictional experiments, Rosenberg saw the world much as Shmarya Richler did: a straightforward battle between the righteous and Satan. This was the world that their grandson Mordecai Richler would initially define himself in and then rebel against, perpetually, even long after the world had disappeared from his vicinity. And although he would come to disagree violently with the content of his grandfathers' beliefs – with what constituted righteousness and what ought to be damned – their vein of moral certainty would never be far from the surface of his life or his writing.

≶

At age fifty-three, with Polish Jews beckoning from Canada, pogroms chasing at his back, Rabbi Rosenberg crossed the Atlantic. He became "der Polisher rebbe." The whole city knew him,[22] and all manner of people arrived at his doorstep with problems – religious, marital, economic. Avrum, Mordecai's elder brother, who used to carry Rosenberg's prayer shawl, remembers the noisy prayer services. Everybody prayed aloud at the same time, with the loudest deemed closest to God.[23] Family and friends say Rosenberg became Chief Rabbi of Montreal.[24] That's a bit of a stretch. In the mid-1920s, he challenged Rabbi Hirsch Cohen's power to regulate kashrut in Montreal – but was unsuccessful. Mordecai, even as a young man, was skeptical of Rosenberg's importance, recognizing that every year Lily made him out to be "a chiefer and chiefer rabbi," impressing the goyim more than anybody else.[25]

After his epic defeat in what became known as the Kosher Meat War, Rabbi Rosenberg still had the support of many Hasidic Jews, including Shmarya Richler.[26] Even when failing health reduced Rosenberg to performing services at home, Shmarya remained among the faithful few.[27] There was an additional reason, besides the spiritual, for the scrap-metal dealer to remain loyal to the aging rabbi. On 18 June 1924, in the middle of the Kosher Meat War and just as Rosenberg stepped to the pinnacle of his writing career by publishing five volumes of his *Zohar Torah*,[28] Shmarya arranged for his eldest son, Moe, to marry Rosenberg's daughter, Lily. Lily wanted no part of Moe, but Shmarya clinched the deal by promising the rabbi that Moe would soon get a share of the scrap-metal business.

A strange reversal: the wily businessman retained enough of the Old Country ethos to want the spiritual prestige of marrying his son into a rabbi's family. Conversely, the mystical rabbi, nearing the end of his days, wanted to ensure the material security of his daughter in what he thought would be a financially prudent union. The wedding was splashy enough, with taxis dotting the street because Rosenberg was a rabbi,[29] but the new couple couldn't even pay the bills. And while both Moe and Lily would influence Mordecai's writing in crucial ways, it would be difficult to find two more ill-matched people. Moe was twenty-one, Lily nineteen; later she would find it convenient to claim that she had been only seventeen and a minor.[30] He, though an eldest son, was neither as ambitious nor as educated as his younger brothers. She, on the other hand, was desperately ambitious and always kowtowed to education after her own schooling was interrupted early. Her lack of French cost her a scholarship, and that ended her education.[31] The future author of *Oh Canada! Oh Quebec!* kept this fact quiet in his many articles on Québécois language battles.

≶

When Norman Levine described her thirty years later, Lily had "a harsh nasal voice," vast energy, and a less noticeable sadness: "she reminded me of a small bright bird; a sparrow. It didn't matter what she said she made it all sound like a comedian telling jokes. As long as she was talking she appeared confident. It was only when she was a listener that one noticed the vulnerability; the melancholy look in the eyes."[32] Others, who knew her better, were convinced that she was mentally unstable. Out of the blue, she would develop intense hatreds and blurt out injurious remarks.

Lily would have liked nothing better than to have become that impossibility for women – an Orthodox rabbi. It was a family joke. Rosenberg used to say that Lily only lacked a beard to be a full-fledged rabbi, and when he took her on a tour of a slaughterhouse he teased that he was training her to be the first woman rabbi.[33] Such humour palled very quickly for Lily. When she wished to continue beyond the local McCaul Street School into high school and university, it was her beloved father who betrayed her and told her that she had enough schooling for a "Mother in Israel." She would eventually teach herself French, too late, and haul herself to lectures and seminars, always hoping to make up for lost ground. In her twenties and again in her seventies, she became an author, and it would be she who urged Shakespeare, as well as the Romantics Byron, Keats, and Wordsworth, on her son, Mordecai.[34] That influence would be very important in his early sense of himself as a writer, though he would eventually come to despise the Romantics.

Despite her father's betrayal, Lily had a close relationship with him, perhaps unhealthily close. He'd walk her to the window and, pointing out the birds, tell her they were chirping "Lily, Lily." She'd washed his hair, beard, and payess (sidecurls). "A king of our people and a king of men," Lily called him, not the easiest standard for any husband to measure up against, and often during her marriage, when she felt that Moe didn't love her, she returned to her father's house, seeking his comfort. Although her sisters weren't so keen on the restrictions and fashion liabilities that came with being a rabbi's daughter, Lily loved the role. She became (to use the title of a memoir she would later write) "the errand runner," a mediator between Yiddish Jews and the English government. She arranged for visas and translated letters,[35] trying to content herself with the crumbs from her father's scholarly table.

≋

Moe ran errands, too, though less prestigious ones. A man who avoided conflict, he lived and worked under the thumb of his father as a bookkeeper and truck driver. He was dark, sharp-featured, and thin.[36] His education, like Lily's, had been stunted, his father pulling him out of school by grade 4 or 5 and setting him to work in the scrapyard.[37] As the eldest son, he felt his father's hand heavy upon him. If Moe so much as stepped into a corner restaurant for a coffee, Shmarya criticized him, since the cup wouldn't be kosher.[38]

He was besotted with the movies. He loved the Don Cossack Choir,[39] burlesque shows, bawdy stories, and practical jokes, and he memorized the routines of comedians. Moe's reading consisted of *Reader's Digest, Popular Mechanics*,[40] *Doc Savage*, and *Black Mask*.[41] Unlike Lily, he had no time for highbrow theatre. The source for Reuben Shapiro's brilliant line about Shakespeare in *Joshua Then and Now* was none other than Moe Richler: "Take away the fancy costumes and the sword-play … and what have you got left? Poetry. I mean what the hell."[43] Science fiction in particular enthused him. His information about the world he got from the *New York Daily News* and *New York Daily Mirror*,[44] and he "swore by these tabloids." Later, when Avrum and Mordecai were adolescents, they acquired his taste. He'd arrive home with several tabloids, and the boy alert enough to cry "*Daily Mirror* first!" got it.[45]

Lily thought him a fool,[46] and a relative have called him "a true, honest-to-goodness ignoramus." His son, Avrum, disagrees vehemently: "He was a wonderful man. He wasn't ignorant; he was very smart … He had a mathematical mind." With the right education, Avrum suggests, his father would have made an excellent accountant or engineer. "I don't know why my mother didn't like him. She felt he was beneath her."[47] At times, particularly in his early teens, Mordecai felt that same contempt, but once he reached a certain level of intellectual maturity he began to revel in his father's bad jokes and colloquial speech patterns and to utilize them as raw material.[48] Moe mocked Lily's intellectual pretensions, and to him Mordecai would owe some of his own anti-intellectual tendencies, as if he were consciously taking his father's side against Lily's pretensions, Rabbi Rosenberg's idealizing, and highbrow culture generally.[49] "What did he want?" Mordecai would ask after his father's death. "Beyond peace and quiet, which he seldom achieved, I have no idea."[50]

≋

In any case, says Lily, "we never had a serious conversation before we were married." What little she saw of Moe struck fear into her, and she told her parents so. She feared that she and Moe had nothing in common. She feared that he didn't seem old enough for marriage. She feared sex. Before the wedding, one of her older sisters took her aside and explained the basics of intercourse. Lily claims that the morning after the wedding Shmarya, according to custom, entered the bedroom to check for the bloodstains that would confirm her virginity. He was mystified because the sheets were spotless. She had, she insists, changed the sheets to thwart him.[51] But the story sounds contrived.[52] In *Son of a Smaller Hero*, Wolf and Leah (characters based heavily on Moe and Lily) don't consummate their marriage for months.[53] Certainly, Lily and Moe slept in separate beds, and Lily admits that Moe was "sexually vibrant" while she was unresponsive.[54]

As for Shmarya's verbal agreement that Moe would be taken into the family firm as a partner, that soon fell by the wayside.[55] Shmarya may well have intended that in the best of all possible worlds he'd make his son a partner, but the Depression struck, and although in 1931 Shmarya was calling himself "S. Richler, President of Metal Smelters and Refiners" the money was shorter than the title.[56] He simply denied making the deal.[57] Shmarya treated the other truck drivers more kindly than he did Moe – Moe was only a son, after all.[58] When money ran short, it was Moe's $20/week paycheques, not those of the other truck drivers, that bounced.[59] Even money aimed at Moe flowed into the path of least resistance, running directly to Shmarya. Shmarya hatched a scheme whereby Moe would manufacture bricks for building houses. Rabbi Rosenberg lent Moe $1,000 for start-up costs, but by the next day the money had found its way to Shmarya's pocket. Lily poured her outrage about such matters upon Moe daily and urged him to cut himself off from his father. "If you don't like it," he retorted, "go back to your parents." Often she did.[60]

What exactly Moe made of his father is unclear. In *Son of a Smaller Hero* Wolf is sorely tempted to drop his derrick's two tons of scrap metal onto his father, Melech, who stalls at making him a partner and denies him a raise; but in short order Wolf mythologizes the event to point that he believes he "saved" Melech from death.[61] Evidently, Mordecai sensed unexpressed hostility in Moe. Any overt rage in the novel, however, comes from Mordecai, not Moe. If Lily gave Mordecai the notion that literature was a holy calling, Moe's kowtowing gave Mordecai the anger and resolve not to end up in his father's position. The motives for much of Richler's writing – the early socialist stance, the punitive satire, the drive to be paid properly for work – many things can be traced to his rage on behalf of Moe against Shmarya. Richler's daughter Emma certainly noticed the iconic quality that Moe's job held for her father. In her novel *Sister Crazy*, the father, based on

Richler, speaks crossly and proudly of his own father: "'He was a junk dealer! A scrap man!' it was like the end of a conversation and not the start of one."[62]

Moe struggled in the scrapyard from 6 A.M. to 10 P.M., salary intermittent.[63] Lily had the idea of turning Moe into an accountant. He balked.[64] At one point he did make a break for freedom by obtaining the distribution of Seiberling tires, but when that fizzled he had to return to his father again, tail between his legs. Rent collectors, water-bill collectors, representatives from the gas company – all found occasion to pay courtesy calls at Lily's door and to use words such as "evict" and "discontinue."[65] At least twice the family skipped out on the rent by changing houses late at night. There were many homes: on Esplanade, Jeanne Mance, St. Dominique, Clark.[66] Mordecai would be too young to recall the more desperate moves of the early 1930s, but once he grew old enough to grasp the situation he would feel his family's poverty and his father's lowly position keenly.

2

A Light Has Gone Out in Israel

IN LATE JANUARY 1931, Lily begged her sister Ruth for $50. Lily was pregnant again, about to give birth, and needed money to pay the doctor. Although it seems that she didn't get it from Ruth,[1] she must have scraped something together, and, on 27 January, Mordecai was born. When Mordecai was old enough to understand, Lily loved to remind him that Moe wouldn't keep watch at the hospital to find out whether the baby was a girl or a boy but ran off to get drunk and watch movies.[2] Avrum was nearly five, and Lily hadn't intended to have another baby. For a long time already she had thought about divorce. Her parents too had warned against having more children, so she felt guilty about her pregnancy.[3] But Avrum was growing up, and she needed someone to touch and to love.

The new child, like Avrum, was circumcised by his grandfather, Rabbi Yudel, just shy of seventy and still allowed to wield the mohel's knife. Yudel also named the child after his old teacher[4]: Mordechai, the biblical hero who refused to bow to Persian gods and who is celebrated during Purim each year because he convinced his cousin Esther, King Ahasuerus's consort, to use her charms and shield the Jews from the first pogrom. Mordechai, hero of the Jews. Or alternatively, as Richler calls him, "the first Jewish pimp."[5] The name held a symbolic poignancy for Lily, who complained that, after she left her father's house, her beloved Purim celebrations – performers singing, dancing, and doing little plays – were over and would never come again.[6]

More usually the boy was "Muttie," "Mottle," or "Mottkele," at least until high school.[7] Mordecai started off left-handed, but given the practices of those years – hard raps on the knuckles – such an eccentricity didn't last long, and he was thumped into ambidexterity.[8] Both Moe and Lily loved their boys, yet commentators have long noticed that in Richler's novels the fathers (Wolf Adler, Max Kravitz, Issy Hersh, Reuben Shapiro) get good press despite their shortcomings, while the mothers tend to be "emotion-ally manipulative, dominant, self-centred, culturally pretentious."[9] Asked about that list of failings, Avrum says, "That's the one ... That's her."[10] Lily admitted it, too. She called Moe a good father who spoke to the children in ways that he never would to her, but she called herself an unfit – often nervous, impatient, and sad – mother. All the same, Mordecai was Lily's darling, and for a long time he was very close to her. As "the dominant party" in the marriage, Lily took care of the discipline, washing Morde-cai's mouth out with soap when occasion demanded it.[11] She also cuddled him often. An affectionate, forgiving mother, she would smile and call him "little bandit."[12] "He was the favourite, there's no doubt about it," says Avrum. "I used to fight with my mother about it when I was older, always accusing her of favouring him." Many years later, when Avrum spoke about it to Mordecai, Mordecai apologized, saying that he didn't realize what was happening.[13]

"I live in my children," Lily said in 1981,[14] a statement just as true in the 1930s and 40s. From the beginning, she heaped her frustrated ambitions on the boys. According to Richler, she would whack him for reading *Tip Top Comics* or listening to the Green Hornet on the radio,[15] and, although Avrum doesn't remember this, he does remember her shredding his comic-book collection, which included the original *Superman* no. 1, worth a for-tune now.[16] Mordecai got the message and learned to become a literary highbrow. For all the eclecticism of his reading, and his vernacular writing, he never really put aside her attitude. He said that she intended him to be a rabbi. In fact, it was Avrum, not Mordecai, whom she pushed in that direc-tion, at least until Avrum rebelled against the script, and she had to settle for optometrist.[17] She had Mordecai reciting poorly understood Hebrew by age three.[18] Eventually Lily became the staunchest supporter of his writing, though the style of writing he finally settled on was in large part a reaction against her. Avant-garde writing and then satire came as disappointments to her; success among the highbrows did not.

Whenever she could, she packed the boys over to Yudel's. He'd tickle the boys' faces with his long beard or draw pictures for them while they sat in his lap. In the summer he'd rent a cottage in the Laurentians at Shaw-bridge or Piedmont, where they all sat on the grass while Yudel read Yid-dish poetry aloud.[19] For young Mordecai it was mostly gibberish. Since Moe and Lily rarely spoke Yiddish at home, Mordecai never picked up more than a few basic words.[20] To Avrum went the bulk of Yudel's attention, and Lily later complained that Mordecai missed a deeper sense of his grandfather's greatness.[21] She evidently felt that a closer acquaintance would have im-proved (which ultimately meant "gentrified") Richler's writing. Rosenberg in his *Discourse on Tefillin* said that the carnal lovers in *Song of Songs* showed how attractive Jews were to God when they dressed up in their tefillin (phylacteries, the little boxes containing scripture and worn on the left arm and the forehead by devout Jews): what could Yudel have said to the novelist who in *Cocksure* wrote of dear old Miss Ryerson rewarding her hardest-working students with blowjobs?[22] The portrait of the zeyde in *The Apprenticeship of Duddy Kravitz* implies that grandfather and grandson eventually *would* have something to say to each other across the years, though that conversation would be strained and often condemning. It would be the close observations and hectoring of Lily, much more than Yudel's idealized voice, that Mordecai would learn. In one of Lily's stories, a woman asks, "Rabbi, how can I Kosher my false teeth?" while the more sophisticated, Lily-like narrator asks – silently – how to make her tongue Pesachdig (Passover-ready) when all year she uses it for chumitz[23] – for leaven, that is, for all manner of sin and uncleanness.

≶

During the warm evenings in the Laurentians, plans were being laid. Lily was in a desperate state about her marriage, and although she had a standing prescription for her nerves, one of her many squabbles with other family members prevented the medication from arriving.[24] But there seemed to be a light in the darkness. Palestine's chief Ashkenazic rabbi died in 1935, and Rabbi Rosenberg believed that he had a line on the job. Back in the 1920s he had already twice bought land (in Haifa and Jerusalem) from itinerant Zionist salesmen and bought shares in the Anglo-Palestine bank.[25] Lily resolved to emigrate with her parents, taking along her children but leaving Moe behind – though as far as the children knew, the whole family was going. She may have even bought the steamship tickets. How much of an escape it would have been is debatable. Mea Shearim was the destination, a section of Jerusalem so Orthodox that many Jews there still don't even recognize the legitimacy of the Israeli state. "Thank God we didn't go," says Avrum, "they're nuts."[26] American visitors find Mea Shearim an astonishing place: "One of the signs … read, 'The Torah commands a Jewish daughter to dress modestly, to dress immodestly in our neighborhood is forbidden.' The entire neighborhood looked like a transplant from eighteenth-century Poland."[27]

If Lily felt that things were bad in Montreal, they were about to get worse. For Simchat Torah that year, the Richlers were invited over to Shmarya's, but Avrum refused to go, convincing the family to visit Yudel instead. So the family walked over to Yudel's, and it proved to be the last time the boys saw him. A stroke felled him. Though he could still make out what others were saying, he couldn't reply. His wife Sarah, youngest son Abraham (who would eventually follow his footsteps as rabbi), and Lily watched

at Yudel's bedside for three days, until 23 October 1935, when he died. His
funeral was indeed the grand one that the mother brags about in Richler's
story "The Summer My Grandmother Was Supposed to Die": many Jewish
businesses closed, a motorcycle guard escorted the hearse, and the newspapers proclaimed, "A LIGHT HAS GONE OUT IN ISRAEL!"[28]

≶

Six weeks later the emigration papers arrived. There could, of course, no
longer be any question of Palestine. While Maurice Duplessis was founding
the Union Nationale – a bad augury for Montreal Jews – Lily's route of escape dried up. To cut costs, she and her family moved in with her widowed
mother at 4587 Jeanne Mance Street,[29] causing some resentment from Lily's
siblings to the tune that she was growing fat off Yudel's money – *their* future inheritance, thank you very much.[30] But within the year a second burden was placed on Lily. Sarah, too, had a stroke. Here, again, "The Summer
My Grandmother Was Supposed to Die" accurately conveys the bones of
the situation: unlike Yudel, Sarah lingered for seven years, all the while fearing that her children would desert her.[31] Sarah was paralyzed and eventually lost her speech, relying on grunts to communicate. According to Lily,
initially Sarah's many children stopped by often to assist in their mother's
care, but after a while they tired of coming. When Lily suggested that they
instead send money to hire help, they proposed a nursing home for Sarah.
Lily refused. Not the most sweet-tempered woman to begin with, Lily entered a soul-destroying time and neglected her boys. "As the years passed,
I became more weary. I ranted and raved against my brothers and sisters,"
she says, "I wanted the mother I loved to die! I raged within myself."[32] Once
she stood on the doorstep and railed at the whole family.[33] Although the
young narrator of "The Summer My Grandmother Was Supposed to Die"
is only obliquely conscious of the suffering, the story's harsh satire against
the family makes it clear that Richler, still identifying closely with his mother,
was of her mind. The events of this time had an important formative influence on Richler's fiction. Running through his novels, from the weakest to
the best, is a vein of brutal honesty about human motives that had its source
in what came out of Lily's mouth, almost against her will: the dark knowledge that despite many fine tributes to Rabbi Rosenberg's spiritual heritage,
no one wanted to do the dirty work of caring for Sarah.

"Very tendentious," says Lionel Albert of Lily's account. After Sarah's
stroke, Ruth (Lily's sister and Lionel's mother) provided support by contributing money and spelling off Lily – moving in for a while to look after
Sarah, Avrum, and Mordecai, so that Lily could get out of the house. Eventually Ruth found a nursing home, and everyone agreed to chip in to pay

for Sarah's room. She really shouldn't have stayed in the house, Bessie Pine (a daughter of one of Lily's sisters) claims, but Lily thought of herself as the martyr who was going to take care of "babashi."[34] More, "she saw her meal ticket disappearing," her excuse to top up Moe's meagre wages.[35] Lily demanded that each of Sarah's children contribute $2 or $3 a week, a lot of money in those days. If you refused to send money, watch out. You might open the door (so Lily threatened) and find baba standing on your doorstep. Some of Sarah's children contributed, some didn't. Bessie Pine's mother, Hannah Hadler, got anxious every time the doorbell rang.[36]

The truth lies somewhere between Lily's account and the accounts of her sisters. Clearly Lily was a schemer and sniffing around for much-needed money, but it's also clear that Sarah wanted no part of a nursing home. For a brief moment Lily did relent and had her mother put in a home, but when Lily came to visit the next day, Sarah refused even to look at her. Within a few days Lily took Sarah back home again. "She wasn't there a week," says Avrum. With Sarah back in Avrum's bedroom, the weight once more fell mostly on Lily to change her mother's diapers and to feed her. Lily occasionally prevailed upon Avrum and Mordecai to embrace and talk to their grandmother, but the biggest help (though Lily never said so) was Moe."[37]

Dictatorial and unhappy, Sarah was hardly an easy patient. She couldn't accept that it was God's will for Yudel to die. For the adolescent narrator of "The Summer My Grandmother Was Supposed to Die," Sarah is little more than death's bogeyman. In the autobiographical notes that almost word-for-word entered Richler's early unpublished novel, *The Rotten People*, the adolescent narrator, Kerman Adler, is even less sentimental: "So the old bitch was finally dead," he thinks, remembering the stink of her gangrenous foot, the "kaka" in bed (and, once, smeared on the wall) that his mother had to clean up, putting her in a nasty mood. Unwillingly, Kerman is sometimes forced to babysit her. When the grandmother summons him with "boiyu, boiyu," he cries and hides behind a chair. The bottom line: "Can you … blame Kerman yet if he was glad when she died."[38]

By the time Richler wrote "The Summer My Grandmother Was Supposed to Die" (nine years after *The Rotten People*), he had become slightly less honest and a great deal more humane. There the middle-aged mother rocks the wailing grandmother in her arms, one of the few times in Richler's fiction that the figure standing in for Lily is sympathetic. A moving incident Richler *didn't* record – he may not have known about it – occurred when Lily bathed her mother. At the time, Sarah was still able to talk. The naked intimacy of the childhood bath for mother and daughter, long left behind among greater joys, returned for Lily amid tears (as it does for many women) when the daughter had to reverse childhood roles and bathe her mother. Embarrassed, Sarah wept and called herself a burden. Nonsense, Lily replied, Sarah had bathed *her* as a baby. Then Lily took her mother's breasts in her mouth and pretended to suckle.[39]

≶

In the early months after Sarah's stroke and before the weight of caring for her mother overwhelmed her, Lily began to write. Whenever Mordecai looked back on authors in his family, he spoke about Rabbi Yudel Rosenberg's work on the Zohar, or about Uncle Israel Rosenberg and his wife Vera – "the Yiddishe Shiksa" – who took to the vaudeville theatre of the Lower East Side, New York.[40] The family labelled Israel as "the communist," and Richler, sensing a kindred spirit, made a point of mentioning him in his first published novel, *The Acrobats*.[41]

But there was a writer of much nearer kin. From the end of 1935 until well into 1937, Lily wrote a semi-regular column called "I Pay a Visit to the Beloved Rabbi" for the *Canadian Jewish Review*. Each column is narrated by an alter-ego of Lily's – a reporter – and describes little incidents in the Rabbi's counselling career, usually segueing into the joyful celebration of a Jewish festival. Readers have been puzzled by the tradition-friendly and almost twee conceits of early Richler stories such as "The Secret of the Kugel," but one look at Lily's work would have clarified the lines of influence.

Lily's gentle and humane Rabbi was of course an idealized memorial of her father, in the soft-focus nostalgia through which she now saw the past after her father's death. More covertly, she also broached the things that made her present life hell – marital strife, the gender roles of the 1930s, her husband's lack of culture – and invented a fantasy life as an unmarried reporter. In the several stories that venture towards divorce, the deck is stacked, not surprisingly, against the husband; and one dispute in particular that the fictional Rabbi settles must have made Moe burn a little around the ears. A man owes another $1,000 dollars and claims that he can't immediately repay it.[42] What did Moe make of the $1,000, so explicit an echo of the money that Lily had accused Shmarya of taking? Clearly, Mordecai Richler wasn't the first one in his family to recognize that fiction could hold a sting and be used to settle private scores.

Lily's happy-ending formula made it impossible for her to approach the problems with anything like realism. Years later, she tried to move beyond formula by writing a few chapters that she hoped (in vain) to expand into a novel about life at her boarding house[43]; and, later still, she published an autobiography. But the Rabbi stories she ended with a sentimental flourish that obscurely prophesied no good between herself and Moe: "Really, I must visit the Rabbi's home again."[44] One story concludes with a seder, the Rabbi nearly Messianic in a white yarmulke edged with silver, the celebrants awestruck. But not everyone responded to the stories in the way Lily had hoped. Moe mocked her writing and her pretensions. Small wonder, given her one-sided treatment of marital trouble and the magisterial seriousness of nominating Rabbi Yudel Rosenberg for Messiah now that he was dead. "[Moe's mockery] did not help their marriage, to put it mildly," says Avrum.[45]

While his wife entered the public world of the CJR, Moe wrote privately: in a diary, in code. "He catalogued injuries and insults, betrayals, family quarrels, bad debts."[46] While Lily turned literature into the place where she could have, sentimentally, ideally, that which she could no longer have in life, Moe catalogued darkness. One senses, in Richler's novels, that this contest for the interpretation of events made an indelible impression on him. In fiction, Lily visited, again and again, the Rabbi's lost home, yet literally Lily *was* now in the Rabbi's home on Jeanne Mance Street, no Rabbi in sight, only a paralyzed Rebbetzin in diapers, wasting slowly towards death. Richler, having witnessed the fissure between the wished-for world and the one that Lily was really stuck in, would slowly follow Moe in taking the more jaundiced view, suggesting in *Son of a Smaller Hero* that Leah (Lily's Jewish name) had a difficult time realizing that she was not a tzaddik's daughter anymore.[47] With Lily's stories as models to resist, it would be eight novels (one unpublished) and almost twenty years into his writing career before Richler would allow himself a full-blown happy ending. Whereas Lily sent Jewish festivals up into the clouds, Richler, contra, would bring them back to earth: "These are the Days of Awe. Tomorrow is Rosh Hashonna, our new year, and like a week later it's Yom Kippur, when if you shit on anybody during the year you got a legal right to repent."[48] In Lily's stories, the individual exists mainly for the sake of the festival, her fiction not so far removed from her father's work, where the individual exists to make an Orthodox theological point. Apart from the work of a handful of writers such as Evelyn Waugh and Flannery O'Connor, in the contemporary novel (including Richler's work, and even the work of, say, Rudy Wiebe) it is the individual life that gives value to the festival, not vice-versa. Heir to Lily's and Yudel's writing, Richler would feel the constant pull between allegory and novel. No allegory? Then a novel is nothing more than a string of anecdotes without larger import. Too much allegory? Then a novel loses whatever life it might have, turning into a political or religious diatribe tricked out in colour. Richler aimed to make his characters lifelike, though when he spoke of such things, it was Hugh MacLennan, not his mother whom he invoked.[49]

And yet ... the *Canadian Jewish Review*, in which Lily's stories appeared, was hardly the Orthodox home that Yudel Rosenberg would have wished for his memorial. With photographs of women in girdles and (despite a fairly conservative editorial policy) the occasional article such as "Was Moses an Egyptian: Freud Searches into the Beginnings of Jewish History,"[50] the CJR measured the shifting currents in a partially assimilated Jewish elite at the same time as it published rabbis who lamented that the Sabbath was being neglected, birth control was being used, and parents were waiting too long to inform little Abie and Sarah that they were Jews.[51] Not many Orthodox children – certainly none in the Richler or Rosenberg families – had to scratch their heads in puzzlement about whether they were Jews or not. According to many accounts, including Richler's own, it was Richler who made the decisive break with the Orthodox past. But it wasn't as simple as that. Rabbi Rosenberg had unwittingly initiated the break by pursuing Russian and fiction; Moe and Lily had widened the fissure, the one via the *New York Daily News* and bawdy jokes, the other by turning towards a non-Orthodox newspaper. In the 1930s, changes were already brewing in Canadian-Jewish public culture to which an ostensibly Orthodox woman such as Lily aspired. Larger changes were brewing, too, for worldwide Jewry and for Mordecai, as the world edged towards war.

3

À bas les Juifs

WHILE LILY WAS WRITING, Mordecai, at age five, began the type of religious education that the Beloved Rabbi had laid out for his male grandchildren. Mordecai went to United Talmud Torah on St. Joseph Boulevard at Jeanne Mance. Mornings, he submitted to the required English curriculum and some French, all taught by "bracingly modern" girls. Afternoons, he was gently led by old men – "ear-twisters and knuckle-rappers" – through the intricacies of Torah and Talmud in Hebrew.[1] A certain amount of Hebrew penetrated his resistant skull, though by 1971 the Hebrew had evaporated.[2] Special ministrations were sometimes necessary. The principal, Mr Magid, repeatedly phoned Lily, saying, "I don't know what I'm going to do with your son."[3] Lily, however, knew what to do. In Mordecai's presence she pretended to call Eaton's, and said, "I want to exchange my bad little boy for a nice girl."[4]

In 1938 the Richlers moved, Grandmother Sarah in tow, to the second-floor coldwater flat that would be immortalized in Richler's fiction: 5257 St. Urbain Street. It's still there, one in a line of row houses, all attached down the run of the narrow street. The jutting balconies, the long sets of rather delicate concrete stairs make the second floors look surprisingly inviting, more so than the first floors, tucked in the dark under the stairs. The flat was a couple of streets from "The Main" where the boys roamed – St. Laurent Boulevard (St. Lawrence in *Son of a Smaller Hero*) – now in the "trendy Mile End district." There one can find Greek grocers, samosas, Hasidim in black hats and sidecurls roaming the streets, but the new immigrant inhabitants are generally still poor, as were the Richlers. Sarah took a bedroom, Moe and Lily another, and Avrum and Mordecai shared a third until Sarah's death in 1942. The back bedroom that Mordecai inherited from his grandmother had a cracked ceiling and a sizzling radiator, "mice scrabbling in the walls, a window looking out on sheets frozen stiff on the laundry line" –

though apart from the mice it's hard to know how these features would distinguish the bedroom from most other bedrooms in Montreal.[5]

Early on, he had an independent spirit, and he made a first, ill-advised bid for freedom at about age seven or eight, after a big fight with his mother. "I'm leaving home," he declared. "Ok, go," she replied, "I'll help you pack." She got him a little box, and he put his valuables inside. It was winter or late fall, pouring rain and already dark. Avrum, twelve years old, was terrified, thinking, "my God, he's leaving home, what is he going to do!" Mordecai packed up his bundle and stepped out into the rain. Avrum started to cry, "What are we going to do? He's gone!" "He'll be back," Lily said. Not five minutes later, the doorbell rang. Mordecai was soaked. Rather harshly, Lily demanded, "What d'you want?" "I forgot my rubbers," came the plaintive reply. It was enough. Mordecai stepped back inside, and all was forgiven.[6]

Also at age eight, Mordecai visited Toronto for the first time, staying with Lily's sister Hannah Hadler. His cousins Bessie and Frances were already in their late teens and early twenties. Everyone liked him and felt sorry for him; they thought him almost an orphan, "a lost kid." Frances took him to his first movie at the Tivoli theatre. It was like going to Wonderland.[7] Looking back, Richler spoke of Toronto as "a latter-day Sodom," where children under sixteen could get into movies and teenagers get their hands on the sunbathing and girlie magazines that were banned in Québec.[8] Technically accurate, Richler's "memory" is deceptive, since it conveys neither the style nor the gusto with which the "darling darling little fellow" approached experience. Young Mordecai, when confronted with a heavy sea that rocked sailors on the screen, rocked along in his chair.[9] It is pleasing to know that the sardonic wag who would pillory Toronto in *The Incomparable Atuk* once rocked along with the boat at his first movie.

If the autobiographical notes that became *The Rotten People* are accurate, Mordecai didn't remain innocent very long. Kerman (Richler's alter ego) finds some condoms in his father's drawer, and his older brother "Abe" (Richler didn't bother to fictionalize his brother's name) laughs at him because "Kerman didn't even know what a screw meant." At the ripe age of thirteen, with the help of a condom and a dirty magazine, the "Abe" of the novel demonstrates to his eight-year-old brother and a friend the proper way to jerk off. Afterwards they smoke cigarettes, but someone squeals on them.[10] Nothing like this actually happened, says Avrum.[11] Whatever the case, Mordecai was no saint. With Avrum he picked cigarette butts off the street to smoke, and, when there weren't enough of those, they'd smoke dried banana peels or the bamboo sticks used to stretch shoes. At Schacter's Tobacco and Candies Mordecai antagonized the old men who played chess in the

back room and stole what candies he could. He liked to pick on the handicapped son of a peddler there.[12]

Closer in age to Mordecai than his female cousins was a male cousin,
Lionel Albert. Whenever Lily was on good terms with Lionel's mother Ruth,
the boys spent a lot of time together. Winters they slept three to a bed in the
St. Urbain Street flat, and summers they roamed Shawbridge, the Laurentian village (now merged with Prévost) where their families holidayed in
rented shacks without electricity.[13] The boys' stole apples together and swam
in the North River. "Mischief-maker," and sometimes "Puss In Boots,"[14]
Lily called Mordecai, the boy who by the end of his teens would set himself
up as something more than a miller's son. Once Mordecai nearly killed himself, inadvertently taking the short way down "their" mountain – dead veg-
etation having less braking effect than anticipated. The boys' main concern
afterwards was how to explain the gash on Mordecai's forehead to Lily. A
tree, yes, that was it, Mordecai had bumped into a tree.[15] In the notes to
The Rotten People, Richler put it more plainly: "he fell off a thirty foot cliff
without dying and when they came home Abe told his Momma he had
bumped into a tree because Abe was scared."[16]

Another Shawbridge summer they stayed at a Mme Lachance's. Avrum
and Mordecai's Orthodoxy, at the time, was very strict. If Mme Lachance's
daughter wasn't around on the Sabbath, someone else had to light the fire,
and Lionel, "being not that religious anyway," was the designated apostate.
It certainly couldn't be Avrum or Mordecai, who were required to observe
the Sabbath exactly. One Saturday, as the boys sat talking in the weedy,
dried-up lawn at the back of a rented place, Mordecai absent-mindedly tore
a leaf in two. Avrum immediately accused him with a cry of "Shabbes goy!"
– literally a "Sabbath gentile," an unclean factotum who is required to do
the Sabbath work that Orthodox Jewish employers and employees shun. It
wasn't as if the boys were little policemen, running to Lily to tell on each
other, but neither was the term meant as a joke. It was a dig, a way of saying, "You're not a real Jew." Lionel wasn't considered "Jewish" enough to
be thus insulted, but he heard Avrum, Mordecai, and David (Shmarya's
youngest son, Dudy) use the term often, the boys always ready to challenge
one another.[17] In many ways, Richler's literary reaction against Orthodoxy
would be a reaction against the social control that surfaced in such moments. He would soon hear the cry "Shabbes goy!" again, from a more powerful source and in more disturbing circumstances.

≷

The arrival of World War II would eventually have a pervasive influence
upon Richler's life and work, his religious and racial outlook. Initially, how-

ever, the war was little more than a vicarious adventure. Mordecai marked
Allied advances on a map of the world posted in his bedroom, and, at the
tail end of the war, participated in a voluntary cadet program at his high
school.[18] According to his memoir, *Back to Ibiza*, Mordecai sat with his family in the living room, listening to an RCA short-wave radio: "We caught
Hitler addressing the Reichstag, Hitler in a rage, cresting waves of *sieg heils*
and static. We were petrified."[19] But in fact (and as Richler says elsewhere)
the family only heard Ed Murrow and J.B. Priestley, the latter broadcasting
from London.[20] Nobody really grasped the full extent of Hitler's genocidal
plans early on. Rumours surfaced by 1942, but even then, as Bernard Richler says, "it was so unbelievable ... we started to hear stories and couldn't
believe it."[21]

At the time of the war, the fortunes of hockey's Montreal Canadiens,
baseball's Triple "A" Montreal Royals, and the boxing heroes at Madison
Square Gardens were as important to Mordecai as the fate of the Allied
troops – perhaps more important. Later he would despise players like Wayne
Gretzky who were all grace and finesse on the ice but could only speak in
clichés off it. He would quote Richard Ford: the athlete is "never likely to
feel the least bit divided, or alienated, or one ounce of existential dread ...
Years of athletic training teach him this: the necessity of relinquishing doubt
and ambiguity and self-inquiry in favor of a pleasant self-championing one-
dimensionality."[22] In Mordecai's adolescence, however, existential dread still
far in the future, the Stanley Cups of Maurice Richard and 1946 pennant
for Jackie Robinson and Montreal Royals were enough.

Richler looked at sports as a way out of the ghetto, says his son Noah:
"It was about getting ahead, about making your way in the world."[23] One
ought to add: it was about pecking order. Always painfully attentive to hi-
erarchies, Richler understood that, in the society of boys, physical prowess
almost exclusively determined social position, and much of his later ambivalence towards athletes is the intellectual's revenge for not being cock of the
walk. He never amounted to much as an athlete.[24] By the time he was able
to afford skates he was too old to catch up to the boys who had learned
young.[25] Boxing, though ... At the YMHA, under the tutelage of a gym teacher,
Mordecai learned to box and thought he might enjoy laying a few people
on their backs. However, a more experienced schoolmate knocked him down
in his first bout and relieved him of that particular vanity.[26]

Bouts of a less controlled nature were taking place on the streets. For
Jews, wartime was proving more and more troubling, less so (at first) because of what was taking place in Germany than because of what was happening in Québec. Many French Canadians aligned themselves against
conscription, pro-Vichy, and against Jews. One of the reasons that Canada
accepted few Jewish refugees during the Nazi reign of terror was that Macken-

zie King feared a violent reaction from Québec – and polls in English Canada showed that anti-Semitism had grassroots support there, too.[27] If Richler after the 1992 publication of *Oh Canada!* could be accused of paying too much attention to Québec in the 1930s and not enough to Québec in the 1990s, his critics were too quick to dismiss the exclusions that nationalism is in the habit of making. In the late 1930s and the early 40s when Richler's responses were being formed, Québécois nationalism wore a sinister face, and, if English-Canadian conscription was an appropriate target for Québécois anger, it was the Jews who bore its brunt.

The racial prejudice went both ways. At his fingertips, Mordecai had apocryphal stories about the sexual aberrations of priests and nuns, and he was convinced that French-Canadians were "abysmally stupid," that their culture could accurately be summed up (as some of his teachers said) by William Henry Drummond's dialect poems: "An' wedder I see to-morrow, dat's not'ing for I don't care."[28] But the more sinister prejudices belonged to the Francophone majority. "We don't attack Jews," Duplessis's Labour Minister Adrien Arcand wrote in 1933, "We simply defend our country against their conspiracy."[29] Some nationalist leaders suggested that Jews would be so much happier in Palestine and should forfeit their Canadian citizenship.[30] In the Laurentians, where a young Pierre Trudeau had for a lark worn a German army uniform while riding his motorcycle,[31] Richler remembers "*à bas les juifs*" ("down with Jews") appearing, painted onto a rock beside the highway. On the Main, a few blocks from Mordecai's home, French-Canadian students terrorized Jews on the pretext of hunting for Communists. A mob marched through the Jewish neighbourhood, chanting "Death to the Jews."[32] Fights broke out on a beach outside of Montreal and beside the YMHA on Park Avenue.[33] Avrum remembers the fights well. One night the Jews, including Avrum, got beat up, and the next night they returned with baseball bats and beat the hell out of the French-Canadians, smashing the windows of their stores. Mordecai, boxer manqué and all-around tough kid, fought too.[34]

≋

Nevertheless, during the war years the Jews moved up, not down. Those years, Richler liked to say, were a time when "my generation" left the cold-water flats and moved in "to apartments in Outremont, duplexes and split-levels in the suburbs."[35] The operative (and deceptive) words are "my generation." In other words: not me. Some of Mordecai's relatives – Joe Richler for one – did indeed grow rich enough to move across Park Avenue, out of the ghetto and into Outremont, a "junior Westmount"[36] at the base of Mount Royal where other relatives – Lionel Albert's family – already lived. Not Moe Richler, however.

Lionel's prosperity rankled. "I sometimes snobbishly rubbed it in to Mordecai," he admits, and acknowledges that Sheldon Leventhal in *Joshua Then and Now* is a satiric and fanciful portrait of him. The portrait contains a characteristic Richlerian in-joke – Sheldon doesn't allow Joshua to run the switch on his "Lionel train engine." Lionel Albert remembers having a one-loop train track with a clockwork handcar, but no contested switch. He doesn't remember his father helping Mordecai out of any scrapes either, as Harvey Leventhal condescendingly tries to do with Joshua in the novel.[37]

As for Joe Richler's rise, rather than being a welcome symbol of bourgeois prosperity, to Mordecai the whole process seemed like a personal insult. Shmarya had already made Joe, six years Moe's junior, a partner in the family firm, and during the war Joe rode the success of aluminium. Moe was the slave labour, Joe "the superior guy," says Avrum. "My father did all the work, and Joe did all the talking." Although Moe seems to have accepted his brother leap-frogging over him, Avrum and Mordecai were infuriated by Shmarya's unequal dealings.[38] Mordecai was learning something he wouldn't forget as a writer: his father's low status was the result of his inability to make money. Richler would never be too fastidious to haggle with editors and publishers over money, and, when he didn't sell enough books to tide him over, he wouldn't turn up his nose at TV and film work. He understood that in cultural productions as much as in the muck of Montreal scrapyards, money conferred status. And no matter how satirically exaggerated, his characters always maintained a surprisingly realist substantiality because they worried about money.

Back to Ibiza tells of an "Uncle Barney Richler," the "first of the Richler brood to quit St. Urbain for the pleasures of tree-lined Outremont," the Joe/Barney who would eventually become Oscar Shapiro in *Joshua Then and Now*. Sly digs at the *nouveaux riches* finding puny public voices would come in abundance from the adult Mordecai Richler, but the animating hostility came from Mordecai's adolescent experiences at Shmarya's shop. There Joe sat behind a desk – in a glorified shack, true, but behind a desk all the same – while Moe drove truck, operated the crane, hustled junk, and walked home every night, "dirty as a miner."[39] "A metal merchant," Lily insisted on calling him.[40] One incident in particular explains Mordecai's hostility towards Joe Richler. Mordecai, off school, was answering phones in the company office. Near him were Moe and "Barney" – "Barney" expounding on the money to be had in aluminium, Moe listening and nodding his head because "Barney" always knew everything. The phone rang and someone asked for "Mr Richler." Mordecai handed the phone to his father. After a minute or two it became clear that the call was for "Barney," not for Moe. Once "Barney" got off the phone, he lectured Mordecai, "If they ask for Mr Richler in this office, it's for me. If they want to speak to your father they ask is

Moe around." Feeling the humiliation more keenly than his father, Mordecai said, "fuck you." "Barney" whacked him. Fictionalized, the incident in
Joshua Then and Now ends with Joshua's father driving the uncle up against
the wall. Thus, the fantasy. Not so the less satisfying result in *Back to Ibiza*.
Alone with his father afterwards, Mordecai must have hoped at least for
tacit approval. "You got off easy," was all Moe said.[41] Many years later Joe,
like "Barney," would go bankrupt, and Mordecai would get an unexpected
revenge when he stepped into a Montreal taxi: at the wheel, Joe.[42]

§

Actually, though Mordecai was almost telepathically sensitive to the un-
voiced insults of greater wealth, he didn't do so badly during the war himself. He learned to combine public service with enlightened self-interest,
going door-to-door to collect metal for the war effort. Sometimes the haul
made it to the depot; other times Mordecai stopped first at a scrapyard, sold
the metal, and pocketed the money.[43] At a grocery, he cleaned, ran deliver-
ies, and stuffed potatoes into 5lb bags. For about a month he did the cloth-
ing-factory job that Duddy Kravitz does in the film.[44] Late in the war Mordecai
became positively wealthy. Using his bike, he collected bills Saturday or Sunday mornings for a kosher butcher on St. Viateur Street. He earned 2¢ on
the dollar – as much as $5-6 for a few hours' work – and, though the fam-
ily was struggling, Lily let him keep the money. He had up to $400 in his
pockets, he claimed, though that seems hard to believe.[45]

Up to this point his reading hadn't amounted to much. "Our mothers,"
Richler says, pushed "us" away from games and into *The Books of Knowledge*.[46] Again, his memory takes a bit of license. The Richlers did not own
The Books of Knowledge; those appeared only in the homes of his rich
cousins and were never made available to the Richlers.[47] Although he later
wrote children's literature, he didn't read any. Instead, comics were the sta-
ple.[48] He read Bible comics and Classic Comics, as well as books such as
Scaramouche, *The Three Musketeers*, *The Count of Monte Cristo*, *Robin Hood*,
Treasure Island, and *The Good Earth*. Perry Mason and Ellery Queen, Kipling
and Henty kept him occupied too.[49]

At Talmud Torah Mordecai's artistic talent was good enough to convince one of his teachers, Evelyn Sacks, to allow him to teach art, a subject
she knew little about. Sacks, who would soon become very important to
him, got him reinstated after a suspension. When a teacher lecturing near
Mordecai's desk accidentally seasoned his Hebrew with saliva, Mordecai
protested, "Don't spit on me." Out he went. Sacks claims that she urged
mercy because of the difficult state in Mordecai's home – civil war, really –
with Lily and Moe on the verge of divorce.[50]

Avrum doubts the saliva story,[51] but it could be true. In fact, a clearly apocryphal story that supposedly happened to Mordecai at his high school, Baron Byng, may have originated in the saliva story. The apocryphal story goes that one day during the last year of World War II the boys of Morde-cai's class, left alone in the chemistry lab, grew boisterous. Enter the teacher, Mr Spracklin. Unhappy with the ruckus, he said, "We need Hitler here to take care of noisy Jews." But Mordecai was always fearless and strode up to Spracklin, asking, "Do you like your appearance Mr Spracklin?" "Yes," Spracklin replied, and Mordecai hit him as hard as he could. Blood was shed, not because of the punch, but because of what ensued. Spracklin stumbled against the sink and hit his head." Mordecai, "white as a sheet," ran to Frances Katz and told her what had happened. She informed the principal. Although the principal immediately wanted to expel Mordecai, Katz warned that she'd file a complaint against Spracklin with the RCMP. The principal relented and instead demanded that Katz take Mordecai into her class of thirty-six girls, a class Mordecai found awkward and rarely attended. The story, attributed to Katz, was published in the *Canadian Jewish News*.[52] However, Richler's former classmates find this story preposterous. Some of them were in Mordecai's chemistry class and remember no such incident.[53] The imagined Nazi-baiting of Richler's *fictional* characters evidently crossed the divide into biography, colouring memories of Richler himself.

According to Evelyn Sacks, Mordecai was already a skilled writer at an early age. He had a stinging wit and was therefore popular, yet often disliked.[54] His early stories, however, bore little wit. Reading a book of short stories, he came upon one called "The Face on the Wall." It takes place in a Kiplingesque club, where one Englishman tells another how frightened he is by a face on the wall. The face disappears; the man dies.[55] The shiver that went up Mordecai's spine at age fourteen convinced him that he should try his hand at writing, too. His first writing attempts, "set in London club-land,"[56] were thus intended to reproduce Romantic eeriness, not satire.

The turning point in his reading came with Erich Maria Remarque's *All Quiet on the Western Front (Im Westen nichts neues)*. He hadn't planned to read it. During an illness that confined him to his bedroom, librarians dropped off books. Who was the anonymous librarian who decided that, deep in the heart of World War II, a young Jewish boy convalescing at home would benefit from a World War I novel written by a German? When Mordecai finally turned to the book out of boredom, the unthinkable happened: he began to identify with the enemy. It was a trivial incident, a bit of cookery, that Richler says affected him most profoundly: "The business, I realized, alarmed – no, *affronted* – was the making of potato *latkes*, a favorite of mine as well as of Paul Bäumer, a dish I had always taken to be Jewish, certainly not a German concoction. What did I know? Nothing." Suddenly the Nazis began to look human, though Mordecai's mind was eased somewhat when he heard that Hitler had banned Remarque's books.[57]

Richler gives various dates for this event: he was either twelve or thirteen.[58] The timing is close enough to a crucial nexus of upcoming events to suggest that reading contributed to his alienation from Orthodoxy, that *All Quiet* made him feel the insularity of his Jewish society. He began to read broadly in the YMHA library[59] and began to listen to CBC radio plays – both to adaptations and to Canadian originals. The homegrown originals he would later find fault with.[60] Yet he also spoke of the "shared excitement" when he and other students discovered the CBC *Stage* series, including the plays of Lister Sinclair and Len Peterson.[61] It was only in better-read retrospect, clearly, that he saw how far European drama towered over Canadian social-problem plays.

≶

Closer to the viscera than literature were the practices and strictures of Jewish Orthodoxy. "The grandfather believes, the father doubts, the son denies" – so goes the nineteenth-century Franco-Jewish proverb.[62] Not true of Moe Richler, says his younger brother Bernard: Moe never doubted.[63] Perhaps – but, if Moe believed, it was a specialized kind of belief. He did put on his prayer shawl and tefillin every morning and say his prayers; yet he had honed the art of prayer to such a keen edge that what should take twenty minutes to half an hour if done conscientiously took Moe all of thirty seconds. Moe wasn't Orthodox, insists Avrum: "My father didn't believe in this. He only did it because it was a routine ... He'd go 'Rrruuurr, Rrruurr, Rrruu.' Finished. Thirty seconds."

"Daddy," Avrum asked, "how can you do it so fast?"

"I do it in my heart," Moe replied. "Don't ask questions! What do *you* know?" Moe pretended to be Orthodox because he had to be, since he worked for Shmarya, says Avrum. More probably, given how strongly Moe would react to Mordecai's marriage to a shiksa, Moe's faith was instinctual – a routine, as Avrum says.[64] Moe was indeed Orthodox, but his real desires lay elsewhere.

Every Sabbath morning, Moe shepherded his boys over to the Young Israel Synagogue,[65] a modest building (no longer standing) that had once been a private residence at 5584 Park Avenue.[66] The sanctuary was nothing more than the double parlour of an ordinary house.[67] Mordecai carried the prayer shawls in "a little purple velvet bag" because he hadn't been barmitzvahed yet and therefore didn't have to be as careful about "work" on the Sabbath. Once there, however, Moe didn't find enough edification in the rabbi's sermons to keep him from stepping out back and gossiping with his friends.[68] Synagogue wasn't a place where Moe could forget his poverty. Wealthier synagogue members bid $25 for the honour of an aliyah (a call to read the Torah in public) before Moses could even bid $2.[69]

Nevertheless, the Torah was obeyed, and Lily kept her house kosher.[70] On the Sabbath, the Richlers didn't turn on lights, didn't light the wood stove, didn't answer the phone. Mordecai's laxer Jewish friends teased him about these restrictions. During Sukkah, Moe would set up a little booth on the balcony of their flat, and, whether it was cold out or not, they ate their suppers there, as Lily complained of how far the celebration fell short of what it had been in her father's home.[71] Several days before Yom Kippur the Richler boys would, as a replacement for temple sacrifice, rotate a live rooster or chicken over their heads and recite the Bnai Adam blessing to release the year's load of sin onto the bird. Occasionally, there were misadventures. "One of them shit on me," Avrum recalls.[72] In later years, Richler would mock Shmarya and the stricter aunts and uncles who unscrewed refrigerator light bulbs and tore off extra toilet paper sheets on Friday so as not to unintentionally make "fire" or "work" on the Sabbath,[73] but the same practice had been followed in Moe and Lily's home, too, though it was discontinued when the boys were fairly young.[74]

Sabbath afternoons, Moe headed out, his boys often trailing, to Schacter's Tobacco and Candies at #24 Laurier[75] to play gin rummy for a penny a point with his brothers in the back room.[76] There kashrut was slightly looser, as they dined on coke and chocolate biscuits.

"How can you eat that?" Avrum demanded of his father, "It's not kosher!"

"What do *you* know?" was Moe's considered reply. "Don't ask questions.'"

This was his favourite expression – "What do *you* know?" – an expression Richler later gave to Reuben in *Joshua Then and Now*.[77] The Richler brothers also listened to the radio, another Sabbath no-no, though they scrupulously waited until after dark to pay their tiny gambling debts.[78]

Not unkosher, strictly speaking, but also falling short of Orthodox ideals was the Gayety Theatre. Moe loved the Gayety and its burlesque show, and he dutifully took his place there Saturday nights. By the time that the boys were "adults" – fifteen or so – he occasionally took them along. Some of the funny scenes in Richler's novels – a character arguing that a blowjob from a prostitute doesn't constitute a violation of the Sabbath – get their bite from these early incongruencies, as Richler tried to square his family's careful observance of the Sabbath with the pleasures of watching Lily St. Cyr simulate intercourse with a swan.[79]

Talmud classes to prepare Mordecai for his bar mitzvah didn't do much to convince him of the essential soundness of Orthodoxy. Twice weekly after school he attended cheder in the back room of Young Israel, learning Modern Hebrew and Hasidic lore from a Mr Yalofsky.[80] Later, Richler would say that he much preferred the weird miracles of the Hasids to the rationalizations of younger rabbis, who explained kashrut as God's way, in overheated Palestine, of protecting his Jews from food poisoning.[81] Still, Mordecai couldn't have been too taken with Orthodox lore either, since he soon bolted with all possible speed from cheder. But he did refine his arguing skills. He began to debate the finer points of the law with his parents, arguing that if Gentile streetcars ran on the Sabbath *regardless* of what the Jews did, how could it be sinful to step onto an already moving streetcar? Lily tried to put a positive spin on this resistance: it was evidence that her youngest son was becoming "a Talmud head."[82]

The failed indoctrination into a literalist approach would, much later, stand Richler in good stead when he burlesqued the biblical stories of Abraham, Job, and Esther in *Joshua Then and Now*. When the poet and editor David Rosenberg urged Richler at age fifty-five to consider the biblical texts as metaphorical – an important intellectual strategy to recuperate the texts for the present, but an emasculation of biblical mysteries and absurdities – Richler fiercely clung to the either/or that had presented itself to him at thirteen: either the Torah was literally true or it was nonsense. He'd remain grateful for a Hasidic childhood – rich in imagery and legends – though he'd be glad to escape the suffocation.[83] All this would amount, eventually, to a joyous and salacious refusal to let the Bible become a grim authority and, at the same time, to a more agonized, perhaps never fully successful, search for a morality that could stand in for his departed Orthodox faith.

For a while during the war years, Shmarya moved to 5244 St. Urbain, directly across the street from Mordecai, putting a point on the question of Orthodoxy, since Shmarya could watch him closely. Sunday afternoons, all the Richlers gathered at Shmarya's. If the boys observed the Sabbath properly, they sometimes got a quarter from Shmarya – "shabbes graft" as Moe called it.[84] Mordecai's closest friend at the time was his Uncle David (Dudy), Shmarya's youngest son – uncle; but only three years older than Mordecai.[85] Shmarya insisted that the boys join him for Maariv (evening prayers) at a tiny Galiciamer synagogue at 136–38 Fairmont.[86] One evening – this may have been after 1942, with Sarah already dead and Shmarya already moved to nearby Jeanne Mance and Groll Lane – the boys neglected to appear at the synagogue at the appointed time. Returning home, Shmarya found the boys in his basement, playing with a little lab they had set up. He smashed up the chemistry set. It was enough to move David to apology. Not Mordecai. A short time later, Mordecai took his revenge by picking a fight with David, but David told Shmarya. Shmarya summoned Mordecai to his study and thrashed him with the belt.[87] A defining moment for Richler: after this, it would no longer be possible for him to approach the questions of Ortho-doxy and the world's "meaning" with any degree of objectivity. Shmarya had defined religion as a battleground, ensuring that the result would be either shame or pride, not compromise. Mordecai would eventually take up the battle in fiction, and use his novels rhetorically – at first with social criticism, later satire – to strike back at Shmarya.

4

Shabbes Goy

NEAR THE END OF HIS LIFE Richler blamed his rebellion against Orthodoxy mainly on pool – he just wanted to play pool on the Sabbath. And listen to the radio. And go to Saturday afternoon baseball games. All this is a bit disingenuous, though it contains a germ of truth: Mordecai was no Spinoza or Saul Ansky, no Enlightenment maskil rebelling for intellectual reasons. He often skipped the final class of the day and raced over to the Rachel Pool Hall to get the first table. With home on war footing, he began to go to the Rachel even on Friday nights, a Sabbath violation, yet not so very different from Moe going to Schacter's. The crucial difference: at the Rachel could be found hot dogs and boys who dated shiksas, treif flashing neon, rather more visible than a bit of pork jelly in a chocolate biscuit.[1]

But it's not as if Mordecai threw aside his tefillin simply because he wanted to play pool. More important was his deteriorating relationship with Shmarya. The lover of the Sabbath Queen, Rabbi Yudel Rosenberg, was no longer around to protest Mordecai's desecration of Her.[2] But Her sergeant-at-arms was. When Mordecai walked through the lane between Jeanne Mance and St. Urbain without a hat or cap on, Shmarya shouted out his disapproval.[3] According to Bernard Richler, Shmarya couldn't show love for Mordecai because of Mordecai's behaviour.[4] It was more than that. Richler claims that he once caught Shmarya cheating "a drunken Irish peddler"[5] at the scrapyard scales, a piece of hypocrisy dramatized in *Son of a Smaller Hero*. There Noah catches his grandfather Melech accepting what he knows to be stolen goods and giving short weight to an Irishman – though it's clear that the Irishman is scheming just as determinedly to cheat Melech. Max Richler, a reliable source, believes the incident to be purely fictional and says that between 1938 and 1942, when he worked for his father, he never saw anything dishonest.[6] Yet Harry Richler's conviction for accepting stolen goods while working for Shmarya gives weight to Mordecai's version. In *Son of a Smaller Hero*, Noah challenges his grandfather. Melech defends his practices by insisting that any "monkey-business" is all for the benefit of his fourteen children.[7] According to Richler, the actual scene ended differently. Mordecai told Moe, who cut him off with his all-purpose answer, "What do *you* know?" and added a clincher: anyway, the Gentiles were all anti-Semites.[8] Shmarya and his oldest sons still had a powerful sense of being inside one community and outside another, with the concomitant understanding that rules that applied inside didn't necessarily apply outside. But Mordecai, drawn to that outside world, was already demanding a wider form of justice that could encompass both worlds – he was, so to speak, a maskil-in-training, and in imagination, he was already leaving St. Urbain.

By itself, a bit of this-and-that with the weights from Shmarya probably wouldn't have heated up Mordecai. He himself shoplifted bats and balls from Eaton's[9] and tried to steal stamps, the shopkeeper lifting him by the seat of my pants and threatening destruction if Mordecai showed his face in the store again.[10] But another incident roused his sense of injustice more viscerally. It happened on a Sabbath, a few months before Mordecai's bar mitzvah, with much of the extended family gathered in Shmarya's living room. As usual, Mordecai had broken the Sabbath by riding a streetcar, and when he entered the room Shmarya began to denounce him as a Shabbes goy.[11] In front of everyone, Shmarya grabbed him by the ear and, all the while clouting him about the face, pulled him to the door and threw him from the house.

The watching family sided with Shmarya. According to Richler, David smirked.[12] Though he had been a bit devilish as a youngster, David took his news from the demolition of Mordecai and turned into the most Orthodox of the Richlers, eventually naming his son "Shmarya." Although he became a man of integrity and some warmth, he would have nothing to do with his wayward nephew and ex-companion. He refused to speak of Mordecai, even to family.[13]

Mordecai hoped that Moe, at least, would commiserate, but Moe had as little patience as Shmarya for his son's transgressions. Moe told Mordecai that he had it coming. Apologize, was Moe's advice. Not likely. Instead, the incident led to Mordecai's final rupture with Shmarya.[14] Lying in bed at night, Mordecai would sound out Avrum, asking if his older brother believed. "No," Avrum told him, and confided that he only put on his tefillin when Lily was watching.[15] Very soon Avrum had a kind of epiphany at Queen's when he saw the local rabbi, Zachariah (Zeke) Gelber having a meal during the Yom Kippur fast. Avrum hadn't been very religious before that, but it was a defining moment. "Fuck this," he said to himself, and when he returned home for holidays he told his mother "I don't believe in

religion any more ... I'll do what you ask me to as far as kosher and everything, but I have tasted lobster now. And it's good."[16] Mordecai did go
through the motions of his bar mitzvah, singing a passage from the Torah
or the Prophets, but the ceremony meant little to him.

⪽

Perhaps the most important factor in Mordecai's rebellion had nothing to
do, initially, with religion. For a time after Sarah's death on 15 July 1942,[17]
the boys had had their own bedrooms, yet in short order Lily decided that
there was money to be made among the Jewish refugees from the Nazis, and
she opened one of the bedrooms for refugee tenants. Moe expected the
refugees to be something like his own parents – "real *greeners* with sidecurls." Instead, most of those who arrived to board at the Richler house
were sophisticated German and Austrians. "My mother was enthralled,"
says Richler.[18]

More than enthralled. Among the fewer than five thousand Jews[19] who
managed to slip through Canada's iron curtain was Julius Frankel.[20] Tall
and dark, "intelligent, talkative and charming, well versed in Mosaic Law
and extremely well-read," he was the sort of man, Lily thought, that she
had always yearned for, a man like her father, a man who'd choose *Rigo-
letto* over Lily St. Cyr's striptease. She met him at a Talmud course held at
the Jewish Library, where she had begun to attend lectures, though it may
have been the other way round: the lectures may have recommended themselves because tall, dark, and cultured refugees could be found there. "My
moral sense would not allow me," Lily later maintained, "both to live with
a husband and have an affair."[21] Her moral sense was given a boost when
Moe discovered love letters that she had written to Frankel.[22]

In the autobiographical notes that with very few changes became the
unpublished novel *The Rotten People*, Richler's alter ego Kerman Adler describes Frankel:

> worst of all Frankel. He was charmed and he was a lier [sic]. Frankel
> was a refugee from Vienna and he stayed in the house long after he
> found a job & left the job & found another job & left that & started
> a business ... Frankel was kind and he was tricky. He was endearing
> and he was malicious. Mrs. Adler fell in love with Frankel & Frankel
> (who was a lot of things but most of all an opportunist) thought Mrs.
> Adler was a good lay.[23]

Matters came to a head in late 1943.[24] Avrum was away at Queen's University. From Lily there came the inevitable letters complaining of one thing

or another that Mordecai had done. But the letter calling him home in late 1943 dropped a bomb. "She was kicking my father out of the house, that's how she put it ... I remember coming home and there was my father, with his hangdog expression."[25]

For Mordecai, without a university sanctuary, there wasn't a lone bomb, but a constant shelling that he couldn't escape. Added to all the old quarrels were newer, harsher arguments:

> Please don't divorce me. Where will I go? What will I do? What am I?
> No I want a divorce.
> So many fights in the house Kerman couldn't sleep nights.
> Leave her alone. Don't hit her. He sobbed. He cried. He went crazy.
> I'm your father. You don't love me. You only think of your mother.
> Leave me alone. Please please please leave me alone.[26]

At times Richler has claimed that when he declared to his father that he was an atheist, the two had a fistfight.[27] However, in *The Rotten People*, it's the divorce that causes the fight. One night Kerman wakes to screaming in the kitchen. His father is beating the table with his fists while Kerman's mother cowers in a corner. Kerman runs to his mother and briefly embraces her, then grabs a kitchen chair and hurls it at his father.[28] Since this incident occurs only in *The Rotten People* and not in the autobiographical notes, it may be fictional, yet so many of the events of Kerman's *early* life are lifted directly out of Richler's life. Richler's later sense that he must tightly control his vicious temper[29] may have been born at such a moment.

In Richler's notes, Kerman's father, wiser than he initially knows, blames the refugees for his troubles: "They put ideas in her head. If not for the refugees she never would have divorced me ... (He always told these things to Kerman as Abe was away at an out of town university) ... The refugees & worst of all ~~Frankel~~ Schnitzer" [*sic*].[30] As this note suggests, Richler changed Frankel's name to "Schnitzer" in *The Rotten People* manuscript – the minimal change necessary to turn real events into fiction.

What Mordecai thought of the affair becoming public around the time of his bar mitzvah he mostly kept to himself, but the boy's anger at the refugee in Richler's short story "Bambinger" may have had its roots in Frankel.[31] More spectacularly in *Joshua Then and Now*, Richler has Joshua's mother, Esther, perform a striptease at her son's bar mitzvah. When Lily read the novel, she was horrified.[32] It's easy to feel her dismay: Richler has spoken of himself as one "who tends to remember slights – recording them in my mind's eye – transmogrifying them – finally publishing them in a code more accessible than my father's."[33]

Summoned home from Queen's, Avrum found the house in an uproar.[34]

"She doesn't want me anymore," Moe told him.[35] Rabbis arrived to reason with Lily. Moe, who had been in the habit of going to sometimes four feature films on Sundays instead of enduring Lily and his insubordinate sons,[36] made an extra effort to please her, buying presents, laying aside movies and card games.[37] But nothing would sway her. Shmarya boiled. He behaved as if Lily were divorcing *him*, not Moe.[38] In a way the patriarch was right, since the much-desired connection to a rabbinical family would be converted into the stigma of divorce. In *The Rotten People*, Kerman's grandfather and uncles want him to blackmail his mother by threatening to live with his father.[39] Much was expected of the boys, for when Avrum entered his grandfather's house, Shmarya turned his intense eyes on him and (though Shmarya rarely spoke English at home) said, "You gotta do something!"

"What can I do?" Avrum asked.

Shmarya had no answer, but hissed, "It's a scandal."[40]

≶

True to her word, Lily propelled Moe out of the flat. Technically she secured neither a divorce nor a get (a Jewish divorce); rather, she had her marriage annulled, a much easier route, on the pretexts – both false – that she was only a minor of seventeen when she got married and that she had married against her *father's* will. Moe was, as Richler says, "Stunned, humiliated. St. Urbain's cuckold." With "a natty straw hat," a new sports jacket, aftershave, and rye whiskey, he hoped, in vain, to become a swinging bachelor. He moved to a flat on St. Urbain in the next block, and although he continued to pay child support,[41] for two years Mordecai refused to have anything to do with him.[42]

But separating the combatants didn't bring peace to Mordecai, and the notes to *The Rotten People* describe a scene that affected him deeply:

> The old man left the house & took a room & she got her divorce.
> Frankel I love you.
> You're a damn good lay ...
> One night – a night that Kerman shall never forget, come rain or
>   come shine – something <u>most</u> horrible happened.
> Kerman shared a room with his mother. He couldn't sleep that night.
>   Late, Frankel came into the room softly.
> Is he asleep (with a slight, cultured Berlin accent).
> He's asleep.
> He got into her bed & kissed her. Kerman trembled & tried like mad
>   to fall asleep but he couldn't because he heard it. A slow, rhythmatic [*sic*] pumping sound in the next bed, like when somebody's
>   pumping the sink, only slushier.[43]

For many nights the boy is unable to escape the sound of pumping, "like a pipe being lowered into a bucket of vomit & out again, in again & out again." One morning he awakes to find his mother gone. He rushes to Frankel's room, crying for his mother. Frankel claims that he had no idea where she is, but Kerman spies a human-shaped lump under Frankel's blankets.[44] In the completed novel Kerman soon dreams of stabbing Frankel/Schnitzer, the usurper.[45]

Although it's possible that the twenty-year-old Richler expanded the scene in order to make his fiction more graphic, Avrum said that, a couple of years before his death, Richler confided a shocking secret about Lily. At first Avrum wouldn't say what it was, but eventually he revealed that Richler had spoken of witnessing his mother and Frankel during intercourse.[46] Because the early life of Kerman is in so many points *identical* to that of Richler (substantiated either by Richler or others), because Richler used a number of real names, and because there is no direct evidence to counter the unsubstantiated points, Richler's notes for *The Rotten People* seem based in fact. Changing his own name to "Kerman" and then "Noah Adler" is mostly cosmetic whenever Richler deals with the early portions of his protagonists' lives in *The Rotten People* and even in the much more fictional *Son of a Smaller Hero*; only late in the chronology of the two novels do Kerman and Noah become completely fictionalized, enmeshed in events that didn't happen to Richler. As much as Richler hated the idea of literature as therapy (and as narrow as such a line of analysis can be), in the beginning literature *was* therapeutic for him, allowing him to dress early wounds. Later Richler became more canny at covering up the wounds, but even in his last novel, *Barney's Version*, he never forgot his early crises, and he never forgot that literature owed its blood to the real world.

Lily miscalculated in the matter of Julius Frankel. He took advantage of her for a couple of years and then moved to Toronto, even though they had planned to wed.[47] She grew embittered over time and resented any allusions to her situation.[48] The divorce and its accompanying soundtrack had profound effect on Mordecai.[49] While he was taking Talmud classes to prepare for his bar mitzvah and was being pressured to keep the Sabbath, his mother was scandalizing the Orthodox community. About the time that Mordecai started at Baron Byng High School, a few months after the divorce, he dropped tefillin, morning prayers, and Sabbath services.[50] As for cheder, he simply stopped going.[51]

※

Baron Byng – "The brown brick building as charming as a Victorian workhouse"[52] – no longer exists, except fictionally as Fletcher Field High School, kept alive in the stories of its most disgruntled graduate. Byng belonged to the Protestant School Division and had a reputation for academic excellence. Over a thousand students attended there, 90 percent of them Jewish, the teachers nearly all Gentile.[53] Alumni included NDP Leader David Lewis, Québec Minister of Justice Herbert Marx, Communist MNA Fred Rose, poets A.M. Klein and Irving Layton, and, at the head of the class, *Star Trek*'s William Shatner.[54] While Canada was finding it too difficult to save Jews from the gas chambers by admitting them as refugees, Mordecai was learning songs such as "British Grenadiers"[55] and the Byng theme song, which asked the student to be "Constant and true in your work and your playing." A homier Yiddish version – *A mentsh zolstu zayn, sai baym spil sai baym arbet*[56] – urged the student to be "*a mentsh.*"

Mordecai was a mouthpiece with a short fuse, and these features didn't fail to cause him problems. He later claimed that he hated school[57] and that he had been a hustler. Others remember a different Mordecai: introverted and bookish.[58] Both versions were true, in schoolmate Jack Rabinovitch's opinion. *Everyone* at Byng was a hustler, says Rabinovitch, "The kids that graduated from Baron Byng either became crooks or outstanding citizens. They didn't become bank managers, *now okay*? ... Everybody was striving, because do you want to go back to the scrap metal business?"[59] Richler says that he had little patience for the classics of British literature and for his "criminally-dull English reader." Again, classmates disagree, insisting that he read every piece of literature on the curriculum before he got to the grade and that he recited British poetry very well. He had a strange relationship with one English teacher, Mr McLetchie, a Scottish veteran, who in the World War I trenches along the Somme had read Milton, Donne, Marvell, and Blake by means of a candle affixed to his helmet. All the boys, and Mordecai too, idolized "Mech" ("Mac" Jewishized with a soft, Yiddish "ch").[60] Yet when things got too quiet, Mordecai would trash the British Empire and McLetchie would blow up.[61] "Mech" would make his literary debut a decade-and-a-half later in *The Apprenticeship of Duddy Kravitz* as Mr MacPherson.[62] What ate at McLetchie, a failed novelist himself, was that Mordecai didn't seem to *enjoy* composition even though he was so good at it. Students had to read their compositions aloud, and everyone was eager to hear Mordecai's.[63] He thought about starting a literary magazine,[64] and, in grade 10 or 11, after he interviewed Toe Blake (captain of hockey's Montreal Canadiens), Mordecai considered becoming a sportswriter.[65]

Frances Katz – Miss Katz – a grade 9 drama teacher and one of Byng's few Jewish teachers, liked, in later years, to invoke the days when she taught Mordecai all he knew.[66] But according to Rabinovitch, she was nothing special, just "a fat, dumpy teacher who loved poetry ... She liked Mordecai because he was literate."[67] For his part, Richler hesitated to look upon her fondly, recalling "good-hearted but inadequate ladies who flushed at the name of Keats" and bemoaning the literary education – Auden, cummings – that he *didn't* get at Byng.[68]

Lily wasn't thrilled with Mordecai's scholarly progress – the boys, particularly her pet, Mordecai, were supposed to make up for her own truncated education, but he did poorly in mathematics and French, and wasted very little effort on subjects other than literature.[69] According to one classmate, learning was the *last* thing in Mordecai's head.[70] Lily had gotten into the habit of pointing to his more scholarly cousin, Lionel Albert, as an example of what Mordecai should do and be. "Lionel's smarter than you," she liked to say. In later years Richler was quite pleased that his success had trumped Lionel,[71] who became a computer consultant and the co-author of a book on Québec separatism. In high school, however, Mordecai was more interested in painting and drawing, and a summer course at an art gallery convinced him that he had potential.[72] He would toy, in *The Acrobats*, with the fantasy that in order to write he had spurned brilliant success as a visual artist. His realistic assessment was less sanguine: "I could have become a third-rate commercial artist."[73]

⧗

Girls, segregated into separate Byng classrooms, were the sum of his desires at that time. He did some "necking,"[74] but later gave no direct indication that he had anything in common with the sexually precocious Duddy Kravitz. In *Back to Ibiza*, Richler claims that his sex education occurred on an outing with Moe, with whom Mordecai was again on friendly terms. Moe would take the boys to a deli, followed by bowling, snooker, gin rummy, or, more often, a movie. Avrum and Mordecai would always let him win, and, though he knew what they were doing, he would slip them each a few dollars.[75] Judging by the notes to *The Rotten People*, Mordecai wasn't impressed with Avrum's changing relationship to Moe and felt that Avrum was cadging money from their father – not at all true according to Avrum.[76] Moe also took them to the Gayety to watch Lili St. Cyr do a striptease. It wasn't unusual for high-school boys to attend the Gayety, especially during matinees when management bent the rules, happy to have any paying customers at all, and when one could get into the third-floor seats for pennies.[77] But it was unusual for fathers to accompany their sons.

"You like that?" Moe asked his boy.

"Yeah," Mordecai replied.

"Me too."

After that, Richler says, he was no longer ejected from the room when the men told dirty jokes.[78]

The notes for *The Rotten People*, however, tell a different story. One of his young teachers at Talmud Torah, Evelyn Sacks, discovered that, across from the school, Mordecai's mother ran a boarding house and that one could take one's dinner there. With Sacks's husband off fighting in Europe, she was depressed and alone.[79] In the completed manuscript of *The Rotten People*, Sacks, like Frankel, is renamed – "Helen," Richler calls her, giving her the name of his later lover on Ibiza. However, in the notes to the novel she is called by her real name, Evelyn.[80] After Kerman's fistfight with his father, he visits her apartment, where she sympathizes with his difficult home life. This is how Richler put it:

> And the same time [as Frankel] something else was going on – Evelyn was going on.
> Evelyn was Kerman's young school teacher.
> Kerman was in love with Evelyn & Evelyn was in love with Kerman. Shame shame.[81]

One's initial impulse is to write off the events that follow as a schoolboy's overheated fantasy. Kerman's mother opens up a boarding house in the Laurentians, where both Frankel and Evelyn (separately) visit. She and Kerman are able to canoe out to a private spot and talk. Although she's nearly twice as old as him, she says that she can talk to him as if they were the same age, and she is, in Kerman's opinion, the most beautiful woman in the world:

> Soft, brown curly hair, & eyes & a nose. But the breasts man, the breasts big, fat & full of things always in a sweater & looking at him. Everybody teased him. So what if she was 8 yrs older than him. Can you imagine those breasts & a 13 year old boy with a capable thing all his own alone. He was afraid to do anything because he loved her … That night, that wonderful summer night, in the woods, lying together on a rock, he dared to rest his head on one of those breasts … He kissed her, so help me. Everything stopped & started again & stopped – like a lead pipe in and out. The next night in the same woods he slipped a nervous hand under the sweater & he must have held on to that wonder ~~breast~~ tit for hours. He kept his knee hard in between her thighs because (fool that he was) he thought she'd be sore if he did her proper.
> On the way home
> She: What if I went to bed with you tonight dearest?
> He: Nobody would know.
> Anyway she didn't. She cryed the next day & went home. [*sic*]

Afterwards, Kerman receives a letter in which Evelyn describes her guilt over what happened – "My dearest ... I'm a grown woman, married & you a child" – nevertheless, she insists that only with him could she sit under the stars saying nothing.[82]

Overheated fantasy – were it not for the fact that in the 1999 Accession of the Richler Papers at the University of Calgary, Richler finally released two letters from Sacks that he had held onto for almost fifty years. The letters do not allow us to say definitely that the affair had a sexual element or exactly what Mordecai's age was. However, they do establish that in his teenage years he had some sort of an affair with Sacks and that *The Rotten People* – in which "Helen" watches Kerman grow up and is forced to listen to him brag of his dates with university girls[83] – at least partially reflects that affair. In 1953, when Richler was twenty-two, Sacks wrote,

> Do you value the great love I have for you, Mordy or does your swollen conceit allow you to take it for granted. Such an affair. It would make others laugh. Never a day goes by, but you are in my thoughts, not always kindly, not always pure – but I do think of you ... And if you want to know how a frustrated woman acts, when she's approaching middle age and desires a very young man who regards as a loving woman – mother and friend – this woman becomes rude and impatient ... My husband is very grown-up, and loves me more than a little ... And I'll continue to deceive him, because I need you – whatever you have to offer ...
>
> All my love, Evelyn"[84]

Richler hadn't allowed this letter to appear in the First or Second Accessions of his papers, but the fact that he neither destroyed the letters nor *The Rotten People*, suggests that he did expect the truth about Sacks to come out eventually and that he believed that the affair had some bearing on his writing.

In *The Rotten People*, Richler renamed Evelyn "Helen" and added a lot of detail, turning her into more of a composite and imagined figure. Certainly the extension of the Helen/Kerman relationship in Europe is entirely fictional. At age nineteen, Kerman invites Helen to Paris. She leaves her present lover, joins Kerman, and he very soon tires of her, going so far as to imagine throwing her off a cliff into the sea. None of this later, imaginary material appears in the notes, where Evelyn is called by her real name. The added details include coitus, before "Helen" cuts him off because she fears ruining his life. He becomes infuriated.[85] Judging by the notes to *The Rotten People* and the hints in *Barney's Version*, there was no coitus, but his interest in sex was both heightened and frustrated, and his subsequent sexual aggressiveness with girls his own age[86] implies that he had some degree of sexual experience before age sixteen. The affair does give new meaning to the sexually precocious Ephraim Gursky and to all the hotcha schoolteachers in Richler's fiction, from Miss Ryerson in *Cocksure* to Miss Oglivy near the end of his life in *Barney's Version*. Preparing for *Barney's Version*, he clipped a couple of newspaper articles about a British teacher who engaged in sex with her teenage students, and he circled (among other things) the judge's considered opinion that the boys hadn't been harmed but had enjoyed the attentions.[87]

Given that Richler, later in life, had no patience for therapeutic interpretations of the self – I'm the way I am "because ... my father was in a hotel room with a hooker somewhere"[88] – Richler evidently "refused" to feel injured by either his mother's affair or his own relationship with Sacks. It seems that Lily's affair helped to awaken a precocious sexuality in Mordecai and to lead him into a relationship with Evelyn. At the same time, the notes to *The Rotten People* – "like a lead pipe in and out"[89] – suggest that his affair with Evelyn raised the spectre of Lily's affair, in a feedback loop of stronger, more conflicted feelings about both affairs. During his own pleasures, he couldn't entirely put out of his mind the repulsive sounds of his mother's pleasure. Still, if he enjoyed his times with Evelyn, why shouldn't his mother be similarly free to enjoy Frankel? Then again, his mother's affair ripped apart their home; in that case, how could he feel entirely pleased about his own affair with Evelyn? Like his eventual hero Hemingway, Richler chose the traditional masculine solution to personal wounds: he'd not blubber, he'd posture. Being picked out by an older woman was slightly disturbing – was there something wrong with her that she desired an adolescent boy? – and of course an immense ego-boost. Mordecai had always had the largest share of his mother's affection, and, if that love had lost some of its exchange value in adultery, he now had a young attractive schoolteacher to announce his worth. No wonder that Richler soon felt the urge to write. He had raw material churning inside, and he knew that he was somebody significant.

As for the non-sexual details in *The Rotten People*, they are difficult to assess. Kerman's battle with his grandfather (found in the notes as well as in the novel) comes directly from Richler's life, but it's difficult to judge whether Kerman's intellectual biography (found only in the novel) draws on Richler's own life. At age twelve, Kerman starts to write a novel and gives up three days later. Next he decides to become a doctor and buys subscriptions to two different medical journals. Stumbling through the first few pages of the first issue, he puts the journal down, not even bothering to unwrap the other issues. Books he reads halfway through, before casting them aside.

As well, Kerman's pre-romance behaviour in Helen's classroom – the account is *not* intended to be satiric – has far too much of the nineteen-year-old writer's self-aggrandizing to be taken as biographical:

> The pale skinny Adler kid who had a reputation in school for being brilliant but uncontrollable, shrewd and possesor [*sic*] of a malicious adult tongue. From the very first moment he stepped in – leering and stooping like an old man – she was afraid of him. First she tried to ignore him, then when this didn't work she tried to reward him with favours, but it was no use. Whatever she did he laughed at her and being in class with him became a horror. He corrected her when she did arithmetic problems on the board and argued with her over the pronounciation [*sic*] of words. Once she heaved him out of the classroom but he smirked so triumphantly she never dared do it again.[90]

The evidence suggests that Richler's surprising, precocious "success" with Sacks stimulated him as a male and as an embryonic writer. About this time he got hold of a pipe and set up shop as "an English literary dilettante" by reading doorstop-sized books such as H.G. Wells's *Outline of History* in public places.[91] He began to write stories, one about an anti-Semitic bully who is rescued from drowning by a stranger. The bully asks the name of his saviour. The answer: "Isadore Lipschitz. But you can call me Izzy."[92] It may well have been Sacks's pangs of conscience that sent Richler packing off to Europe, in search of Bohemia, Henry Miller's Paris, and, as Richler would later claim, girls who "did."[93]

By the time he reaches Europe, Kerman has changed from a boy into "a sicker being, more complex and less uninhibited"[94] [*sic*]; and if we smile at the *Weltschmerz* and the deficiencies in the young novelist's expression ("less *un*-inhibited"), the affair with Sacks certainly added turmoil to a life that already had plenty to spare. For him sex would never be an uncomplicated thing that required little explanation, or a negligible thing that could be dispensed with in explaining male motivations. His early (high school) fiction was formulaic and avoided the things that really disturbed him. Only slowly did he come round to addressing them, yet part of the greatness of Richler's fiction is that he confronted his wounds directly in the early novels, then with increasing literary sophistication and indirection in the later works. With a high degree of literalism, he would address Lily's affair and his own affair in *The Rotten People*, but unsuccessfully so, forcing him to become canny and oblique. He would deal with Sacks again in *Son of a Smaller Hero*, this time putting her in a spot – professor's wife – where she would be incognito. Only in the last novel of his life would Richler place her back in her original spot, as his schoolteacher, and even then the real woman would remain almost unrecognizable because she corresponds so perfectly with a common male fantasy.

≶

In high school, Mordecai became conscious of Zionism too, though by default, in place of Sacks and the unavailable girls. He joined the Labour-Zionist youth organization Habonim, literally "the builders."[95] In the 1930s, politically minded young Jews joined the Young Communist League; by the 1940s, the first resort had become the Zionist movement[96] – Bene Akiva and Mizrachi for the Orthodox, Habonim for Leftists. The Nuremburg trials and the increasing postwar Jewish emigration to Palestine hadn't produced neutral observers in Canada. The British still occupied Palestine as a protectorate; between 1945 and 1947, Jewish terrorists struck not only at Arabs but also at isolated groups of British soldiers. Finally, on St. Valentine's Day 1947, British Foreign Secretary Ernest Bevin gifted the Palestinian problem to the UN.[97] Avrum, in the process of beginning an optometry practice in Montreal, had little time for Zionism, but Mordecai jumped in with both feet.[98]

Habonim's purpose was to help establish Eretz Yisrael, the state of Israel, and to encourage Jews to emigrate there – to "make *aliyah*."[99] Mordecai's group was led by Ezra Lifshitz, an Engineering student at McGill. Richler would later declare less than idealistic motives, saying that he joined because his friend, Murray Greenberg, a star athlete, was a Zionist. No doubt the adolescent's canny assessment of what's fashionable played a role in his decision: Richler in his best writing never forgot adolescent motivations or, indeed, their second life as adult "principles." However, his demythologizing claims come from a period after he had largely rejected Zionism. The evidence suggests that he began quite earnestly, helped along by George Eliot's *Daniel Deronda*, which he received from one of his mother's boarders.[100] The extended Richler family had no direct quarrel with Zionism but tended to support Bene Akiva or Mizrachi over Habonim, whose members could be seen riding bikes on the Sabbath.[101] Richler says that Shmarya complained about the noise that the marching and singing chaverim (comrades) made,[102] but more likely it was their laissez-faire attitude towards Orthodox observance that he resented.

Of course, Sabbath bike-riding wasn't a stumbling-block for Mordecai. In fact, one of the reasons that Mordecai joined Habonim, where he wasn't obligated to pronounce a blessing before meals, was because it would be sure to annoy Shmarya.[103] In many ways, Habonim operated as a social club for young Jews. The chaverim listened to speakers together, sang and danced the hora, and raised money for the future Israeli state.[104] Mordecai helped by stuffing envelopes[105] and, less officially, by making harassing phone calls

to a Jewish doctor who opposed Zionism.[106] At the same time, Habonim
opened up Mordecai's political consciousness. With his friends Greenberg,
Earl Kruger, and Walter Tannenbaum, Richler sat in the clubhouse at 5392
Jeanne Mance and argued about Zionism, socialism, and Communism.[107]

Like the other chaverim, Mordecai planned, someday, to make aliyah.
Some of his friends did; some didn't.[108] North American Zionists, astute
about the quality of their lives – soft, according to one of Mordecai's Zionist teachers[109] – tended to send money but had the lowest freely chosen aliyah
rates in the world.[110] Richler claims that preparing to fight for Eretz Yisrael
he lied about his age and joined the Canadian reserve army, but that an Israeli emissary told him to finish high school first.[111] Avrum is skeptical of
the story: if Mordecai had been in the reserves, Avrum would have known
about it.[112] In fact, it was the Baron Byng air cadets that he joined, Squadron
241, but only briefly. No lies needed about one's birth date. They did target
practice in the school basement and a bit of marching, though it's doubtful
whether Mordecai actually took part in the weapons training. He wasn't really a big one for group activities.[113]

St. Urbain's Horseman may in part be read as Richler's reply to his
younger Zionist self, as an explanation of why it was providential that he
never did immigrate to Israel. And what would Mordecai Richler have done
in Zion? Fifty years earlier, Baron Maurice de Hirsch was already complaining to Theodor Herzl that Palestine needed agricultural workers, not more
intellectuals.[114] An urban person, as far from the kibbutzim as one could
imagine, Richler was on the fast track to becoming an intellectual – he had
the pipe, he had the five-pound books. Within a year, Richler, writing a student newspaper article cheering for the newly formed state of Israel, sensed
precisely this problem: "How long these idealistic intellectuals will be satisfied as mere tillers of the soil is doubtful."[115] Still, Habonim was an important stage in Richler's development and secularization. It made him part of
something larger, part of a yes-saying group rather than just one of a loose
group of Orthodoxy's dissenters at the Rachel.

In 1947 this was especially important. Shmarya died, and Mordecai, at
Lily's request, attended the funeral. There his Uncle Joe told him that in his
will Shmarya had directed that Mordecai, a bad Jew, shouldn't touch his
coffin. On his own initiative, the uncle added that Mordecai hadn't spoken
to Shmarya during Shmarya's illness and had perhaps hastened Shmarya's
death.[116] "Chilling," Richler called the voice that condemned him from beyond the grave.[117] Though he appealed to Moe for help, he got none.[118] Others – his slightly older uncles Bernard and Max, and his brother Avrum –
remember neither the incident nor any such clause in Shmarya's will,[119] and
Bernard doesn't even remember Mordecai attending the funeral. Richler himself got the date wrong, placing his grandfather's death in 1945, when he

was fourteen rather than sixteen.[120] Still, the incident has the ring of truth. Aunts and uncles no longer invited him to family functions,[121] and his closest companion at one time, David, would have nothing to do with him. Only Max (who would eventually officiate at Richler's funeral) and Bernard remained close. In later years, Mordecai's grandmother Esther (Shmarya's widow) was asked what she thought about Mordecai. All the Baba had to say was, *"Ehr drinkt, ehr pisht"* ("he drinks, he pisses").[122]

If Mordecai was being shunned by many of the Richlers, Habonim was a new home, bringing him solidarity and even, on occasion, euphoria. When Baron Byng welcomed Malcolm MacDonald, British colonial secretary and eldest son of former British PM Ramsay MacDonald, Mordecai joined his Zionist friends in refusing to stand or sing "God Save the King." This because MacDonald had placed severe restrictions on immigration to Palestine.[123] At the end of November 1947, lobbied by the Truman administration, the UN voted 33–13 to divide Palestine 50/50 between Jews and Arabs.[124] Although the Arabs turned down the compromise, and the proposed Jewish homeland was almost territorially indefensible, the vote was nothing less than a colossal victory,[125] paving the way for independence six months later. After the partition vote, Mordecai marched with Habonim down St. Catherine Street in downtown Montreal waving Israeli flags, singing "Am Yisrael Chai" ("The People of Israel Lives"), and dancing the hora.[126]

≶

Sometime near the end of high school, Mordecai moved in with Avrum to an apartment behind Avrum's optometry office on Sherbrooke Street West.[127] Nights Mordecai spotted pins at the Park Bowling Academy.[128] Lily paid the rent on the apartment, and on paper she lived there too, but she had bought a guesthouse at Ste-Agathe in the Laurentians and spent most of her time there – which left the boys were pretty much on their own.[129] Mordecai had no patience for the bourgeois life that his brother was embarking on, and the autobiographical notes to *The Rotten People* show Kerman's contempt for his brother's fledgling business, though by the time Mordecai would write those notes, he would be asking Avrum for money.[130]

The guesthouse in Ste-Agathe – Rosenberg's Lakeside Inn – Lily managed to keep afloat for a number of years, until the early 1950s.[131] "A nothing place," Bernard Richler called it. With six or seven rooms, each housing a family, upwards of thirty people could be shoe-horned in on any given summer day. Lily, a highly skilled cook, made meals. Avrum chopped onions and liver and did repairs, while Mordecai, like Duddy Kravitz, waited on tables and, unlike the outsider Duddy, lorded it over the other boys who worked there. Avrum and Mordecai slaved from 5:00 A.M. on. According to Mordecai's friends Avrum was rarely there; according to Avrum, Mordecai took a lot of time off. He loved fishing and swimming, and sometimes when he was supposed to be working he could be found off in a rowboat or getting into mischief with Dave Gursky.[132] The guesthouse clientele consisted mostly of Outremont Jews[133]; in Ste-Agathe Mordecai was again learning (if not quite as graphically as Duddy) what it meant to belong to a lower class. Orthodox Jews, including Max Richler, avoided Lily's guesthouse because it wasn't kosher.[134]

In Montreal, too, Lily no longer tortured her scruples about kashrut or the Sabbath, her views changing as her circumstances changed. Avrum arranged a job for her (1949–53) managing the office of what she called "a nightclub"[135] – the Esquire Show Club to be exact, a strip-joint owned by the "Jewish Mafia." Her jobs "mellowed" her Hasidism, she said. When the working world requested that she ride the bus and work on the Sabbath, she discovered a more liberal attitude in herself, bringing taunts from her sons, "Ma! What are you doing?" "Well, you know," she defended herself, "when you have to you have to." Says Avrum, "She made her own rules."[136] At the same time, Lily tried to convince "her strong-willed boys" to observe festivals. They would decide on a festival but then fail to observe it and instead laid down the law for her: "Behave or we marry out of the faith."[137] Wavering parental control suited Mordecai just fine. He was now often on his own – schoolwork and Sabbath be damned – haunting "the pool halls, bowling alleys, cinemas and snack bars near Baron Byng."[138] For a long time, Mordecai had taken his news from his mother, above all her strong will and her readiness to defy inconvenient rules, and as he became disillusioned with her notion of bourgeois success, he sought ways of plunging into some other world.

5

A Losers' Finishing School

IN JUNE 1948 RICHLER graduated from Byng as president – no one else wanted the job – of his grade 11 class.[1] Grade 11 was enough to get one into a Québec university in those days, but he hadn't studied much, and his marks were too poor to open the doors of McGill (at least until his honorary doctorate in 2000).[2] Jews needed a 75 percent average. With a 65 percent average and a 35 percent in Trigonometry "artificially inflated by cramming the night before," Richler couldn't have entered McGill even if he weren't circumcised.[3] The booby prize for loafing was English Literature at what he called a "loser's finishing school,"[4] Sir George Williams University, now part of Concordia.

In Sir George, Richler turned into the kind of left-wing bohemian that he had been aiming at throughout high school. He bought a blue beret but didn't wear it if anyone was around.[5] He grew his hair longer. A "very skinny" boy with a "great mass of curly hair, like the mother on The Simpsons" is what Mavis Gallant remembers[6]: Kerman's vanity about his long unruly brown hair in *The Rotten People* clearly belonged to the author.[7] Richler fell in with a group of slightly older Gentile friends, his first, who fostered his bohemianism,[8] took him to Italian restaurants, and invited him up to the Orange Crate, an apartment on Côte St. Antoine where ultra-sophisticated women such as Kina Mitchell and Joan Cassidy – *third-year* undergrads – held court.[9] They sat till 4 A.M. reading poetry and listening to classical records. He found out that he could get a laugh with stories of Orthodox drolleries, such as rotating the live rooster over his head or hiding Passover wine lest Gentiles eyes see it and render it treif.[10] According to his Jewish classmates from Byng, Richler no longer even acknowledged them in the halls of Sir George.[11] Angry and intense, he loved to argue at parties, though he felt out of place.[12] He met the principals of *Northern Review* (Canada's foremost literary magazine, even though its circulation was only four hundred) just as editor John Sutherland, who had a flat-bed press in his basement, was consolidating his grip. Poets such as Patrick Anderson, F.R. Scott, and eventually Irving Layton were in the process of divorcing themselves from *Northern Review* in protest against Sutherland's authoritarian and anti-cosmopolitan editorial policies. But what Richler remembered were "rambunctious, hard-drinking evenings."[13]

T.S. Eliot, ee cummings, W.H. Auden, opera: these Richler encountered for the first time through his new friends.[14] It's hard to underestimate the influence cummings, especially, had. For several years after leaving Sir George, Richler would write in lowercase, labouring ever so hard to make his style seem loose and hip. Scraping by in "yurop" as he called it,[15] Richler years later would complain, "i'm just in the mood to get crazy drunk. feel completely sterile, impotent, hopeless. oooooh dos arty blues!!"[16] cummings' style came to represent a kind of beatific response to worn-out educational and political institutions, and it's unlikely that Richler would have ever broken through to his mature style without passing through cummings first. The Romantics dominated literary education in Canada, and even the previous generation of Montreal writers – F.R. Scott and A.M. Klein, for example – had in the late 1940s barely begun the process of shucking that influence. For a young bohemian choked by Romanticism, cummings was just the ticket: Romantic enough to be emotionally comprehensible to a generation schooled in that movement, yet formally modern enough to pass as a revolutionary. He provided Richler a transition into the more austere modernists. For a long time much of Richler's writing would be brash and juvenile, but his early experimentation was a necessary step, a freeing from the dead hand of the past, a launching of him towards the colloquial Jewish style of his maturity.

There's no doubt that Richler's dig at the "good-hearted but inadequate ladies who flushed at the name of Keats" was also a dig at his mother. She loved Keats.[17] Richler would come to see this as an emblem of her literary pretension,[18] but there's little evidence that he thought so in high school. His mother from the beginning was the one who championed his writing.[19] The modernists he hadn't yet read. Indeed, apart from a bit of misdirection, Richler's delightful "Some Grist for Mervyn's Mill,"[20] a satire at the expense of a young romantic who sets himself up as a writer, is autobiographical – inflated and fictionalized, but still autobiographical. Richler wrote it in 1961, when he was thirty. With the father and mother clearly resembling Moe and Lily, one might reasonably expect the unnamed adolescent narrator, their son, to be Mordecai. And so he is. But Mervyn, the young adult boarder from Toronto, is also Mordecai, and in a more immediate way. Affecting a pipe and avoiding books so as not to be influenced, he prepares himself to write, novice though he is, a magnum opus. In Richler's little *roman à clef* touches, the father calls Mervyn "Moitle" behind his back,[21] Mordecai's old nickname. And Mervyn clings to the self-deluding belief that his book has been rejected because of a homosexual cabal, reproducing Richler's own 1951 complaints in France.[22] The mother is happy to slave so that her Mervyn – clearly a genius, since he discusses Shakespeare – can write, while the Moe-like despised father wonders why Mervyn can't *work* for a living.[23] Once the mother, however, discovers that Mervyn hasn't been writing in the style of her father of blessed rabbinic memory and hasn't been following her scrub-editing advice (to replace "whores" with "ladies of easy virtue," for example) her admiration wanes. The uneasiness of Mervyn's relation to his father is the uneasiness that would characterize Mordecai's relation to Moe once Mordecai had attained a measure of success: Does my father have time for me now because I'm writing movie scripts? All told, the story is Richler's jaundiced view of his own younger self.

Despite new friends and exciting new writing, Richler later insisted that "being 17 or 18 is not something I'd like to go through again."[24] "Some Grist for Mervyn's Mill" tells us why. He felt that he was desperately naïve. He wanted to be a writer[25] but had barely begun to read modern writers. He wanted to pass on what he knew, but his marks suggested that he did-n't know very much. Anyway, the sorts of things he wanted to know weren't being taught in university. He wanted to escape the narrowness of his Or-thodox upbringing, but he still couldn't get rid of an earnestness of manner. He wanted to escape his parents' poverty and their tight intellectual hori-zon, but he was still Moitle. His parents' Yiddish accents galled him[26] – strangely, because others don't remember Moe and Lily's accents as partic-ularly strong.[27] In this new world, Richler was being tuned to such a fine pitch by Anglo culture that even the smallest deviation grated on him. Li-onel Albert suggests that what troubled Mordecai was that Moe's accent was common, the sort of voice you'd expect to hear from a taxi driver.[28] Mordecai had no plans to be common. He had told Bernard that he was going to be somebody,[29] and now he was discovering how impossible that might be. A friend, Stuart, particularly, reminded him. Stuart was "scathing" about Richler's "mannerisms" and lack of knowledge of the world.[30] The two young men drank together, and when Stuart was drunk, these things would come out.

Women, too, were still a problem. Once, through a *Herald* interview of a stripper named Candy Parker, Richler got a date for Stuart and himself with two girls who called themselves "The Daughters of Fun." The expected orgy fizzled, and though Richler later made light of it, the two young "men without women" ended up consoling each other over a bottle of scotch.[31]

Whenever the older Richler looks back on the younger, it is with the eyes of Stuart, and what he sees is mostly ignorance, the naïve boy he escaped only with great deal of pain.

In 1948–49 that younger self encountered Truman Capote, Norman Mailer, Tennessee Williams, Graham Greene, Jean-Paul Sartre, Carson Mc-Cullers, A.J. Perelman, and, above all, André Malraux's *La Condition Humaine* (*Man's Fate*). Also the *New Statesman*, which made Richler rage inwardly at prejudice and injustice.[32] Also, he claimed, the *Partisan Review*, *Commentary*, *Kenyon Review*, and *New Yorker*,[33] though one might be forgiven for suspecting that he didn't come to some of these periodicals until he was in Europe. Had he read Mike Gold by this time? There's no conclusive evidence as to the date of first contact, but at some point Richler began to admire him.[34] Among other things, Gold (born Itzok Granich, New York, 1893) had written the kind of socialist literary manifesto, "Towards a Proletarian Art," that the young Richler was inclined to take very seriously: "We cling to the old culture, and fight for it against ourselves. But it must die ... Seeking God we find Man, ever and ever."[35] On a sheet marked "feb 6 1949," Richler had scribbled similar thoughts: "it is mankind that created god, not god that created mankind." Signed "mr mr."[36] And farther down the same, mostly blank, page, "what is good is most times bad and what is alive is ussually [*sic*] dead," again signed "mr." Gold had listed the qualifications required for a new sort of writer: "a wild youth of about twenty-two, the son of working-class parents, who himself works in the lumber camps, coal mines ... He is sensitive and impatient. He writes in jets of exasperated feeling and has no time to polish his work. He is violent and sentimental by turns. He lacks self-confidence but writes because he must – and because he has real talent. He is a Red but has few theories."[37] Gold, of course, meant himself, but he could have been describing young Mordecai Richler. Before Richler wrote anything of value, he had to imagine himself as a certain kind of writer, and what he imagined was a writer ready to overthrow the social order – politically, spiritually, artistically.

In contrast with the undomesticated imaginings of Richler's private self, his public voice was measured. He caught on with the university student paper, the *Georgian*, and, in addition to obligatory articles on the Georgian Ski Carnival, he wrote about Zionism. "Israel is one of the few miracles of modern times," he declares, "the great work of an inspired and fearless people." Some of the phraseology, quite foreign to his own developing consciousness, Richler clearly lifted from elsewhere: "the first monotheists of this world once again pray in the land where Abraham, their father, is buried." Other observations – "a people who have not tasted military victory since the rebellion of Judas Maccabeus ... once more have tasted the dangerous fruits of military victory" – come with similar phraseology, yet capture ac-

curately the ambivalence that the young leftist felt about the Arab-Israeli
War. He meditates on the problem of Stern Gang terrorism, concluding that
in the grand scheme of things the Holocaust carries more weight. In the end,
he predicts an imminent peace settlement between Arab and Israeli.[38]

The work on the *Georgian* Richler managed to parlay into work for the
Canadian High News and for the now-defunct *Montreal Herald*. The new
job paid less than spotting pins.[39] Nevertheless, there was a certain gratifi-
cation at seeing one's name in a citywide newspaper, and he saved the clippings. Richler wasn't a real reporter, more of a stringer passing on small
stories about Sir George, the sort of PR exercise that newspapers run every
so often in order to lure young potential customers. He did whatever story
the full-time reporters felt was beneath them[40] – stories on college basket-
ball, on Sadie Hawkins Day Week, and on lecturers coming through Sir
George to announce that universities were too materialistic or that mate
choosing was getting harder for the modern generation. Democratic family
relations were on the horizon, Moe would have been interested to hear,
rather than "father-is-the-boss."[41]

But there was also considerable leeway for Richler to write about things
that interested him. He reviewed Gayety "comediennes" as well as performances of *The Dybbuk* and Sholom Aleichem's *It's Hard to Be a Jew*,
two of the more significant plays to come out of the Pale of Settlement. He
wrote about Jewish refugees in English classes, where a survivor of Belsen
concentration camp, Mrs Eva Kupfert, showed him the convict number
stamped on her arm. He reported on a lecturer who analyzed the shift of
Chinese youth towards Mao Tse Tung. Richler even revealed some incipi-
ent satire, writing about "smugglers" who capitalized on margarine price
differentials between provinces. Crossing the Ontario border, "Canada's
'margarine curtain,'" one smuggler says, "I was feeling very cocky and sure
of myself, until the train I was on neared the Ontario frontier."[42] By his
second year, Richler opened the McGill door a crack, covering such events
as the "Mr Hillel" contest for the *Hillel McGillah*, the newspaper of the
McGill Hillel Foundation.

More earnest were the leftist pieces he wrote about Sir George's "Red
Dean" controversy. Already in high school, Richler had become militant in
his socialism, painting election posters for a Byng alumnus, the communist
MP Fred Rose.[43] Now Richler joined his older Gentile friends calling for nuclear disarmament through the Stockholm Peace Appeal (later exposed as a
communist front), for an end to the Korean War, and ("God forgive us," he
eventually pled) for the election of US presidential candidate Henry Wallace,[44]
a former vice-president, forced from office by Roosevelt after speaking against
the administration's policy on the USSR. The young armchair radicals in Sir
George's student union, of which Richler was a member, scrabbled their way

into these world events by inviting Hewlett Johnson, the "Red" Dean (not Archbishop) of Canterbury to campus. Although some faculty supported the students, the YMCA Board of Governors (which ran the university) refused permission because Johnson advocated the nationalization of industry and had become an apologist for Stalin. Richler reported on the board's decision and on the three-hundred-signature student petition contra. By the age of eighteen, Richler had mastered the reporter's technique of slanting the news by judicious quotation: "The real issue, claimed one student, is whether we are old enough to make up our own minds about communism."[45] In *The Georgian's* "Student Forum," a high-toned response came from "the activated freshman, Mordecai Richler": "As a student who has grown up and lived in the free environment of democracy, I believe that any suppression of freedom of opinion would not only be adverse to the teachings of democracy, but also a most dangerous sacrilege."[46] Richler's political involvement, like his Zionism, was an important phase, tying him to the larger world that he would never escape, for all his later disillusionments.

Despite his involvement in student life, Richler ultimately grew bored in his second year.[47] He failed in an attempt to become editor-in-chief of *The Georgian*,[48] and many of his friends graduated, including the veterans whose yarns had made Sir George an interesting place.[49] Richler went to a psychologist for some aptitude tests.[50] He'd never be a scholar or a writer, he was advised. Try business.[51] He dropped out of university. Avrum thought that Richler was perhaps expelled over an article he wrote,[52] but that wasn't the case. Richler later maintained that he left because he feared that a BA would lead to an MA would lead to a PhD, the squirrel wheel that certain of his *Northern Review* friends were on.[53] Yet he protested vehemently that he wasn't a dropout in the 1960s sense.[54] Truth be told, he wasn't in danger of being lumbered with a Master's or a doctorate, and the real explanation was much simpler: he didn't know what he wanted to do. Post-facto rationalizations notwithstanding, he *was* a dropout in the 1960s sense, though by the time the 60s actually came round, he had moved on ideologically. In 1949 he wanted to be one of the avant-garde and felt, probably correctly, that university would deaden him with formality and information.

≶

After dropping out, Richler had no idea what to do next. Briefly – he only lasted a week – he wrote copy and did few cartoons for an ad agency.[55] Others were moving on, Moe getting married,[56] Avrum too. Richler stood as best man for his brother. "Can you picture him in tails?" asks Avrum. "White tie with a top hat?"[57] The new developments seemed designed to leave Richler alone with his doting mother, a prospect he no longer relished. He applied for, but didn't get, a job editing a monthly fashion magazine.[58] He was writing but was still too shy to show his work to others[59] – wisely so, judging by "John D. – a Guy with a Rep," a sub-Hemingway story that probably dates from this period: "If you don't know how to play snooker than [sic] one table is as good as another. Then again, if you're a money player, and every stroke means more to you than hot blonde on Saturday night, or even a good bottle of Canadian rye, then when you played at Tony's, you'd insist on the first table from the door."[60] Steely, grey-eyed John D. is goaded into playing a game for $1,000. After some thrilling play-by-play, Richler abandoned the story mid-game.

He wanted to leave St. Urbain Street. From the example of Hemingway, Faulkner, and Callaghan, Richler knew that the proper thing for a young writer to do was to get the hell over to Paris. Callaghan's case, especially, was salutary. He had proved that Canadians could not only write and hobnob with Hemingway and Fitzgerald where the action was but could also, given a chance, punch out macho Ernest.[61] When John Sutherland heard that both Mavis Gallant and Richler were planning for Paris, he invited them to lunch together and introduced them to each other. Gallant, already a journalist for the *Montreal Standard* (later to become the *Star*), was "a glamorous figure" to Richler,[62] and the meeting certainly did nothing to cure him of the Europe bug.

Mordecai had been told that he could write well, and he had enough inspiration from the community and from his parents for any number of novels. The Orthodox community and the extended Richler family had made his father puny – Richler wanted revenge for that, revenge that he at first thought would come when he turned into a Hemingway, but that he later realized could come much more directly by exploring community and familial tensions in fiction. His mother in her affair had betrayed him and had shamefully exposed her privacies, not only to social mockery, but also more directly, to her son's ears. In many ways, especially in his stubbornness and his critical spirit, he was becoming, and feared becoming, a copy of his mother. Writing could solidify the distance between them and reveal that he was a sophisticate, a free male.

He knew that his departure would be hardest on her. First Frankel's abandonment, then Moe's and Avrum's marriages, now Mordecai's departure. The feelings that Kerman in *The Rotten People* and Noah in *Son of a Smaller Hero* have about leaving their mothers for Europe were Richler's feelings. Noah decides, "I'm not going to replace [my father] for her."[63] After the divorce, Mordecai had sided with his affectionate though eccentric mother[64] against his ineffectual father, who had abandoned him to Shmarya's wrath. The fistfight had cemented that identification, but only for a while. Now that Moe, living down the street, had become less of an authority figure, more of a companion and money-source, Mordecai sensed what other men had always sensed: that his lumpen proletarian father[65] was a lot of fun.[66] Occasionally, Mordecai threatened to leave home unless Lily treated Moe with respect.[67] It was Lily, more than anyone, who had nurtured Mordecai's talent; still, in the wake of Frankel, the more he sensed her increasing emotional investment in him, the less inclined he was to reciprocate, and the more he took Moe's side. These shifting alliances, combined with Lily's hectoring about one thing or another, made the break easier.

Still, Avrum was surprised when Mordecai announced that he was going to Europe to write. "Gee, Mottie," Avrum said, "I always thought you were going to be an artist." Avrum predicted that his younger brother would last six weeks in Europe, maximum.[68] Moe wasn't sold on the idea either. At the time, Richler had no inkling of the animal called artistic distance, that in Europe he'd be able to write freely about Montreal. At this point, Montreal just seemed far too mundane. In Europe ... in Europe ... there would be plenty to write about. Wasn't there, Moe prodded his son, enough to write about in Montreal? Richler thought not: "I assured my family that they were small ordinary people, not the sort Andre Malraux would bother about. 'You know everything,' my father said. I could not disagree."[69] The older writer could laugh at such posturing, but it took a while. His first two novels, unpublished and published, would be set in Paris and Spain; his third in Montreal, just to get Canada and childhood "out of his system," he assured his friends; his fourth in London. Although Richler would find his mature "Montreal" voice in his fifth novel, *The Apprenticeship of Duddy Kravitz*, as late as his sixth and seventh novels, he was still hankering to be the cosmopolitan who wrote mainly about places other than home. Only with his four last and greatest works did he fully understand that what other people called The Muse was, for him, no more and no less than St. Urbain Street, and that his experiences in Spain, Paris, and London could be understood only through a window in St. Urbain Street. "That was my time, my place," he would acknowledge, many years later, "and I have elected myself to get it right."[70]

Resigned to a son he never would really understand, Moe nevertheless lent Richler his blue steamer trunk.[71] Richler scraped together the necessary cash – some from a small insurance policy his mother had taken out at his birth, some from Bernard, some from Avrum , and some from Moe.[72]

During that last summer in Canada, Richler again waited on tables at Lily's guesthouse, often disappearing into a little side-room to write.[73] He also begged Sam Stick, owner of the Castle des Monts Hotel, for a job as a busboy and eventually waited on tables for $35 a week.[74] But his mind was already far afield. Every night after work, he says, he lay down on the lawn with a beer.[75] In the Laurentians, where once Yudel and Lily had laid plans – never fulfilled – to escape Canada, Richler now imagined another sort of escape, not aliyah to Palestine, but out of tiefste Provinz and across the Atlantic to the centre of the universe. Armed with his History professor's testimony that he was "keen and alert ... a definite asset in class discussions,"[76] a certificate from his English professor, Neil Compton, declaring him of sound moral character,[77] and a letter from the managing editor of *Montreal Herald* stating that he had been "loyal, industrious, and ... a sober employee,"[78] Richler put St. Urbain behind him and set sail for Liverpool.

PART II

yurop
1950–1972

"o yes, the reason why you probably never heard my name ... is
that prior to my sailing for yurop in 1950 my activities – artistic,
political, etc – were confined to the university and the mtl herald.
i'm only twenty-one."
– Richler, letter to Ted Allen, 1952

6

Bohemia among the Fishermen: Ibiza

RICHLER CROSSED THE ATLANTIC in September 1950, backtracking partway over the Yiddish flight westwards of his grandparents, returning to Europe, continent of pogroms and gas ovens.[1] His Habonim leader, Ezra Lipschitz had made aliyah to Israel that same year, and Richler felt a brief pang of guilt that he might be getting off at the wrong port.[2] He was journeying *outward*. When Robertson Davies, in the late 1930s, went to Britain, he went there to become British; he went "home," to learn how to be. Richler, less than a full generation later, went to Europe as an American revolutionary. This difference would inhabit their novels. Davies allied himself to the past, and his novels made explicit homage, for example, to the Virgin Mary's continuing significance, to Rabelais and his world, to Renaissance artistic practice, and to Arthurian Britain.[3] Richler, in contrast, allied himself to the future; he *wanted* to lay waste to the Jewish tradition, and especially in his early work he tried to bomb his past. This would eventually make Richler a more intense and moving writer than Davies, as Richler struggled in his mature work to articulate a way of being that didn't depend on the Torah but that wasn't entirely sold out to the new.

Richler sailed with Terry McEwen, a fellow Sir George alumnus and fledgling music producer who eventually became head of the San Francisco Opera.[4] The voyage on the steamship *Franconia* was sick-making,[5] and Liverpool no great prize either, everything small and grimy.[6] Within a week, Richler was lonely and miserable.[7]

A couple of weeks later, he pressed on towards Paris. On his first night there, he went to the Café de Flore, sat down at a table, and pulled out his notebook and pen.[8] Mordecai Richler, European sophisticate: the image had been forming in his mind. In one undated TV play, "The Lamplight of Paris," probably written early on in Paris (or in Montreal shortly before his departure), two naïve young Canadians, Tom and Artie, happen upon an older

European, "Monsieur Eric Richler." He whispers of a treasure buried since the war in Mannheim. Because he can't cross the German border, the treasure is inaccessible. Tom and Artie hurry to Mannheim, dig by the light of the moon, and are discovered at the moment that they open the box. No gold inside, only a skull. In the ensuing melee, Tom is shot, while Artie escapes back to Paris. "Yes, I wanted that body found," breathes the elusive Mr Richler when Artie finally locates him. It's the body of Mr Richler's brother, "Hans Richter" [sic]. An ss officer is presently on trial for murdering a subordinate, Mr Richler reveals, but the prosecution had no body.[9] Now they have a body. Mordecai Richler, international man of intrigue, already avenging the six million.

Parisian reality was far less glamorous. Later Richler would mythologize his hotel room in St. Germain des Prés, describing it as a former Wehrmacht brothel,[10] but Richler's acquaintance James Baldwin came closer to the truth: "The sordid French hotel room, so admirably detailed by the camera, speaking, in its quaintness, and distance, so beautifully of romance, undergoes a sea-change, becomes a room positively hostile to romance, once it is oneself, and not Jean Gabin, who lives there."[11] Richler's room was up a dark flight of stairs off a court. It was unheated, requiring sweaters, scarf, and toque,[12] and was infested with mice, their droppings materializing on his sweaters. At the cinema one could contract fleas in the cheap seats.[13] Soon Richler would describe Paris in *The Acrobats*, intending a pithy statement about the new zeitgeist but producing instead an unwitting testament to the loneliness of a young St. Urbain boy: "Only the fifty year old menchildren returning for maybe the first time since the twenties, attempted to renew the calculated idiocy of their youth abroad, only they boozed until 6 A.M. in Montmartre. This newer generation, their children, gazed on the pathetic festivities wearily but indulgently, sitting sad and unknowing in the cafés, sitting, saying nothing and going nowhere, today being only the inevitable disappointment of yesterday's tomorrow, waiting, waiting for something they were at a loss to explain."[14] A few friends and a year on a sunny island later, at least one member of the newer generation would be quite prepared to booze until all hours.

During the first terribly lonely month, he tried to read Sartre's *La Nausée* in French, but found it too difficult.[15] He expected to make contact with whatever passed for Hemingway's Lost Generation now – there'd be existential aimlessness, sure, but mixed in with camaraderie, a good deal of boozing, and women who "did."[16] Inexplicably, however, women seemed able to resist the sad young man gazing wearily on all the spectacle. The only woman he tried to befriend, a young woman he saw reading Faulkner's *Sanctuary*, refused to answer when he spoke to her.[17]

Action there had to be. Henry Miller said so. The novels of Miller and Céline (in English[18]) found their way to Richler now and landed with thunderbolts. Miller: so uninhibited and such a yea-sayer, the latest word in sexual liberation. Compared to tight-lipped Montreal, Miller seemed like a new world, as long as one didn't look for intellectual structure beneath the splash on the page.[19] A taste for Céline and Miller isn't surprising in a young male, but Richler's knowledge, via Lily's affair, that the surface of adult life didn't tell the whole story helped convince him that writers who directly engaged the repressed elements of sex had uncovered The Truth.

Richler cultivated a beard – a little Van Dyke thing[20] – and the required costume of jeans, sandals, and Gauloise cigarettes.[21] But where, exactly, was Miller's Paris? Richler couldn't find it. Perhaps by writing in the style of Céline,[22] he'd lure bohemia out into the open, but the novel floating in his head – *The Rotten People* – didn't seem like such a piece of genius as it began to arrive in clumps on the page. In later years Richler would dismiss Miller as a mythmaker, the hot stuff having aged badly.[23] Céline, despite his malicious anti-Semitism, Richler never repudiated,[24] though he wisely stopped trying to copy him.

By December, still slaving at *The Rotten People*, Richler finally made friends, mostly ex-Montrealers. Mavis Gallant introduced "Mordy" round to Alex Cherney and Bill Weintraub.[25] The expatriate Montrealers huddled together in restaurants and bars, listening to be-bop, another latest thing. According to Gallant, Richler was completely bowled over by the existential climate.[26] Weintraub, five years Richler's senior, was a former *Gazette* journalist, now freelance, Jewish too, but not Orthodox and not raised in a Jewish ghetto. Richler became maybe Weintraub's second Jewish friend. "Cocky but charming – and hopelessly unrealistic"[27] was how Richler struck Weintraub. Theirs was a joking and playful relationship. Both maintained the fashionable poses of the time and took great pleasure in denouncing anyone who didn't meet their standard.[28] Despite Richler's later reputation as a hard nut to crack, he was a congenial companion to those whom he respected. Weintraub and Richler would remain lifelong friends.

Richler also met Sinbad Vail, the editor of a small new journal called *Points*. Unlike all the other publishers of small magazines in Paris, Vail, the son of Peggy Guggenheim and painter Laurence Vail, was never strapped for cash. He'd stand his writers to drinks, even to billiards, in cafés.[29] When it came time to publish the first issue of *Points*, he flung four thousand copies at the unsuspecting public. Only four hundred sold.[30]

Vail accepted three of Richler's short stories, collected as one mood piece entitled "Shades of Darkness." The stories that Richler later called mawkish and foolish earned him $10.[31] He says they were written at age sixteen.

That seems early, given the tone, but they do seem to have been written in Montreal. "Shades of Darkness" consists of brief vignettes from three pitiable lives, while the point of view teeters unsteadily between the sentimental and an objective view-from-above in which the characters are seen ironically and existentially as symptoms of a sick culture. A fat comic, dismissed from his job at a lodge because well-wishers don't want him to joke about his weight, swims out too far from shore; an Italian marries a Jewish girl and becomes a slave in his father-in-law's sweatshop; an abused young Québécois finds self-actualization and social acceptance by clobbering Jews. One is tempted to call the style of the vignettes Hemingway-laconic: "His name was David Disraeli Wallman, his father was a zionist, and he was awfully fat. He was just too goddam fat." Missing, for better or worse, is Hemingway's characteristic emotional restraint, and added is a more pressing interest in social context, signified here by the clever "Disraeli." Knowing that Richler wrote an admiring letter to Morley Callaghan sometime in the 1950s, we may instead detect Callaghan's variation on the Hemingway style – a curious mixture of sympathy and crudity that allowed Callaghan a large, almost sociological perspective while still angling for the reader's (though not always the character's) humanity. Callaghanesque, too, are the ironic open endings, which, without saying so directly, immediately put the characters in degraded positions. Some strains would continue in Richler's later work: the objectifying distance would broaden out into savage caricatures. So would the concern – both sympathetic and unsympathetic – for Jewish experience. Other things would change. Richler's protagonists, at least, would acquire complex and compelling inner lives, their worlds would become flush with detail, and there were signs that they'd be dressed in a far richer vocabulary than Callaghan's one hundred words – "she cried, and kissed her little *boychick*, and she answered him, "Sam, siz shvere tzo zien a yid" ("Sam, it's hard to be a Jew). As for Richler's fan letter, Callaghan never answered.[32]

By the time Richler published his stories in *Points*, the money was already running low and his novel wasn't anywhere near finished. The windfall $10 didn't improve things much. In *The Rotten People*, Kerman remembers being dizzy with delight at stepping ashore in Europe, almost unable to resist kicking his feet in the air – "He was free, unencumbered, unknown!" But within a few months he's full of despair, "tangled in a slew of problems, sufficating. It was aggrivating!" [*sic*][33] At a party a British sculptor told Richler about an island in the sun where one could live for under $100 a month and just write, man. Hadn't Hemingway abandoned Paris for Spain? But the money. Richler alternately begged and demanded that Moe and Avrum wire funds for passage to Ibiza. With a stake extorted from them, Hugo's *Spanish Self-Taught*, and a Penguin *Don Quixote*, Richler boarded the train heading south.[34] For six crucial months he would live and write there, until the Spanish police ordered him to leave.

≶

Sometime in late December, a young Canadian who had lived his life alongside the frozen St. Lawrence, stood on the deck of the *Jaime 11*, watching Ibiza and its main town, San Antonio, floating nearer on the blue-green Mediterranean: "cube-like, sun-dappled white houses rising out of the rock." He only intended to stay a few weeks on Ibiza,[35] a Balearic island about the size of Montreal. By the 1960s Ibiza would become a hippie destination and later the home of ear-pounding nightclubs and *Wild On* cameras, but in the early 1950s it was largely unknown and had the great virtue of being dirt-cheap. It certainly wasn't impersonal Paris, because at the dock a fortyish fisherman, Juanito Tur-Guerra, immediately corralled Richler and escorted him to a waterside bar for a glass of Fundador. Tur-Guerra, called "Juanito Pus" by everyone, owner of two fishing boats and a dockside storage shed, was, so Richler believed, emperor of the waterfront. And Richler was, so Juanito believed, a wealthy American sent by his father to dodge the Korean War. In front of his cronies, Juanito plunked the newly arrived "American" down – by the scruff of his collar, so to speak – and despite Richler's denials in broken Spanish, kept him in the Escandell all evening until he was staggeringly drunk; then, when the party seemed over, dragged over him to Rosita's, a bordello,[36] for what may have been his first experience of intercourse. Later Richler would wonder what Juanito saw in him and why Juanito became his mentor: "I was so arrogant. Such a prick ... Drinking until I collapsed, cavorting with whores had seemed to me the ultimate rather than a truly Rotarian experience when I was 19."[37] But the point was: he was no longer on Orthodox St. Urbain Street.

What did Juanito see in him? Foreignness, probably; considerable energy, almost matching Juanito's own; a drinking companion. In the isolation of Ibiza, Richler – or "Mauricio" as the Spanish called him – suddenly became a curiosity, no longer one of thousands of ghosts who drifted about Paris with a manuscript and a hopeful expression. For his part, Richler had found his bohemia, not among writers and artists as he had expected, but among fishermen. They were all very jolly and funny and friendly, says Bill Weintraub.[38] For some weeks Richler didn't stir from his landing-spot. He took a room in a waterfront hotel, and wrote in the daytime; evenings he roistered about with Juanito Pus and the fishermen.

In a six-week white heat, he says, he wrote a novel, but, on more mature consideration, the thing didn't look at all promising. He rewrote it. It still didn't look promising. He burned it, he says.[39] Not true. It must have been the highly autobiographical (and never published) novel *The Rotten People* that Richler had been working on so feverishly, because the date on an early but substantial draft of the novel reads "san antonio, ibiza, 1950."[40] If the date is accurate, then the first Ibizan weeks (the last few weeks of 1950) were dedicated to finishing that early version of *The Rotten People*. Possibly Richler hedged his bets by burning an earlier draft of *The Rotten People* and keeping the next. He revised ceaselessly, but he was never one to throw work away. He continued to rework the novel throughout his time on the island.

In Paris an ex-GI, Joe Dughi, told him, "You cross the Pyrenees… and you're leaving Europe behind you … On the other side, it's a hundred years ago." Not a problem … at first. When Richler wrote about Spain later, he quoted Roger Fry to the tune that Spaniards lived instinctual, not detached or intellectual, lives.[41] Despite the weakness of such a racial generalization – indeed, the main reason for Richler's hasty exit from Ibiza would be that his life became rather *too* instinctual for the Spaniards – Fry's statement *felt* true: felt true in the whorehouses or bars when drunks were invited to sing an aria, juggle, or dance for a drink, and everybody howled with laughter; or on nights such as the one on which he rode a motorcycle with the anarchist doctor Juanito Villan-Gomez to Rosita's and stayed till 4 A.M., *only* 4 A.M., because Villan-Gomez had to operate the next day; or in the dentist's chair when Richler received cognac as anaesthetic while having a filling done, the dentist himself sampling the bottle, too.[42]

Spain seemed exotic to Richler because there he was able to assume a freer bodily life. Late in March he visited Valencia to celebrate the fiesta of San José and, with Hemingway's *Death in the Afternoon* in hand, to witness his first bullfight. Hemingway notified Richler that the Spanish were more conscious of death. Watching Luis Miguel Dominguin fight bulls, who could argue? The spectacle itself was breath-stopping enough, but when a boy from the audience leapt over the barrera into the bullring, stamping his foot and inviting the bull's charge, Richler's heart pounded. The crowd cheered and laughed, but Richler trembled, not knowing how common it was for boys to get so aroused by the ritual of death that they simply had to join in. In the fiesta daylight he saw the fallas, gigantic papier-mâché effigies, one of a pot-bellied gypsy. At midnight of St. Joseph's Day, the Nit del Foc, came the Crema, when celebrants lit all the effigies on fire. These weren't a few firecrackers on Victoria Day; these were hundreds of human figures, some a few stories high, flaming hot against the midnight sky. The experience was nothing less than revelatory. Later would come the slow retreat from instinctual bodily life, later the recognition that Spain for him was a "dangerous indulgence," but now, Richler said, "those flames in Valencia consumed … a host of personal devils. The most wintry of my Canadian baggage as well as some of the more stultifying Jewish injunctions I had grown up with. Gone with the flames went the guilt acquired by leaving college without a degree ... I'm a slow learner, but walking away from that fire I grasped, for the first time, that I was a free man."[43] In the nineteenth century, the central marks of Jewish assimilation had been Enlightenment scholarship and nominal baptism into Christianity, as typified by people such as Mendelssohn, Disraeli, Marx, and (in more complex ways) Heine,[44] but by the mid-twentieth century, the new mark of assimilation was the flight from Orthodoxy into secularism and the body. A harsh grandfather, snooker on Shabbes, and a divorce hastened Richler's leaving of St. Urbain and Orthodoxy. The burning fallas marked his entry into secular Europe. He immediately began working on a short story, "The Acrobats," to commemorate the occasion, but returning to Ibiza he resumed work on *The Rotten People*.[45] It would be another half a year before Hemingway and the Valencian fallas (seen through Malcolm Lowry's *Under the Volcano*) would give Richler the tragic structure for a novel-length version of "The Acrobats."

Richler mailed stories to *The New Yorker*, *Harper's*, and *Atlantic Monthly*, but nobody wanted to buy.[46] Even on cheap Ibiza, money was evidently required. He sent delicately worded telegrams home to Moe: "IMPERATIVE CHECK SENT PRONTO MADRID C O COOKS WAGON LITS ALCALA NR 32 MADRID. BROKE. MORDECAI."[47] Moe, despite his own lack of money, often came through, but made it clear that what he sent were loans, not gifts, and he kept a little book of Mordecai's accounts.[48] Sometimes, tucked in with the money, Mordecai found a Jewish calendar, a sign of his father's hope that Mordecai would confess his sins and celebrate Rosh Hashanah.[49] Richler also sent dunning letters to Bill Weintraub: "mavis said – god bless you – you might be able to lend me a few bucks until sept. – if so, fine – if not, i know your type!" At some point in Paris, Mavis Gallant had indicated that she might join Richler on Ibiza and split the rent. By the beginning of April, Richler was anxiously trying to reach her and urging her to come posthaste.[50] He couldn't possibly last long on the island spending as lavishly as he did at the Escandell and Rosita's. Some "nights" of leaving Europe behind proved to be more than even the free man Richler could be happy about. One of these began as a drink with Juanito before dinner and ended when the two awoke forty-eight hours later in a fisherman's boat, Juanito's face bruised, Richler's pants torn.[51]

As a result, Richler determined to leave the capital and move ten miles across the island to the sleepy village of San Antonio Abad. There, for one thousand pesetas ($20–$25) a month he could rent a three-bedroom finca (a cottage), with living room, fireplace, kitchen, and "BATH." Throw in another $50 and there'd be drink, food, and a cook to prepare it. Every morning wine would arrive like milk on the doorstep. Removed from Juanito and the temptation of too much instinctual life, he'd be able to live a more Spartan lifestyle. Best of all, the house had a small garden and a shaded alcove where he could write in the mornings. But Juanito wasn't quite done with his young protégé. A week after moving, Richler was roused out of bed at 3:00 A.M. by three ancient taxis with a load of girls from Rosita's, a flamenco guitarist, and Juanito. Richler protested, but Juanito barged in and made himself at home.[52] That Richler would very soon name a pimp in *The Acrobats* "Juanito" may have no significance – the name "Juan" being so common – but it could also signify that in Richler's eyes other reasons than friendship sometimes motivated Juanito.

Mavis Gallant never arrived. Instead Richler began to work on Bill Weintraub: "san antonio is a fantastic place in many ways that are best not enlarged on thru the mails," Richler wrote, tantalizingly. Weintraub made for Ibiza and immediately gloated to Brian Moore: "I have the typewriter out on the patio and the palm trees in the garden are rustling ... Our cook is now preparing dinner." Then he repeated Richler's standard boast, "It's expensive here *not* to drink."[53]

≶

Richler continued to peck away at the new novel, but two developments changed Ibiza completely for him. One was the arrival of a young American woman, Helen. Neither petting Evelyn Sacks in the Laurentians nor cavorting with prostitutes at Rosita's had quite prepared Richler for Helen. She stepped off the *Jaime 11* with three buttons on her blouse undone. *Joshua Then and Now* transforms her into "Monique," a lively young woman but very much an intellectual lightweight, thrilled by the fact that Joshua frequents a brothel and quick to rave about "savage nature." In *Back to Ibiza*, she is "Pauline," probably closer to the real Helen – not nearly so foolish, but still eager to be impressed by anything avant-garde.[54] No doubt Richler allowed Helen to clap hands at the deep thoughts that during these months went into *The Rotten People*:

> Time,
> like a bleeding pus sore on the anus of life,
> comes, and passes.[55]

Helen applauded, but Richler wrote it, so he couldn't have been an intellectual heavyweight either.

Helen was followed, some days or weeks later, by a fierce and protective mother.[56] The mother hoped to curb her daughter's sexual wildness but had few notions of how to do it, and in short order Helen and Richler became lovers, mostly at Helen's urging. As long as she was on Ibiza, Rosita's was apparently on hold. By June, Richler was worrying about her "monthlies."[57]

If he wasn't ready to be a father, neither was he prepared for the second person who radically altered Ibiza for him: a former ss colonel who had fought alongside General Franco and stood under sentence of death in France for World War II crimes. Before Richler came to Spain, he had had some unformed fantasies, arising out of his reading, that his arrival would buck up the left-wing Republicans, losers of the Spanish Civil War. He did make acquaintance on one hand with the anarchist Doctor Villan-Gomez and on the other with a fascist secret policeman (called "Mariano" in both *Back to Ibiza* and *Joshua Then and Now*) who under General Mola had executed POWs during the Civil War. But even though in *The Acrobats*, Richler would try to make the Spanish conflict between left and right seem immediate, he had arrived on the scene too late, and his hopes of revolutionary ferment were disappointed. Whatever had happened twelve years earlier was settled, "the whirlwind elsewhere."[58]

Into this mental geography stepped the ss colonel, a focus for Richler's inchoate anger. Called "Roger Krauss" in *The Acrobats*, "Mueller" in *Back to Ibiza* and *Joshua Then and Now*, the colonel carried himself among the Spanish officers with a worldliness that Richler, conscious of his own naïveté, could only envy at the time. In one of the island bars, "Mueller" challenged Richler to gamble with lie dice for drinks, demanding, "Are you a man or a mouse?" Revenge for the colonel's suavity and for the absent conflict between left and right, Jew and Nazi, supposedly came one evening at the same bar when Richler enticed Helen out from under "Mueller's" nose.[59]

≶

How much can *Back to Ibiza* be trusted as an account of Helen and the ex-ss colonel? Richler writes that he encountered "Mueller" during his second night on Ibiza,[60] but Bill Weintraub, who met Helen, heard nothing about "Mueller" and therefore judges him fictional.[61] Yet among the points that Richler on Ibiza listed for a planned *"letter to Katie"* were rumblings of his changed situation –

10. My ludicrous situation with the army officers in San Antonio.
11. the german cruiser
Mrs. Germany
Many Nazi & Chinese refuggees [*sic*] here....
21 ... the whore who wanted to know if I was a spy.[62]

– and in a 1952 letter Richler said very directly to Ted Allan, "after abt six months i finally ran into trouble. an s.s. colonel – under sentence of death in france, and living on the island – sent in a report on me."[63] In his fiction, of course, Richler dressed up real events and added whatever a good story demanded, but, since there's no evidence that he was dishonest in letters to friends, the ss colonel must have been a real person. Possibly, the crucial events happened in June, after Weintraub left Ibiza. Even without the Allan letter, it's difficult to imagine Richler constructing an obsession out of thin air, an obsession strong enough that, twenty-six years after dealing with the colonel in *The Acrobats*, Richler had to exorcise him a second time in *Joshua Then and Now*.

The differences between the unpublished 1976 memoir *Back to Ibiza* and the 1980 novel *Joshua Then and Now* can partially guide us. 1) If an incident appears in *Joshua Then and Now* but not in *Back to Ibiza*, the incident is *likely fictional*, since it appeared at a stage when Richler was shaping a work of fiction. 2) If an incident appears in *Back to Ibiza* but not in *Joshua Then and Now*, the incident is *likely factual*, because, for a variety of reasons, factual incidents are easy candidates for cutting: real life can be too pedestrian, real life can be embarrassing in ways that the author isn't ready to expose, and real life can work against the artistic effects the author desires. 3) If an incident appears in both *Back to Ibiza* and in *Joshua Then and Now*, the incident *may* be factual.[64] There are a few (non-Spanish) incidents in *Back to Ibiza* that can be identified as fictional, yet because Richler's editor, Bob Gottlieb, regarded *Back to Ibiza,* as undigested non-fiction,[65] because so much of the material is attested elsewhere, particularly in interviews with his extended family, and because Richler uses the actual names of his wife and friends – Florence, Ted Kotcheff, Reuben Ship, Tony Godwin, Bob Gottlieb – the manuscript is (apart from protective pseudonyms and some exaggerations) a representation of Richler's life.

Fictional, clearly, are the ss colonel's second career as a writer of westerns in *Joshua Then and Now*, his menace against Joshua, and a host of lesser details. Making "Mueller" a writer of cowboy stories is Richler's inspired connection between Nazi ideology and American master-race practicum on the frontier – Karl May in a black Stetson. In the novel, when Joshua claims the colonel's regular restaurant table, "Mueller" says, laughing, that with his hands unseen under the table he could easily have shot Joshua's balls off. In *Back to Ibiza*, the scene ends more prosaically, though, one could argue, also more profoundly. "Mueller" joins Richler at the table and (in a passage transferred elsewhere in *Joshua Then and Now*) says, "It's all over for me, a closed book. Chew, nigger, it's all the same to me. I respect a man for what he is."[66] No threats, just the seductions of peace and "Mueller's" expectation of a too-cheap amnesty from the Jews. But *Back to Ibiza* isn't completely reliable: elsewhere this prosaic version is attributed to Richler's hearse-driving landlord in Munich, who says, "For me, enough. For me, a man's a man. A chew, a nigger all the same."[67]

More prosaic, too, in *Back to Ibiza*, are "Mueller's" other doings at the restaurant, run, we discover, by the Freibergs, bourgeois Jews wise enough to flee Germany immediately after Kristallnacht. Max, a relative of the Freibergs, flogs a black-market camera to "Mueller," and, when "Mueller" begins to use veiled threats about Max's racial origins as a bargaining chip, Richler interferes. Some version of this incident may be factual, since it appears in both memoir and novel. But in *Back to Ibiza* there's no indication that Max was once a victim of German anti-Semitic thuggery, and the Freibergs are insignificant. Richler is annoyed by their servility towards their ex-Nazi guest, and he says early on that they are partially responsible for his hasty exit from Ibiza, but they are depicted neither as the mousy Jews that Joshua wants to protect from anti-Semitism, nor as the bourgeois Jews who complain about Joshua making love on the beach.[68] These shifts – the subtle changes in detail and attribution, as well as the more exaggerated leaps – are important signs of Richler's development as a novelist. Both the twenty-year-old Richler and the fifty-year-old Richler hoped for a more direct and tangible confrontation with the systematic atrocities of World War II than the actual 1951 confrontation supplied, hoped for a more direct way in which a Jew could strike out against the Holocaust. The literary changes show Richler grappling his way towards literary seriousness, recognizing that the conflicts he felt in his gut (however unsatisfactorily acted out in real life) would also be felt by others, provided that he could make the conflicts immediate.

Among the things that likely *did* happen (i.e. appearing in *Back to Ibiza* but not in the novel) are Richler's conversations with Helen and her mother's rage upon discovering her daughter's affair. Richler says that he read his short stories to "Pauline" and had long discussions with her about "man and his place in nature." He also reports that someone revealed the affair to "Pauline's" mother and that she, enraged, burst into Richler's room, searching for her daughter and denouncing Richler, complaining loudly that he would give her daughter venereal disease because he frequented a whorehouse. Richler assumes that "Mueller" revealed the affair to the mother, as revenge for Richler enticing "Pauline" away from him.[69] The conversations may be factual, cut from *Joshua Then and Now* because faux-profound discussions between the lovers would have blunted the satire against "Pauline's" role as the young writer's groupie and focused too much attention on the intellectual self-importance of Joshua (né Richler). Similarly, the mother's rage would have dissipated the symbolic battle between Nazi and Jew and raised the issue of sexual responsibility, an issue that Richler was eager to avoid for a very strong reason: Helen became pregnant and her mother spirited her back to France for an abortion. Although Richler wrote Weintraub that the "brave kid" knew about the pregnancy for two months and never said a word,[70] it's also possible that she lifted a finger to test the wind and recognized that she couldn't expect much support from Richler. Certainly he was aware of her fears when she told him that her period wasn't arriving. In all likelihood, he was putting on his own brave face for Weintraub. Why else, at the same time that he was professing love and praising her courage, did Richler call Kerman Adler's unpalatable girlfriend in *The Rotten People* "Helen"? The character "Helen" is partly Evelyn Sacks and partly fictional, but for Richler to place "Helen" on Ibiza and then to have his alter-ego Kerman wish to throw her off a cliff suggests that at some level Richler feared that he'd be trapped by the real Helen. The literary evidence suggests that during this period he wanted to flee.

≷

What is certain is that around the end of June, Richler became the object of a police investigation and that he predicted the outcome to his friends: "i'd hate to be thrown out of spain at this point as i'm broke and can't think of anywhere to go."[71] The police briefly jailed him. Why? Ted Kotcheff says, "The secret police started to hassle him, making it difficult to work, and so he left and returned to Paris." According to Kotcheff, the trouble was a result of Richler consorting with Republicans and attempting to pry literary material from those who knew "Mueller."[72]

But it was an arrest, not just a hassle. In Richler's 1961 account and in *Back to Ibiza*, causes abound: a burglary, the Freibergs, "Pauline" (Helen), a complaint by "Mueller," the rumour that Richler was a Communist and a spy[73] – reasons that also appear in *Joshua Then and Now*. Since the Freibergs figure so little in *Back to Ibiza*, and since Helen had already left in early June with her mother for the French abortion,[74] it's unlikely that the police were still dealing with charges arising from public indecency on the beach, though the earlier accusations of indecency could have exacerbated more immediate factors. It's even possible that "Mueller" had no direct involvement with Helen, that no woman was "stolen" from under anybody's nose. Spy charges, which Richler himself liked to emphasize,[75] seem least likely of all, though police may have used such charges as a convenient catch-all in the absence of direct evidence for other charges.

That leaves burglary and "Mueller." In both *Back to Ibiza* and *Joshua Then and Now*, Richler/Joshua vandalizes "Mueller's" villa. Simmering over Nazism and assuming that "Mueller's" revelations to an angry mother had whisked away Helen, Richler/Joshua breaks into "Mueller's" place, finding Beethoven and Bizet on the shelves, rather than Wagner; Hemingway, Stendahl, and Saroyan rather than *Mein Kampf*. Still, he smashes the records and a lamp.[76] Further complicating questions of fact is that some of the

"Mueller" material, including, notably, this scene of vandalism, appeared first in drafts of the novel *St. Urbain's Horseman*, written in the late 1960s, long before *Back to Ibiza*.[77] In an even earlier 1961 account, "someone" broke into the colonel's villa and he suspected Richler. Richler encouraged the suspicion by commenting on how ironic it was that he had just sold a short story and come into money at the same time as the colonel had been burgled. Richler offered to buy him a drink. The colonel left the table, and the two were no longer on speaking terms.[78] The earliest account of all, in "My One and Only Countess" (written in the early 1950s), tells a similar story, with the colonel swearing out a robbery complaint against Richler. There are no references to vandalism.[79] The most likely scenario: because of his youthful bravado, Richler was accused, possibly wrongly, for breaking into a German colonel's villa, and for this reason the law placed its hand on Richler.[80]

Richler came to Spain hoping to encounter the fascists and communists of the Spanish Civil War, but instead ran into the remnants of German Nazism and discovered that he was a Jew. Thousands of miles from Montreal, despite instinctive fishermen, despite shellfish and unclean women, he was a Jew. In Barcelona he had come across both *Mein Kampf* and "Bubb [sic] Shulberg's"[81] *Porque Corre Sammy?*, the Jewish novel about Hollywood, and he heard stories of the Spanish Jews – the conversos – who had tried to adopt Western personae but who had nevertheless been burned in the Inquisition.[82] What was Richler but a secular converso? At some point Richler also began to read *Guide of the Perplexed*, by the great Spanish medieval synthesizer of Jewish belief and practice, Maimonides. Despite the vast differences between the anti-bourgeois novel *The Acrobats*, written by a sensitive young outsider unquestioningly in love with his own stance, and *Joshua Then and Now* – more cold-eyed, yet much more responsible and profound – the two books separated by twenty-six years share an admiration for Maimonides, quoting his comment that even wise men overestimate the world's evil.[83] Although Richler still had some months of avant-garde *hauteur* to serve out, and although he would never be pleased to focus exclusively on the good things of this world, medieval Jews and ex-Nazi colonels were conspiring to push him out of the anarchic province of youth.

With so little money that he even had to pawn his typewriter, he cabled a request for bail to Avrum and Moe.[84] The police ordered Richler to leave the country within forty-eight hours,[85] and leave he did, though not before one last "whopping party" at Rosita's whorehouse.[86]

7

Mr. Gauche of the *Rive-gauche*: Paris

"COME HOME ... I MISS YOU," writes Reuben to his son in *Joshua Then and Now*. "Come home ... take a job," wrote Moses Richler to Mordecai in *Back to Ibiza*.[1] But in 1951 Richler wasn't ready to surrender to Montreal just yet. Where to go? He had planned to meet up with Helen on the Côte d'Azur, but she would be in the chilling post-abortion company of her mother.[2] Only a few weeks more would see the completion of his earth-shattering novel, now called *The Rotten People*. How to survive through the summer?[3]

He surfaced in Tourrettes-sur-loup, a medieval village between Cannes and Nice. Atop a sheer cliff overlooking the Loup River, the village lies about fourteen kilometres from the Riviera coast. Richler shared a flat with Jori Smith, a forty-four-year-old Montreal artist. She was not his girlfriend; Richler approached her at a café, and, on the strength of a couple of days' acquaintance, asked if she would share the rent at his place. She had to settle for the couch – Richler explaining that, since he typed all night, it was in her best interest that he have the bedroom; he promised that, if she ever went to Spain, he had names of people who would be only too glad to put her up. Smith found him surly and uncommunicative. In later years, she did go to Spain, but when she invoked the name of Richler, people hung up on her.[4]

Helen, who had only finished her convalescence the day of Richler's arrival in Cannes, was able to elude her mother for a few days; she and Richler hitchhiked to Grasse, the Colombe d'Or, and all the Cagnes. Richler remained quite serious about her, while her mother fumed. He even planned to ask Helen to marry him and accompany him to Canada. To Smith's relief, he moved from Tourrettes down to the coast at Haut-de-Cagnes, still starving, not the sort of picture to inspire a potential mother-in-law. Still, the apartment he found was lovely, one window overlooking the hills and the sea, another overlooking, as he put it, "jimmy's bar and existentialist sex."[5]

Some of the expatriate writing and magazine-editing Americans, including the editor of *New Story*, Eric Protter, arrived to summer in Cagnes – drinking till dawn, then running down the hill to the sea.[6] In that crowd was Montreal-born film director Silvio Narizzano, shooting *Twenty-Four Hours in a Woman's Life* with Ingrid Bergman and Rip Torn. Narizzano threw a few crumbs Richler's way by letting him and his friends appear as extras. Richler, who could barely afford food, never mind high-stakes roulette, played one of the diffident high-society gamblers in the Monte Carlo scenes.[7] On Ibiza, the prospect had not looked good for Richler's stories: "nothing from protter the bastard! i wrote him but will you pul-eeze look him up and find out what the fuck happened to my stories. if they've been rejected i'd like to have them back as soon as humanly possible."[8] But the crucial thing was the novel, not the stories. The final draft is dated "August, 1951, Tourrettes-sur-loup,"[9] so it must have been almost complete when Richler left Ibiza; when Richler arrived in France, he began showing it around to his friends.

≋

The novel is more naked than any of Richler's subsequent work, and it's fascinating – not for artistic reasons; it's a very bad novel – but for its revelation of the young Richler. *The Rotten People* begins with rats, Parisian rats tormenting Kerman Adler, who slices open his stomach with a can-opener and decorates a railing with a good length of his "smily [*sic*] in testines." Not to worry – just a portentous hallucination, followed by portentous dialogue: "And after the Styx, and after the Styx, what shape is the soul after that?"[10] Such passages show Richler to be a self-important, romantic petitioner at the doors of the avant-garde. Evidently, after "the Styx" the soul takes the form of laborious puns: the rats stand for the bourgeois "rat race" that Kerman must escape. On one side of the Atlantic waits Kerman/Richler's grasping Jewish mama, begging him to return home to a writing room she's setting up for him, complete with a nice secondhand bookcase. Kerman/Richler's memories of his grandfather's harshness, his grandmother who was supposed to die, his mother's affair with a refugee – all these make it clear what Kerman/Richler is fleeing. On the other side of the Atlantic, Kerman had imagined that European bohemia would solve all his problems, but his screwed-up writer and painter friends – either lousy or the most original artists of their time – are as rotten inside as the effigies of Kerman's childhood.

Kerman's name suggests that Richler envisioned a role for his protagonist that was Jewish and at least partially heroic. "Kerman" evokes one of

Richler's childhood heroes, Kermit Kitman, the Jew who cracked the Montreal Royals lineup, while "Adler" – "eagle" – gives Longinian sublimity, and
also a representativeness, recalling the Canadian Yiddish newspaper, *Keneder
Adler*. Feeling that his own writing is no less rotten than that of his friends,
Kerman is poised between his Jewishness and secularity. He's definitely not
pleased to be a Jew:

> A Jew is something you are lucky not to be born.
> Also, thank God,
> A Jew is not as bad as being a Negro.[11]

At the same time, it bothers him immensely when other Jews accuse him of
trying to erase his past. Thuggish Labour Zionists mock him for acting as
if he were a Gentile; they also mock Larkin, a Gentile who wants to convert to Judaism to allay the fears of his Jewish mistress's family. Rejected,
Larkin turns into a vicious anti-Semite. All the while, Kerman preaches and
theorizes about God, discounting "the Hebrew-Christian tradition" – which
he thinks of as "the tragedy of the great Moral Bribe" – yet wanting to retain the concept of God. A mystical White Russian, Sasha (who seems to be
a fantasy creation, not based on anyone Richler knew) says that everything
is relative except God. Not that God has an independent existence, but He
is humanity's "most beautiful creation and is the point of sanity in our ex-
istance" [*sic*]. Sasha advises Kerman not to waste his time on "the political-
social salvation of man."[12] From the simplistic psychology of Larkin to the
overblown (and too cheaply bought) mysticism of Sasha, this is the work of
an immature writer.

The twenty-year-old Kerman becomes romantically involved with a
twenty-seven-year-old journalist who has separated from her professor husband. She is sophisticated, cynical, and occasionally rough on Kerman. In
the notes to *The Rotten People*, she is listed as "Estelle Connally (~~Mavis~~)."
How much she really owes to Mavis Gallant (who had been a journalist, had
recently divorced her husband, and was twenty-eight at the time) is unclear,
because although Kerman's early life is faithful to Richler's, Kerman's life in
Paris and Ibiza isn't. Kerman begs his former teacher "Helen Perlman (~~Evelyn~~)"[13]
to leave her husband and join Kerman in Europe. Which she does, resulting
in a tangled situation with Estelle. Letters that Richler received from his former teacher Evelyn Sacks in 1953 and 1954 demonstrate that he was still in
contact with her, but nowhere is it suggested that she joined him in Europe.
Clearly, at a certain point, "Helen" became fictional.

Kerman's friends, card-carrying Outsiders, theorize long and hard about
murder and suicide. Kerman, not far behind, thinks that in the twentieth

century, morality is "such an intellectually illegal concept."[14] Feeling that "Helen" is a rope around his neck, he fantasizes about pushing her into the sea. The misanthropy that appears in the novel was the gift of Lily – her real voice that she disguised in her fiction, but that Céline had, so to speak, licensed in Richler. The rigours of avant-garde style evidently convinced Richler to exaggerate his feelings about Evelyn and Helen, but one would be hard-pressed to argue that Richler was reconciled to everything that love and women had brought him. In the end, Kerman's problem is solved by a *deus ex machina*: "Helen" becomes entranced by the ex-Nazi colonel, "Roger Kraus," who acts and speaks very much as he would in *The Acrobats* and even, to some extent, in *Joshua Then and Now* as "Mueller." Yet Kerman's greatest fear is neither of Nazis nor of women but of insanity, the possibility that the rats are only the creations of his sick mind. He is very pleased at the end of the novel, therefore, when, back in Paris again, he makes acquaintance with a big and very real grey rat. In his hotel room – rats on the floor, rats in the ceiling – Kerman, "happy and free as he had never been before," begins to "dance and sing and cry and scream."[15]

Richler received thumbs-up from his fellow would-be writers, not so much from Weintraub or Gallant as from the avant-garde Americans that Richler had cultivated; Protter and his coterie pronounced the novel 500 percent better than the stories. Richler bragged, both about the praise and about the novel's unpublishability: "they think i'm stupendous and young and brilliant but they also think i'll have one hell of a time selling the book (the conventional publishers wouldn't read past page three) ... everybody thinks if i made my next opus a bit more digestible for the tender bourgeois stomachs i should be able to sell."[16] He was right, about unpublishability at least. Later, in another incarnation, Richler would criticize one of his students' writing, saying, "It's pretentious horseshit ... You show unlicensed confidence."[17] This is precisely the criticism that one could make of Richler's first novel. It's clear that young Richler had talent – some truthful descriptions of his own experience got through. But Richler's youthful self-involvement, combined with his intellectual limits and his lack of compassion for his characters, ensured that the worthwhile was mostly papered over by his pious rejection of society. Kerman "sees through" a great many things: the fraud of the university, the bourgeoisie, politics, and morality.[18] Quickly Richler tossed off a story (possibly "Il faut s'agir," which dates from that period but is apparently no longer extant) in the style of the novel, and Protter promised to consider it very carefully.[19] When Richler heard that a Mavis Gallant story had been accepted in a very different quarter, *The New Yorker*, he must have been sick with envy. He, too, had been sending stories there, unsuccessfully. But he made light of her polish, claiming that he didn't like her story very much.[20]

Soon enough, the literary crowd drifted back north and Richler no longer had an overwhelming interest in Helen, even though Bill Weintraub in Montreal was perjuring himself on Richler's behalf, giving Helen a big build-up to Lily and swearing that Richler wasn't drinking much. In August, Richler said he would hitchhike to Italy in September; in September he said he'd go in October with a beautiful Swedish girl, Ulla. By other accounts she was shapely, but "not what you'd call Miss Sweden"; he finally ended up with her in Paris.[21]

⩽

No Left Bank poverty, for the time being. Richler had sold some of his clothes to afford the train to Paris, but lost all the money at a party before he could buy the ticket,[22] and in the end it was his shipmate Terry McEwen, earning a good wage as artistic director of Decca Records, who sent him enough for the trip. McEwen permitted Richler to use his box seat at the symphony, and even allowed Richler and Ulla to move into his Right Bank apartment for a while. Ulla probably contributed some money, too. Her father was wealthy, owner of the GM concession for Sweden. Although he bankrolled his daughter in France, he worried about what kind of mischief she was getting up to, and he deputized his son Arne to investigate. But Arne double-crossed his father and kept mum about her liaison with Richler.[23]

In late October Richler spoke of drinking all day with his bohemian friends and then crawling bar to bar in St. Germain.[24] He spent a lot of time in front of pinball machines.[25] In *Back to Ibiza* Richler wrote that he and "Pauline" had exhausted each other and that he had broken up with her in Haut-de-Cagnes.[26] In fact, however, Helen contrived to follow Richler to Paris, and, according to Lionel Albert, Richler kept two women busy. Make that three, by Richler's own count: "i have fallen out with Helen. (she drops round almost every day.) there is also ulla. and sanki. (i hope this doesn't sound just a bit crude.)"[27] Albert, visiting Paris at the time, says, "We'd leave Ulla at home to wash the dishes, and trot out to the Left Bank and meet all his friends, Terry Southern and co." They'd also trot out to meet Richler's other girlfriend, a petite, dark, and attractive woman in a dark beret and trenchcoat – either Helen or Sanki, Albert isn't quite sure.[28]

Time ran out on Terry McEwen's benevolence. It was probably in this period that Richler got himself a room in rue Cujas, off the boulevard St-Michel. Despite the weakness of the franc, which inflated the Canadian money he could pry out of his parents and friends, Richler returned to the Left Bank and to poverty.[29] After requesting $50 from Weintraub in Montreal, Richler said, "i wouldn't ask if it wasn't pretty bad."[30] A skin rash that he developed briefly convinced him that he had caught syphilis, but it turned out that because he ate so few fruits and vegetables he had developed scurvy. He spent a lot of time in the place de Fürstemberg, off the rue Jacob, sitting there late at night, thinking, worrying that he had made a big mistake by deciding to become a writer.[31] A letter from shameless Sir George Williams University arrived. True, he hadn't completed enough courses to be called "Bachelor," but in view of the courses he *had already completed*, Sir George would be pleased to bestow upon him the title of "Associate in Arts," with all the rights and privileges thereto pertaining. Please send $5.[32] Richler didn't apply. One very banal (and evidently factual) unpublished short story from that period – "Eating" – tells, in a Callaghanesque mode, of a starving young Canadian celebrating Dominion Day by eating the free food at the Canadian embassy.[33]

⧖

"Half the world's poetic misfits are huddled together in Saint Germain des Prés and the language is American," Bill Weintraub had said a year earlier.[34] Indeed, Richler's crowd – David Burnett and the *New Story* gang that Richler had met in Haut-de-Cagnes – had become mostly American, what with Weintraub in Canada and Mavis Gallant keeping more to herself. Gallant wasn't so enthusiastic about a community of young men who drank and blustered like junior Hemingways. Burnett's mother, Martha Foley, had founded *Story* many years earlier to attract new writers; Burnett now decided to do the same with newer, more avant-garde writers. When Jean Genet published a piece in the magazine, *New Story* got its stamp of approval. Young, still unknown writers huddled round the fire – Alan Temko, Terry Southern, James Baldwin, and Mason Hoffenberg – harbingers and, in part, creators of the 1960s. In the popular press it was assumed that these young rebels were existentialists, Sartre's progeny. One rowdy night, however, as Richler and his friends cavorted at a Left Bank café, Sartre apparently put up a sign at his table claiming (incorrectly, as any historian must add) that he had nothing to do with these children. Apocryphal or not, the story does suggest how older intellectuals viewed the unruly swell beginning to push forward a counterculture that would culminate in Swinging London, the Parisian upheavals of 1968, and Terry Southern's face on the cover of the Beatles' *Sgt Pepper*.[35]

The drill was this: terrace-sitting and drinking in the Café St. Germain des Prés or the Old Navy, a cheap bar-tabac, till midnight – if discreet, one could smoke hash at the tables – then writing all night.[36] There was horrified excitement on New Year's Day 1952, when George Plimpton returned from Tangier "loaded with hash."[37] The conversations at the Left Bank cafés weren't especially literary, according to Lionel Albert, though someone did once pass around an open matchbook with some poetry scrawled on it. Only Terry Southern, who afterwards scored his first big success with *The Magic*

Christian, and went on to write screenplays for *Dr. Strangelove*, *Barbarella*, and *Easy Rider*, made an impression on Albert.[38] The Texas-born Southern affected a "mock high-society English-gentry way of talking, complete with little harrumphs ('What? What?'),"[39] and he spoke disparagingly about "the quality lit game."[40] Baseball or anything else from back home – Fibber McGee, the Andrews Sisters, the Katzenjammer Kids – the aspiring writers talked about.[41] Yet they, Richler in particular, insisted that they were vastly superior to "amerkun tourists," ridiculous people all: "wide-eyed, big-assed idiots from hollowhead, Illinois; sophisticated career bitches from nyork and a whole flock of dungareed googoo-eyed lady-birds from the village."[42] For liberated bohemians, the Hoffenberg/Southern circle spent an awful lot of time thinking about suburbia, keeping up a "running ironic commentary on what the squares were up to."[43] Richler couldn't anticipate a larger-bellied self bargaining for slippers in Marrakech thirty-three years later.[44]

"Those who know, do not speak. Those who speak, do not know" – such was the hipster credo.[45] It arose out of American forms of laconic masculinity but also from contemporaneous non-Anglo currents in Paris. How had it come about that glorious bodily fluctuations, delirium, and discharges had been reduced to stereotypes? Isadore Isou and the Lettrists, to whom Richler several times refers,[46] pointed a finger at the guilty party: words. "Letters have a destination other than words," Isou declared. "Anyone who can not leave words behind can stay back with them! ... THE LETTERIC AVALANCHE IS ANNOUNCED."[47] Not necessarily the best news for literature, though it did lead to interesting visual art. The Hoffenberg/Southern circle was a bit more circumspect. "The whole point was not to write a book but to talk one,"[48] says Southern, and his circle pretended to care little about publication.[49] "If it was corny enough and square enough and bourgeois enough to get accepted by some of these asshole editors," Southern wondered, "how could it be worth anything?"[50] Theses and other bourgeois-track labours were frowned upon, but dirty books, such as the ones Hoffenberg wrote for Maurice Girodias, received nods of approbation. Movie-writing, no; script for a Tarzan movie, yes.[51] Judging by *Barney's Version*, in which Hoffenberg provides the model for Bernard "Boogie" Moscovitch, it was mostly Mason Hoffenberg who handed down these and other commandments.

By Richler's estimation, Hoffenberg was the most talented of all the expatriate writers.[52] Small, lean, wiry, and with protruding eyes, Hoffenberg always had a book in his pocket. He was nearly a decade older than Richler. He had marched through Paris with the liberating army, and now, like Southern and many others, he was "studying" there on the GI Bill. His father, owner of a shoe factory in New York, sent cheques, so Hoffenberg could party and stir up debates. He knew everybody – Sartre, Beckett, Henry Miller, William Burroughs – and was game for anything. Deceptively gentle, he had mastered the art of the caustic put-down, with Southern in the role of younger brother/schmuk.[53] "A Nobel Prize-type poet," Southern called him,[54] but judging by his 1949 poem "Divination,"[55] Southern's and Richler's assertions seem exaggerated, the product of nostalgia, an awe of Hoffenberg's conversational rather than literary inventiveness, and guilt that they borrowed his lines for their own work. Tales abound of Hoffenberg ideas charitably distributed in bars, only to reappear as if by magic in somebody's story, somebody's film. Richler's guilt at becoming one of Hoffenberg's literary executors, so to speak, would be expressed obliquely in *Barney's Version*, where Boogie says, "If you want to know what Boogie was thinking yesterday, listen to Barney today."[56]

Even if Hoffenberg was as talented as his friends thought, his lifestyle wasn't conducive to the creation of great literature. In the Hoffenberg/Southern circle it was *de rigueur* to smoke marijuana and hashish, both cheaper than scotch; so Richler smoked, fearful of God and addiction, but more fearful that he might be called chicken-shit.[57] Not everyone was impressed: "What a prick you were… with your goddamn artsy beard and tight-ass blue jeans. Bragging about smoking hashish. Mr. Gauche of the rive-gauche," said one friend.[58] God turned out to be less vengeful than advertised, but addiction Richler had reason to fear. Both Burnett and Hoffenberg had already graduated to heroin, and Richler was sometimes called upon to accompany Hoffenberg, that "model for … hipster perfection," to the bathroom, there to hold Hoffenberg's veins while the poet dug for them with his needle.[59] Later in life, when the fun ended, Hoffenberg moved back home with mom before he died in his early sixties. Instead of writing his own novels, he appeared as a character in Richler's.

"I suffer from a wonky system of values, acquired in my Paris salad days," says the aging Barney Panofsky.[60] Likewise Richler. Had Richler never felt the disdain for bourgeois culture that he acquired in Paris, one doubts whether his writing would have amounted to anything. There's nothing remarkable in his more traditional stories. Nevertheless, in Paris he began to recognize – with some pain – that hipsterdom, later called Beat, was a dead end. Many times in his subsequent career, in *Cocksure* for example, he would write valedictions to that life, valedictions that weren't quite valedictions. Even the bourgeois Barney, who is finally so much more interesting than the quick-burning Boogie, retains a profound affection for the Hoffenberg value system, though he knows that he cannot go forward unless he jettisons it.

≋

Unlike Hoffenberg's father, Moe Richler owned no shoe factories. Mike Gold, an expatriate himself, complained about the Parisian mystique in "Hemingway – White Collar Poet," but Mordecai Richler, blue-collar nov-

elist, waited on tables and tended bar to stay in Paris and keep from starving.[61] Everyone, he lamented, was telling him that he had "IT," but nobody
wanted to publish his work.[62] With $100 from one of his uncles,[63] he vis-
ited Lionel Albert in London and stayed at Cambridge with John Harrison,
a friend from Sir George. Although Richler complained about the hygiene
of the French and mocked, in *Barney's Version*, Clara's aversion to baths, it
was Richler who during that England trip was the subject of complaint. Harrison's wife expressed a "heartfelt wish" that he would take a bath.[64]

In the middle of the Parisian winter of 1952, Richler's thoughts drifted
to Montreal, to free board and room – bookcase included – at his mother's
house and, reluctantly, to gainful employment. Weintraub must surely know
where opportunities hid themselves, since he held that extraordinary thing
in Richler's bohemian world, a good job. Richler asked him to find something that paid well and wasn't too demoralizing. Proofreader, Richler suggested. No driving of cabs. "christ," he exclaimed, "i just realized you're
about the only friend i have who really works!"[65]

He laid aside *The Rotten People* as unpublishable and began a new
novel, which he initially called *Only God Never Dies*,[66] "a clarion call," he
thought, "to retreating liberals."[67] By March it had metamorphosed into
The Jew of Valencia.[68] Near the end of *The Rotten People*, Kerman tells
Sasha, the mystical White Russian, "I never had a father.. .I..I always wanted
him to take me to a parade when I was a child, a parade, a circus even, but
all he wanted to do with his time was play cards. While the world fell apart
and crumbled like a mud pie in the sun my father kept the score on a piece
of paper in gin rummy figures. Poor wretched little man!"[69] Gin rummy was
Moe Richler's game. Living still on the money that Moe occasionally sent,
Mordecai pined for a fantasy father – warm and wise and erudite; a humanist, not an Orthodox Jew. "Maybe you are my father, Sasha," Kerman stam-
mers.[70] Sasha begat Chaim, the Jew of Valencia, who, in a short biography
of him that Richler prepared, arrives in New York from a family of Warsaw rabbis and scholars. A humanist and anarchist, Chaim writes on Cab-
balism, and, even when his Communist bride gives birth to a stillborn son,
Chaim believes that there is a light in man. As a prank, he dabbles in Valencia's black market, where his path crosses Richler's old/new protagonist,
"~~Kerman~~ André," still dreaming of his grandfather's accusations and afraid
that he's going mad.[71] Richler decided to set aside the Jews he knew and give
himself over fictionally to a Gentile self and to elaborately constructed secular Jews. *The Jew of Valencia* would eventually beget *The Acrobats*, Richler's first published novel, but only after much pruning over several years;
and Richler's genealogical sleight of hand would fail over the long haul:
slowly he would tear himself loose from the fantasy father Chaim and make
his imaginative truce with Moe.

"i'm working vurry vurry hard," he reported from England, "and every-one including m'self seems to be thinking i'm writing a damn good book. new story will probably run something of it in the spring." John Lehmann, who had been publishing the journal *New Writing* out of London, turned it down. Richler's stories also bounced back from *Harpers*, *Atlantic*, and *Mademoiselle*, the magazines giving him what he called "the same fuckingold runaround – gee yre great kid! you really shd. be published. like yr. stuff swell, BUT ... signed fiction editor." From very early on, Richler had be-lieved that it was contacts he needed. At Cagnes he believed that had he been a homosexual and slept with "jimmy," New Directions (publisher of William Carlos Williams, Ezra Pound, Tennessee Williams, and soon Céline in translation) would have accepted his novel. Back in Paris again, he com-plained, "SO MUCH OF IT IS CONNECTIONS, BILL, AND IT MAKES ME WANT TO PUKE." After the rejection by Lehmann, Richler queried Bobbs-Merrill in the US, but nothing would come of that either.[72]

In the meantime, he continued to thrust his massive and unruly manu-script at American writers and editors in bars, and his incredible persistence paid off. Just as Richler had predicted, it was a personal contact that finally opened the door. At a Left Bank hotel, Richler met the playwright Michael Sayers, a past Faber & Faber editor who had direct access to the Reverends Eliot and Pound. So what if Sayers himself was having publication troubles ("the pretentious and arty elements who now run the 'reviews' apparently wont touch him," Richler boasted); the important thing was that he read Richler's manuscript and offered the kind of commentary Richler yearned for: "The chcif [sic] thing is that you're going on and through the wilder-ness of that novel of yours, hacking your own path. That's wonderful! ... you're a writer in your blood and bones ... You have this damned and blessed Jewish philosophical-mystical faculty, saved – redeemed by the ruthless old Jewish irony – and your brand of Chassidic lyricism; you'll always tend to exaggerate your experience into universals (to 'minotaurize' your bullocks). ... But – being so deep in this Jewish and alienated mode of being – I feel deeply that you will have to go through a rather painful initiation of explor-ing and learning and mastering ideas." What did the anti-Orthodox Rich-ler make of "Chassidic lyricism"? Still, "the best critic I ever had," Richler called Sayers.[73] Minotaurize your bullocks ... but Sayers also delivered some-thing more than just pretentious commentary, two names: Joyce Weiner, a literary agent in England, and Ted Allan, a Canadian writer in Hollywood.[74]

Having asked for and gotten from Moe a steamship ticket home to Canada to be used in September, Richler had little time to waste. Neverthe-less, he kicked about France, rewriting and keeping women busy. Thinking about Ulla, he asked, "should i get married?" and then answered his own question, "she's a lovely swede. no, i don't think so. abt. helen, we correspond, but all more palsy than passion." He boasted that someone named Dave was waving around a .45 in Montparnasse, swearing that he would get Richler. "i laid his woman, or something," Richler added, with a studied offhandedness. In August he went south to Tourrettes to spend time with Kina Mitchell, whom he had first met when they were both students in Montreal: "i've been fornicating somewhat earnestly since i finished my book, about a wk ago. kina and others have been around to lend a helping hand." "He was a great little womanizer," Albert said.[75]

Why had Richler been considering marriage so soon again? A letter from Ulla just after he left Paris tells why. There was again a price to be paid for all the earnest fornicating, and other cuffs besides lack of money that drove Richler from Paris. Richler wrote Ulla, probably from Tourrettes; her reply is sad and affecting, made even more so by her difficulty expressing herself in English. She missed him terribly; three days after he left she was sick, and after trying to carry his seaman's trunk she felt a harsh pain in her "stomach." The letter contains strong hints that either shortly before or shortly after Richler left Paris, she, like Helen, had had an abortion. For many days, Ulla bled "like a mother who borned their children to the world." She told him, "Many times I was just on the way to faint and felt really like I had borned and would never be able to do it again (not babies anyhow). I like to tell you, and now that you think I am silly but I don't like any idea of killing any thing or stop anything who or who is anyone to leave or to bee there. I don't even like to stop somebody laughing, or somebody crying, less of everything to brake a flower" [sic]. She had returned to school, but she wanted him back and tried to catch his sympathy, telling him that she had seen "some young boy and girl speaking to each other with tender voices, a pregnant cat who slowly moves around still or like always gracious." Alone most days, she spent her evenings sometimes with Hoffenberg, sometimes with someone else. "I wount to tell you everything, what I am feeling or thinking. Do you think it is wrong of me? I leave a new life away from everything, the only as is still the same is, if I hold out my hand in the sun I will feel warm … The mornings and the nights are still strange for me. Nobody kicking me out from bed nobody kissing me goodnight." Even in this difficult time, she continued to promote Richler's book to a Parisian editor that she knew. "Promisse to be onnest," she begged, "and don't write about any Daily news. I don't care about that … Hope your beard will grow out after to months an hope my eyeslashes will that to, because I cut them. God knows why." The letter ended, heart-rendingly, with "Write me soon Mordy, please. Don't you wish to kiss me anymore? Why not? My leaps are warm and soft. Love Ulla" [sic].[76]

But Richler was gone – to London and then Canada. In *The Acrobats*, which Richler was probably already working on, André Bennett discovers that his girlfriend is pregnant and offers to marry her, only fleeing to Canada after she dies from an abortion.[77] Ulla's letter, in contrast, suggests that Richler didn't make any offers of marriage.

Four days before sailing for Montreal, he contacted the agent Joyce Weiner,[78] an eccentric figure by some accounts.[79] Richler came to her in a seedy condition, unshaven and long-haired, and onto her desk he emptied an LP record sleeve crammed full with his manuscript. Weiner described the scene: "it was a hot afternoon in 1952, secretary away, J.W. in need of a holiday, yet another aspiring writer introduced by the merest acquaintance and Mordecai turns up, strange, wild-eyed, diffident with a great big MS under his arm. J.W. severe, will read and report to him in Montreal. Surprisingly the farouche young man stops at the door, turns round and in a (beautiful) voice with great sincerity says 'Thank you – very much.' Hard heart of an agent melted." Richler's own account adds what Weiner glosses over: "She was very dubious about the whole thing, and in fact said that she was sure it was no bloody good." She also warned that she couldn't read it for a long time. Despite her protest, she read the book that very night and claims to have jumped out of her chair at the recognition of both his talent and the impossibility of getting the mammoth published.

The next morning she phoned and said, "Young man you should not know such words at your age."

"How old do you think I am?" he asked.

She guessed twenty-three.

"I'm twenty one," he said.[80]

Years later a more hard-headed author, quite capable of battling percentages with publishers on his own, would trade Weiner in for a more sophisticated model of agent who had more industry contacts, who never knew the "farouche" young man, and who made fewer presumptions when criticizing his work. But in 1952 and for many years afterwards Weiner was something of a mother to him,[81] helping him rein in the excesses of his style and shepherding him into publication.

8

What Do *You* Know about the Circus?

THE SUDDEN HOPE FOR HIS NOVEL made the voyage home much easier to bear, much less of a tail-between-his-legs sort of a journey. After some boozy days on the Atlantic, he disembarked at Québec City. Avrum and his first wife Esther drove their secondhand Austin out to Québec City to meet him. "Here this guy, skinny little guy comes out with a beard," says Avrum. "I started laughing." But "Mottle" as Avrum still called him, hadn't changed much.[1] By the time Richler met Weintraub and started on the job hunt, the Van Dyke was history.[2]

While Richler travelled home, his manuscript, courtesy of Weiner, made its way over to David George, a respected editor at Jonathan Cape. George agreed that Richler was clearly talented, though undisciplined, and that his manuscript was overwritten.[3] In the first shearing, Weiner wanted one or two characters made more loveable and less rage on racial questions. She pushed him to cut many details from the novel's brothel scene[4] and worked hard to reduce the braggadocio of a young writer. Above all, she demanded austerity.[5]

Richler accepted the criticisms – how could he not – but his reply to George bristled with self-confidence. The next draft, Richler promised, would be "less inclined towards the trapeze … God it's not the revising that bothers me but the other books that are not being written! I've got at least three novels buzzing around in my head … and I'm mad to get them down on paper. Honestly, it keeps me up nights." But fears of being tamed came through in his complaints about British critics: "Why almost always the indulgent attitude towards The American Novelist?? As if we were a bunch of ill-behaved, rauccous [*sic*] yahoos caught trying to light up the old man's pipe in the parlour closet. Surely Mailer with all his bungling, and ditto Algren, are doing more sympathetic work than Sansome (and the others) rushing about with their handy brownies, taking their small but only accurate snapshots of suburbia???"[6] Judging by the drafts of his manuscript, Richler the avant-gardist was still immature, and he owes a large measure of his later subtlety to Wiener's editing.

≶

His money gone and his prospects cloudy, Richler stayed at 61 Hallowell Avenue with Lily, who had recently acquired the house as a rental property. Lily retreated from three rooms to two, and then to one, leaving the best for her boarders. For ambience, she acquired new dishes and wall plates with scenes from Dickens.[7] Richler didn't really want to work for his uncles at Richler Industries, but his choices were limited, since the CBC job that he had hoped for via Weintraub didn't materialize at first. Just as well, Weiner said. On the theory that his writing would receive full concentration, she lobbied in favour of a mindless job.[8] Truck company, he had told her, mindless labour. In fact, however, Max Richler had him prepare advertising copy for newspapers and radio. He was competent at the job, yet had no desire to stay.[9]

When CBC radio finally called in the beginning of December,[10] he jumped; CBM, the Montreal affiliate, hired him for the 4 P.M. till midnight shift.[11] Each night he dug through the wire news stories, rewriting material for next morning's broadcast.[12] Very quickly it dawned on him that he was now the conscience of North America, one of the unacknowledged legislators of the world. He did several pieces on Julius and Ethel Rosenberg and one on Reuben Ship – the Byng alumnus and Hollywood screenwriter, later to become Richler's friend – who had recently been deported from the US for his communist views. Richler discovered that if he wrote exactly the 1,200 required words for the morning newscast, the morning man was unlikely to make cuts.[13]

The left-leaning news had a happy, one might even call it a bourgeois, side-benefit, though this wasn't immediately apparent. Just before he got the job, Richler had played the second calling-card that Michael Sayers had given him, this one for scriptwriter Ted Allan. Like Ship, Allan had made the leap from Montreal to Hollywood. Allan had lived on St. Urbain Street a few years before Richler,[14] so why shouldn't Allan's upward literary mobility rub off on Richler? Politicized by the Depression, Allan had defied his parents, joined the Young Communist League, and then tagged along with the International Brigade to Spain in Norman Bethune's blood transfusion unit. Afterwards Allan wrote a novel about the war and a bestselling Bethune memoir, *The Scalpel, the Sword*, which eventually sold 1.5 million copies; also a film treatment of Bethune's life, which he sold to 20th Century Fox in 1941 for a staggering $25,000. Yet despite all this success, Allan was no longer lounging poolside in California. The Cold War had decided to teach him a sharp

lesson on the incestuous relationship between Hollywood and American politics. By the early 1950s, no film with a communist hero could be made in
Hollywood; Allan, blacklisted, might as well burn his $25,000 screenplay.[15]
To put a point on the matter, the US Government concluded that communist screenwriters were in overabundance, and wouldn't Allan like to please
leave the country?

In the fall of 1952 Richler phoned, wrote, and visited the exiled Allan
in Toronto[16] on the pretext of talking to him about their mutual affection
for Spain. What Richler wanted he soon revealed: a job – editing, or script-
ing, since Allan now worked in radio. Richler also left Allan his manuscript
and flogged a one-hour radio play about Canadians in Paris, hoping that
Allan might nudge the CBC to produce it. Bobbs-Merrill, Richler revealed,
had praised his talent but had wondered, "why the rage against things American?" and had complained that ideas controlled his characters. He wasn't
as much of a leftist as the display suggested, but the soft sawder shows that
he was already learning how to cultivate people who could be helpful to his
career. "o yes," Richler added, "the reason why you probably never heard
my name ... is that prior to my sailing for yurop in 1950 my activities –
artistic, political, etc – were confined to the university and the mtl herald.
i'm only twenty-one."[17] No job was forthcoming through Allan at this point.
Indeed, one of the CBC's advertisers, General Motors, had just scotched an
Allan play for "G.M. Theatre" when he stepped far over the bounds of good
taste by *making a derogatory joke about mass production*.[18] Still, Richler
correctly intuited that his CBM reports on the plight of blacklisted Canadian
screenwriters wouldn't hurt him in the long run, and several years later he
did turn the contact with Allan to good account.

At a party shortly after Richler left Toronto, Allan told a young family
friend from Montreal, Florence Wood, about him. She had just missed meeting Richler, but Allan, aware that Wood was a reader, offered her Richler's
manuscript to read that night. She did.[19]

≲

The CBM job allowed Richler to escape Lily again. There was a very pressing reason to move out: Catherine Boudreau. More than once, Richler had
visited Evelyn Sacks, though he didn't renew their relationship on its old
terms. But sometime in the fall Richler got together with Boudreau, who
would receive the dedication for *Son of a Smaller Hero* and become his first
wife.[20] The two joined Lionel Albert in a semi-basement apartment at 1947
Tupper Street, Richler and Boudreau taking one bedroom, Albert the other.[21]

Boudreau was from St. Catherine's, Franco-Ontarian, but more English
than French. She, like Richler, had been raised in poverty. Loud and witty,
she liked to deliver "the odd withering remark" about Richler or about any-

body, a trait Richler admired ... at first.[22] Clara, Barney's loud first wife in *Barney's Version*, bears a trace of Boudreau, but exaggerated 500 percent.[23] Given the easygoing, joking relationship between Richler and Boudreau, not everyone thought they were headed in a serious direction. Albert, at the time, thought, "she was just a handy lay, frankly."[24]

Shocked, upon his return to Canada, at how narrow and provincial St. Catherine Street suddenly seemed,[25] Richler had opportunities to show off his hard-won European sophistication. Arts bureaucrat Bernard Ostry remembers first meeting Richler, sprawled across the floor, a glass of Scotch in one hand and his head resting on the other, in the Montreal flat of Richler's former English professor and job reference, Neil Compton.[26] At a night-club in Dominion Square, Richler watched a comedienne work her way through the audience and get a smile or a laugh from each of the men she teased. She made the mistake of testing Richler. He was no longer a cub reporter from the *Herald*, but a news editor who had duelled with Nazis, hobnobbed with Parisian hipsters, and, any minute now, would have his novel published. His deadpan stopped her completely.[27]

After Richler got off work, he haunted the press club at Mount Royal.[28] It was probably there that Bill Weintraub first introduced him to Brian Moore.[29] Moore had emigrated from Belfast four years earlier and now reported for *The Montreal Gazette*.[30] Although Moore was ten years his senior, Richler didn't look upon him as a surrogate father.[31] In later years, Richler would speak of their shared literary interests – Babel, Waugh, Nathanael West – but the "immediate rapport"[32] between Richler and Moore more likely stemmed from their parallel rebellions against religious orthodoxy – in Moore's case against his mother's fervent Catholicism. Unlike Weintraub, who had been raised in liberal circles, Moore could commiserate when Richler told stories of the price he had paid for defying an unreasoning faith. Moore's departure from *The Gazette* in order to write serious fiction happened about 1952,[33] a departure set into motion by "a fellow" he knew in Montreal whose incredibly bad book was accepted for publication. The "fellow," claims Weintraub, was Richler.[34] Evidently Richler's brash example of setting himself up as a writer at twenty-one had a salutary effect on the older man.

≶

When Richler sent what he felt was a much-revised manuscript back to Weiner in early 1953, the battle of the book began in earnest. Michael Sayers's words of praise still ringing in his head, Richler continued to suppose that *The Acrobats* was slashing a completely new path through the wilderness. Weiner, on the other hand, hoped for a less showy, less avant-garde book. She marked off two pages near the end of the novel and wrote "revolting" over top. There's "still too much of thought processes and display-ing all you know," she said.[35] Richler felt that Weiner was emasculating him. She must want to turn him into a doddering Brit writing about tea-time, whereas Richler knew himself to be young, virile, American. "Dear Mr Rich-ler," Weiner winced, "You are touchy aren't you ... Heaven forbid that you should be a British novelist ... No one wants you to." She agreed that the characters didn't have to be likeable but argued that the reader had to have some faith in them. Then she pronounced on the writers that Richler had paraded as witnesses for his cause: "Sartre is a great writer. Céline I'm not so sure about and Algren I just don't know, but the one Henry Miller I read (and I forget its name) I loathed at all costs. Just an exhibitionist with no talent. But, in any case, all these blokes have arrived – and you have not and our aim is to help you do so."[36] This list makes it clear that at this stage, nothing was farther from Richler's self-perception than Waugh, or satire, or even Isaac Babel. If Richler could convince a publisher to accept the book with all its objectionable passages, Wiener said, she wouldn't stand in his way, but she guessed that publishers would side with her.

That was a bit disingenuous. Jonathan Cape had already decided to re-fuse *The Acrobats*, yet as she had hinted to Richler more than two months earlier, she had a line on a new and young publisher, André Deutsch, a Hun-garian Jew educated in Vienna, who had fled the Nazi-engineered Anschluss.[37] After the war he started a publishing firm, calling it Allan Wingate, advised by his father not to use his own German-sounding name. At a party he hooked up with Diana Athill, who became his lover for a brief period, then his long-time editor.[38]

Art, not the making of money, was Deutsch's prime objective, yet he was a natural businessman. Following early success with former German Chancellor Franz von Papen's *Memoirs*, Deutsch secured British rights to Mailer's *The Naked and the Dead*. Mailer preferred that his soldiers say "fuck" and say it often, as was proper military etiquette. Not yet free to print the word so often, US publishers hit upon an ingenious, though unin-tentionally hilarious solution: they would substitute "fug" and "fugging." Deutsch wanted to champion "fuck," but didn't dare. All the same, some-one took out an injunction against the novel; in response, Deutsch pushed a friend in the House of Commons to stand up and demand whether the at-torney general would ban the book. The answer was a grudging "no." Re-sult: good sales and an overnight reputation as "a brave and dashing little firm, worth serious attention from agents handling interesting new writers." Shortly afterward, Deutsch started a new company in his own name, and in the ensuing years his reputation attracted writers such as Terry Southern, Brian Moore, V.S. Naipaul, Jack Kerouac, Philip Roth (for two books), Mavis

Gallant, Jean Rhys, Geoffrey Hill, Simone de Beauvoir, and eventually Margaret Atwood and John Updike.[39]

In December 1952, Weiner pitched Richler to Deutsch. He was immediately excited, because Richler reminded him of Mailer's debut,[40] but Deutsch's readers were less enthusiastic. Initially, therefore, Deutsch decided to pass on *The Acrobats* and take an option on Richler's next book instead. Weiner refused. Take *The Acrobats* or lose Richler, she insisted. Her gamble worked, and early in March, Deutsch chose to take the book, as long as Richler cut 30 percent of the sex. When Richler received the congratulatory phone call in Montreal from Wiener, Lionel Albert exclaimed, "Do you realize that at the age of 22 you're having a novel published?" Richler didn't even hear the question.[41]

"I consider – with appropriate modesty – that I have performed a miracle," Weiner boasted. "I hope your Mama will think 'that agent woman' some use now."[42] Indeed, Mama was ecstatic.[43] She had told her friends that her son was going to become a famous author, and, sure enough, he was on his way.[44] If Richler's style in *The Acrobats* struck her as alien, the glory of publication she had no trouble cozying up to, and, to top it off, the book was dedicated to her. Moe was less sanguine. When he heard that the title was *The Acrobats*, he asked, "What in the hell do you know about the circus?"[45]

⩞

Reader beware of the early drafts of the circus book: "J.C. doin a soft-shoe dance on the fluff-capped sea, fuggling grenades and whistling Who's Sorry Now ... The Virgin Mary oh yeah doin the bump and grind whilst the Syphilitic Sisters & Saints Chorus, Inc. wiggle their rosy fannies one-two-three on the spinning horizon ... Yowzuh! And up your gigi!"[46] We may thank Weiner and Athill for disabusing Richler of avant-garde pretensions, even though Athill claims that she didn't edit the manuscript much.[47] Not every overheated passage was cut. Torsten Blomkvist, Swedish translator of *The Acrobats*, couldn't help pausing at the line: "the jerk-off Jesuits and the ac/dc nuns raiding the collection plate for the 1-a-month hallelujah." Blomkvist thought he understood what the line *meant*, but didn't quite know what to *do with it*.[48]

After he gained fame, Richler kept *The Acrobats* from being republished, rather surprising for someone notoriously fast to pick up a buck by repackaging essentially the same essay for three or four different sales. But in the case of *The Acrobats*, delicately re-titled as *Wicked We Love* for the American paperback, Richler worried about his literary reputation. The novel was "really very bad," Athill would remember, "Talk about a young man's book!

... What on earth made us take it on?" For one thing, Deutsch was desperate for promising young writers. For another, Athill saw in Richler's work a seriousness and an honesty, though none of his later characteristic wittiness. Richler spoke very little to her, but Athill sensed that he was generous and kind and completely lacking in phoniness.[49]

Deutsch was, as Weiner succinctly put it, "opposed to a mammoth."[50] Richler owed a great debt to her and to Athill who cut juvenile profundities such as "people who like animals are usually so cruel," or – a nice plum for Canada's governor general and for the British audience – "Kultchir is rewarded annually by a pompous soldier – chest always glittering with medals to detract from the tiresome idiot face – who is usually cousin or uncle to a mental defective or *bon vivant* who dozes on the very royal throne of Buckingham Palace."[51] But, really, despite such confrontational passages, and despite Weiner's claims, it was no miracle that Richler was published. The novel told an engaging story in the new earthy style that Mailer represented, and after the editing knives went at *The Acrobats*, it wasn't nearly as bad as Athill and Richler himself later insisted. Compared to the English-Canadian novelists such as Hugh MacLennan and Morley Callaghan who were in ascendancy at this time, Richler had a much more compelling and contemporary voice. Evidently the novel stacked up well against British writers, too, since Walter Allen said, "it would probably be mad to publish it as it stands, but it would obviously be mad to let him get away."[52]

The Acrobats takes place on Valencia's carnival weekend, when fallas – large effigies – are burned. André Bennett, something of a human effigy, who came to Spain to escape his rich bourgeois family and to paint, finds himself hounded by a former ss colonel, Roger Kraus, who desires André's girlfriend, the prostitute Toni. Goodness knows there can't have been many Rogers in 1951 German phone books, and the conflict between Kraus and the revolutionary manqué André ends in murder. Yet even if the ideas aren't fully formed, the melodramatic story is engrossing. Complicating the André/ Kraus/Toni triangle are the still-walking ghosts of the Spanish Civil War, a postwar "Last" Generation,[53] according to young Richler: communists, fascist police, a fallen aristocrat, and a cynical writer, Derek Raymond. A less maudlin figure is cut by the rich Jewish-American businessman, Barney Larkin, whom Richler would later judge the most interesting character of the lot[54] – "He hates the Cossacks; and one day he hopes to dine with their generals." The charmingly common-sense Barney doesn't understand the wastefulness involved in the burning of the fallas, "They spend a whole week making 'em and then they burn 'em in one night ... Why make something only to burn it? It doesn't seem practical." Practical, no, but because of the importance that the burning Valencian fallas held in Richler's personal mythology – the defining moment of his escape from Jewish Orthodoxy –

he wanted to use them in an imaginative way. The fallas show young Richler struggling for a tragic theory of art: his characters are fallas, exaggerated versions of human beings, made for burning, representatives of stances that must be destroyed. Derek says, "we build evil toys and dance around them, later we burn them. Hoping, perhaps, that it will help."[55] It's a therapeutic theory – too therapeutic. According to its logic, instead of calling on his most profound intuitions the writer invites into the text his foolish thoughts and evacuates them in a literary catharsis. *The Acrobats*, like *The Rotten People*, is very much a young man's book, simplifying communism, capitalism, the bourgeoisie, and God. The characters are often clichés – the good-hearted prostitute, the communist who really doesn't love individual people, the idiotic but physically powerful ss colonel, the suffering artist.[56] The artist is foolish to die, Richler implies, but how hip of him to do so!

The novel is fascinating, at times, for reasons that would soon embarrass Richler. One sees the immature Richler who eventually gave birth to the mature artist. Who but an overintellectualized twenty-three-year-old Richler would seriously complain that "I love you" was "such a cliché!"[57] The Anglo-French painter André Bennett resists both communism and decadence and seems like a wish-fulfilled version of Richler himself, though Richler, good enough as an artist to have considered commercial art as a possible career, was neither French ("André") nor English ("Bennett"). By having André's mother run off with a poet to start a little magazine, another romantic thing to do, Richler plastered over the painful edges of Lily's affair with Frankel. Psychoanalytic explanations can give very little insight into Richler. His sense of an adult cover-up helped send him to the avant-garde where he could broach and master such issues, yet one cannot say that Richler was haunted by the affair very far into adulthood. In his new circles, it was rather a feather in one's cap to have had a mother living on the edge. He had dealt directly and emotionally with the affair in *The Rotten People*, and after that its significance slowly faded into the background. Lily's difficult *personality*, however, did not recede, and soon he would deal with her kind of person more harshly in his fiction. *The Acrobats'* dedication to Lily read "with love" in the manuscript version,[58] though by the time of publication Richler left love out of it.

However, in a surprisingly mature stroke, Richler appeals to Maimonides through the death-camp survivor and bar-owner Chaim. Possibly a nod to Israeli leader Chaim Weizmann, who had repudiated violence and become the conscience of the paramilitary Haganah, Richler's Chaim was still, as he had been in *The Jew of Valencia*, André's surrogate father, the kind of Jew that Richler found it easy to celebrate – a humanitarian on easy terms with whores.[59] Even if Chaim is a bit too far removed from a certain *Doc Savage*-reading father, too much the wise, suffering Jew, Richler has him quote

Maimonides to undermine André's tragic force, hinting at ironies that would characterize Richler's mature work: "When a person is in a state of apprehension and cannot make out the cause of it ... Let him jump where he is standing four cubits, or let him repeat, 'Hear O Israel, etc.': or if the place be unfit for repetition of the scripture let him utter to himself, 'the goat at the butcher is fatter than me!'" André isn't fortunate enough to hear this advice, nor would we expect him to learn much had he heard it. The same, almost, went for the intense young Quixote who, though he could quote Maimonides, had recently cooled his heels in an Ibizan prison, waiting for his brother to throw his bail.

The Acrobats was an important step. Richler later said that as derivative as *The Acrobats* was, one could find all his later themes there, mapped out.[60] So what if the scaffolding of Hemingway, Lowry, Sartre, and Céline shows. So what if, as Ramraj points out, the characters are overweighted with ideology yet lacking inner lives.[61] What a triumph: to make a novel of ideas that was, nevertheless, colloquial and visceral and arose out of one's experience. *The Acrobats* shows Richler striving, already, to become a witness to a time and place, even if at that age and in that country – Spain – he didn't really know the time or the place well enough. The trademark themes of Richler's masterworks appear: the Jew rising out of the ghetto; the post-communist struggle for a humane and yet workable politics; the second-generation confrontation with the Holocaust; the existential search for secular moral values. On the dustjacket, Richler announced, "there is only one thing for a serious writer to write about today. Man without God. Man embarrassed."[62] André's skepticism about his intellectual and spiritual leaders looks ahead, if self-importantly so, to *St. Urbain's Horseman*. And some of the passages associated with Richler's intellectual disillusionment are surprisingly poetic, as when Derek expresses skepticism about the communist revolution: "Enjoy yourself madly, because pretty soon the hillbillies are going to storm the Winter Palace. Afterwards, darkness." Richler was already trying to work his way towards an affirmative vision, as the epigraph from Maimonides suggests: "Men frequently think that the evils in the world are more numerous than the good things. Not only common people make this mistake, but many who believe they are wise."[63]

What a triumph, also, for a Canadian to attempt an experimental novel. Long before the great Canadian experiments – Leonard Cohen's *Beautiful Losers* and David Godfrey's *The New Ancestors* – Richler was writing in a colloquial way, undreamed of in the highly skilled but still genteel experiments of Howard O'Hagan's *Tay John* (1939), Elizabeth Smart's *By Grand Central Station I Sat Down and Wept* (1945), and A.M. Klein's *The Second Scroll* (1951). In *Souls What Make No Progress and Souls What Do*, a manuscript of an early theatrical treatment of *The Acrobats*, Richler provided his own blurbs:

> "Too highbrow for me! It must be poetry because I can't understand it ... Could have come right out of the filthy pages of *The Daily Worker*... Anti-American ... Trivial when compared to such problems as vivisection and women sitting in bars ..."
>
> THE KNOCKSHOP NEWS, KURST INC.

Other faux blurbs were less showy, but even funnier, showing the young avant-gardist on the road to satire:

> "This sickly offering when compared to Gorki ..."
>
> THE DAILY WORKER[64]

Not surprisingly, when he found out that *The Acrobats* had been accepted, Richler immediately envisioned himself as a literary superstar. He bought a $30 boat ticket to England so that he could help market the magnum opus.[65] He sent Weiner his unpublished stories, thinking that now, surely, stories from such an important author ought to be worth quite a bit. He told her that he was working on a fantasy. Also a play. He instructed that *The Acrobats* be published already in the fall, not next spring as Deutsch had planned. Couldn't they understand that he needed money desperately?[66] It probably didn't help his sense of moderation that Deutsch asked for a 10 percent cut of film rights.[67]

Weiner, meanwhile, played damper to the fireworks. Around this time Brian Moore asked one of his friends in New York about Weiner's reputation, getting, in response, a smile and silence, then the comment that some writers prefer a booster agent.[68] This was complete nonsense, as Richler well knew. "You won't be able to live on writing for a long time," she warned him. She didn't neglect to praise him – "Of course you're dazed and scared. I would be too. To 'hole in one' is quite an achievement" – but she advised him to hang onto the "trucking" job: "It gives solidity to one's life even if one is a genius (and you are definitely not)." The fantasy story she was in no hurry to see. "Oh dear," she lamented, "everyone goes in for this most unmarketable commodity as they do for children's books." And theatre she considered nearly as hopeless a proposition, saying, "Plays can ditch you quicker than anything but this is something no writer ever takes secondhand ... so by all means forget what I say." She tried her best to stall Richler's stories from arriving on her desk; when that proved impossible, she spoke more bluntly: "I beg you now not to send out stories that are not absolutely tops. You have a reputation to consider, and I have my time."[69] Her immediate cause for complaint was "Beyond All Blessings and Hymns," but the other stories he sent her – "The Secret of the Kugel," "Four Beautiful Sailors Americain," "Mr. Macpherson," "The Shape of the Ghetto," "My Uncle Mendel the Lion" – weren't much better.[70] In "Four Beautiful Sailors Americain," Richler tried to copy Hemingway's style, telling a story about an old Jew trying to sell a camera to American sailors. But *Punch*'s rejection note pigeonholed the story with devastating accuracy: a run-of-the-mill story "of the brand that finds significance in events at Cannes that would pass unnoticed at Cape Cod." By November, Weiner had had her fill and returned the stories *en masse* to Richler.[71]

Not one to waste his efforts, Richler eventually got money from the CBC, the *Montreal Star*, and the *New Statesman* for "The Secret of the Kugel," though he shouldn't have.[72] In the story a young boy discovers that his unmarried Aunt Fanny, famous for her kugel, has been buying kugel from Mrs Miller's bakery and passing them off as her own. Out of loyalty to his mother's supposedly inferior kugel, he plans to expose Aunt Fanny. His eventual decision not to do so is meant to be read as a sign that he has matured enough that his concern for truth and his partiality toward his mother are muted by compassion for Fanny, who, tragedy of tragedies, has never married.[73] The story must have been written by a teenaged and Lily-influenced Richler, one not yet blindsided by Céline. The overly sentimental treatment of family and community, so different from the bitter rejections in *Son of a Smaller Hero*, suggests that early on and despite his personal rebellions Richler attempted to write as the dutiful son of Montreal Jews – in a Sholom Aleichem voice that he would later mock. The price for Aleichem-like compassion, both Richler and his protagonist discovered, was silence about the truth. At the same time, the boy's "betrayal" of his mother suggests that at another level Richler was aware that honest writing might injure community, family, and in particular his mother. Indeed, *Son of a Smaller Hero*, much more autobiographical and much less sentimental, was already percolating, a book that the Richler clan would interpret as nothing less than a betrayal.

9

Cathy, Commerce, and Señor Hoore: London

COME 26 AUGUST 1953, on the strength of his high hopes for *The Acrobats*, Richler left St. Urbain and set sail for Europe again, this time not alone. Cathy Boudreau followed him, booking passage on the same boat – possibly without his knowledge.[1] Evelyn Sacks, during a final visit in Montreal, offered herself to him, though she afterwards insisted that it was only a test. "Bad manners," is how she dismissed her behaviour. "I was upset because you were leaving ... I only wanted you Mordy, even though you never even thought of me ... And if you want to know how a frustrated woman acts, when she's approaching middle age and desires a very young man who regards as a loving woman – mother and friend – this woman becomes rude and impatient." If he shared his laugh with anyone, she promised to hate him.[2]

The voyage on the *Samaria* was "godawful," Richler complained to Weintraub. "Cathy still suffering from a cold. I arrived with a fever, and my ass shot full of penicillin."[3] His original plan was to meet his publisher and his many anticipated readers in England, then on to Austria or Spain, where he could again live cheaply and write his next book. He couldn't afford to live and write in Canada, he said.[4] In truth he wanted to be where the action was – publishing action and action of every other kind. If he was an important writer, what was he doing in Canada? There were also sound career reasons for passing through London. Face-to-face contact, Richler knew, put the kind of pressure on a publisher that even Richler's tireless letter-writing campaigns couldn't.

He never made it to Spain or Austria. Several blocks south of the Thames in Chelsea, at 509 King's Road – what Salman Rushdie called "the wrong end" of King's Road[5] – Richler found a small basement flat to share with Boudreau and a woman named Florrie MacDonald. Their bus stop was appropriately named "The World's End" after the pub down the street.[6]

Boudreau, working as a stenographer-typist, supported him,[7] and again he asked his Uncle Bernard for a loan. That well, however, was drying up. "Dear Muttle … At long last a letter to your favorite uncle. I thought you forgot me," Bernard said. He wished he could lend Richler money, but he was building a house and was therefore short of cash.[8]

Richler wasn't so poor that he couldn't attend plays by T.S. Eliot and Graham Greene, and complain about "Grandma Eliot's latest sermon *The Confidential Clerk*."[9] Perhaps through John Harrison, Richler managed to wangle an invitation to tea with E.M. Forster at King's College, along with a promise that Forster would look at *The Acrobats*.[10] The meeting soon began to seem like a bad idea. Richler found out that Forster disdained the American writers that Richler admired – Fitzgerald, Algren – and, although Forster proved kind, Richler embarrassed himself by knocking back sherry like whiskey.[11] Before the meeting, Richler could snicker at "old boy" Forster, sitting on his balcony with binoculars in hand, waiting to take down the wing numbers of the American military jets so that he could report outrages against his quiet. After the meeting, however, Richler lost some of his optimism about the worth of his own writing.[12]

Still, Bob Amussen of G. Putnam's Sons in New York decided to pick up US rights to *The Acrobats*. Amussen tried to convince Richler to alter the novel's ending so that André wouldn't die, but Richler held firm.[13] In his role as about-to-be-published author, Richler began to take on a certain gravitas. "A bloody impressive document," he called his contract and admitted that he had begun to feel like "A Man of Importance."[14] As befitted his new dignity, he dropped "Mordy" for "Mort." He also decided that it wouldn't be too much of a sellout to the bourgeoisie if he occasionally used uppercase letters, say at the beginnings of sentences and for names.[15] Was it a coincidence that, a week after Richler's meeting with Forster, Weintraub got his first letter in which Richler no longer scorned uppercase? Certainly Weiner and Athill had long been nudging him in a similar direction, though as late as 1955 Richler still called Ted Allan's secretary, "that little mex chic," and signed off "Much merde. Mazel. Cojones. Etc."[16]

In any event, ee richler was beginning to feel the weight of the past. Wandering into Foyle's, London's largest bookshop at the time, he saw a vast table covered with the hundred novels that came out that week,[17] and it suddenly hit him that there were an awful lot of books in the world. "Questions come to you making small wounds. Why are you making this book? Does it matter?" He began to wax philosophical, gazing past all the vain enticements that had once lured him on: "Before I had my first bk accepted and until I began work on my second I wanted to be famous. Have position. Anecdotes told about me … But now I do not want or think about these things very much … And, worse still, there is no fame big enough or money bribery enough to compensate for the pain that goes into the making of a novel ... So why do I write? ... Nearest I can come to it is 'I have to.'" The funniest bit of hubris came late in the letter: wrung out of him came the admission that he could only get so close and no closer to the truth in his writing; "never the orgasm," he lamented. It did little to deflate Richler's self-importance that the printers cried obscenity and refused to print *The Acrobats.* He made the required changes – "tits" to "breasts," "kick you in the balls" to "kick you where it hurts," "bloody Christ" to "Christ" – and, from his lofty perch, pronounced the affair "All most amusing."[18] Yet for all of his pomposity, it was true that Richler had to write: he was still defending himself against the beliefs of Shmarya Richler and Rabbi Rosenberg and Lily. In the end, the changes weren't deep enough for the book chain W.H. Smith, which placed *The Acrobats* on its restricted list after complaints about vulgarity.[19]

Richler's gravitas benefited, though it did not always amuse, his friends. He now felt substantial enough to lobby Deutsch and Putnam's to publish Brian Moore's first novel, *The Lonely Passion of Judith Hearne,* as well as Ted Allan's *The Scalpel, the Sword.* After many – possibly sixteen – rejections, Moore suddenly found that he had a publisher.[20] Richler's tone, however, wasn't always what his friends would have wished for. He'd say things such as, "Brian has wasted a lot of time writing for the slick mags – writing things that embarrass him but give him the kind of income that he is too weak or frightened to give up."[21] Within months Richler himself would be asking Michael Sayers for tips on where one could make quick money writing in London. Sayers, not realizing how nearly he was echoing Richler's very own sermons to Moore, repeated the advice that Tolstoy gave to Andreiev: "Never write for money ... don't write about things that don't profoundly excite you."[22] Much later, in *An Answer from Limbo,* Moore would dramatize what remained unspoken then. Max Bronstein (Richler's alter ego), having published his first novel in New York, tells Brendan Tierney (Moore's alter ego) that he'll put in a good word for Tierney with his publisher. The older and, up until then, senior writer, with six published stories to Bronstein's two, rages inwardly against the upstart crow, recognizing in the gesture both great generosity and preening, the male battle for status. For his part, Bronstein admits that he needs Tierney's jealousy and hates him in a way.[23] Not until 1961 did Moore write about such issues, not until, that is, Richler was having troubles with American publication and Moore had put in a good word *for Richler* with the publisher Seymour Lawrence.

At the beginning of 1954 in London, these jealousies simmered beneath the surface as Moore visited England and the two writers jousted about other writers and about the value of a bourgeois life. Richler had strong opinions, which he made known. He praised the Marx Brothers and (not unreason-

ably) called Jean Cocteau a fraud.²⁴ A little older and less hasty, Moore satirized the contempt that Richler distributed so generously: "Many points in
Mordecai's vocabulary have been revealed to me as jargon. All unliked artists
are 'a trick.' Anything unliked is 'a trick.' People who dance or play bingo
are 'hilarious.' People who drink heavily in the bar are 'tourists.'"²⁵ Moore
defended the values that Richler complained about, prophesying that even
for Richler things would soon boil down to bourgeois values. While Richler's basement flat was not uncomfortable, it was dingy, Moore told his
friends, and Richler's life was disordered, "a confused jumble of pubs," including the Mandrake with its (according to Richler himself) "bearded
Britishers, black Little Englanders," and "phony lit people."²⁶ Even though
Richler still fancied himself a bohemian, Moore commented on Richler's
hopes, pointedly observing that Richler talked a lot about money and sales.
Weintraub concurred. Nevertheless, Richler's arguments evidently carried
some sting, since Moore signed himself "Señor Hoore."²⁷

Despite professional jealousies and seniority, Richler and Moore became
close friends as Richler worked on his second novel, tentatively entitled
Losers,²⁸ and struggled to find ways of contributing to Boudreau's income.
Moore, shrewder about money than Richler and readier to stoop, came up
with an ironclad scheme: Richler would write potboilers. In his longest letter to Richler, Moore drafted a detailed seven-page book outline replete with
much advice. As Moore had done, Richler would slap together a thriller,
publish it under a pseudonym, take the money, and run. Moore? He would
skim a nice 25 percent off the top. Copy my *Wreath for a Redhead*, he suggested, "make the hero a loner, a wisecracker, occasionally nervous but *not*
a deep thinker. Don't for pete's sake try to three dimension him." The plot
didn't have to be intricate, since the publishers worried more about its feel
and how fast it moved. Moore also warned against taking the assignment
lightly: "Don8t [*sic*] be a wise guy and try to parody the genre." To remind
Richler that Moore wasn't a prostitute, that there was good scriptural prece-
dent for this sort of thing, Moore gave an example of the kind of laconic
dialogue that would be required:

"We'll run them right in to the long beach," I told him.
"Take her in now?"
"Sure," I said. "Take her in slow."
We came in slow over the reef and to where I could see the beach
     shine. There is plenty of water over the reef.

In case Richler was inclined to make light, Moore added, "don8t laugh, son,
that's Papa in to have and to have not which I consider a model for this
work" [*sic*].²⁹

Perhaps Moore and Papa Hemingway could churn out pulp such as *To Have and Have Not*, but Richler couldn't. He feared that it would rob from *Losers*. At the same time, the financial pickings from *The Acrobats* were a lot slimmer than Richler had hoped. Translations into several languages notwithstanding, Richler was some seventeen years premature in reckoning on literary superstardom. Canadian publishers, before gambling on Richler, wanted to know whether *The Acrobats* was thick, whether it contained Communists, and whether it was anti-Canadian.[30] Richler ultimately sold two thousand copies of *The Acrobats* in England, but less than one thousand copies in the US and three hundred in Canada.[31] An uncle told him that he could have earned more mowing lawns and been healthier into the bargain. But Lily, Moe, and Avrum were excited, Moe no longer certain that writing was "a nutty idea."[32] The downside was that Moe, who had heard of the great Mickey Spillane, now assumed that Mordecai must be rolling in money.[33]

Evelyn Sacks, too, was very proud of Richler's accomplishments, begging him to send anything he had: news, proofs, books. She wrote that she would continue to deceive her husband because she needed whatever Richler could offer. "Please don't marry Cathy yet. She's not the only one who loves you. Please write me, after you get over the nausea this revolting letter must cause you. All my love, Evelyn." A couple of months later, perhaps sensing that too much clinging would alienate him, she confined herself mostly to publication advice. She feared that he'd have to flatter "all those professional business men in the racket of writing," but only "until you're so well-established that you can snap your fingers, and say to hell with you all. I don't need you morons."[34]

⪍

The first non-English house to pick up *The Acrobats* was Kindler Verlag, a German postwar firm operating out of Munich. Curious about Germany and convinced that Kindler needed his help publicizing the book, Richler decided to go there. He and Boudreau went via Paris. He now complained that the city was too full of literary people, so much so that nonconformism had become the new orthodoxy.[35] In Paris he asked Brian Moore whether he should marry Boudreau, and Moore advised against it on the grounds of incompatibility.[36]

In Munich, where Richler and Boudreau stayed for a couple of months,[37] he was both elated and horrified. Elated, because at age twenty-three a limousine ride seemed to confirm his belief in his talents. He told Weintraub, "This, man, was the funniest evening of my young life. Two men taking down all my opinions, pronouncements, prejudices – ho ho ho … (I'm never coming home – never.)"[38] Richler also wrote Brian Moore, gloating, but softening the gloat a little with the promise to act as Moore's literary agent:

"Will speak to Kindlers abt you next wk. Am getting the big, big treatment here. Last night the big Mercedes convertible pulls up, cahuffeur jumps out and opens door for me. Inside, the Kindlers. There okay people. He cant get States because who used to be a party member ... Maybe, by next yr, we'll both be yelloe bk men in Norway. You, me, Faulkner, Hem, and Tom Wolfe" [*sic*].[39]

Afterwards, Richler would remember mainly "a mixture of terror and hatred,"[40] and, indeed, although he managed a studied nonchalance around the words "party member," he was horrified. He told Moore about going to the American Way Club and about the signs there (signs he would use in *A Choice of Enemies* and in *St. Urbain's Horseman*): "BARN DANCE TO-NIGHT," and, just below, "BUS TO DACHAU EVERY SAT AT 1400. VISIT CASTLE AND CREMATORIUM." He had tried to study a bit of German, but it was Americans with whom Richler hobnobbed. Harlaching, where Richler stayed, was full of US officers. At the American Way Club he found comic books, ping pong, the latest hit tunes, and Coke, though he claims to have made an anti-US speech there.[41]

In his relative isolation he worked on *Losers* and on a correspondence voluminous enough for Weiner to protest that he was draining her. She also felt that he was running around too much, collecting bagfuls of ideas without properly digesting anything. For a few months he'd squat in a conflict zone – Spain, Germany – and then assume that he had a full and deep knowledge of the place. Such criticism didn't sit well with Mordecai Richler, Beat writer. He thought that she was trying to turn him into a grocer. Didn't she know that passionate writing couldn't come out of a bourgeois existence? "Oh, Mordecai, Mordecai," Weiner let some of her exasperation show, "try and lose these pre-conceived notions."

She wanted him to go to university, hoping for a better balance between sensuality and the mind. Richler argued that he could learn more by travel and that, in any event, Sir George and McGill were juvenile places. Fine, countered Weiner, then go to Oxford or Cambridge. Get a tutor in logic, history, philosophy, and political thought. With logic at the head of the list, Weiner's choices implicitly repeated her own and others' complaints about *The Acrobats*: too much undigested emotion, too many naïve philosophical harangues that kept turning the novel into a simple allegory. For now, she wanted him planted in a quiet and dull spot where he could think deeply. Travel could come later.[42] Yet for Richler, though his defense of his actions was naïve, travel did prove important – not that he would become a profound interpreter of Germany or Spain, but that, once he was mature enough to interpret his own secular Jewish experience, he'd have enough sensory detail to stage his own conflicts in a variety of settings.

Rather than follow Weiner's advice, Richler decided to marry Boudreau. It was she who popped the question.[43] Lionel Albert, who had lived with the two, was amazed,[44] but their relative isolation in Munich no doubt played a part in the decision. Weiner, hoping that marriage would be an alternate route to that quiet and dull spot, sent strategically worded blessings – "A sense of permanence will enter into your life" – and she offered to host a wedding dinner in London for Richler's closest associates.[45]

The nuptials were to take place on 28 August 1954. Brian Moore revised his position, writing, "All our blessings and hymns be upon you bridegroom."[46] The night before the wedding, Ted and Kate Allan threw a party for Richler's friends, among them Stanley Mann. Richler had known Mann casually at least since 1949, when Richler had praised Mann's acting in a YWHA production of *The Dybbuk*.[47] In London, Mann, Richler, and other former Montrealers Reuben Ship and Allan got together occasionally for expatriate poker.[48] At the Allan pre-nuptial party, Richler for the first time met Mann's wife, Florence, the woman he had narrowly missed meeting in Toronto when she was still Florence Wood. Working now as a model, she was tall and graceful, with large blue-black eyes, thick black lashes, and long black hair.[49] At the wedding reception he couldn't keep his eyes off her. When he approached her and asked if she had read *The Acrobats*, she said, "Yes," "I liked it, but not enough to want to meet its author."[50] The rebuff didn't stop him. Although Richler rarely spoke about his first marriage in public, he did tell a German interviewer that, when he saw Florence, he realized that he had just made a mistake.[51] After the wedding, Florence became good friends with Cathy,[52] and the Richlers often got together with the Manns.

For very different reasons than Mordecai, the Richler clan also thought that he had made a grave error. Having boasted so freely in Montreal about his European exploits, he must have believed that his father and the more friendly uncles had reconciled themselves to his non-observance of Jewish law. Not, he discovered, when it came to intermarriage with a shiksa. Getting news of Mordecai's plans, Moe had begged him, "Think, think, think, think, think hard before you make this drastic step for after August 28, your fatal day, my door and all that goes with it will be closed to you ... So now it's up to you to choose between the unwelcome woman and your father who has tried to do the best for you."[53] When Mordecai went ahead anyway, Moe and Uncle Bernard both cut off contact.[54] Bernard justified himself by saying that, if he approved of Mordecai's actions, what would his own children and grandchildren do?[55] With two young daughters, he wasn't taking any chances. Some Orthodox Jews go so far as to sit shiva if a son or daughter marries a Gentile – treating the child as dead – and Richler knew that such things could happen. In *The Acrobats*, he had had Barney's father sit shiva after Barney's marriage to Jessie and specify in his will that Barney shouldn't come to his funeral.[56] Avrum isn't sure if Moe actually sat shiva for Mordecai, but Moe claimed that he did.[57] Later Richler would jokingly tell of Moe's warning that when tough times arrived a Gentile wife would call him names, and of his own deft parry, "Did Maw ever call you bad names?"[58] At the time, however, Richler raged. Weiner tried to mediate; she could see his family's point of view and agreed that intermarriage usually didn't work. Be gentle and conciliatory, she urged.[59] But not until a year after the marriage did Marion Magid, a family friend, notice a semblance of objectivity in Mordecai.[60]

As for Lily, she had long heard the boys threaten intermarriage, yet she was nevertheless upset when it finally happened. She immediately asked herself where she had failed. With a selective memory she lamented and struggled to understand how intermarriage could have fallen upon the son whom she had sheltered in the lap of Orthodoxy.[61] Of course, Lily too had shucked Orthodox rules – commandments about the Sabbath and about adultery come to mind. Years later, when Avrum divorced his first wife to marry a Gentile, Lily stopped talking to him for a while, but he doesn't remember Mordecai undergoing the same treatment: "Mordecai was her hero then… He was an established author. He was in *London*."[62] Jackie Moore reported that Weintraub was successfully lobbying Lily: "Mama … is fond of the bride, and there will be no disinheriting from that quarter."[63]

About this time, still working hard on *Losers* (now called *Son of a Smaller Hero*), and with Moe refusing to send any more money, Richler decided to unbuckle his rather strict notion of writerly integrity. In principle, TV, the latest thing, surely ought to be milkable by a writer of sufficient talent and enterprise. Richler's earlier resolve not to bow to commercial pressures had made a virtue of necessity. Now the publication of *The Acrobats* secured Richler introduction to the story editor of a film company. However, instead of a high-powered young producer, Richler met "an emaciated 60-year-old with a disconcerting facial tic" who wanted not film rights to *The Acrobats* but a live body that for two guineas a week could read novels and do five-page synopses, reporting on each novel's film potential. Richler took the work.[64] About the same time, and more promisingly, Richler's contact with Ted Allan paid off when Allan invited Richler to help script the half-hour TV series *Robin Hood*[65] (a show Richler didn't neglect to trumpet in his columns).[66]

Near the end of Richler's life, Bill Weintraub would wonder why Richler, who took a dim view of Allan's literary talents, continued to remain friends with him. Weintraub attributes it to the romance of the Spanish Civil War.[67] To this we could add Richler's intense loyalty to those friends who helped him get ahead. When *The Montreal Gazette* book reviewer Edgar Cohen published one of his several diatribes against the new young writer,

Mordecai Richler, Ted Allan wrote *The Gazette*, hailing the appearance of a major novelist and defending Richler's bleak vision by comparing him to Spinoza, of all people.[68] Many years later, Allan asked Richler to provide a dust-jacket blurb for Allan's memoirs. Say what you like, Richler responded, not at all eager to wade through the manuscript but still in Allan's debt. When Richler saw how literally Allan interpreted the permission, Richler's loyalty received rather a stern test: "I love his book," gushed the blurb. "I wish I had written it myself. Richler." After that, Richler vetted his blurbs more carefully.[69]

Allan and Richler wrote *Robin Hood* under pseudonyms. Richler says that he typed, while Allan paced, acted out parts, and dictated. "Help me. Give me a line," Allan requested at one point. Richler gave him one. It wasn't satisfactory. "Are you crazy? That's real. This is television," Allan said.[70] Nevertheless, Allan became Richler's ticket into series TV. There's no doubt that the experience improved his writing, confirming the sorts of things that his editors were saying. Gone, in *Son of a Smaller Hero*, were *The Acrobats'* long speeches about the human condition. To Bob Amussen, who was overseeing the trimming of *The Acrobats* in New York, Richler wrote, "As far as the political essay and such go, they no longer do anything but embarrass me ... Im [sic] through with that kind of stuff now."[71]

≋

Richler delivered *Son of a Smaller Hero* to Deutsch in October 1954. If *The Acrobats* was Richler's derivative attempt to turn himself into a modern, Gentile writer, *Son of a Smaller Hero* was more of the same, yet couched in a much more honest appraisal of himself as a Jew. Looking back at the early 1950s, he often spoke of Arthur Miller and Paddy Chayevsky hiding the Jewishness of their heroes, but Richler could just as easily have used *The Acrobats* as his example. Saul Bellow's *The Adventures of Augie March*, which won the US National Book Award in 1953, proved that Jewish-American writers were no longer afraid to declare themselves, Richler said.[72] Actually, Henry Roth had already done this much earlier, in 1934 with *Call It Sleep*, where cheder features prominently and David Schearl's companions speak a Yiddish-inflected English. Now Richler, too, was prepared to excavate his dead grandfathers and his living parents. "Is it good for the Jews?" had been the measure of everything for his parents,[73] but he turned the question back upon itself: Who *are* these Jews on whose behalf we ask of everything whether it's good for them?

Richler knew that the novel would create trouble in Montreal, and in fact he accompanied Deutsch to see a lawyer about possible libel suits, so close was the novel to autobiography.[74] Ordered to disguise Montreal people and places, Richler did so, but the camouflage wasn't terribly convincing: the Labour Zionist Youth House on Jeanne Mance Street became the Zionist house on Clark Street. Not good enough, said the lawyer, and unfortunately Diana Athill convinced Richler to scrub further, until the Zionist house had become "the hall of the local youth group."[75] The love scenes he had already cleaned up at Weiner's suggestion to avoid problems that had plagued *The Acrobats* with W.H. Smith.[76]

There are too many real people in the novel, Brian Moore scolded.[77] Indeed, Noah Adler, the novel's protagonist, is based on Richler, and constellated around Noah are figures closely resembling Richler's parents and grandparents. Rabbi Jacob Goldenberg stands in for Rabbi Yudel Rosenberg; Melech Adler, the scrap-metal dealer, for Shmarya Richler; Wolf Adler (Melech's eldest) for Moe; and Wolf's wife for Lily – even bearing Lily's Hebrew name, Leah. Harry Goldenberg and Max Adler are composites of Rosenberg and Richler uncles, with less resemblance to actual individuals.[78]

Son of a Smaller Hero	Original
Noah Adler	Mordecai Richler
Wolf Adler	Moe Richler
Leah Adler	Lily (Leah) Richler
Melech Adler	Shmarya Richler
Rabbi Jacob Goldenberg	Rabbi Yudel Rosenberg
Harry Goldenberg	composites of Richler
and Max Adler	and Rosenberg uncles

Through these figures, Richler attempts a sociology of the ghetto, simultaneously a broad historical and intimately personal explanation of how it came to be that a young Jew in the early 1950s would want desperately to escape close-knit Montreal for a Europe where Jews had recently cleaned streets and suffered pogroms. In a letter, Richler explained his larger purpose: "I'm trying to trace the development of the ghetto from the scholar-poet to authoritarian to liberal to money leadership ... e.g., 50 years ago my grandfather, a Chassid, was a leader of the ghetto: today he'd be a 'character' in the same community. I'm not interested in passing judgments or shouting – I'm simply observing."[79] The sociology articulated by Noah runs slightly simpler than Richler's original plan: first come poets (Rabbi Goldenberg) and authoritarians (Melech); subsequently the ghetto splits into businessmen (Harry, Max) and communists.[80] For lack of an alternative, it is left to the moneymen to hold aloft the Torah, but they prove inadequate. Wolf, though impoverished, displays Richler's harsh allegory. Wolf is so tangled in materialism that he attempts to save a Torah scroll from fire mainly because he thinks that the box contains money. Money first, Torah scroll second: this, implies Richler, is contemporary Montreal Judaism. If Moe wanted to pretend that Mordecai was dead for marrying out of the faith, Mordecai would have his revenge by devising a pointless death for Wolf – the image of Moe Richler – and by a false, posthumous glory for Wolf, who (*like Moe*, Mordecai was implying) is mistakenly praised as a defender of the Torah.

The ghetto's final historical development, the novel's burden, is Noah. Originally he had been called "Nathan," but when Richler lit upon "Noah," with its promise of a deluge and a new world, he couldn't get it out of his head, and seven years later gave the name to his first-born son. Noah Adler's problem wasn't Jewishness, Richler insisted,[81] and, if that seems a bit disingenuous, Richler makes it clear that Jewishness is a symptom of the larger problem of human meaning. Wolf, by his own standards, defines Noah as "a Nothing,"[82] unwittingly prophesying the new Existentialist generation, the first Rosenberg generation without a rabbi, as Richler liked to say.[83]

"I'm not interested in passing judgments," Richler said, but the judgements come, fast and furious. At every step, the novel is the work of a young man defending his freedoms. Melech and Melech's sons, Richler treats melodramatically, as if he felt that the case against the real Shmarya weren't overwhelming enough. Melech/Shmarya must have had, Richler imagines, a moment of choice similar to Noah's moment. The choice for Melech is between Judaism and Helga, an actress,[84] resulting in a simplistic, Freudian explanation of Melech: one must choose either Orthodoxy or desire. And choosing Orthodoxy must freeze all the juices, making one stiff and authoritarian, mustn't it? Melech's two sons, Max and Schloime, are psychologically simple as well: for them the alternatives to Orthodoxy are the crudest sort of money-worship and communist-baiting respectively.

Rabbi Rosenberg receives a gentler but no less firm rebuke from Richler. The novel intimates (though Avrum Richler disagrees) that Lily liked to compare Mordecai to his grandfather Rosenberg,[85] hoping to nudge her son into a writing style that kowtowed to tradition. Rosenberg's story – "How the Maharal of Prague, with the Aid of the Golem, Foiled a Plot by the Evil Priest Tadisch to Convert a Beautiful Jewish Girl to Christianity" – ended with the Duke's son converting to Judaism and donating his father's mansion to a yeshiva. Only then can the Duke's son marry his Jewish Cinderella.[86] Richler, for his part, showed a young Jewish man fleeing Orthodoxy and chasing shiksas. In later years, after twice marrying a shiksa, Richler would reprint Rabbi Rosenberg's story and follow it with Moe and others plotting a stag.[87] But, in Richler's marrying years, Rosenberg's idealized fables seemed less risible and more threatening. Richler allows the popularity of Noah's grandfather, Rabbi Jacob Goldenberg, to fade around 1925, as did that of Richler's grandfather. In what was called the Kosher Meat War, Rosenberg unsuccessfully challenged Rabbi Hirsch Cohen's right to regulate kashrut in Montreal.[88] Richler's important achievement isn't the history of the Montreal ghetto per se, but a larger pattern: the secularization of North American Jewry. Secular education, the tool of Richler's and Noah's emancipation, had been resisted by Rabbi Rosenberg, who complained that Jews, by abandoning religious schools, "make Jewish children into gentiles."[89] During Goldenberg's deathbed delirium in *Son of a Smaller Hero*, he believes that he is speaking to the eighteenth-century founder of Hasidism, the Baal Shem Tob [*sic*], and repeatedly presses Leah on whether she sees the kind of light that was reported at the Baal Shem Tob's death. When she finally gives in and reports a nonexistent light, it's clear that Rabbi Goldenberg has repressed his own existential insignificance, his absurdity – a repression as profound as Melech's.

Both of Noah's parents die, too, and *Son of a Smaller Hero* marked the second time that Richler killed off his mother in fiction. The first time, in *The Rotten People*, the point was to double Kerman's guilt at having left the mother who idolized him and having gone to Europe to write.[90] The troubling aspects of Lily's personality – her willingness to have an affair, her misanthropy and near-constant complaining, so out of keeping with her idealizing tendencies in faith – frustrated and drove and inhabited Richler. The symbolic convenience of Leah's death in *Son of a Smaller Hero* is meant to show how ineffectual Rabbi Rosenberg's and Lily's idealizing finally are,[91] particularly Lily's continual and pathetic harking back to a golden past in which her father ruled the Jews. In later years, Lily would ensure that Rosenberg, rather than being entombed like ordinary mortals, would rest in a little brick house where a perpetual fire would burn as a testament to his (*and her*) worth.[92] For much of his life, Richler had identified with Lily, but he had come to feel that, although he was loved deeply, he was loved by an inadequate person. In *Son of a Smaller Hero* he began explicitly to define himself against her, against not only her unconvincing religious and literary optimism, but against *her*. Yet in his willfulness, promiscuity, and the determination to get what he needed, Richler couldn't so easily banish her personality from his own. Both her indomitableness and her harshness appeared even in his rejection of her.

Son of a Smaller Hero also takes on white-bread Anglo-Saxon intellectuals, typified in Noah's college professor, Theo Hall. Richler based Hall on Neil Compton, his former English professor at Sir George and his former job reference (at whose house Richler had attended parties in 1952–53). Compton's fictional portrait is far from commendatory. Although Hall is not anti-Semitic and has a broad intellectual scope, he is repressed and ineffectual, lacking Noah's passion and losing his wife, Miriam, to the young Jew. In Noah's stealing and then abandonment of Hall's wife, the strain of adolescent fantasy runs strong. Miriam was based on Evelyn Sacks, not on Compton's wife, Pauline,[93] but what better way to show the intellectual virility of the young Jew than to have him cuckold his Anglo professor?

Brian Moore protested that Richler was treating Compton unfairly.[94] Thirty years later in *Joshua Then and Now*, Richler would examine his motives more profoundly when Joshua's similarly "stolen" wife, "Pauline," criticizes him: "Something in you called out for a prize. A golden shiksa."[95] Cathy Boudreau, spunky and poor like Richler, wasn't the sought-for prize, even if he dedicated *Son of a Smaller Hero* to her. The novel reveals Miriam's impoverished origins and French background just before Noah abandons her, not a good omen for Cathy. After Helen, Ulla, Cathy, and eventually Florence, who *was* the prize, Richler would insist that despite appearances he didn't have a policy on shiksa marriage and that he had had a Jewish girlfriend in Paris.[96] Possibly he was reshaping his life to make a point.[97] In 1954, at any rate, his girlfriend stance (both in fiction and in life) did seem programmatically anti-Jewish, a calculated defiance of Orthodoxy in the name of bohemia, evidenced in *Son of a Smaller Hero* when he has Marg Kennedy repeat the conventional wisdom about young Jewish rebels: "Eventually they all settled down with a dreadfully respectable Jewish girl."[98] Not me, Richler was saying, not me.

Someone whispered in Neil Compton's ear that he might want to take a peek at his former student's novel. Compton wrote Richler, "We heard weird rumours about the new novel. Do I have to duck out of Sir George Williams and pretend never to have heard of you, or can I stand up proudly and say this is the sort of thing well – I mean Sir George does for Canadian culch!"[99] There's no evidence that Compton directed any recriminations Richler's way. There's also no doubt that he recognized himself in the novel. Ten years later, when Compton was assigned to write an article on Montreal Jewish writers for *Commentary*, he jokingly warned Richler, "I may take my revenge for *Son of a Smaller Hero*."[100]

The extended Richler family felt even less gratified. Montreal's Jews recognized the people in the book, says his Uncle Bernard, and the family hated Richler for that.[101] A review in the *Jewish Standard* of Toronto came complete with a self-congratulatory warning that Toronto's Jews were fine, but Montreal's Jewish community had gone off the rails. Evidence? It produced people such as Richler.[102] A more astute Jewish reader called the novel brilliantly overwritten, with music-hall yids on one side and the young, who speak like Hollywood hoodlums, on the other.[103] A year after the novel came out, in what may have been a rebuke to Mordecai's version, David Richler (the "Yankel" of Mordecai's childhood) named his eldest son "Shmarya." One reporter, probably quoting Richler, afterwards said that *Son of a Smaller Hero* was read by a lot of people who didn't normally read books,[104] as if, by contrast, it were the habit of sophisticated literati to applaud when confronted with damning fictional portraits of themselves. Bernard spoke for a large segment of the family when he said to Richler, "we don't buy your books."[105]

Astutely, though not without guile (conveniently forgetting Chaim of *The Acrobats*), Richler countered that he wasn't interested in depicting sympathetic, downtrodden Jews who spoke in parables.[106] Richler's words echo any number of emancipist projects, but he went further, saying "I don't find [Jews] altogether cute or lovable or pathetic ... the Jewish-American middle class is plenty corrupt."[107] Although Richler portrayed resourceful Jews, stupid Jews, Jewish bullies, kindly Jews, those who were authorities in the ghetto, and those who were leaving to become movers and shakers in the Gentile world, his family sensed that he was doing more than just shattering stereotypes. It was simply inaccurate to accuse Richler of anti-Semitism, as some were doing[108] – ignoring the wide variety in his fictional characters and demanding that the minority writer be a cheerleader for his community – yet Montreal Jews correctly sensed his unspoken declaration that he wasn't really one of them, that, as he had tried to do in *The Acrobats* and would continue to do for some time, he was attempting to make himself over as a European existentialist writer. To savage the ghetto in the way that he did meant that he was outside it, a "liberated" Jew.

Even his friends complained. Jackie Moore spoke most directly: "In effect, you say, 'the Jews stink; the Gentiles stink; Montreal stinks; Canada stinks.' The end result is an all-pervasive stink."[109] Weintraub, who thought highly of Neil Compton and felt that Richler had skewered Compton because of his general propriety and moderation in alcohol, predicted that Richler's next books would be better ... when Richler became less angry. Weintraub also scolded Richler for the incredible lapse of good taste in calling a drunken Irish character "Moore" and in having a character named Mavis. "I don't think Brian will be annoyed," Weintraub said, "but it's such a bad joke."[110] That wasn't all. Weintraub didn't notice, but, in the novel, Max Adler, wanting to be a success among Gentiles, starts calling himself Mr Allen, just as Ted Allan, né Alan Herman, had done.[111] Other touches Weintraub no doubt noticed but chose to maintain a dignified silence about: for instance, one "Pincus Weintraub" made his fictional debut in the novel.[112]

It must have come as something of a blow to Richler when Weintraub, Jackie Moore, and a new contact at the CBC, Nathan Cohen, all declared that Noah, so closely modeled on Richler himself, was unsympathetic.[113] Only Brian Moore, calling Richler "Noah," brought up the crucial distinction: "The hero resembles you – although I think you a much better man than he is."[114] Other than the Joycean flight from home, Noah finds no clear solutions to his existential and artistic crises, but Richler clearly meant for Noah to be admired. Richler used Ivan Karamazov's famous statement – "If God did not exist, everything would be lawful" – as the epigraph to *Son of a Smaller Hero*. Early on, Noah combines Ivan's fateful musings with Richler's own juvenilia, to come up with "No God, no ethic: no ethic – freedom."[115] If that seems somewhat naïve, by the end of the novel Noah has recognized his similarity to Melech and Wolf and has in fact reached an ethical position. *Answer to Dostoevsky*, one might call *Son of a Smaller Hero*. Dostoevsky ultimately fastens his ethic to God and undermines Ivan, who has unwittingly supplied Smerdyakov with an ideology of absolute murderous freedom. On the contrary, Richler answers, Noah *will* have a secular ethic, cobbled together out of the materials at hand and acknowledged, if not exactly blessed, by an Orthodox grandfather. Richler directly affirms Noah's position when Noah kisses and yet detaches himself from Melech. Melech is Shmarya tamed; and the respectful parting of ways is Richler's fantasy autobiography, recovering in fiction what the intransigence of the real Shmarya had denied him in life. His decision to treat Melech with a modicum of respect probably owed something to Weiner, who had urged him to highlight Melech and the scroll, both of which impressed her as constructive elements in the novel.[116] In subsequent explanations of the writer's task, Richler faithfully used the scaffolding he had set out in Noah. The artist, Richler would insist, must find morality in a world where there is no agreement on values: "We are living at a time when superficially life seems meaningless, and we have to make value judgements all the time, it seems in relation to nothing."[117]

If the novel consistently stacked the deck against Noah's opponents, *Son of a Smaller Hero* nevertheless in several ways marked a huge advance in Richler's writing. Satire, its brilliance in the later novels excusing all manner of deck-stacking, was beginning to raise its head. Noah's landlady in *tiefste Provinz* Montreal assumes that *The Naked and the Dead* must be a medical text. David Lerner, a lampoon of the gifted but (according to Richler) compromised A.M. Klein, discovers that among Canadian Jews his ode to Wolf Adler, the *Torah*-rescuer, circulated much better than did his "Ode to Sacco and Vanzetti." At the same time as Richler was getting funnier, he was also getting more honest. Instead of the idealized artist André who has renounced fame, we have Noah: a tortured, self-doubting writer, hating and loving a mother stuck on Keats, hating and loving a brow-beaten father who holds to Orthodoxy yet skirts Sabbath laws by buying snacks on credit.[118] Because Richler weighted fictional situations with the gravity of autobiography, the novel rings true despite the polemic against Montreal Jewry. Some of those imagined situations – does Wolf jump into the fire to save money or to save the Torah? – capture, with great precision, Richler's sense of his society's contemporary relation to Torah Judaism. In some ways *The Acrobats*, though a reasonably entertaining story, didn't matter. *Son of a Smaller Hero* mattered.

10

Friends and Enemies

SON OF A SMALLER HERO received pride of place in the Andre Deutsch
1955 Spring catalogue.[1] Nevertheless, given the poor sales of *The Acrobats*,
Putnam's in the US declined to publish the new book.[2] In Canada, where
the competition was less fierce, *Son of a Smaller Hero* stood out as a powerful and original work. The judges of a *Maclean's* novel contest chose *Son
of a Smaller Hero* as worthy of first prize, which was to include serializa-
tion in *Maclean's*. Unprintable, the magazine's genteel editors declared – and
vetoed the novel for being anti-Semitic.[3] Richler wasn't impressed by his
country's attitude. "I don't want to be respected, man, I just want to be accepted," he said.[4]

Already in January 1955, and then every few months after that, Richler talked of a return home. "I must get back to Montreal in 56. Figure on
settling there eventually. It's the place I know and can write about best. I
have no choice."[5] But he couldn't put aside the dream of making it in Europe, and it would be another seventeen years before he came home permanently. Still, the acknowledgement was important: he began reworking the
story "Mr. MacPherson" into the novel that would make his reputation. But
because of world events, another novel, *A Choice of Enemies*, would intervene.

Richler took one more stab, his last, at Paris. During February and
March 1955, he rented a three-room apartment in Montparnasse and earned
$80 monthly by writing two articles for UNESCO. Many of his former friends
were gone. The way that Richler phrased it, however, it was Cathy who was
lonely and missed Florence Mann.[6] As he sweated through the outline for
his third novel – his first true original, he believed – Richler tried to put
Cathy to work on a pornographic novel. He knew that they could get 200,000
francs (about $600) immediately from Obelisque Press, with another 300,000
upon delivery.[7] The porn never came to fruition, though the "Mrs Oglivy"
sections in *Barney's Version* suggest that Richler himself had a certain facil-
ity in the genre.

Richler and Cathy returned to London and found a flat at 5 Winchester Road – three rooms, no bathroom, on the third storey of a crumbling Victorian house in Swiss Cottage.[8] She worked; he wrote. What she really wanted was a child, and early in 1955 she suffered a miscarriage, but Richler must have been relieved because he was quick to joke about it and he told Diana Athill that he didn't want a child. If Cathy had a child, Richler feared he'd have to stay with her forever.[9]

The West Indian writer George Lamming, with whom Richler had become friends in London a year earlier and to whose daughter Richler would become godfather, moved in for a while.[10] As colonials, the two men were equally puzzled by the British, and thus drawn to one another.[11] They frequented the Mandrake Club together, waiting on Friday afternoons for their wives to show up with full pay envelopes.[12] When Weintraub arrived in London, he found "a real lit factory with George Lamming batting out a novel in guest room, Mort polishing novel in front room, and Cathy doing scripttyping job for Reuben Ship in kitchen" [sic]. Richler and Weintraub collaborated on an NFB film called *First November*. Richler could laugh about their protagonist Harry Merton, a struggling writer who lives off his wife's earnings,[13] but Richler's own rejection slips knocked on the door with dispiriting frequency

He turned his attention again to writing for money, and CBC Radio came through. Robert Weaver, the young producer who would do so much for Canadian writing, accepted "Benny, the War in Europe, and Myerson's Daughter Bella."[14] The story on which the radio play was based didn't hold much promise. Benny, labouring under his parents' constant comparisons of him to "the Shapiro boy," goes to war and comes home shell-shocked. There's no indication that Richler knew anything about shell shock; rather, he treats it as a clever device to make possible the manifold humiliations of Benny, creating a pathos that works mainly because the reader isn't allowed to see too deeply into him. Yet Richler was writing about what he knew best, Jewish Montreal, and his family: Benny was an exaggerated version of Moe; Benny's pushy mother and pushy wife were both versions of Lily. Most importantly, Richler was developing the rudiments of his style. In lines such as Myerson's "I need him here like I need a cancer" or the exchange between Bella and Benny –

"You feel like a cup coffee?'
"I wouldn't say no."[15]

– Richler was mining cliché not just as comment on the characters' intellectual limits but as their self-display and as trace of a certain Jewish social order. Cliché here begins its Richlerian career as a performance that the characters calculate (ineptly overcalculate) will get them their share of social respect, and as a deep expression of a selfhood that in Richler's terms was *not good enough*.

Even though he apparently turned down an offer of a regular TV-writing job for £100/week,[16] one of his unproduced TV scripts from this period, *A Tram Named Elsie*, shows the positive effects of commercialization. A madman taxi driver, who reads books such as "How to Succeed," takes over a tram on its last day. He is hounded by schoolchildren, despised by women, and harried by a maze of tram rules before he explodes in a rage and takes Elsie on an unauthorized journey.[17] No TV producer could wag a finger here at too much dialogue or too much profundity; the screenplay is an energetic and satirical romp through London. Richler worked on the script with his mentor Michael Sayers, but the final product didn't seem literary enough to Sayers.[18]

≶

By early 1956, Richler's new circle of friends and acquaintances consisted mostly of Americans who had fled the US. They were blacklisted writers and TV people – including Carl Foreman, who had recently written the screenplay for *High Noon* – most of them Communists or leftists. The Rhodesian expatriate Doris Lessing, who lived nearby, befriended the Richlers, and at her parties Richler met *New Statesman* and *Tribune* journalists, as well as veterans of the Spanish Civil War. He was tongue-tied in the presence of John Sommerfield, author of *Volunteer in Spain*. The crowd drank hard and worried about CIA informants, reviling Eli Kazan, Clifford Odets, and anybody else who had bowed under pressure to testify before HUAC (the House Un-American Activities Committee) as a friendly witness. Arthur Miller was their hero for mythologizing their stance in *The Crucible*. No surprise, then, that Richler should be mistaken for a deported US writer and be invited to lecture to a communist writers' group (only a few souls showed up) or that he should imitate Ted Allan in writing about that *de rigueur* leftist subject, the Spanish Civil War.[19] His was a delicate position. Among his TV friends, he held that important post, Authentic Representative of the Working Class, and he depended upon them for TV work. At the same time he was beginning to scoff at their politics.

Two of his best friends were among the blacklisted – Ted Allan and Reuben Ship, both from Montreal. In Montreal, Richler had reported on CBM that HUAC had lassoed Ship for financial contributions to the defense of Madrid. Less sentimental accounts blamed the fact that he had served as the Communist Party's literature director and that he had made a speech arguing that American manufacturers enforced anti-Semitic and anti-labour views on the radio. Summoned before HUAC, he called the members witchhunters and quoted Thomas Jefferson on freedom. In Los Angeles, Ship became front-page news. Patriotic Americans stood up for God and country by phoning Ship at all hours and shouting obscenities. He was deported in 1953, flown to Canada in handcuffs.[20]

Ship immediately wrote a satire on McCarthyism, *The Investigator*, for CBC Radio, and it became an underground hit in the US. The investigator dies and goes to Heaven, where his new committee tries to revoke the permanent resident status of potential dissidents such as Socrates, Jefferson, and, for the benefit of Canadians, William Lyon MacKenzie. Eventually the investigator overreaches himself and decides to subpoena even "the Chief."[21] Unfortunately for Ship, the investigator himself is more interesting than the dissidents with all their pious speeches.

Ship's radio play, performed in Britain, wasn't far from Richler's mind as he began his own politically motivated works of the period. He *liked* the blacklisted expatriates. Ship, in particular, Richler considered light-hearted and, despite what one might expect, not at all obsessed with a sense of tragic betrayal.[22] It also didn't hurt that Ship sent work Richler's way, for example an early Peter Sellers comedy short, *Insomnia Is Good for You*.[23] But despite the friendship, Richler didn't really belong among the blacklisted.[24] By now, he considered communists muddleheaded and was quick to argue politics, even though he, too, supported Labour. His friends scolded Richler for being an apolitical cynic.[25] After Nikita Khrushchev detailed Stalin's crimes in an eight-hour "secret" speech in February 1956, many British communists went into a flurry of self-examination and defensive posturing. Ted Allan, who suddenly realized that he had dedicated his life to a monster, had a breakdown.[26] Not Richler. For years he had noticed the little ironies when the well-heeled martyrs of the blacklist howled about the injustices of the British class system, yet schemed to get their children into the right schools. They (AKA Ted Allan) lived high on the hog courtesy of *Robin Hood*, the richest British TV series, yet made a Jewish tailor doing piecework for the Sheriff of Nottingham chirp, "all property is theft."[27] And Richler himself was acclimatizing: "I learned to … begin any description of a wog or somebody-not-quite-my-class as that 'nice little man.'"[28] Within a few years Brian Moore would be secretly relieved when Richler, too, sold out and sent his adopted son, Daniel, to an expensive school.[29]

≋

The most important political event of the day was the Suez Crisis, and Richler was still enough of a leftist to join in the protests. In 1952, after the Egyptian Revolution, the socialist Colonel Gamel Abdel Nasser had sent British troops packing, and in April 1956 he nationalized the Canal. The Israelis, denied access to both the Suez and now the Gulf of Aqaba, and aware that Nasser had recently formed a joint military command with Jordan and

Syria, feared that Egypt's Russian-made weapons would soon be pointed at Jews. On 29 October, Israel attacked. It mowed a swath through the Egyptian Army, seizing Gaza and the Sinai. Britain and France, who had long called the shots in the Suez, nominated themselves as referees (after consulting Israel) and rushed troops toward the Suez a week later. The UN, including even the US, immediately denounced both the Israeli aggression and the Franco-British "intervention." So did the bulk of the British Labour Party and even forty Conservative MPs. Labour leader Aneurin (Nye) Bevan condemned the use of "epic weapons for squalid and trivial ends."[30]

To many on the left, the choice seemed simple: either resurrect the old and rancid British imperialism or allow the colonies self-determination. So said Brian Moore, remembering the Irish experience.[31] Richler, like other Jews, saw a more complex picture. He supported Labour and particularly admired Bevan, a coal-miner's son who *nevertheless* (as Richler was fond of noting) loved books and fine wines.[32] In principle, Richler opposed colonialism. In practice, however, Egypt had been making commando raids across the Israeli border, so he wasn't about to shed tears when British Conservative Prime Minister Anthony Eden took a pro-Israeli stance. Bill Weintraub spoke for Richler when he said, "I guess it must look a lot different from Tel Aviv ... every Arab screaming that Israel must perish."[33] Compounding the problem of leftist allegiances was the recent abortive uprising in Hungary against Communist rule. After the harsh years of Stalin, Khrushchev's secret speech declared the will to liberalize (in a limited way) and to ease Khrushchev's own conscience. The Hungarians, misled by such talk and by minor reforms in Poland, took to the streets, hoping to break through to an open, multiparty society. Mobs knocked over a statue of Stalin, and corpses dangled from lampposts.[34] Initially, Khrushchev wavered, but at 5:19 A.M., 4 November, he sent in Russian tanks.

Later that same morning, and in an atmosphere now suddenly charged with the blood flowing on the Hungarian streets, British Labourites gathered for a gigantic "Eden Must Go" rally against Britain's Suez intervention, the largest public demonstration since the war, many of the protesters young.[35] Rumours flew that the US was threatening a nuclear strike against the Russians.[36] Carrying signs that said "Law – Not War," about ten thousand people jammed into Whitehall and Trafalgar Square,[37] among them Richler, Bill Weintraub, Bernice Weintraub – and Florence Mann.

Since meeting Florence the day before his own wedding, Richler had become very sensitive to the Manns' movements. Nathan Cohen, evidently responding to a Richler comment, said that he had raked Stanley over the coals because Stanley didn't want to return to England posthaste. "Nothing good can come of his staying," Cohen said, and sensing that Richler would like the news, added that Florence was grateful.[38] At one social occasion

Richler told Ted Kotcheff, "She's mine. I want her." But she's married, Kotcheff replied. Richler wasn't put off, "I don't care. I want her and I'm going to take her."[39] In later years, Richler told Noah, "I didn't win your mother just like that; it takes a little work you know."[40] An understatement: by the time of the huge "Eden Must Go" rally Florence was seven months pregnant with her husband's son, Daniel. Stanley had been philandering, indiscreetly, and Richler had been visiting the Manns alone, though it never occurred to Stanley that Richler might be interested in his wife.[41] In *Joshua Then and Now*, Richler's alter ego Joshua begins his romance by pressing against Pauline in the middle of the march's political turmoil. Weintraub says that Florence wasn't in Trafalgar Square that day,[42] but in fact she was, though she won't speak of what happened there.[43]

The Labour crowd had come to Trafalgar highly incensed by Eden's equivocations. Britain, merely separating the combatants,[44] wasn't really *at war*, Eden had claimed, only in a state of "armed conflict."[45] Bevan set the mass of protesters ablaze with an impassioned speech, shouting, "If Eden is sincere in what he is saying – and he may be – then he is too stupid to be Prime Minister."[46] The crowd chanted, "Eden must go! Eden must go!" in response, and then moved, with Richler and the Weintraubs near the front, down Whitehall. At first the bobbies allowed this, but when it became clear that the destination was #10 Downing Street, where Eden sat in meetings, the mounted policemen tried to halt the marchers. Repeatedly the marchers pushed forward; repeatedly the police forced them back. In the end, the crowd gave up. Slowly people began to disperse, and by early evening Richler found his way home.[47]

This surge of public militancy, along with international opinion and diplomacy, convinced Britain to accept a ceasefire and to save face by giving way to UN forces. My plan all along, Eden insisted in hindsight, and he repeated a bus driver's comment that one could ignore the protest, since "Eighty per cent of the crowd were of foreign extraction."[48] It was a lesson in politics for Richler. He shared the marchers' satisfaction that they could influence British foreign policy, but, given the ambiguity of his own feelings about Israel's actions, what appears most strongly in his later accounts of the march is his relief at the orderliness and restraint of police action. The contrast with the Soviet tanks in Hungary no doubt helped.[49]

≶

During and after the Suez and Hungarian upheavals – perhaps because of them – Richler wrote several politically motivated works: the TV scripts *Harry Like the Player Piano* and *A Friend of the People*, and the novel *A Choice of Enemies*. When Richler had visited England, in 1950–51, near the end of Clement Atlee's Labour Government, he had praised Labour for bringing in

National Health and for raising the living standard of the working class.[50] But not long afterward, Labour began to pall for him. He read Isaac Babel's *Red Cavalry*[51] and shared with the Russian Jew an early faith in socialism, then disillusionment. Babel's old Jew, Gedali, pleased when revolutionaries thrash his Polish oppressors, admits that he is less pleased at what follows, "Then he that has beaten the Pole says to me; 'Hand in your gramophone to be registered, Gedali ... Gedali I will shoot at you, and then you will find out, I cannot do otherwise than shoot, because I am the revolution.'"[52] The continued "shooting" in Hungary in 1956 didn't exactly boost Richler's socialist inclinations or inspire sorrow for the blacklisted communists; although he befriended people who could aid his career, he was never afraid to attack their views ... or them. Richler's three works weren't likely to please his TV mentors Reuben Ship and Ted Allan, but he had ceased to worry about such things.

For some of his TV work Richler used pseudonyms such as John P. Swan,[53] but he must have thought *Harry Like the Player Piano* and *A Friend of the People* good enough (they aren't) to use his real name. *Harry Like the Player Piano* began life as *The Interview*.[54] A reporter named Lou Coleman interviews the Canadian writer Harry Wharton, who feels abused by the left. The left coddled him and his superficial work for years, but then dropped him the moment he began to think more deeply and to question the Party. Critic Frank Lalor told Richler to temper his anger, told him that exposing a few phoney world-savers was hardly worth the candle, that it would be better to find where the real tragedy lay.[55]

Richler tried to follow the advice. He turned the straightforward *Interview* into *Harry Like the Player Piano*: more "documentary" clips, less Harry. Richler made Harry a bit like himself and Harry's father Jimmy a bit like Moe. Of his son, Jimmy says, "He had a grudge against the world ... He didn't like my being a barber. Can you imagine that, sir?"[56] Like Richler, Harry cheered for Henry Wallace's third-party presidential campaign and worshipped at the shrine of the Spanish Civil War. "I know you don't like anybody making jokes about the Spanish trenches," Ted Allan wrote to Richler as late as 1985. But soon the similarities between Harry and Richler break down, and Harry begins to look suspiciously like Ted Allan. Allen was witty, boastful, absolutely confident in his views and his literary destiny. He had long defended Stalin, and in Spain Allan feared that he had betrayed a Montreal acquaintance, Harry Muscowitz, who had been accused of being a Trotskyite and a spy for the fascists.[57] Richler's Harry insists that without the heroic defense of Stalingrad we wouldn't be here. When told that Spanish leftists are shooting Trotskyites, he dismisses concerns, saying, "It's a revolution, not a talmudic discussion." After his first novel, *Let Them Eat Cake*, Harry repeatedly finds reasons not to write – there are more important things in Spain to attend to! When he finally does write, the new novel is so polemical that no one wants it: "This is 1956 ... the workers of the world ... Are saving up for the next installments on their TV sets." Harry's conservative son, whom Richler named Ted, leaves to protest the Soviet intervention in Hungary, but Harry dismisses the anti-communist groundswell there as "a bunch of Hungarian noblemen, Horthy fascists."[58]

Although Richler intends to satirize the inadequacies of ideological writers such as Ted Allan, *Harry Like the Player Piano* is much too ideological itself, too wooden. There are moments of humour, as when Lou declares that Canadian indifference and the capitalist system killed Harry, but Richler's personal involvement in the issues, without a deep involvement in the characters, sabotages the play. Harry is an alternative self, Richler's version of 'what I could have become if ...' As the writer that Richler *refused* to be, Harry demands heavy censure. Yet for all its woodenness, the play does end lyrically, the disillusioned reporter crying, "Those guys who went off to Spain were tall, plenty tall, and they got a very bad deal."[59] *Harry Like the Player Piano* was never produced: too many people on both sides of the Atlantic thought that it wouldn't be understood.[60]

A Choice of Enemies, originally called *Till Break of Day*,[61] was a much more complex approach to the same issues. When Nathan Cohen saw the manuscript, he wondered, as only the imperious Cohen could, what the point was. Hadn't the issue of whether or not to join communism been settled definitively in the 1930s and 1940s? Witness Arthur Koestler's *Darkness at Noon* (1941).[62] But for Richler the questions were very much alive. John Osborne's working-class play *Look Back in Anger* had recently premiered, explosively, at the Royal Court Theatre,[63] and most of Richler's friends "had bet their lives on politics."[64] He argued with them daily.

One might call *A Choice of Enemies* the novel that Joyce Weiner wrote by telepathy. It is dedicated to her, and although she, too, felt that the issues were outworn, she had for years been pushing Richler towards what she called "objectivity." He finally surrendered, and announced that his third novel would be his first "objective" work.[65] He was even able to fool some critics about this,[66] mainly because he didn't show up directly as a character. In fact, he *did* show up, though in disguise.

Not as Norman Price. *A Choice of Enemies* revolves around Norman, a fortyish Anglo-Canadian professor and blacklisted writer who has landed on his feet in London. Norman will not admit to himself that he is sexually attracted to a friend's daughter, Sally, twenty years his junior. He's neither kind enough to let her go, nor assertive enough to declare his love. If Richler had escaped the haze of romanticism that for him once surrounded Anglos, he had absorbed too much Morley Callaghan. Norman is more thought-experiment than man, too naïve, too good for his own good, the Nietzschean caricature of a principled man. Straw men, Brian Moore called the novel's characters.[67] In Callaghan's Catholic universe such partly ideal figures collide with a harsh social order in productive, though scarifying ways. But in Richler's more barren world, principled kindliness amounts to a dangerous lack of self-knowledge, and Norman's wavering ultimately destroys Sally.

Norman's "communism" is similarly fraught with ambivalence. Like US writers of the 1940s and 50s, Richler was attentive to history, and by the time his first novel was published he depended upon realism to suture his work to events. Richler observed Norman's milieu and drew devastating portraits of the expatriate, fellow-travelling Jews in London's film community. The infidelities, the petty jealousies, the jockeying for scripts, the scripts themselves jockeying between correct politics and wit – all of these surface in Richler's delightful and un*literary* party chatter. But it was a troubled realism, never sure when to kick aside hyperbole and allegory. Is Norman a simple allegory of the Party Man, who wilfully forgets Stalin's excesses? It appears so, even though Norman, like Richler, has moved long enough in Hollywood expatriate circles to dread the correct politics that the expatriates substitute for lost artistic (and therefore political) clout. Norman senses that among his friends socialism has become a narrow set of glib responses, not a lived standard. The ultimate indignity: Norman's friends blacklist *him* for his refusal to continue parroting leftist ideals. In later years Richler would come up with his own set of glib responses. Joe McCarthy? Quite the best thing to happen to Hollywood. Cleaned out all the bad and uninspired writers.[68]

At the moment that Norman is blacklisted by the victims of the blacklist he seems like an interesting realist character, capable of growth: he is writing a closet book on John Dryden, the revolutionary poet who turned Royalist when it seemed prudent to do so. But soon Richler packs Norman off into allegory again as he has a breakdown and amnesia descends. Allegory and *roman à clef*: Norman's defense of Stalin and breakdown after Khrushchev's secret speech both pointed directly at Ted Allan, as those in Richler's circle knew.[69] When the Khrushchev revelations about Stalin appear in the press, Norman suspects the US State Department of authoring them.[70] Ted Allan, likewise, had laughed at how ineptly the Khrushchev speech recycled old Trotskyite slanders against Stalin – CIA propaganda obviously. When the speech refused to go away, Allan "realized" that Khrushchev must be a secret Trotskyist. It took months before Allan could admit that Stalin had committed the crimes; then Allan broke down and called his own life "a farce."[71] The name "Norman Price" was Richler's joke … in code. For years, Allan had traded on his former relationship with the famous Canadian communist Dr Norman Bethune, whom he considered a surrogate father, and Allan, ever the showman, had gone so far as to name his son Norman Bethune Allan. Already an adolescent, Norman Allan felt that he was competing with Richler for his father's attention.[72] Of course,

Ted Allan recognized himself in *A Choice of Enemies* and wasn't flattered. For a short time he even broke off his friendship with Richler.[73]

Yet the heart of the novel isn't Norman at all. If Norman is Richler's thought-experiment, Ernst Haupt, the young and rather savage émigré from East Germany, is his *person*. Although one wouldn't expect Richler's sympathy to lie with a former Nazi, Ernst was Richler's way of being the *enfant terrible*, thumbing his nose at those truths held to be self-evident by Allan, Ship, and co. Why not put a former member of the Hitler Jugend in the henhouse and see exactly how far the socialists would extend universal brotherhood? Richler's major narrative miscalculation – that before Ernst comes to London he kills Norman's brother – was intended to put a point on the limits of brotherhood and of Norman's civilized kindliness, but the effect is melodramatic. Not so with Ernst's character. Despite the surface disguises (Ernst's anti-Semitism, his beating of Sally) and Richler's stated antipathy towards Germans,[74] Ernst is Richler: a ghetto boy clawing his way through an alien society.

Repeatedly Ernst enacts Richler's personal circumstances and philosophies, though sometimes in an exaggerated fashion. Ernst plays the role that Richler saw himself playing among leftists: the outsider who tells unpleasant truths, especially at parties. The film-world socialists, who have little patience to hear of Communist repression, hear from Ernst about the political contortions in East Germany, where it was politic to take off one's Hitler Jugend badge and put on the badge of the Freie Deutsche Jugend (the youth wing of the Socialist Unity Party). By the time the novel begins, Ernst has given up on politics,[75] and he rejects the film bourgeoisie. Doris Lessing remembers Richler as a similar odd-man-out among the communists and fellow-travellers. At the same time, he was unwilling (as yet) to make peace with the bourgeoisie: "Mordecai would stand with his back to a wall a glass in hand, inarticulate or almost stammering, lovably modest, genuinely so," says Lessing. "He would confront me, or Ted Allan, or Reuben, all of us weighed down with responsibility and children, with the earnest and urgent query, straight from the flaming heart of the bohemian myth – Do you think an artist ought to get married and burden himself with children? Surely that destroys talent?"[76] Partly this was a function of Richler's naïveté. Partly his anti-bourgeois stance was a symptom of his growing impatience with Cathy, not unlike Ernst's impatience with Sally. The unpleasant little Nazi initially plays the role of uppity young Jew, stealing desirable women from under the noses of Anglo males. After a while, however, when Sally declares that she and Ernst are in love, Ernst agrees wearily, and asks, "But where... where are we going?" Ernst's sense of purpose returns only in moments when he thinks that he has left Sally for good.[77]

Although Richler had as good as dismissed Moe and Lily in *Son of a*

Smaller Hero, familial circumstances, too, tie Ernst to Richler. Like Moe, Ernst's father declares that Ernst is no longer his son, and tells him not to come home again, though that doesn't prevent the father from asking his son for money. Most importantly, Ernst's distrust of metaphysics paralleled Richler's own. Sally says that she believes in God. "Who?" Ernst asks.[78] In a deleted epilogue for the novel, a Canadian truck driver asks whether Ernst believes in God, and, when Ernst replies in the affirmative, the truck driver proposes a version of Pascal's Wager: "If there isn't one believing in Him still won't do you no harm and if there is one it ought to do you some good."[79] But Ernst has fallen asleep. Instead of right and wrong, Ernst (in the published novel) sees only "conditions, rewards, punishments and sides."[80] Responding to the problem of morality in a post-metaphysical universe, Ernst goes beyond Richler, approaching instead the attitude of Karp, Richler's unsentimental portrait of a Holocaust survivor. What Karp arrived at through his concentration camp experience – a belief in nothing[81] – Ernst arrives at by watching politics in operation.

Not the German, not the Jew, not the disengaged intellectual, not the engaged intellectual, not the avant-garde, not the bourgeoisie – no one in the novel provides a viable solution to the problems raised. The deleted epilogue sees Ernst on the road again, fleeing to the US,[82] but Richler cut that too-clear romanticizing of Ernst. The published novel ends bleakly with Ernst blackmailed into marrying the widow Kramer and the amnesiac Norman retreating into the most unlikely of marriages to "Horse-Face" Vivian, intending Voltaire's post-political solution – "*il faut cultiver notre jardin*," ("we must cultivate our garden") – and wishing, with clear futility, that Vivian would have a baby. Meantime, the most refined of the socialists, Bob Landis, explains that Stalin is only a stage in socialism, praises the USSR for the magnificent drop in its infant mortality rate, and almost in the same breath demands that his new mistress, Sally, get an abortion.[83]

At the time of *Cocksure*, Richler began to talk of the writer as "the loser's advocate." Only a few writers, Richler said, live up to this moral responsibility. Rather, most writers labour to "compose paeans of disguised praise of people very much like themselves."[84] Richler had read Moore's *The Lonely Passion of Judith Hearne*, and, looking back at his own works, he convinced himself *post facto* that he, too, had an abiding interest in the downtrodden. Never mind that he found them unsympathetic or laughable. *A Choice of Enemies* was supposed to be one of the exemplars of the theory,[85] but it's difficult to take the hard-headed Ernst for a loser when he forcefully articulates so many of Richler's views, so much of Richler's situation, and survives despite all odds. The real "losers" aren't those who are literally homeless, but people like Norman in *A Choice of Enemies* and Harry in *Harry Like the Player Piano*, who've lost their way. Richler had no patience for such "losers," and we must look elsewhere than "the loser's advocate" for Richler's moral sense.

Richler's third work of the period, the TV script *A Friend of the People* (originally called *Spain*[86]), was his most political, overtly and covertly, a companion piece to *A Choice of Enemies*. *A Friend of the People* occurs during the Spanish Civil War and concerns Norman Price's father, Dr Max Price (briefly mentioned in *A Choice of Enemies*), a hard-drinking, womanizing Canadian doctor on the Republican side. Some reviewers complained about the familiarity of the plot, probably both because Price is that popular literary character, a leftist who falls out with the revolution over its methods, and because of Price's obvious similarity to Norman Bethune. In *A Choice of Enemies*, Richler had cobbled together Max Price and Norman Bethune to come with "Norman Price." In *A Friend of the People*, Max Price, unlike the historical Bethune, dies at the hands of a jealous woman. Some of Richler's ironies already required knowledge of more than one of his works. Norman Price considers his father Max's day a time when the choice of enemies was clear,[87] but to read the TV script alongside the novel is to recognize that Richler doesn't share his character's nostalgia. Thankfully, Richler soon abandoned the rudiments of this white-bread Yoknapatawpha in favour of his true home, St. Urbain Street.

A Friend of the People addresses the betrayal of leftist hopes on a less subtle level, taking its audience directly to propaganda and murder. The title, a Republican password, appears first in the mouth of Jan, whose father was killed by the Fascist leader General Gero's secret police. In an early draft, Richler had made Jan the most promising Spanish poet, who, after the murder of his parents, never wrote another word. The maturing Richler, trying to erase the young romantic who wrote *The Acrobats*, crossed out the bit about the silenced poet, and gave Jan a surname – Lemming – not designed to evoke sympathy, but sure to get a rise out of Richler's house guest, George Lamming. Jan oversees the defection of Colonel Matya Proz and his remarketing as a Man of the People (Proz has some claims to peasant origins). Later, when Proz is suspected of revealing troop positions to the Fascists, Jan has no compunctions about having him assassinated, blaming the Fascists, and then lionizing the newly minted Republican martyr. Jan speaks to his more squeamish comrades in an uncompromising and somewhat clichéd language of political realism: "Oh, you gentle, fastidious people, you sentimental humanists, you parlour rebels, haven't you heard? The meek aren't going to inherit the earth unless they develop souls of iron to take it."[88] Jan's machinations were based on stories that Ted Allan told about the Civil War. Republican authorities had sent Allan, Bethune's protégé, to Bethune's blood transfusion unit to observe and report on the diminishing morale there. While Allan was "spying" on Bethune, Bethune confided that he suspected one of his colleagues, Dr Culebras of being a fascist saboteur. Bethune was right, but Allan didn't believe him.[89] Eventually it was the temperamental and often-drunk Bethune who got sent home to Canada, privately disgraced though publicly a hero.[90]

A Friend of the People received mixed reviews,[91] though reviewers didn't notice what Allan, Ship, and Richler's other friends, so attuned to the worldwide progress of Communism, must have immediately seen: the un-Spanish names of two Spaniards. The medium of TV doesn't usually encourage attention to subtlety, and critics who thought that A Friend of the People wasn't timely had missed the echoes in "General Gero" and "Jan." When the Hungarian protesters threatened Communist rule and called for a withdrawal from the Warsaw Pact, it was the Hungarian hardliners – General Secretary of the Communist party Ernö Gerö, and Prime Minister Ján (János) Kádár – who pushed hardest for Khrushchev to bring in the Soviet tanks. More than thirty thousand people died in Hungary, most of them between the "Eden Must Go" rally on 4 November 1956 and the arrival of A Friend of the People at the CBC the following January.

≶

Thus began a period in Richler's life during which he looked upon politics with a jaundiced eye,[92] though it would soon be Canadian and Israeli politics, rather than the Cold War, that would capture his attention. When a few years later he rang doorbells for the Labour Party, it wasn't out of political conviction, but only in hope of getting some good material for a magazine piece.[93] When Ted Allan, Doris Lessing, and Ted Kotcheff joined the brief flight of Centre 42, a politicized working-class theatre – much experiment, nominal pay – Richler was scathing in his criticisms.[94] For starters, he didn't approve of theatre and couldn't be enticed to go to there, except for Chekhov or Look Back in Anger. Like TV, theatre was a communal art form; therefore it wasn't as serious as the novel and could be hijacked for propaganda.[95] The British Labour Party was tired, Richler announced in 1959, but in fact it was he who was tired of the Labour Party.[96] For the better: Richler's slow divorce from socialism and continuing affection for the work of Evelyn Waugh[97] made his writing freer. The three political works of this period allowed Richler to unburden himself of the earnestness and romanticism of so much leftist writing.

He may have expected his political works to cost him some friends, as Son of a Smaller Hero had done among his relatives. That didn't happen. Reuben Ship remained close and would soon take Richler into his home just after Richler's marriage failed. Ted Allan, not working and in bad shape,[98] came round again. In A Choice of Enemies, the TV crowd made Norman suffer for his political cynicism, but Richler thrived.

11

Florence Mann, the Golden *Shiska*

IT WAS THE HABIT of some in the British film crowd to holiday in the south of France, so in March 1957 Richler, too, headed for his old stomping grounds above the Riviera, Tourrettes-sur-loup. Stanley Mann, Florence, and their baby, Daniel, had gone to Canada,[1] though not before Richler had declared his love to Florence.[2] The Canadian poet F.R. Scott wrote him, "I often think of the Richler-Moore-Surrey combination at Tourrette-sur-Loup [*sic*] with envy. What an opportunity for taking ones-self and country apart."[3] Well ... not exactly. Richler reported to Weintraub that he was going to Juan les Pins for a swim, then to dinner at Cannes with Reuben Ship and co., then to the Crazy Horse Saloon for the striptease.[4] Twenty years later, Richler would joke with Moore about "the historic Chicken Liver Loaf Writers Conference of 1956" (probably 1957) as a seminal moment in the genesis of Canadian literature, but at the time relations had cooled between the two writers, for Moore revealed his misgivings about *A Choice of Enemies* – too many coincidences, poor writing, "full of crap" – and took to calling Richler "the Bard."[5]

Still, parties abounded in Tourrettes, especially after Richler invited Terry Southern and Mason Hoffenberg down. In Paris, Southern had begun a pornographic novel, *Candy*, because with a dirty book one could theoretically make money and strike a blow against bourgeois sexual mores at the same time. But he had gotten bogged down. Why not come down to Tourrettes with your wife? Richler suggested. Why not bring along Hoffenberg – that bag of ideas – as a collaborator?[6] Yet *Candy* proved to be hard work, and Hoffenberg lacked the stamina to write every day.[7] The collaborators struggled to get a few pages of pornography in the can each day so that they could in good conscience join Richler and a new acquaintance for poker.

Eventually, Southern and Hoffenberg would return to Paris to complete *Candy*.[8] It would sell up to 7 million copies, many of them from pirated editions, so the publisher Girodias made money, the bootleggers made money, while the authors got a $500 flat fee[9] and the intoxication of seeing their work in print. Richler, starting in again on *The Apprenticeship of Duddy Kravitz*, watched attentively. He grasped that the pornographic book mill was not quite the gold mine it appeared to be. Based on the first flush of *Candy*'s success, he told his Uncle Bernard that he could easily have written "sexy" books and made any amount of money.[10] Somewhat disingenuous, one might say, but he did realize that pornographic material was a literary dead end. It could bring temporary notoriety, but not serious attention over the long haul. At the same time, however, Richler was filing away for future use the notion that sex could be funny and that sexual content certainly didn't harm sales. At the urging of Weiner and Athill he had turned away from the bourgeois-defying, existential sex of his early work. By the late 1950s and throughout the 1960s he began to let "the sexy stuff" back into his work, less portentously and more pleasurably.

Before Southern left for Paris, Richler collaborated with him on a half-hour TV play, *The Panthers*, about youth gangs.[11] When TV editors subsequently showed no interest, Southern told Richler to impress upon them that the story originated in a Princeton study linking gang violence to media publicity: the irony, intoned Southern, was that the press claimed to deplore *but actually glamourized* gang violence![12] It's hard to tell whether Southern was serious – unaware that his great discovery was banal and that *The Panthers* just might be engaged in the same dynamic it criticized – or whether Southern was simply parodying the sort of high-minded justification that networks trot out to defend sordid material. Given the talent of the two writers, their child delinquents are curiously flat and clichéd. Either serious drama was beyond Richler and Southern, or they weren't going to spend their best material on a co-authored work.

A much more fruitful collaboration, however, was about to begin for Richler. The new arrival at the ongoing Tourrettes poker game was Ted Kotcheff, a Canadian film director. Like Richler, Kotcheff was born to a poor family, Bulgarian immigrants in Toronto's Cabbagetown,[13] and he thought of himself as a "white wog," almost a Jew. Beginning with a BA in English Literature, then CBC work, he had graduated to British TV and London's West End theatres. Eventually he'd make such critically acclaimed films as *Outback* (1971), and films acclaimed in less rarefied circles: Sylvester Stallone's *First Blood* (1982), *Weekend at Bernie's* (1989).[14] Nathan Cohen had urged Kotcheff to look up Richler,[15] but Kotcheff thought he'd hate Richler.[16] They met for drinks one afternoon; Kotcheff talked nonstop for two hours while Richler nodded, spoke maybe ten words.[17]

Kotcheff, courtesy of his parents, was a doctrinaire socialist – which made life easier with expatriate filmmakers, but which wouldn't necessarily recommend him to Richler – and an existentialist, which would. Sartre's *Existentialism as Humanism* was Kotcheff's Bible: reason must be the guide, metaphysical delusions must be stripped away, yet the individual must take moral responsibility for his own actions. Even after Kotcheff found out how much fun Richler could be, he acknowledged that Richler's existentialism was rawer than his own: "Life for Mordecai was like walking on his eyeballs. There was a melancholy sense of life's impossibility, its unattainabilities, its ineradicable injustices." In later years they would make pilgrimages together to their secular Lourdes, the Café Deux Magots and the Café Flore in Paris.[18]

Richler blamed his ten-word afternoon on absorption in *A Choice of Enemies*, and this was partly true. He had heard from Canada and, more importantly, the US that *A Choice of Enemies* wasn't loved by those who mattered.[19] US publishers declined *A Choice of Enemies*, calling its conflicts outdated, and fearing that readers wouldn't identify with Hollywood émigrés.[20] Identification was, of course, hardly the point. However, so badly did Richler want to prove himself in the US that he was tempted to rewrite the novel for the US market. When he dropped this bombshell on Weiner, she protested vehemently. Although both she and Cathy had warned him about the datedness of the political conflicts, the deed was now done. What he had made of those conflicts was "far from negligible," Weiner insisted. Go forward to new material, she urged, don't redo. A rewrite for the Americans would be a fine kick in the arse to his English and French publishers. Weiner had also cautioned against that incestuous and unmarketable habit that so many writers had – of writing about writers. "My protests rang to Heaven last winter," she reminded him. "Now you 'give it back to me' as your own idea. Mordy, oh, Mordy ... I would say – no lobbying, no reviewing, no extraneous publicity anymore for you until you have turned out the kind of book that you yourself can be proud of." Best of all would be a strategic "disappearance."[21]

Richler acquiesced on the rewrite, but, since money was again an issue, he wisely declined to disappear. From Tourrettes he queried Weintraub, who now worked for the National Film Board, about scriptwriting opportunities in Canada,[22] and grilled Nathan Cohen about employment at the CBC.[23] A few months earlier he had prepared a radio piece for the CBC program *Anthology* in his own voice. Almost at the same time as Cohen gushed about how sensational Irving Layton had been on Cohen's show, *Fighting Words*, Robert Weaver informed Richler that he'd never be a first-rate broadcaster. What about coaching, Richler pleaded, wouldn't coaching help? No, and eight years later, when Richler did another trial broadcast, still no. "How come you write so well and read so badly?" Weaver asked.[24] (Judging by a 1965 interview of Lord Thompson one could say, contra Weaver, that Richler was a crisp and witty interviewer, prodding Thompson into all sorts of mischief.[25]) In 1957, on top of everything, relations with Cathy were deteriorating.[26] When Joyce Weiner visited Tourrettes, she remarked that despite the beauty of the ocean and the many parties, everyone seemed so terribly unhappy.[27]

≶

Richler did go to Toronto briefly at the end of 1957, but – no job – he didn't stay.[28] Meanwhile Weintraub had gone into an alcohol-fuelled depression, caused in large part by his comparison of his own novel against the consistent achievements of Moore and Richler. Richler tried to console him: "it grieves me to thk of you sitting there looking out the window all day, and possibly not sleeping at night … I never heard of anyone – Ted Allan aside – who didn't feel punk about his novel after the first and even final draft" [sic].[29] It didn't help that a Richler/Weintraub collaboration, First November, got lousy reviews, all the more stinging because Weintraub considered them justified.[30]

Although the prospect looked grey in 1957, the next year would turn into one of the happiest years of Richler's life, a year of financial, artistic, and personal breakthroughs. He received a Junior Arts Fellowship from the newly formed Canada Council to work on The Apprenticeship of Duddy Kravitz.[31] In later years Richler would manage amnesia about the Junior Fellowship, its renewal the following year, and a Senior Arts Fellowship in 1966, as he waxed eloquent about being the last of the free-market scribblers, and about how Canada bathed and coddled its young writers in all manner of grants.[32]

But bigger things than the fellowship were afoot. When Richler had returned to London, his first order of business had been to write Ted Kotcheff, apologizing for the silence at their first meeting, and asking to meet again.[33] This burgeoning friendship transmuted itself quickly into gold for Richler as he got in on the ground floor of Armchair Theatre, a Sunday night TV drama run by the Canadian producer Sydney Newman on Britain's ABC TV. What a difference, for Richler, between the 3 guineas he could expect for a magazine article and the weighty paycheques that TV already threw around![34]

In 1954 the British Parliament had opened the door a crack to allow independent TV stations to compete with the BBC.[35] There had been immediate demand for TV people, and ABC had lured the CBC's Newman over. Later, as head of drama for the BBC in the 1960s, he would go on to devise The Avengers and Doctor Who.[36] In early 1958 Newman set forth what he wanted on Armchair Theatre. Not talky, elitist drama. No reheated West End hits in the BBC style, please. If a play couldn't speak "to the Bradford mill-worker,

the Clydeside shipwright or the Welsh miner," forget it. Once Armchair Theatre hit its full stride, the average audience ran up to twelve million, and
Newman aimed to keep up the numbers, complaining that during one show,
"owing to a flubbsy opening, 2,700,000 people ... gave us 'the bird' by flick-
ing off within the first seven minutes." The plays must be about people, not
just ideas; must be conflict-driven; and must be strongly visual. As producer,
Newman was also the major-domo who decided how many "damns" could
walk the fine line between unadventurous fare and smut. Also, precisely how
many inches of cleavage was demanded by realism. To his potential writers,
he gave a peppy little essay, outlining his requirements, and as example he
held up Ted Willis's *Hot Summer Night*, a play about a liberal union organizer whose daughter falls in love with a Jamaican. It wouldn't kill you, he
told his writers, if you touched on something that everybody's thinking about.
Nevertheless, he did employ writers such as Harold Pinter and did insist
that, if an author wrote a message play, the characters should not know it.[37]

Money dictated that the whole process from start to finish must be completed in five weeks, with sets and casts kept to a minimum. While the sets
were being built in Manchester, the cast rehearsed in London, and then, on
the final Friday, caught the 5:55 train to Manchester's Didsbury Theatre for
final rehearsals and the live Sunday-night filming. Newman had a notion,
too, of what kind of director the process required: tough as a commando,
disciplined as a Jesuit, and able to move like lightning. "For shock, he'll
hang a camera (and a cameraman) from the grid, even if it means conceal-
ing three microphones to do it. His cameras move ... the television director's trump card."[38] Of course, Newman's imagined superhero inevitably
brought along strong notions of his own. "A perpetual screaming match"
ensued between Newman and his protégé Ted Kotcheff.[39] Kotcheff was quick
to explode but also ready to forget the quarrel in a minute.[40] When Newman recited a list of his own tribulations – critics, actors who have tempera-
ment, writers who can't speak, monomaniacal directors[41] – one suspects that
Richler and Kotcheff weren't far from his mind.

Armchair Theatre found a niche for itself somewhere between no-holds-
barred literature and popular TV, contributing to the northern working-class
realism that was sweeping British theatre.[42] Richler's first original offering,
"Paid in Full" (broadcast May 1958) demonstrated this.[43] Tommy, a working-class child falls down a well and is rescued, but Richler quickly turns
the feel-good story into a tragedy. While Tommy's parents try to milk his
newfound celebrity for money, Dr Logan, the physician who treated Tommy,
finds that he may suddenly be able to build that new clinic for the under-
privileged after all, if only he can keep his stubborn socialist mouth shut.
The milk doesn't flow, and Logan can't. After a newspaper headline – "LAST
RITES IS RELIGIOUS MUMBO-JUMBO SAYS SOCIALIST DR" – and Logan's

unwillingness to budge on Tommy's bill (the family is no longer poor), every-thing crumbles, including Tommy's health. In a final scene, Tommy's mother says to Dr Logan, "I only put him on that last show so I could pay your bill."[44] Tears, curtain. The play could be interpreted as an "uncompro-mising" look at human nature, an indictment of both left and right, of the money-grubbing working class, the apathetic rich, the media. One reviewer rightly classed Richler among the Angry Young Men,[45] those lower-class writers who were taking England by storm with their stories of social alien-ation, though Richler seemed to imagine that he had nothing to do with the movement.[46]

"Paid in Full" lay very much along the political row that Richler had been hoeing in the previous two years, adding the tried-and-true hooks of a child in trouble and the equivalent of a lottery win. "Television is not a serious medium," Richler had declared not too long before,[47] and he set about to prove his claim. Full of exaggerated characters and trumped-up conflict, bearing the predictability of the problem-play genre, occasionally enlivened by humour, "Paid in Full" wasn't very good. Still, exaggerated characters and trumped-up conflict held 3½ million TV sets in Britain.[48] Most of the reviewers nodded approval, though some were pained that *British* writers weren't being used. What was with all the North American settings in *our* commercial theatre?[49]

Richler also did *The House of Bernarda Alba* (an adaptation from Lorca)[50] and *The Trouble with Benny* (based on his own short story) for Armchair Theatre,[51] and London came to seem less daunting, less of a mecca and more of a home. As soon as Richler graduated to the movies, he was quick to complain about the TV form. Serious television drama didn't exist, he as-sured his readers, only social problem plays: "Look here, Archie, would you let your daughter marry a – a nigger?" In Richler's eyes, "the sentimental goo usually served up by Armchair Theatre" was dreary and predictable, owing far too much to yesterday's headlines. The solutions were always sim-ple. Afterwards, staring at poor ratings, the producer would say, "You see, I tried to do a serious play. But it's no use."[52] Of course, Richler's criticisms pretty much summed up "Paid in Full," too.

Later, facetiously, Richler would say that he and Kotcheff were to blame for four-letter words and nudity – for post-1960s TV and movie standards, no less.[53] But Richler's joke held more truth than he intended. Having gone to school with the Parisian avant-garde, he was part of a larger movement that opened up TV for truths that it had been avoiding and, also, for ex-ploitation of audience desire. In one of those quirks of fate, many years later Richler's daughter Emma, working as an actress, would tell him that she had to do "a deeply silly bodice rippy scene" for a director who had once been a cameraman for Kotcheff on Armchair Theatre.[54]

Even more lucrative than Armchair Theatre in 1958 was Richler's job as script doctor for what would become one of the most critically acclaimed feature films of the upcoming year. Richler was called in – anonymously, no screenwriting credit – to add some spark to Neil Patterson's screenplay of *Room at the Top*.[55] The film, like John Braine's original novel, was an attack on the class system; Richler, not so long escaped from the lower orders himself, thought it full of clichés about the warm and colourful working class.[56] He must have sympathized, however, with the working-class Joe Lampton's ambition to get "the girl with the Riviera tan." "[*Room at the Top*] proves," Brian Moore said, "that a good novel may not be possible fare for a good film but a bad one certainly is. I thought I heard your voice in some of the scenes, notably the summer house one."[57] Despite the plaudits, the film is melodramatic. Only the class conflicts, which are real enough, and the wit, presumably owing much to Richler, keep the film from becoming a simple manipulation. In *St. Urbain's Horseman*, Richler's autobiographical Jake Hersh doesn't want to brag about his surreptitious triumph as ghost-director for Timothy Nash.[58] Not so the real Richler. The fact that Richler was supposed to keep mum about his script-rescue only made him all the more eager to hint to everybody just which major motion picture had received a badly needed transfusion from which young Jewish doctor.[59] *Room at the Top* went on to win two Oscars, including Best Actress for Simone Signoret and, more ironically, Best Adapted Screenplay for Neil Patterson. At first, Richler was angry at being denied the glory, but director Jack Clayton was happy, and told everyone about Richler's work.[60] Suddenly, Richler was a feature-film writer.

≶

Not everybody was impressed. Richler's acquaintance, Nathan Cohen, the son of a poor Jewish shopkeeper from Sydney, Nova Scotia, considered himself not just the most important drama critic that Canada had ever known but the only one, and since he had mastered the witty put-down many people bowed before that judgement. A big man, he swung his weight around with a kind of aggressiveness that caused crowds to part before him. His intelligence made him an entertaining friend, but he was also a shameless self-promoter and, when his ego required it, untruthful.[61]

There was bound to be a clash with Richler, who wasn't quite so self-assured in public, but who wasn't overburdened with humility himself. At first Richler was respectful. After all, Cohen liked Richler's work and could be instrumental in the CBC buying it. But Richler began to find him annoying, starting in a September 1956 interview of Richler for the first issue of the new Canadian literary magazine *Tamarack Review*. Cohen arrived in London and expected to be entertained by Richler. The interview went well,

yet Cohen made a point of suggesting that TV writing could poison one's serious writing and thinking. "Not unless you overdo it,"[62] Richler replied.
The criticism was far from valid: even if TV writing encouraged laziness in
ideas, it improved Richler's style. Yet he must have felt that his reply was
lame, because he quickly added that he had used pseudonyms and had turned
down a regular TV job. Afterwards, when Richler proofread the interview
he saw a remark about shoplifting at Eaton's that he wanted deleted. *Tamarack* editor Robert Weaver spoke for himself and Cohen, "We're surprised
to find you being rather timid and bourgeois about this."[63] This, too, must
have stung, because Richler let the shoplifting remark stand.

Worse, Cohen had tried to rewrite Richler's novels. Cohen convinced
the CBC to do a radio play of *The Acrobats*, and then began giving Richler
dramatic advice. Some of the advice was good. A play is not a novel, Cohen
said, *show* the character conflicts from the start. Other advice was less sound
and almost calculated to offend. Cohen suggested that André didn't have to
die, implying that the entire novel was misconceived. Not that Richler had
too much sentiment attached to *The Acrobats* anymore, but the core of the
work was that André must pay for his idealism and that, nevertheless, there
must be hope at the end. This time Richler had his way. After the play was
produced, Cohen grumbled and gave it a niggardly blessing: "Hell, for a
first script, very, very impressive." When the CBC added a TV version of the
play, Cohen was harsher, telling Richler that it was hopelessly misinterpreted
and that too often it had people talking about other people. A CBC scenario
repeated itself several times: Cohen would reject a piece by Richler, but then
others at the station, sometimes against Cohen's advice or sometimes *on* his
advice, would buy the piece. And yet, shuffled in among the harsh critiques
was flattery, Cohen declaring that his own main claim to posterity would be
"I-knew-him-when" books about Richler.[64]

Serving as co-editor of *Tamarack Review*, Cohen judged that the debut
issue in late 1956 had been too dull,[65] and took it upon himself to remedy
this ... by chastising Richler publicly in the first 1958 issue. Cohen wrote
that neither the Jewish middle-class family nor "the Marxist mirage" had
any relevance: the world of *Son of a Smaller Hero* had long disappeared;
the world of *A Choice of Enemies* had never existed, invented by a writer
who hadn't experienced Marxism first-hand. As to whether TV-writing would
undermine Richler, Cohen announced, with a false air of neutrality, that time
would tell, and then stacked the deck with such ambiguously worded sentences as "There is no doubt in Mordecai Richler's mind that he is a serious
writer."[66] In fact, the whole purpose of the essay, judging by the last few
sentences, seems to have been to push Richler away from commercial writing – with its half-baked ideas, its focus on what the audience wants – and
towards serious writing, in which, Cohen argued, the author simply tries to

see the world out of his own eyes. The novels did deserve criticism, but Cohen couldn't have been more wrong about the effects of TV writing. TV writing, more than literary editors, forced Richler to confront the fact that he was writing for an *audience*, that nobody eagerly awaited long soapbox speeches about the horrors of the middle class, that if he wanted to be heard, he'd better learn to tell a good story. Even though his TV work did slide towards the lowest common denominator, it held nothing but good omens for his serious work, packing him off towards *The Apprenticeship of Duddy Kravitz* and all of his later work.[67]

Cohen worried about Richler's reaction to the piece in *Tamarack* and told Richler so.[68] The advice had been delivered with enough rudeness to ensure that someone as tetchy as Richler would be infuriated, and he was. "Nathan Cohen has butchered me," Richler wrote in March, telling Weintraub that Cohen's main accusation had been that Richler heroines had small breasts.[69] Cohen expected the tempest to blow over quickly, and by May he was asking Richler to meet his plane in London.[70] Richler met the plane[71] but didn't forget. He had some measure of satisfaction when *Tamarack* accepted his story "Mortimer Griffin, Shalinsky, and How They Solved the Jewish Problem" for the next issue. He also heard and gleefully reported that the scholar Peter Scott was about to publish "a big pro-Richler anti-Cohen article" in *Tamarack*.[72] Richler's meditation on his injuries didn't end there. When Cohen left his job as story editor for the CBC, Richler would become more explicit in his revenge.

⩍

Courtesy of the Canada Council, of TV work, and of the coming film windfall – "500 quid for three weeks' work" – Richler in 1958 had months of free time to work on his new novel. "Am financially solid now, embarrassingly so," he wrote.[73] He was able to send Lily cash, to make up for the money he had gotten from her over the years, but he suspected that his money was making its way to Avrum's business ventures, and this suspicion deepened his estrangement from his brother.[74] He had ideas for two novels, one set in southern France and the other in Canada.[75] Since his editor at Deutsch, Diana Athill, had encouraged him to write a comic novel in which he would control the farcical element (as he had failed to do in "Mortimer Griffin, Shalinsky, and How They Solved the Jewish Problem"),[76] the comic Canadian novel took precedence.

Richler decided to go to the Riviera again and work there, beginning in June. By then, Stanley Mann, like Richler, was writing for Armchair Theatre,[77] and Richler arranged for Stanley and Florence to share an enormous villa in Roquebrune near the Italian border with himself and Cathy,[78] the arrangement not only recommending itself economically, but also in other

ways. At Roquebrune in the beginning of June 1958, there were two cou-
ples – the Richlers and the Manns. By July, there was one – Richler and Florence. The previous year Florence had been in analysis, struggling to decide
what to do about her marriage. After a separation and an involvement with
a doctor who broke her heart, she had again tried to reconcile with Stanley.[79] By December Richler had reported to Weintraub that Stanley, depressed
and drinking a lot, hardly saw Florence anymore, but that their toddler
Daniel looked fine.[80] It was on the Riviera that Cathy finally noticed Richler's love of Florence, when the four of them dined together at a Monte Carlo
nightclub, and one afternoon after Cathy came home from the beach, Richler told her, "It's over. I'm not in love with you."[81] Stanley had returned to
London, and in short order Cathy left the villa. Florence and Daniel eventually followed Stanley, leaving Richler alone in the empty villa, but not before the romance had flowered.[82]

Richler has claimed that both marriages were already at the point of
breaking up, though he didn't add that he had been pursuing Florence for
years. He wrote Weintraub from Roquebrune: "There was no real incident...
Probably it's simply that we've both been unhappy for a long time." He did-
n't mention Florence, and only spoke of her a month later, nonchalantly
mentioning that he thought that she and Stanley might be getting a divorce.[83]
While setting aside Cathy and pursuing Florence, Richler ploughed ahead
on his novel about a hard-headed St. Urbain Street boy, a schoolyard ring-
leader and tormentor of teachers who isn't given to sentimentality in his relationship with his French girlfriend, and who does whatever is necessary –
legal or illegal, moral or immoral – to acquire the land that will make him
a success. Ted Kotcheff, who had come down to Roquebrune for a short
time, read the manuscript. Sitting on the floor of the villa with Richler and
Florence, Kotcheff pronounced *The Apprenticeship of Duddy Kravitz* the
best Canadian novel ever written and vowed that someday he'd return to
Canada to film it.[84]

Cathy, meanwhile, had no wish for a divorce and was furious,[85] but she
got a job at an American children's camp at Villefranche and stayed there.[86]
Eventually she went to Spain.[87] Richler, with his new wealth, supported her
financially for a time.[88] Stanley Mann seems to have borne no grudge, and
when it came time for Florence to give birth to Richler's son, Stanley sent
his best wishes for an easy delivery: "I don't know how much you will believe me, but I am pleased about it." He wanted to hear from Richler.[89] Mann
remained on friendly terms with Florence and Richler, coming often to visit
Daniel and lamenting that Putney was too quiet when the Richlers in subsequent years began to spend more time in Canada.[90]

Doris Lessing theorized that so many of her friends (Ted Allan, Reuben
Ship, Richler) divorced their first wives because "men have to fight so hard

to free themselves from their mothers, but then circumstances and their natures make their wives into mothers, and they free themselves again."[91] But Cathy Boudreau was hardly the motherly type. One wonders whether Lessing confided her theory to Richler, because when *The Apprenticeship of Duddy Kravitz* went to the printer a year later, it featured Aunt Ida, who, buoyed by a book or two on psychology, diagnoses Duddy as suffering from "The Oedipus."[92]

Florence was just over a year older than Richler.[93] She had been adopted by an Anglican family in Lachine.[94] Tall and graceful, she had little formal education, but had already carved out a lucrative, five-year modeling career with Christian Dior, *Queen* magazine, and the big Knightsbridge stores in London.[95] She had been pursued by Sean Connery and Christopher Plummer.[96] Eventually, she hoped, she'd work her way up to Paris, but not until Daniel was older.[97] In this sense, despite dark hair, despite a poor and unhappy childhood, she was the golden shiksa Richler desired. Lessing remembers Richler as "so anti-romantic, so tough," but when he met Florence, he "stood around mooning after her."[98] According to Diana Athill, the description in *Barney's Version* of Barney's besotted love for Miriam is an accurate representation of Richler falling before Florence.

The contrast with Cathy was striking. Cathy had a sharp tongue, and when she was with Mordecai, there were, no mistaking it, two Richlers in the flat. She also had the elegant habit of calling everybody "Suckerballs."[99] At the beginning Richler was attracted to her feistiness, but as time passed it got on his nerves.[100] The Richlers had learned how to score mean points jokingly against each other,[101] and friends arriving unannounced might come upon her screaming at him. It was very unpleasant.[102] Florence was something else altogether. If "Puss in Boots" (as Lily had called Mordecai) yearned for a titled lady,[103] Florence, with her studied refinement wasn't far off the mark. She had a social dignity and elegance of speech that Richler admired but lacked completely. Within a couple of months, according to Ted Kotcheff, she was attempting a makeover, a sweetening of Richler, gently coaching him after parties on how Amy Vanderbilt would have behaved in his stead.[104] According to Florence herself, she would never have been so bold as to try to remake him. She rarely confronted him directly, though he could sense when she disapproved of his conduct. He would conclude, "I think it's time to go home because I can see Florence's face," and yet, afterwards, he would be amused by her disapproval.[105] Later, according to the children, she would be the only one who held moral authority over him.[106]

Very quickly, Florence won over Brian Moore, who thought her "an awfully nice girl and bright,"[107] and Diana Athill, who, despite being daunted by Florence's beauty, came to love her.[108] Moore worried, however, about Cathy's future. He didn't waste condolences on Richler, who didn't need consoling: "As you know I was never a great booster of that particular union and always thought you foolish to marry for the reasons you told me at the time."[109] Moe, a little more blunt, couldn't help saying, "See, I told you so," and repeating his prophecy that mixed marriages didn't work.[110] About his own marriage – unmixed yet still failed – Moe kept discreetly silent, but Mordecai didn't neglect to rub his father's nose in that particular irony.[111]

Florence would need her "strong inner resources" to put up with Richler's family. Also to put up with Richler and his black moods. Florence admits that he was difficult when he was waiting to begin a book. One senses, in the fiction of their daughter, Emma, for example, that Florence decided to tolerate a lot because Richler was brilliantly talented and because he adored her and because, unlike Stanley, he was faithful. Emma's portrait of the young Yakov Weiss is a good portrait of the young Richler: "You meet a man with a deep frown, a man out of place nearly everywhere, not yet fully formed, spinning wildly, a man with a mess of curls and a twisted collar … He is lean, almost scurvied, if that were possible."[112] Florence says that she had never met anyone with his intensity. He would drop ashtrays and accidentally break things with a fury that made it seem as if the physical world were a malevolent force arrayed against him. Small talk repelled him. At parties he would speak the truth with a bluntness that made people quail. It wasn't just that he demanded the unvarnished truth, but that he judged the lives around him, and found them wanting. "One would wish," Florence says, "that he would leave very soon, so that we could all be our foolish and ordinary selves."[113]

12

The End of the Apprenticeship

BACK IN LONDON AGAIN, the moonstruck Richler trailed Florence around her Dior photo shoots.[1] With Cathy inhabiting the Richlers' flat at 5 Winchester Road, Mordecai's immediate problem was where to park himself. Reuben Ship offered a bed. At the time Ship was living with Elaine Grand, a former CBC television host, while he, too, waited for a divorce from his first wife. Ship's flat became a haven for Richler, first his home for several weeks and then his place of resort for companionship.[2]

Surely the Highest Paid TV Writer in Great Britain (as Richler with some exaggeration called himself[3]) ought to have a place of his own, even "tho," as Richler put it, "I have precociously graduated into the alimony class."[4] It was Cathy, however, who decided to leave Winchester Road behind, opening up their flat for Richler to use, and he quickly found a roommate, Ted Kotcheff. Two gentlemen sharing: Kotcheff had the bedroom; Richler worked and slept in the living room. The place was very much at odds with their heady income levels. Black tarpaper covered the floors, the ceiling in Kotcheff's bedroom sported a hole, and their books sat on planks held up by bricks. Mice and even a rat made appearances. Yet Kotcheff was highly paid to direct, and even Richler's scripts had become lucrative. Such incongruencies delighted them, as they ordered smoked salmon or kippers from Harrod's to be delivered to their door for breakfast, or invited rich film people over. When Richler received his pay for *Room at the Top* – more money than he had received for anything hitherto – he changed it into £5 notes and brought the loot home to ruffle under Kotcheff's nose. "We behaved like characters in bad films," Kotcheff says, "throwing the cash up in the air." Then Richler stashed the money among the books of their library before going out on the town. They forgot which books. When the money in hand ran out, they had to open hundreds of books to find the rest. Their cleaning woman said they lived like pigs.[5]

In the mornings Richler sent Kotcheff off to work with "Have a nice day at the office, dear." At precisely 9:00 Richler reported to his desk. At 9:05, typing sounds. He lunched at noon and browsed through the *Herald Tribune*. Then, possibly, a nap. At precisely 2:00, back to the desk. At 2:05, typing sounds. Of these regular habits, Kotcheff said, "I was in the grip of some silly Hemingway fantasy that writers sat around drunk or drugged waiting for inspiration to strike, and it usually came at midnight and one wrote all night. But the Muse clocking in for duty every day at 9:05 and 2:05?" In fact, Richler had already tried the Hemingway-hipster route. But by now he was approaching his work with the attitude of a serious craftsman. He meant to make a home for Florence and Daniel, which home could only be built through consistent labour. After Kotcheff's day at rehearsals, Richler would welcome him back with a nice rib roast or a cholent (lima beans stewed in chicken fat). Usually, Kotcheff hoped for a quiet evening. Richler, however, had been alone all day, writing, and was revved up to go out on the town. "C'mon Kotcheff!" he'd say, and off they went.[6]

≸

One of Isaac Babel's rabbis says, "The jackal moans when it is hungry, every fool is foolish enough to be unhappy, and only the wise man rends the veil of existence with laughter."[7] It was *The Apprenticeship of Duddy Kravitz*, Richler's first consistently comic novel, which he greeted at 9:05 each morning. He had written most of it in Roquebrune; now he was revising. Because it was the longest and yet quickest novel he had done,[8] Richler was a bit uneasy, but in the interval since *A Choice of Enemies* he had grown younger. Although he had given up trying to be a Hemingway clone after *The Acrobats*, he was still beset in *A Choice of Enemies* by the desire to leave his past behind and to make pronouncements about world affairs; in *The Apprenticeship of Duddy Kravitz* Richler instead dove head-first into the Jewish-Canadian idiom of his Montreal childhood and let any pronouncements arise with less manipulation, so that Duddy's story never feels rigged the way that Norman's at times does.

Richler thought that he had left St. Urbain, but he began to return to it in imagination, and, as a result, he found his voice. Introducing *Innocents Abroad*, he would speak of Mark Twain mastering an American idiom by going to Europe and Israel. One of the joys of *Innocents Abroad* was "watching the young Twain liberate himself, and American writing, from the yoke of the European tradition, doing a necessary demolition job on it."[9] The very same could be said for Richler. "You wouldn't Talk Like That if You Were Dead," a St. Urbain story written in that period, hints strongly at Richler's mature style. To save on funeral costs, Uncle Sol begins a cemetery-plot co-op among his relatives. He gets impatient when two years pass and, tragically, nobody dies. Whenever one person asks another, "How are you?" the other immediately senses vultures. Richler's dialogue is more natural – no longer either hardboiled or self-consciously intelligent. The superior narrative voice is gone, and instead we are left with a collision of self-serving motives – so that the relatives absolutely *insist* on making miraculous deathbed recoveries rather than give Uncle Sol the satisfaction of profiting over their corpses. Richler's carefully weighted appraisal of human folly appears when at long last the first funeral is celebrated: "'Some premiere,' Uncle Sol said, counting the house unhappily. 'Some drawing card.'"[10]

But most of all it was in *The Apprenticeship of Duddy Kravitz* that Richler showed himself to be the first major Canadian voice to step outside the British and French traditions. Earlier minority writers – such as Frederick Phillip Grove, Laura Gudmund Salverson, John Marlyn (Mihaelovitcz), A.M. Klein, and Adele Wiseman – had described the immigrant experience but had done so in an adopted Anglo-inflected voice ... as had Richler in his first three novels. "I started out as a rather earnest and pompous writer," Richler admitted.[11] Until Duddy. Even so, one US editor thought that the novel's title was too specialized and too Jewish. Seymour Lawrence suggested the pitifully straightforward *What's in It for Me?*[12] Yet Richler's style in the novel belied such meddling, for example when Duddy wants to butter up, to shmeer, Hugh Calder without making it look like a bribe: "Usually, Duddy knew, it was safe to send a *goy* booze, but Calder owned a distillery. 'I've got it. You name your favourite charity and I'll send them fifty bucks. A token like.'"[13] In lines such as this, Richler found a seam in language ("*goy*," "token like") and in manners (Duddy's precise outsider's assessment of the kind of bribe that self-deceiving English Canadians would find socially acceptable) that was utterly new to Canada.

Some complained that the novel was derivative of US work – specifically Budd Schulberg's *What Makes Sammy Run?* (1941) and Saul Bellow's *The Adventures of Augie March* (1953).[14] Far from it. The other novels invite comparison mainly because, like *The Apprenticeship of Duddy Kravitz*, they're Jewish variants of that most American of structural forms, the progressive narrative, the story of the man who rose from nothing, and because their protagonists have a liveliness that the great Gatsby could only envy. Bellow's style, still very much within the European tradition of Thomas Mann, couldn't be more foreign to Richler. *What Makes Sammy Run?* – less profound and more formulaic than *The Apprenticeship of Duddy Kravitz* – was admittedly closer, and Richler even allows Duddy's nemesis, Irwin Shubert, to call Duddy "Sammy Glick" after Schulberg's protagonist.[15] No wonder that Richler remembered Sammy, whose problems so nearly matched his own: Sammy hated cheder; so did Richler. Sammy's father died when Sammy was thirteen; Richler, due to the divorce, was estranged from his father for several years at that age. Sammy rebelled against Orthodoxy and therefore wasn't bar mitzvahed; Richler was bar mitzvahed, but it meant little, because of his similar rebellion. Sammy's grandfather said he didn't want to live anymore because his grandson wasn't a real Jew – "He was no different from the little wops and micks who cursed and fought and cheated." Richler's quarrels with his grandfather Shmarya were of the same intensity and had the same religious cause. And Sammy's pursuit of "the golden girl, the dream" – a beautiful, rich, and cultured WASP wasn't something that Richler found at all puzzling.[16]

But it was Richler's *life*, not fiction, that ran parallel to Sammy. Many Jews who left Orthodoxy and acculturated to North American attitudes could tell a similar story. Apart from the name of Duddy's father, Max, *The Apprenticeship of Duddy Kravitz* owes very little to Schulberg. Those who think they see similarities see them because both Sammy and Duddy are Jewish boys on the make. Yet none of the incidents in the two stories resemble each other, and Schulberg's attitude towards his protagonist is much more condemnatory than is Richler's. *What Makes Sammy Run?* is a simple morality tale: run after material wealth too much, and you'll lose your soul. Duddy's story is much more complex and ambiguous. Even when he tries to use his "smart operator" shtik in his love relationship, or when he's figuratively cutting throats, Duddy is so engaging, so concerned for his family, and so able to see through the bullshit, that it's difficult to damn him. When Duddy says, "I am not a British Lord and this isn't my ancestral home," how can one fault his clear-minded, bargain-rate sale of his uncle's library and antique furniture?[17]

Above all, Duddy is not really Richler. Some of the old grads of Baron Byng maintain that, if anyone is Duddy, it's Richler[18] – but neither Duddy's life nor his attitudes ultimately fit Richler. The novel revisited Richler's childhood haunts, but not in Richler's own person. Ste. Agathe, scene of Lily Richler's defeat in the rooming-house business, becomes the place where a higher-class Jew, Irwin, humiliates and fleeces Duddy at roulette, but where Duddy also gains a moral victory and his money back with interest. Unlike Richler, Duddy still retains the minimum level of Orthodoxy (he won't intermarry) and of course he doesn't have the disdain for business that the high-minded young Richler once had. The figure who stands in for Richler in the novel is Hersh: a goody-goody, later an unpublished bohemian writer who thinks that he has "purged" himself of the ghetto and has set his sights on Paris. Max, Duddy's father, resembles Richler's father Moe only in the turnabout both did when they discovered that their sons were successes. At the end of the novel Max mythologizes Duddy's nasty behaviour in school as an early sign of a Boy Wonder, Max's attitude not so far removed from Moe's renewed interest in his son once he found out that Mordecai could

rub shoulders with the likes of Sean Connery.[19] This – that Moe loved Mordecai's image more than he loved Mordecai – was clearly painful, yet apart
from the Boy Wonder dig, the two fathers are dissimiliar. As for grandfathers, in Zeyda Simcha, who advises Duddy to get land, Richler was finally
able to move beyond the judgemental portraits of the Orthodox grandfathers.[20] He was becoming someone *other* than he had been. *A Choice of Enemies* both signalled the wish to belong to a wider culture than Jewish
Montreal and the accomplishment of that wish in penetrating London's film
crowd. When *The Apprenticeship of Duddy Kravitz* returned to Montreal,
it was a Montreal that no longer had Lily at its centre.

One reason that Duddy comes off as sympathetic is that Richler gave
him a background that Dickens might have come up with … had he been a
twentieth-century American Jew. Duddy's is an orphan story for a more cynical age. Duddy's mother is dead, and the implications are that his quest for
social and familial status originate in that primary wound. In drafts of the
novel, one can see Richler steering for a middle course between satire and
emotional manipulation. In an earlier draft the Reform Jewish congregation
Holy Blossom Temple was Lemon Blossom Temple, led by "Rabbi Harvey
Finestone," who "had started out in life as a tap-dancer," "had once won a
prize on the Major Bower Amateur Hour," and who had published a much-
loved article, "I Like Being a Jew – It's Fun." In later drafts, this material
disappears. Richler also changed Jerry Dingleman, "the Boy Plunger" to "the
Boy Wonder": fewer laughs, greater evocativeness – suddenly a role for
Duddy to aspire to. And Yvette doesn't laugh (as in the earlier draft) when
Duddy suggests Lennie as abortion-doctor should she get pregnant. On the
other hand, also deleted was Duddy's weeping immediately after he wishes
Virgil dead,[21] Richler sensing that what might have worked for Dickens
would seem too sentimental for 1959. In his two subsequent novels Richler
would try to subtract the sentiment entirely. As a result, *The Incomparable
Atuk* and *Cocksure* got Richler the knowing laughs he wanted, but readers
didn't care very deeply about the books. Only with *St. Urbain's Horseman*
did he return to the process – difficult for him, *embarrassing* – of giving his
protagonists a full range of emotion and interior life.

Another reason that Duddy comes off as sympathetic is that, despite appearances, he doesn't just chase money. "The Promised Land," Duddy calls
his few acres of snow, Richler hinting that Duddy's coveted land bears a
symbolic equivalence to Zion. Derived from Yiddish poetry, Simcha's phrase
"a man without land is nobody"[22] articulates the emotions behind the Zionist enterprise and perhaps even something of (Richler's grandfather) Rabbi
Rosenberg's lament over the Diaspora.[23] Duddy wants land, that hedge
against ghettoes, poverty, and anti-Semitism. His purposes are thus made
comprehensible in more ways than one; but, of course, we are left with the

question of means, especially when Duddy recognizes that he would be capable of selling a baby to get the land. Rosenberg had gone so far as to purchase land in Zion, but like the fictional Simcha he didn't think about what it might cost, morally, to seize and to hold onto new land. Duddy, searching for a euphemistic way to describe his lying, stealing, and cheating to get land, lights upon the word "unorthodox."[24] It's a profoundly apt term. Many Orthodox rabbis insisted that Jews should wait for God's miraculous redemption, not pre-empt Him by purchasing and seizing land in Palestine.[25] Duddy's scheming and his willingness to step over the crippled Virgil Roseboro to reach his goal are nearer to the "unorthodox" means – bombings and revenge killings – used by the Irgun and the Stern Gang. When Duddy tries to make Simcha a present of the land, Simcha refuses, the logical consequence of rejecting Duddy's methods.

Other, less subtle, objects of Richler's satire than Zionism were also in focus: avant-garde filmmakers, Reform Judaism, and special pleading for minorities, via Virgil's defense of epileptics. Certain aspects of the satire on special pleading – the proposed "Miss Health Handicapper" contest for example[26] – skirt the edge of good taste. Richler cast fear into the hearts of publishers with the gleeful specificity and the seemingly indiscriminate range of his barbs. Nancy Reynold, managing editor of Atlantic, feared possible libel suits: "In particular, on page 51, you imply that Pepsi induces sweating, and on page 61, Johnny Walker gives one a red nose." She also objected to derogatory references to John Huston, Alfred Hitchcock, Charlie Chaplin, and William Lyon MacKenzie King.[27] The publishers' filters evidently didn't catch everything. *Maclean's*, which published a portion of the novel, was threatened with a libel suit by a Montreal lawyer named Sivak, who suffered mental anguish after reading the line, "Sivak goosed Kravitz."[28] Although Richler had gotten beyond the disdain for business so common in intellectual circles, his way of mythologizing the businessman wasn't in terms that most businessmen – particularly Jewish businessmen sensitive to stereotyping – would find congenial. This is true not only of Duddy, but also of the novel's other businessmen, such as Mr Cohen. It is Cohen who gives the fatherly advice that if Duddy lets a thing such as responsibility for Virgil's crippling stop him, Duddy won't be able to contribute to the hospital fund or build Israel. In moments like this (and they are many) *The Apprenticeship of Duddy Kravitz* leaves *What Makes Sammy Run?* far behind. One can neither despise Cohen completely nor accept his moral reasoning.

≸

That Duddy was Jewish rankled many Jews, and Richler loved to recount the time that a woman in a synagogue asked him why he couldn't have given Duddy an Italian name.[29] In fact, Richler *liked* Duddy[30] and wanted to make the "go-getter" sympathetic.[31] Small consolation to Jews who could remember the satiric violence against Jews in the Weimar Republic,[32] prelude to Nazi ovens. Jews were right to feel that *The Apprenticeship of Duddy Kravitz* was an attack, but it wasn't an anti-Semitic attack. To call it that is to ignore the complexity of Duddy's character, the complexity of audience reaction to him, and Richler's refusal to exempt other nationalities from the same kind of satire (the Anglo businessman Hugh Thomas Calder, for example). Non-Jews had very different criticisms of the novel. Brian Moore pointed out that the goys were uniformly stupid and that Richler was "inside" most of the Jewish characters but not inside the goys.[33] More than one reader complained, with some justification, that Duddy's French-Canadian girlfriend, Yvette, functioned not as a person in her own right but simply as a moral conscience for Duddy.[34]

As he was revising *The Apprenticeship of Duddy Kravitz* early in 1959, Richler had a very Jewish TV play done by Armchair Theatre, *The Trouble with Benny*. The ineffectual Benny, working hard to pull his family up into Outremont, is rewarded by his wife's affair with Shapiro's boy and by the reappearance of his own war demons.[35] The *Times Educational Supplement* gave *The Trouble with Benny* a good review,[36] but, even far from Montreal, Richler was beginning to get mail accusing him of being an anti-Semite, as one witty but barbed letter testifies:

> Dear Mr. Richler,
> You will doubtless receive so many enthusiastic letters congratulating you on your play that one more will hardly count, but I really must say that I feel you couldn't have done a better job of anti-semitic propaganda if you had been Oswald Mosley himself. Perhaps you are? It would be a brilliant stroke for any Fascist to take a Jewish nom de plume ... I say you are an anti-Semite of a far more nauseating and ugly order than the ordinary kind. The Jews are not yet sufficiently well-liked in this country to be able to afford spokesmen like you.[37]

For those who accused him of encouraging anti-Semitism, Richler had little patience. "I don't write for the lunatic fringe,"[38] he said, and later, "There's no point in addressing a novel to the Enoch Powells of this world."[39] When a CBC-TV production of *The Apprenticeship of Duddy Kravitz* did poorly in 1960, Harvey Hart, the director, blamed Richler: "This play was conscious anti-semitism on the part of the author. I tried to save it but the script beat me." Richler was livid: "This we call standing up for your work. Loyalty. Courage. Canada. Anyway, he's shorter than me, and not many are, so I fully intend to bop him one."[40]

≶

Looking back at 1959, Richler remembered not good times, but "long nights thinned out by gin, the days thick with hope and excuses." He had three novels to his credit, but little in the way of sales.[41] Yet despite a painful slipped disc that forced him to walk with a cane in January,[42] he wasn't nearly as morose as he later made out. *The Trouble with Benny* featured the direction of Kotcheff (who that year was voted best TV drama director in England by the Society of Film and Television Arts[43]), Ted Allan as narrator,[44] and none other than Florence Mann, now studying to be an actress, in one of the smaller female roles.[45] "Being an actress would be much more stimulating than being a mannequin," she said at the time,[46] though later she spoke of the acting as more of a lark that allowed her to be with her friends. By the end of the year, she knew that choices had to be made. When she was offered a part in the stage version of *The World of Suzy Wong*, Richler hovered around the discussions, ostensibly as her protector, but really, she soon realized, as a jealous suitor. He didn't want her pursuing a career.[47] In choosing Richler, she would have to give up what was a lucrative period in her life: "you could not be married to Mordecai and be a mannequin or an actress or whatever. It was a full-time responsibility."[48]

Meanwhile, script-doctor Richler was called in again, this time to rescue *Faces in the Dark* (1960), a film that had a good plot but wooden characters. "The patient," said Richler, "is a thriller by two tricky Frenchies – the chaps who wrote Les Diaboliques and Vertigo – and the anxious producer is one Sid Box." Richler's "surgical fees," as he called them, had gone up to £1,500 for six weeks. His confidence was brimming, "If thgs break as well as they indicate, next year I will give a grant to the Canada Council."[49] He went under the pseudonym Ephraim Kogan[50] and expected to get sole credit,[51] but in the end he had to share it with the two French writers, Pierre Boileau and Thomas Narcejac.

More importantly, the great majority of readers, especially those who counted, loved *The Apprenticeship of Duddy Kravitz*. Weiner, Athill, Moore, Jack McClelland, and, most pleasing of all, US editor Seymour Lawrence recognized immediately that the new novel was a huge leap forward.[52] Robert Fulford argued in the *Toronto Star* that *The Apprenticeship of Duddy Kravitz* ought to win the Governor General's Award.[53] "Dear Duddele," Moore wrote Richler, "You can come home now and you won't have to speak to Earle Birney again ever. You have left all the Can Lit men far behind so They Won't Do You Any Good Any More."[54] Gladdened by such reactions, Richler announced that *The Apprenticeship of Duddy Kravitz* was to be the first volume in a trilogy. No, a whole series! Next would be *Dudley Kane's First Marriage*. Then "a whole clutch of novels, big and small, about St. Urbain

Street alumni," one about Hersh and a short one about Uncle Benjy. "Briefly, I'm staking out a claim to Montreal Jew-ville in the tradition of H. de Balzac and Big Bill Faulkner."[55] But the return to St. Urbain didn't happen as quickly as advertised. Only one of these proposed novels materialized, and that not for twelve years.

There was at least one person who wasn't happy with Duddy. Cathy, stoked up by Bea Narizzano, who was subletting a flat to Florence, came unannounced to Richler's flat when only Kotcheff was home. Discovering that, after her long support of Richler, *The Apprenticeship of Duddy Kravitz* had been dedicated to Florence, Cathy raged, tried to tear up the book, and threw Richler's Olivetti typewriter out of the window into the mud. She only stopped her rampage after Kotcheff hit her.[56] As far as Richler was concerned, it was Bea who deserved the back of his hand. "Only Stanley, an injured party, had license to say anythg he pleased to Cathy," Richler said, "tho I doubt he was so irresponsible"[57] [*sic*].

Cathy didn't want a divorce, and divorce on the grounds of desertion required a seven-year waiting period – a non-starter for Richler[58] – but there was another potential solution: he could be caught in adultery. Reuben Ship gave Richler the name of the seedy detective that he had used in his own divorce, while Kotcheff arranged for his girlfriend to be discovered *in flagrante delicto*, wearing a frilly negligee in Richler's bed, empty champagne bottles telling the tale. Kotcheff hid in toilet when the detective came, flushing the toilet again and again to cover his laughter, and Richler, too, couldn't help laughing as the detective took his statement.[59] Cathy agreed to come in October for their court hearing, and Richler hoped for the final decree by January. At the same time, the double standard (under which British law still operated) required that for Florence to receive her *Decree Nisi* from Stanley she must forswear sex for six months. According to the law, a Queen's proctor could still surprise the female petitioner in a too-hot embrace and cancel divorce proceedings. The first decree of Florence's divorce was expected on 28 June and the final decree on 28 September, but Florence and Richler were already together every evening by early June. Kotcheff recalls sitting outside Florence's flat in his Austin Healy, ready to alert Richler with three beeps of the horn. Once, when a suspicious stranger entered the building, Kotcheff did indeed honk three times. Richler leapt out of the ground-floor window, and his getaway car raced off into the night.[60] Although he received news that Bill Weintraub's marriage had broken up, too, Richler didn't believe that all marriages were doomed. In fact, soon he spoke of having children with Florence and of a return to Canada with her. In December he wrote Weintraub, saying, "Am in a waiting and party-going period. Brian tells me you thk I'm happy, or I sound happy, or something, and what if I am, man?"[61]

Even the parental situation was rosier because Moe wanted very much to hear about (and, like Max Kravitz, speak about) his son's success. "At times Moe didn't like Mordecai at all and then he got to like him,"[62] Bernard Richler said, "when he became more famous then I guess he liked him." Moe, lover of movies, could by now watch *Room at the Top*, and father and son resumed the contact that had been broken by Mordecai's marriage to a Gentile. From Moe's second wife, Sara, Richler heard about the effect of his renewed correspondence with Moe: "you have brought Dad a lot of '*nachus*' and the man is a new person. He has always been a discouraged type of person. But since you have been writing to him etc. He is so changed" [*sic*].[63] Bernard wrote in the same vein as Sara had, saying that Moe was bragging about Mordecai's accomplishments and showing everybody his letters – "Your father is so eagerly awaiting your return he will probably kill the fatted calf."[64]

At first, the financial promise of *The Apprenticeship of Duddy Kravitz* didn't hold up. Collins, Richler's publisher in Canada, only ordered 750 copies, a figure not guaranteed to impress, and the book would, indeed, sell poorly. Yet at Toronto's Park Plaza Hotel, better things were brewing. Collins rented a suite for the novel's launch, to which Richler brought Daniel, now three. Richler had requested that Jack McClelland be invited, but why would Collins invite a rival to the barn dance? Instead, Richler phoned McClelland to meet him in the downstairs bar.[65] While chintzy Collins celebrated its talented author upstairs, the talented author was downstairs, laying the groundwork for a better deal.

And slowly, steadily, word of mouth spread the news about *The Apprenticeship of Duddy Kravitz*. It helped, too, that in the 1960s and 1970s teachers and professors, knowing that students would love it, began to assign the novel in classes. Much later, wealthy and secure, Richler would pooh-pooh the idea of commanding students to read novels – novels ought to be read simply for pleasure, oughtn't they? – and he managed to forget how much the sales of his later novels depended upon teachers championing *The Apprenticeship of Duddy Kravitz* one class at a time. Also in later years, *The Apprenticeship* began a second career as a hell-raiser, finding itself expelled from the more sensitive high schools. Profane language, sexual references, and the inability of naïve readers to find a straightforward moral all played a part. The Norfolk Board of Education in 1977–78 and the East Parry Sound Board of Education in 1980-81 banned *The Apprenticeship* and also *The Catcher in the Rye* from their senior reading lists. The Norfolk case was initiated by Rev. Harry Strachan of Bethel Baptist in Simcoe. Strachan hadn't read the book, but said, "I'm not here to debate with people … All they have to do is pick a good book and teach it … I don't care if there's a story behind it. That's just humanist thinking."[66]

While Richler, his own apprenticeship over, climbed his way up both the literary and film ladders in 1959, Reuben Ship's comedy series was cancelled, and Ship began to live in the bottle. Richler cared, but not enough, he admits: "We were still in our twenties, immortal beyond question, greedy, self-absorbed, and concerned with our own unrivalled promise and pleasures."[67]

13

Certified Libel-Free

ON THE STRENGTH of his film money, in January 1960 Richler laid his second bachelorhood aside, packed up Florence and Daniel, and together they ran off to Rome for a couple of months.[1] "Things were a little hot in England just then," Richler and Florence later said.[2] She was pregnant with his child,[3] but the couple decided that a wedding could wait until just before the child's birth. For now, the plan was to fly to Paris and buy a car there. However, first Richler had to learn how to drive. Just shy of his twenty-eighth birthday, Richler, kept out of driver's seats by poverty, had to learn quickly, with Kotcheff as teacher.[4]

In Paris, Richler paid cash for a little Renault and couldn't resist combing through the old haunts. But he recognized nobody, and, staying in nice hotels, he was now the bourgeois "tourist" that only a few years ago he had so cheerfully despised.[5] The family drove down along the Rhine. At one German guesthouse, Richler did hear, as he claimed, a group of reunited old soldiers nostalgically singing the song that had rung out spontaneously in German towns when France had surrendered to Germany in 1940 – Horst Wessell's Nazi anthem,

> *Die Fahne hoch, die Reihen fest geschlossen,*
> *S.A. marschiert mit ruhig festem Schritt ...*
> (The flag raised high, the ranks locked tight together,
> Storm troopers march, with steady, quiet pace ...)[6]

Shortly after the Richler entourage passed through Germany, swastikas were being daubed on West German synagogues, possibly by East German agents wishing to discredit Bonn. Honest, I had nothing to do with it, Richler wrote his friends. It was true that he did have his hands full with other matters: blizzards, car breakdowns, a stop to buy a potty for Daniel, with whom Richler was already thrilled.[7]

In Via Biferno, the little family rented an apartment, complete with a garden, an orange tree, and an English au pair for Daniel.[8] Richler, in his letters, made the working holiday sound idyllic,[9] though when he received from one of his poker companions an unpleasant letter with a bill enclosed,[10] he wasn't like the unruffled saints in Paradise who let such things pass. Richler's reply to Silvio and Bea Narizzano is a two-page, single-spaced caustic masterpiece. It begins, "Your rude, kittenish letter to Florence arrived this morning (with enclosures) ... Florence is possibly too gentle and forgiving to reply in kind. I am not." He even had an epigraph – "'Silvio Narizzano is a man who stands up...occasionally' (overheard at a party)" – and praised Narizzano for standing up for his pocketbook and his dog, even if he stood for nothing else. Among other things, the Narizzanos requested five shillings from Richler to cover Ted Kotcheff's phone calls made from their apartment. To which, Richler: "Well, Sir, Kotcheff and I have an arrangement. He pays his bills, I pay mine. So why don't you or Bea phone him for the five bob? As the last time he saw you he brought a couple of bottles of champagne to the house, and the time before he spent some forty quid at a posh restaurant, he might find yr behavior eccentric ... But go ahead." Richler closed demurely: "The Canada Council is giving yr bill every attention and consideration. Dont get on the phone right away. *Your agent may be trying to reach you.* See you soon. M." [*sic*].[11]

Although Richler was pleased about a life that had led to Florence Mann and Roman orange trees, other concerns got him boiling too. Just before Rome, Richler had finished a screenplay of his own, *No Love for Johnnie*, his first solo feature.[12] Now he had no choice but to see how the script-*patients* lived. Richler had been asked to adapt a bestselling novel of political ambition written by Wilfred Fienburgh, a Labour MP, before he died in a car accident in 1958. Through MP Johnnie Byrne, Fienburgh had shown the machinations of power, as Johnnie finds it in his personal interest first to become a tool for a dissident faction of Labour MPs, and then to abandon the faction when parliamentary debate interferes with his love life. The novel's sensibility wasn't far removed from Richler's: working-class boy gets rid of Yorkshire accent, rises, wants more. Richler understood perfectly the emotions behind such a story, including what drove Johnnie's unsuccessful pursuit of Pauline, an attractive model. When at the climax of the film Johnnie must choose between the position of undersecretary to the postmaster general and reconciliation with his estranged wife, Alice, the choice, for an ambitious man, is clear.[13]

Richler stuck faithfully to the novel and put very little original work into the adaptation.[14] But it didn't please Rank Organization producer Betty Box, who had overseen the popular *Doctor in the House* (1954) and whose husband had recently produced the first instalment of the wildly successful *Carry On* ... series. Neither was Box impressed that Richler, considering himself big-time, sent her a restaurant bill for £36 among his expenses. "Please tell him that we don't pay this sort of thing," she told Weiner.[15] More importantly, Box thought that the point of film was to entertain, not to fiddle too much with social messages. She called in Nicholas Phipps to doctor Richler's script.

In the heat of embarrassment, Richler wanted to walk away from his half of the screenwriting credit. No doubt he remembered how, after livening up the corpse of *Room at the Top*, he had crowed so loudly – "They are saying 'that bum [Neil] Paterson couldn't have written Room.'"[16] Weiner calmed Richler down. Keep the credit, she advised.[17] He did, a wise choice because the movie drew praise and even won a BAFTA (British Academy of Film and Television Arts) Award. In the novel and Richler's script Johnnie was a bounder, but Peter Finch, starring, earned plaudits for making Johnnie lovable and was criticized for exactly the same thing. What excited many reviewers were the "grown-up" themes of politics and sex (off-screen), even though leftist papers such as *The Daily Worker* demanded to know why not a single voice in the film spoke for "the political aspirations of the honest socialist." The original novel had helped to sabotage Labour in the 1959 election; Conservative Harold MacMillan, proponent of "The Middle Way" was returned with his second majority. Remembering this, Nina Hibbin declared that Box and director Ralph Thomas had placed "a weapon in the hands of Gaitskellites and their Tory friends."[18]

≷

Instead of doing an anti-war screenplay that he was offered after *No Love for Johnnie*, Richler started another novel, *It's Harder to be Anybody*, which after many years and much rewriting would become *Cocksure*.[19] It began as a story, "Mortimer Griffin, Shalinsky, and How They Solved the Jewish Problem," the story with which Florence began her editing of Richler's work.[20] Shalinsky, a Jew, decides that his night-school instructor, Mortimer, needs help in admitting that he, too, is a Jew (he isn't). Doris Lessing had told Richler that after a public lecture someone had asked her if she was Jewish. No, she had confessed. But Lessing was so literate and witty – infallible signs of Jewish blood, her questioner insisted. She needn't be ashamed of it.[21] Richler's editor, Diana Athill, felt that Shalinsky was merely a puppet and that Richler, attempting to satirize everybody, was in effect satirizing Jews the most. She feared that Richler would be labelled anti-Semitic. "Does this matter?" she asked, and answered, "I don't know." Although she feared losing Richler, the new novel wasn't a worthy successor to *The Apprenticeship of Duddy Kravitz*.[22] Joyce Weiner agreed, and André Deutsch himself delivered the hardest kick: even *The Acrobats* was better than this novel.[23]

Looking at the drafts of *It's Harder to be Anybody*, one must say that Athill, Weiner, and Deutsch had a point. In a long set piece. Mortimer, working for a publisher, leafs through a *Book of Cars*: "[a] black and white study showed a resolute masculine hand grasping a petrol pump, drippy and still vibrant, as it was withdrawn from the dark secret depths of the Mercedes Benz's tank."[24] Good for a chuckle, but at three pages, the joke wears thin. As well, the artificial search for literary ancestors in Canada (epitomized in Frederick Philip Grove, author #1 in McClelland & Stewart's "New Canadian Library") spurred Richler to "discover" the neglected "Angus Wilfred Robertson." The fictional Robertson was an erratic speller – just like F. Scott Fitzgerald! – died of old age – like Dickens! – and his book, *Out Fishin'*, though rejected by many publishers, contained unequalled descriptions of "blackflies, grass snakes, mosquitoes, beavers and marshes."[25] Again: good for a brief laugh. Not so inspired four pages later.

Athill wanted something along the lines of *The Apprenticeship of Duddy Kravitz*. "We are agog for the Canadian book and for the St. Urbain Street stories," she said, trying to soften the blow,[26] but Richler was annoyed and immediately began casting about for a new agent and publisher. He was already cutting his own deals in England and Canada, though he didn't begrudge Weiner her commission even when he did the negotiating. His two-sentence outline for a new play, "Kane's Coming," convinced the CBC to put $500 down. The protagonist, Kane, would run a mystery ad campaign, with only the teaser, "Kane's Coming." Finally appearing, he would walk up and down the street with a blank sandwich board, and people would project their own concerns onto him. Richler offered Sydney Newman British rights: "Ive only gone wrong once in all our dealings. With Peacock. And I paid back ½ for that one. I want a deal that would give me £500 for final, accepted draft. (You paid 425 for Duddy) ... Write me directly, please. Will not put darling Joyce Weiner on to you until we two have agreed. Best that way, I think."[27] Soon Richler signed with the more high-powered agent Monica McCall of New York[28] and explained to Weiner that he needed someone working for him on the scene in the US, while Weiner took care of Britain.[29] In a sad, correct letter, Weiner replied that she didn't for a moment agree with his reasoning, but that she still expected her commissions on the first four novels, plus the option book for Atlantic/Little, Brown, even though "as a gesture" she would forgo commission on his short stories.[30]

He didn't break with Weiner immediately, but made it clear that the end was coming. They had a long conversation in which he complained that she was overbearing, intimidating him; that she was an uncommercial literary agent, not able to get him much script work; that he was making many of his contacts himself. It was a mixture of truth and spin. Several days later,

Weiner wrote him two letters, defending herself. Intimidation? Richler must be oversensitive. She didn't recognize his first complaint for the smoke screen that it was: Richler was no longer at a career level where he could be intimidated by anyone, let alone by an "uncommercial" agent. He had always wanted to write outrageously and had never been very happy reined in by her old-school literary taste. But the tone of her reply makes it easy to see what he found annoying. She still nudged him towards her ideal of the educated, "objective" writer, and although for some time he had been pushing everybody to call him "Mordecai," she and Deutsch continued to call him "Mordy." Not long afterward, Jack McClelland asked Deutsch how he got away with calling Richler that. McClelland recounted an incident at a party when he had introduced Richler to the hostess. She said, "Migod, I can't call you Mordecai. Do you mind if I introduce you to the other people as 'Mort'?" "Yes, as a matter of fact, I do," he replied. "Introduce me either as Mordecai or as Mr. Richler."[31] Weiner and Deutsch, having known Richler for so long, weren't aware that he was getting more regardful of his dignity.

Against the charge of uncommerciality, Weiner defended herself by criticizing Richler's work: "Give me the tools, dear Mordy, and I will finish the job for you … I will go on slogging away at Andre [sic] for you, at earning the few guineas from the magazines."[32] André – ah, but therein lay another problem. André Deutsch was small potatoes, fine for a struggling bohemian, but he wasn't the big commercial firm that Richler now had in his sights. As for Weiner not being able to get script work and Richler making contacts himself, she was the one who had linked him with the producers Sydney and Betty Box, out of which had come *No Love for Johnnie* and *Faces in the Dark*, with other films on the horizon.[33] Yet he was partly right. He was the one setting up deals with Newman and Kotcheff, even going to Toronto and to New York to schmooze with the people who might buy his work.

Richler inflicted the unkindest cut when he told Weiner that he was staying with her out of sentimentality. She replied, "Apart from the fact that this element has been absent from your dealings with me for nearly five years, this cannot be quite true. You knew you would get honest dealing … full value for what you paid me." But his statement *was* true, if cruel. She knew that and was quite prepared to use sentiment to hold onto him, saying, "When your two other agents are roaring away in their Jags, maybe they will spare a passing wave for the 'un-commercial' agent, on whose efforts for a decade they are so happily cashing in." At the same time as she scorned "the plush and chromium boys or girls," Weiner, sensing the rope around her neck, tried to behave like one – awkwardly. One moment she berated Richler for not sending her quality work, and the next she fulsomely praised the new book that he was working on: *The Incomparable Atuk* was "a *tour de force*!" funny, subtle, "just sheer crazy fun"; and when he sent the article "London for Beginners," it, likewise, was "great fun," one of his best pieces of its kind, she said. He was making great strides, though just possibly he ought to branch out to new subjects.[34]

Too late. Were Jags necessarily so bad? In an unpublished article written around the same time, Richler groused about liberal British reviewers who couldn't understand the sensibility of, and therefore panned spunky American novels such as Philip Roth's *Letting Go*. British liberals, Richler said, "will allow Jews everything but vulgar humanity, clannish snobberies, etc ... Not for liberals the happy, cigar-sucking materialist with his Jag or the pushy working-class boy."[35] Norman Levine, with whom Richler periodically did house exchanges,[36] was a cautionary tale. He, too, had come over to England to write, but had made almost no money. With an English wife and three children, Levine went to St. Ives in Cornwall when it was overflowing with writers and artists. After a while, bohemia pitched its tents elsewhere and Levine, too poor to follow, had only the bank manager, the milkman, and the postman to converse with.[37] Buried alive. "What sort of advance," Richler scolded Jack McClelland, "did you pay Norman for his stories, goddamn it! He's got a shoeshine box out on Trafalgar Square and wears a sweatshirt with MCCLELLAND and STEWART printed on the back."[38] With an envious eye to Roth's popular success, Richler hoped that Monica McCall would open the doors of upscale US magazines for him. Shortly he would replace Weiner in Britain as well. She could hardly deny that he was doing a lot of the business himself. She didn't deny it. "You keep a dog and bark yourself, which is hardly an economic practice," she scolded.[39] Richler's point exactly.

Yet was he becoming too much the businessman? He didn't voice these fears directly, but they came through when he objected to the business savvy of Norman Mailer and of the Beats. Mailer, though talented, was far too worried about turning over retail units, said Richler, and not worried enough about writing good books. And now that Richler was no longer a hipster himself, he could reveal a shocking secret: Kerouac, Corso, and Ginsberg were self-promoters![40]

≋

In March 1960, a year and a half before the argument with Weiner, Richler came to Montreal,[41] where he and Florence were married on 27 July. Two days later, Noah was born.[42] Ted Kotcheff flew all the way from England. "It's a hell of a lot of moolah for four days," he initially wrote to Richler, "which same the mostest wedding present could be acquired that ever was but then just how many best friends does one have and how often does he get hitched to Florence" [*sic*].[43] Richler wasn't prepared to entertain excuses. "Ted," he said over the phone, "I don't want my kid born a bastard."[44] The couple settled for a civil marriage, since only the United Church, at that time, would officiate at the marriage of a Jew and a Protestant.[45] Kotcheff stood as best man to Richler and godfather to Noah.[46] Bill Weintraub attended the wedding, too, but no family came, and together the friends had much fun, as Kotcheff's film of *Joshua Then and Now* hints, Joshua's bride so close to giving birth that she can hardly stand up for the little ceremony. Of the Richler clan, only Max arrived afterwards for a visit.[47] Intermarriage was still abhorrent to most of the Richlers, though Lily and even Moe had become resigned to having a Gentile daughter-in-law.[48] Mordecai refused to worry about whether the children would be brought up as Jews or Christians or neither. Still, he was determined that this marriage would work and that he wouldn't give his children the unstable home he had had.[49] He took steps to adopt Daniel formally.[50] Time and again Richler was thrilled by Daniel – by his early ability to read, his curiosity, and his tactile ability. As for Florence, she had already made her choice. With two young children now clamouring for her attention, there was hardly enough time to keep the household running, let alone think of returning to her career.[51]

The year in Canada was supposed to be about resuming touch with the city that provided the raw material for Richler's best writing,[52] but his reports weren't encouraging: "I am seeing Canada. I'm seeing lots of it so that I wont have to come back for a long time" [*sic*].[53] On a rainy day he accompanied his Uncle Max to the opening of a Montreal synagogue, and when the sun broke through, the president of synagogue interpreted the event as a sign of God's favour.[54] Richler's eyebrows rose. "I was appalled," he wrote, "at the lack of humility implicit in the notion that our God, who seemed to be busy elsewhere when six million were murdered in Europe, had the time to indicate his pleasure with this suburban community." It wasn't a fully considered theology, but it would form one basis for Richler's attempt to address the Holocaust in *St. Urbain's Horseman*. A little while after the sun broke through, the rabbi paid tribute to the money that had built the synagogue. Here, too, Richler found reason to fume: "A young moon-faced rabbi rose, and after first assuring us that he had never known the lady in whose memory the ark had been given, he then went on to extol her in such hyperbolic terms that she appeared a saint."[55] What, Max wanted to know, *could* the rabbi have said about a woman who contributed $5,000? Max was somewhat pained but not surprised when he read his nephew's article, recalling how embarrassed Richler had been as a boy that Moe couldn't contribute enough to get his name posted on synagogue boards.[56]

Because of his growing celebrity, Richler was by now being invited to speak at synagogues.[57] Jews came to the Beth Ora Synagogue, hoping to hear about the lofty heights attained by one of their own. Instead, they saw a short, long-haired man with the expression of a sad dog, wearing a yarmulke,[58] telling them that Orthodoxy was kaput, finished, and at the same time that attempts to modernize Judaism were a farce – bar mitzvahs had become "musical comedies," and synagogues "religious drugstores."[59] When he finished, utter silence for a while. Then whisperings. Then rebuttals. You are an angry young man. I *like* our synagogue to be a community centre. I went to Baron Byng, too, and you only presented half of the picture. Do you think you're the Messiah? Even the rabbi hosting the talk felt the need, given Richler's barbs about rabbis, to get on his feet and dispute with his guest. Some in the audience asked Richler about possible corrective measures to the problems that he raised. Sorry, he said, I've only got questions, not answers.[60]

Partly as a result of his personality and partly as a response to the kind of exclusiveness that he despised, Richler began to earn a reputation for being uncompromising at such events. Some Jews, unaware of the extent of his religious disaffection and unaware that in *The Apprenticeship of Duddy Kravitz* he had depicted Reform Judaism as laughable, thought that if they addressed Richler's concerns by making financial contributions voluntary and secret, Richler would leap back into the fold.[61] During one question period a man complained that Richler shouldn't have depicted Jews who called French-Canadians "frogs." The depiction was accurate, the man admitted, but bad publicity.[62] Others denounced him as an anti-Semite. For some audience members, "Jew" was purely a religious, not an ethnic designation. That counts you out, Richler. Bernard Schachter, still confined to the language of the Maccabees, wrote to him that, "A Jew is different because when all the world through dark centuries crept in fear and superstition, in ignorance of God, in contempt for the concept of international oneness of man ... THE JEW marched with head held high and purpose strongly believing in the goodness of man, that each man is truly his brother's keeper, that God is oneness." Anything else, said Schachter, was Hellenization: "If you can brush these differences aside as inconsequential," Schachter informed Richler, "then I must say that you are no Jew."[63] Richler, in response, tended to speak as someone who had been saved from such rank nonsense, speaking not, his audiences soon realized, as an insider bent on reforming the traditions. At the same time he received letters from a different set of readers who invited him kindly to do a little more research, and to *open his eyes* because the *Protocols of the Learned Elders of Zion* gave a historically accurate account of the Jewish master-plot to take over the world.[64] About this time in his career he began to insist that a good satirist wasn't a vendor of panaceas but a naysayer.

In Montreal Richler laid febrile plans to go to Toronto, New York, Miami Beach. As he explained to Sydney Newman, "Richler follows the rich Jews everywhere. A spy."[65] He did get to Toronto. At a Canadian Conference of the Arts there, Richler was no kinder than in the synagogues, telling the four hundred people assembled that a real writer would have nothing to say to them. Serious discussion could occur only between artists. Not quite reconciled to his increasingly bourgeois status, he looked over the audience and saw far too many elegant hats and dresses. It wasn't likely, he said, that there could be many serious artists inside such fancy hats.[66]

His months in Toronto weren't spent collecting dirt on rich Jews, but chatting up CBC editors and studying the predatory habits of journalists and TV producers. Enough to begin what he called "a short satanic novel" about Toronto.[67] Like the still simmering *It's Harder to Be Anybody*, the new novel, *The Incomparable Atuk*, was to be a parody of "special pleading." In order to forestall the criticisms that were bound to be made – that Richler no longer pretended to create living characters,[68] that he was racist, that he was sexist – Richler told everybody that the book was "six feet off the ground" in the tradition of Nathanael West and Evelyn Waugh.[69] True, there was a nod to the deceptive advice columns of West's *Miss Lonelyhearts*,[70] and like Waugh's *The Loved One*, Richler's novel initially revolved around an expatriate Britisher, who, not able to cut the mustard in England, was reduced to stumbling his way through the nonsense that passed for culture in North America. But there any resemblance ended, for *The Incomparable Atuk* utterly lacked the restraint of West and Waugh. It was farce, pure and simple. First of all, Richler hadn't forgotten the injury done him by Nathan Cohen's snide recap of his career in *Tamarack Review*. Now that Cohen had left the CBC to do drama criticism at the *Toronto Star*,[71] Richler needn't worry about offending him. To the script for the CBC program *Q is for Quest* Richler added some – presumably unfilmed – touches, advertising "AN EVENING WITHOUT BELAFONTE … Nathan Cohen sings and plays some Eskimo folk songs."[72] Mild, compared to *The Incomparable Atuk*. The novel featured one Seymour Bone, a fat and self-obsessed drama critic. His wife, evidently on good terms with her Negro gardener, prepares Bone for a soon-to-come wallop by reminding him that they are Jews and sometimes Jews have babies with darkish, call it "Yemenite," skin. You can't do that in a novel, an aghast Jack McClelland told Richler. The coloured baby would have to go.[73] It stayed.

Following what was now becoming standard procedure with Richler's novels, Diana Athill had lawyers prepare a libel report. Though the confrontation between the straight laces of the law and Richler's irreverence wasn't quite as delicious as it would get with *Cocksure*, the report is inadvertently funny nonetheless. Repeatedly the serious British barristers, quite prepared to charge throat-choking fees yet unfamiliar with the Canadian originals, find themselves unable to say for certain whether the characters are potentially libellous or not. Instead Rubinstein, Nash, and Co. can do little but refer Athill to the author: "No doubt you will seek satisfactory assurances from the Author that no-one coming within this category could conceivably claim to be identifiable."[74]

For his part, the Author assured everyone that all manner of thing was well. He did pay some attention to the report. He replaced the "Hudson's Bay Company" with the "Twentyman Fur Company,"[75] though he didn't go as far as the lawyers might have liked. The top British legal talent had reached at least one definitive conclusion: *if*, on the off-chance, a Hudson's Bay Company was still in existence, *then* no change of name would reduce the danger of libel.[76] But as to whether such an organization had actually existed or still existed, they had no firm opinion. (It did, non-Canadian reader; it does.) Richler also changed Bone's rise to fame, which in the early draft was a more realistic portrait of Cohen's advancement through self-published reviews, newspaper columns, and a TV show.[77] The final (certified libel-free) version had Bone accidentally gain the Canadian seal of approval by being mentioned in Britain; never mind that the reference occurred during a satire on Canadian culture.[78] Richler did enough – making Bone Presbyterian, Western-born, and red-headed – to be able to prove that Bone wasn't Cohen, and enough – rhyming the two names, making him a drama critic, making him fat and high-handed – to make it obvious that he was. Cohen's CBC show, *Fighting Words*, on which guests debated contemporary issues, became *Crossed Swords* in the novel. Many years later, Peter Gzowski would ingenuously insist that there were no personal attacks in *The Incomparable Atuk*, so, excellent thing, no one got hurt.[79] In fact, it took more than a year after the novel was published for Richler and Cohen to slowly resume contact.[80] Robert Fulford, seeing his old boss slaughtered, dreamed of a magnificent trial in which Cohen, mistakenly convinced that Bone was a portrait of him, sued Richler for libel. Canadian literary scholars flown in from British Columbia. Robert Weaver, Ken Lefolii (of *Maclean's*) and Fulford as expert witnesses. "It would be," Fulford gleefully anticipated, "the Dreyfus case of modern Canada, the biggest event in all our lives."[81]

One of the fictional panellists on *Crossed Swords*, Rabbi Glenn Seigal, was also a lampoon – skewering Rabbi Abraham Feinberg of the Reform congregation at Toronto's Holy Blossom Temple.[82] Richler measures cultural deterioration when the panellists (including Seigal) are unable to identify the source of the quotation "Blessed are the meek," and Seigal puts a period on it when he dismisses the slogan as lacking appeal anyway.[83] Already with *The Apprenticeship of Duddy Kravitz* one editorial reader had taken offense at Richler's satire against the Reform Jewish service, and had made a copious list of what he felt were Richler's errors, though recognizing that the sermon topic – "Jewish Athletes from Bar Kochva to Hank Greenberg" – was satirical.[84] Several years later Richler would attack Feinberg explicitly, calling him "the Jewish Norman Vincent Peale." Feinberg was for all the

right things – "the workers, civil rights nuclear disarmament, the yellow people, black people, Jewish people, and so forth" – but Reform Judaism led
nowhere, Richler kept repeating.[85] Orthodoxy was "severe, illogical, even
bigoted," but it was also "rich in poetic tradition and ... solidly there."[86]
Richler, unbeliever, still sang the old synagogue songs,[87] but Feinberg astutely guessed that Richler had wandered far enough from Orthodoxy to
have mostly forgotten its lash.[88] Yet Richler was correct to think that Reform would speak for only a small number of Jews.[89] And even young Reform Jews were heading in Richler's direction. By 1965, two years after *The
Incomparable Atuk* was published and four years after Feinberg retired, the
young congregants of Holy Blossom Temple requested Richler's permission
to do a theatrical reading of *Such was St. Urbain Street.*[90]

Other characters in *The Incomparable Atuk* were also more than just
"conceivably" identifiable. Harry Snipes, author of *Ejaculations, Epiphanies, et etc*, preaching *ad nauseam* that Canadians were "too damn conventional"[91] and threatening to expose the glories of his body to one and all,
was clearly the poet Irving Layton. J.P. McEwen was Pierre Berton, then an
investigative reporter for the *Toronto Star.* Like McEwen, Berton relied
upon operatives for his investigations; unlike McEwen, Berton wasn't a
cross-dresser,[92] even though his natty bowties might give one pause. More
eye-catching was Betty Dolan, Richler's lampoon of Marilyn Bell, the six-
teen-year-old who swam across Lake Ontario. Richler held a seemingly gra-
tuitous and cruel grudge against innocent athletes such as Bell (and later
Wayne Gretzky). An early draft of *The Incomparable Atuk* suggests why.
The early draft lets a dissipated Englishman, Lucas Hartley (instead of Atuk)
deflower Betty Dolan. Post-coitum, Lucas wants to apologize, "but what
does one say to Canada after clearing the Jasper woods for timber or draining Niagara Falls?"[93] An old and hallowed theme for Richler, Canadian innocence. In *The Acrobats*, before Weiner and Athill got their hands on it,
he had apostrophized, "The Canadian artists! Mediocracy [sic] draped in a
maple leaf ... Sonnets by the aging virgin grandmothers of tory tradesman."[94]
From the published version of *The Incomparable Atuk* Richler wisely cut
the ham-fisted allegory (Betty = Canada; Lucas = Britain), but not the mo-
tivation behind it. No doubt Richler sensed that the worship of innocent
idols such as Bell and Gretzky stunted the nation's intellectual culture and
left Canadians unable to worship more worldly and cynical artists, say
Mordecai Richler. Thus, while the final novel became much more playful
when Richler cut Lucas out of the picture and left the deflowering to Atuk,
the aggressiveness against Dolan came to seem nastier, no longer tied to political allegory, though in Richler's mind it probably still was.

Atuk himself was fairer game. Since he wasn't based on any individual
and since he is the most complex in a book of cardboard characters,[95] Rich-

ler (following the tradition of Paul Hiebert's *Sarah Binks*) couldn't fairly be accused of racism in his merciless satire on "innocent" art. The mass production of "authentic" soapstone carvings and the hilarious evolution of Atuk from naïve poet –

> I go hunt bear in white dawn
> good spirit come with me"

– to imitative Beat poet –

> Twentyman Fur Company,
> I have seen the best seal hunters of my
> generation putrefy raving die from tuberculosis,
> Massey, you square,
> eskimos don't rub noses any more and the cats
> around Baffin Bay dig split-level houses[96]

– all this is a send-up less of Atuk (who perceives what's necessary to make a buck) than of his white audience, eager to applaud because the poet is Inuit, not because he's good. Richler's knowledge of the Inuit and the Arctic was at this time minimal, and it's likely that he got his idea for an Eskimo art factory from a skit that Robert Fulford and a friend did for *Spring Thaw*, a long-running musical and comedy revue in Toronto.[97]

As Jack McClelland was quick to point out, many of Richler's jokes were local, and the danger was that *The Incomparable Atuk* might not appeal to people outside of the Toronto establishment,[98] something that *The Tatler*, a British magazine, would confirm, calling the novel "a bizarre Canadian in-joke."[99] Richler himself was none too convinced about the book's value and several times decided that it was too frivolous to publish.[100] Names like See-more Bone or Buck Twentyman and characters such as the transvestite RCMP officer certainly appeared to come from some Kiwanis Komedy Revue, but perhaps, too, Richler had the feeling that his very determination to address contemporary issues via satire was suspect. How topical was the novel? *Son of a Smaller Hero*'s epigraph came from Dostoevsky, *The Incomparable Atuk*'s from *Maclean's* magazine, 1960, a nationalist quotation urging Canadians to shut the border to US culture. Thus the "need" for Atuk's art, Richler joked. Thus the Liberal promise of a new Canadian flag (rather than measures against unemployment). But topicality created a double bind: Torontonians seemed to think they inhabited the hub of the known universe; good material, such thoughts, for satire. But, to feature Torontonians centrally in a novel, wasn't that surrendering to their hubris?

Yet its very topicality helped to make *The Incomparable Atuk* important in that curiously roundabout way of satire. When Richler was in Toronto
gathering material during March 1961, Philip Roth, a writer whom Richler admired,[101] published a *Commentary* article that Richler read. Roth contended that US reality had reached a level of absurdity that stupefied and
infuriated, but that also showed up the puniness of the novelist's imagination. The immediate danger was that the novelist would ignore public life
and escape to fantasy or to the self.[102] In short order, Richler was making
very similar statements about his own novels: "It's terribly difficult nowadays to compete with reality because reality is becoming so grotesque."[103]
The Incomparable Atuk took shape, with Roth's unwitting blessing, as a
direct and infuriated response to Canadian public life. Leacock had laughed
at small-town hicks, but Richler savaged the most important urban cultural
and political institutions. With *The Incomparable Atuk*, Richler became
one of English Canada's first truly self-mocking public voices. It's ironic
that a novel that wouldn't stand among Richler's most important could
hold such a pivotal place in the history of Canadian literature. Richler often
spoke of being a witness to his time, but he was far too easily annoyed to
be a plain speaker and instead moved close to what Alvin Kernan suggested
were the roots of satire: formulaic curses against one's enemies.[104] If exaggerated characters pulled *The Incomparable Atuk* away from the real, Richler's concerns were rooted deeply in public culture, and he made Atuk flexible
enough to follow the contours of the Canadian polity, coming at the real
from the back door.

Atuk, the image of the naïve Canadian artist early on, broadens out to
other cultures later on in the novel when he becomes a parody of the rebel-
lious young Jew, duelling with his father about intermarriage. Still later, he
becomes a vehicle for an attack on Zionism, probably as a result of Richler's trip to Israel in 1962, a year before the novel was published. To the
nervous Jew, Rory Peel, Atuk patiently explains that Eskimos would like to
see all other Canadians relocated to a single province, "a sort of national
park."[105] Why? Because their God had promised them the land, and because
the Inuit had suffered terrible hardships. Later yet, Atuk participates in *Stick
Your Neck Out*, a show involving a guillotine and a difficult question, a
show whose intensity *Fear Factor* hasn't yet equalled. In a blaze of glory, he
flares up as a saint-martyr to Canadian nationalism, murdered by an American food company... if we trust the Canadian millionaire and proprietor
of Esky Foods, Buck Twentyman.

Not surprisingly, given its revelling in kitsch and bad jokes, the novel
was dedicated to Moe Richler. Moe could also appreciate the novel's satire
against cultural protectionism – it would pain him should his precious New
York tabloids encounter any difficulties at the border. But there was another,

more troubling reason for the dedication. In recent years, Richler had gotten closer again to his father[106] and had begun to admit how much he owed Moe (especially for the Montreal-inflected voice in *The Apprenticeship of Duddy Kravitz*). Diana Athill put it succinctly: "Your father is splendid – it's sad to think that if he ever tries to claim that you owe a lot to him, he won't know how true that is. But every remark of his you've ever quoted has been really monumental."[107] Richler had said as much, though more subtly in the story "Some Grist for Mervyn's Mill" (1961), which mocks Lily, and also Richler himself via the young writer Mervyn, who thinks he's a budding Shakespeare. The only figure who comes across as halfway sensible is the narrator's father, something of a ghost-writer, it turns out, telling Mervyn a better story than any of Mervyn's, a story much like Richler's "The Summer My Grandmother was Supposed to Die."[108]

Just after Richler left Canada again, he found out that Moe was in the hospital. Instead of quizzing Moe, Richler asked Brian Moore's brother Sean, a Montreal physician, to make discreet enquiries. Moore reported that Moe had had a small cancer of the bladder removed. Whether the tumour was malignant or benign Moore didn't know.[109] Even before the operation, Moe and his wife Sara hadn't been doing well financially, so Avrum and Mordecai sent regular support, Mordecai beginning to return the money that had kept him alive and writing in Europe years earlier. When Lily offered to pitch in $50 a month, Mordecai said that she worked too hard for what she had.[110] Moe kept himself busy with reading and stamps. Sara knitted sweaters for Mordecai's children, and Moe sent them little gifts of money, Hanukkah gelt.[111]

14

Idols of the Tribe

BY THE MID-1960s Richler had become both the *enfant terrible* of Canadian nationalism (the traitor who took potshots at the idols of the tribe) and the poster-boy for Canada (the Canadian who had made an international success of himself). Canada's Ryerson Press, founded by Methodists and still run by the United Church, declined *The Incomparable Atuk*. Editor Robin Taylor thought the novel witty, but uneven, and feared that the issue of libel just might arise.[1] He didn't mention that in the early draft of the novel Richler mocks "a publishing house that was, of all things, financed by a group of clergymen."[2] Down in the US, Seymour Lawrence, befuddled by all the Canadian references, declined the book on behalf of Atlantic-Little, Brown (the publisher of *The Apprenticeship of Duddy Kravitz*).[3] *The Incomparable Atuk* being the option book, Lawrence worried that he might lose Richler, but, cheering up a bit, announced that he still planned to publish the other books in the projected Duddy trilogy.[4] Not likely that Richler would invite Lawrence back to feast when the next book (the "next" book is always a big seller) appeared. In fact, Richler wasn't overly displeased by the two rejections since he had a line on two better publishers. While Joyce Weiner was still dickering with Robin Taylor, Richler had already felt out the non-clergyman publisher with whom he sensed a greater kinship, Jack McClelland. McClelland at first had qualms about *The Incomparable Atuk*, and even enumerated for Richler how many people at McClelland & Stewart didn't like the book, but he wanted Richler badly. Better yet, he had expressed interest in the other pots that Richler had boiling – a book of short stories, a book of essays, the novel *It's Harder to Be Anybody* from which Deutsch and Weiner had recoiled. Seven months and a thorough revision later, McClelland pronounced *The Incomparable Atuk* "terrific" and no longer believed that local knowledge was required to enjoy it.[5]

Perhaps every biography of a Canadian writer who published between the early 1950s and the late 1970s includes a moment of silence before the altar of Jack McClelland, and rightly so. After McClelland retired, Richler left McClelland & Stewart, but he always recognized how much he owed to the godfather of Canadian literature. McClelland accepted writing that didn't belong to the genteel tradition. He, as Richler said, "dragged his father's sobersides publishing firm kicking and screaming into a postwar world of ruffian Jewish scribblers and lady novelists and poets who wrote dirty."[6] Leonard Cohen put it more lyrically in a letter to Jack McClelland:

> you were the
> real Prime Minister of Canada. You still
> are. And even though it's all gone down
> the tubes, the country that *you* govern
> will never fall apart.[7]

Richler and McClelland would get on well at their late-night drinking sessions.[8] Although each was a hardheaded cuss in his own right, and, although McClelland wasn't one to mince when harsh words were necessary, he allowed the writer to be king. That suited Richler, who would rather his publisher curse him than cross him.

On the US front, too, Richler had no worries, because even before Lawrence finished petting Richler in hope of future Duddys, Monica McCall had been on the phone with Bob Gottlieb at Simon & Schuster.[9] All that Richler needed was a better editor, Gottlieb assured him. *A Choice of Enemies*, for example, was full of good things, but wasn't *good*, and a better editor – i.e. Gottlieb – could have prevented Richler from killing off Sally.[10] The rapport between Richler and Gottlieb was immediate – Richler "adored" this man, says Florence.[11] The Richlers, particularly Florence, grew close enough to Bob and his partner Maria for vacations together and for Bob and Maria to become godparents to Jacob when he was born.[12] They shared friends and an irreverent sense of humour. Garish statues of Elvis and the Lone Ranger presiding over his desk,[13] Gottlieb could be found on the floor of his office, lying on his stomach beside an author and munching on a sandwich as they went over a manuscript together. He showed up for work in jeans and sneakers. Having grown up in an atheistic home, Gottlieb was a secular Jew who knew nothing about Jewishness. All fine by Richler.[14]

Reading was Gottlieb's life, and Richler was pleased that Gottlieb read manuscripts very quickly – often overnight, at the most within two or three days. Also, Gottlieb didn't go in for line-by-line editing, and Richler was glad to be rid of it.[15] Florence already gave the first read to Richler's fiction,[16] commenting on the characters and situations, and he wanted the same from the paid help. He didn't want to "rethink" books anymore. For his part, Gottlieb thought that a magazine editor could afford to be imperious, but a fiction editor must either serve the writer or be jilted.[17] A typical appointment at Gottlieb's office: Richler comes in, listens "solemnly" to Gottlieb's criticisms and caveats, and then does "whatever he want[s] to do."[18] Once, during the editing of *Cocksure*, Gottlieb said, "if you don't want to make these changes, don't. Only five hundred people will appreciate the difference anyway." Flattery proved the best diplomacy: Richler made the changes.[19]

≶

The months in Toronto (not to mention *Atuk*'s epigraph) had solidified Richler's standing with *Maclean's*, the foremost Canadian magazine and a source of income not to be despised. His start there hadn't been auspicious: Peter Gzowski had bought his "Making It with the Chicks" in 1960 while managing editor Ralph Allen was on vacation; Allen, on his return, blew up and fumed that the article was nothing more than masturbation behind the barn.[20] Allen had always had a rather decorous idea of what *Maclean's* was. When Ken Lefolii, Peter Gzowski, and Robert Fulford (ranging in age from twenty-nine to thirty-four)[21] began to steer the boat, *Toronto Telegram* columnist McKenzie Porter grumbled that all three were shabby dressers and uncomfortable in society. Prior to their tenure, no *Maclean's* employee could leave the building without wearing a hat – hats being the infallible sign of seriousness. Porter also complained bitterly that the Young Turks made their own little circle at cocktail parties and jeered "at guests of greater worldliness." Richler quickly entered the cadre, a charter member if jeering was the criterion. F.G. Brander, publisher of *Maclean's*, admitted that he never liked Richler's work – too abrasive – but according to Lefolii, Gzowski, and Fulford, the thirty-three-year-old Richler's panache was just what they felt would lift *Maclean's* from a middlebrow imitation of the *Saturday Evening Post* to literary distinction.[22]

   Although Brian Moore called journalism "a dissipater of talent,"[23] Richler didn't consider it an artistic compromise – unlike his movie work.[24] Journalism forced him out of the hothouse inhabited by writers and media types, out onto the street among all kinds of people with all kinds of concerns, raw material for novels. For a week in 1963, editor Blair Fraser sent Richler to the Royal Canadian Air Force base at Baden Söllingen (near Baden-Baden) in West Germany to do a story on RCAF life.[25] Fraser didn't mind Richler mocking the lower ranks, but he tried and failed to delete the gossip that Richler had gathered in the officers' mess. When the story appeared, the RCAF complained bitterly.[26]

In early 1962, *Maclean's* put up money to fly Richler to Israel for a piece on the kibbutzim, and he also laid his own plans to go to Amagansett, Long Island, for the summer. *"L'shana haba'a b'yerushalayim"* – "and next year in Jerusalem" – so ended several Jewish prayers that Richler knew, including one at the end of the Passover meal.[27] Many Jews, among them Richler's mother[28] and Sandra Kolber, wife of Leo Kolber (a later butt of Richler's satire), rhapsodized about approaching Zion –

> From the Mount of Olives we looked down
> To salute you, Oh Glorious Jerusalem.
> Eyes ablaze in transfigured faces,
> We yearned the touch of God ...
> But we have lost the vantage point.[29]

As Richler's plane descended towards Lod Airport, some passengers clapped, some wept, and Richler joined in the singing,[30] feeling, too, the initial thrill of finally arriving in the tribal homeland. Almost every second night he was on the move,[31] but he avoided seeking out his former Zionist companions in Habonim – Ezra Lifshitz, Sol and Fayge Cohen, Gdalyah Wiseman – because he still felt that he had let them down somehow by not emigrating to Israel.[32] He met not only Israeli patriots but also critics of the government, Arabs, and Jewish land developers. The result was less than his mother's reverence. Like Ahad Ha'am, Richler sensed the disjunction between Zion's idealized image and the reality.[33] He felt humbled by people who had come to a barren land and built Eretz Yisrael from scratch, yet at the same time he wondered whether the flowering of the Negev Desert really ought to culminate with the Desert Inn, an eighteen-hole golf course, and nightly dances by ethnic Bedouin. On Kibbutz Gesher Haziv near the Lebanese border, he experienced the Israelis' fear when the alarm shut down and armed guards marched back and forth,[34] but his jaundiced satirist's eye couldn't help noticing that the kibbutzim, zenith of his youthful aspirations, were considered the equivalent of dying hick-towns on the Canadian prairies.[35] Richler didn't *like* the kibbutzim – too communal[36] – and he wasn't overwhelmed by Jerusalem either – too old, too religious. The Labour Zionist compromise with Agudah (the home-land movement of Orthodox Palestinian Jews) had resulted in Sabbath rules, kashrut, and marriage laws,[37] not at all to Richler's taste. He felt most comfortable in Tel Aviv, the most westernized of Israeli cities.[38]

Richler belonged to Diaspora Jews who looked to New York, not to Israel, for their culture. The Israel trip raised an important question: was he an assimilationist? Yes, he admitted. Were he to live in Israel, he'd miss the goys and the productive clash of cultures. The refrain he kept noticing in Israel –

"We're a new kind of Jew here" – was intended as a declaration that Israeli Jews would no longer bow obsequiously before Gentiles, but Richler heard darker undertones; namely, that if there had to be Pharaohs in the land, they would damn well be Jews; and, if there had to be slaves, they might as well be Arabs this time round. Conditions in the Arab refugee camps of Gaza, Richler heard an Israeli say, were deplorable, but Dachau was worse. Infuriated, Richler ended his *Maclean's* articles by drawing a parallel between the present oppression of the Arab minority and past oppressions of the Jews. He imagined that he had less in common with his own tribe than with the winking Arab entrepreneur who sold Certified Earth from the Holy Land in three different packages – Cross, Crescent, or Star of David.[39] In the late 1950s, Moshe Sharett, the former Israeli prime minister, had visited London and at a gathering of Jewish writers had wondered aloud, to Richler's annoyance, why they didn't come to Israel to write.[40] After the Six-Day War in 1967, Richler would be less inclined to easy identifications with Arabs, and on the road to *St. Urbain's Horseman* his understanding of the complexity of the Middle East problem would deepen, but by the end of his Israel trip he was "miserably lonely" and drinking too much in the evening.[41] Whatever Israel was, he recognized already in 1962 that it wasn't home.

≶

Before the Israel trip, Robert Weaver had intimated, without saying so directly, that Richler was writing too much satire on Jews and that the CBC balked at accepting any more for a while.[42] Daryl Duke, a CBC producer, spoke more bluntly, "high time you stopped this obsessive Montreal bit, Mordecai, and looked at the world around you." Yet Duke made it a catch-22 when he added that the CBC valued Richler's work precisely because it didn't reproduce middle-class Anglo-Saxony. Canadians had had their fill of that.[43] Richler's way of dealing with the complaints? He invited Weaver and Duke, as well as Lefolii and Gzowski of *Maclean's*, to join him for a holiday in Amagansett, Long Island, next summer.[44] In New York, Ted Solotaroff, associate editor of *Commentary*, accepted Richler's "Their Canada and Mine" for publication, but not the brilliant short story, "The Summer My Grandmother Was Supposed to Die." Didn't Richler know that these kinds of stories happened in the US all the time? If Richler knew the US scene, why bother pretending that Canadian Jewry was unique? He ought to emphasize the story's typicality and put in US references wherever possible. Richler's way of dealing with the complaint? He invited Solotaroff to join him for a holiday in Amagansett. Solotaroff thought that Richler must be very gracious to invite him on such a short acquaintance.[45]

   Amagansett. Tree-lined streets, houses set well back, the destination for tenement-weary New Yorkers.[46] The beaches were overrun with writers,

painters, TV people, and psychiatrists.[47] The place had been in Richler's mind
for a few years because Bill Weintraub and Brian Moore summered there
and kept inviting Richler.[48] Finally, for the 1962 season, May to November,
Richler arrived with his entire family, now five, in tow. Emma had been born
the previous October. Moore, her gift-bearing godfather,[49] found the Richlers a house and taught Daniel how to ride a two-wheeler.[50] Norman Mailer,
William De Kooning, A.J. Leibling of *The New Yorker*, Peter Matthiessen
of *Paris Review*, and David Shaw (Irwin's TV-writing brother) all holidayed
there. So did novelists Wallace Markfield and Josh Greenfield. Above all,
Philip Roth – the next big thing. "Baby Boy Roth," as Moore called him,
was Moore's neighbour and top pecker in the writers' unofficial pecking
order. Quite prepared to lord it, he wasn't an agreeable fellow, Weintraub
thought. Richler and Moore, on the other hand, found Roth likeable and
funny, but they agreed that "he tends to go on a hell of a lot about P Roth."
Grist for satire, potentially. Soon after Richler's visit, Moore grew apprehensive that his protégé might cost him his holiday destination by skewering all of "NY Jewville," and he warned Richler that one summer there
doesn't make you an expert.[51]

Moore had cause to worry, since he had just finished *An Answer from
Limbo*, in which the writer Max Bronstein looked an awful lot like Richler.
But Richler, for whom six months had more than sufficed to skewer Toronto,
reassured Moore that he had no plans to prick influential Americans and
had no objections if Bronstein was indeed based on him. What he did object to was the passage in *An Answer from Limbo* where Mrs Tierney, the
protagonist's mother, has a stroke while the TV is on. "I knew what was
coming," Richler told Moore, "and hated you for it."[52] What was coming
was Mrs Tierney's long dying, through *The Edge of Night*, through count-
less advertisements for beauty aids, through severe casualties in Vietnam,
through the applause meter for the best "hard-luck-but-I-came-out-on-top"
story – the trivia and danger of the United States.[53] This irked Richler because he had had the same idea and could never use it now. To win a Guggenheim Fellowship, Richler had promised a Duddy trilogy, with the third book
to be called *The Bathtub* because it featured Max Kravitz dying in his bathtub, the TV on and Kravitz forced to share his last intimate moments with
what TV programmers, in their great wisdom, sent out across the continent.
Moore's use of the motif had been sad and profound, Mrs Tierney's Irish
Catholic soul merging with and clashing against the alien USA. Said Richler, "Naturally I thk I could have used this idea better."[54]

Back in London, Richler did more work that was highly paid but offered
small artistic satisfaction: doctoring another Angry Young Man screenplay,
The Wild and the Willing, for Betty Box and writing additional dialogue for
Ted Kotcheff's feature film debut *Tiara Tahiti*, a social comedy. Early in 1963

Richler decided, to the applause of Weintraub and Moore,[55] that he would move to Canada again. But Florence didn't want to go, and when he sent a barrage of letters to Toronto, inviting tenders for his services, he was disappointed. The CBC didn't want to hire him.[56] Robert Weaver also informed him that he wasn't likely to get a job as literary advisor to a publisher for the very good reason that such jobs didn't exist in Canada.[57] Although *Maclean's* promised a few assignments, it wouldn't be enough to live on.

When Richler asked *Maclean's* editor Ralph Allen what he should write on, Allen's suggestions were depressingly sociological: "The general area in which I am most interested is TODAY.NOW.HERE. Do you know anything about the French-Canada-English-Canada relations in Quebec or the Maritimes or the West? Anything about unemployment in Canada today? About the effects of automation on workers? About the pull of the U.S. on talented Canadians, and the counter-pull of Canada? There are hundreds of themes."[58] Hundreds of themes and almost all of them securely tied to the idol of nationalism. No wonder Richler displayed such antipathy towards the patriotic song and dance.

In Britain, he adapted the Russian writer Isaac Babel's brilliant 1926 story and play "Sunset" for the BBC as *The Fall of Mendel Krick*, but it didn't meet Canadian specifications. Obviously not enough of TODAY.NOW.HERE. Partly, the trouble was Richler's own doing. He had turned himself into the Famous Canadian Writer, and what do such personages do but comment on Canadian affairs? The difficulty of selling *The Fall of Mendel Krick* in Canada irritated him, because apparently he was good enough for London, but not for Toronto. And Babel was more than just a paycheque to Richler. Born an Odessa Jew, the short and bespectacled Babel, as far as Richler knew, had seen his father kneel in the mud before a Cossack officer during a pogrom[59] and had decided not to linger among history's losers but to become a non-Jewish Jew. It was a reaction Richler well understood. He had been confronted (secondhand but still insistently) with the brutality of the Holocaust as an adolescent, and had determined to leave Orthodoxy, mostly for different reasons than Babel, but in part because of his father's low status. When his serious writing proved uncommercial, Richler, like Babel, relied upon journalism and film scripts. Babel was tougher than Hemingway, Richler thought, and had so profoundly reinvented himself that he had ridden to war with the Red Cossacks.[60] Such information Richler gleaned from Lionel Trilling's 1955 introduction to Babel's *Collected Stories*,[61] unaware of what Babel's daughter Nathalie revealed in 1964: that likely there had been no kneeling, that Babel's father's warehouse was not targeted during the pogrom, and that Babel had ridden as a press correspondent, not as a soldier, with the Red Cavalry.[62] Babel reported for Gen. Budyonny's *Red*

Trooper, a propaganda newspaper, but angered Budyonny by writing *Red Cavalry*,[63] which detailed Babel's initiation into brutality and which nevertheless recounted moments of surprising tenderness. It may seem a bit ingenuous to compare the Montreal Jews' disgust at *Son of a Smaller Hero* to Gen. Budyonny's wrath, but in both cases the nakedness of the writing angered the writer's former community, a community expecting a salute.

"When a Jew gets on a horse he stops being a Jew," Babel's Levka said, "he's a Russian."[64] Richler saw, in that brief phrase, "the quarrel between the Israeli and Diaspora Jew."[65] But it wasn't quite so simple for Babel. To Stalin, at least, Babel was still a Jew. Worse, a writer. Richler told of how Babel, after witnessing Stalin's crimes and the Soviet restrictions on free speech, gave an ironic lecture to the Writers' Congress in 1934, claiming that now he was going to write in a new literary genre, the genre of silence. If Richler (following Trilling) mythologized that speech, making it much more ironical and defiant than it actually was,[66] nevertheless by 1939 Babel had been arrested and was never heard from again.[67]

"When a Jew gets on a horse, he stops being a Jew" – that striking line moved Richler to begin a little piece called "My Cousin, the Horseman,"[68] the first sign of Richler's masterwork, *St. Urbain's Horseman*. The story was about Joey Hersh, who got a start in juvenile crime, then rode horses, fought for the Jews, and, like Babel, finally disappeared. Thug or hero? The piece wasn't much … at first.

In an essay Richler gave the details of the Soviet writer's life and quoted Babel's literary philosophy: "I have no imagination … I can't invent. I have to know everything down to the last vein, otherwise I can't write a thing. My motto is *authenticity*."[69] Less forthright than Babel, Richler never said as much out loud but proceeded according to the same motto. He never liked to talk of "the imagination," preferring to think of himself as an honest witness to his time, an attitude that confused many readers in whose minds "satire" and "honest witness" never appeared on the same shelf. Unlike Babel, Richler invented much, but his inventions almost always lay on the back of real events. Sometimes, as in the early novels, the fiction formed only a thin veneer. By now, the layers were growing thicker, and although it's not clear whether Richler *needed* to mythologize Babel or whether Richler simply accepted Babel's own self-mythologizing at face value, Joey Hersh slowly began the gestation into a mythical horseman.

The Fall of Mendel Krick was a labour of love for Richler, and he did a beautiful job. It wasn't a difficult adaptation, because with the help of a translator Richler changed the original as little as possible.[70] Krick's sons bash their autocratic father over the head, and he rages, Lear-like. Richler caught all of the original's harsh grace:

Day is day, my friends, and evening is evening. The day soaks us in
the sweat of our labour, but evening offers the promise of its divine
coolness. Joshua, the son of Nun who stopped the sun in heaven was
a madman. And now we see that our friend Mendel Krick has turned
out to be no wiser than Joshua the son of Nun. He wanted to warm
himself in the sun all his life long. He wanted to remain for all his life
on the spot where mid-day had found him. But God has watchmen
on every street and Mendel had sons in his house. The watchmen
come and put things to order. Day is day and evening is evening.
All is as it should be. Let's drink a glass of vodka.[71]

When in 1965 Richler finally turned to *St. Urbain's Horseman*,[72] this incip-
ient awareness of the savage assault of time would deepen his own work.

Ted Kotcheff directed *The Fall of Mendel Krick* for the BBC and received good reviews, but despite Robert Weaver's support the CBC didn't
want it, not for radio, not for its TV cultural showcase, *Festival*. One CBC
producer, unaware of Babel and of how closely Richler had followed the
original, criticized Richler for being historically inaccurate and thus defam-
ing the Jews. No Jew would strike his father in the face with a gun butt.
Cossacks, certainly, were capable of such. Just to be sure, the producer con-
sulted his father, who had come from Russia. His father confirmed the
point.[73] Unfortunately for Richler, the CBC advisor for *Festival* was none
other than Ralph Allen, who, even if he operated under fewer illusions about
Jewish fathers and sons, preferred an original play. He feared that Richler
had been out of the country too long to realize what was bedevilling Canadians: "I'd like a play which has something relevant to say to Canadian
viewers in the winter of 1963-4: that's a wide enough scope for you?"[74]

≷

Instead of returning to Toronto, in December 1963 Florence found a house,
Hillcrest, for sale in Kingston Hill, Surrey.[75] With a little help from Brian
Moore, and banking on the anticipated payday for *Life at the Top* (the se-
quel to *Room at the Top*), Richler finally took the full bourgeois plunge.[76]
Hillcrest, to North American ears, sounded like a country estate, and Ted
Solotaroff immediately asked, "Are you becoming one of those fox-hunting
Jews?"[77] Solotaroff wasn't off-target. Richler had acquired a large treed lot,
with an almost castle-like home crowning the hill. Although a traffic-filled
street ran at the base of his property[78] and the adjoining lot was slated to
become a housing development,[79] to reach the house one had to climb a long
stone pathway through the trees. The new home delighted Florence. Rather
than their flat in Lower Hampstead, with three children crammed into one
bedroom, the Richlers now had a large and distinguished three-storey house

for mortgage payments no greater than what their rent had been. A nineteen-foot drawing room with oak paneling, a large kitchen with a refectory table, and out back a fish pond and garden where the children could play. Florence's first order of business was to furnish the third storey as an office for Richler, a place where he could scatter his papers and could work without interference.[80]

Richler's disc trouble flared up again; he had to be encased in a plaster cast and borne up into the fruit of his labour on a stretcher.[81] After the cast came off, he was forced to wear a surgical belt, what Weiner termed "fancy gents' wear."[82] Even when he was up and about again, Kingston felt dead to him; if he got restless, he'd head back into London and prowl around there.[83]

To compound the physical ailments, Richler had long been bogged down in his writing.[84] He had an old film script, *Reward*, still kicking around. Some time earlier, after a boarder had died at his mother's rooming house, Richler had thought of telling the story of a group of deadbeat boarders who are suspected of murder and who solve the crime themselves. He wrote the script in prose, cribbing bits from his own play *The Trouble with Benny*, the result a serviceable but unremarkable mystery, with a weak payoff. It was old work and nobody was interested.[85] At the beginning of the year he had adapted for the screen another thriller, Lionel Davidson's *Night of Wenceslas*, a low-rent Bond that in Richler's hands occasionally spoofs the genre. Nicholas Whistler, an unwilling British spy in Czechoslovakia lays a hair across the break between his balcony doors so he'll have evidence of secret searches, yet burns his fingers trying to light a cigarette. His communist opposite, Vlasta, reveals a secret hankering for Western decadence because "in London is also the Twist." There are also menacing encounters with the Czech secret police, among them one "Peter Gzowski," a dead eye with a pistol. Eventually Nicholas does make it home to Britain, in exchange for "a second secretary at the Hungarian Embassy who was caught importuning in the gents in the Earl's Court underground."[86] Better than *Reward*, but not original.

Richler had also proposed a series of programs on famous journals – those of Boswell, Pepys, Defoe, Dostoyevsky, Rousseau, Kafka, Sartre, Bellow. Or, alternatively, Josephus, Tolstoy, Gide, Gorki, Fitzgerald.[87] Only Boswell's Dr Johnson seems to have made it to the air. Richler had done *The Fall of Mendel Krick* and sent Armchair Theatre an outline for "Run Sheep Run," a melodramatic TV version of *A Choice of Enemies* – but again, more adaptations, not new work. At the bottom of the "Run Sheep Run" outline he wrote, "And so we come to the end of another strong, meaty drama from ABC's Manchester studio."[88] The self-mocking tone suggests something of his frustration. He even contemplated – Richler? ablaze against the notion

that writing could be taught? – knuckling under and going to the Iowa Writers Workshop, possibly because Philip Roth had recently taught there. A
friend discouraged him: "God, no! – don't go to Iowa unless you're really
desperate for a change."[89]

Bogged or not bogged, Richler wasn't one to take breaks from work,
no Sabbaths or Sundays, and when back trouble laid him out he named his
next work *Sloth*. It was supposed to be a film for actor Dirk Bogarde, the
British Rock Hudson who had recently come out on screen as a homosexual in *The Victim* (1961), though he remained discreet about his private life.
But the fifty-nine-page fragment that Richler managed to produce shows him
venturing into farce, avoiding, again, his Jewish past. He desperately wanted
to mock the British, as he had been trying to do with *It's Harder to Be Anybody*. *Sloth* centres around Lord Harry O'Brien, an aristocrat who briefly
had a job *once*, but the office was five floors up and, tragically, there was
no elevator. Now he prefers to lounge in bed. He has moments of abject self-
assessment, particularly vis-à-vis his nemesis, the Jewish up-and-comer Barney Rosen, and bits of the outside world do pierce through: "Other people
dress themselves. If they have no one to send on an errand they – they go
themselves." His servant, Luther, helpfully adds, "Lots of Germans are like
that." Included among *Sloth*'s characters is a turtlenecked, tight-jeaned writer
named Fulford who babbles in the popular press on Wednesdays, and then
excoriates the idle rich in the quality reviews on Fridays.[90] Writing screenplays wasn't difficult Richler said, on the heels of more successful work,[91]
but *Sloth* was generally limp, and he was forced to lay it aside because he
was contractually obligated to give Ted Kotcheff a screenplay adaptation of
John Braine's *Life at the Top* by 30 April. Just as well. Bogarde and his man-
ager/partner Tony Forwood thought *Sloth* unfilmic and refused to put any
more money into it.[92]

Life at the Top, though not a failure, had less life than *Room at the Top*.
The quick-rising Joe Lampton of *Room at the Top* had been a striver, forced
to choose between love and success. It wasn't a choice that Richler had had
to make, but he could understand the dilemma. The Joe Lampton of *Life at
the Top*, now married to four prime acres and a northern mill owner's daughter, feels trapped among Tory in-laws, who think him a lapdog, and trapped
even among his own pampered children, who despise the lower-class newspaper boy. Bored by his wife, falsely nostalgic for his former poverty, Lampton has no idea what he wants, a dilemma far less comprehensible to Richler.
After *Life at the Top* opened in North America, he acknowledged that it
wasn't always easy to project oneself into characters created by others.[93]
Lampton attempts to escape, renouncing wealth to move in with a London
TV reporter – unfortunately discovering that, nepotism aside, upper-class
employers have no interest in him, and that as a layabout he no longer cuts

a romantic figure for his girlfriend. By film's end the rebel is back home and slippered, sitting in his retired father-in-law's spot as chairman of the board. But *unhappy*. Soon enough Richler would mock the habit of directors tracking in on a "socially symbolic sewer grating,"[94] but for the final shot of *Life at the Top*, Kotcheff did just that, panning to the socially symbolic wrought-iron fence of country estate, visually imprisoning Lampton's homeward-bound car. Despite the serious attention to class difference, it's difficult to sympathize with Lampton moping on his country estate. Richler grumbled – justifiably – that he had gotten stuck with a "hoary plot" and a protagonist who felt too sorry for himself.[95]

Yet in contrast to more sentimental fare, *Life at the Top* pursued adult problems without solving them, and most reviewers applauded.[96] Richler and Kotcheff, the one with Hillcrest, the other with a new house in Highgate,[97] rode high on *Life at the Top*: working-class boys making it big, telling tragic stories of working-class boys making it big.

⩘

Rather than immediately return to fiction after *Life at the Top*, Richler jumped into his homeland's national argument. If editors wanted Canada HERE and NOW, he'd give it to them, and if they wanted controversy, he'd give that, too. Nationalism at issue? Canada should join the US, Richler proclaimed. The best things about Canada are American, anyway.[98] Near-laureate Irving Layton had a new book out? "I can think of no other Canadian poet," Richler stated, "who better illustrates the stylish cliché, the ill-thought-out rebellion."[99]

Layton and Richler duked it out on the pages of *Maclean's* and the US travel magazine *Holiday*, on both personal and political levels. No doubt Layton had been fuming since Richler had lampooned him in *The Incomparable Atuk*. A gifted and often profound poet, Layton was also a grandstander whose tilting at WASP repressions sometimes verged on stand-up comedy. Several years earlier he had written a poem imagining intercourse with Jackie Kennedy and then invited her to a soirée in Pittsburgh where the distinguished author himself could read it to her.[100] Richler carefully steered wide of Layton's great poems and, with the satirist's intuition, zeroed in on the poems that betrayed Layton's immense egotism. *Balls for a One-Armed Juggler*, Layton's latest, had looked down its nose at the unimportant "9-to-5" faces in a restaurant and had derided an English professor whose wit shone at ladies' teas. "Doesn't Layton read his poems at ladies' teas?" Richler innocently asked. And what exactly constituted an "unimportant" face? Richler hadn't been far from such pomposity himself. In *The Acrobats*, Richler's "wise" Chaim had thought, "So many anonymous people ... being anonymously happy on an anonymous night. Why doesn't somebody tell them."[101] But Richler had made the mistake at age twenty-one and had had the good fortune of getting his knuckles rapped by Weiner and Athill.

It didn't smooth Layton's feathers any to see the article accompanied by a cartoon of himself partly in drag. He answered with expected gusto, but Richler's editorial friends at *Maclean's* published only Layton's invitation that Richler return to Sir George Williams University to finish his truncated education. Only in private did Richler get to feel Layton's sharper barbs, aimed at Richler's unease with his Jewish past and at his ambivalence about entering the bourgeoisie: Layton said of Richler, "Years ago he decided it's smart and profitable to retail family skeletons and to caricature Jews ... The trick? How to kiss every distinguished untrousered ass of the Establishment and yet manage to appear a surly rebel."[102]

The political argument took place in *Holiday*, where Richler had suggested that Canada didn't have an identity distinct from the US and that on a cultural level, at least, there were no obstacles to Canada becoming the fifty-first state of the union. Layton alerted readers that "the author of this giveaway program" hadn't lived in Canada for ten years – "Having nothing to give, so to speak, he's prepared to give all." Richler had cut his roots for money, according to Layton, and, as a result, Richler's novels had become "ephemeral puffballs." Layton revealed that Richler's decision to leave Canada "had nothing at all to do with the danger, as he so touchingly and modestly puts it, of his being overpraised."[103] The statement about Richler not living in Canada wasn't quite accurate, as Layton well knew. But in outline, Layton was right. Richler no longer had much of his heart invested in the tribe – whether Jewish or Canadian. If it was witty to guillotine Atuk, through whom the Canadian businessman Twentyman turns nationalism to economic profit, the point looked less appealing when Richler baldly invited Canada to comply with American Manifest Destiny. More ominously on a personal level, Richler's recent work (and dry spell) showed the effects of deracination.

Layton's friend Leonard Cohen leapt into the fray, saying that, if he'd met Richler just after the *Holiday* article, he'd have punched Richler in the nose. According to Cohen (who would soon have his narrator in *Beautiful Losers* nearly reach orgasm during a Québécois separatist rally), it was nationalism that produced art. Only after we worried about our natural resources would we start to worry about our poets. To say that we were like Americans while bombs were exploding in Westmount mailboxes was betrayal.[104] Richler's friends agreed and told him that his proposal to join the US was naïve.[105]

Even Richler the contrarian realized that he couldn't hold his position for long once the Vietnam War heated up. "Yes, we *are* nicer," he allowed.[106] Replying to Layton, Richler said that he didn't want to join the US, but,

parsing his words carefully, he insisted that the differences between Canada
and the US were regional, not national, and since there was no true cultural
distinction between the two nations, politicians shouldn't erect false protectionist boundaries.[107] In 1964, Richler had a very limited sense of what nationalism might mean, and evidently conceived of it (as did Cohen) in the
European and tribal sense – as a racial identity. Later he would become more
pleased that Canada wasn't a "nation" in this old sense.[108] As for the man
who presided over Canada and its deepening French/English rift, Richler
called Prime Minister Lester Pearson "a half-assed fumbler,"[109] though in
the future Richler would pronounce him "the greatest Canadian of our
time."[110] The fact that the country still functioned didn't seem, to Richler,
good enough reason for its existence.[111] Nationalism either existed in the
gut or not at all. His gut told him that he belonged among Jews, but the trip
to Israel had confirmed what Orthodox Montreal had told him – that such
a nationalism cost too much. At the same time, his "Canada" was really only
Montreal,[112] and his sense of culture pulled him, more than most Canadians, to New York and London, not to Toronto, not, God forbid, to Ottawa,
which was nothing more than a backwater to him. He was Europe-Returned.
What value could there be in the colonies?

     With such notions lurking, it was no surprise that Richler couldn't un-
derstand the attraction of a multicultural, jerry-rigged nation such as Canada,
but that he could intuitively grasp Québécois separatism. Up to this point,
Richler had thought and written very little about French Québec. The death
of Duplessis in 1959 had begun a political thaw, and during the election of
1960 Richler, in Montreal at the time, had stayed awake until 2:00 to watch
Jean Lesage and the Liberals squeeze through to inaugurate a new era. Richler happily bid the Union Nationale good riddance but had no premonition
of the FLQ (Front de libération du Québec).[113] He avoided using French
Canadian characters in his books because he has no idea what made them
tick.[114] By 1961 he had threatened to write an article declaring how little he
cared for French Canadians. "Whyinhell don't you," Peter Gzowski had responded.[115] In 1963, when FLQ bombs started exploding, Richler, from the
distance of London, was initially filled with glee. At last something was happening! At last the pompous English were tiptoeing around Québec. His
family's poverty in the Depression had radicalized him in the 1940s, and if
he had lost that radicalism he still felt more akin to the lower-class Pierre
Vallières, FLQ bomber and author of *White Niggers of America*, than to
Lester Pearson.

     Maclean's brought Richler back to Montreal in May 1964 to report on
Queen Victoria's birthday, that unconscionable holiday guaranteed to get a
rise out of Québécois nationalists. Richler watched as demonstrators choked
up Montreal's narrow downtown streets. A bomb on Victoria Bridge failed

to detonate. For eight hours, one thousand policemen on horseback, in patrol cars, and on foot battled to control what the *Globe and Mail* called "gangs of goons and separatists."[116] Nuit de la Matraque – Night of the Truncheon – it was called later; in the end, eighty-five people were arrested. Nevertheless it wasn't bombs or demonstrations that finally staunched Richler's glee: it was graffiti alongside the highway, saying "Québec Libre." Richler recalled the graffiti of his youth, "à bas les Juifs" and remembered that when spray-painted slogans began to appear on the roadside, things inevitably got hot for the Jews.[117] In that conviction he would prove wrong, though his experiences in the 1940s prevented him from realizing the mistake.

15

Cocksure; Spent Worm

RICHLER COMPLETED HIS SPLIT from Joyce Weiner in 1964, replacing her even in England shortly after she propelled *The Apprenticeship of Duddy Kravitz* into the bookstores of Israel.[1] By this time she had resigned herself to his decision.[2] That same year another child, Martha, was born, and, though Richler worried before every birth, all went well.[3] He turned down a $7,000 opportunity to go to Africa and write a screenplay. Courageous! cheered Robert Weaver.[4] Nuts! diagnosed Jack McClelland, "You must have more money than brains."[5]

From many quarters now, Richler received movie offers, some ... unconventional. He didn't want to miss a good opportunity, but he could now afford to be choosy. Martin Stern, a TV writer, offered Richler $1,000 for an option on *The Apprenticeship of Duddy Kravitz* and $4,000 more upon completion of a film. If no film were made, Richler would kindly refund the $1,000. Stern confided that he had had a very personal reaction to the novel and therefore had an aversion to getting agents involved. Richler replied, "I am, of course, touched that DUDDY means so much to you and I'm sorry if you find what follows blunt ... I have no desire to 'borrow' $1000 for one, two, or three years and I would never let film rights on a book go for $5,000 ... If my agent come up with the sort of deal youre offering me I would think she'd gone mad. You are either very innocent or very shrewd" [*sic*]. What films, Richler wanted to know, had Stern done?[6] Stern, in reply, admitted that he had no production credits. In place of a CV, he recited a litany about how difficult it was to get Jewish stories onto film: "Hollywood's producers have outHiltlered Hitler. They have sent 100% of America's Jews to the literary gas ovens by pretending they don't exist." "You are the kind of man," he revealed to Richler, "with whom I (if we lived in the same town) could be friends."[7] Richler didn't waste any more postage.

As Richler's magazine articles became more frequent and more controversial, people responded, often angrily. Richler speculated in print that Hank
Greenberg had held back from breaking Babe Ruth's home-run record so as
not to seem a pushy Jew. Baseball fans, not on friendly terms with irony,
voiced their disagreement: "As a professional athlete in the highest sense of
the word, Hank Greenberg would never have ..."[8] In Britain a reader complained that, even when Richler wrote about French Québec, everything always returned to the Jewish Question and that one couldn't read about
Canadian political or social developments without wading through Richler's Jewish boyhood.[9] In Leeds, the owner of a struggling Jewish restaurant
raised objections to Richler's poetic license. The nation's attention had been
called to wine stains and crumbs on the restaurant's tablecloth, but there
were, the owner reported, no stains or crumbs. He threatened to sue. Accompanied by the magazine's lawyer, Richler returned to Leeds, scene of the
crime, and inspected the contentious tablecloths. They were spotless. The
lawyer offered £50 but no retraction. The owner declined. £100 but no retraction? Deal done.[10]

Lily, then Moe and his wife Sara, visited London.[11] Lily had been coming to London since the mid-1950s when Richler was still married to Cathy
Boudreau. Usually Richler bought the tickets, quietly saving $5 a week with-
out telling Florence, and then suddenly a ticket would appear as if by magic.[12]
Ostensibly Lily came to babysit the grandchildren, but really to see her successful son.[13] The children, who never saw any members of the extended
family, found Grandmother Lily strange, slightly exotic. She'd lug in a suit-
case bulging with gifts, and every day she'd carefully unveil one. Outside
her bedroom door the children lined up, as required, and each received a
slobbery kiss in exchange for, say, Snakes and Ladders. Lily also offered Florence plenty of advice on how to raise the children.[14] Florence tried hard to
be gracious to her but felt that Lily didn't really respond.[15]

When Moe came to London, Richler rented him a flat near a synagogue,
a kosher butcher, and a movie theatre. He gave Florence some quick point-
ers on what was kosher and what wasn't and dragged himself to musicals
that he knew his father would enjoy. Moe's highlight was the opportunity
to shake hands with James Mason. Did Moe have a good time? When pressed,
he allowed, "I can't complain." Given Moe's reticence, his statement was,
Richler knew, "an undreamed of flight of hyperbole."[16] A short while earlier, Richler had trolled through the Catskills at the expense of *Holiday* magazine, seeking drolleries at Jewish resorts such as Grossinger's. He realized
that this would be just the thing for Moe. Moe would enjoy the opulence
and the Jewish comedians, while Richler would snicker at the glassed-in
walks ("so nobody has to get too much mountain air"[17]), taste so bad it was
good. He promised to take his father there soon.[18]

Even though a year earlier Richler had shied away from the lucrative script that would have taken him to Africa, when Jack Clayton, who had directed *Room at the Top*, called with an opportunity to do John Le Carré's *The Looking Glass War*, Richler jumped.[19] He finagled a trip to Warsaw to do research for the screenplay[20] and boasted to his friends about movie life.[21] Ted Solotaroff replied, "It must be nice to be eating that high on the hog ... Does Julie Christie come to you with her troubles to make use of your wise Jewish heart? ... It must be very heady."[22] After a couple of years of trying, Clayton couldn't raise the necessary money.[23] Putting the best spin on events, Richler claimed that he and Clayton had "walked out" when Columbia Pictures asked them to change the central character from a pathetic old Pole to "a very young man with his shirt open."[24] The film was taken over by director Frank Pierson, who did his own adapted screenplay while Richler's languished.

≷

By late 1966, Richler was sitting on two partly done novels, and he didn't like that at all.[25] He still had *It's Harder to Be Anybody*, farcical and rejected. As well, he had begun *St. Urbain's Horseman*, a more autobiographical and humane novel that would return to the territory of *The Apprenticeship of Duddy Kravitz* just as his editors prayed. Although Richler had been offered the screenplay for Twentieth Century Fox's *The Blue Max*, starring James Mason and Ursula Andress, he had refused because he wanted to work on *St. Urbain's Horseman*. Soon, however, he was kicking himself, because the novel wasn't coming together and the alternative opportunities had been lost.[26]

Richler had no intention of letting *It's Harder to Be Anybody* rot, even if it weren't a suitable heir to *The Apprenticeship of Duddy Kravitz*; when he hit the logjam on *St. Urbain's Horseman*, he resurrected the earlier novel.[27] Like *The Incomparable Atuk*, *It's Harder to Be Anybody* was less a narrative than a collection of send-ups. As in the story upon which the novel was based, Shalinsky is convinced that the protagonist, Mortimer Griffin, must be a Jew. Griffin – a Canadian expatriate, a publishing executive, and a "square" – undergoes ever-increasing humiliations while his wife, Joyce, offers herself to progressive causes and while a sinister Hollywood "Star Maker" takes over Mortimer's employer, Oriole Press. The plot exists mainly to allow Richler to mock progressive schools, the counterculture's prostration before "nature," Hollywood, changes in obscenity laws, and, of course, Jewish chauvinism. Richler fiddled with all sorts of new and uninspired names for the book – *The Last Hero, Hero's End, It's Harder to Be a Hero, Limp Hero, The WASP in the Woodpile* – before coming up with a *The Importance of Being Cocksure*, which, though not good itself, would finally cough up an excellent title.[28]

The original title and eventual subtitle – *It's Harder to Be Anybody* – hints that Richler had a very particular literary score to settle. During the question period after Richler's speech at a synagogue, an audience member had made a pointed distinction between the much-loved Yiddish writer Sholom Aleichem (1859–1916) and Richler, who, the audience member offered, wrote garbage about Jews.[29] Aleichem's genial depictions of Eastern European shtetl (village) life in works such as *It's Hard to Be a Jew* and *Fiddler on the Roof* had made him popular among Jews, who yearned to remember a beloved shtetl that had never existed. Tradition, tradition: everyone wanted it, so long as it confined itself politely to the music hall.[30] Richler, however, shed no tears during what he called "the indecently sentimental *Fiddler On The Roof* (ha ha, it's a pogrom)."[31]

Richler had reviewed a B'nai B'rith performance of *It's Hard to Be a Jew* back in 1949[32] and had no doubt had come into contact with Aleichem much earlier. In one of Lily's "Beloved Rabbi" stories, the Rabbi inspects the sacrificial chickens for Rosh Hashanah. "If the chicken is fat and *trefah*, forbidden for use, the women shake their heads sadly and murmur, 'Ah, it's hard to be a Jew!'"[33] Aleichem's *It's Hard to Be a Jew* (*Shver tsu zayn a yid*, 1915), based upon his own novel *The Bloody Hoax* (1912–13), involves a conventional "trading places" scenario during the time of Russian pogroms: the Russian, Ivan Ivanov, who believes that it's *not* so hard to be a Jew, trades identities with his Jewish friend Hersh Shneyerson. Ivanov discovers that an academic gold medal is little help at his city's college if, as a Jew, he doesn't even have the legal right to reside in the city. Harassment and bad will from the police show Ivanov that in fact it *is* hard to be a Jew. Since Aleichem's audience was Jewish and powerless, the play functioned as a steam valve for Jewish complaints rather than as a direct political protest. The light comic entanglements of identity are sharpened for the Jewish audience by the spectre of intermarriage when both the outwardly "Jewish" Ivanov and the outwardly "Gentile" Schneyerson compete for the hand of Betty, daughter of their Jewish landlord. Intermarriage, warns Aleichem, would be polluting. As well, he has Schneyerson predict, "At the first opportunity when the couple will quarrel, that perfect Gentile lover will remind her of her race."[34] The phraseology was familiar to Richler from arguments with his father. The arguments had culminated in Moe sitting shiva for a son whose marriage to a Gentile had rendered him "dead." Lurking behind the geniality of Aleichem, Richler recognized, was a billy club to keep marriageable young Jews in line. In the end, Schneyerson's heroic decision to reveal his identity (so that he, rather than Ivanov, will suffer legal punishment) clashes strangely with Betty's father's joy at the family's "deliverance" from intermarriage. To Richler, Aleichem attacking Russian bigotry seemed strangely unconscious of his *own* bigotry. Where intermarriage was concerned, it was harder to be Ivanov.

The contortions that *Cocksure*'s "Anybody," Mortimer, goes through to prove that he's not a Jew are witty, yet they also stem partly from Richler's own confusion about just what he was. For years and on many fronts, Richler had been trying to elude his Jewish past, and the subtitle *It's Harder to Be Anybody* underscored this. He wasn't a believer, Florence wasn't a Jew, the children were being raised without a religious faith – so why raise the ghost of Judaism on a personal level? "All men are Jews," Bernard Malamud had announced, but Philip Roth, closer to Richler's sensibility, disagreed: "In fact, we know this is not so; even the men who are Jews aren't sure they're Jews."[35] In place of a narrow, sectarian self, these uncertain Jews had substituted a broader liberal humanist self. On the one hand, "Jews" designated a moderately successful but still jumpy minority who feared bigots while seeing no cause to examine their own bigotry. Such is Shalinsky in *Cocksure*.[36] On the other hand, if "Jews" designated those who had suffered in the Holocaust, the term could not properly be applied to Montreal businessmen but ought to apply to anyone who suffered from persecution. The novelist, being the "loser's advocate," as Richler now deceptively styled himself,[37] must broaden his notion of suffering to include all of humanity. This liberal notion, too, appears in the mouth of Shalinsky – Richler felt no call to be consistent – when Shalinsky delivers the novel's punchline to the harried Mortimer: "Don't you see? A Jew is an idea. Today you're my idea of a Jew."[38] If "Jew" is simply another word for "victim" and the world is becoming an unfriendly place for tradition-minded WASPs such as Mortimer, then Shalinsky is correct, and in this way, too, it's harder to be *anybody*. In the story on which *Cocksure* was based, Richler solved the terminological dilemma by having Mortimer marry a woman named Gitel, give up bacon and Christmas, and move in with the in-laws.[39] This overly simple solution of turning Mortimer literally into a Jew disappeared from *Cocksure*.

Like every one of his earlier novels except *The Apprenticeship of Duddy Kravitz*, *Cocksure* thus re-enacted once again Richler's escape from an Orthodox past. He mocked Aleichem's Jewish chauvinism through Shalinsky, and when Richler touched on the Holocaust, he did so in a burlesque manner designed to offend Jews: the Germans at Treblinka once celebrated Miss Fishman's mother, we discover, because she was the one-millionth Jew to be gassed there. Lord Woodcock, with the "forgive and forget" philosophy that he recommends to Miss Fishman after the war, receives an award for fostering Jewish/German amity. Ha, ha, it's a pogrom: in banishing Aleichem, Richler hadn't banished laughter, and he seemed to think that as long as the humour was black it wouldn't dishonour the dead. Certain deleted sections of the novel went even deeper into black humour. In an early draft Lord Gross (later to become Lord Woodcock) recalls days of yore, when "Sturmbannfuehrers and condemned Jews had temporarily put the furnaces behind them, giving their all to [a] soccer game" on the playing fields of Dachau, proving how much the two groups had in common.[40] The satire was ostensibly directed against efforts to move *beyond* the Holocaust. Richler had just read Chaim Kaplan's diaries, smuggled out of the Warsaw Ghetto, though Kaplan himself had gone on to death in the gas chambers. "The Germans are an abomination to me," wrote Richler, "I'm glad Dresden was bombed for no useful military purpose.[41] Nevertheless, like the Jewish Hollywood moguls (though in a different fashion), he imagined his submersion in America. There is an anxiety, a protesting-too-much in *Cocksure*, Richler too eager to show that he doesn't belong with the un-urbane sort of Jew. By treating Jewish experience in a blackly comic way, Richler places himself high above that experience, and by avoiding his own personal experience, Richler makes it appear that *Cocksure* had been written not by a particular Jew, but by a hip, non-sectarian member of an artistic elite, precisely the sort of person that the novel was criticizing, if we are to take it at face value.

Gottlieb applauded Richler's editing of the novel as "the removal of much Jewiness."[42] Mortimer's dismay at being called a Jew, a dismay implicit in the final draft, could invite one to read him against Richler's intention: as a closet *Jew*. The name "Mortimer" did echo Richler's former nickname, "Mort," but in the end Mortimer carries little of Richler. When Daphne Humber-Guest, a trendy novelist (no Isaac Babel) in *Cocksure* says, "I cannot invent. I must know everything I write about firsthand," we are meant to laugh at such a narrow, plodding view of literature and applaud a novelist, who in writing *The Incomparable Atuk* and *Cocksure* had been inventing everything. Surely a gifted novelist could create his greatest work once he fully escaped the strictures of his own life. No, in fact. *Cocksure* proved entertaining but weightless, mostly as a result of Richler's escape from autobiography. "Literature," Cynthia Ozick would say, "does not spring from the urge to Esperanto but from the tribe."[43]

The least convincing aspect of the novel is the subplot concerning the Hollywood star-maker, the too-clever pun unfortunately intended, a simultaneous allegory of religious orthodoxy and of mechanical, solipsistic Hollywood. Richler meant to show that intellectually he owed nothing to the film business. In this he was partly successful, mocking by night the film clichés that buttered his bread by day. He refused, for example, to attach an ending to the thriller in which Mortimer finds himself. As well, before the star-maker sees the literal wisdom in the expression "go fuck yourself," he/she creates stars, American Goy Boys I (capable of a single expression), II, and III (capable of three *different* expressions!), stars suited admirably to

the simple and wholesome tastes of WASP audiences. In an earlier draft, the
robotic Goy Boys I and II had names: Alan Ladd and Richard Chamberlain.
Another Goy Boy had escaped the lab and entered politics, becoming very
big in California.[44] It would have been no great task for readers to puzzle
out Ronald Reagan's name, since the former President of the Screen Actors
Guild had in 1966 been elected Governor of California. But the names were
expunged, and with them much of the wit in Richler's Hollywood subplot.

Richler warned Jack McClelland that selected bits of *Cocksure* might
raise a few eyebrows, but McClelland wasn't worried: "Okay, so make your
book sexy. You can't shake me. We publish Leonard Cohen. We are dedicated to sex."[45] There was more to the problem than sex, even if *Cocksure*
wasn't nearly as graphic as Cohen's just-published *Beautiful Losers*.

At a school concert of Noah's – it being impressed upon Richler that a
father ought to attend his son's concert – Richler arrived with a friend, but
arrived somewhat plastered, and, to Noah's delight, began making faces at
him from the second or third row of the auditorium.[46] What was Richler
thinking at such moments? Not about the baby Jesus, one may guess. In the
novel, Mortimer, too, attends his son's Christmas play. He's somewhat taken
aback to discover that on the playbill at the very progressive Beatrice Webb
House school (a poke at one of the founders of the British Labour Party,
and, as Victor Ramraj notes, Summerhill school) is an adaptation of de Sade.
The Marquis De Sade, the children all know, was imprisoned by Puritans
for being "such a truth-teller," and good students can even cite the French
authorities for such knowledge – Apollinaire and Simone de Beauvoir (the
time not yet ripe for Foucault and Deleuze). Yet Richler's satire becomes
more troubling when children actually speak De Sade's lines: "I have seen
girls younger than this sustain still more massy pricks."[48] Defending Richler, Anthony Burgess argued that *Cocksure* wasn't obscene at all, but that
the novel had to go to the permissive society's limit in order to attack obscenity. "There is nothing in the book," he added, "calculated to deprave
or corrupt."[49] Tony Godwin, passing Burgess's glowing review on to Richler, couldn't resist a sly dig, "I clearly shall have to watch my language in
front of you."[50]

Richler wasn't a spokesman, Godwin knew, for moral conservatism, and
yet Richler was far from championing the sadistic extremes of "Philosophy
in the Bedroom." One might even argue that Richler's satire against the le-
gitimation of the Marquis predicted De Sade's later trendiness. All the same,
Richler wasn't above titillating his audience in other, more acceptable ways.
Defending himself, he made the distinction between obscenity and pornography. Obscenity simply involved the unflinching and graphic depiction of
all areas of human life, while pornography was intended to arouse one sexually. With some exaggeration he called *Cocksure* "a shatteringly moral

book," obscene but not pornographic.[51] (He wasn't even necessarily against pornography as long as it didn't try to parade as high art.[52]) His delicate parsing was only faintly sincere. True, Richler, quoting De Sade, meant to mock and irritate. Yet *Cocksure* dealt out plenty of four-letter words, innuendo in names like Lord Woodcock and Hyman Rosen, and sexual frisson. Visiting from Canada and hearing "f-dash-dash-k" on British TV,[53] Mortimer's former teacher Miss Ryerson (another shot at Ryerson Press) decides that the mother country needs her, and she finds work at Beatrice Webb House, hoping to raise academic standards. In this she succeeds, though she is reduced to methods other than handing out gold stars: top students receive blowjobs. The principal, as one might expect, is horrified, recognizing immediately that this could lead to unhealthy, capitalist-style competition. Miss Ryerson ought to blow everyone in the grade or no-one. Wanting to moralize, to pass judgement on the passing scene, Richler was at this point too much indebted to the times, and so came across (not completely against his intentions) as a temporizer. Arnold Davidson called *Cocksure* "an impressive allegory of sin and damnation," but even he felt that the humour was often sophomoric.[54] Clearly, the novel belonged securely within the hip culture that it affected to satirize.

Some writers, such as Leonard Cohen, jumped into the 60s all the way. Richler, of whose film work it can be said that he helped to *make* the 60s, went in only up to his waist. In some senses Cohen was a "deeper" writer than Richler: he went further into the sources of Being, where there were no lifeguards. Cohen's refused to worry about the viability of his experiments with the psyche, and *Beautiful Losers* seems significant not purely because of the artistic result, but in part because Baby Boomers have been prejudiced in his favour by rock & roll, sexual freedom, and the avant-garde. Ultimately, Richler would become the more measured observer, for better and worse. The weakness, or indecisiveness, of *Cocksure* was that it tried so hard to forget that the writer had a family moving around, two floors below. If Cohen went deeper, building a "house" in the desert, Richler was on the verge of embracing a much wider life. All the while, during the writing of *Cocksure*, Richler was conscious of the gap between the mundane London he lived in and media hype about "Swinging London": "Orgies? *Where*? I haven't been to one and nobody I know has been to one either."[55] Possibly, he allowed, he wasn't in the right clique. *Cocksure*, with its ambivalent attitude towards the sexual revolution went out of its way to mock those who thought they were ushering in a new, liberated society, and yet the novel did little to dispel the myth. With writers such as Philip Roth, Richler had become part of an artistic elite that defined itself largely by its rejection of traditional canons of taste. "When they tote up our contribution," Luke Scott would say in *St. Urbain's Horseman*, "all that can be claimed is that we took 'fuck' out of the oral tradition and wrote it plain."[56] One evening, at a small dinner party, Richler and Roth had a contest to see who could deliver the most obscene story, defending themselves afterwards by calling it a necessary activity of the times. Some wives were appalled; Florence found the whole affair humorous.[57] When *Cocksure* came out, Robert Fulford called it the dirtiest book of the 1960s.[58] Neil Compton – *Son of a Smaller Hero*'s goat, who was nevertheless kindly trying to arrange a university job for Richler – asked, "How are we going to push outrageousness much farther than you have done here? Is this going to be the end of satire?"[59] *Portnoy's Complaint* would, in short order, become the climax of these changes, but, heady as the newfound artistic freedom was, Richler couldn't help feeling uneasy. *Portnoy's Complaint* and *Beautiful Losers* wouldn't show much abashment in their celebration of the sexual revolution; *Cocksure* would.

Certainly Richler didn't want his young children reading his book,[60] and a "visit" from Mason Hoffenberg also pushed Richler up against the darker aspects of 1960s liberation. Hoffenberg had been freeloading in London at Marianne Faithfull's luxury flat, but he wanted to quit heroin, not easy surrounded by Rolling Stones groupies. He asked Richler's help. He told Richler that he hardly ever went to the bathroom anymore and that, when he did, his stool was rock-hard. Getting hold of some methadone, the heroin substitute often used in treatment programs, Richler helped him shoot up. It was difficult to find a vein. Hoffenberg's veins, perhaps wiser than Hoffenberg himself, shied from the needle. Richler brought him home, transferred one of his children to another bedroom, and moved Hoffenberg in for the weekend. Florence and the children had heard enough anecdotes about Hoffenberg over the years to expect witty conversation, but, except for a silent half hour in the garden, Hoffenberg remained holed up in the bedroom. After two nights, Hoffenberg gave up and asked Richler to drive him to Leicester Square for a fix.[61]

From what position was Richler laughing in *Cocksure*? Was he *for* the freedoms of the 1960s or *against* them? Readers couldn't tell. "Liberated" members of his audience could feel smug about the uncensored style, yet uneasy that Richler was laughing at progressive schools and potentially advocating a return to censorship. Leslie Fiedler, wanting badly to be on the cutting edge of culture said that *Cocksure* demonstrated the nihilism of all popular culture, but that Richler's movie savvy stopped the book short, alas, of true obscenity.[62] At the other end, the more conservative audience members might initially nod their heads to see progressive schools under fire, but would soon be appalled by the novel's sexual license. Philip Toynbee rightly noted that the book continually approached moral judgements and then balked at the last moment.[63]

Misunderstood, cried Richler. He had been on Mortimer's side all along and was making the case for "that much-abused man, the square."[64] It would be more accurate to say that, at this time in his life, Richler was a man divided. He still had the instincts of the avant-garde and wanted to sell *Cocksure* as a creature of its time – metafictionally playful, boundary-testing, hip. Yet he had read enough of Waugh to want *Cocksure* to be an antidote to its time, showing the pitfalls of the 1960s' freedoms. In this impossible double task of temporizing and moralizing the novel fails. Richler couldn't precisely go forward, and, unlike Waugh, he couldn't go back. If conservative satirists saw the present as a general disaster, Richler had lived long enough in Jewish Montreal not to feel nostalgic about a return to "tradition, tradition," the world of the fathers. In some ways he was still striking out ineffectually against Lily. *Cocksure* proclaimed that he would make no truce with the Hasidic traditions that she held dear, and yet, ironically, one of the forms that his rebellion took – literary sexual license – still owed something to *Lily's* instinctive resistance to Orthodoxy. At the same time, Lily's affair may have helped Richler subsequently to rein in his desires: he didn't want to *be her*.

With *Cocksure*, Richler still wrote as if he had no family. The children were small enough for him to think of them as extensions of himself. Authors were special cases; they could moralize without moralizing; they could tease with De Sade and still expect their children to say *please* and *thank you*. *Cocksure* wasn't nihilist, but neither did Richler declare his allegiances. By the time of *St. Urbain's Horseman*, he began to understand that his children were separate beings and that he must declare his allegiances, that he could write nasty characters, but that he must eventually punish them, just like any bourgeois novelist. He wanted to be a satiric moralist, especially to those round about him, but where to ground himself? Unlike Hoffenberg, Richler was on the road to domestication, and it wasn't a bad thing. The difference between the young man who urinated in the sink and the middle-aged man was striking. Florence bore a measure of responsibility, though she has tended to deny it. Anarchic youth; bourgeois father: it would never entirely disappear, this division in Richler, but it would become more muted and lend depth to his mature work.

By contrast, on the issue of political correctness Richler was never divided. Partly this stemmed from his early anti-bourgeois perceptions. He had proven himself independent by snubbing the Orthodox community; were he to enlist in the liberal intelligentsia, he'd be just another apostate Jew who had sold out his birthright for a seat among the scoffers. At a deeper level, he may have convinced himself that to court political incorrectness was to avoid choosing a ground on which to stand. If he shot at everybody, didn't that bespeak a kind of principled objectivity, a ground almost? In his defense, he had also begun to recognize how difficult it was even for a fiction writer to speak freely, how quickly readers would holler for censorship if they detected ridicule against their own cause. Richler mocked Mortimer's wife Joyce's Labourite preoccupation with being on the correct sides of all the issues – supporting Oxfam, supporting the Anti-Apartheid league. He mocked not because the causes were suspect, but because correctness, rather than humaneness seemed to be the overriding concern. In fact, he donated to the same causes he mocked, and he marched to Hyde Park Corner to protest apartheid, marched reluctantly, for he didn't expect his protest to change anything and he knew that he'd feel like an idiot, embarrassed by posturing companions. Nevertheless, he declared that he'd march every Sunday afternoon if he thought anything concrete would come of it.[65] At home, the children were certainly aware that their parents held Labour views in support of Harold Wilson and National Health. During the 1966 election, which returned Wilson, Daniel Richler needed to do an election poster to fulfill a school assignment. At his upper-crust school, everybody did blue Tory posters. So Daniel, swayed by peer pressure, did a blue poster as well. Ashamed afterwards, he scribbled over it and threw it out, but he must have been aware of his parents' political conscience or he wouldn't have felt any shame.[66]

A little incident a couple of years earlier may have played a role in Richler chafing against correctness. At a party in the Richler house, playwright David Mercer had been chatting up Ethel, an anti-apartheid South African Jew, when George Lamming came up behind him, grabbed him by the ear, and said, "It's my wife you're trying to get off with." Mercer, furious, started yelling at Lamming, and Richler restored peace by asking Mercer to leave.[67] A few days later Mercer apologized to the Richlers, not for the content of what he had said, but for the disturbance. He stated, "I demand the right to love or hate George, or any other negro, as a human being first – not as a kind of deformed white man."[68] Standing in Mercer's liberal position, Richler satirized liberals: if whites and blacks shared a common humanity, then blacks must have equality but no special privileges. Margaret Laurence, who had had an affair with Lamming and who was at the same party – quietly suffering (she still loved Lamming), drinking heavily – recognized something of herself in Joyce and applauded Richler's refusal of sentimentality in *Cocksure*: "[Mortimer's] wife reminded me of myself, not so much in the progressive-sex bits as the progressive-race bits, and if you have ever once been a white liberal, you never forget how it was, way back when, even when you have changed and no longer can imagine yourself agreeing with people just because the colour of their skin was different from yours."[69]

Richler's attack on political correctness in *Cocksure* was anything but measured and verged on libel, according to Oswald Hickson Collier and Co., lawyers for Richler's new publisher, George Weidenfeld. The novel takes Richler's old friend James Baldwin to task for howling whenever Negroes are called more musical or athletic that whites, and yet proclaiming that

Negroes have bigger penises. How does Baldwin know? Mortimer wonders.
By comparison-shopping? He concedes that possibly the knowledge is "in-
tuitive … like Mailer's discovery that cancer in America was caused by Protestants."[70] The lawyers' report on such passages is delightful reading: "Messrs.
Baldwin, Mailer and LeRoi Jones will almost certainly not like the description of their writings given in the fourth paragraph. It is recommended that
this and the ensuing paragraph should be deleted." Wildly cautious, one
might call the report's tone: "Bernard Levin may well object to the statement that 'he had gone out of fashion.' It is recommended that his name be
deleted." Best of all is the reference to the great Jewish artist, Marc Chagall.
Finicky care over legal niceties, but only baby-steps into art and history: "It
is believed that Chagall is dead and if this is so, then there is no danger with
the reference to him as a myopic mystic." Chagall lived until 1985, almost
eighteen years after the preparation of the libel report, but the pseudo-ob-
jective "it is believed" and the escape clause "if this is so" would protect if
not the publisher Weidenfeld then least Oswald Hickson Collier and Co.[71]

Two names that didn't worry the lawyers were "Joyce" and "Lord Woodcock." There is nothing in *Cocksure* explicitly linking Mortimer's easily
offended wife Joyce to Joyce Weiner, but in *It's Harder to Be Anybody*,
Mortimer's wife was called "Dauphne," a more modish, fitting name.[72] Richler had broken with his long-time agent, and now, in his new book, renamed
the major satiric butt *Joyce* … it's difficult to imagine Richler doing this innocently. Without other identifying features, however, libel couldn't come
into consideration, and indeed the joke wasn't that Joyce Weiner was *like*
Joyce Griffin, but that the modest Weiner was the very *opposite* of Mortimer's lascivious wife. One senses a certain misanthropy here, a tendency
to burn all one's bridges, just in case Weiner continued to think of him as
dear Mordy. For "Woodcock," there were, of course, sound figurative reasons for having a character so-named in a novel called *Cocksure*, but just
to be careful, Richler, through Weidenfeld, queried the lawyers whether Canadian literary critic George Woodcock could take offense. Woodcock had recently written a good introduction to the New Canadian Library edition of
Son of a Smaller Hero, though not quite to Richler's taste. Richler thought
Woodcock a plodder. But again, "Lord Woodcock" presented no danger of
libel because nothing explicitly linked him to George Woodcock.[73] Four years
later Woodcock published a slim book on Richler, and, in the chapter on
Cocksure, referred to "the saintly Lord Woodcock." Woodcock also reversed
the scales, referring to the "smugness" of those who recognized themselves
in *The Incomparable Atuk*'s lampoons and to the jealousy of those who had
been overlooked. No resounding affirmations from Woodcock for *The Incomparable Atuk* ("amusing but insubstantial") or *Cocksure* (he wasn't smit-

ten with the sex jokes),[74] so later Richler unfairly added "humourless Puritan" to the list of Woodcock's defects.[75]

As for possible obscenity charges, Oswald Hickson Collier and Co. cited the obvious touchy spots – the de Sade excerpt, Miss Ryerson's student incentive plan – and a host of lesser passages, including the blasphemous suggestion that Jesus might have had an erection. The lawyers noted that obscenity could be justified if a book added to the public good in the interest of literature or learning. "It is envisaged," the lawyers wrote, "that this particular defence will not be available."[76]

Richler later claimed that he had rejected all the cuts suggested by the lawyers.[77] That isn't technically true: he did delete John Osborne's name after the lawyers warned that Osborne was "sensitive of his reputation" and, more to the point, that he wouldn't hesitate to sue.[78] But other than that, Richler changed little. For all its faults, what a limp piece of lettuce *Cocksure* would have been had Richler followed the solicitors' advice. Calculated to offend just about everybody, *Cocksure* remained both Richler's and Florence's favourite among the novels,[79] and he would keep returning to the problem of political correctness right up to his death.

≋

Even as Richler was polishing *Cocksure* and trying hard to be a deracinated "anybody," a death and a war in 1967 would cast him back among Jews. In 1966 he had had a scare about possible cardiac disease. A false alarm, but enough for him briefly to follow the doctor's "no smoking" regimen.[80] For his father, however, the alarm was real. By autumn, Moe had new cancerous tumours again and needed an operation. He came through in good spirits, and his wife Sara felt sure that the tumours were benign. So did Moe's brother Max until Richler let him know different. Max, who saw to it that Richler Brothers made up the difference between Moe's insurance and his regular salary, promised that the brothers would take him back on at work to make him feel useful and keep him occupied.[81] When Bill Weintraub announced that he was turning forty, Richler, five years shy of the same age, countered, "You can't be 40, my father is 40."[82] Within a few months, Nathan Cohen had a heart attack while on holidays and, unaware of what exactly had happened, kept wandering around Europe for another three weeks.[83]

In spring 1967, Moe had another operation for cancer, and Richler flew over to visit him during Passover. To keep out of Lily's clutches and to avoid having to "booze surreptitiously in the john," Richler stayed with Weintraub.[84] Avrum, in the process of leaving his Jewish first wife and marrying a Gentile, had fought with Moe, and the two were no longer speaking. The estrangement from his father greatly disturbed Avrum, who loved his father but couldn't say so. Mordecai arranged for Avrum to visit Moe. A charitable deed, Max Richler thought: "You may not realize what you did – bringing Avrum and the kids to visit – but it was the type of thing that proves a person's worth." Before Mordecai left, he and Avrum went to Moe's little room and celebrated a Passover seder.[85] Twenty years later Avrum would still dream about Moe a lot and would ask Mordecai where his fictionalized account of that last seder was (it's in *St. Urbain's Horseman*), taking the fictional account as a good reflection of what actually happened.[86] Whether the author who had just pranced through *Cocksure* saw "his father's penis curling out of his jockey shorts. A spent worm" – the sight that strikes Jake so forcefully in *St. Urbain's Horseman*[87] – or whether Richler got the image from Babel's *Red Cavalry*, where the dying Ilya's penis is "the wilted, curly virility of a Semite worn to a shadow,"[88] whatever Richler saw told him that he and Moe would be making no father-and-son trip to the Catskills. It was a very difficult time. Moe would try to speak but could press out only a few words, often impossible to understand. He lay and watched while Avrum and Mordecai asked the ritual questions:[89] "Why is this night different from all other nights? ... For on all other nights we eat any vegetable, but tonight – bitter herbs."[90] With Moe on the verge of death, Mordecai returned to London, and Sara encouraged him to write Moe cheerful letters.[91]

That same spring, Egyptian President Abdel Nasser re-militarized the Sinai, blockaded the Gulf of Aqaba, and signed a military agreement with Jordan, vowing on Radio Cairo, to "drive the Jews into the sea" either by force or by economic strangulation.[92] The World Jewish Congress sent *The Sunday Times* an open letter, signed by many Jewish intellectuals, including Richler, asking the British Government to break the Egyptian blockade.[93] But on 5 June Israel struck first, destroying the Egyptian air force on the ground. When Jordan and Syria, supporting Egypt, counterattacked, Israel speedily conquered Old Jerusalem, the Left Bank, the Golan Heights, and the Sinai Peninsula in what became known as the Six Day War, hailed by many devout Jews as God's miracle. Suddenly Richler grew reluctant to sign a second letter from the Writers for Israel Committee. This angered chair Louis Marks: "The conclusion [Richler] seems to invite is never protest when your cause stands a sporting chance of success, lest you appear foolish."[94] That was a distortion, since the Six Day War had given Richler a renewed sense of Israel's fragility, and he rejoiced at the victory. Yet it was true that military success worried him, as those Israelis who had spoken about "Greater Israel" and of Israel's biblical right to all Palestine now began to seem highly credible.[95] One might even call Richler prescient, given that the new conquests resurrected the Israeli right wing. Was the Six Day War only self-defense or had the Jews mounted horses, become aggressors?

On the first day of the war, Moe died. Richler flew home again to attend the shiva of a father who had once prematurely sat shiva for him. His father dead, Jews under attack. By the time Max met him at the airport, Richler already had a bottle of liquor in his hand. In those years people didn't go to movies or listen to the radio while they sat shiva, never mind drink alcohol,[96] but, amid his grandmother, seven uncles, six aunts, and brother,[97] Richler sat on the floor and drank a bottle of scotch.[98] He refused to put on his tefillin. Everybody was offended. At the shiva and then every morning at the synagogue for eleven months, Avrum said Kaddish for Moe.[99] Mordecai doesn't appear to have followed suit. Instead, said Mary, Bernard Richler's wife, "he listened to what everybody had to say and then he wrote it in a book."[100]

According to Bernard, Mordecai was an alcoholic; according to Lionel Albert and Avrum, he wasn't. But he did drink an awful lot. Once, Albert visited the Richlers and in the drift of conversation mentioned that he sometimes liked to skip a day, having no alcohol at all. Florence immediately looked very wistfully at Mordecai. Max, who once heard Richler say, "I want to be loaded before I get on the plane," speculates that Richler drank in order to cope with difficult situations, while Kotcheff traces it to Richler's tortured relationship with his mother.[101] Late in life, an interviewer wanted to know what Richler did when he wasn't writing. "I drink," he said.[102] A joke, but not completely inaccurate. He usually had a few drinks before dinner, and when he had to meet people he drank more.[103] Three double-scotches didn't send him to the cleaner's, according to one anonymous dining companion, and Richler contended that after three drinks he was still competent to drive.[104] When Avrum asked his brother why he drank, Mordecai replied, "If I don't drink, I can't write."[105] Or, as he succinctly put it when speaking of Graham Greene. "No booze, no Muse."[106]

After the shiva, Sara gave Mordecai Moe's talith and Lily's love letters from Julius Frankel, but Moe's diary, which Mordecai desperately wanted, she wouldn't let him have.[107] Perhaps she anticipated what a writer might do with such material. Apparently the diary ended up with Bernard Richler, who wouldn't allow Avrum even to see it.[108] Nevertheless, Mordecai continued to support Sara financially,[109] even though Max didn't think she was Mordecai's responsibility.[110]

The double blow – Moe's death and the Six Day War – reminded Richler forcefully that as alienated as he was from Orthodoxy, he was no longer just its rebel son, but a father – what kind of a father? – and that "Jews" didn't begin and end with secure, bourgeois truck-parts manufacturers in the west end of Montreal. The uncles doubted that he approached his father's death with proper seriousness, and some Jews felt that Richler was trying to disown his race. Was he? *St. Urbain's Horseman* would provide an answer.

16

Mortimer Square and the Counterculture

RICHLER DIDN'T SHOW *Cocksure* to Athill and Deutsch because there had been, he told Athill, a loss of "rapport" about his work. Translated, that meant Richler had asked for a £50 advance, been given it, then had asked for another £50 and been turned down. Deutsch's reasoning was simple: Richler hadn't made the firm much money, so he couldn't expect to get much.[1] Richler, on the contrary, suspected that he hadn't made much money precisely because he wrote for Deutsch.

When it came to palace intrigues and mutinies, Richler didn't go in for half measures. He contacted Tom Maschler at Jonathan Cape and began to hammer out terms. Then he began to whisper rebellion into the ear of Brian Moore, whose work Richler had secured for Deutsch more than a decade earlier. About to work on *Frenzy* for Alfred Hitchcock – it would be a torturous experience, though Moore didn't know it yet – Moore, too, thought he was destined for bigger things than "Deutschland" could afford. He also had a bone to pick, namely that Deutsch had held back one of his books and then published it in the same week as a Graham Greene. Moore swore fealty to Richler: "I, with you am secretly planning schism. Tell Maschler I am willing to turn Trotskyite." Deutsch, of course, cried foul.[2] But there was little he could do except carry on an ineffectual word-of-mouth vendetta against his former authors.[3] Athill composed a diplomatic letter (which Deutsch, too, signed), wishing Richler and *Cocksure* the kind of success that would make herself and Deutsch look silly for balking at the novel.[4]

The intrigues didn't end there. While dickering with Maschler of Jonathan Cape, Richler also met Tony Godwin, the pixie-like editor for Weidenfeld and Nicolson. Godwin called himself "a hothouse degenerate Englishman – efete [sic] as they come" – and on those credentials refused, years later when planning a Canadian vacation, to be enticed into such a thing as a lake. Pixie-like; but he could be dour and impatient with fools.[5] After Richler and

Godwin concluded their tête-à-tête, Richler reeled in a £1,000 advance to sign on with Weidenfeld, and Maschler was left holding the bag.[6] Deutsch, hearing the sum, could only gasp and breathe heavily.[7] Richler understood that a good advance was the *whole* point: it signified that the publisher was going to work hard on advertising and that the book wasn't just a prestige publication intended more to bolster the letterhead than to sell. In Tony Godwin, he found a more worldly, less inhibited audience than Joyce Weiner had been. *St. Urbain's Horseman*, when it finally made its appearance, would be dedicated to Godwin.

≶

For some time, Neil Compton and others had been working to get Richler back to Canada, more specifically to Sir George Williams University.[8] That way Sir George, little sister to McGill, could score PR points. On Richler's part, it was a chance to get paid for minimal work, a sort of reverse sabbatical.[9] Mavis Gallant warned that "in the wake of Le Grand Charles" (de Gaulle, who had in July of 1967 visited Montreal and declared "*Vive le Québec Libre*") the city was full of nationalist rhetoric. According to the media, oppressed French Canadians couldn't afford to eat meat, she reported. Pro-Vichy Québec had been forgotten, but older memories still rankled, because, Gallant read, the Québécois were "'forced to live in houses built by the Conqueror.'" Since the houses weren't suited to the climate, unfortunate Québécois froze.[10] Richler returned because, firstly, he sensed that leading up to *Cocksure*, a projected book of essays, and a projected book of stories, he needed Canadian publicity; secondly, he recognized that to write *St. Urbain's Horseman* he needed to revisit the headwaters of his fiction in Montreal.

With four children and pregnant again, Florence wasn't eager to go.[11] But go she did. In spring 1968, Bill Weintraub found the Richlers a house in Wildwood, near Vaudreuil and not far from Montreal. To keep Lily at arm's length, Weintraub promised not to mention the looming stork.[12] "Coach House," as the Richler manor was named, palled quickly. It was filthy, there were leaks, mattresses with springs broken through, a live wire, a foul odour. The final straw was mice, making Florence afraid to nurse the new baby, Jacob, at night.[13] Richler moved the family to 1 Malcolm Road in Westmount.

He popped over to Sir George once a week to teach creative writing and signed on as a regular columnist with *Saturday Night*, where Robert Fulford had just become editor. At Sir George, Richler serviced all of ten students, all the while proclaiming, "Writing is unteachable." He wanted to tell many of his students "Go home, you can't write," but such honesty was frowned on at universities. His office he kept tidy by avoiding it, and he later joked that he considered subletting it to a bookie. "A year-long party," he called the time. Little work got done, and he felt like an impostor. Although he had an immediate offer to be writer-in-residence at Carleton, he turned it down, acknowledging that he wasn't social enough to be a teacher. "I'd never do it again," he vowed. That resolve would last exactly three years.[14]

He continued to pay close attention to the worth of his services. When Peter Gzowski had asked for advice about staff firings at *Maclean's*, Richler had told him to go ahead, "they're taking my money."[15] As editor for the *Star Weekly* in 1968, Gzowski sent Richler books to review and wasn't particularly happy when the reviews showed up in the *New Statesman* first, or when Richler reused ideas. But Gzowski couldn't do much about it. "I <u>know</u> we need you more than you need us," he lamented. "You sneaky, double-selling, strip miner, I caught one of your thoughts about Berton in one of the two new pieces (both of which are fine) and thereby selling us the same phrase twice. Coddled? What the hell does that mean? Of course I think you're coddled, and will continue to be."[16] Richler's zeal in making sure that he was paid what he was worth exposed him to ribbing from Jack Ludwig, University of Toronto's writer-in-residence, who arranged for Richler to speak at the university: "About that matter, Mordecai. I thought I was dealing with a white man, or knowing you have been a resident of England, a white Jew, and so, naturally, omitted in a gentleman's context your kikey considerations." After the visit, Ludwig posted the cheque, "Here is the money. Take. As a recognizable parameter an expense account establishes you are 2? to 3 times the writer Brian is, a fact you may quote should objective standards come in handy."[17]

≷

Richler, who now claimed that he read reviews of his books only as market reports,[18] was in a strange position amid the student radicalism and campus upheavals of the late 1960s. People assumed that the author of *Cocksure* must surely sympathize with the rebels and with all that the Age of Aquarius had to offer, particularly after W.H. Smith in Britain refused to sell *Cocksure*, calling it a book that didn't suit the Smith image. The firm sold girly magazines, *Valley of the Dolls*, and soon *Portnoy's Complaint*, but balked at the often-libellous *Private Eye*, *Penthouse*, and *Cocksure*.[19] Because *Cocksure* therefore wasn't stacked in train stations or airports, and because in many towns W.H. Smith was the only bookseller, Tony Godwin estimated that Richler's sales were cut in half. Explaining the decision, spokesman Leonard Cotterell argued that, like a grocer, W.H. Smith must be regardful of its image.[20] One might laugh at such a defense, but how could Richler, who had satirized the permissive society in *Cocksure* and claimed to be upholding Mortimer Griffin's right to remain a square, complain about a bookseller making an independent decision about where the limits of good taste lay? When it came to real, live Mortimers, Richler wasn't quite so keen to take up their cases.

Richler's attitude towards censorship was repeatedly tested in the late 1960s and early 1970s. He came out as grand defender of free expression, but his attitude depended very much on who was doing the censoring. John Metcalf asked to use "The Summer My Grandmother Was Supposed to Die" for a Ryerson high school anthology, but English education consultants in Toronto balked at the words "shit" and "orgasm" and requested that Richler cut one paragraph.[21] He was immediately outraged:

> Golly!
> Jeepers!
> Holy cow!
> Is there a ten year old left in Ontario who doesn't say 'shit'? … for me to say yes, wd be to agree the passage is in doubtful taste. Which it isn't. So I must say no. Emphatically no.[22]

Instead, he gave Ryerson the much less distinguished story "Bambinger."[23] He also lit into Robert Fulford when Fulford presumed to delete a passage involving fellatio and false teeth from one of Richler's columns without consulting Richler. Fulford apologized and pled cowardice.[24]

On the other hand, when *Maclean's* editor Walter Stewart cut Richler's comments on Andy Warhol's sexual proclivities, Richler surrendered.[25] In the face of potential libel charges, Richler's acquiescence was understandable. Less so in the case of excerpts from *St. Urbain's Horseman* for *Chatelaine*. The editor, Doris Anderson, was eager to publish Richler but requested that he cut a few "salty" words, in particular "pig shit" and "Old Lady Dry Cunt." Although Anderson didn't object to the words herself, she had no desire to answer letters from a few hundred outraged readers, so she proposed "manure" and "Old Lady D."[26] Strangely, no cry of injury and outrage from Richler. The pieces were quietly printed according to Anderson's specifications, Richler even submitting to the deletion of "crap" and "Oh God."[27] It's not difficult to divine why. Ryerson Press had had the bad sense to be run by a United Church board, so Richler felt that it was his duty to take the old maid for a spin around the red light district. Furthermore, "The Summer My Grandmother Was Supposed to Die" had already been published in *The Street*, and the additional royalties from Ryerson would be miniscule, divided among many authors. *Chatelaine*, on the other hand, was a big magazine, able to pay well and pay again in the future. Most important of all, an excerpt in *Chatelaine* would be a great advertisement for *St. Urbain's Horseman*.

The W.H. Smith ban on *Cocksure* in 1968 immediately perked up Jack McClelland. He assumed that the buzz would turn the book into a Canadian bestseller; he was disappointed when this didn't happen.[28] Bringing the novel out three weeks before a federal election, what did McClelland expect? Nevertheless, *Cocksure* did gain fans among the intelligentsia and, along with Richler's book of essays, *Hunting Tigers Under Glass*, went on to win a Governor General's Award in the strangest year in the history of the awards. Beforehand, a young CBC producer, interviewing Richler on radio, explained that in these bold anti-establishment days the Governor General's Awards were obviously an anachronism. Since literature was passé, shouldn't folk singer Gordon Lightfoot get the Governor General's? Richler, about to ascend to the pinnacle of his craft in Canada wasn't amused. Give Lightfoot another award if you must, Richler snapped, just don't confuse Lightfoot's work with literature or with the Governor General's Awards. "But you're all in the business of communication," the interviewer pressed. "I am not in the business of communication," growled Richler, "I am a writer."[29] At the awards, novelist Hubert Aquin and sociologist Fernand Dumont won in two of the French categories. Aquin, a former member of the radical *Rassemblement pour l'independence nationale* (which merged into the Parti Québécois), refused the award. Dumont accepted, then donated the prize to the Parti Québécois.[30] Leonard Cohen, a Montrealer and the winner for poetry in English, arguably Canada's greatest poet at the time, had no idea what to do. Already the hippest among the hip, he couldn't very well quarrel with the tide of the times, especially since he had allowed Separatism its full orgiastic possibilities in *Beautiful Losers* (1967). But of course he was English, and his fans primarily English. He hit upon an ingenious solution. He announced that couldn't accept the award; when asked why, he grew very solemn, "Much in me strives for this honour, but the poems themselves forbid it absolutely." Richler, too square for such a gimmick, was infuriated. He could see his day in the sun slipping away. The evening of the awards, Jack McClelland threw a party at Ottawa's Chateau Laurier. When Cohen showed up, Richler herded him into the bathroom and bawled him out.[31]

Richler won too, but strangely. The award categories had loosened up: depending upon the quality of the contenders, there might be two winners for poetry and none for fiction, as in 1967. Nevertheless, the award was *not* given for a body of work, but for *one* book. For her short story collection *Dance of the Happy Shades*, Alice Munro won in the fiction category. Richler, however, won both for *Cocksure* and for *Hunting Tigers Under Glass*. The category? There was no category. He was cited for "Fiction and Essays," but such a double category didn't exist under the terms of the awards.[32] Later Richler would chuckle that the stodgy GG officials couldn't very well give the prize to a pornographic book, so they included *Hunting Tigers Under*

Glass.[33] There is an alternative explanation: it's just possible that the judges considered Munro's work more profound, but didn't want to seem too square for a book as hip as *Cocksure.*

For all that, *Cocksure* sales weren't taking off. "Fat books sell, skinny books don't," the US novelist Josh Greenfield consoled Richler.[34] But Richler estimated the situation more astutely, recognizing that satire gives up the reader's sympathy. *Cocksure* simply didn't have enough humanity. Given the award and the tastes of the permissive society, Richler expected a *Cocksure* film on the double, but his screenplay, too, died on the shelf.[35] As much as filmmakers wanted the property, they also feared the censor: they didn't want to cut much from the novel, but who was eager to risk a costly obscenity trial? Richler's children, old enough by now to be aware of the whispers around *Cocksure*, though not old enough to be allowed to read it, heard from friends that their father had written a dirty book. "My Dad read your dad's book," one boy told Daniel Richler, "*My Dad* says I'm not to even name the name."[36]

≶

Yet on Canada's seething campuses, as in the bathroom of the Chateau Laurier, Richler looked and sounded like a feistier Mortimer rather than the author of an unnameable book. He noted that countercultural rebellion seemed to involve a very specific fashion in clothes, and, harassed by bell-bottoms,[37] he skewered those professors driven to bind their potbellies in "punishingly tight Nehru jackets, ceramic pendants swinging from their knotted necks,"[38] their conversation sprinkled with "It's not my bag" or "outasight."[39] "Be true to the slang of your generation,"[40] he reprimanded them. Conservatively dressed, Richler was in no danger of being mistaken for a hippie; yet, permanently rumpled, he wasn't about to be confused with the Chairman of the Board either. Later it would become common to label Richler a conservative, but despite his occasional support of the Progressive Conservatives and free-market economics, and despite his admission that satire ran with small "c" conservatism,[41] he was never a genuine conservative. Richler was a true countercultural figure: when it was unfashionable to flout the system, he flouted the system. When flouting became fashionable, he defended Joe McCarthy,[42] yet in such a way that one could not mistake him for a right-wing ideologue. His specialty was the counterblast.

Materiel for counterblasts wasn't hard to come by. Patrick Lyndon, chairman of the Centre for Communications and the Arts at Simon Fraser University invited Richler to SFU for a lecture in November 1968,[43] a week after 114 students were arrested for a sit-in. The students wanted to stop the freeze on British Columbia's education budget and wanted the right to transfer between colleges without losing credit.[44] When Richler reported on the sit-in for *Saturday Night,* he ignored the issues in favour of the personal ironies. After the sit-in, the students requested that SFU's acting president convince BC's attorney general to wipe out their criminal records. Hearing this, Richler wrote, "In the heat of the battle, then, what roused Simon Fraser's red guards most was the fear that five years hence, when they applied to the Hudson's Bay Co. or Shell for a job, they might be compromised by an old police blotter."[45] The put-downs betrayed something of Richler's own ambivalence about his political position. On the one hand, he still sensed the pull of his early years – high and selfless political ideals – so he still made exaggeratedly idealistic demands of the radicals. And when the impossible demands weren't met ... satire. On the other hand, he had by now moved far from any sort of radicalism.

Richler also complained in *Saturday Night* that a student film, "a moderately horny skin show" according to Richler's rating, was treated by the attendant SFU professor as if it were the work of Ingmar Bergman.[46] Richler's ex-host, Lyndon, summoned now to the defense of his university's programs, rued his invitation to the celebrated creative artist. "Mordecai Richler has always been splendidly impervious to all the arts except his own," Lyndon recanted, and then explained that while professional filmmakers and theatre artists had emerged from SFU, there might nevertheless be good reason why many students had not yet attained "that level of efficiency and avoidance of excess which the author of *Son of a Smaller Hero* now appears to think is the root of art."[47]

Richler's view of student radicals was confirmed in the winter of 1969 by the Great Computer Fire at Sir George. In the year before Richler arrived, West Indian students had accused Biology Professor Perry Anderson of being a racist and had succeeded in having him suspended. With the administration's investigation slowed to a crawl, however, and battles continuing about the composition of the investigating committee, protesters decided to occupy the faculty lounge early in 1969. Richler talked to their leaders there and agreed that, if Anderson was racist in the assigning of marks, he'd have to be fired. Yet Richler was also wary of the railroading that could occur when an individual espoused views counter to the prevailing orthodoxy. "Racism" was a nebulous charge, unless the accusers could point to specific improper actions. Since the students also accused Anderson of missing twenty-one lectures, why not, Richler suggested, nail him on that more objectively provable charge? And if they couldn't make that simple charge stick, how could they expect to prove racism? But this didn't capture the imaginations of the protesters. Tiring of the Faculty Lounge, approximately 150 students moved to occupy the campus's ninth-floor computer centre. When even that didn't sway the semi-judicial process, impatient students torched the rooms, using axes and fire to do $2 million damage. Police arrested ninety-seven people for conspiracy to commit arson. Richler happened to be in Ottawa that day but immediately commented that the protests were keyed by a few adventurers and supported by a lot of callow young people who knew very little of the world.[48]

On campus as he had in the synagogues, Richler refused to sail with the prevailing winds. He argued with students on the CBC's *Under Attack*.[49] He told students at the University of Calgary that Dr Timothy Leary's "Turn On, Tune In, and Drop Out" reminded him of "There's a Ford in your Future."[50] Leave, if you think that the university is a compromised institution, he taunted protesters, and when they sensibly replied that they wanted their degrees, Richler unholstered his satire: in twenty years' time they'd be utilizing the same pressure tactics at Progressive Conservative conventions. He confessed that he liked the Beatles and the Stones but insisted that they weren't important and wouldn't be remembered. To the Sir George newspaper, fashionably titled *Inner Space*, he recounted a world student conference at which a leader of the riotous May 1968 student protests in Paris, Daniel Bendit-Cohn, and other Western student leaders had advocated socialism and student control of universities, while Eastern Bloc students had cried, no, no, we've got that and it doesn't work.[51] Against the Sir George protesters' demand that a Department of Black Studies be created, Richler argued that Canada didn't have a colour problem and that Canadian students were simply mimicking the more valid demands of their US counterparts. Americans had reason to take to the streets. Although he thought that writers were citizens, nothing more, he said that if he lived in the United States he'd find it obligatory to protest for Civil Rights and against the Vietnam War,[52] and indeed, he told his children a lot about the Civil Rights movement, drawing parallels between the Jewish experience in Europe and the black experience in America.[53] As for Vietnam, a couple of years earlier, he had written a brief satire, "Preparing for the Worst," based on a *Time* magazine article about US recruits preparing for possible POW conditions. In General Richler's army, recruits had to crawl head first through a bottomless offal barrel, then endure torture. The four who survived the training, including a Jew, were threatened to be shot if they didn't talk. They didn't. They were shot.[54] In interview, Richler agreed that Americans who burned their draft cards were engaging in a true and necessary subversion of the state, and certainly Americans ought to demand Black Studies programs at university. But Canadians, anxious that they had no issues of similar weight, were protesting because protest was modish.[55]

⅀

Richler wasn't the most impartial commentator on black frustrations. A short time earlier, he and black author Austin Clarke had gotten into a public dust-up as Richler staked out the same liberal but politically incorrect position in life that he had in fiction. *The Canadian* had profiled Clarke and allowed him to air his manifold complaints: he despised Canada's racist immigration policy; he disapproved of intermarriage because the children of such unions were inevitably less black than the black parents; he didn't like to be called "a Toronto Negro novelist" because the tag implied patronage; he didn't feel appreciated by the white publishers McClelland & Stewart or by the CBC; and he hadn't been asked to appear on *Front Page Challenge*, that rousing Canadian game show in which four panellists are asked to identify a mystery celebrity.[56] Hearing Clarke badmouth their mutual publisher, Richler had no compunction about sideswiping him in *Saturday Night*. Richler hadn't appeared on *Front Page Challenge* either, he confessed, and added, "Until now, I was comparatively sanguine about this." He pretended to "suspect" that Clarke's victory in a *Saturday Night* short story contest, Sidney Poitier's victory at the Academy Awards, and a recent honour for Martin Luther King had been rigged by paternalistic whites. Then Richler went on to serious matters, such as Clarke's opposition to intermarriage, which Richler interpreted, just as he interpreted Jewish opposition to intermarriage, as a form of reverse bigotry.[57]

Clarke, perhaps realizing that his own diatribe protesting the many instances of discrimination against one Austin Clarke was dictated more by emotion than by logic, didn't reply publicly. Privately, of course, he was livid, and his letter to Richler made it clear that this wasn't a forum on racial discrimination but a contest of alpha males:

> You are running out of ideas and imagination, baby, if you have to peddle all that shit, to the extent of four columns. I was going to reply to your thing, but I decided that there was nothing to reply to. I was going to challenge you to a fight, (the pen is irrelevant in this case), and possibly kick your little arse, but again, I have this advantage over you. I am not running out of ideas, baby. You dig it? ...
>
> Man, why don't you get on with your own creative thing, instead of writing an article on an article which was written on me?
>
> Was I informed truthfully, that you too entered a story for the first Belmont Short Story Award?
>
> Salaam and love,
> Austin C[58]

Was Richler a racist? The term is imprecise and sloppy in such a case. True, Richler was never overly fastidious about racially demeaning jokes. When a friend conveyed Clarke's "greetings" after the incident, Richler responded, "Oh good, Florence has been trying to reach him. She wants him to wait on table tonight."[59] More seriously, by ignoring the root causes of black anger – consistent discrimination in housing and employment, especially in Toronto and Montreal, where black populations were growing[60] – Richler distorted the issues, suggesting that black rage was senseless. As for Canada not having a colour problem, Richler simply didn't know what he was talking about. His satire against blacks was nothing that he hadn't already hit the Jews with, but, since he was himself a Jew and since the Jews by the 1960s suffered little of the bigotry that they had endured in the 1940s, the social dynamics weren't comparable.

Yet in one sense he was right to ignore causes: to draw a direct line from black anger about housing discrimination to the $2 million damage in the Sir George computer room or to a perceived snub by *Front Page Challenge* was tendentious at best. At worst, it invited a politics of victimhood, according to which the oppressor's discrimination would excuse any illegal or foolish action by the victim. One couldn't demand social responsibility of the perpetrators of discrimination while exempting the victim from responsibility whenever things got hot. Moreover, Richler's fiction *wasn't* racist. Alongside the racist jokes – nothing could kill fiction more quickly than sermons or the scrubbing of all unpleasantness – Richler consistently mocked racism.

And if Richler's put-downs were demeaning, they were common as water in his circles. One might even say that the ability to give and take sharp little put-downs was an entry ticket into those circles. This can be seen in letters from his friend Kildare Dobbs and from Jack and Haya Clayton, who had received the dedication of *Cocksure*. In one letter to Richler, Dobbs drew a swastika in the margin and signed himself, "Yours in Christ."[61] Jack Clayton was planning to film *St. Urbain's Horseman* long before the novel was complete,[62] but the Claytons' letter to Richler within six months of the Richler-Clarke bout used the same hired-help put-down that Richler had used on Clarke:

My dear Mordecai,
    Find your continual abusive letters intolerable. Who the hell cares when or whether you come back to this country: we have a new set of friends now, and a much better *class* mob.
                        Lots of love to Florence and the family.
                                    Love, Jack and Haya.
PS Please bring chef's hat and apron in order that your appearance operating our BBQ might be more formal.
                        Haya.
PPS Please improve your appearance generally.
                        J.[63]

This was free speech *à la Richler*, requiring one to distinguish between real bigotry and jokes, the former causing physical or material injury, the latter testing the receiver's broadmindedness, demanding a witty counter-jab, not angry shouting.

≶

Richler's politics no longer included any utopian hopes that the artist was in the vanguard of a better world. The best one could hope for was to keep one's freedoms, to make small improvements, and to be governed by reasonable people. "Biliously liberal," *The Observer* had long ago dismissed his *No Love for Johnnie*, and, give or take the adverb, *The Observer* wasn't far off the mark.[64] The summer just prior to his tenure at Sir George, Richler's affection for the establishment had been cemented when Pierre Elliott Trudeau took over as leader of the Liberal Party. Jewish Quebeckers had long supported the Liberals provincially and federally, in power and out, probably because the Jews' minority status sent them leftwards, towards parties that favoured minority rights, but the Jews' hopes of integration prevented them from going too far left.[65] Just before Richler came to Canada Max Richler told him about how Trudeau, Jean Drapeau (mayor of Montreal), and Daniel Johnson (premier of Québec) had faced nationalist Québécois rioters. When the bottle-throwing began, Johnson had retreated, but Trudeau and Drapeau had stood their ground, Trudeau "calmly smiling."[66] Richler had already met him in the home of Bernard and Sylvia Ostry when Trudeau was Justice minister.[67] A politician who could discuss Dostoevsky's Grand Inquisitor, Céline, and Malraux! Richler was immediately impressed.[68] "Trudeau," said Richler, "strikes me as a rich, elegant, highly-cultured, assimilated Jew, with an aristocrat's impatience of the Quebec ghetto and its chief rabbi and advocate, Rene Levesque [*sic*]."[69] With that flair and English Canada's hope that a federalist French intellectual might best be able to stare down the separatists, Trudeau soon captured the Anglo intelligentsia. Peter Gzowski wrote Richler, "Trudeau might *win*. Jesus! Pierre Trudeau as prime minister! Lefolii as head of the CBC! Fulford takes over culture! Richler becomes president of the Mount Royal Club! Concentration camps for westerners ... the whole thing."[70] Richler hopped aboard the wagon.

Although Richler doubted that "Mr. and Mrs. Frontporch" would elect an intellectual, he praised Trudeau in a *Star Weekly* article, "A Man for Today." Richler tried to add satire by mocking Trudeau's attention to the cheese industry, but only succeeded in showing his impatience with the details of the economy. Throughout his career as a controversialist, Richler would ignore the day-to-day economic business of government; but social policy intrigued him, and in later years he would praise Trudeau for making divorce easier and abortion and homosexuality legal.[71] When it came to estimating leaders, their potential and their follies, Richler was in his true métier. NDP leader David Lewis he marked out as a tragic figure. The moral and intellectual superior of everybody in Parliament (and a Baron Byng alumnus), Lewis led a party that wasn't going to win a national election. Among the Liberals, Richler singled out Jean Marchand, John Turner, and Trudeau as worth taking seriously.[72] Peter Newman, after reading Richler's article, immediately offered him directions to the Trudeau headquarters.

In June 1968, even Mr. and Mrs. Frontporch succumbed to Trudeaumania, and the Liberals won the election by a landslide. A few months later, Richler speculated that Trudeau had let his name stand only in order to promote his less-than-peppy book, *Federalism and the French Canadians*, but near the end of the whimsical column, Richler grew uncharacteristically serious, "Pierre Elliott Trudeau embodies a level of hope and honour for this country that must not be betrayed."[73] A cultural liberal, Richler voted as a political Liberal too, a compromise position that he defended on campus and in his columns. He agreed that social justice was more important than art,[74] yet his stated view of protest and the writer's role was growing more subdued at the same time as his social power (measured by the *Saturday Night* column and the Governor General's Award) was increasing. One protests, he sighed, "out of a radical politesse, as it were and not with any hope of effecting change. You go through the motions, that's all."[75] Not writers, but politicians were responsible for changing society – "I pity the writer who thinks he's going to effect political changes."[76] Then he reversed himself and insisted that writing had a political purpose, to shape the world, no less. In later years, Richler would report with approval that Saul Bellow, once a young Trotskyite, called himself "some sort of liberal."[77] Richler's earlier novels, including *The Apprenticeship of Duddy Kravitz*, had revealed what Richler was against, but not what he was *for*. *St. Urbain's Horseman* would make it clear: even though he still called himself a socialist,[78] he had become some sort of a liberal.

17

Horseman

IN 1970 RICHLER SAID THAT throughout his career he had continued to think of serious writing as founded on truth and moral purpose. Entertainment was secondary, he claimed.[1] An odd way to characterize his recent satires: in no way was entertainment secondary in *The Incomparable Atuk* or *Cocksure*. But there were reasons for his backtracking. Richler had again said no to "filmsville," resolving not to adapt anybody else's work again unless he were in a financial crisis, and he had resumed work on the most complex novel he had ever attempted, *St. Urbain's Horseman*.[2] The material raised questions. How true to his own life should Richler let his fiction be? How far should a moral purpose guide him? And, as Richler re-entered his imagined St. Urbain Street, another stumper: what is a Jew? The question was both fictional and real. With Daniel and Noah on the verge of adolescence, Florence and Richler wondered whether they should pass on anything of Judaism to the next generation.

It would be a stretch to call Richler, as Peter Gzowski has, an old-fashioned gentleman and family man. Richler adored but wasn't very close to his children.[3] He drove his boys to school each day,[4] but the children soon realized that if they wanted to know about their father's life, the best bet was to hang around when Jack Clayton, Ted Allen, or Ted Kotcheff came by to drink and tell stories late into the night. One day, courtesy of *Time* magazine, Noah discovered that his father had been married before. Noah, age seven, said, "Dad, you never told me you were married before." "You never asked," Richler replied.[5] Overaffectionate displays Richler associated with his mother Lily, and he had no plans to imitate her by turning into a hugger and a kisser. Far above emotional display, he valued fairness, loyalty, and a more measured love. He would sit quietly, not aloof, but watching his children as they played. He was, as Florence said, very patriarchal.[6] Seven days a week he worked, expecting from her tea and a clean ashtray. The children, barred from upstairs during working hours,[7] walked around on tiptoe and, unless they were in their own rooms with the door shut, spoke only in hushed tones. This was, of course, most difficult when the children were young. Afterwards, it made for individual pursuits. Florence remembers one of the children coming back from a friend's house with a shocking discovery, "Do you know in other houses, the children don't tiptoe around as we do?"[8]

Using his own family, Richler tried to write a children's book, *The Last Plum in the House*, a mystery in which Emma's plum is eaten and suspicion falls on the other family members. In the story Richler reveals that if the children were loathe to step outside during the London winter, he'd rehash, yet again, accounts of epic Canadian winters: walking to school through blizzards and five-foot snow drifts; sifting the ashes nightly and stoking the furnace. No car, no maid, no TV. The children learned to keep complaints to themselves. Evidently Richler only wrote seven pages of the story, a delightful beginning, as good as *Jacob Two-Two and the Hooded Fang*, but not something that children's editors, even in the liberated 1960s, would snap up. In the first chapter the children know that, with the Kotcheffs and Jack and Haya Clayton coming to dinner, their parents would go to bed "very, very late, and get up very, very, very late, and be in a bad mood." Daddy will have a headache. No matter how quiet the children are, he will complain of the noise, and when Emma starts chanting, "I want my plum, I want my plum,"[9] he'll say, "Will you give the child her bloody plum." An honest story, a story about children, but not a story *for* children.

The Richler children were Florence's responsibility. The father in Emma Richler's second novel has the following way of dealing with unruly children: "Hey! Cut that out! What do you want? What is that? Ask Mum! I'm reading!"[10] At times Florence resented caring for the children while Richler was off thinking his great thoughts,[11] but she was good at homemaking.[12] Given his own upbringing, Richler didn't expect family harmony, and he was grateful to Florence for creating it.[13] As an adopted child, Florence had had her own familial difficulties, and felt alienated from all but one sister. Neither Florence nor Mordecai wanted to repeat the failings of their parents, so, relying mainly on their love for each other, they sequestered their own family off from the extended family.[14] Emma's excellent novels, *Sister Crazy* and *Feed My Dear Dogs*, highly autobiographical in their descriptions of the narrator Jem's family, point to "Mummy" as the family's emotional core. Mummy knows what the children are thinking. Her day job, homemaking, "is very tense and demands physical strength, mental circumspection, and refined behaviour." The danger of that job – "a sort of lonely, startled and wayward look, like in a lost animal or maybe a thirsty plant" – can be averted by means of champagne and meursault; "art, especially

paintings featuring her friends;" beauty, especially starry skies; acts of
thoughtfulness.[15] Martha, too, paints a picture of Florence as a sympathetic,
natural teacher. When they had problems, the children couldn't go to Richler, because he'd drop a stack of books outside their doors and imply that
buried somewhere in one of those books was the answer.[16] In *Feed My Dear
Dogs*, Jem's father thinks that he can sort out her depression by shouting,
"One! Two! Three! ... IS SHE OUT FOR THE COUNT? Six! Seven! ..." Jem
perks up, mostly to pacify him, no credit to his psychiatric method.[17] When
she has a bad day, it's Mum she needs, and she imagines Mum in a Fra Fil-
ippo Lippi painting, gathering up on her knee all the saints, in this case her
five children, plus Dad.[18]

To forestall potential identity crises in the children, Richler tried to hide
newspapers featuring him, but unlike Florence he wasn't big on quality time
with the children. Daniel remembers him saying, "I'm not the kind of father who takes his son fishing but I can't wait until you're old enough to go
out for a gin and tonic."[19] If he was bored, Richler didn't hide it, even with
the children.[20] Martha, as a young girl, feared him and felt that when he
was talking to her his mind was elsewhere. A cloud of darkness and silence
surrounded him, and it was difficult to pierce through his self-absorption
and get his attention. "I've been quite a distant father," Richler admitted.[21]
Instead of talking to them, he assigned weekend essays in which he required
that they use words such as "alacrity," and "parochial."[22] He took Noah to
Paris once and tried to broach a birds-and-bees discussion. The results weren't
far removed from Moe's abridged version of sex education for Richler a generation earlier (though without Moe's audio-visual aid, the Gayety Theatre).
The author of *Cocksure* asked Noah, "You know how ...?" and Noah quickly
cut him off with a lie, "Yes." That relieved Richler of the awkward duty,
"Right. Good."[23]

Richler and Florence agreed that the children would be raised in a completely secular fashion – "I'm okay, you're okay; no hang-ups, but no magic,
either; too bad."[24] Richler's and Florence's *modus vivendi*, he revealed, consisted of Florence allowing him to sing old synagogue and Zionist songs,
while he let her play Christmas carols,[25] but how this differed from mere
tolerance, it would take a very subtle dialectician to sort out. It was hardly
a rapprochement between two faiths. In England the boys had gone to King's
House, an Anglican school, and Noah, "a promising fascist," Richler joked,
had been appointed vice-captain there.[26] In both England and Canada, Florence chose to send Emma and Martha to convent schools because the schools
had excellent reputations. Florence realized that what the children would
hear from Richler would contradict some of what they heard in school, but
she was confident that this could only enrich their education: "the good part
of it was extremely good and what was corrupt would become apparent to

them."[27] King's House featured a Christmas carol service,[28] which Richler duly attended, silent and observing.[29] Yet, as St. Urbain's Horseman, Sister Crazy, and Feed My Dear Dogs imply, Richler grew anxious that his children might abjectly surrender to Christian superstitions, such as making the sign of the cross. At the same time, among many of the Richler relatives, Mordecai was still persona non grata for what they considered attacks on the family and Judaism. The few times that he showed up for the family gatherings that still occurred on Sunday afternoons at the house of Shmarya's widow, he sat in a corner chair and hardly anybody talked to him. When his young cousin, Sam Orbaum, asked to have him invited to Sam's bar mitzvah, Sam's mother said, "He won't come, we're not having a bar."[30] What to do now that Richler's own children were approaching bar mitzvah age?

Young Emma thought she had a workable solution to the half-breed problem: "You guys are Jewish," she told Noah and Daniel, "but the girls aren't."[31] Still, were Richler to hand the boys over to the rabbis for training, he'd undermine his own escape from religion. Yet were he to ignore Judaism altogether, he'd help assimilate his boys directly into Anglo culture in a way that even he had never fully been assimilated, and, incidentally, he'd prove right those uncles who had predicted just such a future when he had intermarried. Richler's assimilationist nightmare would appear in St. Urbain's Horseman when at Jake's funeral his son, "Lord Samuel Hersh," wonders what the hell Kaddish is, and asks, "I say, what shall we do with the old fart's ashes?"[32] Richler's parental answer to assimilation was a brief salute to religion, once, maximum twice a year: for a number of years, he celebrated Passover seder and took the children to synagogue on Yom Kippur.[33] The suggestion initially came from Florence, who wanted them to learn about as many religions as possible. She asked Richler if something couldn't be done about this. He looked thoughtful for a moment and then said, "Alright, we'll have a seder." It wasn't easy for him. Nevertheless, as Florence says, "he never did anything he didn't want to do." The seders began in the late 1960s or 1970 in London – Noah says the family still has a Haggadah somewhere with Jack Clayton's spilled wine on it. In Canada the seders continued, and ended about the time that Noah left for Oxford in 1978. For the Richler catechism, the main idea was to step into history, and when he came to the verses praising God, he ran through them quickly, pro forma. Inevitably there would be comical moments as Richler battled with the Hebrew, and as Florence drew the time out with highly intelligent questions while the children chafed to escape.[34]

Telling the children that they were Jewish was, as Richler called it, "breaking the news."[35] At school in Britain, Noah thought that the one Jewish boy he knew was odd.[36] Later, in Canada, Richler would also call up Max, who took his faith seriously, and ask Max to arrange for the children to witness a Simchat Torah. Together they all trooped to the synagogue. However, these nods to Judaism didn't last long. "Heritage stuff," Max called it,[37] and Richler didn't disagree, admitting that he was nostalgic for synagogue prayers but didn't yearn for them. His grandfather, Rabbi Rosenberg, had complained in 1924 that Jews desecrated the Sabbath by skipping synagogue services, pushing baby carriages, and turning electric lights on and off. For 25¢, one had been able to read in his *Letter from the Sweet Mother Sabbath Queen* ... that to eat bread baked on the Sabbath was like dining on Jewish blood. Richler had dismissed such beliefs, and although in *St. Urbain's Horseman* he would let his autobiographical character, Jake, be stirred on Friday evenings by the arrival of the Sabbath like a bride,[38] Richler's moral code was existential-humanist. In the absence of God, humans must accept responsibility for their own conduct.[39] When it first came time for Noah to attend the bar mitzvah of a friend, he dressed up in clothing that he had no reason to expect might not be adequate to the occasion: a windbreaker and Adidas runners made of pigskin. Richler saw him leave the house but said nothing. And Richler chortled at the upshot – it was his idea of a good joke – when Noah returned and reported having gotten into a fight at the synagogue.[40] There would be no bar mitzvahs for the Richler boys.[41]

Still, Richler worried about assimilation, whose danger Cynthia Ozick articulated so well: "if we choose to be Mankind rather than Jewish ... we will not be heard at all; for us America will have been in vain." "*Amerikanergeboren*" ("American-born") was her grandfather's disdainful term for Jews who had lost their moral compass.[42] Richler discouraged his children from sentimental identifications with the Jewish nation,[43] and his real – impassioned and moral – Jewish education for his children he gave via history: lessons on the Depression, the Spanish Civil War, pogroms, the Holocaust. The children were only allowed to watch one hour of TV per day, unless the show was of cultural importance. That meant *The Grapes of Wrath* and World War II documentaries. When Emma's Jem in *Sister Crazy* is allowed to stay up late to watch a movie, she predicts that there will be Nazis in it.[44] Although Richler used his children sparingly in his writing, one signal "Jewish" incident in *Joshua Then and Now* seems to have had a biographical basis: when the children laugh at a film of Hitler dancing his victory jig after the fall of Paris. Angry, Richler ordered them to shut up and watch. In another incident, one of the boys, possibly Noah, brought home a Messerschmitt model to build, and Richler ordered him to take it back. Tears. To soften the blow, Richler recited his sacred stories: about Bethune, about the 1937 Fascist air raid on Guernica when Messerschmitts slaughtered a thousand Republicans. Although Noah doesn't recall the incident himself, he put it this way: "We were never going to get a Volkswagen ... That was not going to happen."[45] Unwittingly, Jacob put his finger on the new religion.

Hearing Richler sing the Spanish Republican song "*Los Quatro Generales*" in the bath, Jacob asked if this was one of his Hebrew songs. Indeed, for Richler, it was comparable to his other bath song, "*Adon 'olam*" ("Master of the Universe").[46]

≶

Approaching puberty and bar mitzvah age, Daniel and Noah were turning into *people*, with their own tastes and attitudes. One of the most strongly held of those tastes worried Richler: James Bond. The boys didn't just want to watch 007; they wanted to *be* him, unaware that according to Ian Fleming they, Jews, were the villains of the stories.[47] Out of Richler's anxieties grew one of his most ambitious and most problematical essays, a 1968 *Commentary* piece called "James Bond Unmasked," which not only tied literary criticism to racial issues, fiction to biography, and Richler's own youth to that of his sons, but also, as Richler's original title, "England's Golem"[48] indicated, provided one of the many routes into *St. Urbain's Horseman*.

Richler's own youth: as a boy he had read and enjoyed John Buchan's World War I spy-adventure novel, *The Thirty-Nine Steps* (1915). Now, however, he (rather simplistically) considered that its description of "a little white-faced Jew ... with an eye like a rattle-snake" had poisoned his attitude towards his own grandfather Shmarya.[49] The youth of his sons: Fleming gave Bond villains stereotypical Jewish traits, so Fleming, like Buchan, was anti-Semitic. Because Buchan eventually became Canada's governor general (as Lord Tweedsmuir) and founded the Governor General's Awards, Richler later declared that had Buchan still been governor general, Richler would have refused his GG.[50] Scudder, Buchan's character, delineates a Jewish plot for world control very much like the one described in the *Protocols of the Learned Elders of Zion*, that transparently fabricated conspiracy theory used by Russian autocrats to oppose all democratization and to incite violence against the Jews. Admiring readers of the *Protocols* have been many, from Henry Ford to Nasser to the Ayatollah Khomeini, to, in recent times, Malaysian Prime Minister Mahathir Mohamad, who received great applause at a summit of Islamic leaders after he recited material that originally came from the *Protocols*.[51]

Yet it was a mistake to count the flag-waving Buchan among these admirers.[52] A respondent to the Bond essay, Rabbi Noah Gamze, defined anti-Semitism as expressions of hostility or agitation against Jews, not as a racial dislike. By such a definition, Buchan wasn't anti-Semitic.[53] Buchan had supported a Jewish homeland, even turning up on a Nazi hit-list because he was believed to be too pro-Jewish, though it is possible that his Zionism may have originated in the wish to keep the Jews out of Canada.[54] More importantly, Richler's critics also cautioned against taking the characters' pronouncements as the author's pronouncements. Late in *The Thirty-Nine Steps*, Buchan's protagonist, Richard Hannay, calls Scudder's story of a Jewish conspiracy "eyewash" and "an odd bias."[55] Indeed, anyone with blinders and a pair of scissors could have gone to *Richler's* three most recent novels and easily have cobbled together an anti-Semite.

Fleming's xenophobia, however, Richler placed convincingly in the mid-1950s context of a diminishing England, bereft of its colonies and enduring the revolt of its own lower classes. Briefly Richler even envisioned writing a nonfiction satire on England, *Reflections on the Anti-Jews: Ten Years on an Offshore Island*, in which he would force Fleming to eat his own tail. Why did the British always act as if *they* were Chosen People? Obviously, just as the eccentric British Israelites preached, the British were descended from the Jewish "lost" (i.e., "dumb, inefficient") tribes. Many things suddenly made sense: British hostility towards the new pharaoh, Nasser; Britain's Masada-like island mentality; the horror of marrying out of one's class; the assimilationists' eagerness to enter the Common Market with its "Restricted Clientele"; the Colonial Office's uncanny similarity to the Elders of Zion; the Jewy greed of press baron Lord Roy Thompson, who said "The copy is the stuff you put between the ads."[56]

Editors weren't eager for a one-joke book and *Reflections on the Anti-Jews* never came to fruition, but "James Bond Unmasked" Richler considered his best essay,[57] and Weintraub joked that his friend was trying to ingratiate himself with Shaar Hashomayim, Montreal's upper-crust congregation.[58] Richler's daughter Emma shrewdly observed her father's attitude towards anti-Semitism, and in *Sister Crazy*, Jem's father forbids Enid Blyton books, "due to prejudiced views expressed in dodgy writing."[59] The key: dodgy writing. One respondent to the Bond essay sensed Richler's vulnerability on precisely this issue, asking why Richler didn't include Graham Greene among the anti-Semitic thriller writers.[60] The answer wasn't difficult to guess: in Richler's view, Greene had talent. Nevertheless, for all its shortcomings, the essay was indeed Richler's best. He was right about Fleming's anti-Semitism, and he had arrived at questions that would haunt *St. Urbain's Horseman*, questions central to liberalism. How far do we tolerate politically incorrect expressions of hate? At what point do we call them crimes?

≶

All this – his anxiety about the children, his apprehensive backward glance at anti-Semitism and the Holocaust, his need to articulate some kind of a post-religious faith – boiled into *St. Urbain's Horseman*. Bond was England's golem, but the golem was a Jewish invention, a Jewish avenger often imagined fighting against the pogroms of Eastern Europe. Richler's grandfather, Rabbi Rosenberg, had written golem stories; why couldn't Richler invent a contemporary golem to address the Holocaust, the creation of Israel, the Six Day War? He had tried out golems in *Cocksure* with the Hollywood Goyboys and Hyman Rosen, but only farcically.

In *St. Urbain's Horseman*, instead of trying to write at a constant fever pitch, as he had in his last two novels, Richler wanted to return to the naturalism of *The Apprenticeship of Duddy Kravitz*, not an easy proposition. The new novel took five years of work, on and off, including several depressing months during which he wrote perhaps two pages.[61] In 1969 he collected some of his stories and a few genial sketches as *The Street*, giving him another payday while he continued to slave on the novel. His publishers were much more eager for a novel than for repackaged short stories. Tony Godwin praised *The Street*, but asked why Richler hadn't welded the fragments into a single storyline. "I can loan you 'Plots' if you're stuck," Godwin offered, "283 entirely different plots GUARANTEED."[62]

Richler in fact had an excellent plot awaiting his attention. He hoped to write a screenplay, *The Survivor*, based on Ken Lindenberg, one of the seven thousand Jews whom Danish citizens had smuggled into Sweden during the Nazi occupation of Denmark.[63] Richler bought an option on Lindenberg's story and planned to go to Sweden to meet him.[64] It's unfortunate that Richler never wrote *The Survivor*, because the extant seven-page outline that survives is compelling, though it's not clear how much of the story is Lindenberg's and how much is Richler's. The escaping Lindenberg is thrown together with an Aryan deserter from the German army, Kurtz, who realizes that, once they arrive in Denmark, he won't be able to expect mercy from Lindenberg or the Danes. He therefore begs Lindenberg to teach him how to be a Jew. Lindenberg catechizes him, but sardonically, mixing vicious stereotypes among the received truths and creating, as Richler puts it, "his very own golem." Eventually they fight for the single set of Lindenberg identity papers, Kurtz winning, but getting a strange welcome at a synagogue when he unwittingly curses where he should be praising. Wrapped around the essential story is another, contemporary plot, in which a mysterious man dogs the elderly Kurtz/Lindenberg.[65] In Richler's hands, it could have made a compelling movie, but *St. Urbain's Horseman* intervened.

Not until September 1969 did *St. Urbain's Horseman* begin to really flow.[66] After returning to London from his reverse sabbatical, Richler finished the novel in ten months.[67] Twenty years later, Saul Bellow got himself into hot water by asking, "Who is the Tolstoy of the Zulus? The Proust of the Papuans?" and disappointed Richler by apologizing for that "zinger."[68] Yet in the 1960s, the same question could have been asked of Montreal's Jews or of Canadians, and it would be Richler, more than anyone else, who would begin to attempt novels of sufficient scope to answer that question. For *St. Urbain's Horseman*, he sutured much of his autobiography onto a suspenseful and non-autobiographical rape trial. Co-accused are the culpable Harry Stein, and the not-so-culpable Jake Hersch, who reflects on his rise from St. Urbain Street to prominence as a film director and contrasts his own compromised life with the mostly imagined and therefore exciting life of his older cousin Joey Hersch. To Jake, Richler assigned everyday life, while to Joey – Jake's golem, the Horseman – Richler assigned the more fantastic historical encounters. Finally, in Jake, a character with whom readers could sympathize! Richler and his friends acknowledged that in most ways he was Jake.[69] As with any *apologia pro vita sua*, there was the danger of self-indulgence, and Kerry McSweeney criticized Richler for letting Jake off too easy.[70] But a huge majority of readers agreed with Brian Moore, who wrote to his friend, "You're there man, you're there."[71]

Richler's friends immediately recognized real people behind the novel's characters. Novelist John Fowles said, "I loved a number of scenes for strictly non-literary reasons. I can think of a couple of faces I'd like to be watching when they come round to reading them too."[72] Joyce Weiner had great fun identifying London's literati and film crowd.[73] But these were minor games. The important *roman à clef* was constellated directly around Richler: the wife, the best friend, the father, the mother. Nancy, Jake's wife, Richler made a saint. Among the thirty to forty thousand words that he cut were Jake's exaggerated concerns about Nancy's fidelity and his troubles with his previous wife, Carol.[74] Richler's editor, Tony Godwin, noticed that there was a great deal of idealization in the depiction of Jake's marriage.[75] Partly this was Richler's inability to imagine Florence out of control, even given a rape trial, and partly it was, as Richler admitted, "a congenital weakness" in creating women.[76] The early novels had paid scant attention to women, and there's little evidence that Richler's perception of love was much more sophisticated than the rather limited perceptions of his early main characters. Women were often the innocent (Sally in *A Choice of Enemies* and Yvette in *The Apprenticeship of Duddy Kravitz*) or unfortunate casualties (Miriam in *Son of a Smaller Hero*) of the far more important male characters. Their character styles were chosen as much for their symbolic Anglo-Saxon or Canadian or Québécois qualities as for anything else. In *Cocksure*, Joyce – robust, liberal, and utterly unlikable – was even more of a symbol and even less human than the earlier, less powerful women.

As Richler began work again on *St. Urbain's Horseman*, Margaret Atwood published her first novel, *The Edible Woman*. The differences between Atwood and Richler recapitulate the differences between much female and male writing. Richler's use of gender remained conventional, and his female characters often unconvincing, while Atwood soon showed herself capable of writing believable male characters. There would be nothing in Richler's oeuvre to match the inventiveness of *Oryx and Crake*, yet who could make

an *evaluative* choice between two *Künstlerromane* as great as *Cat's Eye* and
St. Urbain's Horseman, each succeeding brilliantly on its own terms – the
one female, the other male. Atwood's criticism would regularly be directed
at traditional gender roles, yet that criticism would also mark her limit. In
Alias Grace, for example, Atwood's allegiances to "women's history" prevent her from submitting Grace to a full moral analysis. Atwood went more
astutely into whatever controlled the subject's social existence; Richler more
astutely into race and polity. Atwood would demand justice first of all between individuals; Richler would demand it in the law, the state, and (despite his atheism) before God. With *St. Urbain's Horseman* women took the
place that they would hold, for better and worse, in Richler's later corpus:
as moral ground. His women began to imitate Florence's role as homemaker,
the centre of the family. With that, the progress of love and of the male protagonist would be measured in how well he could fulfill his responsibilities
to his family, responsibilities defined by his wife.

The best friend, Ted Kotcheff, Richler transformed into the writer Luke
Scott in *St. Urbain's Horseman*: Richler the famous writer became Jake Hersh
the famous director; Kotcheff the famous director (but with a BA in English
Literature) became Scott the famous writer. In Kotcheff's case, the trans-
position was merely structural, since Scott retained very little of Kotcheff's
character or background. Richler jettisoned Kotcheff's poor Hungarian ancestry in favour of WASP and OBE (Order of the British Empire) anoint-
ments, allowing more opportunity for Anglo/Jewish counterpoint. Jake's
parents Richler made much like his own. Through Jake's father Issy – "Isaac"
was Moe Richler's middle name – Mordecai resurrected Moe's love of kitsch
and his opposition to Richler's first marriage. Issy's dying became one of the
most intimate pieces of writing that Richler had attempted, an unsentimental yet moving tribute to Moe. No tribute in Issy's wife however. One could
hardly expect Lily to be flattered by the portrait of Mrs. Hersh, a controlling and nosy mother who comes to London to babysit her son's grandchildren.[77] The fact that he was living in Europe had made the traumatic aspects
of Lily's affair recede into the background. She was no longer a psychological force to be reckoned with, as she had been in *The Rotten People* and
Son of a Smaller Hero; she could instead be stereotyped as a nosy and in-
trusive Jewish mama. Mrs. Hersh was a fictional character, says Florence
Richler, but if Lily *wanted* to identify with her, why then …[78]

According to some accounts, the quarrel that would estrange Richler
and his mother for over twenty years originated in his portrait of Mrs.
Hersh,[79] but that's inaccurate. The final estrangement began later, dating
from Richler's behaviour towards Lily at the 1974 film premiere for *The Apprenticeship of Duddy Kravitz*.[80] Nevertheless, *St. Urbain's Horseman* did-
n't help, especially since one of Lily's babysitting trips had cost her some

embarrassment. She had told Avrum (who had an optometry practice in St. John's, Newfoundland) that she could no longer make long trips to babysit Avrum's children. Arriving in London on business, Avrum had decided to look up Mordecai and had been surprised when his mother answered the door, saying that Mordecai and Florence were in Canada.[81] Reading *St. Urbain's Horseman*, Lily received a rude jolt to her perception that she was the kindly grandmother come overseas to help out a grateful son.

Other Richler family members fared even worse in the novel. An uncle, Chaim Shimshon Hershcovich, as stern as Shmarya, had a son, Yidel, who was an easy-going fellow and wanted to fit in. Avrum and Mordecai would say, "Yidel, run around the block." And he did. Shimshon and Yidel are the originals for the novel's Uncle Abe and his son Irwin, the ice-cream-licking clown whom Abe holds out to Jake as a model of filial devotion.[82] For Richler, writing and vengeance were cousins: "one does, on the coarsest level, get even with the world for slights imaginary or real," he admitted.[83]

Where vengeance and idealization and defensiveness fall away is in the portrayal of Jake's co-defendant, Harry Stein, and in Jake's attraction to Harry's way of thinking. Harry is Richler's unregenerate male – always sexually aroused; intellectually subtle, especially when it comes to his social subordination and poverty; aggressive whenever he doesn't get what he thinks he deserves (and that's often); filled with contempt for the classes above him, yet less interested in equality than in power. Harry is for Jake (and was for Richler) an acceptable outlet for Jake's (and Richler's) misanthropic tendencies, particularly their fears as young men that they weren't getting enough of whatever was going around. What man could disavow Harry Stein completely?

For the first time, Richler did serious research for a novel. John Ponder, the Chief Crime Reporter for *Evening Standard*, arranged for him to sit among the visiting barristers in the privilege seats at the Old Bailey and absorb British courtroom procedure.[84] Richler also obtained a membership application and sample test paper for Mensa. Mensa eventually wrote (though not the delightful letter that appears in *St. Urbain's Horseman*![85]) and asked Richler to return the sample test, but he had written his own answers directly onto it. Most of the answers appear to be correct.[86] Jake can't complete the test, though Harry can. Even beyond intellectual capacity, the offensive Harry is treated with a good deal of sympathy, Richler's performance for the first time matching his stated intention of making a case for the loser.[87] Harry's wonderful trademark line – "For the purposes of census, taxation and pogroms ... I am a Jew" – Richler lifted from Greta Nimiroff, an English teacher at Sir George Williams who complained about one of his articles.[88] On the other hand, the scene in which Harry brings up Elizabeth Taylor's toe jam to mock the chiropodist to the stars came from Richler's own experience, imaginatively heightened. Richler had spoken to an "obscenely overpaid" star about a film on the Trotsky assassination while a chiropodist "reverently" snipped the star's nails.[89] There is a consistent ambivalence in Richler's scatology: he often delights in the spoor of the human animal, yet also reveals a disgust that people are so despicable as to produce toe jam. Although Richler didn't name the star, Richard Burton played Trotsky in *The Assassination of Trotsky* (1972).

What makes Harry compelling is also what makes him disturbing: his witty, politically incorrect expressions of hate. Jake's befriending of Harry is a self-imposed penance for his newfound wealth and social status,[90] a way of maintaining contact with his earlier poor self. More broadly, at the borders of liberal pluralism Richler opens the question of how much of Harry's nastiness should be tolerated. Richler himself had, as he put it, "a perverse taste for coarseness in others," and that taste – no doubt an asset for a novelist – kept him in touch with people who would be more quickly shunned by those not in search of raw material. Harry was based on a man named Benjamin Franklin Levene.[91] A Navy deserter, Levene had several bomb hoaxes to his credit, including threats against two embassies and a four-hour shutdown of busy Victoria train station, where he claimed to have placed radioactive material. Somehow he latched onto Richler's acquaintance, the prominent film director Silvio Narizzano. A Levene-Narizzano friendship ensued; then indecent assault, rape, and buggery charges, pressed against the two by a Swedish au pair girl.[92] Richler attended the July 1963 trial. As in the novel, the judge concluded that Levene was guilty and deserved seven years in jail, while Narizzano was more or less in the wrong place at the wrong time and deserved only a fine.[93] Levene, believing that journalist David Roxan's articles were responsible for his jail time, sent hundreds of harassing postcards to Roxan and to Roxan's neighbours, slandering him as "a consort of criminals, a pimp and a homosexual." Police eventually caught Levene at a post office in the act of mailing his cards.[94]

Richler, too, began to receive a great deal of "mail" that showcased a witty but very black sensibility: cards with stamps depicting Jesus, children's cards that said "Happy Birthday Grandad," "Sincere Sympathy" cards from "your Sweet Heart Harry Stein," issues of *Capital Gay* (a British Gay newspaper), and the fascist *New Frontier* ("Voice of the NEW National Front"). The mail came for years, and at a certain point Richler stopped showing it to Florence. Often the cards bore rather eccentric addresses:

Morty Richler:
"<u>Author</u>"
c/o Chief Rural Constable
    <u>Montreal</u>

Quebec, Canada

and to

Chez   de la
Madamercai Rubenstien-Richler
Sherbourn St West, Montrel
Montreal, Canada [*sic*][95]

and from "Harry Fitznorman Stein" to

Morticia Richler
Secatary
Labour Zionist Movement
c/o Goverment House, Ottawa [*sic*][96]

Intrepid Canada Post got the mail through, and then asked Richler to please give his correspondents his proper address. Not necessarily the soundest advice, since one letter read, "Silvio NARATZANO *your* Friend presumably is a Nausiating piece of Human shit apart from a vicious homosexul – who put one up that Swedes Arse-Hole and got poor Harry 7 years Jail Well let the stench Rise Canadian Filth that is wouldent you say remember the Walks on Hamstead Heath – late Eh rather late competing with the most competent flashers in Merry England, Haw Haw Haw what times we had in the 50s" [*sic*].[97] Levene, obsessed with his imprisonment, sent an "In Memoriam" card with "Harry Stein 1963–68" penned in: "Harry Stein Died at the infamous Hands of Jake et Freinds 1963 – Resurected 1968" [*sic*]. Most of Levene's wrath was reserved for Narrazano and Roxan, but Richler – whose breakthrough novel, *St. Urbain's Horseman*, had used Levene – didn't escape notice: "you created me, so live with Harry Stein ... Your bowles and bladder must have given way when *you realized* We Found out *And* read the Book??? Whos idea was it did you get a lot 'a laughs, And a lot More cash??? Whose *idea* was it to try and kick me in the *balls*; while I was undergoing the Treatment?? 7 years a crime your sidekick commited" [*sic*]. In 1993, twenty-two years after *St. Urbain's Horseman* was published, it suddenly struck Levene that he had been unfairly maligned in the novel. He sued Richler, as well as the publisher Weidenfeld & Nicolson for damages and requested an injunction against further publication of similar libel, but nothing ever came of the suit.[98]

≸

Although Richler worried aloud that he couldn't depict the British class system accurately enough in *St. Urbain's Horseman*,[99] he must have meant the subtle markers that distinguish people of similar classes, because he had no difficulty imagining either lower class rage (in Harry) or the guilt that accompanied upward mobility (in Jake). Harry treats expensive cars to the edge of his key, while Jake agonizes over just how hard he should make his gardener work. If Richler didn't have his own chiropodist, nevertheless he was no longer on a milkman's salary, and Jake's guilty socialist conscience had its origins in Richler's upward mobility. On Kingston Hill, Richler was once mistaken for a gardener.[100] In fact, he was already employing a live-in au pair and soon brought in a gardener for an hour or two a week.[101] The problem of conscience had been defined for him by Kotcheff, who, some years earlier, had hired a maid in Torremolinos, Spain, and had reported to Richler, "Old sentimentalist Ted gets upset as poor young thing scrubs tile floors on hands and knees, old leftist Ted rushes up to the terrace and allows deck chair to envelop him in bourgeois comfort."[102] Jake's moral solution to the guilt problem – firing the gardener – is hardly flattering in a novel so near to autobiography, but Richler wasn't so sentimental as to disdain the perks that his work had brought him.

What helped push Richler towards autobiographical self-revelation was Saul Bellow's *Herzog*. Bellow would go on to win the Nobel Prize for literature in 1976, but already in January of 1965, Richler called *Herzog* "a song of praise, chassidic in its intensity and delight in life" and pronounced Bellow the greatest living American novelist.[103] Bellow's early work Richler was very familiar with. Front-rank novelist, assimilated Jew, Bellow had as a child even lived in Richler's old stomping grounds, Montreal's Main, 1918-24. He was one of those Americans against whom Richler measured himself. And Bellow declared, "Jews stand apart from the prevailing nihilism of the west."[104] Richler, who as early as *The Acrobats* had sensed that negation was a cheap solution to the post-religious problems he had set for himself, didn't need to be reminded. Still, his satire had edged closer and closer toward negation – wittier and wittier negation, but negation nonetheless. *Herzog* gave Richler not a style, not material, but the inkling that he could do something larger in scope and more compassionate than the satires.

A year before he published *Herzog*, Bellow had explained his literary goals in *Encounter*, a magazine that Richler read.[105] A vast public life tended to dwarf the writer and to drive private life into hiding, maintained Bellow, but the novelist must resist this, must give a full expression of the humanist self – both public and private.[106] *Herzog* delivered on that promise. Whereas Richler had been retreating from autobiography in *The Incomparable Atuk* and *Cocksure*, Bellow had moved towards autobiography (fictionalized, of course), believing that in his own emotion, his own stupidity, his own knowledge he could find the larger tides of American life. Richler was impressed. He said that Bellow showed "how to be plain and awkward ... among the Filthy filthy too, and in his own weak person ... suffer dully all the wrongs of Man."[107] This was more than satire's political incorrectness. Unwittingly, Naim Kattan may have punctuated Richler's musings on this subject and nudged him towards *St. Urbain's Horseman*. In an assessment of Richler's career that surfaced among Richler's papers, Kattan acknowledged Richler's skill but said that Richler's fight against his own Jewishness had overpowered his comprehension of it. Yet the article's final sentence held out hope that Richler would follow Bellow and Malamud and not content himself with Herman Wouk. Strong criticism – Richler hated the middlebrow Wouk – and yet potentially high praise.[108]

Despite Kattan's warning and despite the lure of the movies, middlebrowdom was never the real danger for Richler. Farce was. Grasping that his future didn't lie there, Richler began melding his private life with public concerns about the Holocaust and the state of Israel. He claimed, now, that one of his reasons for writing was "the historical impulse ... to see things as they are."[109] Perhaps he also saw, again at Bellow's prodding, the fallacy in the belief that "writers can be both bureaucrats and bohemians, they can be executives but use pot, they can raise families but enjoy bohemian sexuality, they can observe the laws while in their hearts and in their social attitudes they may be as subversive as they please."[110] In "that rare creature," Bellow's "many-sided vulgarian,"[111] Richler saw that he didn't have to choose between adolescent humour and seriousness, that he could use his own vulgarity in an expansive way, not just to score cheap points against Toronto media types or British progressive schools, that he could revisit the recent Jewish history that had so mesmerized him as a younger and less-skilled writer.

Not just the Holocaust and Israel, but World War II in general mesmerized Richler. He had read Sir Harold Nicolson's diaries and therefore made Harry Stein one of the verminous children whose evacuation from London to the country Nicolson had described,[112] Richler giving a human face to the wards who had so disgusted their benefactors. But the Holocaust did loom large. It was, Richler said, what bound Malamud to Bellow.[113] "If you want to know the character of any nation, ask the Jews. They know the character of every nation" – Richler read this in Chaim Kaplan's diaries, smuggled out of the Warsaw ghetto.[114] When asked about Germans, Richler didn't equivocate: "I don't especially care for Germans, no." He admitted that such an attitude was wrong but felt that it was too soon for his generation to be reasonable.[115] Yet in *St. Urbain's Horseman*, his attitude had a subtlety and complexity that bespoke a greater objectivity than his expressed feelings. On one hand is the novelist's equivalent of Simon Wiesenthal's Jewish Historical Documentation Centre: stark reports of concentration camp conditions, which Jake gleans from the Frankfurt trial of Auschwitz guards, the longest jury trial in German legal history, December 1963–65.[116] These reports Richler lets speak for themselves; about these there is no moral ambiguity. On the other hand, the novelist's unique contribution: the tangle of guilt and innocence among Jake, Harry, and the other characters who apprehend that genocidal history twenty years later.

Richler's only license in the Levene-Narizzano case, according to David Roxan, was to make the Swedish au pair girl less innocent than she was and to turn her into a German.[117] Only? The change was of profound symbolic import. For Harry and Jake to lay Germany's crimes at the foot of the au pair girl, Ingrid Loebner, is at once absurd and fitting. She is too young even to have been in the *Hitler Jugend*. Her father, she claims, saved Jews. Yet her offhanded dismissal of the past and Jake's Jewishness – "it's a drag"[118] – makes her precisely the sort of Holocaust bystander who requires explanation. In *Writers on World War II*, Richler included a pointed excerpt from Martha Gellhorn's travels in postwar Germany: "No one is a Nazi. No one ever was. There may have been some Nazis in the next village, and as a matter of fact, that town about twenty kilometers away was a veritable hotbed of Nazidom … Oh, the Jews? Well, there weren't really many Jews in this neighborhood. Two maybe, maybe six. They were taken away. I hid a Jew for six weeks. I hid a Jew for eight weeks."[119] Of course, without the active help of millions of Germans – Paul Johnson cites the nearly 1 million in the S.S., the 1.2 million working for the railways, as well as the large number who received possessions expropriated from the Jews[120] – and without the acquiescence of further millions, the Holocaust couldn't have happened. Richler was, Brian Moore recognized, raising questions that Hannah Arendt had raised about the banality of evil in the context of Adolf Eichmann's trial.[121] Ingrid is *not* guilty of the Holocaust … but had she been alive and of age during the war, she would, like Eichmann, have acquiesced. At the same time, her lower-class bluntness and her willingness to bend over for Harry as long as she thinks he's a famous film director won't score many points in a courtroom cued to upper-class refinement. Had Richler made Ingrid absolutely innocent, he would have discounted the Holocaust: twenty years later, it turns out that the nasty and lascivious Jews are the oppressors; how ironic. Conversely, had Richler absolved Jake entirely and allowed a *guilty* Nazi into the novel, Richler would have courted melodrama: poor innocent Jews, the Holocaust just goes on and on. In fact, for a while Richler did experiment with a guilty Nazi. He originally had Jake going to Spain, there to encounter the ex-Nazi Colonel "Mueller."[122] Too many subplots, commented Tony Godwin,[123] so Richler deleted the Spanish material, saving it for his next novel, where he would wrestle with the question of how to depict a former Nazi without falling into melodrama.

As complex as Richler's invocation of the Holocaust was, the novel sat awkwardly beside his decisions about his children's secular education. Repeatedly, Jake fears that a pogrom will arise and break the bodies of his children. In Nazi Germany, the chief medical and racial officials decided that those with only one Jewish grandparent were Germans, while those with one Jewish parent were Jews. Wherever Jewish ancestry was half or more, the Jewish side "predominated," so to speak. In such a regime, Jake's whole family would have been doomed. But the German civil service, which wrote the laws, decided that only *religious* half-Jews and those married to Jews qualified as Jews.[124] In the Holocaust, therefore, Jake and Nancy (and Richler and Florence) would have perished, but (depending on whether the intent or the law were followed) Jake's fictional and Richler's real children might have survived, their secular education saving them. Whatever personal relief such knowledge might afford, it wouldn't necessarily be the best of news to a secularized writer who, his children in no danger, was under fire from religious quarters for presuming to speak on behalf of the Jews. If Jewishness could still be a liability long after one had ceased to believe in Judaism, nevertheless in marginal cases (i.e., of one Jewish parent) it was religion, not hooked noses, which stood out as the most "reliable" feature for anti-Semites to latch onto. The greater the intermarriage and the less direct one's identification with Judaism, the less the danger of anti-Semitism.

That Richler was profoundly aware of the contradictions in his approach (though perhaps not of the details of Nazi race law) can be seen in the Horseman, Joey Hersh. Very early in the novel, Jake remembers the line that stirred Richler in Babel's "Sunset": "When a Jew gets on a horse, he stops being a Jew."[125] But it hadn't been that simple for Babel, and it wouldn't be for Richler. Is Joey, who has clearly gotten on a horse in more ways than one, still a Jew when in 1948 he fires upon his fellow Jews to prevent them from surrendering Jerusalem to the Arabs? Is Jake, who idolizes Joey and goes down the road of assimilation? And what of Richler, who created Jake and Joey, and who loved Westerns?[126] About the time that *St. Urbain's Horseman* was published, Richler's daughter Emma decided that she, too, was going to be a writer,[127] and many years later, when she published her first novel, she had her character wonder, "Can you be a cowboy if you are Jewish? ... One day I'll ask my dad, who is Jewish and a cowboy, maybe the only one that ever lived."[128]

The character Joey, and Jake's quest to find not just a cousin but a Jewish Horseman, arose out of Rosenberg family stories and A.M. Klein's *The Second Scroll*. The mundane face of Joey came from a story that Lily probably told Richler. Although Rabbi Yudel Rosenberg had arrived in Canada with most of his children, his eldest son, Baruch (Benjamin), had remained in Russia and died in 1919, fighting for the Communists on the Ukrainian front. After Baruch's death, his widow Helen Rosenberg, who had held a post at the Commissariat of Foreign Trade but was nonetheless very poor, suddenly showed up in Canada with her daughter Suzanne (Shoshana) and an illegitimate son, Shurri. Lily, then sixteen, met them at Montreal's Windsor Station. The Rosenberg extended family immediately cared for, even loved, the immigrants who for a while lived in Rabbi Rosenberg's home. But when it became apparent that Helen would remain an irreligious and vocal communist, tensions rose, and she had a run-in with her father-in-law. Penniless, she left the house. She broke away from the Rosenbergs, and put up side-by-side portraits of Lenin and Trotsky in her new place. Suzanne attended Baron Byng, where she fell in love with Irving Layton.

By the early 1930s Helen decided that Canada didn't fully appreciate her, and she took her family back to the USSR. In the Stalinist paranoia after World War II, Suzanne and her husband were arrested and sent to a Siberian labour camp. Shurri, blacklisted from employment, took to alcohol and in the end threw himself under a train about 1950. For a time the Canadian Rosenbergs lost all contact with Suzanne. In the 1960s, however, Lily attended a lecture by Irving Layton and discovered that in Moscow he had met Suzanne, now a translator at the Moscow Library. When Lily told Richler the news, he paid for her trip to Moscow. Lily's visit paved the way for the families to be reunited and, eventually, for Suzanne Rosenberg and her daughter Victoria (now Zinde-Walsh) to defect to Canada.[129] Richler had a brief contact with Suzanne when she, evidently unaware of his unpatriotic views, invited him to speak at a London conference on US economic and cultural domination.[130]

It was the whole Helen Rosenberg situation, not so much the individual characters that Richler used. Of "Baruch's bunch"[131] (as Jake calls them in the novel), three – Hanna, Jenny, Arty – have parallels to Helen, Suzanne, and Shurri respectively. Onto the bones of the situation Richler mapped his own characters, so that Hanna and Arty bear only superficial resemblance to Helen and Shurri. Jenny seems slightly closer to Suzanne since both are intellectuals and both unwillingly take a large share in the raising of the younger brother. As for the fourth person in "Baruch's Bunch" – Joey Hersh – he was purely an invention, though he does carry the freight (atheism, communism) that came between Helen and the Canadian Rosenbergs.

Tales of the Soviet Rosenbergs' "disappearance" cued Richler on what to do with the Horseman, but he leaned on a literary source as well: *The Second Scroll*, the 1951 experimental novel by Montreal poet A.M. Klein. Twenty years later Richler would savagely lampoon Klein in *Solomon Gursky Was Here*; one reason, arguably, was Richler's resentment over how much he owed Klein for the metaphysical quest that drives *St. Urbain's Horse-man*.[132] Richler owed nothing stylistically. Where Klein was Joycean and formal – sometimes overformal and pompous – Richler was colloquial and direct. But structurally he owed a great deal. *The Second Scroll* is a spiritual detective story, Uncle Melech variously passing as a teacher of Jewish law, a Bolshevik, a Catholic, an Israeli social reformer. The narrator searches for his mysterious uncle but always arrives too late on the scene. A Messianic quest ultimately, though it was too late in the day to expect a particular human being to incarnate the spirit that Klein's narrator sought.[133] Richler saddled the skeptic Jake with a similar quest. The historical cusps at which Jake finds evidence of the Horseman – the Spanish Civil War, Mexico during Trotsky's day, Munich (the Nazi birthplace, ten minutes from Dachau), Israel in 1948, the Argentinean border near Paraguay (where Mengele hid) – all raise the same ghosts that Uncle Melech's destinations did: pogroms, Communism, Israeli independence.[134] Klein's suggestion, too, that the photograph of Uncle Melech may be a graven image, influenced *St. Urbain's Horseman*, where Jake senses that he has raised the Horseman as a golden calf in contravention of the Second Commandment.[135] In the novel's final draft, the mystery surrounding the Horseman became greater as Richler eliminated long sections involving Joey.[136] Of course, Joey's incarnations – baseball star, gangster, Zionist fighter, country and western singer – run much farther afield than Klein's Melech. More canny than Klein, Richler knew that a Messiah who could pass for Bugsy Siegel would make a bigger dent on the literary market than one who sounded like Gershom Scholem.

According to the Talmud, a ba'al shem (Master of the Name) could, if righteous enough, create a world,[137] so it was a small matter to create a servant from clay and give it life by breathing God's name (JHWH) into it. The golem supposedly created by the Maharal in Prague and "reported" by Richler's grandfather Rabbi Rosenberg defends the Jews against pogroms (even though Gershom Scholem complained that Rosenberg's golem was a "tendentious modern fiction," not a true legend).[138] Joey Hersh (JH),[139] unlike Rosenberg's golem, has sexual desire, but like Rosenberg's golem Joey defends the Jews and yet proves dangerous to his own people, as rogue golems sometimes do. The best evidence for Rosenberg's influence on Richler's golem is that some of Rosenberg's material gives the golem a name – Yosele Golem – the Yiddish diminutive of Joseph. If, as Bettina Knapp argues, the golem is a saviour archetype, then he performs that role unambiguously for Rosenberg but ambiguously for Richler: out of Jake's obsession with the Horseman, Jake is given Ruthy, who sends him Harry, who serves him Ingrid.[140]

In some ways, Rabbi Rosenberg's disguised fiction was remote from the boys of St. Urbain Street, whose golems, as Richler had argued, owed more to Superman and Captain Marvel.[141] When Jake is pushed to describe a golem, he reverts to his native language, calling the golem "a sort of Jewish Batman."[142] Despite his ironic views, Richler even as an adult was very keen on heroism, telling Daniel and Noah stories of sergeants who said "Follow me" and led their men into battle.[143] One of Richler's early models as a writer, Mike Gold, hoped as an adolescent for a Messiah who would give the Gentiles a good thrashing. That hope transformed itself into left-wing utopianism.[144] So, too, for Jake, vis-à-vis Joey. In the original story that gave birth to *St. Urbain's Horseman*, Jake is a writer (not a film director), and when editors and Orthodox Jews frown on his books he compensates by fantasizing that the Horseman will read his books with understanding and admiration.[145] *St. Urbain's Horseman*, of course, is far more complex. Harry, not so nice, embodies Horseman-like qualities and also Richler's own obsessions. At the same time, Jake can play Horseman to Harry – aiding a Jewish "victim," so to speak. Asked if the Horseman was good or bad, Richler refused to answer.[146]

It is the Horseman Joey Hersh who articulates Richler's spiritual response to the Holocaust. In *Writers on World War II*, Richler included some of the main lines of Jewish response. From the Orthodox, he reprinted the Hasidic tale of a Rabbi and his follower who were ordered by Nazis to jump across a pit of corpses. Impossibly, they reached the other side. How? "I was holding to my ancestral merit," the Rabbi reveals, "the coattails of my father, and my grandfather and my great-grandfather, of blessed memory." And the follower held onto the Rabbi.[147] Richler, who had long ago abandoned the coattails of his father and grandfathers, was of course conscious that such fables willfully forgot the gassed millions who also grabbed ancestral coattails but whose leaps fell short all the same. Since Richler could have easily chosen a Hasidic tale of martyrdom,[148] which in the present secular climate would have reflected better on the Orthodox, his choice of a miracle tale was a way of discrediting the Orthodox response. Why is the Lord God One? asks Joey in *St. Urbain's Horseman*, then supplies the answer himself: if One God has such a tapeworm inside him as to chew up six million Jews, then Two … "Two we couldn't afford." Rabbi Irwin Meltzer's reply – "do not question the Almighty, or He might call you up for an answer"[149] – is an utterly inadequate counter. Jews such as Chaim Bermant who leaned towards Orthodoxy suggested that Richler habitually let stock figures speak for Orthodoxy and that Richler had a more convincing notion of what it was to be a liberal than what it was to be a Jew.[150]

The pressure of Joey's question was in keeping with Richler's sensibility: no God watched over these events. A secular position, ultimately, but not completely outside the currents of Judaic thought. The positive audience reaction to *St Urbain's Horseman* suggests that a great many American Jews saw in Joey and Jake their own struggle to comprehend the place of God in

the Holocaust. Joey's question could be interpreted as less determinedly secular than it really was, as initiating a debate with God rather than denying
Him completely. Unlike Richler, the majority of non-Orthodox American
Jews believed in God. Like Richler, however, most of them didn't believe
that God *did* anything.[151] Jews who wanted to maintain faith after the Holocaust often spoke, sometimes ambiguously, of God's hiddenness in human
affairs.[152] In *Writers on World War II*, Richler also reprinted Primo Levi and
Elie Wiesel. Wiesel, in particular, was the source for Joey's religious revolt,
although Wiesel articulated the problem in a less blasphemous fashion than
Joey did. Watching a boy die on the gallows in *Night*, Wiesel hears a man
ask "Where is God now?" and then hears the answer from within, "Here
He is – He is hanging here on this gallows."[153] This answer, like Joey's, can
be taken in two ways. First, in the way that Rabbi Yudel Rosenberg's *Zohar*
took it: "In all their affliction he was afflicted, and the angel of his presence
saved them ... He determined in advance to partake of their sufferings."[154]
Second, in the way that Rosenberg's existentialist grandson took it: God is
dead. Wiesel accuses God directly for the creation of Auschwitz and finds
himself alone "in a world without God and without man,"[155] though he
mutes this rebellion later on by continuing to pray to God.[156] From Wiesel's
memoir *Night* comes Joey's account of how in Auschwitz on Yom Kippur
some Orthodox Jews for the first time in their lives refused to fast.

Richler didn't go as far as Theodor Adorno, who said that after Auschwitz
poetry was barbarism, but he did agree with those – Wiesel, Richard Rubenstein, Emmanuel Levinas – who argued that after Auschwitz theodicy was
impossible, in other words that God's ways could no longer be justified to
men.[157] For a Reform scholar such as Rubenstein, the concept of a Chosen
People must be jettisoned, though the rituals of Judaism could still hold importance, not for their mythological, but for their psychological content.[158]
Richler was more thorough-going about the end of transcendence, an attitude which fit with his insistent focus on bodily life. Like Rubenstein, he
mocked the belief that Israel was a chosen nation, but though he took his
boys to Yom Kippur services without believing, he had no use for Rubenstein's attempt to continue rituals under a winking metaphoricism that did-
n't take Jewish belief literally.

In some Jewish accounts (including *The Second Scroll*) the state of Israel is a decisive, nearly theodic response to the Holocaust, potentially justifying God's "ways." By asserting their right to Palestine, Israelis had gone
a long way toward preventing any repetition of the Holocaust, so went the
argument. The idealized version of this was preached in Leon Uris's *Exodus*,
which became a 1961 epic film starring Paul Newman. A western, Arnold
Band called it, with the Arabs as Indians.[159] An appropriate frontier, one
might add, for a Jewish cowboy such as the Horseman, whom Richler places

in Old Jerusalem, where King Abdullah's Arab Legion had success against the Jews and where the fighting was hottest shortly after David Ben Gurion read out Israel's Scroll of Independence. Richler did feel the tug of the Zionist-theodic position, a world in which everything fit.[160] In the wake of the Six Day War, he cringed when Moshe Dayan and the Israelis were caricatured, particularly in the leftist press. One facile cartoon in the *New Statesman* showed an impoverished old Egyptian – with women, children, and a tent village huddled in the background – watching an Israeli bomber. "Who is a Jew?" the caption asked. Richler's response was impassioned, though equally facile, "Well now, if these *are* the alternatives, I'd rather we had the bombers and they made do with the sticks this time out."[161] The point was important. Richler would never forget the Enlightenment rigour that had made him suspicious in *Cocksure* of "his own kind," but after the horrors of the Holocaust and the threats of the Arab League, Israel must have the right to defend itself. At the same time, for him there was no way that *Eretz Yisrael* could compensate for the six million.

Writers of the Jewish Diaspora have turned the "pilgrimage to Israel" into an important literary device. Even Portnoy, whose demythologizing cry is "LET MY PETER GO," strikes out for Israel. The new kind of Jew that he finds there is dishearteningly pure, and as long as Portnoy remains in Israel he can't get an erection. Richler loved *Portnoy's Complaint*[162] and agreed with Roth that, as necessary as Israel was, it didn't solve all Jewish problems. For a while already, Richler had been leaving Theodor Herzl's Zionism for a counter-current represented by Ahad Ha'am. Around the time of his 1962 visit to Israel, Richler had read Hans Kohn's introduction to a new English edition of Ha'am[163] and was intrigued by Kohn's evocative phrase for the Israelis: a "new type of Jew." Ha'am had opposed military solutions to the Jewish problem and had declared that to restore the old national boundaries of Israel was to confuse messianic hope with politics.[164] It wouldn't be hard, then, for "new" Jews to commit atrocities in the name of God and nation; it wouldn't be hard for them to forget the *Palestinian* Diaspora; and it wouldn't be hard for other Jews who saw this to become disillusioned. In the face of anti-Semitism, Joey asked, "what are you going to do about it?"[165] and Richler had a great deal of sympathy for the national self-assertion that answered such a question aggressively. At the same time, Richler distrusted the nationalist rhetoric that issued from Israel. Whether Richler actually heard "We're a new kind of Jew here" in Israel as he claims,[166] or whether he just borrowed Kohn's phrase, he sensed that it resonated uneasily with Babel's "When a Jew gets on a horse, he stops being a Jew." Already in *The Acrobats*, Richler had shown skepticism by having Barney point proudly at Israel as if Israel somehow made up for his personal failings.[167] Using his experiences from the 1962 trip for *St. Urbain's Horseman*, Rich-

ler has Jake – Jacob, son of Isaac – consider and ultimately reject the hope
that the new name and state, Israel, was a final reply to the Holocaust. Neither Jake nor Richler was prepared to concede that Diaspora Jews had to
choose between *Eretz Yisrael* or assimilation.[168] And if Joey joined the Irgun-
Stern Gang massacre of 250 Arab civilians at Deir Yassin (a massacre praised
by Menachem Begin and cited by Lehi ideologue Dr. Yisrael Eldad as necessary to the survival of Israel),[169] Jake/Richler's conscience wasn't quite so
fogged by nationalism. Against Vladimir Jabotinsky, the Revisionist Zionist leader, who declared, "We Jews, thank God, have nothing to do with the
East," Richler implies a troubled kinship: like American Jews, Palestinian
Arabs have loyalties outside their country.[170] Richler's complex, moral attempt to address the state of Israel moved him far beyond the temporizing
games of *Cocksure* into a broader, humane vision. *St. Urbain's Horseman*
was Richler's way of saying what Hannah Arendt had said, "I do not 'love'
the Jews, nor do I 'believe' in them; I merely belong to them."[171]

If the Horseman, God, and Israel provided no full answers to Jake,
what did? At first Richler hedged. His editor Tony Godwin wasn't satisfied.
Doesn't matter what conclusion or philosophy you come to, Godwin prodded him, but you must come to a conclusion.[172] Richler therefore articulated, with great skill, his species of humanism. He wouldn't grant that the
religious logic embedded in the Ten Commandments explained either the
Holocaust or Jake's troubles – these were not, Jake insists, events whereby
God was "visiting the iniquity of the fathers upon the children unto the
third and fourth generation."[173] Having Jake call himself "Aaron" signi-
fies, in an immediate sense, Jake's idolatry of the "Horseman," the golden
calf that Jake necessarily builds in imagination when a divine being and a
divinely authored set of commandments no longer seem available. If Jake
is Richler's imaginative autobiography, then Richler was outlining the role
of the novelist in the Jewish tradition: against the definitive Mosaic epic of
the Israeli past (a stance too closely identified with Shmarya Richler anyway) stands "Aaron" the novelist, forced, in the absence of the divine word,
to build a golden calf that in the end can't be worshipped; yet the
novelist/Aaron knows, in a way that the lawgiver Moses would never admit,
that he has built an idol.

The golden calf: possibly a false and harmful image of the divine ... but
not as harmful as advertised. Jake's discovery that the Horseman's hidden
gun is only an actor's gun comes as a great relief, the gangster receding. No
doubt it helped that Saul Bellow's Herzog instead of firing his father's gun
had hollered about justice. Metaphorical violence is not the same as the real
thing, and Jake's decision that the Horseman is not dead but "presumed
dead" ensures that the golden calf isn't overthrown completely. In admitting that his image of the Horseman is in some ways illusory, Jake stands

intellectually able to separate the actual violence of Harry from the Horseman's storied violence. A separation of great significance if he is to love
Nancy and his children, and if he is to ensure that his own obsessions don't
destroy his family. Yet in refusing to let the Horseman be overthrown completely, Richler maintains a kind of faith, clearly a humanist faith. Jake to
some degree incarnates the Horseman, accepting moral responsibility for the
creation of his own gods, and, therefore (the Horseman being a fiction after
all), for his own actions.

Faced with the question that issues from Joey even after his death, "What
are you going to do about it?" Richler can no longer merely laugh in the
style of *Cocksure*, and Jake can no longer offer the adolescent's version of
the Horseman but can only bow to human mortality: "He wept, that's what
… He wept for his father, his penis curling out of his underwear like a spent
worm."[174] In part this was Richler's recognition of what the age of forty
meant, the birthday that haunted him even into his 60s: "I don't believe in
Consciousness I, or Consciousness II, or Consciousness III," he told an interviewer. "That belongs to *Vogue* magazine, like McLuhan. Forget it, it's
yesterday's newspaper. Really. We're all going to die, and most things haven't
changed."[175]

This was territory far removed from *The Incomparable Atuk* and *Cocksure*, but it's not as if Richler suddenly converted to an empathetic correctness. Among his papers are a letter from the Mouth and Foot Painting Artists
of London, soliciting his business, an article on "The Young Artist Who
Broke the Sight Barrier,"[176] and a letter from a young Melfort Saskatchewan
woman who had had a piece rejected by Toronto's *Star Weekly* and wanted
Richler to tell her why. She said that she had recently survived a series of
strokes that, compounding her other physical disabilities, had decimated her
vocabulary and spelling. Still, she said, "my only hope of getting back into
life … is through my writing, and if I can't sell what I have writen, I might
just as well take a over-doze of something or other right away" [*sic*]. She
also had a political beef that explained why the *Star Weekly* was so reluctant to publish her: "I, like most western poeples, feel that our western views
and opinions are not given coverage by the so called 'National magazines
from the east'" [*sic*].[177] Richler delighted in the arrival of such mail[178] and
turned these bits of special pleading – publish me because you feel sorry for
me – into satire of the most unsentimental sort against the emotionally manipulative way that the wife of Jake's lawyer sells handicapped art, and
against the blind, crippled boy who believes that he is employable. Still, when
a well-dressed woman thrust a letter upon Richler and others outside of
Macy's, he used the material in a less expected way. The woman wanted
help in recovering "five (5) million dollars" of her father's money from Hersz
Cukier, Hersz Sztern, Jankiel Totelbaum of New York. She alleged that the

three were trying to kill her with super sonic waves and had installed radar to track her every step.[179] Instead of taking this in the direction of satire, Richler converted it into the scene in which Jake, on the train to New York, meets a similarly afflicted old man. Jake laughs, but only until he sees the concentration-camp tattoo on the old man's arm.[180]

≶

Intellectually and emotionally, *St. Urbain's Horseman* was by far Richler's most ambitious book up to this point, and he decided that it must have an appropriately symbolic publication date: his fortieth birthday, 27 January 1971.[181] Jack McClelland was dismayed. "It's a very sick and depressing plan," he groused, and instead suggested October 1970, for the Christmas market.[182] In the end, publication had to wait until late spring of 1971, as Richler worked through the editorial process, but his initial plan reveals just how important the novel was to him. There could be no going back. No more acerbic little satires. Each novel hereafter would be a big compendium of his life and times and human folly, and capped by a refusal to despair.

Critical reaction to *St. Urbain's Horseman* was celebratory,[183] so much so that Robert Fulford reported that the novel was fast becoming a touchstone. Knowing that Richler cared as little for Hugh MacLennan's fiction as for "Canadian identity," Fulford added, "I'm afraid that inadvertently you have written the *Two Solitudes* of the 1970s. How does that feel?"[184] Eventually *St. Urbain's Horseman* won Richler another Governor General's Award, and, more important to him, was celebrated in Britain as well, receiving a nomination for the most distinguished prize of all, the £5,000 Booker. Among the other nominees were Richler's old friend Doris Lessing (*Briefing for a Descent into Hell*) and V.S. Naipaul (*In a Free State*), who still published with André Deutsch. Richler must have liked his chances at winning: of the five judges, Philip Toynbee had been highly critical of *Cocksure*, but John Gross (the chair) and Saul Bellow were Jewish, and the novelist John Fowles had made no secret of his love for *St. Urbain's Horseman* when the question had arisen about whether it should appear on the *Times* review list. "It deserves that goddam list – or better, the list needs it," he wrote Richler, and vowed to make sure that the book was eligible for the Booker.[185] Brian Moore certainly liked Richler's chances: "Never mind you'll get the booker prize. Booker is a jew, Bellow is a jew, Mascler is a jew, Richler is a jew … it'll WELL KNOWN! FIXED!" [sic][186] In fact it was Naipaul who won. Richler and Lessing didn't attend the ceremony, and the most excited person in the audience was probably André Deutsch, who called it a wonderful night for his firm.[187]

PART III

Home Again
1972–2001

"It's good to be home again, and firing at close range."
– Richler, "Playing the Circuit," 1972

18

Return to Avonlea

As RICHLER WAS REVISING *St. Urbain's Horseman* in London, all hell broke loose in Montreal. The Front de Libération du Québec kidnapped British Trade Commissioner James Cross on 5 October 1970, and, a few days later, Québec Minister of Labour Pierre Laporte. Prime Minister Trudeau invoked the War Measures Act and deployed 7,500 Canadian troops, many of them in Montreal, but on 17 October Laporte's strangled body was discovered in the trunk of a car. *Life Magazine* dispatched Richler to the scene, although he couldn't get out of London until early November.[1] In the meantime, he deputized Bill Weintraub to photograph Montreal under siege. Weintraub initially demurred, for the city was too edgy.[2] Arriving in Montreal, Richler interviewed Trudeau and Parti Québécois leader René Lévesque, both of whom he admired.[3] That admiration didn't change during the October Crisis, especially when Lévesque called the FLQ "those bums" and repudiated their violence,[4] yet in subsequent years Richler lost his admiration for Lévesque when he heard that during the bombings of the mid-1960s Lévesque had called the FLQ cells courageous,[5] emboldening them for their 1970 crimes.

"The October Crisis frightened the hell out of me," Richler admitted, what with the danger of Montreal turning into Belfast,[6] yet even these appalling events Richler saw through the satirist's eyes. He noticed that many VIPs were insulted that in a city on war footing, they didn't rate high enough to have soldiers posted outside their doors.[7] Writing his article for *Life*, Richler couldn't help fiddling with the words of David Molson, president of the Montreal Canadiens. In interview, Molson had tried to emphasize English-French bridge-building by telling Richler that his family had always been close to the Québécois and that his children were learning French from a Québécois couple that served in the Molson home. Richler fine-tuned the quotation, so that Molson now said, "Of all the old WASP families in this province, ours has always been closest to the natives ... We have a French maid in the house and the children take advantage of it. They're learning."[8] Molson sent an outraged letter to Richler but otherwise ignored the fabrications.[9]

After finishing *St. Urbain's Horseman*, Richler was pleased and confident. "No critic has anything to tell me," he trumpeted. "I'm a great believer in everyone ultimately finding their own level. The fevers and telegrams die down and guys who've had too much are found out two books later."[10] But soon he felt adrift, nothing to do.[11] There was plenty of bad news to cast a pall over the novel's success. Early in 1971, Nathan Cohen died of a heart attack, and his widow, Gloria, felt unable to cope. Robert Weaver urged Florence to send her a short note from time to time.[12] Within a month, Neil Compton, Richler's former mentor and recent host at Sir George, fractured his skull in a gruesome accident and ended up in a wheelchair. At the same time, Richler received word that his former wife, Cathy Boudreau, had been diagnosed with breast cancer in Taipei,[13] where, calling herself by the Buddhist name "Jhānānda," she had joined the Yung Ming Temple. Although she spoke much about "peace of mind," she was lonely and anxious, hoping to avoid an operation. Her sister Tess and the Canadian affiliate of Cathy's Buddhist group sent her money; it appears that Richler did as well.[14] She eventually returned to Toronto.[15]

Less troubling, but irritating nonetheless, Richler ran into hassles about a possible musical version of *Stick Your Neck Out* (the US title for *The Incomparable Atuk*). Producers Steven Sharmat and Sandy Baron had taken an option and signed up composer Jerry Schwartz and Bob Hilliard, lyricist for "Bongo Bongo I don't want to leave the Congo ... Bingle, bangle, bungle, I'm so happy in the jungle." The writers abandoned Richler's satire and aimed solely at over-the-top farce. As of September 1966, the book for the musical was steaming ahead in its fifth rewrite. Rehearsals by July, Sharmat promised in 1967, but over the next few years, he couldn't raise the necessary money. He strung Richler along, and when Richler raised questions, placated him by tossing around the names of stars. Phil Silvers might well take the part of Buck Twentyman, Ringo Starr as Atuk. Richler's agent, Monica McCall, repeated the mantra that she thought would mollify him, "the end result might horrify both of us, but *might just* make a lot of money."[16]

By the summer 1971, Richler was fed up. His friend Norman Jewison said he'd like to film *The Incomparable Atuk*, but couldn't let a musical steal his thunder. Since Sharmat had failed to hire a director and lead actor by 15 June 1971, Richler notified Sharmat that the option was void. Sharmat responded that it would be laughably easy to sign a star and a director, thus (in his mind at least) validating the option, but that, if Richler was agreeable, Sharmat preferred to wait until he had cast Twentyman. McCall, unwilling to burn any bridge, injected her own note of urgency, "If you have immediate profitable picture deal no more to be said, but unless we proceed now theatre will be lost season will be lost actor will be lost …"[17] This after five years of Sharmat's foot-dragging.

Richler wasn't agreeable.[18] But Baron and Sharmat had the last laugh: no film of *Stick Your Neck Out* was made, even though Richler kept hounding Jewison. A few years later – on *Jesus Christ Superstar* stationary – Jewison praised a screenplay of *The Incomparable Atuk* by Don Harron,[19] author of the excruciating Charlie Farquarson books but a friend of Jewison. Florence's ex-husband, Stanley Mann, who got to see Harron's screenplay, countered with bad news to a Richler who was handcuffed by contracts and by his own hopes: "I think it leaves something to be desired – like a total rewrite."[20] Jewison had long before this transferred most of his hopes to *St. Urbain's Horseman*, but United Artists refused to buy that property for him, and in January 1972 Richler was forced to watch not one, but two film deals for *St. Urbain's Horseman* fail – one with Jewison, and one with Alan Pakula.[21] All the while Jewison kept extending *The Incomparable Atuk*'s option. By 1975 he still hadn't solved the problems with the script,[22] and in the end he never did do a film with Richler.

≶

Already in spring 1971, Richler was negotiating a permanent return to St. Urbain. "No more teaching!" had been the epitaph on his stint at Sir George Williams University a few years back. However, when President A. Davidson Dunton of Carleton University came a-courting, Richler not only asked for a two-year contract but also floated the possibility of a more lasting relationship.[23] In Canada he hoped to move among a more eclectic group of people than his English circle of literary, TV, and film types.[24] Also, as much as he liked to think of himself as a cosmopolitan writer, Richler couldn't avoid the bald fact that two-thirds of *St. Urbain's Horseman* sales were in Canada, Booker nomination or not.[25] And the most important consideration: he recognized that he owed the *artistic* success of *St. Urbain's Horseman* to his re-immersion in Montreal. Perhaps with Doris Lessing in mind, he spoke of his terror at seeing other expatriates (from South Africa and elsewhere) write novels set in mythical countries or in the past or in the future.[26] In Britain he still didn't really know what people thought about when they came home from work in the evening.[27] Later Noah would interpret the move as simply a wish to return home,[28] but Noah never had to deal with the many letters that arrived after every magazine article, letters saying that Richler really didn't know what was going on in Canada. Gone from the country for so long, he feared that the lives of Canadians were becoming increasingly shuttered to him, as his critics loved to insinuate. Several years earlier he had proposed an irreverent anthology about Canada as seen by non-Canadians, from Voltaire to Steve Canyon. This never became a book,[29] and instead Richler smuggled a few of the putdowns into *St. Urbain's Horseman*. But to write well about *tiefste Provinz*, he'd have to live there again.

Richler's transformation into provincial had been underway in recent years, and it was painful. In the late 1960s, both because of his Canadian journalism and because he was editing a book of recent Canadian writing, Richler had been forced to come to terms with the heart of the heart of the country. Scoffing at the colonial scrawniness of the Grey Cup and the Saskatchewan Riderette cheerleaders, he had also made what he thought was a reasonable enough complaint about Ottawa's Lansdowne Park, namely that he was forced to urinate with two hundred other men at a trough, rather than having his own private urinal.[30] A fan wrote in to laugh at that bit of snobbery: "Mordecai's indignation at taking part in mass urination really tickled me! It takes a 'mincer' like Mordecai to be a 'wincer' at the trough!"[31] When the article "Bedlam in Bytown" was reprinted, years later in *Home Sweet Home*, Richler's complaint about the trough had discreetly vanished.[32]

Canadians had already embraced the prodigal son: whenever he visited Canada, they wanted to hear him speak. During March 1970 Richler went west, testing the "campus vaudeville circuit."[33] In Brandon, Manitoba – which Canadians more sensitive than Richler recognize as the spiritual centre of the nation – Richler spoke of his western trip as a foreign experience.[34] Hosts beat their breasts. The great writer was stranded on an alien shore, they admitted. Would he please excuse the provincialism of the questions directed at him?[35] At times Richler displayed the requested equanimity: "No Flower Child could have acted with greater gentleness," one observer raved about him after a particularly inept question at the University of Calgary.[36] At other times, fortified by alcohol, Richler was less Aquarian. When Jack McClelland hauled him up through Northern Ontario up to Elliot Lake and deposited him in front of a convention of high-school teachers,[37] Richler declined to give his speech and offered instead to entertain questions – *but no stupid ones*. According to one report, silence descended; eventually the chairwoman got up, thanked Richler, and the meeting was over.[38] That account must be exaggerated, because the organizer afterwards wrote Richler, thanking him for his "informality" and "honesty," a welcome change from speakers who merely parroted the texts of others.[39]

On his western trip, Richler drove through Rockies with the Canadian publisher Mel Hurtig. The weather was foul, and Richler's mood likewise, in Hurtig's opinion. The upshot was a less than enthusiastic article, "Endure, Endure."[40] Despite Hurtig's subsequent grousing, the piece was witty, though not all of it survived when Richler trimmed it for *Home Sweet Home*: in the original version, Richler claimed to be seeking "the Shining Mountains of legend" but discovered only the Banff Springs Hotel, where "old and de-serving Protestants, blessed by God and the Investor's Growth Fund" make their last stand." Predictably for an urbane satirist he found the Rockies more conducive to silence than to literature.[41] Although it's possible to find unintended self-criticism in Richler's approach – witness him a few years older and wiser complaining that, when he spoke to Americans about the Arctic, their eyes glazed over with boredom – the truth is that his putdowns were often clever and apt: "Tomorrow Winnipeg will bedazzle like Byzan-tium. Meanwhile, it's cold. We're getting older."[42]

Hurtig, who helped found the Committee for an Independent Canada (CIC) to keep Canada economically and culturally independent from the US, wasn't laughing. He tried to awaken Richler's hardened conscience to the sins of anti-nationalism. By now Richler was grateful to be a Canadian,[43] and he often did champion Canada, most notably at this time through a Penguin anthology, *Canadian Writing Today*.[44] Nevertheless, although other of his friends, such as Jack McClelland and Peter Newman, joined the CIC, Rich-ler was prepared to sail against the wind. The CIC's agitation resulted in the establishment of FIRA (the Foreign Investment Review Agency) and the CRTC (the Canadian Radio-television and Telecommunications Commission), which established Canadian content rules for broadcasters,[45] but Richler, not ready to support cultural protectionism, argued contra. The loss of Ryerson Press to US interests couldn't bring tears to his eyes, though he did concede that the loss of McClelland & Stewart might.[46] Hurtig told Richler that his jour-nalism on Canada was full of old thinking. How could Richler, living in London, know Canada sufficiently well to write about it? Visits weren't enough.[47] What greatly irked Hurtig, as it had Layton and other national-ists, was that outside of Canada Richler had become a *de facto* spokesper-son for the country. On behalf of the Canadian tribe, Hurtig made the same complaints that the Jews had made and that the Québécois soon would: Richler is a turncoat; he doesn't understand us. For a while Richler contin-ued to speak favourably about the publishing that Hurtig was doing in Ed-monton,[48] but not for long.

≋

All of Richler's Canadian business in the late 1960s and the early 1970s led up to his decision to accept Carleton University's offer and return home. On 21 June 1972 Richler packed everyone up (except Daniel, who stayed be-hind to finish his O-levels), and, since there were no longer any Canadian passenger ships, boarded the Soviet ship *Alexander Pushkin*, "a sort of float-ing communist pleasure palace," as Richler called it.[49] Richler, Florence, four children, a maid, a car, and much baggage set sail.[50] Leaving home – that was how the children saw it.[51] Jack McClelland tried to ease the passage by telling Richler's Soviet hosts, "It could add a great deal to the pleasure and ease of his trip if he is recognized as the international celebrity which he in fact is."[52]

Richler's decision to return wasn't made lightly, especially because Florence was so opposed.[53] She had put Canada behind long before she met Richler, and when they married she had no reason to expect a return,[54] given his ties to Armchair Theatre and to the Rank Organization. Florence felt that she and Richler had created a home and a wonderful family; to move would break the continuity. "I didn't want it to end," she says, "It was a childlike response to a moment of happiness."[55] Making matters worse, Florence had been down with hepatitis, which involved a fourteen-week incubation period during which she was depressed without knowing why.[56] This had passed by the time of the voyage, but Florence was allowed no alcohol for a year, and on board the decadent *Alexander Pushkin* she was forced to make do with Georgian mineral water that smelled like Javex.[57]

Beside Florence's opposition, there was the children's education to consider. Richler worried that a Canadian education might stunt them, and that aggressive Canadian youngsters might trample upon his gentle and considerate children.[58] For insurance he rented out the house on Kinston Hill instead of selling it.[59] London, Richler thought, was "the most agreeable and civilized city in the West," but ultimately the decision couldn't be based on his wife's or his children's or even his own wishes: the danger of drying up as a writer loomed too large.[60] And why not flee a country where his children said "graws," while he insisted on saying "grass"?[61] He thought that they were embarrassed of his accent. Not so, they said.[62]

When he lived in England, patriotic Canadians demanded why Canada wasn't good enough for him; when he returned to St. Urbain, they asked, gleefully, why things weren't working out for him in London.[63] Although he was slated to teach at Carleton, there could be no question of living in Ottawa, which Richler spoke of as "six blocks of sophistication and a cowtown."[64] It didn't help his estimation of Ottawa that at the National Press Club everybody knew who broadcaster Larry Zolf was but nobody knew Richler. Zolf said, "Here he is in the nation's capital, and no one knows him. The f——rs don't read" [sic].[65] Often he was bored in Ottawa and therefore spent a lot of time at the home of Bernard and Sylvia Ostry.[66]

If the return to Canada were to be of any literary value, Richler would have to live in Montreal.[67] No objections from Carleton's President Dunton: the job would cost Richler no more than two days a week in Ottawa.[68] Searching for a place to live in Montreal, Richler and Florence noticed a *For Sale* sign in front of his old house. On TV, a couple of years later, he'd be coy, pointing off-camera and saying, "that, as far as I can make out, was my house,"[69] but of course he knew exactly which piece of St. Urbain he

had left behind. Florence leapt at the idea of his coming full circle and buying the old home. She could fix the place up. Can't do it, Richler informed
her. Already mulling over the wisecracks and cartoons that would surely
appear, he said, "You have to realize that publicly, I could never live that
down."[70] He ascended, rather, to Westmount, at 218 Edgehill, all the while
protesting that Westmount wasn't a dream come true for him.[71]

As for teaching, Richler proposed a course on the Principles of Book
Reviewing. Dunton quickly nixed that.[72] Unbecoming to a university, though
Dunton never said so to his prize catch. Instead, Richler would function as
"mythical resource person" for Rob McDougall's senior seminar, contributing to such topics as literacy, the reality principle, criticism, literature and
film, and the teaching of literature.[73] But no heavy lifting, according to James
Downey. Richler sat in on the classes and contributed when he felt like it,
which turned out to be "occasionally."[74] He returned to the seminar the following year, along with Jack Healy, who specialized in the influence of abo-
riginal life on Australian consciousness.[75] In addition, Richler taught the
unteachable as he had at Sir George: Creative Writing. He warned Dunton
that the students would be assigned a stringent reading list and would be
expected to work hard, "Not so much middle-class group therapy, then, as
a discipline."[76] It must have warmed Dunton's heart to hear the nature of
university education dismissed so confidently by his fledgling appointee.

Twelve students, and Richler interviewed them all before admission to
his class.[77] What Richler thought of his students is well known. He loved to
tell of the "aspiring Hemingway" who, put on the spot to name the most
recent novel he had read, stalled for time by throwing a question back at
Richler, "Fiction or nonfiction?"[78] Richler's lack of astonishment at the literary gifts of his students was justified, according to John Aylen, one of their
number.[79] During the pre-admission interview, Richler felt obliged to inform
students that their hopes for the upcoming class were ill-founded. Writing
required talent, and nobody could teach that. At most he could thrash them
each time they relied upon clichés or overused themes.

The classes themselves, according to one student, Henry Makow, weren't
much more promising: Richler was not a teacher. Uneasy in a role that he
felt was futile, and uneasy in public generally, Richler couldn't relax at the
front of the room. During the first class he gave a long spiel, correct enough
in its main point, that in order to write well the students must be well read.
He repeated this verbatim in the second class when two new students appeared. *Encounter, Tamarack Review, North American Review*, and Cyril
Connolly: this was his recommended reading. Who among the students read
these? More than anything the spiel was a lament about the poor reading
habits of would-be writers – and don't imagine that oral gifts can compensate! Good writers, he cautioned, were often lousy at small talk. He meant

himself, of course. During class breaks he had little to say, and though he
offered to meet with students individually, they, having undergone his initial grilling, were predictably reluctant. He did little to encourage their in-
trusions. The one topic that might have broken the ice – his own writing –
he immediately declared out of bounds, since even with his close friends he
had never been eager to discuss his work. By the end of class he was always
ready to flee to the waiting taxi.[80]

There was nothing wrong with the literary advice that Richler gave: show,
don't tell; never use five words where one will do; don't moralize; forget the
trick O'Henry ending. But on a scale of 1 "Poorly Written" to 5 "Outstanding" Richler would in short order check off 3 "Good" for Margaret Laurence's *The Diviners*. What could a critic so demanding say to undergraduates?
Not so much group therapy as discipline – and there was plenty of discipline.
Richler, not one to butter up students, told one girl that her story was "good
material, clumsily handled, eight drafts away from a story but promising."[81]
That, though the students possibly didn't recognize it at first blush, was about
as warm and fuzzy as Richler was likely to get. He was judging them by professional standards, he continually reminded them. After a very self-confident student read a story aloud, the class gave mixed comments. Then Richler
weighed in, "It's pretentious horseshit ... You show unlicensed confidence."
"I don't think I deserve this abuse," the student protested. "We disagree,"
Richler replied.[82] At the end of the semester, he took them all to the Faculty
Club for drinks and outlined each student's strengths (limited) and weaknesses (grave). None of your work deserves publication, but I've enjoyed
working with you, he said. Silence. This time Richler kept his vow not to
teach again. Had the money been right, he might have swallowed his vow,
but his proposal for an extension proved too rich for Carleton.[83]

≋

To celebrate the end of his final year at Carleton, Richler gave the 1973
Plaunt Lectures. His thesis was a shocker: just because art was Canadian
that didn't mean it was necessarily good! As he had many times before, he
declared that cultural nationalism was out of line. So was Mel Hurtig's Committee for an Independent Canada. Hurtig fired off an angry letter to Richler, lumping him with bankers, manufacturers, Chambers of Commerce, and
"Neanderthal politicians." To cure Richler of his old thinking, Hurtig sent
one of his own speeches and advised Richler to study it carefully. No hard
feelings: Hurtig invited himself to a Montreal Expos baseball game, Richler's treat.[84] But another trip together and continued disagreement on a topic
so dear to Hurtig ended the friendship.[85]

Even Richler's friend Jack McClelland couldn't keep quiet this time
round. McClelland agreed that cultural nationalism could get out of hand

if the CIC's propositions resulted in books being published not on merit but because they were Canadian. However, Richler had granted that Canada must have control over its own economy,[86] and McClelland warned that the man on the street was incapable of distinguishing between cultural nationalism and economic nationalism. In particular, McClelland objected to Richler's statements that the Canada Council shouldn't support Canadian publishers, but should only support Canadian authors – wherever they chose to publish. Why, countered McClelland, should Canadians subsidize Oxford or Doubleday? All in all, McClelland said, Richler's comments were harmful: "There are enough U.S. lovers in Canada without you appearing to support them. Oh well, to hell with it, I guess I am past caring." A year later, McClelland outlined his predictions to Richler: without government subsidy, book publishing in Canada would be controlled by foreigners, who, since they operated purely on a profit basis, would strangle Canadian cultural growth.[87] What McClelland knew well was the precarious financial state of his own company, a company dedicated to the publication of serious Canadian fiction. What he perhaps didn't know was that Richler had also received a letter from a CIC nationalist, Peter Thompson, demanding to know why Richler and other writers used a foreign publisher. Not likely to cheer a writer who had struggled for twenty years to make his novels pay and whose money had come from the screen, not from literature. Richler tore Thompson's letter in half.[88]

Nevertheless, McClelland wasn't about to make an enemy of a good friend and one of his best authors. Instead of arguing over nationalism, McClelland secured an invitation for Richler to join the Book-of-the-Month Club in August of 1973 as its first Canadian advisor.[89] BOMC was both loved and hated by publishers: loved, because it really did sell books; hated because BOMC could set its own terms, usually a 15–20 percent discount that the publisher had to swallow. Sometimes, enraging nationalists such as Mel Hurtig, BOMC imported US editions of *Canadian* books to Canada. In the early 1970s, BOMC had 125,000 members; by the mid-1980s 2 million. BOMC judges in the late 1970s were choosing fifteen main selections and two hundred alternates from among four thousand books submitted by publishers. It was a determinedly middlebrow operation, in theory bringing highbrow books to the middle class, but usually unwilling to do so because such books wouldn't sell. Also in theory, judges were supposed to choose what they liked, not what they thought members might like, but any judge with half a brain knew enough to choose both.[90]

Richler's job was to recommend, from among the more than one hundred books that he read every year, Canadian alternatives to the BOMC's largely US list.[91] In earlier years he had mocked the BOMC,[92] though he had also recognized that there was something far too fashionable about the intellectual's disdain for popular literature.[93] Brian Moore thought that his joining BOMC was a mistake,[94] and, if Kerry McSweeney was to be believed, Richler now spent his days "writing fatuous paeans to tawdry bestsellers."[95] Nothing could be further from the truth. Richler carefully distinguished between books of merit and books that he thought were bad but that had mass appeal. Asked about Hugh MacLennan's *Rivers of Canada*, Richler said it was "Polonius on a canoe." The book, with its glossy photos, would sell, Richler knew, so he recommended it on the basis of popularity, not on quality. He declined to write a blurb himself, and suggested that BOMC instead approach Pierre Berton.[96] The trouble for critics such as McSweeney was that Richler didn't kneel before the books that academics held sacred but showed regard for popular nonfiction. He recommended *Drifting Home*, Pierre Berton's trip with his family down the Yukon in a rubber raft,[97] but panned Rudy Wiebe's *The Temptations of Big Bear*, winner of the Governor General's Award, saying, "This is an over-earnest, largely unreadable novel ... It is a self-conscious, windy attempt at Canadian myth-making. Creative writing 102. Dense, pseudo-Faulknerian, and bloody slow. No." Sometimes Richler discerned a better novel inside an existing, too-baggy novel (W.O. Mitchell's *The Vanishing Point*); sometimes he simply trashed books, as in the case of *Riverrun*. "Frightfully embarrassing," Richler called this elegy for the massacred Beothuk of Newfoundland. In an attempt to get inside the native mind, Peter Such had written, "Waves rock blue glow purple as the sky spills pink," and Richler felt that as a reviewer, he must add, "Reader headaches black as novel bleeds prose purple."[98] *The Temptations of Big Bear* and *Riverrun* are far from bad novels, but it's hard to remember that after Richler's only-too-accurate thrusts.

Like *The Temptations of Big Bear*, many of the novels that Richler panned were published by the man who got him the BOMC job, but Richler wasn't about to play toady to McClelland. McClelland wrote to the author of *Cocksure*, recommending the talented but eccentric Sylvia Fraser's *The Candy Factory* as "a fine piece of writing and an extraordinary novel."[99] Richler called it "bad ... uncommonly nasty ... pretentious, soft-core porn ... I can't remember when I liked a novel less." Richler panned books by literary writers (Adele Wiseman, Morley Callaghan) and bestselling authors (Charles Templeton, Don Harron) alike. *Charlie Farquarson's Jogfree of Canada* by Harron, the follow-up to a book that sold nearly 100,000 copies in hardcover, appalled Richler. It wasn't just the book itself, but what such sales figures said about the intelligence of Canadian readers. What about the Royal Canadian Air Farce's Dave Broadfoot? Definitely no. More reluctantly, he refused books by Roch Carrier (*They Won't Demolish Me*), Ray Smith (*Lord Nelson Tavern*), and Matt Cohen (*The Disinherited*).[100] These writers had talent, he admitted, but the books under consideration were flawed.

Put a satirist on book reviews … if the senior editors at BOMC wanted entertaining reports, they clearly knew what they were doing when they hired Richler. Praising a book, Richler wrote pedestrianly, but damning a book he was brilliant. Of Hugh Garner: "He has all the faults of Nelson Algren, but none of the virtues, which is to say, he doesn't write very well." Then the final clout, which, at least until the final three words, one might nearly mistake as praise: "At his most engaging, [Garner] has the charm of a neglected club fighter." One bit of stylistic shorthand that wormed its way into Richler's prose, always just before a beheading, was the phrase, "to come clean." Up against his acquaintance Margaret Laurence's *The Diviners*, Richler began, "To come clean, it's not my sort of book." "A fattie," he called it, "A menopausal fattie," and added, "There's a lot of embarrassing stuff about the writer's occupational hazards, and it is also flawed by commonplaces about women's lib. Mrs. Lawrence [sic] is far from being an original writer. But she is concerned, honest, warm, and a good storyteller." He was mistaken about Laurence's literary merit and originality, and indeed, in his verdict, he recognized that not everyone would agree with him. He urged that *The Diviners* be a Full Selection, since it would sell and would be enjoyed, "especially by women readers."[101]

Although he selected (and praised) Joanna Glass's *Recollections of a Mountain Summer*, Dennis Patrick Sears's *The Lark in the Clear Air*, and Dennis Lee's delightful book of children's poems, *Alligator Pie*, mostly Richler turned away from fiction.[102] The student who had dropped out of Sir George Williams in 1950 and the writer who was always nosing around for background material turned to nonfiction. If the BOMC course in CanLit didn't take, the courses in Canadian politics, history, and geography did. Books about Canadian fascism in the 1930s, MacKenzie King, Lester Pearson, newspaper baron Lord Thompson, Canada's north, and World War II: all these Richler loved. Reviewing Grant MacEwen's *Sitting Bull: The Years in Canada*, Richler made it clear that he was quite happy to put up with mediocre writing, so long as the material, as in MacEwen's case, was rich.[103] If the *Alexander Pushkin* had brought him to this country physically, one might argue that these books let him enter Canada spiritually.

≶

In *St. Urbain's Horseman*, Richler had had Duddy Kravitz plan a class reunion because Duddy was a millionaire and thought it might be nice for his ex-classmates to choke on this piece of information.[104] Close to St. Urbain for good now, Richler's thoughts returned to his alma mater. Beginning in 1972 and continuing until Baron Byng was closed in 1980, he contributed to a bursary for needy students.[105] When he was invited to speak at the twenty-fifth anniversary of his Byng graduation in 1973, he leapt at the opportunity.

But the honour curdled. Since Florence had no great urge to consort with the Duddies of her husband's childhood, Richler invited his former school-mate, Trizec chairman Jack Rabinovitch. Rabinovitch said no, but Richler prevailed upon Rabinovitch's wife, Doris Giller, to lobby her husband. Rabinovitch called Richler up and said, "I will go only on one condition – that you don't create havoc." A couple of minutes into Richler's speech, however, someone began to heckle, and Richler heckled back. "Mordecai had guts," Rabinovitch says, "He saw shit, he said shit … and he didn't take guff from anybody." Richler walked off the stage in a huff and sat down. "Do you want to go?" Rabinovitch asked. "No – *fucking – way*," said Richler. "They are not kicking me out of my school." They stayed for another hour, until honour was appeased, and then left.[106]

19

Hollywood North

BY 1974 RICHLER MADE IT BACK into the movies, this time on his own terms – or very nearly so. Two films with Richler screenplays were released that year: a TV film that the CBC almost suppressed because it contained a joke that reflected poorly on Israel, and a feature film that not only netted Richler an Oscar nomination for Best Adapted Screenplay but also became a landmark of Canadian cinema.

The TV film nearly killed by the censor was *The Bells of Hell*. CBC producers Fletcher Markle and George Jonas, mindful of Richler's commercial success, invited him to do something for *The Play's the Thing*. Richler had done films for the CBC in the 1950s and 1960s, but he was no longer a struggling writer, and he worried that on a limited CBC budget the result might now embarrass him. For their part, the higher-ups at the CBC were no longer quite so enamoured of Richler either. They had promised to put money into a feature film of *The Apprenticeship of Duddy Kravitz*, and then reneged. Markle and Thom Benson had initially offered $100,000 for a percentage and first TV rights eighteen months after the premiere, but when push came to shove, silence. Prodded, CBC Vice President (and later *Ideas* man) Lister Sinclair maintained that he didn't want to burden an incoming director with such a large investment. Richler claimed to be profoundly insulted: "Hell, we shouldn't have to plead ... People who have seen the early rushes feel that this may be a breakthrough film for Canada." His "usual" fee for a feature screenplay was $50,000, but, he told the CBC, he had done the adaptation of his own novel for a bargain $5,000. Possibly the CBC didn't see quite as much altruism in this as he did.¹

Still, Richler wrote the TV film *The Bells of Hell*. It was about the middle-aged Manny Berger, whose world seems designed to frustrate him sexually and to remind him at every turn of death's approach. Manny hears, but doesn't find a great deal of comfort in,

O, death where is thy sting-a-ling-a-ling
O, grave thy victory?
The bells of hell go ting-a-ling-a-ling
For you, but not for me.[2]

When Manny spends a half-hour at a massage parlour and emerges with a modicum of compensation for death, a CBC crew, filming a documentary, captures his guilty face for the national evening news. *The Bells of Hell* wasn't Richler's best work, coming from the scraps of a new novel that Richler was trying to write about a man obsessed with the Bronfmans. The novel wouldn't blossom until the late 1980s, and *The Bells of Hell*, even in its funny moments, was little more than a retread of *Cocksure*, this time with the much-abused Mortimer transformed into the Jewish Manny. Nevertheless, *Bells* was an original film, and at first Richler fantasized that Kotcheff or Jewison might be enticed to direct. But they were busy, so the job went in-house to Jonas, who had expected to do it all along. The rough cut neither elated nor depressed Richler: faithful to his intent, yet the acting wooden and the low budget apparent.[3] Hollywood North it was not.

Rabbi Jordan Pearlson, Chairman of the National Religious Advisory Committee at the CBC, caught a preview of *The Bells of Hell* and was immediately appalled, not by wooden acting, but by what he took to be a whiff of the old, anti-Semitic blood libels that led Russians to slaughter so many Jews in the late nineteenth and early twentieth centuries. In the film Dr. Schwartz blackmails Manny into making charitable donations to the United Jewish Appeal, reminding Manny that another patient, "Siggie Frankel, may he rest in peace, didn't honor his community obligations."[4] Didn't Schwartz's implied threat bear strikingly resemblance to tales of Jews slaughtering innocent gentile babies and draining their blood to use in matzohs? And to Stalin's false accusation in 1953 that nine *doctors*, six of them Jews, had plotted to poison him?[5] Pearlson's analogies were absurd, but anxieties about the recent Yom Kippur War (in October Egypt and Syria, backed by troops from other Arab nations, had launched a nearly successful surprise attack on Israel during the high holy days) weighed on the CBC. They weighed on Richler too, since his son Noah had become quite anxious, desperately wanting to believe that the fight between Arabs and Jews was twenty-five years old, not hundreds.[6]

In his account of Richler's sins, Pearlson took care not to mention the specifics of *The Bells of Hell*, where the matter of the UJA contribution arises as Dr. Schwartz coats his gloved finger with Vaseline for Manny's rectal examination.

Schwartz: You see, Manny, this year they gave me your United Jewish
    Appeal card.

Manny: What?

Schwartz: You know why? Because last year you cheap momzer, you
only came in for twenty-five hundred dollars. (pause) Aren't you
ashamed?[7]

Schwartz reminds Manny of the "burden" that the Israeli state now carries
in having to develop the new territories (particularly the West Bank) and
recommends a donation of $5,000. When Manny has the gall to venture
that perhaps Israel has bitten off more than it can chew, Schwartz's index
finger, possibly not as gentle as it could be, makes a lunge at Manny. Clearly
the territory of farce, but with Richler's serious political purpose of mocking the tendency of Zionists to find traitors wherever Jews didn't blindly
cheer Israeli military conquests.

Despite the weakness of Pearlson's accusations, Thom Benson, head of
CBC drama, wanted to maintain the broadcaster's virtuous reputation, and
he cancelled the film even though he had already dropped $40,000 on it.[8]
Luckily Richler was not without his own insiders. Robert Fulford, now at
the *Toronto Star* but with friends at the CBC, arranged a screening. He immediately broke the story and announced that the CBC had canned the best
TV drama of the 1970s.[9] In newspaper editorial offices and at the CBC's head
office pressure came from The Writers' Union of Canada[10] and from heavy-
weights such as Pierre Berton. Berton asked Vice-President Lister Sinclair,
"Must we forever be penalized by the out-dated morals of small prairie vil-
lages?"[11] Richler blamed the National Joint Community Relations Committee of the Canadian Jewish Congress and B'nai B'rith, but in fact these
organizations seem to have had no part in Pearlson's original complaint.[12]
At the same time Benson felt the sting of Richler's wit. Benson, granted Richler, was amiable but better suited to sell TVs than to make moral decisions
about what got shown on them. As for the venerable wellhead of Canadian
public life, the CBC, Richler offered a parable. In a dream, he had seen the
CBC burning, and all of its executives poised to leap from the building. But
a quandary: who ought to leap first? Each jumper might potentially offend
a different minority. Everything ended happily, Richler said. They all died.[13]

In the end the CBC felt vulnerable to the charges of self-censorship and
broadcast the film in late January. Richler, with encouragement from Jewison,[14] demanded that it be shown without any cuts.[15] Otherwise he wanted
the rights back so that he could sell it to the BBC, which, he was certain,
would only be too thrilled to have it. Nevertheless, the CBC cut the worst
of the profanity, attached a warning that some viewers might be offended,
and, while Golda Meir's new minority Labour Government in Israel argued
with Likud over who was a Jew and whether civil marriages should be allowed, *The Bells of Hell*, possibly anti-Israeli, debuted on Canadian TV.[16]
The airing proved anti-climactic. Viewing audience and critics were divided

about whether the show was good or not. Some mail did come in accusing the CBC of a history of anti-Semitism. Evidence: news commentary unfavourable to Israel, the cancellation of *Exodus* on the evening of the Yom Kippur War, and now *The Bells of Hell*. Answer me this: why was the talented Jew Sydney Newman *only* head of the National Film Board but not of the CBC?[17] In the end, the CBC took flak from all sides. Liberals had cried censorship; Zionists cried anti-Semitism; and advertisers, sensing that the property was too hot, drew back and gave the CBC the privilege of airing *The Bells of Hell* commercial-free.[18]

⧩

Richler's other, much more successful movie production had begun far earlier, though it wasn't released until after *The Bells of Hell*. When Richler returned to Canada in 1972, he was invited to write an *All in the Family*-style TV series. He seethed.[19] His country evidently wanted to reduce him to Archie Bunker with a Canadian accent. Richler was much more pleased when New York film-maker Alan Pakula bought an option on *St. Urbain's Horseman*,[20] but it would be Canadian producer, John Kemeny, who would bring a Richler novel to the screen.[21] Kemeny had a rather varied background, having worked on *Cash Advances for Prairie Grain* (1961), *Ladies and Gentlemen, Mr. Leonard Cohen* (1965), and the sex film *7 fois ... par jour* (1971; *Seven Times a Day*). Now he had his heart set on a prestige film that would also make money.[22] All those years ago in 1958, under the French sun, Ted Kotcheff had promised to film *The Apprenticeship of Duddy Kravitz*.[23] It had been a long haul. Kotcheff had filmed a small section of the novel (the Ste. Agathe portion) for CBC-TV in 1960, and in 1966 Kotcheff and Richler had begun to speak seriously about a feature film collaboration. Not until 1972 did the talk become concrete. During the interval, Kotcheff made a name for himself in Britain, particularly with *Edna, the Inebriate Woman* (1971) and a film about the dark side of Australian desert life, *Outback* (1971), even though the scenes of kangaroo slaughter weren't calculated for commercial profit. *The Apprenticeship of Duddy Kravitz* would make his name internationally, combining serious purpose with commercial success.

Kotcheff had the rights to Richler's novel and allowed Lionel Chetwynd – a neophyte writer, Cockney-born, Montreal-bred – to adapt it. The script got them in the door at the Canadian Film Development Corporation (CFDC) but wasn't good enough to actually fetch any CFDC money. Richler decided to do a new script; Chetwynd, however, refused to dissociate himself from the final product, even though Richler and the producers dangled an extra $10,000 in front of him. There were no real financial implications to a shared on-screen credit, yet prestige was at stake, so the case went to the Credit Arbitration Committee of the Writers Guild of America. The committee ruled that the credits should read "Screenplay by Mordecai Richler" and "Adaptation by Lionel Chetwynd."[24] Kotcheff obeyed – Richler's credit at the top of the frame in large letters, Chetwynd's, tiny, at the bottom. Richler, who in later years would mock Québec nationalists for measuring whether the English on signs was half the size of French (as required by law), was no stranger to the semiotics of public display. Subsequent events conspired to enrage him at even this small concession to Chetwynd.

Money wasn't easy to get, but Richler's name and Kotcheff's persistence helped. At Cannes in 1972, Michael Spencer (the head of the CFDC), Kemeny, Kotcheff and Richler worked out a deal.[25] All told, they would have to hire fifty speaking parts and five hundred extras.[26] The CFDC kicked in $300,000 of the $900,000 it took to shoot the film[27] – this for a film by a writer who had written a magazine piece highly critical of the Canadian film industry[28] and who had argued so passionately that nationalistic support for the arts was wrong-headed. "You pricks," Paramount Pictures President Frank Yablans complained, "if only you'd set this in Chicago we all could have made a fortune."[29] The money wasn't enough, and it fell to Montreal businessman Gerry Schneider to herd in the rest ... and then to find more when costs escalated.[30] Schneider had made his money in land development. He had had no interest in moviemaking but had gone to Baron Byng a year behind Richler, and although he had barely known Richler, when the opportunity came to immortalize the school and his former classmates, Schneider couldn't resist.[31] One of his colleagues maintained that Schneider wasn't in it for the money but that he was afraid to admit that. Schneider disagreed, stating, "Emotion is wonderful, but we don't invest on emotion." If he or Richler noticed the irony of a Montreal land developer making a movie about an immoral Montreal land developer, they never said so in public. Certainly Schneider wasn't the original Duddy. Exaggerating only slightly, Kotcheff revealed that thirty-six different men had claimed that honour.[32]

For his pains, Schneider got to appear in several scenes as an extra and was able to reward family members and business associates with movie immortality too.[33] But being in the movies wasn't as glorious as Schneider's rich friends had imagined. Roused out of bed at 7:00 A.M., they were squeezed into bathing suits and (since it was summer in the script but fall during the shooting) sent out to enjoy the chill, autumnal air. A shivering few were even plunged into a Laurentian lake. Some of the women, made up in 1940s bright red lipstick, tried to soften its effects with pastels, eye shadow, and eye-liner, much to the dismay of the make-up artists.[34]

Twenty-five-year-old Richard Dreyfuss at the start of his career – he had just come from *American Graffiti* – starred as Duddy. Some people wondered why Kotcheff avoided Canadian actors, but it was difficult to get quality Jewish actors in Canada.[35] Dreyfuss was perfect. He was Jewish, highly

talented but not widely known, could pass as a nineteen-year-old and yet
play poker with Kotcheff and Richler.[36] If Dreyfuss made his character a little too lovable,[37] he possessed Duddy's manic energy. As intended, Dreyfuss
stole the show – chattering, scratching his head, chewing his nails, moving,
moving. Not all of the actors were as successful. One astute viewer, Michael
Samuelson, complained that none of the actors acted like the people he knew
on St. Urbain Street, least of all Duddy's grandfather, played by Zvee Scooler,
a veteran of the Yiddish theatre. "They could get a better zeyda in a Cote
St. Luc production of Fiddler on the Roof," Samuelson groused, adding that
in the movie the same four Chryslers kept circling the block and that Kotcheff had used a 1973 model sewing machine.[38]

In the early part of the movie the abridgement is too tangible; in later
scenes, however, Kotcheff found a rhythm that didn't rely only on brief vignettes, and he even created affecting moments, winding down the roulette
wheel and Duddy into slow motion, as Duddy's bankruptcy wrenches him
out of his frenetic pace into something almost verging on introspection.
Kotcheff, in order to meet the two-hour limit set by his backers, unfortunately had to cut much of the bar mitzvah party, as well as scenes involving Cuckoo Kaplan, played brilliantly, according to all reports, by the old-time
Jewish comedian Mickey Eichen, who had been lured out of retirement.[39]
Richler originally made the movie's conclusion slightly darker than the book.
One CFDC reader applauded; another insisted that the book's ending was
better.[40] In the end, Richler and Kotcheff decided to trust the novel's ambiguity, restoring Duddy's sudden ego-uplifting realization that although he
had helped to cripple Virgil for life, on the bright side Duddy had also become enough of a k'nacker to get credit at Wilensky's lunch counter.

September to November, filming took place, eleven weeks in all. Trot-
ting along behind the film crew, Richler revisited his adolescent haunts, notably Wilensky's and Ste-Agathe. At Castle des Monts Hotel, now dilapidated,
where Richler had bussed and waited on tables as a teenager, the eighty-
three-year-old owner, Sam Stick, suddenly recalled (or convinced himself)
that he had once been like a father to Richler.[41] Kotcheff had the hotel re-
furbished and filmed Duddy's restaurant scenes there. In Montreal, Kotcheff shot the gravestone of Duddy's mother by taping over the surname on
an existing stone. But the tape was carelessly left on the stone, and when
the son of the deceased found out that his mother's memorial had been
treated with less than full respect, Kotcheff had to cut the shot, an important one, under threat of lawsuit. One rich Montrealer offered his mansion
to the film crew – until he discovered that it was Richler's novel being filmed.
Suddenly, the mansion was off bounds.[42] Getting a synagogue was just as
difficult for similar reasons. On the other hand, Moe Wilensky remembered
Moe Richler and his brothers coming to the lunch counter without money

on Saturdays, but paying their Sabbath bills dutifully every Monday. Although Wilensky praised the very religious Shmarya and the quiet and well-behaved brothers, he nevertheless consented to the black sheep Mordecai's movie, letting film crews cart away the new meat slicer and pull the store back into the 1940s; Wilensky's reward: a cameo.[43]

After the film's completion, there were those who urged that it open in New York. But Richler wanted Montreal, where his books sold and where he was somebody. The premiere at Montreal's Place des Arts was a black-tie, $50-a-plate affair, attended by Québec Premier Robert Bourassa, Montreal Mayor Jean Drapeau, Israeli Ambassador Dr. Theodor Meron, and Secretary of State Hugh Faulkner.[44] Kotcheff and even Richler rented tuxedos. The story has been repeated many times about how the two friends were stationed with their drinks in the foyer when liquor baron Sam Bronfman's wife Saidye – "the Dowager Queen herself," in Kotcheff's words – stepped over. "Well, Mordecai, you've come a long way from being a St. Urbain Street slum boy," she said. "Well Saidye," he returned, "You've come a long way from being a bootlegger's wife."[45] Florence told him afterwards that Saidye hadn't intended to put him in his place, but nevertheless the comment rubbed Richler the wrong way.[46]

Less well-known and without a smart punchline is another story, which apparently occurred that same evening. For a long time, relations between Richler and his mother, Lily, had been deteriorating. Richler could not in all conscience isolate his children from their grandmother, even if she weren't the sort of person he wanted them to associate with. From the distance of London, which allowed only relatively short visits every year or two, Lily could be endured … and then laughed about. On Richler's return to Canada, however, Lily proposed a more immediate haunting: she conceived the idea of moving in with him. He demurred. At some point, she wrote him a nasty letter, and he returned the favour, revealing what he had witnessed as a boy between her and Frankel.[47] After that, she no longer visited the Richler house. Intermittently, on Sunday evenings, however, Richler dropped the children off at her place on Stayner St. in Lower Westmount. Mesmerized by North American TV, the kids could watch their fill there. She'd ply them with food and Adams Wild Cherry chewing gum and cousins, who considered the Richler children, with their British accents, very strange. To the children, who rarely saw any members of their extended family, it was Lily who seemed slightly exotic.[48] Richler himself wouldn't set foot inside her house. In London, he had put up with her manipulative personality and unpredictable outbursts, but seeing her so often in Montreal, he could no longer abide her. Sometimes Lily was merely unintentionally funny. Once when Emma tried to move an armchair, Lily rushed forward and waved her arms, "Don't! You're in pubberty!" [sic][49] Mostly, however, Richler was dismayed by his mother and didn't want her to influence the children.[50] According to Noah, his father even tried to keep the filming of *Duddy* from her.[51] When she surprised him and showed up at the *Duddy* gala premiere, he gave her the snub – stuck her in a corner and ignored her.[52] After that, for the last twenty-three years of Lily's life, she and Richler would have nothing to do with one another, and she would say of say of her life, "It is so sad, you see I am very lonely."[53]

If *The Apprenticeship of Duddy Kravitz* wasn't the "breakthrough" film that Richler had assured the CBC it would be, that was only because there weren't a horde of Canadian films capable of following in *Duddy's* footsteps. Audiences loved the film, and it was nominated for the Best Screenplay Oscar. Of course, if Richler won, he'd have to smile and share the award with Lionel Chetwynd. Galling – time for Chetwynd to feel Richler's wrath. For *New York Magazine* Richler wrote an article claiming that he and the filmmakers had chosen – not naming any names – a certain screenwriter because they had no money to hire an established writer and that, when Richler rewrote the screenplay, he could only "salvage" seven pages of the first version. The Credit Arbitration Committee of the Writers Guild wrote Kemeny to express dismay that Richler seemed intent on subverting the arbitration and harming Chetwynd's reputation. The Guild insisted upon a retraction and a written promise that Richler would behave.[54] I can't control Richler's freedom of speech, Kemeny replied, and Richler, in his next salvo, wasn't quite as guarded as he had been in *New York Magazine*. Writing to *The Montreal Gazette*, Richler said that, true, Chetwynd had gotten an adaptation credit, "which is to say, he ripped out a good many scenes from my very own novel before I did, and by the convoluted reasoning of the screenwriters Guild they became his property ... Had his screenplay not been so sadly inadequate there would have been no need for me to step in and rewrite it." John Kemeny had refused to put money into the film with the Chetwynd script, but the real credit that no one could steal from Chetwynd, Richler conceded, was for taking scenes from the novel and typing them out neatly.[55]

Nevertheless, *The Apprenticeship of Duddy Kravitz* launched the leaden Chetwynd, who afterwards would refer back, without qualification, to his "Best Adapted Screenplay" Oscar nomination.[56] Chetwynd went on to a screenwriting career, and became, *rara avis*, a conservative activist in Hollywood. Among his many docudramas is a film about President George W. Bush on 9/11. "If some tinhorn terrorist wants me," cries Chetwynd's Bush, "tell him to come and get me! I'll be at home! Waiting for the bastard! ... We start with bin Laden. So let's build a coalition for that job." Then Bush prophesies the Iraq War, still a few years in the future, "Later, we can shape different coalitions for different tasks."[57]

As for Richler, *The Apprenticeship of Duddy Kravitz* made $2 million in Canada alone. At the Berlin Film Festival it won a Golden Bear, the top prize. Kemeny got his prestige film, but not much money because Paramount and Famous Players netted most of the profits.[58] Kemeny, Kotcheff, and Richler got their original salaries plus the right to turn another Richler novel into a movie.

Richler expected *The Apprenticeship of Duddy Kravitz* to resurrect the old charges of anti-Semitism, but the charges came from surprising places. Montreal Jews, if they had any misgivings, generally kept quiet, but one anonymous complaint did arrive: "Duddy Kravitz is a disgrace to all Jew [*sic*]. You who went to Baron Byng, belonged to Habonim, belong to that good Richler family, how could you? To show it *erev* Yom Kippur! May God punish you. Judas! May you rot in Hell!"[59] Some members of the American Jewish intelligentsia arrived at the same conclusion, even if they were able to phrase their misgivings in a more sophisticated way. At one special screening for opinion makers, the movie was applauded, a rarity.[60] At another screening, a couple of US journalists called the movie anti-Semitic, John Simon of *Esquire* magazine saying, "It will do very well in Saudi Arabia."[61] *The Apprenticeship of Duddy Kravitz* was slated to go to Cannes, but the chef of the Cannes Film Festival, Maurice Bessy, too, decided that the film was anti-Semitic. To guard against racism, the sensitive Bessy deleted a talented Jewish author and an excellent Jewish film from the program and replaced them with Michel Tremblay's *Il était une fois dans l'est*.[62]

20

Kiddie Author

IF THE SUCCESS OF *The Apprenticeship of Duddy Kravitz* movie was predictable – brilliant novel, good director, and reasonable budget – Richler's next success was not. How did it come about that the author of *Cocksure* suddenly revealed himself as a writer of children's books? His wife Florence said that she started the ball rolling with an offhand request. Usually the one who read to the children,[1] she felt the load of her work pressing on her one evening, turned to Richler, who was lying on the sofa, and said, "Do take care of Jake for a minute. Tell him a little story." Richler sat Jake, the youngest, on his stomach and began to invent. Until that moment, Florence hadn't thought of her husband as a children's author, but when she heard the story unfolding, she suggested that he write it down.[2]

Richler had long thought that there might be money in kiddie-lit. Back in 1959 he had already tried to sell Jack McClelland on the idea of a children's book, and in 1966 or 1967, he had begun *The Last Plum in the House*.[3] So it wasn't a big stretch that as his two oldest boys pulled away from their parents, Richler turned toward the audience that little Jake presented. Florence read her husband's drafts of the children's book to the younger children, passing their responses on to him,[4] and the "little story" became *Jacob Two-Two Meets the Hooded Fang*, a short, clever book for all ages. In the story, Jacob, who must repeat everything twice because he's the smallest and no one pays him attention, is accused of behaviour insulting to a BIG PERSON and is sentenced to rot in the children's prison. The usual tale of a child overcoming fears is welded onto distinctively Richlerian material: Richler satirizes adult platitudes about punishment ("this is going to hurt me more than it will hurt you") in a way that is comprehensible to both children and adults, but also, more cannily, mocks *children's* solutions to problems. Jacob's attorney, casting about for a strong legal defense, suddenly hits on one: "I've got it!" exclaimed Louis Loser triumphantly,

"*I'll cry.*"[5] It's true, as Perry Nodelman argues, that *Jacob Two-Two Meets the Hooded Fang*, somewhat subversively, gives children the power to create and enjoy paranoid fantasy,[6] yet at the same time, Richler, like many conventional children's authors, requires that Jacob renounce wailing and work constructively to address his problems.

Superficially, the book refers to the Richler family: mother preparing dinner, father on the couch reading a newspaper and hankering for tomatoes, Noah and Emma playing elaborate war games, Daniel and "Marfa" named though unaccounted for, and the baby of the family, Jacob, eager to join his siblings' games but dismissed as too little. Although Richler says that he modeled the seeming villain – the Hooded Fang – on an engaging wrestler he met doing a *Maclean's* documentary,[7] one might be forgiven for suspecting that the Hooded Fang's fearsome persona and distaste for mushy emotion, yet secret love of children, had a nearer model: Richler himself. The revelation that the Hooded Fang is in fact childish – "he's one of us" – comes very much against the Fang's will.[8] After Richler's death, there would be a Jacob Two-Two cartoon featuring characters that even looked like family members, but in fact Richler avoided saying too much about the inner workings of the Richler family. He had exposed his parental family to the world via fiction; his own family he wouldn't. As for Jacob Richler, he wasn't much traumatized: he didn't remember repeating things to get his family's attention, and therefore felt that the book hadn't much to do with him. He says that in later years he used the book as a come-on line to get dates.[9]

Richler's sense of irreverence made him a natural ally to the child who has subversive longings but no opportunity to dispute the terms set by adults. However, becoming a children's author was no easy matter. Richler's first two readers at McClelland & Stewart were divided, one calling *Jacob Two-Two Meets the Hooded Fang* tedious, the other saying that it brilliantly merged James Thurber, Jules Feiffer, Abbie Hoffman, Jonathan Swift, Spike Milligan, and John Diefenbaker.[10] Abbie Hoffman? John Diefenbaker? In England, Richler gave the book to his old publisher, André Deutsch, who immediately asked for Canadian rights as well. Richler admonished him, "Let's not resume a professional relationship by reverting to where we ran into trouble twenty years ago."[11] In New York, Knopf seemed reluctant about the book, and Richler immediately concluded that he had wasted his time writing it. Jack McClelland calmed him down: "a hard-bitten New York kids editor" might balk initially, but with a little revision the Americans would no doubt come round.[12] Richler merely had to learn a few of the trade secrets of children's writing. Children don't get involved with protagonists younger than themselves, Lily Poritz Miller, the McClelland & Stewart editor, informed him, so a four-year-old protagonist was a non-starter. Besides, Jacob at four was too precocious to be believable. Further,

Miller told him not to shift to an adult point of view and cautioned him to avoid lecturing children on pollution.[13] His children's editor in New York, Nina Bourne, also had advice: don't wink at other adults over the children's heads (Richler had used words like "*cojones*," Spanish for "testicles"); don't use "children's book" vocabulary (Richler had written "he set about merrily ...") ; try, instead, to get rid of "grown up Mordecai" and (in Bourne's memorable phrase) "write an absolutely straightforward narrative – one infant Cervantes to another."[14] Originally, at the novel's climax, Richler had Child Power troops arriving from all over England to liberate Jacob and the other inmates of the children's prison, but astute editors ventured that stuttering machine guns at the climax weren't absolutely essential in a children's book,[15] so Richler let Noah and Emma perform the rescue, Jacob assisting.

For most of his life, Richler had been prejudiced against children's books and "tiresome Eskimo or Indian legends." Didactic, he thought them. As a child he'd read superhero comics, but not children's books,[16] and in *The Incomparable Atuk*, he had mocked J.P. McEwen who "published the bedtime stories she made up for her nieces."[17] But when *Jacob Two-Two Meets the Hooded Fang* outsold his most successful adult novel, *St. Urbain's Horseman*,[18] Richler found himself in McEwen's position. Suddenly Richler, always regardful of his dignity, had to participate in autographing parties such as the "Child Power Popsicle Party" dreamed up by McClelland & Stewart publicity flaks.[19] He found himself besieged by short people who, according to convention, shouldn't be managed with cynical putdowns. Children at a Richler reading found the newly minted children's author rather tight-lipped, unable to enjoy himself. When a twelve-year-old attempted an interview, all she got was "yes," "no," and "ugh"[20] – the Hooded Fang wasn't prepared to renounce his gruffness, except with his own children. Despite this, there would soon arise a generation of Canadians who knew nothing of *St. Urbain's Horseman* or *Solomon Gursky Was Here*. Mordecai Richler? He writes books for kids, doesn't he?

≋

Richler had always thought of himself as a resolutely urban person, but in 1974, courtesy of his BOMC paycheques,[21] he bought a piece of the country, a cottage on Lake Memphremagog in the Eastern Townships. More than a cottage: seven bedrooms, two storeys – decorated with Terry Mosher cartoons[22] – and eventually a large sunroom where he could put not the demotic pool table of the Rachel Pool Hall but its upper-crust cousin, a full-size snooker table.[23] He was now a wealthy member of the squirarchy, having graduated from St. Urbain Street to gentlemanly living. Outside, forest and lake, lake and forest, the Canada with which Richler wasn't so familiar, but which would increasingly appear in his fiction. To Lake Memphremagog he

invited friends, such as his editors Tony Godwin and Bob Gottlieb. Godwin
did his morning yoga exercises on his head, while the Richler children made
faces to try to topple him.[24] When journalist Ian Mayer ran into difficulties
caused by his battle with alcohol, Richler invited him over. Afterwards, Mayer
recognized his friend's generosity, "Thanks is a totally inadequate word for
a weekend that did me more good than any bloody psychiatrist."[25] It was
nothing new. Richler and Florence had always been very hospitable to their
friends, finding room for them even in the early 1960s when the Richlers
had a tiny flat and three children.[26] Of course, Richler expected similar treatment flying into town and imposing himself on friends at all hours.[27]

Richler bought a motorboat and occasionally buzzed around Lake Memphremagog; several times a year he deigned to step in for a swim.[28] Coming
home in the dark with Florence, and inspired by a movie of *The Turn of the
Screw*, Richler rattled the windows to terrorize the children a bit. Lake Memphremagog offered good opportunities for such antics, especially when Emma
and a friend tented near the water.[29] At cottage parties he would in later years
pick up a useful fund of political gossip and meet other of Canada's self-in-
vested aristocracy: Québec Premiers Jacques Parizeau and Jean Charest, Conservative financier (and eventual jailbird) Michel Cogger, Peter White (Conrad
Black's lieutenant), Black himself, Royal Bank CEO John Cleghorn, newspaper columnist Lysiane Gagnon, Tory lawyer John Lynch-Staunton, and Trizec
chair Jack Rabinovitch, the latter two becoming Richler's good friends.[30]

Lake Memphremagog was a good place to write, offering a new locale
for his next novel and offering quiet, but not absolute seclusion. If the difficulties of rural life appeared in, for example, the rigmarole caused by trouble with the Richler well, nothing could gild his tongue better than anger.
He wrote the plumbing company: "Dear M. Montmigny, I thank you for
your shifty letter of May 28. Alas, I cannot prefix my own letter "WITHOUT
PREJUDICE" because unlike you and the equally adroit Mr. Glenn Bennett
(whose fine hand I detect here), I have never written anything without prejudice. Or style, for that matter. Which is not to say that I fail to appreciate
your guile." Richler promised that if he got a new well with good water,
he'd give Montmigny's company a full release, adding, "I also acknowledge,
if my water supply is restored, passing the required health tests, that you
have done this, not because you were responsible for the original spill, but
out of sheer good will. In fact such is the fabled good will of BP that I take
it even tonight you and Mr. Bennett will be out ringing door bells up and
down the Townships, saying, 'Hi, anything wrong with your well? We're the
good will fellows from BP and we'd be just thrilled to fix it for you – provided you allow us three years of trial and error and meetings.'"[31]

Lake Memphremagog was a good place for the children. They needed
a good place. While Richler published and toured *Jacob Two-Two Meets*

the Hooded Fang – where judges are murder on bubble-gum smugglers and all ends well – Richler's own children moved into the teenage years, difficult years. The children had been raised to be courteous: "Bright, attractive, polite, almost ideal children," one house-guest called them.[32] They also had a great deal of independence. At age twelve and acting in a film version of *Jacob Two-Two Meets the Hooded Fang*, Martha commuted from Lake Memphremagog alone, staying by herself in the Richlers' Montreal quarters.[33] But the children had been raised without burning convictions in areas that define the soft underbelly of liberalism: substance abuse, censorship, sexual freedom. As a nine-year-old, Noah was deemed too young by his father to read *Cocksure*.[34] When Noah picked the book up again as an adolescent, Richler again told him that he was too young but didn't take the book out of his hands.[35] The children could swear with impunity – as long as they knew what they were talking about and used their imaginations.[36] Once, Richler saw a love letter of Noah's that relied upon the word "fuck" in every sentence, and Richler commented not on obscenity but on style: the word would be much more effective, he counselled his son, if you used it less often.[37] The Richlers were casual parents, ahead of their time, Martha would say later,[38] and indeed, to hear the eleven-year-old Martha speak was to be astounded at the articulacy fostered by Florence and Mordecai.[39]

Noah and Daniel were now going through prickly years, and although their father had travelled a similar road, he wasn't too sympathetic. "You did get the sensation slightly," says Noah, "that he left you at 12 and you met him again at 19." Richler and Daniel rarely argued directly, but in his embryonic political awareness Daniel blamed his father for the wrongs in the world – the generation gap, global warming, unemployment. Richler wasn't a good ear for Daniel's girl problems either. One of the difficulties was that there was no fresh ground left for Daniel to break, since Mordecai and Florence knew about *everything*, it seemed. The Rolling Stones? Richler had met them. The Cannes Film Festival? Richler had been there. When Daniel appeared in ripped pink jeans, Richler told him he looked like a horse's ass. Daniel started his own punk band, the Alpha Jerks, and Richler condescended to watch them once, but he wasn't as impressed as Daniel hoped he'd be. With an amused grin, he simply said, "You're pretty rough boys." In *Kicking Tomorrow*, the novel that Daniel eventually wrote, Robbie Bookbinder's rebel yell, "All parents must die," is an exaggerated version of Daniel's own punk-inflected teenage years. "I was starting to be a thorn in my family's side," Daniel admits. When Passover came round, Richler entertained himself by having his boys read the wicked son's portion of the *Haggadah*.[40]

As for Noah, school bored him. After King's House School in England, he had landed in a less demanding place and was convinced that he knew everything being taught. He began to find the kids who used drugs more in-

teresting than those who didn't. Along with some friends, he got into trouble for blowing things up in Westmount Park, and at fifteen he landed in
court on a vandalism charge – for cycling stoned through Lac aux Castors
on Mount Royal. His father accompanied him to court, and as the judge
lectured Noah for being a bad citizen, Richler abruptly started in on the
judge, berated him for wasting taxpayers' money on frivolous prosecutions.
Both the judge and Noah were amazed at the "*wall* of articulacy" coming
from Richler. "Sir, you're right," the judge admitted. But playing lawyer was
the easy part. The boys didn't have Richler's work ethic. Asked to rake the
leaves back in London, Noah and Daniel had once raked them into the words
"ON STRIKE." Richler, looking down on the yard from his office on the top
floor, grew distressed, says Daniel, "by what our middle-class upbringing
had wrought. We were spoiled middle-class kids."[41]

Richler soon noticed a certain amount of mental doddering in Noah:
leaving the taps on; making a lunch, packing it, then forgetting it. Knowing
now that his son was using drugs,[42] Richler burned white-hot on the sofa.[43]
He had been no angel, and was still very fond of alcohol, but he nevertheless yelled at his son, and would have taken harsher measures, were it not
for Florence holding him back. He gravitated towards Florence's methods
because she was ("*ostensibly*," she says) a gentler person, and he saw the
effectiveness of her way of doing things. His anger, a seriously bad temper
that Florence rarely saw, he controlled tightly. When she asked him how he,
who got himself into so many volatile situations, managed not to explode,
he replied, "I dare not." Strange, this suppression of emotions in someone
who was praised and blamed for saying exactly what he thought – "The
Last Honest Man" in some appraisals. But this was another way in which
he continued to react against his mother, whose giving way to anger and desire had proved costly for him. To watch him was to see that for all his bluntness, his manner was *not* unguarded. Instead he sublimated his considerable
anger into stinging books.[44] At the same time, he was a very generous man,
says Daniel,[45] and Noah credits his father with helping him quit drugs. Help's
initial stage came from a series of journeys that Richler made, not to his customary haunts, but far afield: to the Arctic.

The first time, Richler flew with Mel Hurtig, as guests of Stuart Hodg-
son, the friendly Commissioner of the Northwest Territories. Richler initially saw only functionality and sleaze in Yellowknife but insisted that the
place was "absolutely wonderful."[46] That may have been hindsight. In Hurtig's view, the trip wasn't auspicious, especially when they were stranded on
Broughton Island (off the east coast of Baffin Island) with Richler in an ugly
mood. Richler wasn't impressed by the people of the North, and said, "Everyone up there is either a drunk or a runaway or a disaster." The Inuit he called
"stupid people" for living as and where they did. He abandoned the trip

halfway through.[47] But it was always easy for grievance hunters, or those, such as Hurtig, with a grudge, to trot out some politically incorrect statement that Richler had made. Outraging people was his specialty. To annoy Florence, he'd call the Japanese "Nips."[48] If he sometimes went too far, his words had far less to do with racism than had the reactions of his critics to do with censorship. Despite his rudeness about the Arctic, Richler felt its attraction, not least because of the interesting people in Northern bars. It wasn't an easy crowd: "if they think you're a phoney or pretentious, you may as well go home."[49]

He soon returned north and started research for a book, quizzing people all over Yellowknife about Martin Hartwell, a bush pilot who had survived in the Arctic for thirty-two days in 1973 after his four-person Beechcraft strayed off course and crashed. A nurse and two Inuit patients from Cambridge Bay died. At the inquest, evidence of cannibalism. Hartwell didn't want to speak to Richler but, after two months of negotiations, invited Richler to his home.[50] On his itinerary, Richler made a holographic note: "H's house mementos everywhere. A life measured out in souviners flags, trophies, cig lighters.. like bars in a ski resort" [sic].[51] Richler says that he almost decided to skip his Oscar date (for his screenplay of *Duddy Kravitz*) in order to attend a murder trial involving an Inuit man. But since there was another trial upcoming, Richler felt that he could sacrifice a few days in the Arctic for some time in the sun.[52]

≶

What arose from Richler's northern trips wasn't a book on Hartwell – that fell to the wayside early on. Deborah Rogers, who became Richler's British agent just before the publication of *St. Urbain's Horseman*, was disappointed. Already in 1973 she was counting the money from Richler's next novel and speaking of the fun she would have with all the publishers who would vie for Richler's hand. "I see you in the role of some Virgin Bride," she laughed. When Richler informed her that instead of a novel she'd get a book called *I Ate Nurse Judy*, Rogers didn't miss a beat, "I shall expect you to arrive complet [sic] with all your tarts gear, and hopefully a brilliant sales pitch on the new novel – lots of tit and mafia for instance!"[53] No Joyce Weiner, she. Possibly Richler was scared off *I Ate Nurse Judy* by Piers Paul Read's *Alive*, a book about Uruguayan rugby players who, after their plane crashed in the Andes, ate their dead teammates. Or perhaps Richler simply realized that the Arctic material cried out for novelistic treatment. In any case, he abandoned the project.

The novel wouldn't come until fourteen years later, when the fictional Isaac Gursky and his father crash in the Arctic, and Isaac dines on a horrifying, yet technically *kosher* meal. Instead of a novel, Richler made the contacts that would allow him to send Noah to the Arctic. If he could extract Noah from his Montreal circles, Richler reasoned, and set him in a more austere environment, there'd be fewer chemical temptations. Richler prevailed on his friends to find Noah a job in the Yukon as a prospector's assistant. Rather than attempt long counselling sessions, Richler – who had little patience for teenagers, and who found galling their limited rationality, their moroseness – loaded his son down with thirteen great books, to be read up north: *The Brothers Karamazov, Crime and Punishment, Darkness at Noon, The Red and The Black, Scoop,* and *The Art of Kissing* – but no Richler novels. When Noah returned to Montreal with a shaved head and an earring, Richler worried briefly that his son might be gay.[54] The Yukon didn't solve the drug problem, but Richler hoped, with some justification, that the hiatus might begin the process of weaning Noah from a drug-centred lifestyle.

⧖

The fallout from the Oscar nomination arrived far more quickly than the Arctic fiction, briefly making Richler a marketable property. Richler had initially phoned his British editor, Tony Godwin, to tell him about the nomination. Godwin, master of the sly putdown and aware that Richler thought that movies were overvalued,[55] asked, "Wouldn't it be embarrassing if you won?"[56] In the event, there was no danger of embarrassment, since the blockbuster *Godfather, Part II* won both Best Picture and Best Adapted Screenplay Oscar for Mario Puzo and Francis Coppola. But the duo of Mordecai Richler and Lionel Chetwynd did win a Writers Guild of America comedy screenplay award. From different tables, the twain converged on the podium. Richler, well-oiled, said, "I've never seen this man before." The black-tie audience howled with laughter, unaware that Richler was simply telling the truth.[57]

When Kotcheff landed the directorial job for Columbia's big-budget comedy *Fun with Dick and Jane*, he naturally turned to Richler for highly paid help on the screenplay adaptation. Richler in Hollywood: the rich cultural and intellectual life of the movie capital handed him material for his novels. In November of either 1975 or 1976, he was flown to Hollywood with Kotcheff and was wined and dined at the Malibu mansion of a producer whose butler brought out Acapulco Gold and cocaine on a trolley. To the amusement of Hollywood debauchees, Richler asked that his wife be given a ticket to join him.[58] Richler was introduced to Jane Fonda, the movie's co-star. They got on well, but when Richler turned in his rewrite, she quickly voiced her artistic and philosophical qualms. She had looked at the screenplay, counted her lines, and discovered that the new version gave her forty-three fewer lines.[59]

Fun with Dick and Jane tells the story of an upper-class husband and wife who, when the husband loses his aerospace job, turn bumblingly to robbery. Richler, the ex-angry young man, was now writing at $50,000 a pop about upper-class people anxious over the fate of their swimming pool. Dick and Jane are self-obsessed cardboard cut-outs, purposely so, and yet the audience is expected to cheer shamelessly for them at the end when they rob a corrupt aerospace executive of his kickbacks and escape with money hidden under their clothes. Much of the film is pedestrian, though occasionally the satire does subvert materialism and does rise to inspired levels, as when Jane's wealthy father answers her request for a loan by giving her a sermon on self-reliance. "Ralph Waldo Emerson is like a god to me," he prefaces his remarks, and then asks her to look at it this way: "It's a monsoon and you're soaking wet. Take money from me and you'll be wet for the rest of your lives." Dick and Jane's sudden poverty is, he concludes, the best thing that could have happened to them. Jane's mother chirps in, "I'm so happy for the both of you."[60]

It isn't clear whether Richler wrote these excellent lines, since five different screenwriters worked on the adaptation of the Gerald Gaiser novel.[61] A moment that doubtless bears the Richler stamp, comes when Dick and Jane, hurrying through the back corridors while aeronautics executives chat up their foreign customers at a reception, pass by a 3-ft x 4-ft photograph of Moshe Dayan: the most recognizable face of Israeli expansionism and a valued military customer, no question, to have his face blown up to poster size. Another Richlerian bit – satire against Jewish exceptionalism – occurs when a lawn and garden company repossesses Dick and Jane's newly installed shrubs and turf. "You're a Nazi!" Jane cries at the foreman. "I can't be," he clips his syllables sweetly, "I'm a Jew."[62] This in late 1975, when the embattled UN General Assembly had just passed a motion that called Zionism a form of racism.

Neither of the two endings of the film that appear among the Richler Papers is the inconsistent ending that Columbia finally settled on. It's likely, though by no means certain, that the most satiric of the manuscript endings is Richler's work. In this ending, Jane's bra-strap snaps, dollars fall out, and Dick and Jane are caught with their ill-gotten money. But they get very good press. The owner of a store they robbed finds that simply by posting their thank-you note he makes his store popular, recouping far more money than they stole. When a reporter asks the owner, "What about the morality of it?" the owner, suddenly inflamed, turns on the reporter, "I thought you said no trick questions." An evangelist whom Dick and Jane robbed preaches on "Forgive and Prosper," and discovers, just as his sermon declares, that a heart-warming story brings in a flood of donations. This screenplay ends, as it originally began, with a Dick-and-Jane storybook: see Dick and Jane playing cards and tennis for nine months at a minimum-security prison. See Dick and Jane posing in front of the new house bought from the proceeds of their tell-all book. These are not the anti-heroes of the film's final cut, but figures of mockery, images of a culture sold out to celebrity.[63] But Richler, soon to skewer poet A.M. Klein for selling out to liquor baron Sam Bronfman, learned the precise artistic trade-off for big film money. Richler's ending was changed and his satiric cut-outs were turned into heroes.

In the end, Richler was thrust into something approximating Lionel Chetwynd's position. Cap in hand, he had to apply to the Arbitration Committee of the Writers Guild, the committee that he had mocked three years earlier when Chetwynd was petitioner.[64] And there was more. No story conferences, Richler had insisted before Columbia flew him to Hollywood.[65] The executives agreed, and after Richler submitted his three weeks of writing, Kotcheff and producer Peter Bart pronounced themselves happy. Less happy was Stan Jaffe of Columbia, so Kotcheff called Richler in for another week. Kotcheff promised $7,500 and offered to pay Richler himself. Richler countered that, if none of his material was used, there'd be no charge, but, if some was used, he wanted not Kotcheff but Columbia or Peter Bart or Max Palevsky (another producer) to pay. Bart agreed. Ultimately, some of the new material was used, but Richler wasn't paid. Bart prophesied that someday, somehow, Richler would see the money. If Richler insisted on raising a ruckus, Bart would order the new material cut from the film. Infuriated and a couple of sheets to the wind, Richler wrote in protest, accomplishing nothing, perhaps – there's no evidence that he ever sent the unsigned and undated letter – but proving that even when sodden and inarticulate, he could be articulate:

> several weeks before the northern ground hog
> A few weekd alter, Bart finally surfaced ...
>
> furtherm e bart, a fancy foot work, imporerly claims kotcheff never told him he wd have to pay ... Does art believe i write
> without fee for film makers in the dim hope that sometime in the fute they might take me 1to dinner. do other writers who workfor me
> I am, to come clean, seething over this matter. I have been treated like a supplicant subjected to indignities, and have found xxxxxxxx ...
> I wish to know what action I can take.[66]

Even the Hooded Fang, sweet-tempered beneath the gruff exterior, couldn't keep his composure against the machinations of Hollywood.

21

Back to Ibiza

BY 1976 IT WAS FIVE YEARS since Richler had published a serious novel. He made do with pieces such as "Witches' Brew," a witty account of the "Third Annual Gnostic Aquarian Festival of Astrology, Mind Power, Occult Sciences & Witchcraft in the New Age," which could fetch an excellent dollar from *Playboy*,[1] even though afterwards he would hear from readers who placed no value at all on a *layman's* report about such esoteric matters. If he got conflicting psychic advice from different astrologers, no doubt at a medical convention he'd get conflicting diagnoses, wouldn't he? "You may not realize now," wrote one reader, "but you had an astrological reading by one of the greatest astrologers in our time, Marc Edmund Jones. Did you really listen to his interpretation? Did you really hear what he said?"[2] The *Duddy* movie and the *Jacob Two-Two* book had been successful far beyond Richler's expectations and had made him famous even in the eyes of his own children.[3] But he knew that these latest achievements didn't constitute his real work. Bits of flotsam sailed through his head – Arctic cannibalism, Manny Berger hearing hell's bells at mid-life, stories about the Bronfmans' rum-running days. Already in 1972, Richler had envisioned a novel called *Gursky Was Here*,[4] which he promised to finish in 1977 and from which he published an "excerpt," "Manny Moves to Westmount." Deborah Rogers applauded furiously, hoping that if she applauded hard enough, she'd prime the pump for a saleable novel.[5]

"Manny Moves to Westmount" appeared in *Saturday Night*, but no novel ensued. What set all of Richler's plans aside was a call from Jack McClelland, wondering whether Richler could recommend someone to write the text for a book of Spanish photographs. Richler supplied a couple of names. Very quickly, however, it became apparent that the most enticing name to McClelland was Richler's own. Enticing to Richler as well, since he longed to see whether the ghosts of the past still roamed the streets of

Ibiza, and whether he could finish his aborted business – "Are you a man or a mouse?" – with the ex-Nazi colonel "Mueller," who, rumour had it, ran a nightclub there. In *Joshua Then and Now*, Joshua flees to Spain alone, his marriage troubled, but Richler took Florence along. The description in *Feed My Dear Dogs*, of the father's need for his wife points at Richler's attitude: "When he wants Mum, which is just about always, and she is not there right before his eyes as he enters the house or a room he expects her to be in, he loses his mind and starts calling out her name over and over in the manner of King Arthur avenging the stealing of his Queen by the traitor Sir Launcelot."[6] Florence offered to let Richler go to Spain alone, but he was becoming less and less eager to globetrot without her, and he convinced her to come along.[7]

What he found on Ibiza was depressing, but salutary. Commerce had overwhelmed the island – new hotel after new hotel, acid rock in the bars and raw sewage in the sea. Everywhere Germans and Japanese tourists. Of course Richler had changed, too. A burger now, he could stay in those new hotels and travel like a German or a Japanese in a style that the younger Richler had despised. He worried about whether his former companions would recognize him and whether he'd have anything to say to them. He managed to locate Juanito "Pus," the partying fisherman who had taken Richler under his wing twenty-five years ago. Juanito said that the fishing near the island had failed in the early 1960s and that he had of necessity gone to sea with a fishing fleet. Now he was retired. "Yesterday's furnace" had forsworn drinking, and every night he tucked into bed early. The Casa Rosita was gone. The cockfights were over.[8]

As for Colonel "Mueller," Richler thought he might resume their old quarrel, this time not as an easily intimidated nineteen-year-old. In *Joshua Then and Now*, Juanito turns querulous when he hears that Joshua is less interested in him than in "Mueller." In *Back to Ibiza*, the more autobiographical account, Juanito is merely baffled. But "Mueller" had died of cancer five years earlier, no battle resumed. Richler felt foolish and homesick.[9] Spain told him: appreciate your family and your home; the past can neither be recovered nor corrected. He was scheduled next to go to Halifax with Jacob and Martha to promote a film of *Jacob Two-Two*. Martha had acted in it, while Jacob helped with publicity.[10] A seemingly tongue-in-cheek postcard to Jacob hinted much about Richler's state of mind with regard to his family, though not, perhaps, with regard to Halifax: "I think of Madrid, Seville, Granada, Ibiza, etc. as no more than a prelude to EXCITING FANTASTIC HALIFAX … I hope that you have made no other plans."[11]

Back home at Lake Memphremagog, Richler started into *Images of Spain*. Instead of a 10,000-word travel piece, however, he surfaced with a 30,000-word memoir. When Florence saw it, she said that he'd be crazy to bury all the rich material in a photograph book. On her advice, he chiselled out most of the personal stories and converted it simply into a travel book. Early in 1977 he reworked the memoir into *Back to Ibiza*, this time showing the 180 manuscript pages to Florence and to Bob Gottlieb. The two still weren't convinced that Richler had found the most appropriate form, and he deferred to their intuition. The best parts of the memoir, Richler decided, were the lies, so why not a novel?[12] By 1978 he was hard at work combining *Back to Ibiza* with the Spanish outtakes from *St. Urbain's Horseman* and with some of the follies that he had witnessed in Hollywood. He called his work-in-progress *Joshua Bloom*. "I won't ask what happened to *Gursky Was Here*,"[13] his friend Michael Darling promised.

Before Spain, Richler had served on the committees for the 1974 and the 1975 Governor General's Award for Fiction. The 1974 award to Margaret Laurence's *The Diviners* was uncontroversial, but because Brian Moore was his friend he took some heat when the 1975 award went to Brian Moore's *The Great Victorian Collection* instead of to Farley Mowat's *The Snow Walker* or Robertson Davies's *World of Wonders*. There were a few nationalists who felt that the ultra-nationalist Mowat should have won easily over a writer (Moore) who resided in California. Literary merit won the award, Richler insisted.[14] He wasn't about to badmouth the other finalists, however, and though in Yellowknife bars such as the Hoist Room and the Gold Range Farley Mowat was now called Hardly Know-It, Richler loved *The Snow Walker* and pitched to have it chosen as a prominent Alternate for the Book-of-the-Month Club.[15]

Richler was tapped again in 1976, this time to chair the Awards, with two other past winners, Alice Munro and Margaret Laurence, rounding out the committee. Munro, who had earlier solicited his advice on selling her papers to the Canadian Literary Archives at the University of Calgary,[16] got on well with Richler but found the meetings in the spring of 1977 a strain, mainly due to Laurence. An informal bar meeting turned unpleasant when Laurence drank too much and began to browbeat the others because they didn't agree that one particular novel was absolutely brilliant. Laurence, planning her own novel (she never wrote it) about her 1940s experiences in North Winnipeg with the Communist Party and with fundamentalist Christians who thought they had all the answers (and who were presently trying to ban *The Diviners* and *The Apprenticeship of Duddy Kravitz* from high schools[17]), recognized the irony of her position. She admitted, "maybe I only have to look inside myself to understand how people can sometimes feel *they are right*, damn it, and *others must be made to see*."[18] Her drink-fuelled rant didn't fluster Richler, who was not unfamiliar with the protocol in such moments, but Munro suffered.

To Richler, Laurence afterwards said, "You were splendid, calming, etc, although you must have been in fact mad as hell at me for my sermonizing."[19] To Munro, Laurence apologized. Munro told Richler, "The good sensible sober Margaret Laurence phoned up apologizing for the bad drunk Margaret Laurence and said, maybe we should have another meeting? I said no." Munro also told Richler that she wanted *Small Ceremonies* on the short list, to encourage Carol Shields.[20] However, no short list was publicized.[21] Despite Laurence's act of contrition, she clearly had the final say. "A banal book, not in contention," W.H. New had written to Richler when informed that Marian Engel's *Bear* stood among the finalists, alongside Margaret Atwood's *Lady Oracle* and Jack Hodgins's *Spit Delaney's Island*.[22] Neither *Bear* nor its set of concerns – female self-actualization, the Canadian wilderness – engaged Richler. But it won. Evidently Munro was made to see things Laurence's way.[23]

Other of Richler's involvements with the CanLit crowd were also less than fulfilling. A year later in February 1978, Jack McClelland overruled Richler's objections and dragged him to the University of Calgary, where, under the guidance of Malcolm Ross, "CanLit diagnosticians" gathered to announce the one hundred best Canadian novels. *The Apprenticeship of Duddy Kravitz* (#3) and *St. Urbain's Horseman* (#15) placed and showed. Laurence's *The Stone Angel* reigned at #1, and sneaking in through the back door at #100 was *The Incomparable Atuk*. "Obviously, next time out I'm going to try harder," said Richler.[24] No injustice there, though one could find strange sights if one wanted: Frederick Philip Grove's clunky *Settlers of the Marsh* up at #23, while David Godfrey's difficult and brilliant *The New Ancestors* languished at #70.[25] Richler thought the conference joyless, and he pointed out the interesting fact that McClelland & Stewart held reprint rights to most of the titles.[26] Purists considered a Top 100 list vulgar, but Jack McClelland argued that the list was needed because high-school teachers and university professors "really don't know a goddamn thing about Canadian writing."[27]

22

Lily, Round 3

RICHLER'S LIFE WAS, for the most part, quiet. By 1976 he had moved from BOMC reader onto its editorial board,[1] and by 1980 his BOMC salary alone was enough to live on.[2] For a year and a half Richler did a *Maclean's* column. He again had visions that a $4 million movie would be made of *St. Urbain's Horseman*, George Segal starring, Kotcheff directing. Although newspapers reported a firm contract, the financiers proved reluctant.[3] But a *Jacob Two-Two* musical opened in North and South Carolina and waltzed through London, Washington, and Toronto.[4] Since Lake Memphremagog seemed to be working out well, Richler gave up the house in Westmount in favour of a large suite in Montreal's most prestigious apartment building, Le Château on Sherbrooke West, the kind of building that in *Barney's Version* he called "a rich old fart's castle … A fortress for besieged Anglophone septuagenarians."[5] Most days, work started shortly after 9:00 A.M. and finished at 4:00 p.m. if the day went well. After 4:00, or earlier if literary pickings were slim, he'd repair to the bar, the Ritz Carleton when he was in Montreal. He'd watch the National News and be in bed by 11:30. Because he worked every day, Richler had little sense of the weekends, though he could give a reliable account of which evening *The Muppet Show* and *Hockey Night in Canada* were on.[6]

Inside that quiet daily round, the novel set in motion by Ibiza was finally beating. Richler imagined Joshua Shapiro, a middle-aged Jew who had worked his way up from poverty to a golden shiksa and renown but who was under a cloud – possibly jail, or, worse, the loss of his wife and family.[7] Critics eager for structural experiment, new themes, or political radicalism, couldn't help but be disappointed. While other Canadian writers such as Michael Ondaatje (*Coming through Slaughter*, 1976) and Robert Kroetsch (*What the Crow Said*, 1978) experimented brilliantly with new forms, and while a more conventional writer such as Alice Munro (*Who Do You Think*

You Are?) approached realism with such austerity that one could not reduce her work formally to comedy or tragedy, Richler stuck resolutely to Dickensian conventions. In his bigger novels, he turned to a basic comic structure – the wish to "show an affirming flame" – for moral reasons: Richler's early tragedies and satires could potentially invite a quietist position, absolving the reader from having to act morally, and Richler was unwilling to let this excuse stand. Ungenerous readers would complain of repetition – Toronto film producer William Marshall said, "I love his book. I buy it every time he writes it"[8] – but that's misleading. Richler's overall structure did become repetitive, yet within the framework would always be a feast of wit and imagination, a jaundiced eye on the passing scene and a revelling in its myriad forms. Whereas Robertson Davies had in the last decade begun writing novels structured by myth, new versions of older stories, Richler's novels were often structured by his life, as Munro's stories were by hers.[9] The individual episodes and actions show a wandering realism in that they are governed not by previous stories but by Richler's sensibility and experiences.[10] *Joshua Then and Now* is a densely layered world, filled with class and racial tensions, barbs against WASP culture, Canadian nationalism, Québécois separatism, identity politics, and Hollywood – a very funny and worthy successor to *St. Urbain's Horseman.*[11]

This time, Richler claimed, he wasn't being so autobiographical. That's not true. Most of what the characters did and said seemed distant from Richler's life, but in fact he had simply grown more canny in how he *used* his life. Even as exaggerations pulled satire away from realism, Richler was never abstract, but worldly and specific with a vengeance. The first target was Lily Rosenberg.

Erna Paris called *Joshua Then and Now* round 3 in Richler's battle with his mother, following on her unflattering portrait in *St. Urbain's Horseman*, and then their estrangement.[12] One could as easily call it round 4 (were one to include *Son of a Smaller Hero*) or round 11 or 43 (were one to include less public conflicts beginning with Julius Frankel). Whatever the number, when Joshua's thirteen-year-old friends in the novel grow bored at his bar mitzvah, Joshua's mother, an exotic dancer, does a striptease, enlivening the proceedings considerably. Reading this, Lily immediately felt implicated and refused to hear Avrum's objections that it was only fiction.[13] As Lily did, Joshua's mother cheats on her husband. "Esther," Joshua's mother is called, the Biblical courtesan whose name immediately evokes "Mordecai," and if Lily hadn't literally done a fan dance for thirteen-year-olds, she had, at the time of Mordecai's bar mitzvah, come close enough. It was a sly and broadly funny kind of satire, but deceptive. By now, the significance of Lily's affair had faded; what hadn't faded was her gift of misanthropy and Richler's sense that she was an inadequate person, so her reappearance in his life during the 1960s and early 1970s entailed her reappearance in his fiction, in *St. Ur-bain's Horseman* and *Joshua Then and Now*. Richler no longer tied the mother of his alter ego (now Joshua) to any realistic image. Still, the roman-à-clef impulse never left Richler, and the characters' psychological incon-gruities that critics sometimes puzzle over[14] can be explained not just by speaking of satirical set pieces, but by noting their autobiographical con-tent. Given Richler's life, it made perfect sense for Joshua's mother to do a bar mitzvah striptease. Taken generously, Esther is a witty take on Lily's job at the Esquire Show Bar and on her ability to conveniently adjust her moral code to accommodate the job. Taken less generously, Esther is a satiric take on Lily's coitus with Julius Frankel, reluctantly witnessed in the next bed by the thirteen-year-old Mordecai.

Within a year of the publication of *Joshua Then and Now*, Lily had her own book out, *The Errand Runner: Reflections of a Rabbi's Daughter*. Re-viewers instantly jumped to the conclusion that the book was Lily's coun-terattack against the portrait of the mother in *Joshua Then and Now*,[15] but that's impossible. Lily's letters to her sister, Ruth Albert, show that already in 1978–79 Lily was writing her memoir and complaining about her sons: "do not derive pleasure from the way my dear children treat me, I love them and they love me and when I need them they will come running so fast no one will be able to catch up with them."[16] In one letter Lily spoke of a visit to Ruth's home, saying, "The visit went very well till you found out that I was writing, but why were you so upset by my writing? You became like a woman demented ... Why were you so frightened."[17] Ruth was frightened because she feared that in the book Lily would settle her lengthy list of griev-ances against family members, including Ruth.

Lily's book did air some of her grievances, but possibly because she had a decorous notion of publication, her autobiography was far less aggressive than her private words. In a sense, *The Errand Runner* was a larger and more revealing version of her 1930s stories, "I Pay a Visit to the Beloved Rabbi," as Lily continued, this late in the day, to worship at the shrine of her father while becoming more candid about the failings of everybody else. She wrote under her Jewish maiden name, Leah Rosenberg. To avoid libel suits, she altered some names in the book, but she made it quite clear who was who. Pinchus Willensky was Shmarya Richler, her father-in-law and Mordecai's grandfather: a Machiavellian scoundrel, in her opinion. Aron Willensky was Moe Richler, her husband: not nearly so culpable – he did love his boys and it wasn't his fault that he was incompatible with Lily – but, come to think of it, a scoundrel too. On her siblings, including Ruth: they could have done a lot better, especially during those difficult years when Richler's grandmother was supposed to die.

And Mordecai? Here Lily surprises. Mordecai comes under only the most oblique criticism. Incongruously she calls him a "Talmud head," and only small cues hint at the depth of their rift. "Moishe," she names Mordecai, subtly equating him with the bawdy sensibility of her incompatible husband Moe, and the book is dedicated to her parents, grandchildren, and great-grandchild, but not to her sons. When questioned about her famous son, she always ingenuously asks, "Which one? I have been endowed with two sons, both prominent and distinguished in their respective careers."[18] Such a response was meant to put Mordecai in his place, but gently. Even in her letters to Ruth, Lily said, "Did you ever for one moment think that this nothing like myself would produce two very gifted children may G-d bless them."[19] In private conversation she was less guarded, referring ("with laboured sarcasm," says Lionel Albert) to Mordecai as "my genius."[20]

At some point Lily found a few of Mordecai's old newspaper cuttings and, hoping they might broker a reunion, asked Victoria Zinde-Walsh to send them to Mordecai.[21] Avrum, who himself had seen almost nothing of Mordecai, wrote him shortly after the publication of *Joshua Then and Now*, praising the novel and saying that Lily wanted to mend fences – though she still expected Mordecai to apologize. "She will soon be at the 'end' of her days and guilt is not pleasant," wrote Avrum.[22] But, as *Joshua Then and Now* predicted, there would be no reconciliation. Mordecai was a man of limited emotional resources. He was prepared to be generous to those close to him, but if you were out, you were out – and Lily was out. She would live for another seventeen years, enough time to harass family members by threatening to broadcast their chintziness if they didn't contribute to the refurbishing of her father's mausoleum.[23] On the fiftieth anniversary of his death, Rabbi Rosenberg got a new home, a handsome little brick building about the size and shape of a garden shed. Lily had no friends, reported Avrum, who eventually took her into his home for about ten years, "If you can imagine it, she is even worse than ever. She never had a good word for anyone … The poison that drips from her mouth is horrible. But, she is my mother."[24] At some point she made two tapes, full of hate, one for each son, and said, "I don't have two sons – I have two stones."[25]

Rather than replying to *Joshua Then and Now*, *The Errand Runner* had included a polite nod to her sons' escape from Orthodoxy. The grand pattern of Lily's own life, she felt, was an Exodus from a strict and loving but bigoted Orthodoxy to an "integration" of her Jewish faith with a secular world – Lily (with self-satisfaction) handing out Jewish calendars to her Gentile neighbours and talking incessantly about Jewish festivals.[26] Mostly the change came about through her sons, so it pained her that while she was writing comparatively gently about her younger son, he, far from endorsing her new persona, depicted the mother in *Joshua Then and Now* as progressing from a stripper to foul-mouthed feminist.

With Richler and Lily estranged, neither McClelland & Stewart nor Knopf were likely to touch *The Errand Runner*. Initially Lily took it to Mel Hurtig, who, though he insisted that he appreciated Lily's charm and wit, didn't think himself the appropriate publisher either. But he encouraged her and helped line up John Wiley & Sons.[27] At the age of seventy-six, Lily had her first book launched in Montreal. Still vivacious and articulate at that time, sporting an orchid, she entertained booksellers, members of the media, and family, including Avrum, who flew in from Newfoundland. Mordecai, who lived in Montreal, didn't attend.[28] In fact he was furious, believing that she was trading on his name.[29] At one time, Mordecai told Avrum that he hadn't read *The Errand Runner*,[30] but Florence had the book on her shelf, and after a long while he finally read it.[31]

Months before the book was published, when news of it became public, a letter arrived from "Aaron Goldberg" of Spelling-Goldenberg Productions offering Richler the opportunity to write the screenplay for *The Errand Runner*, its movie potential obvious: "The memoir reads like a novel by, who else – Mordecai Richler." Ted Kotcheff could direct, though in all honesty, 'Goldberg' conceded, in the starring role he might have to go with a younger actress than "the present Leah Rosenberg." Presuming to speak on behalf of *The Errand Runner's* author, "Goldberg" closed by saying, "Mrs. Rosenberg herself feels that it would be an honor for her if you would consent to become a part of this exceptional project."[32] Who wrote the letter? Brian Moore? Moore was certainly in the habit of writing joke letters to Richler and knew his novels well. The sly dig involved in "Gold*e*nberg Productions" (not Goldberg) reminded Richler of Leah Adler, née Goldenberg, the see-through pseudonym he had used for Lily in *Son of a Smaller Hero*. One wonders whether Richler frowned or laughed at this little missive. Fifteen years later, in *Barney's Version*, Richler would use part of *The Errand Runner's* subtitle for a projected volume in Girodias's dirty book series: *The Rabbi's Daughter*.[33]

⅏

If *Joshua Then and Now* pained Lily, others were less sensitive. Lionel Albert, Richler's cousin, recognized himself in the portrait of Joshua's cousin, Sheldon Leventhal. Richler had already satirized Lionel's youthful sophistication in "The Summer My Grandmother Was Supposed to Die," where "Cousin Jerry" informs the narrator that "Grandpappy" (i.e., Rabbi Rosenberg, who had spoken against a kosher bakers' strike) "was a prize reactionary."[34] In *Joshua Then and Now*, Lionel is both the young Sheldon, who flaunts his wealth to poor Joshua, and the older Sheldon, who has become

Joshua's inferior, Sheldon never having quite lived up to his stellar promise. One quiet afternoon in the mid to late 1970s Albert arranged to meet Richler at the Ritz Hotel Maritime Bar. There, Albert drew Richler's attention to articles and letters that Albert had published in *The Montreal Star* and *The Montreal Gazette.* Hoping that Richler, with his wide publishing experience, could be of assistance, Albert said something like, "I want to become a pundit." Fictionalizing and exaggerating, Richler turned this scene into Sheldon imploring Joshua for help and being sent packing, a just punishment for having lorded it over his cousin as a youth. Indeed, Richler never assisted Albert in punditry, though Albert went on to co-author a book on separatism – *Partition: The Price of Québec's Independence* (1980).[35]

With his own family, Richler was circumspect. He expected great things of his children. Later, when Emma did some costuming for the London theatre, he would complain, "I didn't bring up my daughter to be a *shmatteh!*"[36] a sentiment attributed to the Weiss father in Emma's *Feed My Dear Dogs.*[37] By the time of *Joshua Then and Now,* Daniel had dropped out of university, and Richler told him, "I think now you should go strike out on your own."[38] But it was mostly Noah about whom Richler worried, and in Joshua's difficulties with his son Alex, Richler hinted, tentatively, at some of problems that he had been facing with his own son. He lobbied his new friend, Justice Bill Morrow of Alberta's Supreme Court to try to send Noah north again, on a $5-an-hour job as a freight handler for Northwest Territorial Airlines in Yellowknife.[39] That never happened. Possibly trying to outdo his father's youthful adventures, Noah instead took off for a year, much farther afield than Ibiza – to Afghanistan and India. Back in Montreal by early 1979, he worked at Ben's Delicatessen and had "a very druggy summer," hanging around L'Air du Temps jazz club, procuring and supplying drugs for friends. Noah was painfully aware that he had a problem, and, driving out to Memphremagog from time to time, he intimated that he was trying to wean himself slightly. Not good enough for Richler. Richler, Florence, and Noah held what Noah calls his "Camp David meetings." Florence handled the situation with tact and restraint, but Richler found himself unable to cope. Invariably, things ended up in tears.[40]

Trying a different tack, Richler took Noah to the Lexington Hotel in New York and reasoned with him there, conjuring up Mason Hoffenberg and the devastating embrace of heroin. Noah had met Hoffenberg very briefly in 1966 as a youngster, when the Richlers were still living in London and Hoffenberg was trying to kick heroin. Now, in New York, Richler went into the graphic details that Noah hadn't been privy to at the time – dirty needles, reluctant veins, the horrors of constipation – and appended his own sense of Hoffenberg's wasted promise as a writer: "If you saw what happened to Mason ... He was so talented. I don't understand why you do it."

Richler then confessed to Noah how much he loved his life – he loved Florence, had wonderful children, and was allowed to do a job he was good at. The talk affected Noah deeply.[41] Of these matters, the only hint to surface in *Joshua Then and Now* was Joshua's probably mistaken fear that his son Alex is on drugs,[42] though perhaps some of Joshua's guilt about leaving Pauline to go to Spain originated in Richler's fear in autumn 1976, just after Noah's return from the Yukon, that Richler shouldn't leave Montreal while Noah was still struggling with drug addiction.

To Joshua's wife Pauline, Richler gave Florence's passion for gardening,[43] but in other ways Florence was very different from Joshua's promiscuous, high-strung, Westmount queen. Florence had little contact with her family, the Woods, associated with the historic St. Stephen's Anglican Church in Lachine. One of her nephews was amazed, at age twenty-seven, to discover that Mordecai Richler was his uncle.[44]

Still, Richler did address some of the passions that set him afire, in particular the notion that for a young working-class boy to make it, he had to have a "golden *shiksa*."[45] "The last of the Angry Young Men novels," Marshall Delaney accurately calls *Joshua Then and Now*.[46] There are two Richlers in the novel: the likeable up-and-comer, Joshua, and the sordid up-and-comer, Jack Trimble, who as a poor and unnoticed youth decided that he would "get his dirty fingernails underneath Jane Mitchell's skirts."[47] The same animus, though not the same vulgarity, had driven Richler.[48] Trimble gets what he thinks he wants, then finds that he still doesn't belong on Westmount, because he can't help wallowing, mind and soul, in the dirt. Richler sympathized. Intellectually and achievement-wise Richler could stand beside anybody on Westmount, yet he never felt completely at home there. So quick to spot contradictions, Richler had once sent a note up to the Archbishop of Canterbury sitting in a VIP lounge on a plane – "Would Jesus fly first class?"[49] But Richler had long flown first class himself[50] and now he could afford two homes. After Richler bought the cottage at Lake Memphremagog, but before he wrote *Joshua Then and Now*, he mused on what he saw as two distinct kinds of socialism: "one, life-enhancing; the other, contaminated by bile." As an example of the first, he cited British Labour Leader Nye Bevan who enjoyed "witty companions, fine books, first-rate feed and wine, weekends in the country" and fought so that everybody could have these. As an example of contaminated socialism, Richler cited a hypothetical Parisian *concierge*: "Day after day, seething in her foul-smelling caretaker's cubicle, she watches people with more style, a better life, passing to their handsomely appointed apartments upstairs and ... dreams of sweet vengeance."[51] *Both* were Richler, but in *Joshua Then and Now* he recognized that he no longer had reason to seethe. If Harry Stein exorcised Richler's darker juvenile impulses, Jack Trimble did the same for class disaffection.

For all that, Richler's sensibility would never become sanitized to West-mount specifications, as is evident in one of the less obvious lampoons in the novel. In 1971, Richler had written a piece for *Saturday Night* about Montreal's first (and, for a long time, only) Jewish policeman, Ben Green-berg. Greenberg had started on the force in 1928, when there was still a lot of anti-Semitism, but he had lasted for thirty-six years by creating a congen-ial work environment: "I was very aggressive, not pushed around by the goyim and had a reputation as a fighter."[52] By the time Richler caught up with him, he was director of security for the Montreal Expos. Richler sensed a great story, made even better by Greenberg's way of talking. He wore a tough-guy persona, yet seemed curiously unpretentious because of his un-laundered speech. Of his time on the Morality Squad, he said, "Everybody wanted to be on morality ... I mean you dropped into a whorehouse they always served you a nice wine and a piece of tail." He described to Richler whorehouse madams who gave police a peek at unwitting clients through glory holes, grocery-store owners who paid protection, and police who took criminals down to the basement of the station to get them to "open up." When Richler pressed him on how exactly he "opened up" perpetrators, Greenberg shied away from specifics, only saying, "I got ways and means how." He admitted that after retirement he felt naked without a gun, and that he had finally managed to secure a permit to store firepower at home: "Somebody comes in there, boy, if he wants to I'll air-condition him, sure as hell" [*sic*]. It's not clear what Greenberg expected a journalist such as Richler to do with their interview, but Greenberg must have expected him to dress the truth up at least a bit. Instead, Richler quoted Greenberg di-rectly and often.[53] Greenberg responded by threatening to bomb Richler and, for good measure, cut his balls off.[54]

When Richler needed a rogue policeman to harass Joshua in the novel, naturally Greenberg – tough, foul-mouthed, vindictive, not too bright yet nobody's fool, and, above all, colourful – came to mind. The name Richler gave him, Det. Sgt. Stuart McMaster, wouldn't identify him. Later, in *Bar-ney's Version*, Richler gave Izzy Panofsky all of Greenberg's best lines, but in *Joshua Then and Now*, Richler merely gave McMaster the Greenberg style, plus the advantage of some existentialist reading:

"... so we break down the door," McMaster continued as the Sony whirled, 'and this little Pepsi runt ... Scrub that. This disadvantaged habitant – he's a holy terror with a gun, but he hasn't got it now – he's cowering in the corner. A rat at bay. Trembling from head to foot. And Sweeney, he was my partner in those bygone days, he's moving in, ready to pistol-whip him. I step right in there, stopping him. I say to Sweeney, quote, We are not vigilantes, but officers of the

law. I cannot, in conscience, acquiesce to violence. It does not be-
hoove me. We should endeavour to dig to the roots of this miasmic
problem. Social injustice, unquote. And that little punk, he's still shit-
scared, he trips and falls down all the stairs, head first. And how's this
for irony? Afterwards, his lawyer claims it was us who marked him
up so badly. Well, I tellya. That's when I became cognizant of the
veracity to be found in the works of that well-known French writer
Albert Camus. Our lives are absurd. Hoo boy, are they ever.'"[55]

McMaster's bully of a partner is called "Sweeney." It wasn't a name that
Richler found by chance in a phone book: during summer 1979, literary
critic Kerry McSweeney published an essay in *Canadian Literature*, pointing to "a certain deconstructive energy ... a dark negating vision of human
existence" that undermined Richler's constructive concerns as a satirist and
moralist.[56] There was some truth to this, but McSweeney meant it as a rep-
rimand – Richler working at cross-purposes to himself, at once imposing
morals and not being moral enough. What Richler needed, McSweeney suggested, was both that negating energy *and* a humane depth informed by the
psychoanalytic tradition. McSweeney had it backwards: Richler wasn't a
satiric moralist blindsided by his own unconscious negations; Richler as a
young writer had been a friend to negation – the gift of Céline et al. – but
now Richler, as a satirist and moralist and human being, was looking for
ways to bridle negation, to make it serve. Richler understood that he had
amoral tendencies, used those tendencies in his writing, and yet distrusted
both the philosophical basis for amorality and the notion that psychoanalysis could deliver up some dark *new* secrets about human beings. Instead of
replying directly to the critique, Richler split McSweeney's name between
two rogue police officers.

≷

Nine years between novels – the forty-year-old writer of *St. Urbain's Horseman* was suddenly on the doorstep of fifty. He owned a stationary bike but
didn't ride it,[57] and he despaired of giving up smoking or drinking.[58] His age
began to invite the criticism that he was old-fashioned, reactionary. Eleanor
Wachtel, eventually to become the engaging host of CBC's *Writers and Company*, was uncharacteristically graceless when commenting on Richler, calling him outdated and phallic, complaining that he loved men (Joshua's father
Reuben, Seymour the philanderer) but hated women (Joshua's mother).[59] Of
course there were strong autobiographical reasons for this, reasons that had
hardened now that he was estranged from Lily and that the distance from
his father's death allowed him to idealize Moe.

The feminist criticism that remains after autobiography is taken into consideration can be broken down into questions of taste and of social form. With respect to taste, Richler did admit that the phallus had a mind of its own, and he didn't mind repeating its adventures, though that wasn't to praise its every move – certainly Joshua recognizes that to commit adultery would be to betray his wife. Richler's narratives were becoming important versions of the history of the male, narratives that appeared at the moment when Western civilization, by inventing the pill and striking down numerous sexual restrictions, had opened up a great deal of sexual freedom. At the same time, with the movement towards greater equality for women and their increasing power in the public sphere, male discourse didn't go entirely unchallenged, but some shame and some restrictions were maintained. This was the situation that Richler explored and is one reason why his novels are fascinating and revealing of masculinity.

If Richler's novels expressed the reproductive drive, biology, of course, always takes a social form, and here Richler's feminist critics were on surer ground. The female characters who carried value in his novels were tied closely to the home and were subordinate to male desire. Outside of the novels, he mocked legal challenges by feminists against men-only clubs,[60] and some acquaintances have spoken of a separation between male and female spheres in the semi-public life of Montreal or Township bars, as well as in Richler's private life – men, hard liquor, and poker in one room, women in the other.[61] Yet it's a mistake to speak of his work as simply "phallic." The wives of the main characters in his major novels became progressively *less* stereotypical. He opposed retrogressive measures that would limit the rights of women. He had no difficulty dealing with women in roles of authority in business or politics. In part, the separation of spheres was due to Richler's knowledge that the more vulgar aspects of his humour would go down better among men. Certainly he knew that "political correctness" – such an elusive term, at times an accurate term to describe the emasculation of free speech, at other times a stick used to beat anyone who stands up against sexism – was always in danger of shutting him up.

Critics also trotted out Richler's satire against Gay Pride as another sign that he was outmoded. Here one must differentiate between heterosexism and identity politics: Richler supported homosexual civil rights, though he had little patience for identity politics. "Grim injustice-collectors," he called those who monitored the public sphere for derogatory comments.[62] It puzzled him when Jane Rule and Marie-Claire Blais lent their considerable talents to *Body Politic*'s Great Canadian Lesbian Fiction Contest, a contest he considered parochial. Richler's separation of female and homosexual rights from identity politics may have been somewhat naïve, but it was of a piece with his continuing stance on racial and national identity politics. A Great Jewish Fiction Contest would have elicited the same Richler howl. In his humanist stance the affiliation of human to human must trump any lesser affiliation. Homosexuals deserved rights because they were human, not because they, like Jews, could trade on a lineage of suffering.

Richler's personal feelings about homosexuality evolved somewhat over time, with help (not that he'd admit it) from the "injustice-collectors." In the 1951 manuscript of *The Rotten People*, Richler's alter ego Kerman tolerates his homosexual friends but feels revulsion when he discovers them in embrace.[63] Later on, just after Richler wrote about Detective Inspector Ben Greenberg in 1971, it seems that Greenberg told a researcher that Richler must be gay. Robert Fulford reassured Richler, "As for Sgt. Ben Greenberg, I persuaded the researcher not to listen to Ben on *that* matter. In fact, I pointed out, you are very hard on queers and would just as soon punch one in the nose as look at him."[64] Likely Fulford was both remembering Richler's earlier attitudes and exaggerating for his friend's amusement, because in articles of the time, Richler suggested that homosexuals had valid grievances, though it didn't disturb him that rabbis refused to perform homosexual marriages, or that adoption agencies refused to let homosexuals adopt children.[65] By the late 1970s, when the cultural changes arising out of the Stonewall Riots had begun to take root, *Joshua Then and Now*'s Seymour wails, "now I find out that Auden, my Auden, has been a cocksucker all these years."[66] The passage isn't likely to be praised by gay readers, yet Seymour's views are not Joshua's, and it was Auden who gave the epigraph to *Joshua Then and Now* (as he did to *St. Urbain's Horseman*). This time round the epigraph was erotic. "Lay your sleeping head, my love," applies both to Joshua's relationship to Pauline, and less comfortably, though not in the end homosexually, to Joshua's relationship with Murdoch. In a magazine column, Richler supported the rights of homosexuals to be teachers, yet admitted that he might not send his sons along on a camping trip supervised by a homosexual teacher.[67] In the novel, this voice is given to McMaster and inflated: "You're a faggot today, and you want it written in the bill of rights that you got the right to teach gym in elementary school and soap the boys down in the shower room."[68] Letting McMaster say it allows Richler a more visceral (and funnier) expression of prejudice, yet McMaster's attitudes aren't endorsed. Here, too, Richler was a small-l liberal. He approved of Trudeau's social policy, including the decriminalization of homosexuality.[69] When Timothy Findley asked Richler to support an attempt to get a Canada Council Senior Arts Award for the aging and struggling gay writer Sinclair (Jim) Ross, Richler didn't hesitate.[70]

Ultimately, Richler was a temporizer in regard to same-sex relationships: when the times frowned, he frowned; when the times loosened up, he loosened up … uneasily. In his final novel, Richler would treat homosexuality and feminism as if they were inherently in need of correction, a disciplinary attitude that sometimes makes the satire fall flat: is the reader invited to laugh at human folly or at attempts to put women and homosexuals on equal footing with heterosexual men? Yet even if some of his social views were being superseded, Richler found reasons for his satiric barbs. His Norman Charnofsky agrees that, because he's uncomfortable with homosexuals, he must, as the other academics sternly inform him, be "insecure" about his masculinity.[71] In effect, Richler doesn't deny that homosexuals have been subject to social prejudice, but by wittily overdetermining Norman's self-abasement Richler satirizes the notion that "homophobia" is a psychological disorder.

The homosexual frissons – Joshua writes faux homosexual letters to his friend Murdoch, a photograph of Joshua kissing Murdoch becomes public, Joshua is discovered wearing women's panties – impinge surprisingly little on serious gender issues. These twists were not only suggested by Greenberg's slur and by the draft-avoidance letters that Richler had written in Haut de Cagnes in the early 1950s, but also by more recent wit that surfaced in letters to Brian Moore and Knopf editor Gordon Lish. With Richler as reference, Moore had applied to the English Department Chairman Peter Thorslev, Jr. for a creative writing job at the University of California, Los Angeles.[72] Richler had recommended Moore, but had also sent Moore a hoax letter, which pretended to be that very recommendation. Moore replied with a prank letter, too, purportedly from Peter Thorslev, Jr., saying, "I was distressed by the offensive anti-Gay tone of the p.s. and, indeed have made a private comment on it to Mr Clifton Fadiman, who, as you may not be aware is extremely sympathetic to our movement."[73] Fadiman, Richler's friend on the BOMC board, was gay, as Moore knew. Gordon Lish, who valued Richler's friendship a great deal and perhaps all the more so because Richler made him act foolishly, also joked about a homosexual relationship with Richler. Pretending agony, Lish wrote Florence a very funny letter:

> Flo, he just sent me a letter again. Please God he didn't make a copy of it and leave it around the house where the children could maybe see it. Well, Flo, I don't know – a man gets to be a certain number of years, things maybe didn't work out so wonderful for him, this kind of thing happens, who can tell? Believe me, nobody should point a finger. What we all have to do is to take it all with a grain of salt and meanwhile, comfort, comfort. That's right, Flo – comfort is what this person needs, not finger-pointing. So I am only writing to keep you posted, God forbid it should all go on behind your back and you never know until the last minute … I myself will personally have to

have another "date" with him. Flo, I swear to you, the last time we
were "together," I begged him to listen to reason and to let me go my
separate way ... But Flo, it's for the good of Alfred A. Knopf, yes? In
other words, Flo, what is good for Knopf is good for the Jews, and
this is why this one last time and then, I swear to you, no matter how
his heart breaks, never again. For you and for the children, never, I
swear! (Burn this letter.)

Yours like a sister,
Gordy[74]

Whatever one might want to say about "performing identities," such jokes,
mutating their way into *Joshua Then and Now*, were neither heterosexist
nor a real challenge to gender boundaries.

Much more significant was the tribute that lay behind the Joshua/Mur-
doch kiss, a kiss that is Joshua's declaration of love for his friend, dying in
Hollywood, land of *Fun with Dick and Jane*, land where death is "just a
sour-grapes rumour out of the East, bad word of mouth, something that
used to figure in grainy European-made films, which everybody knew were
bum grossers."[75] In *St. Urbain's Horseman*, Jake had worried obsessively
about his own mortality; in *Joshua Then and Now*, Joshua worries more
about the mortality of his friends. About the time that Richler had visited
Spain in 1976, had come the news that his British editor and friend, Tony
Godwin, had died.[76] Two years later, another of Richler's good friends, film-
maker Jack Clayton suffered what appears to have been a minor stroke.[77]
Clayton survived another seventeen years, but Richler's sorrow at Godwin's
death and Clayton's collapse registered strongly through Murdoch.

≶

On a less personal level in *Joshua Then and Now*, Richler for the first time
began to allow the Canadian polity, particularly Canadian Jewish history
and the debate about Québécois separatism, to play a significant role in a
novel. He had dealt with the Canadian polity often in his essays, but, living
so long in London, he had in his fiction generally shied away from Canadian national issues. After five or six years in Canada, Richler knew the
polity well enough to allow it to figure in Joshua's story.

The diaries of W.L. Mackenzie King, the prime minister who presided
over Richler's youth, were made public in 1977. Greatly interested, Richler
cut out and used newspaper articles revealing that King had received messages from beyond the grave, specifically from his little terrier, Pat II, and
that King considered Pat's death on par with that of Jesus: "I felt as if [Pat
II] had died for me, that my sins might be forgiven."[78] A potentially affecting report – but not for Richler, who remembered that King, to placate

Québec, had allowed very few Jewish refugees into Canada in the years lead-
ing up to World War II, when the refugees so desperately needed a home.
Commenting on C.P. Stacey's biography of King, Richler said that the prime
minister had a relationship with his dog that was "just this side of sodomy
... Pat died in his arms in the summer of 1941, as King, ever the campaigner,
making promises he couldn't fulfill, sang aloud to him, 'Safe in the Arms of
Jesus.'"[79] Out of Richler's impotent anger, as well, came the William Lyon
Mackenzie King Society in *Joshua Then and Now*, a society that looked back
at the war with both nostalgia and rage and that parodied King by singing
"Safe in the Arms of Jesus" in Yiddish.

The WMLK Society wasn't a structure through which one might effect
political change, at least not directly. The society likely took its cue from the
Corvine Society in A.J.A. Symons's *The Quest for Corvo*, where a few literary men meet to speculate about the impostor who styled himself Baron
Corvo and to give papers on topics such as the post-Einsteinian forms of
measurement, "rectilinear and corvilinear."[80] Critics would eventually chas-
tise Richler for *Joshua Then and Now*'s apparent withdrawal from political
engagement. Richler's suspicion of national governments and his favouring
of merely private solutions left the field wide open, said Frank Davey, for
"*laissez-faire* internationalism." Davey argued that Joshua finds his own national history less important than the Spanish Civil War and that Joshua's
burglaries display a self-made individual transgressing in order to succeed.[81]
True, as far as it went. Richler supported efforts to recognize the MacKen-
zie-Papineau Battalion (part of the International Brigade) as veterans for
their service in Spain.[82] He also had great faith in the corruption of party
politics, and although he deplored Reaganomics, his response was not to
join a counter-party but to seek joy with family and friends. The small ci-
vilities were important, and the purpose of life, he said, was to enjoy oneself without harming others.[83] If in *A Choice of Enemies* young Richler had
laughed at Voltaire's "*il faut cultiver notre jardin*," he wasn't laughing any
more. Within a few years he would be blowing the horn for free trade.

But Richler's sense of history and politics was much more finely tuned
than Davey gave him credit for. No other Canadian fictional oeuvre stuck its
nose into so many historical crannies: the clash between Montreal's Jewish
ghetto and the French-English "founding" races, Anglo-conformity, the anti-
Communist blacklist in Canada, Canadian "innocence" as typified in Marilyn Bell, Inuit art, Irving Layton, *Maclean's*, Pierre Berton's investigative
reporting, the colonial inferiority complex, the CBC, Mackenzie King's legacy,
anti-Semitism in Canada, the Canadian class system or "Vertical Mosaic,"
Canadian content regulations, A.M. Klein, the rise of the Bronfman business
empire, the Franklin Expedition, the Barr Colony fiasco, the CFL, the Canadian counterculture, Québécois separatism, the Montreal Canadiens, lan-

guage laws, the Americanization of Canadian popular culture – one loses one's breath. Richler didn't just dutifully plod over to history, sentenced to social problems in order to atone for the novelist's habit of making things up. Rather, he approached history with wit and invention. At a conference after Richler's death, Davey would play "Provocateur" on a panel entitled "Is Richler Canadian Content?"[84] It's not a question that one can seriously entertain, unless by "Canadian" one means "someone with a protectionist attitude towards Canadian culture." Richler was born and grew up in Canada; he lived here for fifty-one years; except for *Cocksure*, his ten novels centred on Canadian characters; each of his five major novels featured Canada and its culture prominently. Except: national sovereignty didn't hold the same sentimental value for a Jew who saw his race turned back at Canada's door.

Before *Joshua Then and Now* was written, from a source far less sophisticated than Davey, came a sharper barb: "How many Jewish causes do you support?"[85] It tickled Richler to no end that the letter writer signed herself, "A Fellow Jewess," but the question was nonetheless important. Richler had no confidence that Jewish political parties or the Jewish state were more honourable than their Canadian counterparts, and he urged his children to read Edward Said's *The Question of Palestine*,[86] which, despite making a very one-sided case for the Palestinians, had the virtue of questioning the pro-Israeli stance that after World War II understandably dominated the Western media.[87] Eventually, "progressives" of all sorts jumped on the PLO bandwagon, calling Israel just another colonialist state, but Richler adopted a more complex stance. He confessed a sneaking admiration for Israeli Prime Minister Menachem Begin's toughness even though Begin had been one of the architects of the Deir Yassin massacre,[88] and in *Solomon Gursky Was Here* it would be to Solomon's credit that he supplied the fledgling Israeli state with fighter planes and had a hand in the 1976 freeing of the PLO-hijacked airplane at Entebbe. Yet when, after a number of Palestinian attacks, Israel invaded Lebanon in 1982 to create a "security corridor," Richler wasn't supportive.[89] More immediately, in *Joshua Then and Now*, Richler satirized the Bond Drive Dinners through which Israel raised funds in North America. Elie Wiesel wasn't amused when one of Richler's fictional characters reported that Wiesel had lectured at his Bond Drive Dinner for $5,000. Wiesel copied the offending page and wrote across it, "I have never spoken for a Bond Drive ... As for the fee, I wish it were true."[90] All the same, Richler didn't avoid Jewish causes. In 1978 he appeared at a twenty-four-hour hunger strike held by B'nai B'rith and the Student Struggle for Soviet Jewry outside the Soviet Consulate, protesting the harsh sentences given to Anatoly Scharansky and other dissidents. Richler called on the government to stop cultural and athletic exchanges, such as the Canada Cup of hockey, until the USSR began to treat its Jewish dissidents more humanely.[91] Along with many other Jewish writers, he signed a letter calling on Ronald Reagan to stop selling F-15 fighter planes to Saudi Arabia, one of the main supporters of the Palestinian Liberation Organization.[92]

Richler's most important way of supporting Jewish causes, however, was his writing. Despite Davey's criticism, *almost all* novels have "individualistic" resolutions. To argue against this is to demand propaganda (political ends steering individual experience) and to assume that individualized responses have no communal-political meaning for readers. In all of his novels, Richler forced readers to become attuned to injustice and racial discrimination. Although his touch was becoming lighter, it was no less serious. Instead of the dangerous Nazi colonel of *The Acrobats*, Richler turned *Joshua Then and Now*'s "Mueller" into a former Nazi propagandist and writer of Westerns – a more complex and less melodramatic entanglement for Joshua.[93] Richler may have been aided by the refusal of his children to take his rants with full reverence. During a Richler diatribe against Wagner, Emma stepped over to Florence's enormous collection of German operas and symphonies, began to pull them out – they were nearly half her height – and took them in a showy way to the garbage bin. Richler was able to laugh at himself.[94] At Mueller's villa, Joshua finds no incriminating Wagner records.[95]

In *Joshua Then and Now* Richler satirized both Nazi anti-Semitism and Mackenzie King's polite but deadly refusal to accept refugees. The cure for anti-Semitic nationalisms? Internationalism. And yet Richler didn't avoid the Canadian polity. Although he didn't *set out* to mythicize Canada in the manner of Margaret Laurence's *The Diviners*, in effect he did so. Bringing together the races and classes, Richler bound not only Joshua to Pauline – the St. Urbain Street corner to the Westmount princess – but also the two fathers-in-law – the Jewish ex-boxer to the WASP Senator. If love and a shared set of generational attitudes bind Joshua and Pauline, the union of in-laws is more witty, as Richler imagines how an unreconstructed lower-class Jew might liberate an uptight, wealthy Anglo.

Richler's "imagined community," to use Benedict Anderson's phrase for the nation, included mainly Jews and the English. He spent less energy on visible minorities or the French, though he didn't leave the French out of the novel completely. The 1976 election of the separatist Parti Québécois alarmed many Anglophones: 133,000 of them, including more than 13,000 Jews, left the province.[96] Richler hadn't voted PQ, but at first he didn't lament their election. He liked the PQ's no-fault auto insurance, its protection of green space, and wasn't upset, initially, when the infamous Bill 101 made French the official language of Québec, humbling the mighty Anglo castles of Westmount.[97] Joshua doesn't worry too much about the declining value of his home, though Richler did worry.[98] He had supported Trudeau's vision of national bilingualism[99] and began, in his journalism, to turn his attention to minority English language rights in Québec, noting

that Bill 101 violated Section 133 of the BNA Act, which guaranteed English in the courts and legislature.[100] He didn't mention that Manitoba had
been in de facto violation of Section 133's protection of French-language
rights for more than a century, a fact that somehow never pained Anglophones. Richler's 1977 *Atlantic Monthly* article on the situation, "Oh
Canada: Lament for a divided country," was, unlike some of his later pieces,
a balanced assessment of separatism. However, he made the mistake of confusing the PQ election theme song, "*Demain nous appartient*" ("Tomorrow
belongs to us"), written by Stéphane Venne, with "Tomorrow belongs to
me," the Hitler youth song from *Cabaret*, written a few years earlier by
John Kander and Fred Ebb. "Sloppy research," Venne scolded Richler, "may
in fact lead to paranoia."[101] His mistake heated things up for Premier René
Lévesque in the United States, as one president of a prominent US university with a large Jewish population declined to meet him. No apology from
Richler. A few months later, Lévesque apparently passed on Venne's greetings to Richler, saying, "When the author of our song catches up to you,
you'll receive a punch in the face."[102]

The "reconquest" of Québec by the French made it into *Joshua Then
and Now* mostly as background. There were no significant French characters in the novel, nor (apart from Duddy's girlfriend Yvette) in any of Richler's novels, a fact that Québécois nationalists would later pounce on. One
thing Richler called attention to: the new power structure. When the new
premier, René Lévesque, accidentally ran over and killed a street person, the
Montreal police, "who used to gleefully crack separatist skulls with riot
sticks," now "escorted the distressed premier and his mistress from the scene
… and booked the offending corpse."[103]

⧖

For many readers, Reuben's somewhat unorthodox monologues on Judaism
were the most memorable aspect of *Joshua Then and Now*. Paraphrasing
rather loosely from what he was taught as a child, Reuben explains to the
young Joshua that Yom Kippur is the day "when if you shit on anybody
during the year you got a legal right to repent." God, Reuben later adds, is
a gambling man, and the message of the Book of Job is that "if you continue to believe in God when you're up shit's creek, it can pay off double at
the window."[104] *St. Urbain's Horseman* had been fairly respectful of the Judaic tradition, but beginning with *Joshua Then and Now* Richler began to
tilt at sacred history.

Possibly Richler's cue was provided by his hero Isaac Babel who in *Red
Cavalry* has the painter Pan Apolek do a series of lively portraits of the Holy
Family: "Josephs with grey hair centre-parted, Christs smeared with poma-
tum, rural Marys who had had many children, sitting with their knees wide
apart."[105] Alternatively, Richler may have gotten his cue from a rather cu-

rious fan letter. A man named Arthur Rawet wrote about an argument he had had with an Orthodox acquaintance in a restaurant, an argument that included an assessment of Moses, the purported author of the Torah: "I let him know that his #1 hero circumsliced himself because he was suffering from an advanced case of V.D.. I gave him a few more of my interpretations on the Good-Book and he hit the ceiling" [sic]. Rawet enlarged on some of those interpretations: "Abe a compassionate prince in his own right took his first born and together with his mother kicked them out without a drachma, because his #1 ZSA ZSA demanded it. Even the Almighty compassionate one who lives UPSTAIRS rentfree whispered to Abram to do Sarah's will ... A singer by the name of Valachi told Jake that Esau is shopping for rope and the minute Isaac becomes a D.D. (dearly departed) the rope will be used on his neck as a necklace."[106] Rawet wrenched sacred history from its idealized, odourless distance, and made it disturbingly and entertainingly contemporary. Richler learned the lesson well, borrowing not Rawet's words or examples, but his attitude and his engaging style.

To desacralize the Biblical stories, to merge sacred history with secular as Reuben did: this could kill Judaism, the nineteenth-century Rabbi Samson Hirsh had warned.[107] Richler, by the end of the 1970s, had for the most part given up the impulse that made him take his children to the synagogue. Once in a while he still went to say hello to his uncles. But, as always, he didn't feel sheltered by faith. Death was final; given the Holocaust, there couldn't be a God in any traditional sense; life was absurd, though to be lived honourably in the face of that absurdity.[108] And yet, and yet ... there was a great deal of ambivalence in Richler about spiritual matters. Richler clearly wished that the Horseman and Solomon Gursky be something more than Jews-with-an-attitude, that there *be* a kingdom of Prester John. This wish for larger patterns of spiritual meaning was a holdover from Richler's Orthodox past, and he didn't entirely abandon it, especially in his exaltation of familial love and in his return to Maimonides, who said "Men frequently think that the evils in the world are more numerous than the good things."[109] If Richler used Reuben to defend the flesh and material concerns against Orthodox notions of purity, Reuben's attempt at a larger pattern of meaning suggests that Richler hadn't fully reconciled himself to the absurd.

In later years Richler would speak of the competition in first-century Judaism between the school of Shammai, with its careful and detailed obedience to the Torah, and the school of Hillel, with its focus on the *spirit* of the Torah.[110] It might seem odd for the determinedly secular Richler to point at Hillel, and odd for Richler to identify a debt collection enforcer – Reuben – with compassion. Nevertheless, like Richler's praise of Hillel, Reuben was intended, on one level, to mark the difference between a loveless observance of the Torah and a more humane, if eccentric, creed. On another level, he, like the novel as a whole, was also just plain fun.

23

Last of the Free-Market Scribblers

IN THE DAYS LEADING up to the Sovereignty Referendum of 20 May 1980, René Lévesque opined that, given Pierre Elliott Trudeau's middle name, Trudeau couldn't be a true Quebecker. Trudeau thundered back that his name was Québécois *and* Canadian. While Trudeau delivered the *coup de grace* by reeling off all the "Canadian" names that would have to be expunged in a chauvinistic Québec,[1] *Joshua Then and Now*, with its own little dig at Lévesque, arrived on the bookshelves. To the tune of 60 percent, Québec voted to remain in Confederation, and *Joshua Then and Now* topped Canadian bestseller lists everywhere, though Jack McClelland tempered the celebration somewhat by remarking, "there is no great fucking rush on for books at the moment."[2] Even before the publication of *Joshua Then and Now*, Richler was invited to become an Officer of the Order of Canada.[3] He declined, noting that Hugh MacLennan, Margaret Laurence, and Gabrielle Roy had all been invested as *Companions*, not as lowly *Officers*. Possibly stung by the McSweeney article that had questioned his place in the Canadian canon,[4] Richler told the director of the Honours Secretariat that he interpreted the offer as "more put-down than salute." A tough negotiator, Richler, but he'd have to wait another twenty-two years before the Honours Secretariat saw things his way.[5]

The growth of Richler's celebrity didn't always have the most positive effect on his character. His anger, suppressed and channelled for the most part into his writing – indeed powering what was most honest in his work – had never disappeared. But his continuing success confirmed his long-held feeling that most people were frauds and that it was a courtesy to tell them so. He told popular author Richard Rohmer at a party, "If you cared anything at all about letters, you'd never go near a typewriter."[6] During an interview with Paul Soles on *Canada after Dark*, Richler didn't like Soles's direction, and interrupted, "Don't ask me those questions. Ask me your *own* questions." Soles, a Richler fan, was forgiving afterwards, but the *Canada after Dark* staff were furious. Even Peter Gzowski, Richler's friend and one who knew better than anybody how to play the interview game, had a hard time interviewing Richler. Gzowski dared not ask any question to which Richler knew that Gzowski knew the answer, fearing that Richler would tear him to shreds. For those outside of Richler's circle wanting to converse with him, rule #1 seems to have been don't talk about his work unless he initiates the conversation. Rule #2, don't talk to him *at all* unless he initiates the conversation. Obedience could result in a rich exchange. One member of the literary community said that Richler didn't *want* to let people into his circle, especially people who might try to interpret him. Others called him rude: "he refuses to communicate, so the onus is on you to do it. Before you know it, you are babbling on like an idiot and you can feel his derision."[7] *Cocksure* had been misanthropic. *St. Urbain's Horseman* and *Joshua Then and Now* had sequestered most of that misanthropy into characters such as Harry Stein, Jack Trimble, and Sgt. McMaster. The novels knew more than Richler knew. Or, rather, the novels *did* more than Richler did to mitigate misanthropy: it wasn't so easy to sequester misanthropy in real life. Richler fought with his mother, reviewers, nationalists, socialists – with anyone not ready to take him on his own terms.

Bev Slopen, who worked for Book-of-the-Month Club in the late 1970s, felt that Richler hung her out to dry. Used to thinking of himself as an independent operator and unused to working inside corporate structures, Richler didn't consider that Slopen, staffing BOMC's Canadian office, worked for him. Al Silverman, the head of BOMC, considered that she did. Throughout Slopen's four years, Richler didn't return her calls, keep her informed, or even include her when BOMC appointees came to Toronto. In the end, Richler's slighting of her convinced the New York office that she was expendable, and New York decided to assess Canadian manuscripts itself. Richler, of course, found little to complain about in this literary application of the branch-plant economy. But neocolonialism wasn't Slopen's main complaint. She simply wanted Richler to sympathize and say "tough luck," or to offer a letter of recommendation. When she wrote to him explaining her feelings, he brushed her off.[8]

Richler's friends attribute his occasional surliness to shyness, to his grave expression, and to his dislike of crowds.[9] Florence says that all he had to do was enter a room and sit down for people to tremble and worry about what he was thinking. At a surprise party that she gave for him, the family doctor came over to her later and confided that he had seen Richler seated in his chair, a serious expression on his face. Not knowing what kind of mood Richler was in, the doctor had skirted around him. Florence, however, knew that Richler was anxious because he was missing the baseball game and wanted to know the score. "That was very much Mordecai," she says, "he would look just grave pondering on a baseball score."[10] Another report of the party tells of Richler walking into the surprise and then running immediately to his bedroom, ostensibly to change his shirt.[11] One might guess that Bernard Gursky's panic when his friends and family yell "Surprise!" in *Solomon Gursky Was Here* had its origins in Richler's ambivalence about such a situation – that for Richler a sudden shock and a loud group of people tearing him away from his anticipated baseball game was a concept with limited appeal. Shyness is a form of arrogance, a self-confident former psych major tells Moses Berger in *Solomon Gursky*.[12] As laughable as this confident assertion is, it wasn't so far off the mark for Richler. Of course, people often sought him out solely on the basis of his celebrity and for their own advantage, a game that Richler detested.

Richler's children weren't exempt from the rudeness. He took pride in his children's educational achievements, but when he visited Martha at Harvard in October 1980,[13] he informed her that the university was just a playpen. He remained convinced that unless one trekked through the Mordecai Richler School of Self-Education, from "Broke in Paris" to "Scratching Out a Living in London," one couldn't learn much more than smug pieties. "Trying to impress him is the road to hell," Martha said, "so you just have to get on with your life." At the same time, when Martha wanted to work on a friend's boat, Richler wouldn't let her – she was a girl. In 1987, she boiled over a bit. To her displeasure Mordecai suggested a spell as a waitress in "the university of life" (his words) instead of going on to a PhD. She put it to her father that the phrase "ambitious young men" rolled off his tongue rather more easily than "ambitious young woman." He had been speaking of writers Adam Gopnik and Roger Kimball; Martha doubted very much that he would have recommended that *The New Yorker*'s Gopnik wait on tables.[14]

It probably didn't make things easier for Martha that Daniel had become the cultural correspondent for the CBC's flagship news program, *The Journal*.[15] Robert Fulford had told Richler that in hip Toronto circles Richler was now known as "Daniel Richler's father, you know, the one who writes."[16] Richler didn't mind hearing such things at all. What Martha feared was that Richler didn't take her seriously enough, that he saw her Art History education as merely a bauble with which to capture a male. As such, he evidently thought it was time for his financial role in her university education to end. Unhappy that Martha wasn't advancing quickly enough, Mordecai infuriated her by asking, "So what do you do all day?" She reminded him that when scholarship funds at Columbia had run out, she had worked as a cashier, juggling two jobs plus courses at university – familiar, then, with his "university of life." But she couldn't be expected to deny her privileged upbringing and become her father, who, after all, had spent a healthy chunk of time "reflecting" in Paris and on Ibiza. Since she was no longer wasting *his* money on health clubs, but was for the most part self-sufficient, she expected a little more emotional support. "So long as you do not believe in my future," she declared, "I cannot be happy."[17]

Yet he was by no means a harsh father and his children clearly loved him, Emma often giving him birthday head rubs,[18] and Martha starting her difficult letter to her father thus: "it goes with saying that I adore you."[19] His friends enjoyed his company immensely, in part because he could be warm towards those whom he respected and in part because he didn't pander to them. The nickname the children, especially the girls, gave him – "Rex" – was an endearment and also a recognition of his primacy. By now, only Jacob was left at home, and Richler took him on salmon-fishing expeditions.[20] Richler spent more time with Jacob than he had with the others, and Jacob, with a precocious understanding of politics and a wicked wit, always seemed more comfortable in his father's presence than the older children had been.[21] According to Jacob, Richler was an even better father than he was a writer.[22] When Jacob began to do poorly in school, treating other students and his teachers rudely,[23] Richler pulled him aside and warned, "Leave your brain stuck in second gear too long and it might get stuck there." He could be loving. Once, after a gruff Richler speech, cartoonist Terry Mosher saw him kneel in the middle of Peel Street to gently fix Florence's broken heel.[24] When Ted Allan suffered his breakdown in the 1980s, Richler came across the room, awkwardly embraced him, and wept.[25]

Perhaps Richler described himself best when he wrote an introduction to *The Best of Modern Humour*, a book he edited in 1983. Ostensibly speaking of comedy in general, his remarks were actually a self-portrait in quick strokes. Humorists, he said, were often melancholy. They drank a lot and liked to hide in corners at parties, fearing the intrusion of strangers prone to ask them to say something funny.[26] There's a defensive strain of elitism in this fear of being caught out, of having always to live up to the wit of one's writing, and of having to sail above the criticisms that one habitually made of others. Yet the fact that humour could hide pain – cliché or not – was fundamental to Richler. He didn't start out as a funny writer, but as a romantic, confronting the experiences (especially with his mother) that so troubled him. To say, as he did, that "the best revenge on experience is writing well"[27] was to admit that the early wounds hadn't diminished in the comedy of *Joshua Then and Now*; they had only gone underground.

≶

As Richler got richer in the early 1980s and turned into a brand name, his views on money changed. He wasn't "gifted" at handling money, but he loved to make it,[28] rendering him a candidate for industrial sponsorship. No longer was it *Maclean's* sending him to report on the political situation in Israel, but posh magazines such as *Signature* (which boasted that its median reader pulled in $86,211 per anum[29]) sending him in 1982 on a tour of Kenya's Great Rift Valley and the Masai Mara Game Reserve,[30] with guides and cooks – a crew of nine – so that the St. Urbain Street boy could flog luxury travel. The crew went ahead to set up tents in a small clearing; then followed Richler, Ted Kotcheff, Richler's lawyer Bob Shapiro, and their wives. At night, one could hear the baboons, very territorial, as they urinated on the tents. The sense of adventure and fear was augmented for Florence because Richler had planned ahead, acquiring a Warner Brothers tape of animal sounds and arranging for one of the crew to turn the tape on after they were tucked into bed. Florence was frightened and told Richler that she wasn't altogether pleased to be in Africa under such conditions.[31]

These trips did harbour certain ironies. The author who wrote fearlessly when confronted with pomp and circumstance suddenly found it in his interest to be gentle and to obey the marketing demands of the travel genre, whispering: "Go, go, before it's gone. Before ... the Masai herdsman who approaches across the plain has his ears plugged into a Walkman."[32] Richler was conscious of the irony, and defended himself, saying, after a pampered trip to Paris, also courtesy of *Signature*, that he had lost his appetite for lumpy mattresses and wondering if it was really necessary for today's young bloods to dress quite so scruffily.[33] Indeed, though Richler himself hadn't really covered all that much of the ground between "scruffy" and "presentable," by the fall of 1983 he was writing a column for the doyen of male style magazines, GQ, *Gentleman's Quarterly*.[34] Asked about his favourite writers, he'd speak of Waugh, Walker Percy, Cheever, Bellow, Le Carré[35] – not a new crew for Richler, but none of them Célines either. When Peter C. Newman accepted the task of editing *Debrett's Illustrated Guide to the Canadian Establishment*, the colonial equivalent of *Debrett's Peerage*, he naturally looked to include Richler and wrote him, asking for particulars.[36] Richler obliged. Yet as pampered as he had become, he couldn't help poking fun at the self-satisfied assumptions of the upper crust. To the request that he list all the exclusive clubs to which he belonged, Richler gave a reply that caused no little consternation in the editorial room. In the end, Newman decided to deliver Richler's information as given, but to deliver it in a sneering tone: "He belongs to no club more distinguished than the Canadian Automobile Association and something called the Owl's Nest Society of Mansonville, Quebec."[37]

The Owl's Nest Society: Richler's friends at the pub of the same name, near Lake Memphremagog. As highly as Richler thought of himself, one thing hadn't changed from his days with Juanito "Pus" on Ibiza: he found people from all walks of life interesting. The previous owner of the house at Lake Memphremagog, Mrs. McIntosh, gave Florence a list of handymen because Florence needed a painter. "Oh yes and there's Roger George," McIntosh said, about to cross a name off, "but you wouldn't want to call him. He drinks too much." Florence, however, asked to meet him. He came to the house in his Sunday finery, on his head a little baseball cap, which he removed to say "How do you do?" She was immediately taken. George – or "Sweetpea" or "Pea" as everyone called him – had a trembling hand, generally not a primary qualification for a house painter, but amazingly, says Florence, as he touched the wall with the brush, the tremble disappeared and he painted very well.

Working under Florence, George only saw Richler to nod at for the first couple of years, as Richler came down and passed through the dining room to refill his teapot. Florence, meantime, went out with Jacob to explore the territory, returning with stories about the local people, knowing, as Mordecai listened, that he would go to the pub one day to meet all the fellows.[38] Despite the grave looks from *Debrett's*, soon Richler did resort to the company of the Owl's Nest Society every afternoon. He also drank at The Thirsty Boot in Knowlton and, in later years, at The Caboose. He was once thrown out of The Thirsty Boot for being rude to owner Gerry Wood's daughter. After the ejection, Richler was unfailingly polite.[39] He sponsored a recreation league baseball team and used the sponsorship to lever himself briefly onto the pitching mound, good news for opposing batters. It cost Sweet Pea a super-size bottle of scotch to lure Richler back onto the bench.[40] In the mid-1980s after the children's education had been mostly paid for, Florence had a cedar-and-glass addition built onto the Memphremagog house, and Richler bought a snooker table. He hung up Moe's old chisel, with its motto in yellow chalk: "Moses Isaac Richler – No Success!" Every Boxing Day, Richler hosted a snooker tournament for his children and his Eastern Township drinking buddies.[41] Those companions eventually appeared, with few alterations, in *Solomon Gursky Was Here*,[42] and Sweetpea George, transformed into Strawberry Watson, was delighted.[43] Mythologizing Canadian origins, Richler insisted that Canada's soul (if it had one) was not to be found on Parliament Hill but in tacky little bars, such as the Owl's Nest, strung across the country.[44] Richler's world: one night he'd be at a Montreal party whose guests included Pierre Trudeau; the next day in the Caboose, slapping at a pinball game that had "Mordecai" written on it, George watching.[45]

≶

In 1984, Richler pulled together a number of his essays, particularly those on Canada and its soul, into a book initially called *Hambourgeois*. He changed the title to *North of Forty-Nine*, then finally released it as *Home*

Sweet Home.[46] In his quest to squeeze every profit from his work without compromising his artistic integrity, Richler hadn't overlooked musical theatre. Over a drink, so the story goes, Richler sold impresario and fellow St. Urbainite Sam Gesser the musical rights to *The Apprenticeship of Duddy Kravitz* in 1984 for $1. Another offer lay on the table: a US producer wanted to do *Duddy* as a TV series, only not so Jewish, not set in Canada, and not set in the past.[47] Better to go with Gesser who wanted songs by Jerry Leiber and Mike Stoller, with the book by Richler himself. The musical opened in Edmonton – not the likeliest home for a Jewish musical – and plans were that it should march through nine Canadian cities before ascending to Broadway. Of necessity it was advertised to subscribers at Edmonton's Citadel Theatre as a finished production, but in reality it was a workshop ... a panicky workshop, with scenes and songs changing right up to opening day. Most of the seats sold because they were included in the season ticket subscription, but reviews were terrible, and many of the songs by Leiber and Stoller, including an ode to friendship sung by Duddy and Lenny in longjohns, were deemed inadequate.[48] Richler's downbeat ending didn't help, since audiences of musicals expected a wedding at the end. Only star Lonny Price consistently drew praise from the critics.

Richler had no experience writing musicals, but Florence urged him to do it, and he learned the craft on the run. When director Brian Macdonald complained about a scene, Richler would go down to the bar, write two pages, and come back with a funnier scene. Richler and Lonny Price soon formed a mutual admiration society. Although Price screamed at Leiber and Stoller, he thanked Richler effusively: "You're the reason I took the part.... Through all this you always seemed to know when *I* needed support or a compliment and I appreciate that."[49] From Edmonton, the production limped to Ottawa, but after four performances in the three-quarter-empty National Arts Centre, the show died. Gesser and his partners lost $1 million. Leiber and Stoller blamed Richler's book, and at times even Richler blamed himself,[50] but Macdonald and the cast blamed Leiber and Stoller. Three years later the show was very briefly revived in Philadelphia with new music and a much-edited book.[51] Canny producers wanted to reconcile Duddy and Yvette in the end but Richler held his ground, and thus scotched the chances of the new version going to New York. One audience member who had no doubt seen many musicals gave advice for improving Richler's novel, advice straight from the burning heart of musical theatre: have Duddy put his brother Lennie through medical school, and then Lennie can come up with a cure for Virgil's epilepsy in the final scene![52]

For Richler the time spent in Edmonton didn't translate into love of the city. Years before Richler's controversial work on Québec's language issue, Edmonton readers gave him a foretaste of what it meant to challenge a group's conception of itself. In a *New York Times* article he called Edmonton the boiler-room of Canada and (having interviewed the Edmonton hockey icon) intimated that Wayne Gretzky might not be Einstein. Gretzky had told Richler that he was too busy to read books that weren't real – i.e., fiction.[53] After Richler's article, the *Edmonton Sun* published his telephone number so that Edmontonians could vindicate their honour by making obscene telephone calls to Richler and his family. When a reporter from the *Sun* called to interview Richler, Richler asked for his editor's phone number. Sorry, it was against the newspaper's policy to release such information.[54] Those more innocent, but likewise unable to take a joke, wrote earnest letters: "you must know we are very proud of Wayne Gretzky and that we will stand up for him. He is one of the few real heroes today. He is well-mannered, considerate of others ... It's unfortunate that merely being a superior world-class athlete is just not good enough for the likes of you."[55] A group of Edmonton businessmen threatened to invoke a mysterious "Plan B" that would bring the *New York Times* to its knees unless it retracted Richler's lies.[56]

Mel Hurtig, Richler's ex-friend, waded into the battle. The anti-Edmonton article by the "rude little wimp" disgusted but did not surprise Hurtig. Wasn't Richler, after all, "the perfect obsequious colonial," who chose only one Canadian writer for *The Best of Modern Humour* and who didn't select enough Canadian books for BOMC? Hurtig reminded everyone that discriminating Edmonton audiences and critics had given a thumbs-down to the *Duddy* musical.[57] This wasn't strictly true: Edmonton critics had indeed panned *Duddy*, but Edmonton audiences had bought tickets. Tit-for-tat, Richler revealed that he had turned down Hurtig's request to write articles for *The Canadian Encyclopedia* and that Hurtig kept sending him speeches, hoping to be named in a Richler article. Eventually, he would be mentioned, though not by name. In *Solomon Gursky Was Here*, the pilot Riley complains to Moses Berger of being pursued by an Edmonton publisher, "one of your brethren ... A smiler born, awfully fancy, he sits down at your table and you're surrounded."[58] As for Edmonton, Richler professed gratefulness that the Citadel had staged *Duddy*. Yet Hurtig's notion gave Richler pause: "Why not punish cities where my plays weren't applauded, my books weren't written about with unstinting praise?" But, he lamented, the list would be too long. In the end, a harrowing guilt must have overwhelmed Richler, for he repented: "Edmonton, Edmonton, I apologize. Ever since the article appeared, I have suffered a crisis of conscience, haunted by the damage I may have done. In my nightmares I see those tens of thousands of tourists who were bound for Edmonton in January, eager to gawk at its architectural marvels and stroll down its elegant boulevards and dine in its fabled restaurants, canceling out because of the lies I had written."[59]

≶

The work that mattered most at this point was the film of *Joshua Then and Now*. At a forum several years earlier, Richler had attacked the Canadian film industry and the Canadian Film Development Corporation (CFDC) for financing schlock provided it was Canadian schlock. Was it really necessary to spend Canadian "culture" dollars on *Meatballs* or *Shivers*? Saying that Canadian producers were "snivelling little greasers" got Richler into a name-calling exchange with producer Bill Marshall. Audience members, straight-faced, explained to Richler that without cheap exploitation films by Francis Coppola or Martin Scorcese, there would have been no *Apocalypse Now* or *Taxi Driver*[60] – as if progress from money-making schlock to art were a genetic quirk in filmmakers, rather than the effect of the Hollywood system. Jack McClelland laughed about Richler tilting at rich and powerful producers ("that poor defenceless chap," McClelland called Marshall[61]) but Richler seems to have been less worried about repercussions than about pushing the CFDC into more responsible projects.

Preparing for *Joshua Then and Now*, Richler put his hand out to the CFDC, and, surprisingly, the money came. He had attempted a film version of Thomas Berger's *Reinhart in Love*, but Hollywood producers refused the screenplay.[62] With *Joshua Then and Now*, however, he thought that he was in the driver's seat. Kotcheff would again direct. His fee per movie had risen since *Duddy*, reaching $1 million after his huge successes with *First Blood* and *Uncommon Valour*, but for Richler he agreed to charge half price and take a percentage of the profits instead.[63] Compared with *Duddy*, *Joshua Then and Now*'s far bigger stakes – a $9.2 million budget – would bring along correspondingly bigger profit expectations. Another problem was the novel's length. Even *Duddy*, so much shorter, had resulted in a screenplay that at times seemed episodic. *Joshua Then and Now*, planned as both a two-hour movie and a 3.5-hour CBC-TV mini-series was in danger of being turned into a sitcom, or, rather, in the words of Toronto film critic Jay Scott "a sitcom dressed up as a satire,"[64] à la *Fun with Dick and Jane*. On the other hand, the financial compensations would be substantial, and the novel would be reissued, gaining a whole new set of readers.[65] To get a film made, he'd chop up the novel, and then, in the next novel, he could always chop up Hollywood.

The problems began early. Duddy's life had been about what he *did*, whereas Joshua had a rich inner life, harder to translate into visual terms. Hollywood's major studios, including 20th Century Fox, declined Richler's script. Kotcheff and Richler finally landed Canadian producer Robert Lantos, who, though not yet the industry force that he was to become, had the drive and enough connections to plan for the most expensive Canadian movie ever made. Through the back door, on the strength of Lantos's wheeling and dealing, came $2 million from 20th Century Fox. Through the front door came CFDC money and attendant restrictions. Only one actor was supposed to be non-Canadian. *Joshua Then and Now* was given a special dispensation for two but really needed four.[66] Although Cybill Shepherd agreed to play Joshua's wife Pauline,[67] Canadian content rules dictated otherwise. To comply, Kotcheff hired Gabrielle Lazure (daughter of the former PQ Minister for Social Development, Denis Lazure) for her first English-language role.[68] Lazure had the golden shiksa beauty to play Pauline but lacked strong acting skills and a WASP accent. As a result, Kotcheff was forced to cut her scenes down and eventually dub her voice.[69]

Many of the Canadian actors proved weak, especially Michael Sarrazin, who played Joshua's brother-in-law as if he were a music hall dancer, and it didn't take long before Richler was complaining loudly about CFDC restrictions. Yet James Woods, the highly intelligent US lead, didn't come across much better. His patrician air and chiselled looks made it difficult to take him as a Jewish grober, and his performance lacked passion, especially when the script called for him to break down into tears. Only Alan Arkin, as Joshua's father, shone.

Running close to 2.5 hours, the script had to be cut drastically – the Mackenzie King Memorial Society, the Spanish intrigue with the ex-Nazi Colonel, all gone.[70] The film kept many of the novel's great lines, but, wrenched from their contexts, they seem curiously enervated. This, of course, can't be blamed on Canadian content. Among the CFDC script-readers was Richler's former boss at ABC-TV, Sydney Newman, and he, like all the other readers, told Richler that the narrative would have to be straightforward, with few flashbacks, so as not to disorient skittish film audiences.[71] In this matter, too, Canadian content played no role. The great advantage of Canadian money was that Kotcheff got the final cut, which would never have happened in Hollywood.[72] Had Richler forgotten *Fun with Dick and Jane*, where his satiric ending had been gelded to make Dick and Jane heroes? Could an actress with a better accent make up for a loss of control over a film's ending?

Some of the Canadian restrictions had to do with the fact that the movie was being simultaneously shot for TV. (Joshua's father) Reuben's profanity had to be reigned in.[73] By investing in the timidity of TV, Kotcheff lamented, the CFDC was "protecting its downside while compromising its upside."[74] The film/TV co-production made writing and filming tortuous, requiring a fat script and a thin one, 180 pages for TV and 150 for the feature, with the added restriction that the TV production couldn't cost much more and so had to rely on the same actors and locations.[75] The result was a continuity nightmare, most of all in terms of character development. Kotcheff worried frequently about the inconsistencies of character development, particularly in Richler's usual blind spot, the female lead: "one minute [Pauline] is stabbing scissors into her hand, the next, she's back home." Some pain and bloodletting at the end might solve the problem, Kotcheff thought.[76]

Filming started in summer 1984 outside Brockville, Ontario, with the St. Lawrence River standing in for Lake Memphremagog.[77] Montreal locations included a former synagogue which, though it was now being used for other purposes, still had Hebrew lettering out front, saying "This is God's Gateway: The Righteous Will Enter Therein."[78] For the Ottawa scenes, Assistant Producer Julian Marks asked to film in Canada's Senate chambers.[79] Sorry, replied the chair of the Senate, Maurice Riel. The chamber must at all times, even Sundays, be at the disposal of senators, who could call a session at the drop of a hat[80] – in theory at least, since no one ever hauled the senators up during vacation time. Richler suggested a reply, beginning, "Dear (enter the nonentity's name here)," and begging Riel to allow an unobtrusive shoot in the parliamentary corridors. We're trying to make a film about bloody Canada, Richler said, though not in those precise words, and mentioned his Academy Award nomination and two Governor General's Awards.[81] They made no impression. Stymied, the filmmakers realized that the best plan was to sidestep Riel and speak to his superiors. Richler & Co. armed themselves with a letter from Employment and Immigration Minister John Roberts, declaring that it was important for Canadians and the world community to view Canadian institutions in as many ways as possible and asking the sergeant-at-arms of the House of Commons to facilitate Richler's attempt to film in the hallways.[82]

But the real production headache was money, with cost overruns and wastefulness constantly threatening to sabotage, even close down, the film. A crew of seventy (including Richler's daughter Emma, who assisted Kotcheff[83]), 120 actors with speaking parts, and 1,500 extras: the cost quickly shot up to $11 million, and even then the crowd scenes still looked empty and staged. Douglas Leiterman, the CEO of Motion Picture Guarantors, threatened to seize the film's production, cancel the planned London shoot, and finish the film as cheaply as possible.[84] In December Leiterman did take over the film, but after savage fighting and the infusion of more money Lantos regained control three months later.

This time round, Richler's new film was deemed fit for Cannes, although it was much weaker than *Duddy*. The continuity problems had never been solved. Awkward leaps from one scene to the next and from one year to the next diluted audience sympathy not only for Pauline but also for Joshua. Weaker films had been rescued from continuity problems by a moving musical score, but Kotcheff's sudden cuts from syrupy strings to jaunty carnival music did little for the film. Still, Lantos, fellow producer Stephen Roth, and many Canadian officials formed an honour guard, escorting *Joshua Then and Now* to the Riviera. Nobody thought to invite Richler. "I'm grateful," said Richler, "that the producers, between making such soft-core block-busters as Heavenly Bodies and Bedroom Eyes, were able to take time off from their busy schedules to travel first-class to Cannes with their wives ... I assume if my work on the film wins anything, they will be good enough to bring it back to me."[85] *Joshua Then and Now* didn't win anything. The black-tie audience cheered during Reuben's (Alan Arkin's) unorthodox monologues on Judaism and gave the film a standing ovation,[86] but critics were understandably less enthusiastic, questioning the credibility of the love story,[87] the same complaint that Kotcheff had made since the beginning. At the Berlin Film Festival the movie fared better, receiving a nomination for a Golden Palm.[88]

⧢

In the 1960s Richler had taken on film work in order to buy time for his real work, the novels. With *Duddy* and *Joshua Then and Now*, the lines were becoming blurred. In one sense he was publicizing his novels; in another sense, he was dicing them up for mass consumption. The $480,000 he got for the screenplay[89] loomed very large. For a long time, he had spoken of himself as a cottage industry, "the last remaining one-man businesses, with the shop over the house, literally."[90] The more successful he became and the more money he made, the more he protested that he was a small businessman – hardy, independent – and the more he was able to forget that the huge corporate enterprise of the movies allowed him to work above a very fancy cottage indeed. By 1994 he was calling himself "one of the last free-market scribblers."[91]

The language of entrepreneurship expressed Richler's ideological shift: his socialism was fading. It still held a rhetorical value, but he now thought of himself as an entrepreneur who had risked all his capital and therefore deserved his reward. He would continue to do high-end travel pieces, reporting from, say, Scotland, where a gentleman traveller could have a rod and the services of a gillie (an expert fisherman) at the Spey River for a mere $170 a day and where waiters trotted to the river at noon with scotch and a hot lunch.[92] When Richler heard that Kotcheff had gotten a free case of scotch for displaying the label in a film, Richler grew jealous. At a New York party he struck up a conversation with the president of a wine and spirits company. It's not clear who broached the subject, but Richler ended up with a couple of cases of Macallan, and Macallan got product placement throughout *Solomon Gursky Was Here*. This gave new meaning to the rest of his declaration: "I am one of the last free-market scribblers, dependant [*sic*] on my pen to keep me in Macallans single malt and Davidoffs."[93] The company employee charged with sending Richler the liquor initially begrudged this gift to someone who could afford the full price, but after seeing *Solomon Gursky*

Was Here he grasped the wisdom of his president's action.[94] Richler, meanwhile, complained of other writers "luxuriating in foundation vigorish."[95]

That's not at all to say that Richler, in pursuit of wealth and free booze, lost sight of his real work. However, since his name could be counted on to move product, neither did he invest too much labour anymore into minor work that was intended primarily to generate money. Case in point: *Jacob Two-Two and the Dinosaur*. Whereas *Jacob Two-Two Meets the Hooded Fang* had been a carefully crafted fiction designed to entertain his own children, *Jacob Two-Two and the Dinosaur* bore all the hallmarks of a rush job designed to put money in his purse. Scrapping an earlier idea for a children's book starring Peter Plasticine[96] and a planned book on the relations between Canada and the US,[97] Richler instead wrote about a dinosaur egg inadvertently brought back from a Kenyan safari. When the egg turns into a Diplodocus, Jacob Two-Two must protect it from adults who want to destroy the oversized beast. In particular, Jacob must protect "Dippy" from Prime Minister Perry Pleaser who has been told that his popularity will rise if only he can slay a dragon. The story has its witty moments, including the satire against Pleaser, an obvious nod to suave Conservative PM Brian Mulroney, who had been elected in 1984. Richler said, again, that he had no patience for preachy children's books trying to teach children manners and hygiene,[98] and he included references to Jacob's dad's glee club, poker buddies who drink beer and sometimes sing old songs.[99] However, the preaching in children's books of the 1940s and 50s had been overtaken by stories of blameless children rebelling against evil authorities, and there's nothing much in *Jacob Two-Two and the Dinosaur* to distinguish it from other examples of this genre. The stories of a child loving an animal and rescuing it from scheming adults initiated a new kind of romanticized preaching: don't trust authority, trust yourself. Richler wasn't so sentimental as to make his young rebels entirely virtuous, but he did include that omnipresent character, Aunt Ida (Aunt Good-For-You), who criticizes the pleasure principle – Richler's cigars, Daniel's pin-ups, Noah's Bowie, Marfa's red nail polish, TV violence – and must therefore be regarded as an unremitting prude. Against Aunt Ida is set the Florence and Mordecai parenting style: encourage promiscuous reading while emphasizing good manners. Richler wouldn't be caught siding with Aunt Ida, but he hadn't laid aside social control. Rather, he used ridicule, mocking Daniel's interest in punk music.[100]

The weaknesses of *Jacob Two-Two and the Dinosaur* weren't helped by Richler's decision to take his upcoming novel away from McClelland & Stewart and sell it to Penguin. In 1985, Jack McClelland sold his undercapitalized company to Toronto real-estate developer Avie Bennett.[101] Suddenly the company was on solid financial footing, owned by a man who had read Richler's work *in toto*, and Richler signed a contract, receiving a $50,000 advance for his upcoming novel, tentatively called *Gursky Was Here*.[102] Yet with McClelland out, Richler felt less attached to the company. A year later he wanted to move, and he asked what McClelland thought. McClelland replied that he didn't *want* to recommend that anybody leave McClelland & Stewart, but his advice made it easy for Richler to leave. McClelland had no sentimental attachment to the McClelland & Stewart name, he admitted, and he gave Richler the names of all the publishers that Richler should consider. Auction your book, McClelland suggested. You'll probably get $300,000.[103] Although there have been suggestions that Richler left because Bennett proposed an editorial role for his wife Beverly,[104] that seems unlikely. Richler's initial willingness to sign a contract, followed by his decision to move after McClelland threw a much higher number into the ring suggests that the move to Penguin was an economic decision.

Even before this, Richler realized that not only could his children's books make money on relatively little effort, but that he could also toss them as bones to his old publishers. André Deutsch was still bemoaning the loss of Richler.[105] Richler's solution: Deutsch would get the children's books. Similarly, Avie Bennett and Adrienne Clarkson at M&S lost the long-awaited novel (Richler returned the $50,000 advance), but in exchange for being understanding in an awkward situation, they'd get a saleable children's book and a promise from Richler not to bad-mouth the firm.[106] For fear of Richler taking even the leftovers away from them, the children's book publishers tiptoed around him, no longer daring to be too critical – in other words, the new editorial status quo was Richler's loss. The Jacob Two-Two books also ensured that Richler's "former" publishers heeded his wishes. A couple of years later Douglas Gibson tried, without telling Richler, to revert the paperback rights for *The Street* back to McClelland & Stewart when Penguin's contract for the book ran out. But any attempt to lead Richler around by the nose was doomed. He responded,

> Further to yr sly-boots letter of March 16.
> Whether discourtesy was intended or not it was certainly delivered, which is to say, in
> all my yrs w M&S, & other publishers abroad, nobody disposed of my pb rights without
> > a. informing me
> > b. seeking my approval.
> As for appropriating it without an advance, well, don't be ridiculous. So
> this is to inform you that it is my wish that you renew the Penguin license on THE STREET ASAP.
> > I await yr confirmation.[107]

Other Canadian writers would probably have forgiven Richler's commercial endeavours and internationalist stance were it not for his very public support for the Free Trade Agreement (FTA) with the US. At least as far back as 1968, Richler had said that making money was a feat of the imagination,[108] and he continued to take that line. On 18 November 1987, at a time when Canada's intelligentsia was almost unanimous in opposition, Richler gave testimony in favour of Free Trade before the Canadian Parliament's Standing Committee on External Affairs and International Trade. His testimony was quite balanced, far less forceful than some Progressive Conservatives on the committee wanted it to be. He touched on old (and somewhat tired) themes – Canada is a client state; don't waste tears over that fact; Canadians are slow to cheer the accomplishments of their own. What Richler wanted was motherhood and apple pie, the same as most voters: if he could be guaranteed 350,000 new jobs with absolutely no threat to social programs, he was all in favour of Free Trade. When it came down to specifics, he wanted, reasonably enough, a carefully negotiated deal that would protect Medicare, the Canada Council, the CBC, and Equalization Payments.

Richler had more jokes than he could use for his parliamentary coming-out, one senses, and he strained to confine himself to rational argument.[109] In one draft of the speech, he began thus: "I had hoped to appear here in style, accompanied by a lawyer. Each time I was asked a barbed question he would cover the microphone with his hand and whisper in my ear. Then, I would begin my answer, 'to the best of my recollection, at that point in time ...'" Richler thought better of pretending that he had been called before HUAC, and he cut the preamble, but he couldn't stick to arguing in favour of the deal on economic grounds. Instead, he recommended the deal on the basis that it might screw Ontario, especially the makers of dubious Niagara wines. Although he claimed to want protection for Canada's fledgling film industry, by the time he was done talking about the "tax jiggery-pokery" of Canadian film producers, it sounded as if he hoped that Canadian film would be strangled, mercifully, in its bed. His anxieties in the literary field extended to writers (who, despite noises off, weren't in much danger from Free Trade), but not to Canadian publishers. "Foreign-owned cultural imperialists" such as Penguin or Doubleday brought out more first novels by Canadians yearly than did Mel Hurtig, "Captain Canada himself," over a lifetime, testified Richler.[110] Not difficult, of course, since Hurtig didn't publish novels.[111] In the main, Richler's support for the deal wasn't based on economic nuts and bolts, but was really a general stance against protectionism. His friend Bernard Ostry said that Richler didn't believe in Free Trade in the way that an economist would describe it – he just didn't like the idea of people controlling things.[112]

The questions put to Richler were fairly gentle, and when NDP MP Bill Blaikie suggested that the cheery metaphor of a level playing field could come back to bite Canadians, Richler didn't argue. Even this late in life, speaking as a small-c conservative, Richler still agreed with social democratic ideas about taxation. Egalitarianism, yes; the political correctness of socialists, no.[113] It was a Progressive Conservative MP from proud Edmonton, Bill Lesick, who pressed Richler hardest, trying, strangely, to convince him that he must not only support Free Trade but must have no worries at all about it. Lesick's crown-prosecutorial style and his attempt to make Richler say that the PCs were giving Canada its best government in decades prodded Richler into reminding Lesick that Mulroney had opposed Free Trade four short years ago and that the Mulroney government wasn't universally trusted, a fact that Richler hoped wouldn't come as a shock. What Lesick's questioning revealed, however, was that Richler hadn't read the actual text of the FTA.

Mary Collins, another Conservative MP, took a more conciliatory line, telling Richler that after so much antagonism from the cultural community, she found Richler's support reassuring. My position isn't very popular, Richler warned. It certainly wasn't. Farley Mowat, fierce and sometimes unthinking nationalist, prefigured the logic of Jacques Parizeau when he complained that Richler's Jewish identity trumped his Canadian identity.[114] Mowat was right but evidently believed that a description of *how* the "ethnics" voted was the equivalent of a reasoned *argument* against their position.[115] Margaret Atwood and Rick Salutin, arguing against the FTA, spoke for the majority of Canadian culture workers, who perceived the deal as a betrayal of national sovereignty and a Conservative pandering to large corporations. When Richler appeared on CBC's *The Journal* to debate Salutin, Salutin called him a lapdog of the Conservatives: a powerful army of writers was strafing the Tories, and Tories, trembling, had called in Richler. A strange tactic, Salutin's, unwittingly casting Richler as St. George. Salutin, who *had* read the FTA, complained about the specifics of the deal, and yet, after mentioning the clause against cultural subsidies, had nothing to say about any other specifics. Instead, in broad strokes, he warned about the US ethos, implying that US writers were spokespersons for their government and saying directly that Canadian writing would disappear under the FTA. Quoting Atwood, he suggested that if the deal went through, the Canadian government would soon disappear. Richler countered that he didn't think that the obsessions of individual writers were dependent on trade deals.[116]

What Richler and many others on both sides of the issue lobbied for did come to pass: the FTA was placed before the electorate. Brian Mulroney called a federal election in 1988, staking his government on the deal, and won. In hindsight, one would be hard-pressed to criticize Mulroney and his ambivalent supporter Richler: Free Trade instituted an unprecedented economic boom in Canadian exports – including Canadian writing – to its largest trading partner.

For Richler, Mulroney's electoral success didn't automatically lead to cartwheels of joy. Arguably, it was Richler's support for Free Trade that would cost him the 1989 Governor General's Award for Fiction. As well, although he believed the FTA necessary, Richler grew more and more irritated by what he perceived as Mulroney's dishonesty and bad faith. "Fool's Gold," a satiric squib that didn't find its way into *Solomon Gursky Was Here*, tells of the incomparable Herky Tannenbaum, first Canadian to win the Booker Prize. Sadly, a urinalysis reveals that Herky had been drinking, a clear violation of Booker policy and a tragic blow to the millions of literature-loving Canadians who had danced in the streets the moment they had heard of Herky's victory. With the help of the NDP, the Jewish Defence League, and cries of "REMEMBER THE SIX MILLION," Herky prevails, becoming a cause célèbre, and signing a seven-figure book deal with a US publisher. Of particular interest is the "achingly sincere" Canadian prime minister who offers the nation his condolences during the trying days after the urinalysis. Although Mulroney isn't named, it's impossible to picture anyone else "surrounded by many of his old classmates from fabled St. Francis Xavier U., each one now a senator. They were helping him load sacks filled with thousand dollar bills for the flight over Quebec's north shore. The weekly billion dollar drop."[117] Despite Richler's support of Free Trade, he was no fan of Mulroney, and if Mulroney, a skillful negotiator, almost brought Québec back aboard the Constitution at Meech Lake, Richler wasn't impressed. Richler believed that the "distinct society" clause and the limits to federal spending power, for which Premier Bourassa and Mulroney fought so hard, might be less about national unity than about Mulroney giving the federal shop away in order to ensure a strong PC vote in Québec. Richler ran in behind Trudeau's anti-Meech salvo by declaring that, to placate Québec, Mulroney was allowing too many federal powers to devolve to the provinces, potentially building a new Canada in which citizens' fundamental rights would differ from province to province. During the 1990s, Richler, making himself over into a major political pundit, would have many opportunities to point his guns at Mulroney.

And, lastly, Richler couldn't fully rejoice because in short order he, too, felt the heavy hand of corporate America. For twelve years he had enjoyed the perks of his position on the BOMC editorial board. He was paid handsomely to fly to New York every so often to debate about which were the best recent books. Richler, with his utter faith in a literary meritocracy – if he was on the BOMC, it was because he deserved to be – never saw the wrecking ball approach. In September 1988, BOMC decided to restructure its jury. Three of the five judges were fired; only two, including Richler's friend Clifton Fadiman (who had been with BOMC for forty-four years), were kept on. It didn't matter an iota that John Hutchens called Richler one of the most discerning judges during Hutchens's quarter-century on the board,[118] or that BOMC head Al Silverman was pleased with the judges' performances. It was simply that BOMC's main competitor, the Literary Guild, operated without a board and could therefore make decisions with greater "flexibility."[119] Translated, that meant that Time-Life had bought BOMC and demanded a rubber-stamp board. In the past, judges' verdicts had been final; now they'd be advisory.[120] If the corporate people at the Guild didn't have to run to a bunch of literary people to ask if the books were worth acquiring, why should BOMC? Richler was particularly disgusted because he had considered the executioner, Silverman, a friend, but Silverman hadn't even informed Richler personally of the firing. "The man is weak," Richler said.[121] At times, afterwards, Richler implied that he had *quit* BOMC.[122] No: Richler received a termination agreement and a lump sum payout specifying that he had to keep quiet about the BOMC, its subsidiaries, its products, and its personnel for two years.[123] The eighty-five-year-old Fadiman, upset by the dismissal of his friends, wrote Richler and the other judges, "I don't understand it, I don't like it, and I have said so to Al. Were I even 15 years younger, I would have been inclined to say No to Al's offer to keep me on." A couple of years later, Fadiman lobbied unsuccessfully to make *Solomon Gursky Was Here* a BOMC Main Selection. "I miss you," he told Richler. "We do our work – but there's no *play*, no fizz of the intellect. You can easily get along without us, but the reverse is not quite the case. Please don't acknowledge. I just wanted to get this letter off my chest. At my age it's time to thank those who have made my life more interesting."[124]

24

The Bronfmans Are Gathering

WHILE RICHLER WAS DEBATING Free Trade, he was also forging
ahead on his old/new novel, *Solomon Gursky Was Here*. Begun in 1972, resumed in 1986,[1] it was finally turning into something that many readers
would call his greatest work. That could be said of any of his four roomy
masterpieces, but *Solomon Gursky* was aesthetically more complicated than
anything he had attempted – Dickensian in scope and brilliantly eccentric
as an enquiry into Canadian origins. Bert Smith, the novel's bedrock Canadian hails from the British pioneer colony, Gloriana, Richler's parody of the
real Barr Colony of Lloydminster, Saskatchewan.[2] At Gloriana's supposedly
purebred heart stands "Ishmael Horn," who is the Jew Ephraim Gursky,
passing as an Anglican clergyman. Richler's wily Jew shows up all over
Canada's nineteenth-century map. In the Meech Lake 1980s, as multicultural latecomers to Canada wondered why the eternal fuss about two founding races, *Solomon Gursky* came as a timely and witty reinvention of Canadian
history, and if some Canadianists, mostly urban, were now cheering what
they called the postcolonial "unsettling" of the land, Richler's novel steered
clear of such mottos. The novel's voices are wonderfully multiple, ranging
from parodies of the nineteenth-century formal English that the con man
Ephraim successfully employs, to the chatty diaries of rich sybarites, to a
credible imitation of Robert Service. "I never had a map,"[3] Richler said,
and, elsewhere, "It's not a minimalist novel, or a little novel about adultery."[4] The maplessness shows. *Solomon Gursky* was a novel one could get
lost in, at once the story of a liquor baron's rise and also a postmodern fable.
Even Richler, who refused to work with profile charts and family trees to
keep his multitude of characters consistent,[5] got lost. His agent Monica Mc-
Call had to draw up a five-page, single-spaced chronology to keep the time
sequences straight.[6]

The seeds of the novel lay in Richler's abandoned biography of Martin Hartwell, the Arctic bush pilot who of necessity had eaten his dead passengers, and in Richler's long-time fascination with the Bronfmans, the Jewish billionaire owners of Seagram distillery. When Richler taught at Sir George in 1968–69, he rented a Mount Royal house that overlooked Sam Bronfman's place.[7] Initially Richler had hoped to continue the story of Duddy Kravitz, a sure-fire route to bestsellerdom,[8] but Richler's interest in the Bronfmans trumped that. With Duddy, Richler would have had to start a plot from scratch; the same went for Manny Berger, the protagonist of *The Bells of Hell*, around whom Richler constellated "Manny Moves to Westmount," another false start. With the Bronfmans, however, a basic plot was already in place: western grober – Sam – rises to become King of the Jews in the holy city of Montreal. Richler called Sam "Bernard Gursky" and gave him Manny's wife, Libby. It's more than a Duddy-story: because Sam Bronfman scrubbed himself clean of his bootlegging days to become a leading Jewish philanthropist, to hold the long-time post of president of the Canadian Jewish Congress (CJC), and (the peak, I believe) to receive an honorary Doctor of Laws degree from Brandon University, his story is laced with a much more complex moral dimension than Duddy's story was. The size of the Bronfman clan made room for any number of additional subplots – some historical, some invented, some both.

In "Manny Moves to Westmount" Solomon Gursky is dead; there's no mystery-vapour surrounding him. What matters most is the process of moving into upper-class Anglo enclaves. Manny Berger, upwardly mobile like Richler, but a lot more anxious, fears that he might not be able to carry off his new role. Already before Sam's death in 1971, Richler had a notion of the narrative richness and moral complexity of the Bronfmans/Gurskys, climbers far bolder than Manny. While Richler for his honesty was being called "a stinker" in synagogues, more dutiful Jews such as Rabbi Stuart Rosenberg (*The Jewish Community in Canada*) were telling fairy tales about the Bronfman rise to power through sheer hard work. No whisper of bootlegging. No shady deals and certainly no dead bodies along the roadside. In Richler's eyes Rosenberg's offense wasn't just moral: it was a literary crime, too. According to Richler, the Bronfman story was natural material for an Isaac Babel, but Rosenberg had whitewashed it to nothing.[9]

Because of Richler's increasing celebrity, Edward Bronfman (the son of Sam's brother Alan) took an interest in him. The Richlers were invited to Bronfman parties,[10] and for a couple of years the Bronfmans sent New Year's cards with Montreal Canadiens hockey tickets. In 1977 they invited Richler to their son's bar mitzvah at the upscale synagogue, Shaar Hashomayim.[11] Richler read the entrails: in the old days Sam Bronfman had co-opted the

talented A.M. Klein as his literary lapdog; the younger Bronfmans, if Richler let them, would do the same with him. The poisoned memories of his
rich Uncle Joe lording it over his father in the 1940s didn't encourage Richler to be respectful. As a matter of fact, the Bronfman interest, slight as it
was, gave Richler his old fire back. Up on the podiums stood the Bronfmans,
speaking for the Jewish community on the basis of wealth not on the grounds
of learning or sensibility,[12] while Mordecai Richler, great writer, stood at the
community's periphery. No matter that by now he was far richer and more
important than Uncle Joe had ever been. To the Bronfmans he was small,
and he recaptured his notion of himself as the underdog, trading blows with
the Kings of the Jews. Also, by the mid-1980s, Richler had probably read
Irving Abella and Harold Troper's book, *None Is too Many*, which not only
damned Mackenzie King's refusal of Jewish refugees from the Nazis but also
described the ambiguous roles of Jewish community leaders, especially CJC
president Sam Bronfman. Bronfman had gotten a few Jews admitted into
Canada,[13] yet he had also consistently kowtowed to Anglo authorities and
had shushed the angry Canadian Jews when Canada kept turning away desperate refugees.[14]

Probably the biggest spur to write *Solomon Gursky Was Here* was Peter
C. Newman's *Bronfman Dynasty*, published in 1978. *Bronfman Dynasty*
doesn't appear on Richler's list of sources, but he reviewed the book for
BOMC and relied extensively on it. Newman did the opposite of Rabbi Stuart Rosenberg, dismantling the fairy tales that the Bronfmans had cultivated
and resurrecting many colourful and less than complimentary anecdotes
about Sam. In a footnote Newman also delivered a highly provocative nugget:
the only previous Bronfman biographer, Terry Robertson, had discovered
unwelcome facts about the family, had had his life threatened – he would-
n't say by whom – and had vowed to do the job himself. He was found dead
of barbiturate poisoning.[15]

Michael Marrus, a University of Toronto History professor whom the
Bronfmans hired to write Sam's official biography, claimed that Robertson's
biography was never suppressed. It was merely "a hopeless, uncompleted
hagiography," and Richler, by alluding to the mystery surrounding Robertson's death, misrepresented Robertson's work.[16] Marrus was mostly wrong.
Stories that blamed the liquor bottle for Robertson's decline were probably
true[17] – and Richler used those stories for Moses Berger, his Gursky biographer – but Richler possessed his own copy of the Robertson manuscript,
and, although Robertson tried to be generous towards Sam, Richler knew
very well that the manuscript was no hagiography. Not the most elegant of
prose stylists, Robertson nevertheless detailed, for example, allegations that
Harry Bronfman had attempted to bribe customs officers in order to keep
"medicinal" liquors flowing into the US throughout Prohibition. Harry's

own account, which Richler also possessed, was blatant propaganda. According to crime writer James Dubro, "Richler the novelist comes closer to the truth about Sam Bronfman's criminal activities than does [Marrus] the historian."[18] Indeed, when Richler began to read portions of the new novel in public, it drew interest at the headquarters of a certain whiskey distiller. Greg Gatenby told Richler that Seagram officials had asked for a transcript of his 1982 Harbourfront Festival appearance.[19] Later reports that the Bronfmans were building a massive house on Lake Memphremagog, caused Richler's friends to joke about potential skulduggery: "Are they keeping an eye on you?"[20]

Nevertheless, Moses Berger's paranoia in the novel about the Gurskys wasn't Richler's. "Moses" was the pseudonym that Lily had given Mordecai in *The Errand Runner*, and Moses Berger shared some of Richler's history, attitudes, and physical features – not least the single testicle.[21] As well, Tim Callaghan's estimation of Moses in the novel sounds like Richler's dispassionate assessment of his own shortcomings: "too nimble, ever ready to rush to judgement, and ... too much self-display there, born of insecurity perhaps, but tiresome all the same."[22] Yet among the protagonists in Richler's major novels, Moses – aimless, unable to make a career, failing Beatrice – was least like Richler. (Neither, despite his name, was Moses the image of Moe Richler.) Berger's drinking has sometimes been equated with Richler's, but in fact Richler had to go to his old friend Ian Mayer, a bright and tormented Montreal journalist, for information on the depths of alcoholism – Antabuse, AA meetings, and such.[23] As Richler wrote *Gursky*, he was also trying to convince his son Jacob not to booze so much. Richler told him, "Obviously, I like a drink now and then myself. But I've never found it necessary or all that enjoyable to be drunk all the time."

Richler worried briefly that the Bronfmans might hit him with a libel lawsuit,[24] but it helped that apart from Bernard/Sam, the fictional Gurskys didn't consistently resemble the Bronfmans. The person with the best case for mental anguish was Senator Leo Kolber, Sam Bronfman's former lieutenant. Kolber's wife, Sandra, had portrayed her husband in *Bitter Sweet Lemons and Love*:

> My husband's a hard-hitting driver
> of mortar and money and man,
> and underneath the firm of him
> my husband is a lamb.[25]

But Richler lampooned him as Harvey Schwartz, a fawner who wore paper-thin soles so as to appear shorter than Bernard and whose wife publishes a book called *Hugs, Pain, and Chocolate Chip Cookies*.[26] In private communication, Richler called Leo Kolber "that twitchy midget,"[27] even though Richler had known him, had introduced Max Richler to him,[28] and had been on superficially friendly terms with him, as Kolber's reply to a Richler letter suggests: "I received your bigoted letter of April 10th and note that time and fortune have not mellowed you at all ... I have shown your letter to my good friend, Harry Belafonte, and my advice is not to come to this continent."[29] According to Sam Gesser, in the early 1980s, when McClelland was still running McClelland & Stewart and Richler had published an excerpt from the novel in *Saturday Night*, Leo Kolber showed up at McClelland's office and told him not to publish *Gursky Was Here*. Not meeting with the response he had hoped for, Kolber had to be ejected from the office.[30]

Although the Bronfmans asked Saidye's nephew, entertainment lawyer Michael Levine, to check if anything was actionable,[31] no lawsuits materialized. Instead, Levine surfaced as Richler's new lawyer. Complaints about the novel's treatment of the Gurskys were limited to the *B'nai B'rith Covenant* crying anti-Semitism and charging that Richler had ignored all the Bronfmans' philanthropic and Zionist activities,[32] a false accusation, since in the novel Israeli Prime Minister Golda Meir appears at a Bernard Gursky testimonial – though perhaps showy self-praise wasn't what the Covenant had in mind. A couple of years after the novel was published, Charles Bronfman's CRB Foundation hired Richler to do two half-hour programs based on Heritage Minutes, one on Joe Shuster, the co-creator of Superman, and another on Jacques Plante, inventor of the hockey mask. Very forgiving of the Bronfmans, noted the chair of the CRB Foundation, who happened to be: Michael Levine.[33]

If Sam Bronfman's power and pretensions had made it unlikely that too many people outside of Seagram would be disturbed by Richler's lampoon, not so with the lampoon of L.B. Berger, Richler's savage (but very funny) portrait of poet A.M. Klein. Probably because Klein's lengthy mental illness before his 1972 death added an air of pathos to his distinguished literary output, Richler friends such as Bill Weintraub and Robert Fulford thought that Richler had gone too far in slaughtering Klein.[34] As Sam Bronfman's speechwriter, Klein had lent his eloquence to a cause dear to him – Zionism – while earning the sort of money that poets usually have no right to expect. Richler's prostration before the movies wasn't so very different, yet by making L.B. Berger/Klein the father of the present-day writer, Moses Berger, Richler was doing two important things. He was acknowledging the crucial role that Klein had played in the genesis of Jewish writing in Montreal and even backhandedly confessing how much his own writing owed to Klein. As in *St. Urbain's Horseman*, so in *Solomon Gursky* Richler turned to Klein's brilliant metaphysical detective plot structure in *The Second Scroll* – the search for "I Am That I Am." Secondly, and against that debt, by treating

L.B. Berger harshly, Richler was declaring emphatically that he was not Klein, that the elevated spiritual quest in Klein's work must be overcome so that a writer unafraid of human vulgarity could flourish. Klein was Lily Rosenberg – larger vocabulary, greater erudition, but still Lily Rosenberg. The devotion to Jewish causes was there, the sentimentality, the literary refusal to deal with muck despite her own prodigious messes. Richler's literary ancestors (Lily, Rabbi Rosenberg, Klein) and non-literary ancestors (his weak father Moe, his hot-tempered grandfather Shmarya) were profoundly unsatisfactory to him. In their place Richler once again invented wished-for ancestors, this time Ephraim and Solomon Gursky: smart and tricky, ruthless, vulgar, humane.

≶

Richler's reinvention of the personal past extended for the first time into a brilliant reinvention of Canadian history. While Rudy Wiebe and others mined the past with painstaking archeological care and perhaps too much seriousness, Richler charged through the china shop. Possibly he had caught the fever from the novel that beat out *Joshua Then and Now* for the Governor General's Award, *Burning Water*, a strange, purposely unhistorical, and yet fascinating revision of the story of explorer George Vancouver. There's no direct evidence that Richler read George Bowering's novel, but he did what Bowering did: combined serious research with a devil-may-care willingness to knock the research aside whenever fiction demanded it. Bookish research was another first for Richler.[35] He read all he could about the Franklin expedition and charged *The Beaver*'s editor, Christopher Dafoe, with the impossible task of finding a Franklin expedition cookbook.[36] The research was at first obtrusive,[37] yet he quickly made it serve the fable, as he "revealed" that kosher salami and schmaltz herring were privately stashed on Franklin's ships for two unlisted Jews aboard, who, with their specialized menu, didn't succumb to lead poisoning like the rest of the crew. Shortly after publishing *Joshua Then and Now*, Richler had grumbled about the trend in which novelists would put imagined dialogues into the mouths of historical characters. A fad, he called it. Then, changing a name here and there to protect the guilty,[38] he did exactly the same in *Solomon Gursky Was Here*, enquiring into a real enough past but, like postmodernists, mediating the past through fantasy, fable, and purposely incomplete allegories – a surprising step for a writer who had no sympathy for postmodern philosophical skepticism.

He did the same with Jewish history. Bernard Malamud, for his Pulitzer Prize-winning *The Fixer* (1966), had reconstructed nineteenth-century Kiev, scene of a blood libel, where prosecutors had argued that Jews had slaughtered a defenseless Christian child, drained its blood, and used the blood to make matzohs for their devilish rituals. Richler admired the novel, yet felt that it had no inner life.[39] He went in the opposite direction, defying history by having Solomon/Hyman Kaplansky, eight years after World War II, invite British anti-Semites to a nosh, during which Kaplansky tricks them into eating bloody matzohs. In crafting such a scene, Richler wasn't so far removed from his grandfather, Rabbi Rosenberg, who had added the blood libel in his retelling of earlier legends.[40] Richler's "false" use of the blood libel is imaginative and stirring. At the very moment that the libel seems be confirmed – the Jew Kaplansky *does* use blood in his matzohs – Richler's aesthetic effect reverses the libel. The bloody matzohs point not to a Gentile child-victim but to the Jewish blood spilled so many times in the Holocaust. A reviewer who interpreted this grotesque moment as just a bit of blasphemous comedy, as the author's "cackling,"[41] completely missed Richler's tone.

Comedy appears rarely in Solomon and his confrontations with anti-Semitism, but it appears often in the Jewish practices and rituals elsewhere in the novel. Ada Craniford has astutely called *Solomon Gursky Was Here* a rewriting of the Torah.[42] This is true in a host of ways, from Bernard Gursky's calling of L.B. Berger – "the summons from Sinai"[43] – to Solomon's declaration in court, "I AM THAT I AM."[44] Most of all, it's true of Ephraim, who makes life comfortable for himself among the Inuit by setting himself up as Yahweh: "Thou shalt not bow down to Narssuk, whose prick I have shriveled, or to any other gods, you ignorant little fuckers. For the Lord thy God is a jealous God, visiting the iniquity of the fathers upon the children unto the third and fourth generation of them that hate me."[45] In *Barney's Version*, Richler would parody "a rap *Haggadah* inspired by the poetry of Ice-T," and also a feminist *Haggadah*:

> This is the Seder plate.
> The plate is flat. Woman is flat, like a plate
> Flat in the relief of history ...[46]

Lines such as these depend, for their parodic effect, on the assurance that, despite Richler's skepticism, there was once a serious, original *Haggadah* whose ancient cadences have been lost in a smugly innovative modern world. But in *Solomon Gursky Was Here* the possibility of blasphemy enters because this isn't merely Ephraim's degraded *parody* of the first Torah but also a potential *image* of that first Torah, a more skeptical account of what Moses might have been up to among the Israelites. In this, Richler falls in line with one of the early forms of satire, the Greek silloi, which made pro-scientific attacks on the gods.[47] Easy for Henry Gursky to distinguish between "the original Moses" and the inadequate present-day "Uncle Moses" Berger;[48]

not so easy for the reader, for whom acidic parody corrodes the idealizing tendency of the original Torah.

While Richler was working on *Solomon Gursky*, he was commissioned by poet and editor David Rosenberg to write an essay for *Congregation: Contemporary Writers Read the Jewish Bible*.[49] Richler chose to write on Deuteronomy, the last book in the Torah. The result horrified Rosenberg. Interspersed between anecdotes about how Torah had been "banged" into him, Richler cherry-picked some of the more troubling commandments given by God – the requirement to stone false prophets (a sign, Richler commented, that authors were already jealous of rivals) and the law that allowed Jews to charge interest to Gentiles but not to fellow Jews. He retold an anecdote about Randolph Churchill, who, after reading the Old Testament for the first time, said, "I never realized that God was such a shit."[50] God barred Moses from the Promised Land, Richler said, because once or twice Moses gave in to doubts.

After Reuben's discourse in *Joshua Then and Now* about "fucking and the Jewish Tradition,"[51] Rosenberg shouldn't have been surprised, but he was. Rosenberg, who had a great deal invested in the continuing symbolic validity of the biblical texts, thought he'd give Richler guidance and sent him a letter almost as long as the article itself. The cross-purposes of Rosenberg and Richler are entertaining. "By not leaving the adolescent world, not taking a step back," Rosenberg lectured Richler, "you wind up with a one-dimensional reading that rivals the Falwells in its fundamentalism." Rosenberg wanted to know why Richler ignored Deuteronomy's literary qualities, why he didn't interpret "God" as a character rather than an actual supernatural being. Also, perhaps Richler ought to comment upon the thousands of years of Talmud and Midrash commentaries on the text.[52] Isaac Bashevis Singer's "Genesis" was evidently what Rosenberg had in mind, Singer beginning with the consciousness of a grand narrative of space, time, and eternity, then falling prey to doubts, and finally mistrusting even the certainties of science, returning full circle with a new love and greater intellectual complexity to Genesis. Richler balked at such returns, even though he hadn't fully lost his Orthodox sense of the residual mana in the Bible's literal dimension.

After listening to Rosenberg's editorial pleas, Richler didn't change a word. He wasn't about to start parsing the Talmud that he had escaped at age thirteen. One of Richler's driving purposes was to satirize and fight against Judaism's control over Jews. If the Bible was still used among the Orthodox as a book of rules, one couldn't treat it simply as a literary text. At the same time Richler believed that the modernization of the religious text emasculated it. Real emotional feeling arose out of his religious past, yet he wanted to escape the rules completely, not set up a secondary religious adherence in which he had to think too deeply about which Deuteronomic rules still made sense and which didn't. And of course there were sound literary reasons for Richler's stance. Real events, real Gods: weren't these always more appealing than Rosenberg's bloodless "authorial intention"?

Failing to sway Richler, Rosenberg, in a catty introduction to *Congregation*, dissociated himself from Richler's "Deuteronomy" and other pieces of like sensibility: "Their response to my editorial criticism was often a pugnacious adherence to the bagels-and-lox Judaism that may have been all they were familiar with." Rosenberg had "wrestled" with these stubborn writers, he reported, but they had insisted on comments related mainly to "minor sects of the contemporary ultra-Orthodox."[53] Afterwards, the success of *Congregation* convinced Rosenberg to do a sequel, this time asking contemporary Jewish writers for personal comments on the Holocaust,[54] but Richler declined to participate.

In Richler's imagination the "minor sects of the contemporary ultra-Orthodox" weren't so minor. Large portions of his family on both sides were Hasidic and Orthodox. Some, such as his Uncle Bernard (his favourite uncle when he was a teenager) and Baruch Rosenberg (who had recently embarked on a translation of Rabbi Yudel Rosenberg's works), had ties to Lubavitch.[55] In *Solomon Gursky Was Here* Richler satirized Orthodoxy in general and Lubavitch in particular. He mocked the literalist adherence to the Torah, which, if strictly applied above the Arctic Circle, would require a rather deadly Yom Kippur fast of several months. Although Richler doesn't name Rabbi Schneersohn, Lionel Gursky's slighting reference to Henry Gursky having been schooled under "the mighty Oz, the Rebbe who ruled the funny-farm at 770"[56] points directly at Chabad Lubavitch World Headquarters, 770 Eastern Parkway in Crown Heights, Brooklyn. There Henry hears talks more bathetic than profound:

> "We look into the mirror ... and what do we see? The self, of course. You see yourself, I see myself, and so forth and so on ... Looking down, what? The feet. You see your feet, I see my feet and so forth and so on. The Rebbe has pointed out to us that on Simchas Torah one does not dance with his head – he dances with his feet."[57]

Henry's Inuit Jews, who demand "WE WANT THE MOSHIACH NOW!"[58] are proto-Lubavitchers, although they may also owe something to Richler's grandfather, Rabbi Rosenberg, who believed that his translation of the Zohar would hasten the coming of the Messiah.[59] After *Solomon Gursky* was published, Lubavitch Headquarters offered no comment.[60]

Notwithstanding the farce in Ephraim's new/old Torah and in Henry's fundamentalism, Richler, in *Solomon Gursky*, moved beyond the narrow confines of his "Deuteronomy" piece. Henry's rescue mission, bringing the Inuit Jews south so that they don't have to choose between breaking faith or dying on a fast, has a kind of pathos. "That good shepherd," Richler calls him, finding Christian Messianism in the same phylum as Lubavitcher Messianism, culminating in Isaac's ghastly communion, in which he lunches on his father, even if Henry didn't exactly say, "Take, eat: this is my body." And yet, Henry's easing of Jewish law also invites sympathy for him, who can neither set aside his religious past nor allow the full weight of the Torah to overburden the faithful. Seen alone, Henry looks rather pitiable, harnessed to a Jewish and Christian apocalypticism that must reject nearly all of contemporary society. Turned away from modernity, and an ice age on his radar, it's no surprise that he falls headlong into the insufficiently examined past. The three-masted ship, the ark that is supposed to save him, returns him not to the days of Noah but to John Franklin, icebound in the Canadian Arctic. Yet seen in relation to the power-hungry Lionel – who says, "Henry ... You're into things that really matter. God and eternity and shit like that" – Henry's simplistic piety seems preferable. Richler himself saw the rise of fundamentalism as a search for magic in the teeth of an absurd world. Even Ephraim isn't merely a blasphemous con man. He employs his medical skills to set broken bones, and one senses that his self-election to the Godhead occurs partly because God doesn't appear, that Ephraim wants to but cannot repeat Moses' encounter with God at Sinai. "Face to face," Ephraim rages into the lashing wind, "I want to see you face to face just once."[61] Partially because of this layer of complexity and partially because Richler's community had matured culturally, Jewish attacks on his work became less frequent.

≲

As with earlier books, however, Richler was called to task in some quarters for stereotyping the Inuit and for turning women into playthings, buffoons, or saviours.[62] Because he was increasingly trying to avoid stereotypes, the criticisms had little merit. Three of the significant female characters – Beatrice (Moses's sometime companion), Diana McClure (Solomon's love interest), Nialie (Henry Gursky's Inuit wife) – don't fit into the plaything-buffoon-saviour pattern at all. Beatrice and Diana are *interpreted* by their men as saviours, but the narrative makes it clear that the two women are wise to refuse such roles. As for the Inuit, Richler hadn't given up satirizing simple cultural forms and the hushed worship accorded them by Romantics. Cape Dorset throat singers produce something "rather like dry gargling," which a Professor Hardy in the novel likens to "the sounds of great rivers." But Richler's satire against throat-singing, and, later, shamanism, is not a wholesale dismissal of Inuit culture, just as his satire against bloodletting and against the cultural arrogance of British doctors isn't a blanket condemnation of

Western medicine.[63] Instead Richler melds Torah with Inuit realities, most obviously through the figure of Raven, provider for Elijah, Noah's messenger, and also Amerindian Trickster. Richler had seen ravens gathering everywhere on his 1975 trip to Yellowknife, and the Arctic Society, which Richler joined, informed him that the raven, a clever, adroit bird, was among the few birds that wintered in the North.[64] Haida (not Inuit) legends, retold by Bill Reid and Robert Bringhurst, added that in a number of native cultures Raven was the Trickster, not fully explicable by a rational cosmology. Solomon Gursky, the figure associated with the Raven, is the least susceptible to rational explanation. In his Hyman Kaplansky avatar, wise old scholar of the Jewish condition, Solomon harked back ("Hyman" being an Anglicization of "Chaim" – "life") to the wise old father-philosopher in Richler's first published novel, *The Acrobats*. But Richler had come a long way in literary complexity from wise old Jewish souls. It's not finally clear whether Solomon is an elusive Yahweh, a shadow cast by Moses' imagination, or a Trickster who (like Raven) steals the light only for his own purposes. Richler echoed a book he had loved as a teenager,[65] A.J.A. Symons's *A Quest for Corvo* – relying not on the story of Frederick William Rolfe of Cheapside, who tried to pass himself off as a Baron, but more on the mystery that Symons and the Corvine Society (i.e., a dozen or so of Symons's friends) had made of Rolfe. "Solomon Gursky is too complex a hero to be a hero," Richler acknowledged. "I think Canadians are too skeptical to believe in heroes anyway."[66]

Solomon Gursky Was Here was massive, but, with the help of Chatto & Windus editor Alison Samuel in Britain, Richler cut a lot.[67] At her urging, he made Isaac less monstrous and more credibly human. Samuel convinced Richler that names such as "Bobbykins," "Bubbles," and "Poots" appealed to a less sophisticated audience than his.[68] Richler also cut a set piece, "The Dental Academy Awards Night," a seven-page account of a "documentary" film in which Richler again tested the boundaries of good taste. The Past President of the American Society for Dental Aesthetics, Wayne "Overbite" Haliburton, goes on a cross-USA skateboard run to raise money for the Dental Anti-Defamation League. Overbite, a double amputee, rests underneath his support truck when the rain gets too strong. All is well until the awards night, when Overbite reveals that he is gay. The "documentary" wasn't connected with the rest of the novel; to make a connection, Richler simply appended "Raven Productions" at the documentary's end.

Florence tells of having only one major argument in her editing of her husband's work. She wanted a large chunk of a particular book cut – bringing on a sulk in Richler. For the first time, he left the house without giving Florence his usual affectionate kiss and headed for New York, where he hoped for a less critical response. He did let Florence know that he had arrived in New York but remained emotionally distant on the phone. Very late in the evening Bob Gottlieb called Florence and laughed: "I hear we've both made the same criticism, and I thought you'd enjoy knowing this." Soon Richler recovered from the blow and was amused by the unanimity of his two most valued readers.[69] Florence won't say which book it was, but Richler admitted that at Florence's request he cut twenty thousand words from *Solomon Gursky Was Here*.[70] The fact that Richler's editors in Britain didn't address "The Dental Academy Awards Night" suggests that Florence cashiered it and similar passages before the manuscript crossed the ocean.[71] One must dispute Florence's claim that she never cut on the basis of outrageousness or irreverence.[72]

Reaction to the novel was almost uniformly laudatory. Yet come Governor General's Award time, judges Robert Harlow, Sharon Butala, and Kent Thompson left *Solomon Gursky Was Here* off the shortlist.[73] Nine years earlier *Joshua Then and Now*, despite its crowded, bounteous canvas, hadn't made the GG shortlist either, but the winner that year was George Bowering's witty *Burning Water*, and because Richler had already won twice before (for the undeserving *Cocksure* and for the highly deserving *St. Urbain's Horseman*), nobody took much notice. But in 1990 howls of outrage came from Robertson Davies, Greg Gatenby, Alberto Manguel, and others. The winner turned out to be Paul Quarrington's *Whale Music*, and Gatenby lamented that the geopolitics of jury selection had triumphed over aesthetic considerations.[74]

At the same time that the novel was frozen out of Canadian awards, it was shortlisted for the much more prestigious Booker Prize. Because the average age of the Booker finalists was sixty-one, younger reviewers called the contest "an old farts' raffle."[75] Richler attended the dinner, ill at ease in a tuxedo, and an hour before the award announcement, he realized, from the way the BBC placed its cameras, that A.S. Byatt would win for *Possession*.[76] He would have to make do with the Commonwealth Writers' Prize awarded later in Australia. At the Booker dinner, Richler saw Brian Moore, with whom he had had no contact for a number of years. Each writer too proud to make the first move and resume their friendship, it would be the last time they saw each other before Moore's death nine years later.[77]

25

Tongue Trooper

BY THE TURN OF THE DECADE, Richler's children were all out of the house. He tidied up some essays and published them as *Broadsides*, went fishing and drinking with Saskatchewan writers David Carpenter and Guy Vanderhaeghe,[1] and rummaged around for materials on World War II, long an interest of his. With assistance from Martha,[2] he soldered together a disparate group of extracts, mostly British and American, that showed the war through the lens of fiction and nonfiction writers: *Writers on World War II*. Briefly he joined a group of investors who attempted to buy the *Sherbrooke Record*, until negotiations with its owner, Quebecor (controlled by Pierre Péladeau), went nowhere.[3] But mainly Richler turned his focus onto Québec's irritating new language laws.

"The country outgrew him, there's no doubt about it," announced broadcaster Larry Zolf in 1981.[4] Far too hasty, such an assessment. In the late 1980s and throughout the 1990s, *no* fiction writer was more significant in the Canadian polity than Richler. Many times he had written about Québec and separatism, mostly in a neutral fashion, but he turned polemical and fiery around 1988. He had seen, in 1977, the PQ introduce Bill 101, the law requiring that Québec signs and education be predominantly in French and that companies with fifty or more employees do all their internal business in French. The law had been challenged, and in 1988 the Supreme Court brought down two rulings: firstly, the Constitution's guarantee of freedom of expression meant that Québec (now Liberal, under Robert Bourassa) could not prohibit anyone from using English; secondly, the province could require that French be *dominant* on all signs. Premier Bourassa pledged a compromise bill to reflect this simple and fair solution, but in the event, he tested the wind and promptly invoked the Constitution's "Notwithstanding" clause for a new Bill 178, which changed very little of Bill 101's thrust. Extorted from Trudeau by the provincial premiers during the negotiations leading up to the Constitution Act of 1982, the "Notwithstanding" clause allowed any unhappy province to escape a constitutional clause for a renewable term of five years.

Bill 178 required French-only signs *outside* on commercial buildings and allowed other languages only on *inside* signs, so long as French predominated. Like many other Québec Anglophones (including three of Bourassa's cabinet ministers) Richler was infuriated, particularly because Bourassa had promised Anglophones that he would allow bilingual signs. In Bourassa's new position Richler saw the long arm of Meech Lake's "distinct society," and he was probably right to say that Bourassa's use of the "Notwithstanding" clause helped kill Meech Lake, giving Canadians a very precise notion of what exactly a "distinct society" might mean in practice.[5] For their support of Meech Lake, Richler denounced Bourassa, Mulroney, federal Liberal leader John Turner, *The Montreal Gazette*, the *Globe & Mail* ...

As in the Free Trade debates, Richler's political stance couldn't be reduced to a particular party. He was very political, very ideological, his friends agreed, but he couldn't be categorized.[6] Says Jack Rabinovitch, "His real leaning was detecting and writing about bullshit."[7] When journalist William Johnson called on Richler to sign a petition against Meech Lake and the devolution of powers to the provinces, Richler declined, saying that he could do more by writing.[8] He threw his support behind a new English-rights party – the Equality Party – mostly made up of Jews and headed by Robert Libman. Traditionally, Québec's Jews had supported the Liberals en masse,[9] but Richler took great pleasure in flouting community leaders, who warned that a vote for anyone else would be bad for the Jews.[10] He predicted that the innocent EP-ers would soon be corrupted by the political process, with Libman eventually surfacing as a Liberal cabinet minister; nevertheless, Richler donated money and apparently even did some door-to-door campaigning for lawyer Richard Holden, who ran for the EP in Westmount.[11] It helped that Richler's friend, *Gazette* wag and city councillor Nick Auf der Maur, was Holden's campaign manager and that Holden drank with them at Woody's Bar. "A dear friend of mine," Richler called Holden.[12] Richler would eat those words before too long: Holden, alongside three other EP MNAs, was elected, but his *final* political stripe neither voters nor his dear friend Richler could have predicted.

I can do better by writing: the first blast of the trumpet was "Inside/Outside," a long extract from his forthcoming book, *Oh Canada! Oh Quebec!*, published in *The New Yorker*. He did make passing reference to the origins of French resentment, particularly of Anglophone control over the business sector, control that had made English the de facto language of the workplace and had kept the Québécois out of managerial positions. But mostly the article centred on the enforcement of Bills 101 and 178. He ridiculed the language inspectors who had to do the PQ's dirty work of uncovering Anglo non-compliance. "Tongue troopers," Richler and others called these inspectors, tying the image of the menacing Nazi storm trooper around their necks. To tell the truth, however, Richler turned into something of a tongue trooper himself, pouncing on purist attempts to replace the Franglais "une bande" with "un corps de musique," and "hamburger" with "hambourgeois." He didn't neglect to mention Education Minister's Claude Ryan's hilarious explanation of why he was withdrawing grants from French schools that taught English as a second language earlier than grade 4: "we've long understood that premature exposure to English might not be compatible with the best development of the child." Richler also reported Bourassa's attempt to increase the French-speaking population with a "cash-for-kids" policy, possibly inspired by former PQ Cabinet Minister Lise Payette's documentary film, *Disparaître*, which showed a happy Québécois family, the Tremblays, and then melodramatically warned, "The Tremblays are in danger! The nation also!" The most contentious part of Richler's article was his accusation of Québécois anti-Semitism, an accusation that dovetailed nicely with "tongue trooper." He repeated the story of how in the late 1980s Outremont city council, led by former FLQer Gérard Pelletier, had denied a routine rezoning application when Hasidic Jews tried to build a synagogue on a vacant lot and of how the columns of *La Presse* had been slanted against the Hasids. He also reminded readers of the recent comment made by Pierre Péladeau (whose *Sherbrooke Record* Richler and friends had tried to buy), namely that Jews took up too much space. But mostly Richler focused on 1930s comments made by the father of modern Québécois nationalism, Abbé Lionel Groulx.[13]

In the US, the article was regarded as merely funny, according to Bob Gottlieb,[14] but in Québec it was explosive, made worse by having been published in New York and thus, in the opinion of the Québécois, ridiculing them in the eyes of the world. The reaction of Francophones wasn't so different from that of Montreal Jews to *Son of a Smaller Hero*, or of Canadians to Richler's articles about Canada: they felt that Richler had little sympathy for their community, but here he was, making authoritative pronouncements about it on the international stage.[15] French ripostes came in many forms. A number of Québécois misread or misquoted him to the effect that he had called Québec women "sows." "Would you like it if I said that your mother was a pig?" said Bloc Québécois MP Louis Plamondon.[16] In fact, Richler had spoken in *defense* of women and against the former practice of having up to a dozen children: "This punishing level of fertility, which seemed to be based on the assumption that women were sows, was encouraged with impunity from the sidelines by the Abbé Lionel Groulx."[17] Other ripostes were based on history: Bills 101 and 178 were appropriate counterblasts to the long tale of Anglo domination. Québécois writer Jacques Godbout told

Richler that, if the signs in question weren't commercial, he would fight like hell to have them in French, English, Japanese, or whatever. Because your family was here for three hundred years, Richler asked, does that give you more rights than someone here for five years? Yes, responded Godbout, many immigrants are cheap Americans tied to a low culture.[18] Some respondents, such as *Le Devoir* publisher Lise Bissonnette, completely ignored Richler's attack on the language laws and only discussed his comments about Québécois "tribalism," as if his rhetoric had nothing whatsoever to do with the substance of his complaint. In "Vu du Woody's Pub," Bissonnette wondered what would happen if a white Chicago writer approached *The New Yorker* with a satire against American Negroes in which he called Negroes tribal and said that their women were reproducing like sows. Better yet, what about an Arab writer from Jerusalem spewing vitriol against the Jews.[19] More sophisticated critics maintained that language wasn't a right, arguing that compared to freedom of speech or habeas corpus the choice of language hardly mattered.[20] They added that North Americans simply didn't understand that in French societies the state had a history of intervening in linguistic matters.[21] Of course, neither of these latter arguments squared very well with the passionate way that Francophones defended their *own* language.

There were appeals to pity. Lysiane Gagnon, a journalist who had been friendly with the Richlers, coming to the house at Memphremagog for dinner,[22] said that things were bad enough in Montreal without Richler making them worse. Unemployment was high, downtown stores boarded up, shopping centres deserted, new offices empty. After eighty-seven years of operation the Angus CPR repair shop in the East End had recently closed, losing Montreal 820 jobs. And now, to top it off, Richler's *New Yorker* article with its slanderous charges of anti-Semitism.[23] Why *Richler* should take the heat for a Montreal that had been emptied by PQ promises of independence she left unanswered. Likewise, she didn't say why it was suddenly the job of Richler and other Anglos to alleviate fears, to do the clean-up work after a ham-fisted language bill had curtailed their self-expression, and after a separatist party had threatened their Canadian citizenship. No doubt Gagnon was irritated because she herself had opposed Bill 101,[24] and Richler had quoted her extensively, putting her in danger of being seen as a traitor by the Québécois.

Yet Gagnon and other far less reasonable commentators were correct to condemn Richler's baseless and inflammatory charge of anti-Semitism. Behind Richler's battering-ram lay a Canada-wide survey by Joseph Fletcher, a University of Toronto political scientist. Fletcher had asked whether Jews used shady practices to get ahead: 17.8 percent of Anglophones and 34.8 percent of Francophones said yes. Asked whether Jews had made an important contribution to Canadian cultural life, 69.3 percent of Anglophones agreed, compared to 41.5 percent of Francophones. Were Jews pushy? 24.9 percent of Anglophones said yes; so did a whopping 72.1 percent of Francophones. Finally, 32.5 percent of Francophones and 15.8 percent of Anglophones, felt that Jews didn't care what happened to non-Jews. Fletcher concluded that Canadian anti-Semitism was highest in Québec.[25]

Some defenders of Québécois language rights claimed that because the surveys weren't published they were inadmissible as evidence[26] – very much a head-in-the-sand approach. The most balanced approach came from Pierre Anctil, a Francophone scholar who knew Yiddish far better than Richler, well enough, in fact, to help translate Michel Tremblay's *Les Belles-Soeurs* into Yiddish and to translate the work of Yiddish poet Jacob Isaac Segal into French. To each of the three primary markers of anti-Semitism – laws hostile to the Jews, discriminatory hiring practices, and the attempts to eliminate Jewish references from the national culture – Anctil declared Québec not guilty. If one enlarged the definition of anti-Semitism to include mistrust and hostility, there was some anti-Semitism in Québec, Anctil admitted, but it was neither organized nor unusually high when one compared, for example, the thirty-six acts of anti-Semitic vandalism or harassment in Québec during the previous year to Ontario's 106. Fletcher's survey results, as well as the problems in Outremont, Anctil attributed to the historic chasms between the two communities. Because Anctil could pass among Jews as an Anglophone, he was quite aware that biases ran both ways, that privately Jews said, "Les francophones n'aiment pas la démocratie, n'aiment pas les droits de la personne, sont prêts à violer des règles élémentaire en démocratie." ("Francophones don't care for democracy, don't care for individual rights, and are prepared to violate basic democratic principles.")[27] Anctil and many others contended that Lionel Groulx's anti-Semitic views no longer had any role in Québécois nationalism.

Richler countered that if Québécois saw fit to name a Montreal metro station, a CEGEP, and a mountain range after Groulx, and if Claude Ryan (former editor of *Le Devoir* and Liberal leader) called him "the spiritual father of modern Québec," Groulx's views must be pretty important.[28] Whenever pressed, Richler kept returning to Groulx, and to the 1930s and 40s, the time when Richler's own attitudes had been shaped. It wasn't a very convincing argument, since it demanded the very political correctness that Richler fought so hard against elsewhere. Should literary people forget T.S. Eliot or Céline because of their repugnant opinions about Jews? Should Mackenzie King's name be expunged from public buildings because of his crucial role in denying a haven for Jewish refugees before World War II? Richler understandably scoffed at contemporary attempts to whitewash Groulx but couldn't admit that contemporary Québécois revered Groulx for reasons other than Groulx's anti-Semitism. A 1984 survey of Canadian anti-Semitism (which Richler would soon quote in *Oh Canada!*) confirmed both Fletcher's findings of some anti-Semitism and the PQ's insistence that nationalism did *not* equate to anti-Semitism. The 1984 survey found anti-Semitic attitudes in Newfoundland, Québec, and New Brunswick to be much higher than in the rest of Canada. Richler quoted this survey's results on Québec but kept silent on its other interesting conclusion: that a PQ affiliation was no greater than a Liberal affiliation as a predictor for anti-Semitic attitudes. The factors that *did* have a high correlation with anti-Semitism were French Catholic affiliation, low income, and low educational attainment.[29] It's noteworthy that, when Richler visited Israel again and was urged to admit that Israel was the only place for a Jew, Richler explained that anti-Semitism was no longer much of a problem in Canada.[30]

That said, Richler's more general point throughout the language debate was convincing: nationalism of *any* stripe – German (most notoriously), but also Anglo-Canadian, Québécois, Israeli – always spelled trouble for minorities. Anti-Semitism wasn't banging at the door, but Québécois nationalists, like most nationalists, had little inclination to respect the aspirations of any minority except themselves. Street demonstrations during which Francophone Quebeckers chanted "Le Québec aux Québécois" didn't strike Richler as calls for universal brotherhood.[31] Repeated references among the Québécois to the rights of the "collectivity" alienated Jews who tended to hold a more individualistic conception of rights.[32] And as soon as Richler challenged Québécois nationalism, he was given to understand that he was an unwelcome guest in the province of his birth,[33] a feeling that was a more intense version of what many Anglophone and allophone Quebeckers had felt since the introduction of Bill 101.

The rise in temperature generated by Richler's article proved too much for Equality Party MNA and Richler drinking companion Richard Holden. Holden at first couldn't understand the Québécois reaction, but at a gala 145th anniversary of Shaar Hashomayim, he suddenly saw the light. Richler was being too harsh. Richler mocking sign laws was like a Palestinian mocking Israeli Prime Minister Yitzhak Shamir. "Assume that a Palestinian author made fun of Zionism, and the valiant sacrifices of sons and daughters of Israel to defend their homeland?" Wouldn't Jews be outraged? So, too, were Quebeckers. Holden could feel Québec's pain, though he also apologized to his largely Jewish constituency should the Israel/Québec analogy offend anybody.[34] Informed of Holden's remarks, Richler countered, "Anybody who knows Mr. Holden would not take anything he says after 2 P.M. seriously." Reporters wanted to know if Holden would sue Richler for defamation. "How can I?" responded Holden, "I'm his lawyer."[35]

Oh Canada! Oh Quebec! – far from a balanced book, yet informative and entertaining – appeared in spring 1992, a few months after the offending article, and kept the kettle on the boil. The book sold very well among Anglophones. At Montreal's Paragraphe Bookstore, about 250 people showed up to get their books autographed by Richler. Also showing up was Pierre Brassard, with microphone and cameramen. Better-known as "Raymond Beaudoin" of the French comedy show *100 Limite*, he specialized in surprise interviews of celebrities. According to some reports, "Beaudoin" harried Richler to the point that Richler simply fled the signing. In fact, however, security personnel gave "Beaudoin" the bum's rush from the store, forcing him to lie in wait outside until Richler snuck out the back door.[36] Even Free Trade hadn't raised so many hackles against Richler. Occasionally Francophones had bought Richler's bigger novels, but you might as well forget about translating nonfiction from English, Claude Hurtubise, president of Les Éditions La Presse, had told him back in 1976: it took a miracle even to get such books reviewed in the newspapers.[37] With *Oh Canada! Oh Quebec!*, however, French translation rights sold quickly, and at a good price. The translator, Daniel Poliquin, had confidently hated the book before reading it. Afterwards, he called it an eye-opener about the lack of freedom in Québec, though he didn't think Richler even-handed.[38] André Beaudet of Les Editions Balzac, who had published *Gursky*, thought that the time might be right to translate *Cocksure* as well.[39] But despite the demand for Richler's work, a number of French bookstores owned by nationalist intellectuals refused to stock it, having no desire to disseminate the "Conqueror's" point of view.[40]

Richler had a rough time of it on the streets of Montreal. People glared at him.[41] Anti-Semites sent their regards, for example one letter writer who denied the Holocaust one moment and yet threatened a second Holocaust: "If you do not shut up the next supposedly Holocaust will take place in the U.S., not Quebec." Since Richler was Jewish and Nazi-hunter Simon Wiesenthal was also Jewish, the letter writer assumed that they must know one another: "Tell Weisenthall [*sic*] to stop chasing old men – the Germans are more civilized."[42] Others, who professed not to be anti-Semitic – "when young I remember welcoming poor jews into our home buying things from them. We accepted that they slept into our home, you see!!!" [*sic*] – nevertheless recommended that Richler leave the country – "Beat it to Israel if you are not happy here."[43]

More disturbing, however, was the official reaction of certain Québec legislators who ought to have had a soft spot for the notion of free speech. Senator Solange Chaput-Rolland said that the French and English press should never have allowed Richler to publish his findings.[44] Laying the foundation for his future party leadership, Bloc Québécois MP Gilles Duceppe

stood up in the House of Commons and declared that, if Jewish and Anglophone leaders didn't immediately denounce Richler as an "artisan of racism,"
then they were his accomplices.[45] Several days later, another Bloc MP, Pier-
rette Venne asked the government to ban *Oh Canada! Oh Quebec!* under
Section 319 of the Criminal Code for inciting hatred. Constitutional Affairs
Minister Joe Clark replied that the Progressive Conservatives would only
act if a law were broken and wondered about the BQ policy on free speech.[46]
Lise Bissonnette declared that it was attitudes such as Clark's that provoked
Québécois nationalism. The BQ shouldn't invoke the Criminal Code, Bissonnette conceded, but Clark, by keeping silent on Richler's book and making insinuations about the BQ, was blaming the victim.[47] Clark, who had
often been on the sharp end of Richler's pen, now received no special thanks
for defending him. Meanwhile, BQ Leader Lucien Bouchard also distanced
himself from proposals to ban the book, saying that, as detestable as Richler's opinions were, they must be tried in the court of public opinion. He
called Joe Clark a demagogue,[48] perhaps the only time Clark has been so
named. In Richler's opinion, the real threat of demagoguery came from
Bouchard – highly intelligent, ambitious, and angry – a more dangerous
threat than the rest of the BQ/PQ brain trust.[49] The BQ didn't escape Richler's satire. Probably thinking of Duceppe, who took over the party leadership eight months before the publication of *Barney's Version*, Richler allowed
a BQ leader to make a brief appearance in his next novel. Richler named
him "Dollard Redux," punning on "dullard" and on Dollard des Ormeaux,
the seventeenth-century French military adventurer whom Lionel Groulx
had turned into a hero-martyr.[50]

The Québécois commentary on *Oh Canada!* wasn't anti-Semitic, but
often came in the form of personal attacks on Richler. *Richler wants the
good old days back, "when 'frogs' kept their place."*[51] This was completely
untrue – he had no nostalgia for the days of the Union Nationale. *Richler's
Solomon Gursky was anti-French-Canadian.*[52] Not true either. Richler had
described the flight of Anglo capital out of Québec, criticized Bill 101, and
created a delightful satiric gem by inventing the book *Qui a tué Martineau*,
in which it is concluded that a debt-ridden, suicidal Québécois painter was
really murdered by Anglophone indifference. But at the same time Richler
mocked Russell Morgan, K.C., who thinks that he needn't know French in
order to represent Montreal in parliament. And Richler also laughed at
staunch Anglos who coughed up money as long as con men pushed the correct buttons:

HELP ANGLO FARMERS
LAST OF A DYING BREDE.[53]

Richler doesn't put French characters in his fiction even though he lives in Quebec.[54] Lise Bissonnette put this most pointedly, saying that in public forums it was always Richler's work that counted, not that of the Québécois, who were only *"vague décor de son grand drame"* (the vague background of his grand drama).[55] Her criticism had some validity. Richler had French characters in minor roles – for example, the corrupt Francophone judge in *Solomon Gursky Was Here* – but only in *The Apprenticeship of Duddy Kravitz* was there a significant French Canadian, Duddy's girlfriend Yvette.

If Richler was under personal attack, the truth was that he hadn't been too squeamish about making personal attacks on Québécois leaders himself. He called the new PQ leader, Jacques Parizeau "a sybarite of considerable girth," and party Vice-president Bernard Landry the party's "Rottweiler-in-residence."[56] At the same time, Richler had never been accepted in Québec.[57] He was a Québec writer, but his books had been published in Paris fifteen years before they were published in Québec, and he had been invited to European book fairs ten years before he was invited in Québec. Part of the difficulty came from Richler's lack of comfort in French. Richler had ensured that his children would be fluent by sending them to French schools,[58] but his own French was weak, even though he studied it at Baron Byng for several years.[59] His reading comprehension was fine; conversation not so fine. Whenever he could, he avoided speaking French.[60] Jack Rabinovitch, who heard him use French in southern France, felt that because Richler was gifted in English he was shy about his lack of fluency in French. He could get by,[61] but on French TV he relied on interpreters.[62]

On English-language TV he was eloquent – too eloquent. During a Barbara Frum interview on CBC's *The Journal*, Richler compared *Le Devoir* to *Der Stürmer*. Bissonnette turned apoplectic. She had a good case – moral, if not legal – for defamation, because Richler kept implying that *Le Devoir*'s anti-Semitism of the 1930s was somehow applicable in 1992. Rabidly nationalistic, the paper hadn't been anti-Semitic for fifty years. But Bissonnette spoiled her case by declaring that Anglophones in Canada were like Rhodesian whites, moaning predictably at tea-time about the ungratefulness of the servants: "One gives them everything, one even lets one's children play with their children (Mr. Richler confides that he put his children in a French school), our laws are civilized, but nothing helps. They remain tribal, resentful, and keep trying to free themselves."[63] (She could have added, had she known, that Richler encouraged his children to read French Canadian history and Pierre Vallières's *White Niggers of America*.[64]) Her metaphor wasn't surprising: it was a favourite analogy among Québec nationalists – from André Larendeau's "roi nègre," to Vallières's "white niggers," to René Lévesque's "Westmount Rhodesians,"[65] – and Bissonnette so loved its ring and its dramatic possibilities that, like Richler invoking *Der Stürmer*, she didn't recognize how absurd the hyperbole was. After all, Quebeckers *made* the laws.

The most conflicted reaction to Richler's new tack came from Québec's Jews. Many rank-and-file Jews flocked to Richler's banner, not a surprise given that 99 percent of Jews supported federalism.[66] About a third of Canadian Jewish Congress (CJC) members disagreed with his stance, a third felt that he was right but had oversimplified matters, and a third felt that he had hit the problem bang-on.[67] No scientific surveys were done, but given that 52 percent of Jews spoke French well or fairly well, and that 30 percent (generally younger Jews) used French in the workplace,[68] it's not hard to deduce who felt what. Older Jews, least likely to speak French well and familiar with the anti-Semitism of the 1930s and 40s, tended to agree with Richler.[69] Members of the extended Richler family, who through eight novels had seen no reason to cheer, suddenly found themselves in Richler's corner. One aunt, Anne Richler, told him, "I want you to know that in this instance we all heartily agree with what you had to say." It was a backhanded compliment – "in this instance" meant "*only* in this instance." She added, if the "*Je me souviens*" crowd kept remembering Wolfe and Montcalm, why couldn't Jews bring up the bad old days before and during World War II?[70]

Jews more fluent in French, most of them younger and far less likely to have encountered anti-Semitism directly, found Richler shrill. Some Jews resented Richler's books because his views were "very typically Anglo ... all the French Canadians are held down by the church, they're all prejudiced."[71] One forty-something Jew wrote, "I base my information on numerous daily contacts with French Canadians," and noted that Richler seemed to find all his references in newspaper articles.[72] It was the letter writer's parents' generation with which Richler had greater affinity. One might point at the irony, however, that young bilingual Jews were also the ones most likely to leave Québec, while their aging, often unilingual parents stayed home to tend the shop. All the Richler children, for example, had by now left the province. They would still gather at Memphremagog for Christmas, or "Richlermas" as they called their secular celebration,[73] the scene caught in *Sister Crazy*, where the family patriarch "a bit bleary-eyed himself, sipping single malt," wonders "who are these people getting so busy and high, who are these big kids in his house ... these bagel-eating carol-singing kids ... keeping him up way past his bedtime?"[74] It was precisely the older generation's stubborn insistence on bilingual schooling for their children that had opened the road for them to be successful in Toronto and the US. Although Jews were among the best-educated and richest Quebeckers, they were an aging population that soon would be overtaken by Montreal's fastest growing group: Arabs.[75] Within a year, speaking at an Association for Young Jewish Adults dinner,

Richler counselled young Anglophones to flee Québec, forcing the AYJA to do some quick damage control.[76]

After the Barbara Frum interview, reporters besieged the CJC for a pronouncement on Richler's work. CJC Québec Executive Director Michael Crelinsten and Community Relations Chair Frank Schlesinger found Richler's comments reprehensible, particularly his imputation that the racism of 1930s Québec was still operative.[77] Since no one in the US asked Jewish organizations to denounce Philip Roth or Woody Allen,[78] why, Richler wondered, did the CJC even feel it necessary to comment on my book? "It's possible that the government of Albania or the SPCA or Black and Decker Tools don't agree with what I say, but they don't feel compelled to comment on it."[79] He was quite pleased when B'nai B'rith national chairman Stephen Scheinberg refused the bait and declined comment. However, it's hard to credit the Richler/Scheinberg position. Roth and Allen hadn't laid anti-Semitism charges against the State of New York. If one made accusations of systemic anti-Semitism, it was quite reasonable to ask the CJC to comment on the accuracy of the claim.

Richler met with Crelinsten, Schlesinger, and Jack Jedwab over lunch – a four-hour lunch. According to Schlesinger, Richler went ballistic, calling them "court Jews" and insisting that they had no right to tell him what to say.[80] In his own account, Richler asked what exactly was reprehensible about the comments on *The Journal*. I don't know, Schlesinger replied, I haven't seen the transcript.[81] Richler thought that Crelinsten hadn't read the book, but Crelinsten insists that both he and Jedwab had read the book and had briefed Schlesinger on its contents.[82] Earlier, reacting to the *New Yorker* article, Crelinsten had uncritically repeated the false accusation that Richler had called Québec women "sows,"[83] but by the time of the lunch meeting, Crelinsten had a clearer sense of Richler's stance.

Silence would have endorsed Richler's claims, said Schlesinger.[84] According to Crelinsten, Richler could say anything he wanted because he wasn't speaking for a constituency, while the CJC executives had to keep open a dialogue between Jews and Québécois sovereigntists, to encourage moderate elements in the PQ.[85] In fact, the CJC response was not "mealy mouthed" bureaucratese as Richler characterized it, but a balanced discussion of the Québec situation.[86] Crelinsten simply stated that *Le Devoir* had published anti-Semitic articles in the past, but that under editors Claude Ryan and Lise Bissonnette it had left that past behind. Even *La Presse* under Alain Dubuc and the highly nationalist Société St-Jean-Baptiste under Jean Dorion were getting better.[87] Crelinsten's comments, however, allowed the PQ's Bernard Landry to go a step further – to pretend that the Jews had hammered Richler. Québec Jews, barked Landry, had absolutely nothing in common with Richler, and had rebuked him as loathsome. Why some Jews still feared Québec nationalism, Landry couldn't understand. After all, there were only two places where Jewish schools were subsidized by taxpayers: Israel and Québec.[88]

Richler and Landry took their battle to the Ritz Carleton bar, which boasted customers from among both the Anglophone and Francophone elites. Richler liked to keep Parizeau and Landry under "surveillance" when they showed up.[89] The PQ luminaries would glare, and Richler would glare back. One afternoon, he ran into Landry in the lobby. They had never been introduced, but Landry started shouting: "I hate you. I hate you. You are a racist!" "You're nothing but a provincial bumpkin," Richler offered. "I have a university degree," countered Landry, certain that this must silence Richler.[90]

Another time, as Jack Rabinovitch was passing by the Ritz, Richler collared him. He said, "Come on in and have a drink." Rabinovitch said, "Mordecai I'm starved." "You'll eat later," Richler promised. "Landry is in the room and they're staring at me, and there's no fucking way they are going to push me out of the Ritz." To keep Rabinovitch from leaving or getting angry, Richler entertained him with personal stories that Rabinovitch had never heard before, such as the time that Isaac Bashevis Singer had made a pass at Florence. Three hours later, Landry finally left and Rabinovitch was paroled for supper.[91]

In English Canada, a group of twenty-five leftist intellectuals, among them Pauline Jewett, to whose election campaign Richler had once contributed,[92] wrote an open letter to the *Toronto Star*, "distancing" themselves from *Oh Canada! Oh Quebec!* and warning that it would incite hatred against the French.[93] These intellectuals were never close to me, Richler responded, so how can they "distance" themselves?[94] One might be forgiven for seeing the open letter as righteous posturing, since none of the intellectuals lived in Québec, and since they didn't address Bill 178. In their defense, they were mostly concerned with the reaction of the rest of Canada to Richler's book. Sam Bronfman's daughter Phyllis Lambert, too, weighed in, reminding Richler of what he had conveniently forgotten: that bilingualism in Canada was *de jure*, but hadn't yet become *de facto*; that in 8.5 provinces (New Brunswick being split) English-only signs prevailed. She saw no tragedy in French-only legislation.[95]

He hadn't forgotten. He professed to be dumbfounded by the strength of the anti-Québécois sentiment in the West,[96] yet he had also spoken of "a very ugly anti-Quebec feeling" in the rest of Canada.[97] After the anger that greeted Trudeau's official bilingualism, it wasn't hard to predict that Richler would be feted in English Canada. Apart from letters that grade-school teachers assigned their classes to write to the author of *Jacob Two-Two and the Hooded Fang*, *Oh Canada!* provoked by far the biggest response of all Richler's books. Letters of support arrived mostly from Anglophones out-

side of Québec, some complaining that he was too soft on the French. In
many quarters, *Oh Canada!* was perceived as a manifesto of English "rights,"
and, to Richler's consternation, shouts of "Give those Frogs hell" greeted
him in restaurants.[98] He had mocked extremist Anglophones who considered bilingualism the vanguard of a French takeover of Canada, but he had
offered no real defense of bilingualism. Richler, gadfly to all sides, was no
demagogue, yet with his witty jabs at Bill 178 he was in danger of becoming one. In Toronto, nine hundred people showed up to hear him.[99] When
he spoke at the University of Western Ontario, the five hundred students in
attendance laughed even when there were no jokes.[100] At the University of
Manitoba, the auditorium filled to the rafters, Richler went through some
of the material in *Oh Canada!* In the question period that followed, one audience member – more attuned to history than to satire – had the temerity
to doubt Richler's figures that one in six Quebeckers were descendents of il-
literate soldiers and prostitutes (Richler's gloss on *"les filles du roi,"* the
king's "daughters" who had been sent to help populate New France). At the
end of his rebuttal, the audience member revealed that he was an Anglo-
Montrealer.

> Richler: A politically-correct Anglo-Montrealer? What are you doing here?
> Audience member: I'm a professor.
> Richler: That's obvious.[101]

The crowd hooted with laughter, as Richler knocked aside any semblance of rational debate. In fact, the audience member was right, even if he
was a professor. The myth that the *filles du roi* were mostly prostitutes had
been debunked years earlier,[102] but, like most satirists, Richler loved to recount our base origins – a truth almost above history. He had done so for
Jewish origins with Ephraim Gursky. As the new constitutional spokesman
for English Canada, elected by popular acclaim, Richler played well all across
the country, especially on the prairies. Resentment about Québec's special
status within Confederation, about federal jobs that favoured the bilingual,
about Western alienation from power, turned into a tide of support for Richler, as Westerners cheered what they thought were his attempts to slay the
French dragon. He didn't want to be used as a stick to beat Québec with,
he protested,[103] but he was.

Some of Richler's friends – Peter Gzowski, for example – were embarrassed by his stance on French.[104] Others, such as Robertson Davies, defended him.[105] Guy Vanderhaeghe, Richler's friend and the "prairie goy" on
whose behalf Richler had put the international Jewish literary mafia to
work,[106] greeted the whole affair with a chuckle. Richler was the second
writer of his acquaintance, he revealed, to have been rebuked in a Canadian

legislature. The first was Lorna Crozier, whose line "The carrots are fuck-ing the earth" from "Sex Lives of Vegetables" had offended the sensibility of a Manitoba MLA. But Vanderhaeghe felt quite exalted now that he knew not just "some mere piddling, dime-a-dozen pornographer" but "a genuine hate-mongering racist."[107]

Richler played two roles in the separatism wars. Firstly, as a satirical polemicist he helped galvanize public opinion sharply into English and French camps. His focus on the tyranny of the majority and on outrages against common sense provoked a strident reaction from many Québécois nation-alists and an unthinking applause from the less flexible of Anglo-Canadians. Canada has little for which to thank Richler in this role. He was still oper-ating within World War II categories – "*à bas les Juifs!*" and gang fights on Park Avenue. By pointing so insistently to the old anti-Semitic Québec, Rich-ler was, as his critics complained, confusing the old defensive French-Catholic nationalism with the new linguistic nationalism. In the old regime, Québec saw itself as a small island harried on all sides by a vast army of heretics. If one couldn't rout the Protestants, one could at least make things hot for Jews and Jehovah's Witnesses. That world, however, was mostly gone. The new nationalism, predominantly secular in character, had no interest in ha-rassing Jews or even in keeping out foreigners. It just demanded that they speak French.

Richler's second role, *inseparable* from the first, had a more far-reach-ing, if less public, effect. At the same time as he pushed his audiences into extreme positions, his satire against the excesses of nationalist self-congrat-ulation helped to tone down the enforcement of the sign laws. Nobody wanted to be the object of ridicule. While some commentators felt that Rich-ler's writing on language simply widened the gulf between Canada's two solitudes,[108] others argued that by pointing out the foolishness of the lan-guage laws he had single-handedly saved the country from breaking up. Who could forget, for example, the Twice As Much Society, formed by Richler and his friends at Woody's Pub, lobbying for a Bill 178 amendment that would require French to be spoken twice as loudly as English?[109] A more re-alistic assessment of Richler's role is that he, along with Alliance Québec and the Equality Party, made it difficult for the PQ and provincial Liberals to pursue extreme measures.[110] Nobody from the PQ or the Liberals was going to acknowledge that the sign laws were eased because of Richler, but eased they were. As the "Notwithstanding" clause expired for Bill 178, Bourassa retreated to Bill 86, which allowed outdoor bilingual signs, and eased access to English in schools, hospitals, and businesses.[111] When the PQ returned to power, Parizeau and Bouchard mostly kept their hands off Bill 86, angering some hard-liners.[112] Instead, the PQ ensured that new immi-grants would learn French.

In his writing on Québec, Richler also took aim at sovereignist weak spots and attacked them vigorously. Joe Norton, chief of the Mohawks at Kahnewake, argued that, if Canada was divisible, then Québec was divisible too. When Parizeau argued against this, Richler chirped up: "Torn between embarrassment and delight, I find myself in total agreement with bumbling Jock Parizeau for once ... 'The right to property,' he said, 'the right to use ancestral land – all that exists. But it doesn't mean you can cut a country in two.'"[113] On a forty-five-minute TV piece that he did for the BBC in September 1992, Richler made much of the divisibility issue, highlighting the satirical song "Anglophonia," premised upon the notion that because the English were populous in the Eastern Townships, they should declare independence.[114] The BBC show again frustrated Quebeckers, because once more Richler had been asked to interpret them internationally.[115] *La Presse*'s Jean-Pierre Girerd did a front-page cartoon linking Richler to Hitler. It was meant as a dig at the BBC, which had said that Richler had been chosen to do the piece because he was well-known. Hitler is also well-known, Girerd shot back. No surprise: after all the posturing on both sides – Richler calling *Le Devoir Der Stürmer* and the BQ calling Richler a racist – the logical next step, as in all correctness battles, was to invoke the name of Hitler. The kerfuffle ended in *La Presse* offering a weak apology.[116] After Richler's death, Richard Martineau, the editor-in-chief of *Voir Montréal*, a cultural weekly, would say, "We won't be crying hot tears here like in the rest of Canada,"[117] and the similarly dry-eyed *Le Journal de Montréal* would report on page 15, "Richler the cursed polemicist, succumbs to cancer."[118]

While his stance alienated many Québécois, his federalist political involvement made him a truly national figure, in a way that no mere novel could do. Montreal's Jews began to invite him to Jewish book fairs,[119] and even to father-and-son breakfasts. Once the prodigal son of Montreal Jews, he now starred on the "lox-and-bagel circuit."[120]

26

VIP's Israel

STILL TAKING FLAK FOR *Oh Canada!*, Richler, in autumn 1992, convinced Bob Gottlieb at *The New Yorker* to give him a new journalistic assignment: Israel. He had been in San Francisco at a birthday party for long-time friend Percy Tannenbaum and got to talking about their old days in the Habonim Zionist youth group.[1] Wondering about the fate of Habonim members who had made aliyah (emigration to Israel) Richler sensed an article in the making. Although Lise Bissonnette and Richard Holden had had identical epiphanies about the similarity between Israeli and Québécois nationalisms, Richler thought more along the lines of Marx's famous dictum, "History repeats itself, first as tragedy, then as farce": Israel the tragedy, Québec the farce. Before his second visit to Israel, Richler had a fairly set view of the Middle East conflict. He favoured a demilitarized Arab state, with Jerusalem as an "international" city.[2] Terrified of Likud Defense Minister Ariel Sharon's military approach to Palestinian dissension – an approach that encouraged attacks on Arab civilians in the early 1980s,[3] including, infamously, the Sabra and Shatila massacre in South Lebanon – Richler (using Sharon's nickname) had had Moses Berger call "Arik Sharon" a "self-satisfied thug" in *Solomon Gursky*.[4] Richler considered Sharon "the closest thing we've got to a Jewish fascist."[5] Israel, Richler admitted, needed a strong defense force, and in *Solomon Gursky* it's hinted that early in the nation's existence Solomon was heroically running guns and supplying military aircraft to Israel. Yet even in his teenage Zionist phase, Richler had feared that a militaristic approach wouldn't solve the Palestinian problem. He supported the "Peace Now" group[6] and donated money to it rather than to the United Jewish Appeal.[7] A movement, not a party, Peace Now advocated trading "land for peace," urged that a Palestinian state be created within the territories captured in 1967, and opposed Jewish settlement in the West Bank

and other contested areas. Although Peace Now has been called "an Ashke-
nazi elitist protest movement,"[8] Labour Prime Minister Yitzhak Rabin,
elected a few months before Richler arrived in 1992, was already following
the "land for peace" policy, which would culminate in the Oslo Accord,
holding out great hope for a peaceful resolution.

On their way to Israel, Mordecai and Florence spent a week in Egypt,
where Richler's stomach rebelled and he felt lousy.[9] Barely arrived in Israel,
Richler got a sense of the strain that Israelis lived under. He had become
friendly with Conrad Black, the magnate who owned, among other newspapers, the *Jerusalem Post*. Black arranged for an employee to pick up Richler at the airport,[10] but between the driver and Richler they managed to
forget his new electric typewriter there. Before Richler could have it picked
up, Israeli security forces, on perpetual guard for bombs, blew it up. Black
offered to replace the typewriter, but Richler declined, saying that the story,
embellished a little, was worth more than the typewriter.[11] While Richler
was in Israel, the *Post* carried a tribute to cartoonist Noah Birzowski (AKA
Noah Bee), and one cartoon, called "Final Solutions," depicted emaciated
concentration camp Jews in one panel; in the next a Jew being married to
a Gentile. Sensitive to such polemic, and with his Gentile wife Florence in
the next room, Richler noted that if Bee had been a Catholic who feared a
Catholic genocide every time a Catholic married a Jew, the B'nai B'rith would
have pounced on him.[12]

During the 1962 trip, Richler hadn't visited his former youth leader Ezra
Lipshitz and friends Gdalyah Wiseman and Sol and Fayge Cohen. This time
he sought them out. All were still glad that they had emigrated, and all were
still Labour Zionists. They supported Rabin's peace initiatives, including the
plan for a Palestinian state. Yet when Richler visited his mostly Orthodox
relatives, he got a very different picture – of Israelis who felt that any concessions of land would give terrorists a stronger base from which to stage
killings. Some of what he saw disturbed Richler. Among Jews Richler felt
the anxiety that accompanied the simplest public tasks, the constant worry
that the friendly Arab in one's office might turn out to be a suicide bomber.
Among Palestinians, he saw the devastation wrought by the Israeli Army.

Richler spoke with common people and politicians across the country
on both sides of the Israeli/Palestinian divide: hearing their legitimate complaints; also noticing signs of fanaticism. Interviewing hardline Israeli politician Eliyakim Ha'etzni (a veteran of Hebron/Kiryat Arba'a, the first Israeli
settlement on the West Bank), who felt no compunctions about state brutality against Palestinians,[13] Richler listened to a defense reminiscent of his
own position in *St. Urbain's Horseman*: "what a Jewish state is all about is
to enable us to be the same as everybody else. Why must we prove to be
better? We were rewarded for that with Auschwitz. So I needn't excel any

more."[14] Richler didn't hesitate to report that as a lawyer Ha'etzni acted for Arabs who demanded better health standards and equal pay for equal work. At the same time, Richler noted that Ha'etzni carried on his conversation at a near-shout, giving him a less-than-rational air. Among the Palestinians, Richler recognized grievances about poverty and evictions from their rightful property. Yet he also noted that one widow whose husband died in an accidental security killing refused to allow an autopsy because she "knew" that "the Jews use the body parts." Shades of the blood libels, Richler immediately thought. By the end of his visit, he yearned for the comparatively bloodless farce of Canada's civil war.[15]

The manuscript that Richler presented to *The New Yorker* in May 1993 was rambling, lengthy, and incomplete. He had promised to write about the Jews who had made aliyah, but that thread had become intertwined with autobiography and history. I wouldn't be surprised, Richler told the editors, if you reject the manuscript. He wasn't worried – in effect he was *asking* them to reject the piece, knowing that with a little more work and the addition of one of Rabbi Rosenberg's golem stories, he'd have a book. Whether a *good* book, he had no idea.[16]

It *was* a good book, interleaving the human stories of former Habonim members with a compact history of Zionism and of Israel. Richler also set the opinions of Israelis and Palestinians about their tortured country beside his own stories – his youthful plans for aliyah and his later sense that he could only ever be a Diaspora Jew. Throughout, he avoided caricaturing those he disagreed with. Most controversial was not his recounting of atrocities on both sides of the conflict, but his ability to find parallels between Palestinian nationalists and early Zionists; parallels between the rhetoric of Palestinian terrorists and the Jewish rhetoric of Stern Gang members, terrorists of the 1940s who now (Yitzhak Shamir, for example) led the nation; parallels between the keening mothers of Palestinian martyrs and the St. Urbain Street grandmothers with their tales of Cossacks killing the Jews. Careful to cast the braggart Jerry Greenfield rather than himself as the skeptical anti-Zionist, Richler nevertheless went so far as to say that, were he a Palestinian youth, he hoped he'd be brave enough to join the stone-throwers.

Reactions, even among his friends, varied greatly. Jack McClelland found the book boring, except during the Rabbi Rosenberg story, and advised Richler to put a sign on the cover, "For Jews Only."[17] Predicting that his views wouldn't be considered Zionist enough, Richler said, "[*This Year in Jerusalem*] may lose me whatever Jewish establishment readers I have left."[18] Academic friends in Israel, Fayge and Sol Cohen, felt the opposite, anticipating that the book would put to rest Richler's reputation as a "self-hating Jew" and "Israel Basher."[19] But Zabam, the Israeli publisher who had bought *Solomon Gursky Was Here*, didn't want *This Year in Jerusalem*. Israelis, certain that nobody from outside knew anything about Israel, didn't buy books by foreigners who presumed to lecture them about their problems.[20]

The reaction of the late Sam Orbaum, Richler's cousin and a journalist for the *Jerusalem Post*, explains much about the Israeli readership. Orbaum had admired Richler ever since Orbaum was a teenager, when to show an interest in "that shegetz" Mordecai was to anger one's parents, aunts, and uncles. Orbaum made Richler comfortable in Israel, and when Richler afterwards needed someone to check his Israeli details, it was Orbaum who scurried around.[21] Despite his admiration for Richler, Orbaum wasn't impressed by *This Year in Jerusalem*. Richler didn't know enough about Israeli complexities, only got surface impressions from the trip, and his viewpoint was that of almost every visitor to Israel, complained Orbaum: "They all mouth the same damn catchphrases ... It's like they're given a pamphlet at the airport, a VIP's POV, provided by the UN, perhaps." After interviewing all sorts of people, Richler didn't budge at all from his original position of a demilitarized Arab state, an impossible position, according to Orbaum, because Israel was a sliver of Western democracy in sea of Arab anti-Enlightenment mentality. To apply Western logic to the situation was "maddeningly stupid – like finding yourself face-to-face with a lion and offering it cash if it'll leave you alone."[22] In the West, a number of Jewish reviewers similarly complained that Richler was too sardonic, too glib, or too prepared to see all things as equal[23] – all criticisms in a Jewish code that, translated, meant "he sympathizes too much with the Arabs."

Back home, Richler ran into shelling from the Jewish establishment in Montreal, but not for *This Year in Jerusalem*: he made the mistake of criticizing Steven Spielberg's film, *Schindler's List*. Jewish women in concentration camps, Richler hazarded, probably hadn't worn "eyeliner and foundation cream," and the scene in which an expected gassing turns out to be merely a water shower, Richler called a "colossal blunder."[24] This put him on the radar screen of Rabbi Ira Grussgott and Dan Nimrod. The former was the new Shaar Hashomayim rabbi in Montreal who was trying to steer the congregation away from Conservatism and towards Orthodoxy; the latter was a former Irgun fighter who wrote, edited, and published the *Suburban*, a little Jewish magazine issuing out of Dollard des Ormeaux, near Montreal. Grussgott carried on a word-of-mouth campaign against Richler,[25] while Nimrod fired away in print. If Spielberg had the women wear eyeliner and foundation, he must have had his reasons, offered Nimrod.[26]

Grussgott didn't get far – within a year, Shaar Hashomayim invited Richler to give the Sternberg Lecture for a lavish $6,500.[27] The lecture was standing-room only, everyone hoping to hear about Québec and language. Instead Richler read from his upcoming novel, *Barney's Version*, choosing the passage in which Barney's father dies on a massage parlour table just after ejaculating. Many in the audience walked out. You don't read material like that in a shul [synagogue], but Richler was always "in your face," said Rabbi Alan Langner, an audience member.[28] Langner probably wouldn't have been gratified to know that, prodded by Michael Levine to give a reading at his fifteen-year-old daughter's school, Bishop Strachan, Richler favoured one thousand girls with the same passage.[29] As for Nimrod, he wasn't upset when he heard that a Kach supporter, Dr. Baruch Goldstein, had slaughtered twenty-nine Palestinians and wounded one hundred at the Ibrahim mosque. Instead of lamenting, Nimrod decried the "warped morality" that made Israelis shy away from doing the necessary to destroy their enemies. While Nimrod asked for Lebensraum for the Jews and accused Yitzhak Rabin of doing the Nazis' work,[30] Richler offered condolences to his Israeli agent at the "stunning setback to peace prospects."[31]

⋛

Meanwhile, the farce in Québec hadn't let up. Richler leapt in again and took an active, but far from straightforward, role in the 1994 provincial election and the 1995 Sovereignty Referendum. The Equality Party, which had never had much of a platform besides English language rights, bickered and fell apart. As Richler had predicted, leader Robert Libman offered his good name and political clout to the Liberals, but they declined.[32] Equality Party MNA Richard Holden, for whom Richler had campaigned, came up with a better idea. Hadn't he wept with Québec, that North American Israel, during the Richler Oh Canada! crisis? Holden contested and won the PQ nomination for Montreal Verdun, a Liberal stronghold. Best not to run in Westmount, where Anglophones might remember his face.

According to fellow Equality Party MNA Neil Cameron, Holden's rebirth as a PQ candidate was maddening, but not so strange ideologically. Federally, Holden had been a Mulroney Conservative. However, fluently French, he had also been close to the old "bleu" Francophone nationalists such as former Union Nationale Premier Daniel Johnson Sr., so he had always sympathized with Québécois hopes for sovereignty. And Richler hadn't been all that kind to Holden after Holden dumped on Richler's New Yorker article. For Oh Canada! Richler added an extra sentence to the section in the New Yorker article where he had spoken of Holden. If Holden had a fault, Richler wrote, "it was that he never met a reporter he wasn't eager to stroke with a quote, especially if it presented him with the opportunity to violate a confidence."[33] Richler felt that in campaigning for Holden he had been played for a fool. A story that made the rounds in the pubs of Montreal told of Richler lunching at Grumpy's Bar when the still-cheery Holden entered. Richler retired to a more distant chair. Pretending that nothing had changed, Holden hailed his former campaign worker,

"Mordecai! I hear you're going to Israel!"

"Why are you interested?"

"Oh, well, I don't know ... I'm interested in Israel. We could exchange some letters."

"Oh, do they allow you to write?" growled Richler in return. Richler then left the bar. Contemplating evil, as subsequent events would show.

Revenge came during the 1994 election campaign. A couple of drinks to the west of prudence, Richler, Terry Mosher, and possibly Nick Auf der Maur[34] hit upon the idea of a special contribution to Holden's campaign. On a broadside poster, Mosher drew a cartoon of Holden wearing socks, shoes, and a flasher's trenchcoat. Chubby, grinning, Holden exposes himself and reveals, where his genitals ought to be, a strategically-placed fleur-de-lys, held in place by a G-string. "Boo!" he says. Richler added the script, "When the blind Diogenes set out with his lantern in search of an honest man it was obviously Richard Holden he was seeking. Support integrity. Vote for Holden." The same in French letters twice the size of the English.[35] Richler hired two youngsters who were to distribute the flyers in the Verdun subway station the next day,[36] and he leaked his scheme to the *Gazette*.

Election officials didn't find the joke so very funny, and directed police to stake out the subway. When the perpetrators appeared, police swooped down and seized the contraband posters as criminal evidence.[37] The Directions des affaires juridiques advised Richler that the posters would be considered an election expense under Article 402 of the electoral laws and that, under Article 413, only the official agent for a candidate could incur such expenses. The fine for contraventions ranged from $100 to $1,000.[38] It was a hard lesson for Richler, one reporter intoned.[39] But in fact Richler wasn't charged, and the more the authorities threatened legal action, the more Richler revelled in the game. He was disappointed that they didn't go through with a trial – "he would have had a ball," says Florence.[40] In any case, under Jacques Parizeau, the PQ stormed back into office, though without Diogenes of Verdun, who lost to the Liberals. The confiscation of the Mosher/Richler posters wasn't enough to swing the riding in Holden's favour.

When bookseller John Mappin afterwards put up signed copies of the poster for sale, Holden's lawyer, Serge Sauvageau, threatened a libel suit.[41] Mappin settled out of court. Richler couldn't believe it, saying to Holden, "you and Serge have pulled off the sting of the season, frightening the intrepid Mappin into parting with two big ones."[42] Flush with success, Holden thought that Mosher and Richler ought to apologize as well. "Fuck it," said Mosher.[43] Richler was only slightly more diplomatic, though technically he did "apologize": "For the record, I abjectly apologize for suggesting that you were lacking in appetite before, during, or after your understandably brief mandate as Westmount's tribune for, in turn, the fulminating Anglophone minority or tribal collectivity. Instead, I prefer to think that, like Uncle Walt Whitman, you were, and remain, large enough to embrace contradictions."[44] On occasion, Richler could again be seen at table with Holden,[45] though in 1996 Richler received – from Holden? – a rough draft of a possible lawsuit, "Holden c. Richler et al." It's not clear whether the draft was Richler's parody of a lawsuit (least likely, given the non-ironical language), or a Holden prank (unlikely, since no other pranks of his appear), or (most likely) a serious attempt by Holden, following a threat by Richler, to prevent Richler from skewering him in a novel:

2. That defendant, who claims to be a friend of plaintiff, has written, and caused to be published by defendant nnn, a book entitled "zzz" in which he has created a character named "xxx";
3. The said xxx is, by defendant's own admission, based on the likeness, background and personality of plaintiff;
4. That defendant, erroneously believing that he could avoid the present libel action, portraying the said xxx as being a homosexual;
5. That defendant arrogantly assumes that he can write or say anything about persons, living or dead, with impunity simply because he fictionalizes and invents characteristics, intended to cloak the truth; which is a malicious intent to defame and bring into disrepute those persons who he uses as models for his supposedly fictional characters.
6. That, because of his double-standard as to what he can say and write about others, defendant laughingly urged plaintiff to sue him in order to increase sales of his new book, zzz;
7. That the present action is not instituted to inflate defendant's royalties but rather to seek reparation of the damages caused by his false, malicious and libelous depiction of plaintiff in the book, zzz;

The damages sought were $1 million.[46]

If such damages were rhetorically high, they were no longer out of Richler's league. He ensured that his employers coughed up as much money as possible, and he didn't neglect per diems, non-taxable. When doing his Québec assignment for the BBC, he made it clear that he needed £71 every day for two weeks, not the measly £30 that had been offered: "Were I a murderous vegetarian ... I might be able to get by on that sum. But I'm an unredeemed carnivore. I never met a pig that didn't look better as bacon ... Look at it this way. For 30 q. a day, my only affordable nightcap a Babycham, you'll be getting one ill-tempered, unobliging, hard-to-find writer." A writer who, Richler swore, would in all likelihood parade in front of Broadcasting house with a placard, "The BBC brought me to London. Feed me."[47]

In fact, however, Richler was living somewhere above subsistence level. By 1993 he had three homes: his upscale apartment in Montreal, his property at Lake Memphremagog (valued at $548,000[48]), and a flat in London. Were it up to Florence, they'd stay in London year round. As it was, they wintered there for 6 months of every year,[49] to visit with Emma (and eventually Martha) and to enjoy London's cultural life – especially the ballet and opera, which Florence loved.

Not long after buying the London flat, Richler helped Jack Rabinovitch set up the Giller Prize – at $25,000 the richest literary award in Canada – in memory of Rabinovitch's wife, the literary journalist Doris Giller. Yet not all of Richler's recent efforts were philanthropic. Journalist Stevie Cameron was in the process of writing her controversial book *On the Take: Crime, Corruption and Greed in the Mulroney Years*, and Richler, his ear to the Montreal ground, sketched political alliances for her and told her where the bodies were hidden.[50] In Conrad Black's *Saturday Night*, Richler also wrote his own assessment of the Mulroney reign, "Hail Brian and Farewell," an almost dispassionate slaughter of Canada's CEO. Many Canadians blamed Mulroney for Free Trade and for the much-hated Goods and Services Tax, but Richler had no quarrel with those: it was Mulroney's manuring of his allies' bank accounts and his courting of Québécois nationalism during the Meech Lake and Charlottetown Accords that raised Richler's ire. Later on, Richler found out that Mulroney still had enough clout to get Black's lieutenant Peter White to show him "Hail Brian and Farewell" prior to publication. Mulroney asked White to delete certain phrases, but White held firm on that score at least. Making it through the gauntlet was one of the funniest and most devastatingly accurate sentences ever written about a Canadian politician: "All politicians lie, but few as often, or as mellifluously, as did Sincerely Yours, Brian Mulroney, who lied even when it wasn't necessary, just to keep in shape, his voice, a dead giveaway, sinking into his Guccis whenever he was about to deliver one of his whoppers."[51] Richler, edging towards the Conservatives ideologically, was partly responsible for the infamy that descended upon them after Mulroney's tenure.

⧚

In 1994 Richler decided to jilt Penguin Books and sign with Knopf. Possibly, Richler wasn't thrilled that Penguin had decided not to publish *This Year in Jerusalem*, which everyone correctly predicted wouldn't be a big seller. He expected better support from a publisher, even on leaner books. Well-fuelled, he wrote editor Cynthia Good an apologetic fax, possibly never sent:

"last yr, hoping to simplicfy my lige in my declining eyars, I
considered two publishing possibilities. movign everythg to viking

or knopf. and i decided on knopf ...
i hadhoped
hoepd we wd get togehtrer in lodnon and i wd be able to tell you
about this move there ...
we have had a good and prlfitable ride together
there s nothing eprsonal in this, anbd i do hope we can remain
friends, and meet fordrinsk when im in tronot in mid june. we have
done three books togeher nciely and i want to leave ti at that,
and will yo uwill soo nget jacob iiiu which im eorking oin now
and hope to delvier at end of june. i will return my 50,000
dolalr advance agians the novel within a month" [*sic*][52]

As promised, Richler whipped up his third "Jacob cutie-pie book," *Jacob Two-Two's First Spy Case*, which he finished by the end of summer 1994.[53] It was much better than *Jacob Two-Two and the Dinosaur*. Although Richler wasn't prepared to put too much effort into his children's books, he did lace it with enough satire, including some directed at himself ("Daddy's Hard Times Tour" through his old neighbourhood[54]), to make the book interesting and to win the Mr. Christie's Book Award – best English book for ages 8–11. This time he pitted Jacob against the principal of his elite school, Mr. Greedyguts, who, in exchange for kickbacks, foists bad cafeteria food on the children. Richler's idea of children's rights ran in line with his idea of adult rights: the right to high-quality food. Villains are punished with soggy french fries and other culinary abominations. The conflict with the principal was rooted in Jacob Richler's teenage run-ins with school authorities over an act of vandalism and more generally over his lack of respect. Asked why the law grinds Jacob Two-Two down so much, Richler said, "I got caught for shoplifting when I was 12,"[55] but in fact it was his son's run-ins that he used as a starting point. Richler could mine his son's life since Jacob wasn't too sensitive. "If I thought they were hard for him," Richler said, "I'd give them up. But he just floats with it."

There was another reason for having the law grind children down: it made for an easy book to write. In his mature novels, Richler had grown far beyond elementary conflicts, but the simplicity of his children's books he defended on psychological grounds, that children *liked* to see adults revealed as vicious and greedy because adults stood in authority over them and frightened them.[56] The adults in *Jacob Two-Two's First Spy Case* tend to preach abstinence and moderation to children while enjoying the very things they caution the children against.[57] Funny and true-to-life: but by Richler's logic one couldn't say why children shouldn't indulge in *every* pleasure that adults enjoy. Strangely enough, the nearest model for Richler's children's fiction in this sense was a book like *Cocksure*, with its insistent laughter at both repression and indulgence. The end result is that one can easily say what the author attacks, but not what (apart from little Jacob) he defends.

Nevertheless, the lightness of Richler's satire keeps one from pausing too long on such puzzles, and diminishes the seriousness of the world around Jacob Two-Two. In a delicious inversion of some of the more cloying aspects of children's literature, one of Richler's bad guys, Leo Louse, keeps a few mementoes of sentimental value: a photograph of "the Bad Witch of the North, who was unjustly murdered by Dorothy" [sic]; "the real whip that was used to beat lazy Black Beauty"; and the actual gun aimed at Bambi. Such jokes at the expense of sentimentality could be appreciated by both adults and children. There was even room for a bit of self-referential whimsy: "Every morning I come up here," Jacob's father says, "toss these letters up into the air, and when they come down again I sort them out, and then there's enough money to buy hot dogs, cross-country skis, ice cream, red roses for Mummy, and maybe enough left over for a bottle of decent single-malt whisky ..."[58]

27

The Bourgeois Trickster

DESPITE THE OCCASIONAL JOKE, *Oh Canada!* and *This Year in Jerusalem* were fundamentally serious works. Personally, however, Richler was aiming his life in the directions suggested by *Jacob Two-Two's First Spy Case* and *Solomon Gursky Was Here*: never less serious. He had begun to take up something of a Trickster persona. When one of the translators for *Solomon Gursky Was Here* sent Richler a series of questions about the novel, Richler answered many of them straightforwardly, explaining such puzzlers as "Montreal Piss Quick." Soon, however, he began to change his tune:

> 'straining Winnebagos.' What does the adjective 'straining' in this context mean?
> *exactly what it says*
> a wet T-shirt girls' basketball league in which he held the rights to the Miami Jigglers' This could as well be Chinese to me.
> *I'm afraid, deeply afraid – too much seems like Chinese to you – think harder.*
> ... 'the future Mrs. Middle-Aged Spread.' I don't understand this.
> *Oh, come on. Do you really understand English?*
> What is 'the Corgi'?
> *I'll give you a hint. "Woof, woof, woof!"*
> Where is 'Vail'?
> *Look it up.*
> ... 'The boy with two belly buttons: everybody looks like that coming out of the swimming hole.' I don't understand this.
> *In Canada a boy's penis tends to retract coming out of water. In [___] it must be different.*[1]

Most of the translator's questions were legitimate. Compared to many other writers, Richler's work was filled with brand names, idiomatic expressions, a dense layer of details. They helped make his work great, but he was heedless of the difficulties that they posed for translators.

Richler had always been a voluminous and often a witty correspondent. Once, in a letter, he had posed as a struggling twenty-two-year-old literary "thematicist" who wanted to prove to herself that she could "do more than just win beauty contests" and who wished to meet Brian Moore in regard to "the historic Chicken Liver Loaf Writers Conference of 1956" that apparently took place at Cagnes sur Mer.[2] After the advent of the fax machine, he realized that as faxster he could dispense with the semi-formal occasion of a letter and instead throw off bits of pseudo-information to amuse his friends, knowing that they'd get his missive immediately and might amuse him in return, maybe even the same day. When his son Jacob interned at *Saturday Night*, Richler sent a fax marked "PRIVATE AND CONFIDENTIAL," thanking Jacob for all the stamps he had acquired for Richler at half price. He told Jacob not to worry about what was probably a harmless rash but recommended that he wear gloves at the office until he checked it out.[3]

Richler laughed at imaginary rashes; he could also laugh at his own looming medical problems, brought on by smoke and alcohol. For years, Richler met with Rabinovitch, Peter Gzowski, and others at (usually) Bregman's Bakery in Toronto for a "prayer breakfast" on the last Friday of every month, and, despite the protests of waiters, he lit up cigars anywhere, non-smoking sections be damned.[4] Around the time of his sixtieth birthday in 1991, a cancer alarm – either a spot on his lung or a growth on his bladder – was enough to stop Richler's smoking for about a year.[5] Richler told cartoonist Terry Mosher the news; Mosher treated the revelation flippantly, trying to joke Richler out of his seriousness.[6] Afterwards Mosher had misgivings, fearing that he'd been insensitive. He apologized, saying that he had masked his own fears.[7] No offense taken, Richler faxed back. "However, be advised, my new novel features a short, overheated cartoonist, actually a failed shortstop, who flees down the 401 to Toronto once his beautiful wife discovers that he is a fag. I call him Merry Tosher."[8]

Richler especially loved to trade prank faxes with those who could give as well as they got – and no one better than Guy Vanderhaeghe. Acting as Richler's proxy in a female United Church minister's attempt to stage *Jacob Two-Two Meets the Hooded Fang*, Vanderhaeghe received Richler's offcolour jokes about the minister. In response, Vanderhaeghe reported that United Church feminists had declared a fatwah on Richler, that several had volunteered to tape plastic explosives around their waists and become suicide bombers. Vanderhaeghe's advice: "If any woman who looks pregnant gets near you, knock her down and run like hell."[9] Another time, after a

Saskatchewan librarian asked Richler whether he could spare an autographed book for a charity auction, Richler faxed Vanderhaeghe, "Dear ... [he inserted her name], I was abt to send you an autographed book, signed and all, but then I contacted Guy Vanderhaeghe, my Saskatchewan maven, and he wrote back to say you were a notorious nymphomaniac who screws high school boys behind the stacks." After mentioning her drug-dealing and coke habit, Richler signed himself, "Outraged father of 5, Mordecai Richler." "Copy to Guy Vanderhaeghe."[10] Vanderhaeghe replied that a disgusted librarian had phoned him: "I had to explain to her that this was Mr. Richler's idea of a joke. She thought about this for a while and then she asked me did I think perhaps your letter to her was a disguised appeal for help, a plaintive cry for spiritual healing issuing from the void of an empty life given over to consorting with movie producers and starlets who would suck a cock quicker than you could say Jimminy cricket? I said I never met a more perceptive person." Vanderhaeghe, not unfamiliar with Miss Ryerson in *Cocksure*, reported that she was on her way to London to stay with Richler for nineteen days. Also that she used a walker and was rather elderly.[11]

In 1995, former *Saturday Night* editor John Fraser, whom Richler had welcomed to that job in a congratulatory fax addressed to "Joe Fraser, editor *pro tem*,"[12] became Master of Massey College at the University of Toronto. Richler ensured a warm atmosphere at Massey for his friend, faxing, "Dear John: I assume that filling your new office of college master you will nevertheless continue to act as our group's campus distributor of coke, smack, and other mind-bending candies ... Re your query about placing 3 girls you have spoken to in Madame Seymour's Belgravia Knocking-Shop, we cannot proceed further until you submit more nude glossies. Those you sent were blurred ... Sincerely, Mordecai Richler. P.S. I'm sorry to report that so far we have been unable to find a client interested in college silverware, but we haven't given up." More of the same followed. When Fraser suggested that Richler become Massey's writer-in-residence, Richler thanked him but confessed that he was troubled by Fraser's demand for a 20 percent cash kickback of Richler's salary.[13]

⧰

In the months leading up to Québec's 30 October Referendum on Sovereignty Association (or "Referendum II, The Sequel" as Richler dubbed it), Richler kept up a barrage against separatism. When Bernard Landry decided to visit London early in 1995, Richler happened to be not only in the city, but also possessed of a contact in Britain's foreign office. Richler reported that Landry requested a meeting with "his, um, opposite number here," Foreign Secretary Douglas Hurd. Hurd knew enough not to provoke Canada by meeting with Landry as if Québec were an independent nation, and Hurd sent one of his underlings instead. Richler, hoping to sabotage Landry, begged for an invitation too, but evidently didn't get one.[14]

As Referendum Day drew closer, Richler reminded his readers of the wit and wisdom of Pierre Bourgault, Parizeau's special advisor on communications. Bourgault had once said that an independent government in Quebec might have to control the news media and that, if Anglophones thwarted the will of the majority by voting "No," there might be a civil war.[15] The implied threat riled Richler, but Bourgault's analysis of the situation didn't, it seems, since Richler feared much the same thing. A close vote, no matter which way, would inflame the losing side.[16] If the No side won, nationalists would be angry, particularly the discontented young, who, he later said, might give up on democracy altogether and opt for direct action.[17] If the Yes side won, Richler (illogically) predicted that the rest of Canada wouldn't allow the new Prime Minister Jean Chrétien to negotiate with the province of his birth, but would demand someone else, perhaps the far less malleable Preston Manning, leader of the Reform Party.[18]

In articles Richler pointed out that Québec would need to shoulder its 22 percent of the federal debt and that, on 31 October, sixteen thousand Québécois federal civil servants would be knocking on the door of the new nation, looking for jobs. He also mocked PQ assurances that an independent Québec would retain Canadian currency and passports. If Parizeau wanted to "appoint" Québécois from the new country to a shared Canadian parliament, Richler wasn't necessarily opposed. He suggested that they call the joint parliament "C——a" and that a free Québec should be represented by 75 MPS. Since nothing would actually change, Richler said that he intended to vote "Yes" in the referendum.[19] Of course, much *would* change, and in other forums, Richler blasted *indépendantiste* leaders for soothing the 25–30 percent of Québécois who assumed that Québec would still be sending MPS to Ottawa.[20]

The Referendum question was a masterpiece of evasion. Instead of asking a straightforward question – "Do you agree that Quebec should become independent?" or "Do you agree that Quebec should become sovereign?" – the PQ authorized a question that hedged its bets, carrying a lullaby promise of partnership for those nervous about independence, and a mysterious reference to the government's enabling legislation. The question read, "Do you agree that Quebec should become sovereign after having made a formal offer to Canada for a new economic and political partnership within the scope of the bill respecting the future of Quebec and the agreement signed on June 12, 1995?" This meek question was a far cry from the take-no-prisoners bill – Bill 1 – which few Quebeckers had read, but which announced: "We, the people of Quebec, declare it is our will to be in full possession of all the powers of a State: to vote all our laws, to levy all our taxes ..." Richler, mocking the PQ's gilding of the Referendum, offered his own questions. Given that the PQ wanted to sneak in the contentious word "sovereignty," and yet to convince moderate Quebeckers to set aside their fears, Richler offered the following:

> Are you in favor of doubling the old age pensions, winning the 6/49, enjoying an annual paid vacation in Florida, and, oh yes, a sovereign Quebec. Answer Yes or No.

Alternatively, given the PQ's waffling about what exactly it meant by sovereignty, he had a fallback question:

> Are you in favor of an economic and political union with Canada, sharing an army, post office, blizzards, national debt, etc. but also allowing that Quebec is a distinct society and that from now on it can consider itself hemi-semi-demi sovereign if only during Montreal's traditional Happy Hour. Answer Yes, No, or Maybe.[21]

Meanwhile, the federal government's ineffectual campaign against separatism dismayed Richler. Chrétien was a washout, Richler thought; the federalist TV-ad campaign was weak; the Reform Party, belting out "Oh Canada" in parliament, was ineffectual and ridiculous. Only Jean Charest, the feisty Progressive Conservative leader brought any intelligent passion to bear. Richler laughed at Bernard Landry warning the US that Québec would be angry if the US dared support Canadian unity, but five days before the vote Richler saw an image that frightened him. At a big Yes rally in Verdun, a young woman with closed eyes repeatedly kissed a fleur-de-lys flag as Bouchard spoke. A new religion, Richler thought. Three weeks before the Referendum he had predicted a 57 percent / 43 percent split in favour of the No side, but two days before the vote he realized that the result would be much closer.[22]

On Referendum night, Federalism survived with the narrowest possible margin, 50.6 percent against sovereignty, 49.4 percent in favour. No great comfort: in the future, Richler prophesied, separatists would win because Anglophones were voting with their feet, leaving the province.[23] He did, nevertheless, feel vindicated when a despondent Parizeau blamed the defeat of the Yes forces on "money and the ethnic vote." Richler had always claimed that Québécois nationalism was tribal; here, he felt, was proof.[24] Some commentators suggested that with such a close vote, it was Richler who had made the difference, saved Canada, so to speak.[25] He had defused some of the intellectual might of Quebec separatists, argued John Fraser. "He robbed them of the purity of their righteousness."[26] Yet since he also irritated moderate Quebeckers, his new role as Captain Canuck was decidedly ambivalent: he didn't really have a broader vision of a Canada in which French and English could live together. No wonder that a few months after the Referendum, when one hundred Québec writers were wined and dined in Canada's Paris embassy at the *"Belles Étrangères"* ("Beautiful Strangers") celebration, Richler wasn't invited. Maybe I was #101, Richler mused.[27] Alberto Manguel and Mavis Gallant withdrew from the fête to protest Richler's exclusion, but no-one else followed suit.[28]

≶

In Parizeau's comment about the evils of the ethnic vote, Richler saw an opportunity to take satire to the streets. Since everything in Québec seemed to be geared towards Francophone, long-established, *pure laine* Québécois, Richler and friends decided to form a dark twin of the nationalist Société St-Jean-Baptiste: the Impure Wool Society. It would offer the "Prix Parizeau," named after its great exemplar, to the best work of fiction by an ethnic or impure wool Quebecker. Richler put up some of his own money and leaned, not always successfully, on friends such as entertainment lawyer Michael Levine, media mogul Moses Znaimer, and McClelland & Stewart publisher Avie Bennett for donations. "It's Parizeau Prize time," Richler informed them, "so drop everything and write me your cheque, please."[29] As a media stunt – its primary intention – the Prix Parizeau caught the imagination of reporters and newspaper editors across the country. And also the imagination of grim Francophones: federalists who found it hard to teach Quebeckers the joys of patriotism, and separatists who saw in the prize yet another humiliating slap delivered by the English Conqueror.[30] College teacher and vice-president of the *Mouvement pour la Souveraineté du Québec*, Gilles Rhéaume, not unfamiliar with media stunts himself, announced his intention of dragging Richler before the Québec Human Rights Commission, since Article 10 of the Quebec Charter of Human Rights and Freedoms forbade the kind of preference that the prize was giving to a particular language and ethnic origin.[31] He didn't explain the precise fit between Article 10 and the penalties against English under Bill 178. "We are no longer the white niggers of America," Rhéaume hotly insisted, and added that Prix Parizeau rules were as racist as swastikas on a Jewish cemetery.[32] His anger came as no surprise, since Richler had mocked him in *Oh Canada!* for walking from Montreal to Québec City to protest René Lévesque's soft-sell approach to independence. His intent, Rhéaume had disclosed, was to urinate on the statue of General Wolfe. Arriving in front of the statue, Rhéaume got cold feet. Afterwards, he said that he had *felt* like urinating but had restrained himself, asking Québécois to consider the deed done – symbolically.[33]

The Human Rights Commission declined to act on Rhéaume's Prix Parizeau complaint, arguing that there was no evidence that Richler was actually going to follow the stated rules. Rhéaume celebrated as if he had achieved a victory. Richler had better watch out, Rhéaume warned, because, if he did go ahead under his racist rules, the Human Rights Commission would nab him.[34] Richler scoffed, and went ahead with the award anyway, noting that male Francophone writers were also ineligible for Britain's Orange Prize (awarded to female writers) and that he himself was ineligible for Toronto's discriminatory Miss Italia pageant even though he had sent contest organizers a saucy photo of himself in his "Ralph Klein underwear."[35]

The Prix Parizeau award ceremonies allowed Richler another podium from which to mock the contortions that Québec language laws required. At the Prix Parizeau ceremonies, books were strictly second fiddle to politics. During his inaugural speech in 1996, Richler spoke about an event that he called "Matzohgate." Earlier that year, investigators from the Office de la Langue Française had entered stores carrying specialty Passover foods and seized foods that hadn't been labelled in French – i.e., nearly everything. The food companies (mostly from the USA) considered the market too small to warrant extra labelling costs. The Canadian Jewish Congress argued on behalf of the food companies, and the PQ government, in a spirit of munificence, exempted unilingual specialty foods forty days before and twenty days after Passover. Year-round kosher foods were not exempted.[36] Richler made the most of this in his speech for the Prix Parizeau ceremony. Heroin was banned year-round, but "the lucky Jews," he grinned, could get away with eating unilingual matzohs for sixty days. And Jews brave enough to pull the blinds and down a matzo on the sixty-first day could feel kinship with Spanish conversos, Jews who had practiced their religion in secret after the Inquisition.[37]

As a literary prize, however, the Prix Parizeau was a washout. Richler prepared a letter, "Dear Publisher, Good news. The recently formed Impure Wool Society of Quebec is pleased to announce a new literary award, the $3,000 Prix Parizeau."[38] But publishers, loathe to alienate the Québécois, didn't leap at the proffered money and at Mosher's signed portrait of Parizeau. In the second year, prize applications were distributed to one hundred publishers, but, a couple of weeks later, not a single book had been entered.[39] Eventually four books crept forward,[40] David Manicom's *Ice In Dark Water* winning. At the award ceremony Richler apologized that Parizeau couldn't attend; thanked the Prix Parizeau's legal advisors, who preferred to remain nameless; and thanked the Prize's financial backers, who also preferred to remain nameless.[41]

28

Absolut Barney

POSSIBLY AS A SMALL BONE to Cynthia Good for having pulled his novels from her company, Richler had proposed that he edit a Penguin book of literary feuds.[1] Richler packed Emma off to do research for the book,[2] and, for four years afterwards, Richler sent an annual fax to Good, predicting that in the coming year he'd finish the book.[3] He never did. More important work held him: *Barney's Version*, a novel in which, after the many middle-aged Richler protagonists who had yammered so movingly about aging and death, Richler finally created an old man who really was near the end of his days. Even to Florence, Richler seldom talked about death,[4] but in *Barney's Version* these things came out. An aging Barney Panofsky looks back over his life, from his salad days in Paris to his success as a producer of schlock-TV, and finds little to regret except that his third wife, Miriam, has left him. After finishing *Solomon Gursky Was Here*, Richler had again considered writing Duddy II. Both Kotcheff and Richard Dreyfuss had lobbied him to do it.[5] Richler, however, realized once again that a non-Duddy would give him wider scope. In the early 1960s, Richler had confessed that from his derivative first novel, *The Acrobats*, the only character who still interested him was the businessman Barney Larkin.[6] Barney had been mostly a figure of ridicule, a piece of revenge against his uncle Joe Richler for lording it over Moe, but even in 1952 Richler had dimly sensed the dramatic possibilities of throwing a businessman among the bohemians and had allowed Barney a human solidity that the other "acrobats," creatures of Richler's youthful romanticism, lacked. The name changed – Larkin to Panofsky – as did the place – Ibiza to Paris – but the essential Barney remained: an insecure, unassimilated Jew, pathetically grateful to hobnob among artists; the seething man against whom Richler measures artists and finds them wanting.

In three years, *Barney's Version* came together.[7] Structurally it was a much simpler matter than *Solomon Gursky*: Barney wanders through his memories, including the accusation that he has murdered his friend Boogie. The posthumous answer to the mystery is disappointingly circumstantial, and there are moments in which Richler seems to be programmatically abrasive, threatening to become yesterday's man, repeating himself by striking at a customary checklist of targets – radical feminism, gay pride, racial correctness, vegetarianism, anti-smoking laws. Unlike Atwood (and unlike contemporary satirists such as Russell Smith or Edward Riche), Richler wasn't interested in nesting his critiques inside narrators who must be taken ironically. Yet *Barney's Version* has the same beautiful forest of detail, the same precise satiric missiles as all of Richler's major novels, and the digressions whereby he chronicles Barney's slow descent into Alzheimer's give the novel emotional depth.

In an interview twenty-five years earlier, Richler had denied the basic premises of psychoanalysis: one couldn't say, "because ... my father was in a hotel room with a hooker somewhere, I am like this." That, Richler scoffed, was Arthur Miller, Ibsen, TV writing.[8] It also happened to be Richler's own story – thirteen-year-old boy wakes to find his mother in the arms of her boarder – and Richler was having none of it as an explanation of his own being. In *Barney's Version* he gives fictional weight to an existentialist and anti-psychological notion of free will. Barney finds his father Izzy dead on a massage-parlour table, but nothing in Barney's subsequent behaviour can be blamed on this shock. Neither can he blame his mother's simple-mindedness or her (shades of Moe Richler) greater love for tap-dancing matinee idols than for him. Richler's favoured characters are capable of all kinds of mischief, evil too, yet the great unalterable facts of their lives are not childhood trauma but illness and death. As for everything else, Barney's life and missteps can be summed up in two words: he chose. Even Barney's experience of the great existential chasm between human beings isn't always fully confirmed by the novel. That favoured existential trope – the false accusation – is no impediment in *Barney's Version* to a well-lived life; although Richler considered Kafka's *The Trial* to be the book of the century, Richler was too full of fun and mischief to be Kafka.[9]

Louise Dennys, Richler's editor, praised his inventiveness, especially in regards to Barney's father, calling Izzy Panofsky a formidably wonderful and unforgettable character.[10] A double-edged compliment, since Dennys wasn't aware that Richler didn't beget Izzy. Instead, Izzy was conceived maculately and directly from Montreal's first Jewish policeman, Det. Insp. Ben Greenberg, who had once threatened to cut Richler's balls off. Det. Sgt. McMaster in *Joshua Then and Now* had been a fictionalization of Greenberg; Det.

Insp. Izzy Panofsky *was* Greenberg in a more immediate way. From his own 1971 article in *Saturday Night*, Richler simply lifted all of Greenberg's best politically incorrect quotations and gave them to Izzy. And, winking, Richler gave Greenberg's surname to Miriam. With Ben Greenberg deceased, Richer no longer had to fear a libel suit or castration.

Barney's self-serving friend Boogie was a version of Richler's old Paris companion, Mason Hoffenberg, who had never lived up to his high promise as a writer. Richler invented Boogie's tryst with the Second Mrs. Panofsky and his disappearance but not Boogie's essential character. Hoffenberg, because of his heroin addiction, had turned himself into "a professional freeloader" who had sufficient energy to complain long and loudly about how Terry Southern had swindled him, but not enough energy to write much. By 1978, Hoffenberg had moved back into his mother's home, and, whenever friends ran into difficulties, he recommended heroin as cure-all. By June 1986, at age sixty-four, he was dead of cancer. Richler hadn't spoken more than a few words to Hoffenberg since 1966, when putting him up in London.[11]

Barney's son, Saul, initially follows in the Boogie hipster style and becomes involved in the Great Computer Fire at Sir George Williams. Back in 1969, Richler had told students that he wouldn't use the aborted revolt in a novel,[12] but the material proved too enticing as satire, as a measure of the generational differences between Barney and his son, and as a way of expressing ambivalence about the cultural changes that Richler and people like him had wrought. Saul was also partly inspired by a Marxist-firebrand phase that Richler's son Noah went through just after he left Oxford.[13] Daniel Richler, on the other hand, worried that Barney's eldest son, the punctilious and vegetarian Michael, might be Daniel himself, even though it was one of Daniel's girlfriends, not he, who was the vegetarian. But he didn't challenge his father on it. Daniel says that his father only had one life, so you had to cut him some slack, and allow him to use it for his work, knowing that he wouldn't betray you.[14]

By mocking juvenile rebellion in Boogie and Saul, Richler defended his increasing conservatism and his resistance to the post-structural experiments of the 1960s, even though he was, by now, prepared to grudgingly acknowledge that "those cultural ruffians" who spoke about Eurocentrism had a valid point.[15] But his tolerance of campus radicals had limits. Via Cedric Richardson, Richler lampooned Amiri Baraka (formerly known as LeRoy Jones), particularly for Baraka's cozying up to the Nation of Islam and for his anti-Semitic comments. After Baraka's recent poem on 9/11, one might venture that satire corrects nobody. In "Somebody Blew Up America" (still proudly displayed on Baraka's website) it turns out that the USA has a lot more to answer for than the invasion of Iraq:

Who set the Reichstag fire

Who knew the World Trade Center was gonna get bombed
Who told 4000 Israeli workers at the Twin Towers
        To stay home that day[16]

Despite the satire against Richardson/Baraka in *Barney's Version*, it's clear, when state troopers beat up Richardson, that Richler has no wish to deny the evil of racism.[17]

The novel is, Barney readily admits, an "*Apologia pro Vita Sua*."[18] Was it also an apology for *Richler's* life? To a large extent, yes. In interviews Richler was coy about his relationship to Barney, the first of Richler's protagonists to tell his story in the first person. I'm not Barney, Richler insisted, "when I wrote the novel, I was Barney Panofsky, but not before and not afterwards ... I'm a much nicer guy than Barney; or "the details aren't close. Some of the attitudes maybe."[19] Some of the attitudes *definitely* – Barney's recommendation of Céline's *Mort à credit* (*Death on the Installment Plan*), his wish to be "a reliable witness," his purposeful boorishness to remind people where he came from (an attitude that Florence admits wasn't far from the surface in Richler), his battles with feminists.[20] One could go on. It's possible, for example, to read Barney as an allegory for Richler's relationship with academia: the witty old sinner, once beloved by his audience (Miriam) is cast out for his refusal to be correct and, okay, for one or two venial sins. The beloved Miriam takes up with the scholar Dr. Blair Hopper né Hauptman, who panders to her feminist aspirations and whose anti-Americanism would be revealed as fascism if it weren't so perfectly in tune with the temper of the age.

Not only were some of Barney's attitudes Richler's, but *details* too, in disguise. His daughter Martha certainly considered Miriam, the great love of Barney's life, to be a very strong echo of Florence.[21] Even if professionally Miriam is more like the genial Shelagh Rogers (host of *Take Five*, a CBC-Radio classical music request show at the time), Miriam has important ties to Florence: Miriam's grace and culture, Barney's continuing infatuation with her through middle age,[22] and above all the fact that Barney pursues her on the eve of his wedding to another woman. This incident finally told, exaggerated and in code, what happened to Richler in London on the eve of his wedding to Cathy Boudreau in 1954. The main focus of love in Richler's novels had been, not unexpectedly in male writing, the male pursuit of women. In *Solomon Gursky Was Here* and *Barney's Version*, that pursuit goes awry in its latter stages, as Richler tries more seriously to allow his female characters (Beatrice, Miriam) independence from men, and as Richler accounts not merely for his protagonists' desires but for the equality that women demand. The breakup of Barney and Miriam, of course, had no parallel in reality: Mordecai and Florence remained committed to one another. Richler simply exaggerated those qualities in himself – his drinking, his taste for barroom companionship, his addiction to *Hockey Night in Canada* – and those anxieties in Florence – her anxiety about being considered *only* a homemaker – that could potentially have led to a divorce. Barney's failed quest to get Miriam back can be read as a tribute to Florence, Richler's way of saying how much she meant to him.

The Second Mrs. Panofsky was pure invention, Richler's revenge against the Jewish yenta. But Barney's first wife, Clara, was a curious amalgam of Cathy Boudreau and Sylvia Plath. "Reader, I married her," Barney begins, but then strays slightly from *Jane Eyre*: "Given that I was a horny 23-year-old at the time …"[23] *Barney's Version*, after all, is a male novel. It's likely that Richler began Clara with memories: a pregnant girl had been mercilessly teased when he was young in Paris and had slit her wrists.[24] Possibly, Richler also remembered Ulla's predicament. Clara is pregnant, briefly considers an abortion, and ultimately refuses it, but her child is nevertheless stillborn. Richler gave her some of Cathy's shrillness and combativeness, partly justifying his own decision to leave Cathy for Florence. But he did more, exaggerating those qualities to the point at which Cathy Boudreau is no longer recognizable, and adding in Sylvia Plath, who, rather shaky about feminist dogma while alive, was adopted as a feminist saint after her suicide. Clara justifies herself in confessional, blame-assigning poems, yet Richler doesn't stack the deck against her completely. All of Richler's important characters, those whom he hadn't created just for a laugh, share Barney's anti-psychological psychology. Childhood trauma has its place, but mostly the characters act the way they do out of desire and obligation. As a satirist Richler paradoxically had both a strong pessimism about the possibility that people could change and the unwavering belief that they were free to do so. Clara, wrecked by her own desires, only senses her obligations just before her suicide. Hard upon her shriek to Barney, "Now you get the hell out of here," she utters a plaintive cry down the stairwell, "Why couldn't we start over again? Answer me that."[25] The dinner she cooks is a belated attempt to return Barney's love, though he doesn't seem to realize that the latkes were intended for him. Barney spurns Clara's cry, and the subsequent guilt never leaves him, the true guilt that persists underneath all the false accusations of Boogie's murder. A tragic scene, the final one with Clara, yet who could blame Barney for preserving himself? The instinct for self-preservation, Barney's posthumous acquittal of murder: Richler would have hated a psychoanalysis of his own actions, but it's hard to ignore how Clara, as highly fictionalized as she is, justifies Richler's own past. Ulla and Cathy

Boudreau had both resisted Richler's wish to leave. The fictional apologia exceeds what Richler was prepared to admit in public.

With some reason, Richler considered that in *Barney's Version* he had finally written well about women, crediting the fact that he had been married to the same woman for nearly forty years.[26] Martha Richler agreed. Certainly Miriam defies Barney's plans for her. As well, it probably didn't hurt that, in developing Barney's full-blooded daughter Kate, Richler had made use of Martha's "feminist" letter, the one that criticized Richler for expecting less from her than from "ambitious young men."[27] If the female characters aren't quite as full-blooded as Barney, they are certainly ambitious. By the mid-1990s, after coming through a difficult divorce, Martha was closer to Richler than ever before. She felt that he had mellowed and was less intimidating, that (like Kate vis-à-vis Barney) she could tease her father out of his dark moods.[28] Richler couldn't resist stagy and sometimes awkward satire about the feminist correctness politicking in the Clara Charnofsky Foundation for Wimyn, and the name "Kate" uneasily recalls *The Taming of the Shrew*, yet her independent character and her demand that Barney finance a film on the suffragette Nellie McClung sets a less one-sided tone. Against allowing female reporters into male locker-rooms, and against sexual harassment suits when, in his opinion, a simple slap in the man's face would have done the trick, Richler was nevertheless pro-choice and he cheered the US Equal Rights Amendment.[29] He added the reference to McClung at the behest of Dennys, who felt that with all of Barney's misogyny, Richler ought either to show *why* Kate loves Barney so much, or to show that Miriam and Kate "never put up with his schtick." And Richler cut the more condescending of Barney's statements to Kate, such as "Don't worry your pretty little head."[30]

The problem of making the lovable sinner, Barney, palatable to women engaged Dennys. She considered the novel a great love story, and she recognized that Barney had to have great failings – she even encouraged Richler to make Barney's failings more substantial so that Miriam would have full reason to walk out on him[31] – but she also sensed that Richler, hankering for the outrageous, was in danger of making his curmudgeon sinister. Pondering Miriam's abandonment of him, Barney imagines her being arrested for shoplifting and himself refusing to be a character witness ... "Let her rot in the slammer."[32] In manuscript he had added, "Gang-raped by moustachioed dykes in the laundry room. No, I take that back."[33] Hard to take that back once it's out, Dennys realized. A very good editor, Richler called Dennys, except that her middle-class upbringing sometimes got the upper hand and she tried to make Barney "nicer than he was inclined to be."[34] Richler also claimed that he liked to give his editors two or three "redundant outrages" so that the editors would keep their prying hands off the rest of his mate-rial.[35] In actuality, however, Dennys approached Barney's nearly misanthropic outrages very gingerly, always urging that cuts be made for reasons other than the obvious ones. On her Post-it note about the imaginary gang rape, she wrote, "Goes on a mite long ... one or two too many ideas for doing her in."[36] Clearly, she was reluctant to say, "Bad taste. You're savaging your characters, as you used to do in *Cocksure*." Joyce Weiner, in a position of power early on, could insist on good taste, sometimes an overscrubbed good taste, but ever since Richler had escaped into the freedom of *The Incomparable Atuk* and *Cocksure*, he had guarded his vulgarity. Instead of cutting questionable material, Richler could easily be provoked in the opposite di-rection, so Dennys was reduced to euphemisms to persuade the enemy of euphemism. Doubly ironic, then, that Barney would soon become a big hit in Italy for his political incorrectness: Italian men praised the incorrectness of a book in which Richler was trying to write well about women and was grudgingly recognizing the value of a few euphemisms.

In everyday life too, Richler guarded his position as an honest – and civ-ilized – vulgarian. He had become friendly with former Ontario NDP pre-mier Bob Rae (a colleague of Richler's lawyer, Michael Levine). When Rae's wife Arlene planned a book in which celebrities would discuss a special child-hood book that stirred their souls, she asked noted children's author Rich-ler for a contribution. She had in mind books such as *Charlotte's Web*, *Anne of Green Gables*, or *The Secret Garden*.[37] No such sentimental favourites sprang to Richler's mind: "The book that moved me most when I was still a shining morning face was acquired, under the counter, from a newsagent corner of Fairmount and Park Ave. It was illustrated and cost 75 cents and it was called DICK TRACEY'S NIGHT OUT, and showed the detective com-mitting unspeakable acts with Tess Trueheart. I also enjoyed GASOLINE ALLEY GANG BANG, also 75 cents, also illustrated." He was referring to the "Tijuana Bibles," which featured cartoon characters in short erotic story-lines. Nevertheless, he promised Rae that he'd come up with a more re-spectable selection.[38]

≶

On Dennys's advice, Richler did cut Barney's gang rape comment from the novel, but in many other instances, he simply ignored her.[39] His editors wanted him to cut a few of Barney's practical-joke letters (another of the ways that Barney mimics Richler) but couldn't agree on which ones.[40] He left almost all of them in. Generally Richler's instincts about when to listen to his editors were sound – he rarely cut colour or humour, but he did edit for clarity and for character. Barney himself is a brilliant creation. Less suc-cessful, perhaps the novel's only serious miscalculation, is the contrived and

O'Henryish exoneration of Barney after his death. All of Richler's editors –
Dennys, Bob Gottlieb, Alison Samuel – urged him to do something about
it. "A <u>touch</u> too contrived," wrote Dennys, with her usual circumspection.[41]
Nearly a sledgehammer, said Samuel.[42] Given Barney's witty comment in jail
– "I'm not the only innocent man here. We've all been falsely accused"[43] –
one *could* make a case for Barney's guilt. His trial is little more than a series of rhetorical gestures, and if Barney, who says, "I am not the son of a
detective-inspector for nothing,"[44] knows enough to dispose of potentially
incriminating typewriters, why wouldn't he know enough to plant water-
bomber references in his autobiography to hook Michael? Nevertheless, it
appears that Richler did want Barney to be found innocent in the novel's
last paragraph. Gottlieb tried to play author, suggesting an alternative ending that Richler found even more contrived than his own.[45] Richler stuck to
his ending, and when a reader buttonholed him, saying that no water bomber
in existence could pick up a body in the way that Richler had suggested, he
responded, "Well, in my book, there is that kind of plane."[46]

Dennys didn't know that one editorial cut she recommended was going
to stay in the novel no matter what. About two-thirds of the way through
the novel, with Dennys on the edge of her seat, dying to know what happened in the love (?) triangle of Barney-Boogie-the Second Mrs. Panofsky,
Richler threw in one of his many digressions. Barney "remembers" his schoolteacher Mrs. Oglivy taking him on a drive into the Laurentians for sexual
highjinks. Although Dennys claimed that she had a soft spot for Mrs. Oglivy,
Barney's reliable masturbation fantasy, Dennys felt irritated for once, because the digression was taking her away from the main story.[47] She could-
n't have known that Mrs. Oglivy owed something to Richler's youthful
relationship with Evelyn Sacks. In his research, Richler also clipped articles
on a forty-one-year-old British music teacher who had sexual encounters
with boys aged thirteen to fifteen. He circled several passages, including one
in which the presiding judge explained his reasons for acquitting her: the
boys had enjoyed the relationship and hadn't suffered psychological problems as a result of it.[48] Barney, reading about the music teacher, remembers
his affair with Mrs. Oglivy.[49]

The section to which Dennys objected contained a number of curious
features, almost as if Richler were playing hide-and-seek with his readers.
In the prior chapter, Barney has just given a page-long excursus on literary
biography, an excursus directly counter to Richler's many complaints that
biography destroys fiction, tearing one's focus away from what is important
– the literary work – and placing it on what isn't – the author. Barney, in contrast, admits that nothing delights him more than a tell-all biography in which
the great man or woman proves to be "an absolute shit," and he even quotes
Samuel Johnson to the tune that biography has the great moral purpose of

keeping us little people from despair by retailing the faults of the great. At the end of the excursus, Barney says, "I'm willing to swear that what follows is the truth." What the reader *expects* to follow, of course, is Barney's alibi for the disappearance of Boogie. But what actually follows is Barney and Mrs. Oglivy driving into the Laurentians for sex. Hence Dennys's complaint about digression. To please her, Richler cut a bit of Barney and Mrs. Oglivy's I-Spying, but left in most of the scene, including a curious speech during which Mrs. Oglivy debunks Barney's hot fantasies: "But you got no further than groping me in your greedy, inexperienced manner ... You made up the rest, because no woman worth her salt will even give you a look any more, you filthy-minded, shrinking, liver-spotted, sunken-bellied old Jew."[50] Was Richler revealing the limits of his teenage affair with Sacks? Or was he laying a trap for biographers? With Richler one can never count out a complex practical joke – namely that years earlier, in the midst of his mother's affair with Frankel, Richler could have invented the affair with Sacks and, looking back, could have spiced up those elements that a meddling biographer might mistake as fact. But this would have required an unlikely level of preparation: writing a letter to himself from Sacks – writing it in the *1950s* – and then dropping it into the 1999 Accession of his papers. Rather, the 1953 letter from Sacks, referring to their affair, is the crucial piece of evidence declaring that Mrs. Oglivy is in fact the ghost of Evelyn Sacks – exaggerated, turned into a titillating fantasy, but at its base, just as Barney swears, the truth. Why, instead of using the Eastern Townships where Richler had been rooted now for almost twenty years, did he set Mrs. Oglivy in the Laurentians? Because that's where it happened.

≋

Into *Barney's Version*, Richler also dropped both lampoons and serious memorials of his friends. John Lynch-Staunton, a lawyer and the Tory leader in Senate, became Barney's faithful lawyer, John Hughes-McNoughton. Lest Richler be accused of stroking egos, he left a barb or two in his friends even as he honoured them by giving them fictional life. Barney reveals that Hughes-McNoughton, "born into Westmount affluence, misplaced his moral compass years ago."[51] On the more serious side of the ledger is Hymie Mintzbaum. Hymie's position as World War II survivor beside Barney and the young know-nothings in Paris owes something to Joe Dughi, survivor of Normandy and Battle of the Bulge.[52]

The death of Hymie was Richler's way of saluting the deceased friends he named in the dedication – Jack Clayton, Ted Allan, Tony Godwin, Ian Mayer – and, more immediately, Nick Auf der Maur. Auf der Maur, in his fedora, pea-green shirt, and Donald Duck tie,[53] had in the absence of Moe Richler become Mordecai's source for knee-slappers and stupid jokes.[54] Long since retired by voters from city council but still writing for *The Gazette*, Auf der Maur in late January 1997 was being ravaged by throat cancer as Richler finished revisions to the novel.[55] Life and art intermingled. Into the final darkness of Barney's Alzheimer's, Hymie Mintzbaum, having survived a stroke, sends a barely legible note that gives Barney one of his last moments of tearful lucidity, a note that Richler scrawled rather than typed into the published version of the novel, "Hang in old friend."[56] The fifty-four-year-old Auf der Maur at the time was slated for surgery. If all went *well*, the operation would rob him of his saliva glands and taste buds.[57] Afterwards he could look forward to twice-daily radiation. From the distance of London, Richler wrote the words of his character to a very depressed Auf der Maur, "hang in, old friend, because we're betting on you here." Trying to offer some diversion, Richler reported that in Jeffrey Meyer's biography of Edmund Wilson, Richler had found (he hadn't, of course) the sentence, "In her teens (Marie-Claire Blais) had had an affair with her mentor, the Dominican monk Rene Levesque, who later became premier of Quebec." More seriously, Richler also told Auf der Maur that Alzheimer's had overtaken Iris Murdoch and she couldn't remember her novels anymore. "Sounds great to me," Richler added ruefully. And then more personally: he spoke about the malignant sprouts that had been discovered on his own bladder five years earlier, about his operation, his fifty-fifty chances (like Auf der Maur's), and his yearly visit to the clinic, where, he said, "they poke a fishing rod, with a flashlight on the end, up my cock to look over the territory."[58] He phoned and faxed Auf der Maur often during that difficult time. In addition, since *The Gazette* continued to support Auf der Maur, Richler kept owner Conrad Black apprised of Auf der Maur's state, encouraging Black to keep up Auf der Maur's salary, because he was far from affluent. In August Auf der Maur would have a thirteen-hour throat and cheek surgery, at which point Richler and his friends at Ziggy's Pub raised $4,500 so that Auf der Maur could have a private room.[59] He lasted into spring of the next year, when brain and lung tumours killed him.[60]

It was a bleak time for Richler. He told an interviewer, "There's just one trip around the block and you better have as good a time as possible without hurting anybody else. But beyond that, that's it."[61] Before his final descent, Barney tells his son that "life [is] absurd and nobody ever truly [understands] anybody else."[62] Mavis Gallant, when she read this, cried, recognizing that Richler still held the austere and comfortless beliefs from their existentialist days in Paris in the 1950s.[63]

A less important death occurred in March 1997, shortly after Richler finished the novel: his mother's. Lily had long suffered, like Barney, from Alzheimer's, having endured memory lapses since at least 1981.[64] After she died, Avrum called Richler in London, and said, "Muttle, we're orphans."

Richler wasn't moved. "Oh, she died," he said. Avrum ventured, "I don't suppose you're going to come to the funeral?" Richler started to laugh. In the end he received a few bonds and a small inheritance, which he didn't acknowledge, and that was that. Because Lily had wanted to be buried near her father and mother, Avrum had the body transported from St. John's back to Montreal. On a – 30° day, Avrum and a few relatives buried her. Even in death, she had hoped to borrow her father's reflected glory: she had bought her grave in the belief that it would be near Rabbi Rosenberg's mausoleum. But she had been fooled, and wound up one hundred feet away, closer to her ex-husband Moe Richler than to her father.[65]

⋛

Just before *Barney's Version* came out, Richler, in summer 1997, raised a small storm by having an excerpt, "Barney's Wedding," published in *Saturday Night* with the last page set around an empty space shaped like a bottle of Absolut Vodka. The caption, in big block letters, read, "Absolut Mordecai." Critics charged him with selling out and with blurring the boundary between fiction and advertising. *Saturday Night* editor Ken Whyte showed "Barney's Wedding" to Absolut officials prior to publication, a betrayal of journalistic and fictional integrity, though understandable from the Absolut point of view – why wouldn't the company ensure that showering Richler with money and whiskey would reap the expected dividends? Company officials noticed a reference to Johnny Walker Black in the excerpt and asked Richler to change it to Absolut Vodka. In the interest of the corporate image, they also asked him to delete the reference to Boogie "sucking some substance into his nose with a straw." Once upon a time, in 1959, Richler had mocked product placement: "Think of all the more money Colin Wilson could have picked up if he had told reporters that *Outsiders* prefer Jaeger's turtleneck sweaters ... In the past novelists have erred by having their characters drink any old kind of whisky."[66] Now, however, Richler made light of his commercial forays, telling Whyte:

> You have a choice. You may substitute 'the nearest bottle of Scotch' for the 'the nearest bottle of Johnnie Walker Black'
> or insert the follwowing:
> "...reache for the nearest bottle on the bar.
> 'Oh my God,' I said, 'that's vodka.'
> 'What's wrong with vodka?'
> 'It leads to blindness, impotence, and cancer. Only Communists drink it.'" [*sic*][67]

In the end, Richler changed "Johnny Walker Black" merely to "Scotch," and the reference to cocaine was left as it stood.

Of course *self*-censorship at a far earlier stage in the writing process ensured that no real stain on Absolut would appear. Doug Smith accurately pointed out that nothing in Richler's fiction could offend a vodka distiller.[68] When criticism of his sell-out reached the daily newspapers, Richler tried to laugh his critics off. Responding to Val Ross, he said, "I do have my principles. Had Ken Whyte come up with a sponsor for my novel excerpt who was a yogourt [*sic*] or crunchy granola maker, I would have said absolutely no. But I'm always proud to be associated with a distiller."[69] If Richler wasn't precisely A.M. Klein, writing birthday odes to Sam Bronfman, he wasn't so far behind: unknown to him, Seagram held Canadian distribution rights to Absolut.[70] In a column that same summer, Richler pilloried the author of *God Wants You to Be Rich*: "If you were brought up to believe a person couldn't serve both God and Mammon, forget it ... The truth is, God, who was possibly snoozing during the Holocaust, has been born again a jolly free-marketeer."[71] But since Absolut Mordecai didn't claim divine authority, more was permitted to him. Richler, thirty-six years after Joyce Weiner complained about hot-shot literary agents roaring around in Jags, was finally in a position to ask his son Jacob's advice about buying one.[72]

29

A Few Parting Shots

THE MOMENT RICHLER finished revisions to *Barney's Version*, he had a reserved spot at a restaurant table with Conrad Black to negotiate a new deal with the Black newspaper empire. For three years Richler had been writing monthly for *Saturday Night*. Although Ashok Chandwani coveted him for a weekly column in *The Montreal Gazette*, Chandwani was surprised to get him. But Richler wanted a voice in Québec. Affiliated papers in Vancouver, Edmonton, Calgary, Ottawa, and Toronto chipped in for Richler's salary. When Black arrived to bargain face-to-face, Richler's asking price sky-rocketed.[1] They split the difference between demand and offer, and, with Black mulling over the considerable expense, Richler made the most of Black's hesitation, "Should Conrad decide my fee is too rich, I still hope to squeeze some pleasure out of our negotiations. For the rest of my life, I will collar strangers in bars and say, 'Conrad couldn't afford me.'"[2] Black did afford him. Thus, when Black launched the *National Post* in 1998, he already had in his stable at least one columnist of national stature.

Richler was in an enviable position. Nobody dictated to him. His *Saturday Night* column, he informed editor Ken Whyte, would focus mostly on books – nonfiction, no reviews of other people's novels: "I just haven't got the heart to do that anymore."[3] When an editor wanted to change a sentence in one of his articles, Richler threatened to quit. The sentence stood.[4] When his book of essays, *Belling the Cat*, came out in 1998, he had a captive publicity machine. He knew in advance that his articles would be accepted and that he could use the Black network to publicize his books. Rather than politely querying editors, he could send tongue-in-cheek messages to *The Gazette*'s Chandwani: "Dear Mr. Chandwani, I am a free-lance writer living at present in London on a Parti Quebecois scholarship. This June my Toronto publisher, Knopf/Canada, will be bringing out a collection of my essays, Belling the Cat. I wonder if you would be interested in running one of these pieces … I don't wish this to influence you one way or another, but may I say that I am a long-standing admirer of your people. Sincerely yours."[5]

More and more he began to act like a man of power. In early October 1997, two and a half months before *Barney's Version* was set to come out in the US, he sent the names of people who should receive review copies to Paul Bogaards at Knopf. By mid-November Bogaards still hadn't sent the copies out. Richler chewed him out, then added, "Hey, I've got an even better idea. Why don't you wait until my fucking novel is remaindered and send out copies then?"[6] To ensure that the message didn't get lost, he also wrote Knopf's senior editor, Jon Segal, and told him, "If you run into that hockey flunk-cum-PR fuck, Paul Bogaarts [*sic*], in the hall, bash him one for me."[7] Shortly afterwards, Richler, Martha, and her partner Nigel Horne could be found holidaying at Segal's chateau in France.

Richler had been very conscious of pecking orders ever since he had been a child watching Moe eat humble pie in Uncle Joe's office. As much as he had rejected bourgeois power early on, he hadn't forgotten status. Mostly it was the venue that had changed – from hipster Paris to the political bars of Montreal. The point, of course, was not to cozy up too much to the powerful, but to behave as their equal, which occasionally required him to tell them where to go. Steve Jarislowsky, a lawyer who had handled some transactions for Richler, thought that his client was sufficiently part of the elite to feel their pain when the Mount Royal Club needed $1 million to redo its building on Sherbrooke Street. He asked Richler to donate his services as a speaker for a fundraising dinner. Richler professed to be deeply touched by the plight of the rich men's club but proposed a tag day instead: "Various CEOs could take their begging bowls to the Main, the North End, St Henri, and NDG. The arrogance of the truly rich continues to amaze me." Stung, Jarislowsky replied that although the meek would inherit the earth, it was the wealthy who created jobs and prosperity. And if the wealthy were arrogant, so were great authors. He was looking, he said, for someone with a feeling for Montreal culture.[8] Richler didn't respond. When Conrad Black hired Richler, Black knew that he was getting a good bet rather than a safe one, someone who shared a number of his attitudes, but not a toady. Advertising a nonexistent "euphemism contest" in one of his articles, Richler offered Black's memoirs as a booby prize.[9] Still, whenever reporters canvassed him for a quote on his employer, Richler was discreet, describing him as right-wing, but insisting that he was also literate and original, qualities that Richler felt were at a premium.[10]

Richler's outspokenness on politics, surfacing now in the *Calgary Herald* and the *Edmonton Journal*, didn't always endear him to westerners, despite their cheers for his stance on English language rights in Québec. Back in 1976, hinting at his slow ideological shift, Richler declared that he wasn't a Tory, but that the NDP was going nowhere, and with Gordon Fairweather and Flora MacDonald on the front bench, the Progressive Conservatives weren't all bad. He added, "I suspect that if we continue to deny the Tories office they will go bananas, falling into the hands of know-nothing cowboys, and then, my fellow Canadians, the arrogance of the Liberals will really be something to behold."[11] If Richler didn't exactly predict the Reform Party (or that a *Conservative* prime minister – Mulroney – would be the unwitting midwife to the rebirth of western populism), Richler nevertheless understood the country's political dynamics. Once the Reform Party showed its strength in 1993, he kept up a barrage of satire and invective, attempting to make Reform intellectually disrespectable so that his Conservative friends – their number was increasing – wouldn't be tempted to join. After the federal election in summer 1997, when Reformers became the Official Opposition, Richler suggested that had Reform won, Hitler's birthday would have become a national holiday, and only white Christians would be allowed to immigrate to Canada. Furious Reformers working for the *Alberta Report* expected that since Conrad Black's lieutenants (Ken Whyte had worked at the *Alberta Report*) and Black himself had Reform leanings, surely Richler's head must roll.[12] But Richler continued to harry the far right from the pages of right-leaning newspapers. When the unite-the-right movement began in 1998 under the name "The United Alternative," Richler took to calling it "The Desperate Alternative" or "The Pathetic Alternative," and had Preston Manning make imaginary speeches: "I have been misquoted again by the atheist left-wing press. Ours is a big tent and all the sour, overlooked folks are welcome ... We do want to bring back the noose in the name of family values, but we are not inflexibly right wing ... we will bring together everybody who could never get a date on Saturday night or has yet to be asked to an A-list party."[13]

Still obsessed with the Mulroney betrayals, Richler followed the Airbus scandal and amassed a big stack of papers entitled "Brian Mulroney Lawsuit Clippings."[14] Dining with Bill Weintraub at Mas des Oliviers, a Montreal restaurant, Richler saw Mulroney walk in. Weintraub was in favour of sneaking out, but, despite Richler's very public attacks on Mulroney, the former prime minister greeted Richler like a long-lost pal.[15] When Richler came out with a collection of essays, he wanted to call it *Bye-Bye Mulroney and Other Celebrations*,[16] but he settled for *Belling the Cat*.

To Conservative friends and associates who might be contemplating the merger of the two political parties, Richler envisioned Manning as the next prime minister – "Faggots beware."[17] Reformers didn't know what to do about Richler's satire; the gay community did. After reading *Barney's Version*, in which Barney is interviewed by and tries to seduce a woman from the community radio program Dykes on Mykes, the show's Johanne Cadorette wrote him, "Naturally we talked about this on air! It was even the Final Jeopardy question on our Lesbian Jeopardy Fundraising party last November." She asked Richler for three copies of *Barney's Version* to give away during CKUT's fundraising drive.[18] Similar results occurred when Richler joked in the *National Post* about the newly formed National Gay and Lesbian Journalists Association and pretended to fear discrimination against "me and my kind." No need, since Jared Mitchell immediately proclaimed a one-year honorary membership for Richler. "Welcome sister," Mitchell greeted him, and invited him to First Fridays at Pegasus Billiards in Toronto, signing off, "Best wishes, fellow gay jay."[19]

≶

As *Barney's Version* hit the bookstands, Richler hoped to do another children's book, *How Jacob Two-Two Saved the Stanley Cup*.[20] To John Aylen, Richler wrote from London that he was planning a new novel and needed Aylen to go into the gay bars of Montreal to gather information. Aylen returned in kind, "I must say it is rather pathetic of you to enquire about the Montreal gay community and lifestyle under the guise of literary research. Many illustrious writers have had the same bent, so to speak. I recommend that you 'come out' immediately rather than continue the family-man façade that has been your public persona for so many years."[21]

Richler, a bigger and bigger celebrity, was no longer willing to do whatever it took to sell his novels. He predicted that, because the showbiz aspect of writing had become so central, within a decade or two publishers would audition novelists instead of reading them.[22] But the reception for *Barney's Version* was enthusiastic. For a long time the book was #1 in Canada,[23] yet for the third time in a row, Richler was left off the shortlist for the Governor General's Award. Carol Shields thought the reason might have been Barney's political incorrectness.[24] Yet, because of the critical acclaim for such shortlisted books as Sandra Birdsell's *The Two-Headed Calf* and Jane Urquhart's *The Underpainter* (the eventual winner), there was no outcry as there had been in 1990. As for the $25,000 Giller Prize that Richler had helped found, *Barney's Version* not only made the shortlist but also won. Here the potential for bias was far greater. His friend, Jack Rabinovitch was the prize's donor, and the three-person jury included two of Richler's friends: Mavis Gallant and Peter Gzowski. But the novel's satiric wit and the emotional impact of Barney's decline made the selection uncontroversial. When Gallant announced the winner at Toronto's Four Seasons Hotel, there was an emotional moment.[25] Richler brought everyone back down to earth, saying "Thanks, but the award I really wanted was the Cy Young."[26]

Almost immediately there was a film offer on the table for *Barney's Version*, the offer coming from Robert Lantos, whom Richler's lawyer, Michael

Levine, had been chasing as recently as 1995 for funds relating to *The Ap-prenticeship of Duddy Kravitz.*[27] Richard Dreyfuss still hadn't ceased hounding Richler to make Duddy II and had involved both Ted Kotcheff and Lantos in the pitch, something of a reversal of Hollywood practice: normally the writer crawls on hands and knees across scattered glass to the producer's office. Richler got round to making conditions for Duddy II – he wouldn't take part if there were Canadian content quotas with regard to actors, and "the money would have to be lavish, or the hell with it"[28] – but he didn't get as far as writing a screenplay. *Barney's Version* took precedence.

Although he had had his heart set on Norman Jewison as director of *Barney's Version*, Richler was nevertheless happy when Ted Kotcheff offered his services instead, but Richler wouldn't accept Laifun Chung, Kotcheff's wife, as producer. Richler warned Michael Levine, "on no account will I accept Lee Fun (sp?) as, um, producer. She is hyper, aggressive, coarse, speaks to people in an appalling manner (especially those she adjudges less important), and would drive me crazy. Please convey this as delicately as you can to Robert [Lantos]." By now Richler was relying heavily on Levine, whose dexterity and long arm made him capable of negotiating on equal terms with almost anybody. Asking Levine to renegotiate a particularly sensitive point with Lantos's Alliance Atlantis, Richler said, "I like to think of Big Mike out there in the canyon, cooking beans over a camp fire in the mornings, ever on guard for hostile injuns. Wearing his ten-gallon hat to the Saturday night barn dance." Yet when Levine made the mistake of charging commission on the GST, Richler pretended to cry foul: "Scoundrel! Shyster! Double-dealer! ... It's enough that your Bronfman mispocha is trying to stiff me on DK musical royalties, but my trusted lawyer?"[29]

≶

In 1998, at the age of sixty-seven, Richler finally became a zeyde and, in his words, "my lovely Florence a bubba," after Jacob's partner Leanne Delap gave birth to a boy, Max.[30] Barney Panofsky's son marries a non-Jew, which, surprisingly, matters to Barney.[31] Daniel says that such things didn't matter to Richler,[32] and certainly he didn't try to constrain his children from marrying Gentiles. But racial choice must have mattered a bit, because he thought it worth declaring that most of his children had Jewish partners. He was reportedly a bit disappointed that not all of his children were married to their partners,[33] and he was pleased when Martha and her partner, British editor Nigel Horne, decided to get married early in 1998.[34] Although Martha sought her father's help in writing a children's book, she soon realized that he was an uncompromising editor, judgemental she felt, and she stopped showing him her work-in-progress.[35]

In summer 1998 all work was postponed for a while. Richler's cancer had returned, this time in one of his kidneys, and he was admitted to the Montreal General Hospital for surgery. "Bye bye right kidney," he said.[36] When it was revealed that he was at the General, hate mail began to arrive. The police, anxious for his safety, asked if he wouldn't mind moving to a different hospital. But he had no interest in hiding. Find the guys who wrote the letters; don't bother me! he fumed.[37] Brian Moore, too, sent a note, wishing him well, and Richler wept over their broken friendship.[38] Moore himself died in Malibu seven months later.

Among the factors that drove his daughter Emma to fiction in October[39] may have been this, her father's skirmish with mortality. In her story "Angel's Share," Emma reproduced some of the difficulties in her relationship with Richler, the love, and the oblique ways in which love must be approached on the sickbed, "Always have some sports news at hand for when your dad is in the hospital after a scary operation to do with a fatal disease."[40] Noah described the scene more directly. On morphine, dreaming awake, Richler refused to let a nurse put an oxygen mask over his face, but sat upright and cried, "No! ... No. I won't – it's an anti-Semitic machine." And later, with Noah unsure over whether his father was talking about the 1948 recognition of Israel or his own life, Richler lamented, "Oh dear, oh dear. Who would have thought it would all end so badly?" "It's not over yet, Pa," Noah replied.[41] By then Richler was already onto further topics – the woes of Canada, and the merits of Don Cherry, though the hockey playoffs, for which Richler had rented the TV, no longer held his attention.

Once out of the hospital, he felt that he had been granted a reprieve.[42] He told his friends that to make up for the missing kidney he was supposed to drink doubles only,[43] but that wasn't quite the message that he was getting from his children. Emma recommended wine in place of scotch and cognac, told him to throw out his cough syrups and to eat fewer saturated fats – to make peace with his remaining kidney. She said that despite his protestations he didn't need a walking stick. What he really needed was to stretch and exercise.[44] The operation scared Richler enough to stop him smoking and drinking again, but only for a while, since this form of celibacy drove him crazy.[45] After a spell of only two cigars nightly, he'd fall off the wagon and chain-smoke, a very difficult thing for Florence to watch. "It was probably too late. Fuck it. He had a very kind of fuck it attitude," Martha says.[46]

After his convalescence, he finished the screenplay of *Barney's Version*. Although he could have sold the option and saved himself the work, he preferred to be the butcher himself.[47] Also, though he didn't say it, he loved the glamour and attention and the hobnobbing with producers, not so much for their company but because he found the wheeling and dealing highly entertaining. Lantos loved the screenplay, and promised a $25 million Canadian budget, with shooting to begin in Paris and Montreal by summer 2000.[48] "Unless I get hit by a truck, I will make that film," Lantos promised in late 2003,[49] but no film has been made.

The last half of 1999, when the screenplay was done, Richler spent in Toronto. His friend John Fraser, Master of Massey College, had convinced him to spend the fall term at the University of Toronto's Trinity College as "Distinguished Visiting Associate." Not a lot was required. He had to speak at two formal events and take part in "fireside chats" with students and faculty. Mainly he and Florence wanted to be near to their children – all their sons were in Toronto – and grandchildren.[50] Initially Richler thought he'd need parking space for his Jaguar. If anybody asked about the flashy car, he directed administration officials to reveal that he bought it on "a Canada Council automobile grant, available to old fart writers." But then he bethought himself, fearing that a conspicuous show of wealth would lead honest professors astray, that they'd start scribbling novels.[51] Richler did his duty at the University of Toronto, but he never felt comfortable. At Montreal or Lake Memphremagog he had worked with Florence always in reach. At the university he had to walk over to his office, while Florence went off about town, visiting. Not knowing where she was at all times, with nowhere to smoke his daily cigar, no happy hour, Richler couldn't write anything more than newspaper columns.[52]

≷

Early in the new millennium, Richler discontinued his regular newspaper column, though he still wrote for *Saturday Night*. When he visited Jack Rabinovitch in Toronto, he had a vodka but sipped it through a straw. "Look what I've come to," he lamented.[53] In some ways he mellowed during these declining years. He spoke of visiting Israel again and also of going to Poland to trace his family's roots.[54] He had occasionally seen his brother Avrum in Montreal, but now Richler decided to trek out to Newfoundland for a reading, and a visit. Avrum hadn't seen Florence in over thirty years. They had a wonderful time at dinner, and Richler treated Avrum to very expensive bottle of champagne. Later that night, Richler divulged his family secret,[55] probably his witnessing of Lily's unfaithfulness.

Richler hadn't, however, mellowed so much that he had lost his power to offend. He could still get people up in arms about his political writing. Were Canadians to elect him prime minister, he had a few solutions for longstanding problems. He'd kill the Constitution's "Notwithstanding" clause. He'd collapse the three prairie provinces into one so that cry-baby farmers could be supported by Alberta oil sheiks. Hadn't farmers chosen their jobs? Why should city people constantly subsidize them, as opposed to, say, shipyard workers? He couldn't buy Maritime votes with the promise of two weeks of work yearly and fifty weeks of welfare, so he'd sell Prince Edward Island to the Japanese and give Newfoundland back its independence. PEI Premier Pat Binns found such comments unfair towards Atlantic Canadians.[56]

When Pierre Trudeau died in 2000, Richler felt that Canada had lost its greatest leader, yet he wasn't impressed by the sentimental obituaries that appeared in the newspapers – the lone heron that took flight as Trudeau's funeral train passed, accounts of Trudeau's last canoe trip down the Styx, or of Trudeau searching for his son, Michel, who had died in an avalanche.[57] Instead, Richler wrote a more measured account of Trudeau, "The Man behind the Mania," for which Richler won a Silver at the National Magazine Awards. The ascent of his old enemy Bernard Landry to the premiership of Québec Richler greeted as the best possible news for federalism, because Landry was "a proven foot-in-mouth performer."[58] Richler mocked Gilles Duceppe, who insisted that if Québec opted out of Canada, it could always opt back in by calling another referendum. And when the characteristic Landry hyperbole went into action – "Basically we have for centuries been a bit like the firemen in the heart of Chernobyl, at the center of a cataclysm, but still standing" – Richler reminded him that Québec wasn't Belfast. Richler continued to argue (echoing Trudeau and Chief Joe Norton) that if Canada was divisible, so was Québec, yet he had been down Shankhill Road in Belfast, and the new, mellower Richler no longer wished partition on Montreal. If he had the say, he'd oblige everyone to go to the same primary schools, half a day in French, half a day in English. It was a classic liberal humanist solution: rational, fair, making no concessions to history or to the aspirations of minorities, and designed to placate no-one.[59]

For the tragedy unfolding in Israel, Richler no longer had solutions, though he continued to sift the ashes. The old solution of a Palestinian state, now partially operative, seemed less and less likely to produce anything but more violence, he concluded, because the Palestinian Authority was a brutal dictatorship. On the one hand, Israel was vulnerable to suicide bombers; on the other, Israeli courts were lenient to Jewish extremists, as in the case of Nahum Korman who had to do six months of community service for kicking and beating to death a twelve-year-old Palestinian boy. Richler looked with equal mistrust on the intifada, in which Palestinians used stone-throwing children to shield gunmen (dead children making good media PR), and on the Israeli army, which still tortured prisoners and violated international standards of human rights at every turn. Israel, confiscating land and blockading towns, with one-third of Israelis wanting the government to deport all Palestinians from the country, *wasn't* a liberal democracy. All Richler could say about the Israeli conflict in the end was, "It's heartbreaking."[60]

Early in 2001, Richler celebrated his seventieth birthday in London with friends and family, his sons having flown over from Canada. He drank his Macallan, rubbed his hands together with some relish, and announced, "Overtime."[61] Noah, judging by the books that his father wanted and by the covetous attitude towards Noah's Apple laptop, suspected that a new novel was brewing, a novel covering such diverse ground as the Cathars (a venture into Umberto Eco country), plastic surgery, and strange fruit hanging from southern US trees.[62] But the overtime period wouldn't last long. In his final months Richler managed to finish a memoir-cum-sports book, *On Snooker*, and courtesy of *Barney's Version* he went to Italy to be feted there, explaining to friends, "I'm suddenly big with the wops."[63] *Barney's Version* would sell 200,000 copies in Italy (up to June 2002). His tour of Italy was a victory parade, and *Il Foglio*, a conservative paper, provided daily reports. Allowing for perhaps less irony than Richler intended, Giuliano Ferrara, the editor of *Il Foglio* called *Barney's Version* "a complete modern theology of love and wisdom."[64] An uncharitable translation of this would be to say that Barney was sexist but still lovable. At its most pandering, the novel dealt (wittily enough) in female stereotypes: the shrew (Clara), the-wife-who-doesn't-understand-me (the Second Mrs. Panofsky). A more balanced interpretation of the Italian reaction would be to say that the novel appealed because it contained enough of traditional gender roles – male as pursuer, female as pursued, marriage as a fully serious commitment – to please traditionalists. Yet by resisting Barney, Miriam maintained enough freedom so as not to completely alienate female readers. In some ways the novel is structured as a romance. Although the pursuit fails, there *is* a pursuit, and it didn't hurt Italian sales that the scale of Barney's passion is operatic. At its best, *Barney's Version* did not require masculinity to disguise itself. Barney is required to demonstrate a certain amount of maturity, but in his inner life he isn't required to pretend to be more sensitive than he is.

After Richler left Italy, *Il Foglio*'s reports on Richler segued into "Andrea's Version," a regular column that annoyed feminists and gathered a large audience of Italian males.[65] Andrea Marcenaro, the columnist, felt (as had many Canadians) that Barney gave him a voice with which to attack the political left without being mistaken for a right-wing fascist. His declaration of how much his own writing was indebted to Richler and to *Barney's Version* would be among the most gracious: "You steal from the beautiful Version, you put a signature on it, and you take it home."[66]

Yet things were not going well for Barney's creator. Cancer surfaced in his only remaining kidney, and he had to cut short his winter in London, rushing home to Montreal for treatment.[67] After having so many years ago refused the second rank, he was finally appointed to the Order of Canada as a Companion, the highest rank. What seems to have pleased him more was that Emma published her interconnected stories, *Sister Crazy*, an obser-

vant and stylistically beautiful work. While Emma cautioned against identifying the Weiss father with Richler, the stories convey Richler's impatience
with Emma's depression. They had had a fight over it – "He didn't believe
in it for me," she says, "and therefore he didn't believe in it at all."[68] Her
novel was ultimately elegiac, mourning the "Weiss" family – once very tight,
but each member eventually spinning into a separate orbit[69] – and mourning also the Weiss patriarch, whose cancer meant that he wasn't going to
live forever. Richler thought the book "wonderful."[70]

To everyone's surprise, in the weeks before his death – May 2001 – having
started on what was supposed to be a six-month regimen of chemotherapy,[71]
Richler showed up at the shiva of his Aunt Celia (Zipporah) Hershcovich,
an Orthodox woman who had had no use for him.[72] In the last year or two
there had been small signs that he was mellowing towards Judaism as well,
but small signs only. His 1999 article "Son's prayers" included a review of
Kaddish, by Leon Wieseltier, who had left Judaism for twenty years but had
returned and stayed when his father died. Wieseltier took up the task of saying kaddish for the required eleven months. Richler, never far from *St. Urbain's Horseman*, mentioned harsh verdicts against the Kaddish – such as
(father of the Zionist Revisionists) Vladimir Jabotinsky's hatred of the prayer
because it didn't speak of loss and it instead exalted God, who, in his infi-
nite power, had after all sanctioned the death. Remarkably, Richler ended
with an inscription found in a Kovel, Ukraine synagogue, from a Jew waiting to be shot: "I, Yeruham ben Shlomo Ludmirer, was here on the fifth day
of Tishrei, 1942. If any of my relatives survive, I request they say *kaddish*
for me." To that, Richler added his own "Amen."[73]

Richler hadn't fundamentally changed his beliefs, because a few months
later, when Grove Press in the US planned paperback editions of fourteen
books of the Bible, Richler was chosen to introduce *Job*, and he took a less
conciliatory line. Theologian Eliezer Berkovits, speaking for those who had-
n't directly experienced the Holocaust, had said that we were not Job but
were Job's brother, and therefore couldn't accuse God as Job had done. Deborah Lipstadt went a step further, insisting that at most we were Job's nieces
and nephews.[74] In counter, "Rabbi Richler,"[75] as he styled himself, argued
that the villain of *Job* wasn't Satan, but Jehovah – what would Job have
done had he known that all his suffering was the outcome of a bet God had
made? Still taking the literalist position that had once so annoyed David
Rosenberg, Richler said that Jehovah had much to answer for, that Job's
God was possibly the first ethnic cleanser, trying to wipe out the Canaanite
population.[76] In the months before his death, Richler satirized a populariza-
tion of the Kabbalah and also Israeli Interior Minister Eli Yishai who had
a task force checking into allegations that leavened bread was being used
during Passover.[77] When a Rabbi complained that an Orlando theme park,

"Holy Land Experience," turned Jewish rites, such as the high priest pray-
ing on Yom Kippur, into Christian imagery by connecting them to the na-
tivity of Christ, Richler offered suggestions that would both encourage
tourism and yet remain faithful to the biblical texts: Sodom and Gomorrah
discos, a place where tourists could stone an adulteress, another where they
could see Lot making out with his daughters, and a peek-a-boo spot where
a model, playing Bathsheba, bathed "starkers."[78]

If Richler had forgotten neither the wellsprings of human behaviour nor
the darker side of the biblical texts, his appearance at Celia Hershcovich's
shiva stunned the extended Richler family. He had kept contact with his
uncle Max and a few others – quietly, because even his children were surprised to learn of the ongoing relationships.[79] But Celia, the second oldest
of Shmarya's children, and Richler had hated one another. Merely to mention Richler's name could heat her up with invective. Sam Orbaum, her
grandson, would occasionally throw Richler's name at her and watch her
sputter, until Orbaum realized that he was being cruel. Orbaum speculated
that Richler warmed to him in part because of the irony of having Celia's
grandson as an admirer. Yet when Richler, drink in hand, showed up a couple of days into Celia's shiva, it seemed to many family members that he was
making a gesture at reconciliation, and they welcomed him back. Unlike the
old days – Richler in a corner chair with no one to talk to – this time everyone, even relatives who hadn't spoken to him for many decades, gathered
round him, talked, and laughed with affection.[80] The animosity had sub-
sided and there was even, claims Sam Orbaum, a sense of pride at Richler's
accomplishments.[81] Not everyone was impressed, however. "Without
whiskey he wouldn't come ... he sat and drank," said Bernard Richler, the
uncle who had been closest to Mordecai when Mordecai was young.[82]

In his cousin Sarah Snowbell's opinion, Richler didn't look sick, but neither was he very comfortable with all the Orthodox Jews at the shiva. Rumour had it that he asked one of the uncles to make a mishebairach, a prayer
for the sick, for him,[83] but that seems unlikely, and Florence says that, if an
uncle did pray, it would have been at the request of the uncle, not Mordecai. Florence worried that her husband, in his weakened state, was confronting so many people who had been hostile to him throughout the years.
But the passage of time had eased some of the conflicts, and it was no longer
necessarily a shameful thing to have been related to him.[84]

As reconciliations were occurring, Richler's cancer metastasized, spread-
ing to his lymph nodes, where it was inoperable.[85] By the time that Jacob
came to take his father and mother to Lake Memphremagog in June, he
knew that his father's diminished weight didn't bode well. Worse, Jacob saw
that, for the first time ever, his father's office was neat and tidy – no open

books, no newspaper articles, no manuscript pages strewn about. The desire to work had fled.

Too weak to stay at Lake Memphremagog with only Florence to look after him, Richler returned to Montreal when Jacob went home to Toronto. As they parted, Richler squeezed his son's hand – too hard, Jacob thought, fearing the worst.[86] Richler still hoped to "beat the rap," as he put it,[87] and a little more than a week before his death he managed to visit his usual haunt, Ziggy's Pub,[88] but soon he was in the hospital again. A blood problem arose, possibly caused by the chemotherapy, and on 3 July 2001, as doctors were debating whether surgery might help, Richler died.[89]

≋

Many years earlier, Richler had had an idea of what he might like to see in his obituary: "Yesterday the literary world mourned the passing of devastatingly handsome, incomparably witty Mordecai Richler, taken from us in his prime, at the age of 969."[90] If that obituary never came to pass, the family's press release, as sad as the news was, didn't neglect to speak in Richler's voice. Donations, it said, could be given in Richler's name to the Canadian Cancer Society, Centraide, Doctors Without Borders, "or, say, the Montreal Canadiens, a true lost cause."[91] Barney Panofsky's will had directed that no rabbi speak at his funeral.[92] Richler had similarly directed that, in place of a rabbi, Max Richler, the uncle who had stood by him throughout his life, should conduct the service. Religious ceremony was kept to a minimum. Although he had slowly grown friendlier with his brother Avrum, Richler had nevertheless also directed that Max, not Avrum, say the kaddish.[93] From *Joshua Then and Now*, Noah read Richler's comic take on the Bible, and Max chanted, "May his repose be in paradise."[94] Afterwards, Richler was buried high on Mount Royal, overlooking not paradise but St. Urbain Street.[95]

Notes

INTRODUCTION

1 Hynam, "The Scene," Richler Fonds Acc. #582/153.19.
2 *St. Urbain's Horseman*, 122.
3 Victor Ramraj, *Mordecai Richler*, 1.
4 *St. Urbain's Horseman*, 209.
5 Welbourn, "I Get Up at 10 A.M., Richler Fonds Msc 36.54.14.
6 Avrum Richler interview.
7 *Shovelling Trouble*, 18.
8 Weiner to Richler, 15 August 1971, Richler Fonds Msc 36.6.31.
9 Draft of unidentified manuscript, Richler Fonds Acc. #582/110.1.
10 Peter Bailey, 126.

CHAPTER 1

1 *Geyt, yidelech, in der vayter velt/ In kanada, vet ir ferdinen gelt.* (Go, little Jews, into the wider world / In Canada, you'll earn your gold). Quoted in Richler, *Barney's Version*, 381. Author's translation.
2 Halberstam-Rubin, 21.
3 Paul Johnson, 364–5, 432.
4 Richler, "Goy," 1997, 2.
5 Paul Johnson, 370.
6 Dansereau and Beaudet interview, 95.
7 *Street*, 20.
8 "Mordecai Richler: St. Urbain's Meistersinger" [unidentified ms] Richler Fonds Acc. #582/135.18, 3–4. Shmarya (Stuart), Richler website, 1. McNay interview (Richler Fonds Msc 36.55.1). *Back to Ibiza*, Richler Fonds Acc. #582/65.4, 17.
9 Avrum Richler interview. Max Richler, email, 10 September 2002. R. v. Richler, [1939] S.C.R.101, Supreme Court of Canada, 1939: 27 February 1939: 21 March on Appeal from the Court of King's Bench, Appeal Side, Province of Quebec.
10 Bernard Richler interview. Avrum Richler interview. *Errand*, 93.
11 *Home Sweet*, 62, 64.
12 Suzanne Rosenberg, 20. *Errand*, 22. N. Baumoil, 14.
13 Robinson, "Forgery," 4; Robinson, "Sabbath," 104.

14 Hayim Leib Fox, quoted in Aaron Brody, 4.
15 Robinson, "Sabbath," 105; *Errand*, 66; Richler in Nathan Cohen, "A Conversation…" *Tamarack Review*, 8. The Zohar, a redaction by the thirteenth-century Spanish writer, Moses de Leon, purports to be a series of second-century discourses. Zohar, ix–x. Rosenberg's translation focused on the exegetical portion of Zohar that connected to the Bible, because he thought that "the esoteric Kabbalah" shouldn't be revealed to "the simple folk." Roskies, 24–5.
16 Robinson, "Kabbalist," 49.
17 *Errand*, 67.
18 Richler, "On Being Jewish," 4, Richler Fonds Acc. #582/110.20.
19 Aaron Brody, 3. Robinson, "Tarler *rebbe*," 58–60; "Forgery," 11, 8; "Kabbalist," 50–2, 55. N. Baumoil, 2. Rosenberg Souvenir.
20 *Solomon Gursky Was Here*, 432.
21 Shnayer Leiman, 31. Robinson, "Sabbath," 106. Ira Robinson, presently working on a biography of Rabbi Rosenberg, has in a series of articles carefully detailed his career, including his fiction.
22 Bernard Richler interview.
23 Avrum Richler interview.
24 Max Richler interview.
25 Richler, Notes for *The Rotten People*, 3, Richler Fonds Acc. #582/102.2. Richler, *The Rotten People*, August 1951, Tourrettes-sur-loup, 116–17, Richler Fonds Acc. #582/102.7–8.
26 *Errand*, 93.
27 Bernard Richler interview.
28 Robinson, "Kabbalist," 55.
29 Bernard Richler interview.
30 Posner incorrectly gives Moe's age as nineteen and uncritically accepts Lily's word that she was seventeen (Posner, *Last*, 2, 19). In fact, however, Moe was born on 25 December 1902, Lily in 1905. Later, when she wanted a divorce, she claimed that she had been only seventeen and that she had married against her father's will. She continued to report this revised version of her marriage late in life. See *The Errand Runner*, 95.
31 *Errand*, 63.
32 *Canada Made Me*, 31–3. Levine's trip through Canada took place in 1956.
33 *Errand*, 13, 65.
34 *Errand*, 9, 49, 63, 93. Paris (Richler Fonds Acc. #582/160.7). Albert, "Richler." Lionel Albert interview.
35 Marchand, "Oy," Richler Fonds Acc. #582/134.8, 64. *Errand*, 88, 97, 51, 69, 79.
36 *Errand*, 95.
37 Avrum Richler interview.
38 Max Richler, email, 3 Sept 2002.
39 *Home Sweet*, 66. *Back to Ibiza*, Richler Fonds Acc. #582/65.4, 9.
40 Richler Fonds Acc. #582/110.20, "On Being Jewish," 4. Avrum Richler interview.
41 *Home Sweet*, 58.
42 *Back to Ibiza*, Richler Fonds Acc. #582/65.4, 9. The line appears, slightly altered, in *Joshua Then and Now*, 226.
43 Avrum Richler interview.
44 Rindick interview, Richler Fonds Acc. #582/39.3.
45 Lionel Albert, email, 24 September 2002.

46 *Errand*, 93.
47 Avrum Richler interview.
48 Diana Athill to Richler, 1 April 1960, Richler Fonds Msc 36.1.25.17.
49 Lionel Albert interview.
50 *Home Sweet*, 59.
51 *Errand*, 95–7.
52 Avrum suspects that she made the entire story up. Avrum Richler interview.
53 *Smaller*, 91. Leah Adler is inordinately proud of her dead father Rabbi
   Goldenberg, and Wolf Adler is submissive to his father who owns a scrapyard. *Smaller*, 20, 30–3.
54 Avrum Richler interview. *Errand*, 98.
55 *Errand*, 95.
56 "Mordecai Richler: St. Urbain's Meistersinger" [unidentified ms], Richler
   Fonds Acc. #582/135.18, 4, 8.
57 *Errand*, 98–9.
58 Max Richler interview.
59 Bernard Richler interview. *Errand*, 99. Max Richler interview.
60 *Errand*, 97, 99–100, 107–8.
61 *Smaller*, 60, 62–3, 111.
62 Emma Richler, *Sister Crazy*, 196.
63 Peritz 2001, A4. *Errand*, 99.
64 *Errand*, 95, 98–9, 108.
65 *Errand*, 111, 99.
66 Avrum Richler interview. "Mordecai Richler: St. Urbain's Meistersinger"
   [unidentified ms], Richler Fonds Acc. #582/135.18, 9.

CHAPTER 2

 1 Lily Rosenberg to Ruth Albert, 27 June [1978 or 1979], private collection of
   Lionel Albert. It's not clear whether Ruth lent her the money or not, but the
   tone of Lily's letter implies that Ruth didn't.
 2 *Home Sweet*, 67.
 3 *Errand*, 101, 110.
 4 *Errand*, 102.
 5 *Joshua Then and Now*, 288.
 6 *Errand*, 43.
 7 Lionel Albert interview. Avrum Richler interview.
 8 Florence Richler interview.
 9 "Mordecai Richler: St. Urbain's Meistersinger" [unidentified ms], Richler
   Fonds Acc. #582/135.18, 7.
10 Avrum Richler interview.
11 *Errand*, 103, 107, 97. Florence Richler interview. Richler Fonds Acc.
   #582/110.19, Richler, "On Turning 50," 3.
12 Lionel Albert, email, 24 September 2002.
13 Avrum Richler interview.
14 *Errand*, 12.
15 Richler, *Leaving School*, 140.
16 Avrum Richler, email, 3 July 2002 .
17 Avrum Richler interview. Mordecai said, "This is the first generation in our
   family with no rabbis. I should have been a rabbi." Nathan Cohen, "A
   Conversation ..." *Tamarack Review*, 14, Richler Fonds Acc. #582/129.8.
18 Marchand, "Oy," Richler Fonds Acc. #582/134.8, 147.

19 *Errand*, 103.
20 Lionel Albert, email, 19 September 2002. Avrum Richler, email, 21 October 2002.
21 *Errand*, 104.
22 "As soon as the soul becomes a partner with the body, then it becomes filled with deceit," Rosenberg had written. Rosenberg, *Commentary on the Book of Jonah*, 19.
23 *Canadian Jewish Review*, 3 April 1936, 7.
24 Lily Rosenberg to Ruth Albert, 27 June [1978 or 1979], private collection of Lionel Albert.
25 Avrum Richler interview. Lionel Albert interview.
26 *Errand*, 114–15. Avrum Richler, email, 26 August 2002. Avrum Richler interview.
27 Shatz.
28 *Errand*, 115, 117, 118. Lionel Albert, email, 31 October 2002.
29 "Mordecai Richler: St. Urbain's Meistersinger" [unidentified ms], Richler Fonds Acc. #582/135.18, 9.
30 Lily Rosenberg to Ruth Albert, 27 June [1978 or 1979], private collection of Lionel Albert.
31 Avrum Richler interview. *Errand*, 117. Richler, introduction to "The Summer My Grandmother Was Supposed to Die," unpublished, intended for a Ryerson anthology, 1970, Richler Fonds Msc 36.11.55.14b. "The Summer My Grandmother Was Supposed to Die," written about 1960 (Ted Solotaroff, Associate Editor of *Commentary*, to Richler, 18 November 1960, Richler Fonds Msc 36.3.46), appears as chapter 2 of *The Street*, 38–52. Sarah Gitel (Greenberg) Rosenberg died at the age of seventy-seven on 15 July 1942 at the Richler home. Lionel Albert, email, 31 October 2002.
32 *Errand*, 121.
33 Lionel Albert interview. Lily Rosenberg to Ruth Albert, 27 June [1978 or 1979], private collection of Lionel Albert.
34 Pine interview.
35 Lionel Albert interview.
36 Pine interview.
37 *Errand*, 121, 116, 119–20. Avrum Richler interview.
38 Richler, notes for *The Rotten People* (small blue notepaper), 1, Richler Fonds Acc. #582/102.2. Repeated in Richler, *The Rotten People*, August 1951, Tourrettes-sur-loup, 115–16, Richler Fonds Acc. #582/102.7–8.
39 *Errand*, 116.
40 Nathan Cohen, "A Conversation…" *Tamarack Review*, 8, Richler Fonds Acc. #582/129.8. Lionel Albert letter to *The Montreal Gazette* (unpublished), 1 May 2000. *This Year in Jerusalem*, 99–100.
41 Avrum Richler interview. *Acrobats*, 105.
42 *Canadian Jewish Review*, 11 December 1936, 44–5.
43 Avrum Richler, email, 25 June 2002.
44 *Canadian Jewish Review*, 20 December 1935.
45 Avrum Richler, email, 25 June 2002.
46 *Home Sweet*, 60. Noah Richler, "Family," 3.
47 *Smaller*, 60, 94.
48 *Joshua*, 65.
49 *Hunting*, 19.
50 *Canadian Jewish Review*, 23 Septmeber 1938.
51 *Canadian Jewish Review*, 20 December 1935, 6–7, 34–5.

CHAPTER 3

1 "Mordecai Richler: St. Urbain's Meistersinger" [unidentified ms], Richler Fonds Acc. #582/135.18, 10. The Talmud Torah has been torn down and is now the playground of École Primaire Nazareth. "On Site" [unidentified ms], Richler Fonds Acc. #582/135.18, 17. *Street*, 10. *Home Sweet*, 109. Richler, "School," 2–3.
2 Nurenberger interview, Richler Fonds Msc 36.54.6.
3 Avrum Richler interview.
4 *Snooker*, 5. Avrum remembers her doing the same to him. Avrum Richler interview.
5 "Mordecai Richler: St. Urbain's Meistersinger" [unidentified ms], 9. "On Site," Richler Fonds Acc. #582/135.18, 24. *Street*, 60. *Smaller*, 14. Hanes, "Homecoming," 1. *Broadsides*, 25.
6 Avrum Richler interview.
7 Pine interview.
8 Richler, "French," 1964, 41 (Richler Fonds Acc. #582/163.5).
9 Schwartz interview.
10 Richler, Notes for *The Rotten People*, 1 [overleaf], Richler Fonds Acc. #582/102.2. Richler, *The Rotten People*, August 1951, Tourrettes-sur-loup, 115–16, Richler Fonds Acc. #582/102.7–8.
11 Avrum Richler, email, 11 February 2004.
12 Herman Silver and Avrum Richler, quoted in Posner, *Last*, 8, 12.
13 *Oh Canada! Oh Quebec!*, 80, 98.
14 Lionel Albert, email, 12 September 2004.
15 Lionel Albert interview. Avrum letter, 2 (Richler Fonds Acc. #582/36.34)
16 Richler, Notes for *The Rotten People*, 3, Richler Fonds Acc. #582/102.2. Richler, *The Rotten People*, August 1951, Tourrettes-sur-loup, 116, Richler Fonds Acc. #582/102.7–8.
17 Lionel Albert interview. Lionel Albert, email, 9 September 2002.
18 Richler, "Foreword," xxiv. *Broadsides*, 21. Jack Rabinovitch interview. Richler, "Foreword," xxiv. *Broadsides*, 21.
19 *Back to Ibiza*, Richler Fonds Acc. #582/65.4, 24.
20 Avrum Richler, email, 3 July 2002. Richler, "Foreword," xxiv.
21 Bernard Richler interview.
22 *Snooker*, 2, 177.
23 Noah Richler, "My," B2.
24 Jack Rabinovitch interview.
25 Noah Richler, "My," B2.
26 Kealey interview (Richler Fonds Acc. #582/152.1). Avrum Richler interview. *Hunting*, 47.
27 Abella, 17, 41–2, 142, 161–2.
28 Richler, "The French, the English, the Jews," 11, Richler Fonds Acc. #582/163.5. *Home Sweet*, 38. *Street*, 30–1, 63–4. William Henry Drummond, "The Log Jam," *The New Oxford Book of Canadian Verse in English*, ed. Margaret Atwood, Toronto: Oxford University Press, 1982.
29 Joe King, 190.
30 M. Brown, "Zionism," 5.
31 Richler, "Man," 2.
32 *Home Sweet*, 37. Richler ,"Canadian Conundrums," 3. Richler, "The French, the English, the Jews," 10, Richler Fonds Acc. #582/163.5.
33 Richler, "The French, the English, the Jews," 10, Richler Fonds Acc. #582/163.5.

34 Avrum Richler interview.
35 *Street*, 69.
36 Lionel Albert interview.
37 Lionel Albert interview. *Joshua Then and Now* 21. Lionel Albert, email, 14 October 2002.
38 Avrum Richler interview.
39 *Back to Ibiza*, Richler Fonds Acc. #582/65.4, 15.
40 Geoffrey James et al., "The Expatriate Who Has Never Left Home," *Time* (Canadian edition), 31 May 1971, Richler Fonds Msc 36.30.12.
41 *Back to Ibiza*, Richler Fonds Acc. #582/65.4, 15–16, 131. *Joshua*, 324. Avrum Richler interview. In *Home Sweet Home* Joe is called "Uncle Solly," Moe's "pompous younger brother" (62).
42 *Back to Ibiza*, Richler Fonds Acc. #582/65.4, 131, 179. The same thing apparently happened to Avrum.
43 Richler, "Foreword," xxiii.
44 "Mordecai Richler: St. Urbain's Meistersinger" [unidentified ms], Richler Fonds Acc. #582/135.18, 12.
45 Richler "In his own words." "Mordecai Richler: St. Urbain's Meistersinger" [unidentified ms], Richler Fonds Acc. #582/135.18, 11. Kealey interview, Richler Fonds Acc. #582/152.1.
46 Richler, "School," 3.
47 Avrum Richler, email, 3 July 2002.
48 Richler, "Writing *Jacob Two-Two*," *Canadian Literature* 78 (Autumn 1978), Richler Fonds Acc. #582/18.38.
49 Richler, "Innocents," 4. *Broadsides*, 20.
50 Evelyn Sacks, quoted in Posner, *Last*, 13–14.
51 Avrum Richler, quoted in Posner, *Last*, 14.
52 Migdal, "Frances Katz," 39, Richler Fonds Acc. #680/10.19.
53 Kurtz interview. Cadloff interview. Barbarash interview. Schecter interview.
54 Evelyn Sacks, quoted in Posner, *Last*, 13.
55 Nathan Cohen, "A Conversation ..." *Tamarack Review*, 8, Richler Fonds Acc. #582/129.8.
56 Richler, "School," 5, 7.
57 Duhm, 30, Richler Fonds Acc. #582/161.1. *Broadsides*, 21–4.
58 Richler Fonds Acc. #582/18.38. Richler, "Writing *Jacob Two-Two*," *Canadian Literature* 78 (Autumn 1978); *Broadsides*, 19.
59 Kealey interview, Richler Fonds Acc. #582/152.1.
60 Richler, "Q Is for Quest," 2, Richler Fonds Msc 36.40.15.
61 Richler Fonds Acc. #582/113.22, "Eye on Books/Canada."
62 Paul Johnson, 564.
63 Bernard Richler interview.
64 Avrum Richler interview.
65 *Errand*, 103. Bernard Richler interview.
66 Lionel Albert interview. "Mordecai Richler: St. Urbain's Meistersinger" [unidentified ms], Richler Fonds Acc. #582/135.18, 30; *Street*, 17.
67 Lionel Albert, email, 11 December 2003.
68 *Home Sweet*, 59.
69 *Broadsides*, 10.
70 Richler, "Not Keeping," 1.
71 *This Year in Jerusalem*, 10, 124.
72 *Snooker*, 81. Avrum Richler interview.

73 Richler, "On Being Jewish," 4, Richler Fonds Acc. #582/110.20. *Snooker*, 81. *Street*, 135.
74 Avrum Richler, email, 22 October 2002.
75 "On Site" [unidentified ms], Richler Fonds Acc. #582/135.18, 17.
76 Kealey interview, Richler Fonds Acc. #582/152.1.
77 *Joshua*, 68.
78 Avrum Richler interview. In *Son of a Smaller Hero*, Melech isn't impressed with their casuistic reasoning and berates them.
79 *Home Sweet*, 67.
80 Avrum Richler interview. Nathan Cohen, "A Conversation ..." *Tamarack Review*, 15, Richler Fonds Acc. #582/129.8. *Broadsides*, 11. Richler, "School," 4.
81 *Broadsides*, 17, 11.
82 *Errand*, 104.
83 Todd, 19.
84 *This Year in Jerusalem*, 16.
85 *Home Sweet*, 63. Richler calls David "Yamkel" in his non-fiction.
86 Congregation Kehal Yeshurun. "Mordecai Richler: St. Urbain's Meistersinger" [unidentified ms], Richler Fonds Acc. #582/135.18,11,26.
87 *Home Sweet*, 64.

CHAPTER 4

1 Todd, 17. *Snooker*, 3, 5–6, 82.
2 Jews who neglected the Sabbath, Rosenberg had written, were nothing more than gentiles. Robinson, "Sabbath," 106, 108.
3 Max Richler interview.
4 Bernard Richler interview.
5 *Home Sweet*, 63.
6 Max Richler, email, 10 September 2002.
7 *Smaller*, 18–19, 62.
8 *Home Sweet*, 63–4. Avrum Richler interview.
9 Nathan Cohen, "A Conversation..." *Tamarack Review*, 7, Richler Fonds Acc. #582/129.8.
10 Val Ross, "Excusing," C12.
11 "Mordecai Richler: St. Urbain's Meistersinger" [unidentified ms], Richler Fonds Acc. #582/135.18, 6. *Home Sweet*, 64. Richler, *The Rotten People*, August 1951, Tourrettes-sur-loup, 115, Richler Fonds Acc. #582/102.7–8–8.
12 *Home Sweet*, 65.
13 Sam Orbaum, email, 2.
14 "Mordecai Richler: St. Urbain's Meistersinger" [unidentified ms], Richler Fonds Acc. #582/135.18, 6, 11.
15 Avrum Richler, quoted in Posner, *Last*, 23.
16 Avrum Richler interview.
17 Lionel Albert, email, 31 October 2002.
18 *Street*, 68–9. *Home Sweet*, 60–1.
19 Abella, x.
20 Avrum Richler interview. Lily calls Frankel "Reuben" in her autobiography, *The Errand Runner*.
21 *Errand*, 122–3.
22 *Home Sweet*, 60.

23 Richler, Notes for *The Rotten People*, 5 overleaf, Richler Fonds Acc. #582/102.2.

24 "Mordecai Richler: St. Urbain's Meistersinger" [unidentified ms], Richler Fonds Acc. #582/135.18, 11.

25 Avrum Richler interview.

26 Richler, Notes for *The Rotten People*, unpaginated, Richler Fonds Acc. #582/102.2.

27 Wong interview, 2. Marchand, "Oy," 147, Richler Fonds Acc. #582/134.8.

28 Richler, *The Rotten People*, 206, Richler Fonds Acc. #582/102.7.

29 Florence Richler interview.

30 Richler, Notes for *The Rotten People*, 3 overleaf, Richler Fonds Acc. #582/102.2.

31 In 1978, when Richler was in the middle of *Joshua Then and Now* and the editor of an anthology asked Richler to explain the genesis of the story, he grew hostile: "A writer's method of work, his address, his disposition, drinking problems, love life, calorie-intake, should be of no concern to anybody but his family and friends. What is the proper concern for the reader is the actual story, no more ... I wrote this story some 20 years ago, on the other side of the moon and I can no longer remember how or why." Richler to Edward Peck, Commcept Publishing, Vancouver, 27 February 1978, Richler Fonds Acc. #582/14.13.

32 Avrum Richler interview.

33 *Home Sweet*, 62.

34 In the notes to *The Rotten People*, "Abe" takes his mother's side in the divorce. Richler, Notes for *The Rotten People*, unpaginated, Richler Fonds Acc. #582/102.2. Avrum denies this, saying that he didn't take anyone's side. Avrum Richler, email, 11 February 2004.

35 Avrum Richler interview.

36 *Back to Ibiza*, Richler Fonds Acc. #582/65.4, 18.

37 Richler, Notes for *The Rotten People*, 5 overleaf, Richler Fonds Acc. #582/102.2.

38 *Errand*, 123.

39 Richler, Notes for *The Rotten People*, unpaginated, Richler Fonds Acc. #582/102.2. Richler, *The Rotten People* 206, Richler Fonds Acc. #582/102.7.

40 Avrum Richler interview.

41 "Mordecai Richler: St. Urbain's Meistersinger" [unidentified ms], Richler Fonds Acc. #582/135.18, 11, 6. *Errand*, 95. Avrum Richler interview. *Home Sweet*, 61, 58, 56.

42 Wong interview, 2. Marchand, "Oy," 147, Richler Fonds Acc. #582/134.8. *Home Sweet*, 67.

43 Richler, Notes for *The Rotten People*, unpaginated, Richler Fonds Acc. #582/102.2.

44 Richler, Notes for *The Rotten People*, unpaginated, Richler Fonds Acc. #582/102.2.

45 Richler, *The Rotten People*, 181, Richler Fonds Acc. #582/102.7.

46 Avrum Richler interview. Avrum Richler, quoted in Posner, *Last* 21.

47 Bernard Richler interview. Avrum Richler interview.

48 Lionel Albert, email, 10 November 2002.

49 Max Richler interview.

50 "Mordecai Richler: St. Urbain's Meistersinger" [unidentified ms], Richler Fonds Acc. #582/135.18, 11. *This Year in Jerusalem*, 16.

51 Nathan Cohen, "A Conversation ..." *Tamarack Review*, 15, Richler Fonds Acc. #582/129.8. Avrum Richler interview.

52 *Snooker*, 2.

53 *Today Magazine*. "Beginnings," Richler Fonds Acc. #582/160.8.

54 Joe King, 105.

55 Richler, "School Days," 7.

56 Baron Byng Room 41 Class Reunion notebook, 6 October 1996, Richler Fonds Acc. #680/45.1.

57 Beaudin, 3.

58 Marci McDonald, Richler Fonds Acc. #582/154.2.

59 Jack Rabinovitch interview.

60 Richler, "School Days," 1–2. Jack Rabinovitch interview.

61 Barbarash interview. Cadloff interview.

62 Jack Rabinovitch interview.

63 Blankfort interview.

64 Kurtz interview.

65 Jack Rabinovitch interview.

66 Boone, 2.

67 Jack Rabinovitch interview.

68 Richler, *Leaving School*, 138. Richler, "School Days," 2.

69 "Artist with a Message," *New/Nouvelle Generation* (Baron Byng), 1:3 (May 1965), Richler Fonds Msc 36.54.14. Barbarash interview. Cadloff interview. Blankfort interview.

70 Schecter interview.

71 Lionel Albert interview. Lionel Albert, email, 24 September 2002, 10 June 2004.

72 Richler Fonds Msc 36.30.12 (*Time*, 9a). "The Author," *Smaller*, 206.

73 Nathan Cohen, "A Conversation..." *Tamarack Review*, 8, Richler Fonds Acc. #582/129.8.

74 Richler, "Bad boys," 1. *Home Sweet*, 113.

75 Avrum Richler interview. *Home Sweet*, 67.

76 Richler, Notes for *The Rotten People*, unpaginated, Richler Fonds Acc. #582/102.2. Avrum Richler, email, 11 February 2004.

77 Blankfort interview.

78 *Back to Ibiza*, Richler Fonds Acc. #582/65.4, 148. Avrum Richler interview.

79 Evelyn Sacks, quoted in Posner, *Last*, 13.

80 In one of the notes for *The Rotten People*, Richler listed characters, with the names of real people in brackets beside their fictional counterparts. He then crossed out the real names, though beside Helen, one can still make out "(Evelyn)." Richler, Notes for *The Rotten People*, unpaginated, Richler Fonds Acc. #582/102.2.

81 Richler, Notes for *The Rotten People*, unpaginated, Richler Fonds Acc. #582/102.2.

82 Richler, Notes for *The Rotten People*, unpaginated, Richler Fonds Acc. #582/102.2. In *The Rotten People* itself, the affair ends somewhat differently, with the postwar return of her husband. Richler, *The Rotten People*, 234, Richler Fonds Acc. #582/102.8

83 Richler, *The Rotten People*, 234, Richler Fonds Acc. #582/102.8. Avrum says, "I think that she had a thing for my brother, even more so when he got older and was at Sir George Williams." Avrum Richler, quoted in Posner, *Last*, 14.

84 Evelyn to Richler, 27 November 1953, Richler Fonds Acc. #680/1.5.

85 Richler, Manuscript of *The Rotten People*, 125, 127–8, 234, August 1951, Tourrettes-sur-loup, Richler Fonds Acc. #582/102.7–8.

86 Pearl Babins (Née Zipporah Stillman), quoted in Posner, *Last*, 26.

87 Joanna Bale, "Judge frees music teacher accused of sex with boys," *The Times*, 25 January 1996, 3, Richler Fonds Acc. #680/47.3.

88 Cameron interview, 124.

89 Richler, Notes for *The Rotten People*, unpaginated, Richler Fonds Acc. #582/102.2.

90 Richler, Manuscript of *The Rotten People*, 320, 232–3, August, 1951, Tourrettes-sur-loup, Richler Fonds Acc. #582/102.8.

91 *Broadsides*, 19. Jack Rabinovitch interview.

92 Jon Anderson interview. Richler Fonds Acc. #582/5.51. *Broadsides*, 3.

93 *Hunting*, 24.

94 Richler, Manuscript of *The Rotten People*, 127–8, August 1951, Tourrettes-sur-loup, Richler Fonds Acc. #582/102.7–8.

95 *This Year in Jerusalem*, 3.

96 *Back to Ibiza*, Richler Fonds Acc. #582/65.4, 103.

97 Paul Johnson, 524.

98 Richler, *The Rotten People*, 321, Richler Fonds Acc. #582/102.8.

99 "Mordecai Richler: St. Urbain's Meistersinger" [unidentified ms], Richler Fonds Acc. #582/135.18, 11.

100 *This Year in Jerusalem*, 17, 95. *Street*, 131. Posner identifies "Jerry Greenfeld" as Murray Greenberg. Posner, *Last*, 26, 28.

101 Snowbell interview.

102 *Street*, 135.

103 *This Year in Jerusalem*, 21, 31.

104 *Hunting*, 133.

105 Richler Fonds Acc. #582/115.20 "Looking for Work," 1. Richler Fonds Msc 36.30.12 (*Time* 9a).

106 *Street*, 140. It's possible that Richler was again using that specialized collective "we" that didn't include him personally. On the other hand, according to Jack Rabinovitch, the overwhelming sense of Jewish nationalism in the 1940s made those who resisted that nationalism seem like collaborators with the enemy. Jack Rabinovitch interview.

107 Walter Tannenbaum, quoted in Posner, *Last* 28.

108 Nathan Cohen, "A Conversation…" *Tamarack Review*, 7, Richler Fonds Acc. #582/129.8.

109 *Street*, 134.

110 M. Brown, "Zionism," 7.

111 Gefen, 1990, Richler Fonds Acc. #582/159.1, 32. *Hunting*, 133.

112 Avrum Richler interview.

113 Kurtz interview. Cadloff interview.

114 Paul Johnson, 398.

115 *The Georgian* (4 November 1948) "A People Come Home! Israel Today," 5. Richler Fonds Acc. #582/163.9.

116 *This Year in Jerusalem*, 182. In *Home Sweet Home* (65) the statement is attributed to "Uncle Solly," another mask for Joe. The prohibition appears in *Son of a Smaller Hero*, but there it is spoken directly by the grandfather to the grandson (157).

117 Todd, 16.

118 *Home Sweet*, 66.

119 Bernard Richler interview. Max Richler interview. Avrum Richler, email, 17 May 2003.

120 "Mordecai Richler: St. Urbain's Meistersinger" [unidentified ms], Richler Fonds Acc. #582/135.18, 11. Todd, 16.

121 Max Richler interview.

122 Sam Orbaum, "Make," 19.

123 *Home Sweet*, 111. Stanley Cadloff and Phil Kurtz don't remember MacDonald coming to the school but do remember Richler refusing to stand for the anthem. Kurtz interview. Cadloff interview.

124 Paul Johnson, 525. Joe King, 247.

125 Arnstein, 341.

126 *Street*, 140. *This Year in Jerusalem*, 33, 276.

127 "Mordecai Richler: St. Urbain's Meistersinger" [unidentified ms], Richler Fonds Acc. #582/135.18, 12.

128 *Home Sweet*, 112.

129 Avrum Richler interview.

130 Richler, *The Rotten People*, 42–3, 35, Richler Fonds Acc. #582/102.7.

131 Avrum Richler interview. *Today Magazine*, "Beginnings," Richler Fonds Acc. #582/160.8.

132 Bernard Richler interview. Avrum Richler interview. Dave Gursky, quoted in Posner, *Last*, 47.

133 *Smaller*, 171.

134 Max Richler interview. Some Jews, with less precise notions of *kashrut*, considered the place kosher. See Jack Basiuk, quoted in Posner, *Last*, 47.

135 Colleen E. Gregory to Richler, 24 October 2002.

136 *Errand*, 124–6. Avrum Richler interview. Lionel Albert, email, 24 October 2002.

137 Avrum Richler interview. *Errand*, 141.

138 "Mordecai Richler: St. Urbain's Meistersinger" [unidentified ms], Richler Fonds Acc. #582/135.18, 12.

CHAPTER 5

1 Donnie Goldberg, quoted in Posner, *Last*, 32.

2 Joe King, 292. Avrum Richler interview. Jack Rabinovitch interview.

3 Richler, "School Days," 5, 7. Rabinovitch, "Mordecai," 25. *Home Sweet*, 107.

4 Richler Fonds Msc 36.30.12 (*Time*, 9a).

5 *Broadsides*, 24.

6 Knelman, "Icon," 3.

7 Richler, *The Rotten People*, 61, Richler Fonds Acc. #582/102.7.

8 Richler, *Leaving School*, 145. Steve Kondaks interview.

9 Jack Lieber, quoted in Posner, *Last*, 42.

10 *This Year in Jerusalem*, 41–3.

11 Donny Goldberg, quoted in Posner, *Last*, 4.

12 Bernard Dubé, "TV and Radio," *The Montreal Gazette*, 18 May 1967, Richler Fonds Msc 36.54.14.

13 Richler, "Afterword," *The Moslem Wife*, 248.

14 "Mordecai Richler: St. Urbain's Meistersinger" [unidentified ms], Richler Fonds Acc. #582/135.18, 13. Nathan Cohen, "A Conversation..." *Tamarack Review*, 13, Richler Fonds Acc. #582/129.8.

15 Richler to Ted Allan, 24 October 1952, National Archives 20.15.
16 Richler to Weintraub 21 March 1952, Weintraub, *Started*, 87.
17 *Home Sweet*, 58.
18 Marchand, "Oy," 147, Richler Fonds Acc. #582/134.8.
19 Max Richler interview.
20 The story forms chapter 9 of *The Street*, 102–30. It first appeared, combined with "Bambinger," in 1961 as a CBC radio play, "The Spare Room," and then in the *Kenyon Review* 24, Winter 1962, 80–105, Richler Fonds Msc 36.31.8.
21 *The Street*, 105.
22 Richler to Weintraub 30 August 1951, Weintraub, *Started*, 71. *Street*, 117.
23 Max Richler interview.
24 Richler Fonds Acc. #582/19.45d.
25 Kealey interview (Richler Fonds Acc. #582/152.1).
26 "Artist with a Message," *New/Nouvelle Generation*, (Baron Byng), 1:3 (May 1965), Richler Fonds Msc 36.54.14. Duhm-Heitzman, 28, Richler Fonds Acc. #582/161.1.
27 Avrum Richler interview. Lionel Albert interview.
28 Lionel Albert, email, 21 September 2002.
29 Bernard Richler interview.
30 Richler, *Leaving School*, 146.
31 Richler, *Leaving School*, 148–9.
32 *Oh Canada! Oh Quebec!*, 100.
33 Richler, *Leaving School*, 148; *five cent Review*, December 1968, 16, Richler Fonds Msc 36.54.3
34 Richler, "Evelyn" (Richler Fonds Acc. #582/163.4).
35 Mike Gold, "Towards a Proletarian Art," 62–3.
36 Richler Fonds Acc. #582/110.1.
37 Mike Gold, "Intro," 8–9.
38 *The Georgian*, 4 November 1948, "A People Come Home! Israel Today," 5, Richler Fonds Acc. #582/163.9. Richler also worked for *Focus: A Magazine for Jewish Youth*.
39 *Home Sweet*, 112. Richler, "Looking for Work," 1, Richler Fonds Acc. #582/115.20.
40 Richler, "Looking for Work," 1, Richler Fonds Acc. #582/115.20.
41 *Montreal Herald*, 17, 19 February; 1, 14 March 1949, Richler Fonds Acc. #582/163.10.
42 *Montreal Herald*, 5, 17, 19, 25 February; 1, 2, 14, 16, 16, 17 March 1949, Richler Fonds Acc. #582/163.10.
43 Jerry Brown, quoted in Posner, *Last*, 38.
44 Richler, *Leaving School*, 147.
45 *Hillel McGillah*, 18 November 1948 (Heshvan 5709), Richler Fonds Acc. #582/103.3.
46 *The Georgian*, 28 October 1948, Richler Fonds Acc. #582/163.9.
47 McCormick interview, 22 August 1971, Richler Fonds Acc. #582/152.16.
48 Trevor Phillips, quoted in Posner, *Last*, 44.
49 "Mordecai Richler: St. Urbain's Meistersinger" [unidentified ms], Richler Fonds Acc. #582/135.18, 13. Nathan Cohen, "A Conversation…" *Tamarack Review*, 8, Richler Fonds Acc. #582/129.8.
50 Richler, *Leaving School*, 137.
51 Richler Fonds Msc 36.55.2.
52 Avrum Richler interview.
53 Nathan Cohen, "A Conversation…" *Tamarack Review*, 8, Richler Fonds Acc.

#582/129.8. St. Urbain's Meistersinger" [unidentified ms], Richler Fonds Acc. #582/135.18, 13.

54 Cameron interview ms (10 June 1971), Richler Fonds Msc 36.54.1.

55 Richler, "Looking for Work," 1. Richler Fonds Acc. #582/115.20. Nathan Cohen, "A Conversation…" *Tamarack Review*, 8, Richler Fonds Acc. #582/129.8. McCormick interview, 22 August 1971, Richler Fonds Acc. #582/152.16.

56 Moe married Sara Werb of Winnipeg on 10 January. Avrum Richler interview. She seems more commonly to have been called Sara Hendler.

57 Avrum Richler interview.

58 Richler, "Looking for Work," 2, Richler Fonds Acc. #582/115.20.

59 Mordecai Richler: St. Urbain's Meistersinger" [unidentified ms], Richler Fonds Acc. #582/135.18, 13.

60 Richler, "John D., A Guy with a Rep," Richler Fonds Acc. #582/103.3.

61 Richler Fonds Acc. #582/123.16. This item seems to have been a speech Richler gave at a Callaghan celebration. *Snooker*, 169.

62 Richler, "Afterword," *The Moslem Wife*, 248. Knelman, "Icon," 3.

63 *Smaller*, 181, 95, 96, 191.

64 Lionel Albert interview.

65 *Back to Ibiza*, Richler Fonds Acc. #582/65.4, 42.

66 Max Richler interview.

67 *Errand*, 123.

68 Avrum Richler interview.

69 *Back to Ibiza*, Richler Fonds Acc. #582/65.4, 42.

70 *Shovelling Trouble*, 19.

71 *Home Sweet*, 62. Richler, "On Being Jewish," 4, Richler Fonds Acc. #582/110.20.

72 [Richler] "Biographical Notes," Richler Fonds Msc 36.55.2. Richler, "Q is for Quest," 1, Richler Fonds Msc 36.40.15. Nathan Cohen, "A Conversation…" *Tamarack Review*, 8, Richler Fonds Acc. #582/129.8. Max Richler interview. Avrum Richler interview. Bernard Richler interview.

73 Jack Basiuk, quoted in Posner, *Last* 47.

74 Press Kit for *The Apprenticeship of Duddy Kravitz*, Richler Fonds Msc 36.32.5.

75 Richler, "Home," 5, Richler Fonds Msc 36.32.5.

76 Gordon O. Rothney, professor of History, Sir George Williams University, letter of recommendation, 23 August 1950, Richler Fonds Msc 36.12.23.

77 Registrar, Sir George Williams University, 18 August 1950, Richler Fonds Msc 36.12.23.

78 Johnathan Yardley, "Richler: Humane Vision, Healthy District," *Miami Herald*, 22 September 1974, *Home Sweet*, 4–5.

CHAPTER 6

1 *Back to Ibiza*, Richler Fonds Acc. #582/65.4, 42.

2 Tina Srebotnjak interview, *Midday*, CBC-TV, 12 September 1994.

3 In *Fifth Business*, *The Rebel Angels*, *What's Bred in the Bone*, and *The Lyre of Orpheus* respectively.

4 Weintraub interview (2002). Richler, *Leaving School*, 149. "Terence McEwen Dies at 69," *New York Times*, 23 September 1998, B12.

5 Richler, "Innocents," 2, 6.

6 *Back to Ibiza*, Richler Fonds Acc. #582/65.4, 43.

7 Richler, "London Province," 42.

8 Richler to George Plimpton, Richler Fonds Acc. #680/31.58.

9 Richler, "The Lamplight of Paris," TV play, n.d., 1–17, Richler Fonds Msc 36.39.1.

10 Richmond interview, 4 February 1970, Richler Fonds Msc 36.55.1. *Shovelling*, 29.

11 James Baldwin, *Notes of a Native Son*, 127.

12 Mavis Gallant, quoted in Posner, *Last*, 60.

13 Lionel Albert, email, 16 September 2002.

14 *The Acrobats*, 29.

15 Richler to George Plimpton, Richler Fonds Acc. #680/31.58.

16 Richler, "Cures for Homesickness." Nathan Cohen, "A Conversation..." *Tamarack Review*, 9, Richler Fonds Acc. #582/129.8. *Hunting*, 24.

17 Nathan Cohen ,"A Conversation..." *Tamarack Review*, 9, Richler Fonds Acc. #582/129.8.

18 Richler to George Plimpton, Richler Fonds Acc. #680/31.58.

19 Richler, "Miller's," 8 October 1965, Richler Fonds Acc. #582/163.7.

20 Weintraub interview (2002).

21 Richler, "Q Is for Quest," 30 May 1961, 3, Richler Fonds Msc 36.40.15. *Back to Ibiza*, Richler Fonds Acc. #582/65.4, 14. "Eating," Richler Fonds Acc. #582/103.2, 3. *Shovelling*, 25.

22 *Back to Ibiza*, Richler Fonds Acc. #582/65.4, 43.

23 Richler, "Miller's," 8 October 1965, Richler Fonds Acc. #582/163.7).

24 Dansereau and Beaudet interview, 89.

25 Weintraub interview (2001). Weintraub, *Started*, 12. Richler Fonds Msc 36.30.12 (*Time*, 9b).

26 Knelman, "Icon," 3.

27 Weintraub, "Callow," 30.

28 Weintraub interview (2001).

29 Richler Fonds Acc. #582/107.1 "Minders," 10. *Snooker*, 10.

30 *Shovelling*, 35.

31 [Richler], "Biographical Notes," Richler Fonds Msc 36.55.2. Kealey interview, Richler Fonds Acc. #582/152.1. *Shovelling*, 35.

32 Richler, "Shades of Darkness," 30, 32. S. Martin, "Insult," Richler Fonds Acc. #582/160.7, 4.

33 Richler, *The Rotten People*, 190, Richler Fonds Acc. #582/102.7.

34 *Back to Ibiza*, Richler Fonds Acc. #582/65.4, 43.

35 *Images of Spain*, 21. Richler, *The Rotten People*, Richler Fonds Acc. #582/102.6.

36 *Back to Ibiza*, Richler Fonds Acc. #582/65.4, 48–9. Noah Richler interview. Rosita was apparently the madam's actual name. Kotcheff, "Afterword," 216.

37 *Back to Ibiza*, Richler Fonds Acc. #582/65.4, 113.

38 Weintraub interview (2002). *Images of Spain*, 20. Weintraub, *Started*, 58. *Back to Ibiza*, Richler Fonds Acc. #582/65.4, 51.

39 Nathan Cohen, "A Conversation..." *Tamarack Review*, 10, Richler Fonds Acc. #582/129.8. Brian Moore to Bill Weintraub, 8 January 1957, Weintraub, *Started*, 187.

40 Richler, *The Rotten People*, Richler Fonds Acc. #582/102.6.

41 *Images of Spain*, 31.

42 Richler to Weintraub, 9 June 1951, Weintraub, *Started*, 57. *Back to Ibiza*, Richler Fonds Acc. #582/65.4, 45, 52.

43 *Hunting*, 46. *Images of Spain*, 26, 22.

44 Paul Johnson, 311–12, 342.
45 Draft of *The Acrobats*, Richler Fonds Msc 36.15.4. Nathan Cohen, "A Conversation..." *Tamarack Review*, 10, Richler Fonds Acc. #582/129.8.
46 Richler "Intro," *Street*, xii. *Back to Ibiza*, Richler Fonds Acc. #582/65.4, 9.
47 *Home Sweet*, 57.
48 Kotcheff, "Afterword," 214.
49 Haberman.
50 Weintraub, *Started*, 46.
51 *Back to Ibiza*, Richler Fonds Acc. #582/65.4, 114.
52 MacGregor, 49, Richler Fonds Acc. #582/157.4. Richler to Bill Weintraub, 1 April 1951, Weintraub, *Started*, 46–7. *Back to Ibiza*, Richler Fonds Acc. #582/65.4, 74, 114. Weintraub, "Callow," 30.
53 Richler to Bill Weintraub, 1 April 1951; Bill Weintraub to Brian Moore, 15 April 1951, Weintraub, *Started*, 47, 51.
54 *Back to Ibiza*, Richler Fonds Acc. #582/65.4, 149–55. *Joshua*, 282–3.
55 Richler, *The Rotten People*, 76, Richler Fonds Acc. #582/102.7.
56 Weintraub interview (2002).
57 *Back to Ibiza*, Richler Fonds Acc. #582/65.4, 137–48, 54. Richler to Bill Weintraub, 9 June 1951, Weintraub, *Started*, 57.
58 *Back to Ibiza*, Richler Fonds Acc. #582/65.4, 167d, 78, 10, 50, 108. *St. Urbain's Horseman*, 87.
59 In *Back to Ibiza*, Mariano informs Richler, "his name wasn't Mueller." *Back to Ibiza*, Richler Fonds Acc. #582/65.4, 167d, 41, 114, 150–5.
60 *Back to Ibiza*, Richler Fonds Acc. #582/65.4, 76.
61 Weintraub interview 2001, 2002.
62 Richler, Notes for *The Rotten People*, Richler Fonds Acc. #582/102.2.
63 Richler to Ted Allan, 24 October 1952, National Archives, Ted Allan Fonds M630 D388 R2931-0-4-E Box 20.15. Richler repeated the claim on the CBC (Richler, "Q Is for Quest," 30 May 1961, 4, Richler Fonds Msc 36.40.15) and in a 1980 interview. Adele Freedman, *Globe and Mail* (17 May 1980), Richler Fonds Acc. #582/157.4.
64 According to Richler, Florence and Bob Gottlieb read *Back to Ibiza* and agreed that "the best parts in it were the lies, or the fiction, not the journalism." Goodman interview, Richler Fonds Acc. #582/157.2.
65 Michael Ryval, 56, Richler Fonds Acc. #582/161.1.
66 *Back to Ibiza*, Richler Fonds Acc. #582/65.4, 79. *Joshua*, 159.
67 Richler, "Goldberg, Gogarty and Ko," 21.
68 *Joshua*, 193–5, 160–1, 285, 308. *Back to Ibiza*, Richler Fonds Acc. #582/65.4, 109–12, 77, 46. Bill Weintraub says that he never met any prototypes of the Freibergs. Weintraub interview (2002).
69 *Back to Ibiza*, Richler Fonds Acc. #582/65.4, 158, 156.
70 Richler to Bill Weintraub, quoted in Posner, *Last*, 67.
71 Richler to Weintraub, 26 June 1951, Weintraub, *Started*, 59. Richler, "It Was Fun," 51.
72 Kotcheff, "Afterword," 216.
73 Avrum Richler interview. *Back to Ibiza*, Richler Fonds Acc. #582/65.4, 46, 177. Richler, "It Was Fun."
74 Richler to Weintraub, 9, 26 June 1951, Weintraub, *Started*, 56–7, 59.
75 Richler, "It Was Fun," 51.
76 *Back to Ibiza*, Richler Fonds Acc. #582/65.4, 174.
77 Richler, Draft of *St. Urbain's Horseman*, Richler Fonds Msc 36.25.1. Draft of *St. Urbain's Horseman*, Richler Fonds Msc 36.30.6. It is therefore possible

that the account in *Back to Ibiza* was already "novelized."

78 Richler, "It Was Fun," 51.

79 Richler, "My One and Only Countess," 7, 9, Richler Fonds Msc 36.48.1.

80 Florence didn't ask Richler what was factual and what was fictional about the incident, respecting his privacy and knowing that to grope clumsily in the place where his inspiration lay might demystify the experience. Florence Richler interview.

81 *Joshua*, 189, 144. *Back to Ibiza*, Richler Fonds Acc. #582/65.4, 74, 43. Budd Schulberg, not "Bubb."

82 See Andrew Wheatcroft, *Infidels*, 104, 123.

83 *Acrobats*, 50; *Joshua*, 161. *Back to Ibiza*, too includes this quotation. *Back to Ibiza*, Richler Fonds Acc. #582/65.4, 116.

84 Avrum Richler interview.

85 *Back to Ibiza*, Richler Fonds Acc. #582/65.4, 177. *Joshua*, 308.

86 Richler to Weintraub, 3 July 1951, Weintraub, Started, 60.

CHAPTER 7

1 *Joshua*, 256. *Back to Ibiza*, Richler Fonds Acc. #582/65.4, 138.

2 *Back to Ibiza*, Richler Fonds Acc. #582/65.4, 178. *Joshua*, 309.

3 Richler to Weintraub, 9 June, 3 July 1951, Weintraub, *Started* 57, 60.

4 Jori Smith, quoted in Posner, *Last*, 67–9. Weintraub interview (2002). Richler to Weintraub, 3 August 1951, Weintraub, *Started*, 62.

5 Richler to Weintraub, 3, 30 August 1951, Weintraub, *Started*, 62, 71. Richler to Weintraub, quoted in Posner, *Last*, 67.

6 Richler, "Countess," Richler Fonds Acc. #582/103.2.

7 Richler, "Countess," 122, Richler Fonds Acc. #582/103.2; "Apprenticeship of Richler," 1961, Richler Fonds Acc. #582/163.5.

8 Weintraub interview (2002). Richler to Weintraub, 9 June 1951, Weintraub, *Started*, 57.

9 Richler, *The Rotten People*, 411, Richler Fonds Acc. #582/102.8.

10 Richler, *The Rotten People*, 6, 11, Richler Fonds Acc. #582/102.7.

11 Richler, *The Rotten People*, 219, Richler Fonds Acc. #582/102.7.

12 Richler, *The Rotten People*, 132, 134, Richler Fonds Acc. #582/102.7.

13 Richler, notes for *The Rotten People*, Richler Fonds Acc. #582/102.2.

14 Richler, *The Rotten People*, 296, Richler Fonds Acc. #582/102.8.

15 Richler, *The Rotten People*, 411, Richler Fonds Acc. #582/102.8.

16 Richler to Weintraub, 30 August 1951, Weintraub, *Started*, 71.

17 Makow, "Master's," Richler Fonds Acc. #582/135.9.

18 Richler, *The Rotten People*, 248, 296, 134, Richler Fonds Acc. #582/102.8.

19 Richler to Weintraub, 30 August 1951, Weintraub, *Started*, 71. The "Unidentified Manuscripts" (Richler Fonds Acc. #582/110.1) at the Richler Archives include a reference to the story "Il faut s'agir," but there is no copy of the story.

20 Richler to Weintraub, 21 September 1951, Weintraub, *Started*, 73.

21 Lionel Albert interview. Lionel Albert, email, 16 October 2002. Weintraub to Richler, 25 August 1951; Richler to Weintraub, 30 August, 21 September 1951, Weintraub, *Started*, 64–5, 71, 73.

22 Richler, "It Was Fun," 51.

23 Lionel Albert interview. Richler, "Countess," 122, Richler Fonds Acc. #582/103.2. Richler to Weintraub, 28 October 1951, Weintraub, *Started*, 74.

24 Richler to Weintraub, 28 October 1951, Weintraub, *Started*, 74.

25 Lionel Albert, email, 16 October 2002.
26 *Back to Ibiza*, Richler Fonds Acc. #582/65.4, 168.
27 Richler to Weintraub, 14 November 1951, Weintraub, *Started*, 76.
28 Lionel Albert, email, 16 October 2002.
29 Richler, "Down and Up in Paris" 21, Richler Fonds Acc. #582/125.6. Lionel Albert, email, 16 September 2002. Kealey interview, Richler Fonds Acc. #582/152.1.
30 Richler to Weintraub, 11 January 1952, Weintraub, *Started*, 82.
31 *Shovelling*, 40. Richler, "Down and Up in Paris," 24, Richler Fonds Acc. #582/125.6.
32 Richler, *Leaving School*, 150.
33 Richler, "Eating," Richler Fonds Acc. #582/103.2. Kotcheff, "Afterword," 214.
34 Bill Weintraub to Brian Moore, 15 January 1951, Weintraub, *Started*, 14.
35 Hill, *Grand Guy*, 34. *Shovelling*, 26, 36–7. Ann Duncan, "Richler Then and Now," Richler Fonds Acc. #582/157.3. Richler, "Q is for Quest," 30 May 1961, 3, Richler Fonds Msc 36.40.15.
36 Mike Golden, 228. Hill, "Interview," 3. Richler, "Q Is for Quest," 30 May 1961, 3, Richler Fonds Msc 36.40.15. Hill, *Grand Guy*, 38. *Shovelling*, 27.
37 Ron Bryden to Richler, 29 December 1980, Richler Fonds Acc. #582/10.23.
38 Lionel Albert, email, 16 September 2002.
39 George Plimpton, 2.
40 William Styron, 217.
41 *Snooker*, 83. *Shovelling*, 32.
42 Richler, "Eating," 2. Richler to Weintraub, May 1952, Weintraub, *Started*, 87.
43 Hill, *Grand Guy*, 38.
44 *Belling the Cat*, 144.
45 Hill, *Grand Guy*, 36.
46 *Shovelling*, 37.
47 Isou, "Selections from the Manifestos of Isidore Isou," 1, 3–4.
48 Terry Southern, "I Am Mike Hammer," *The Best of Modern Humor*, ed. Richler, 279.
49 Hill, *Grand Guy*, 36.
50 Hill, "Interview," 4.
51 *Shovelling*, 28. *Barney's Version*, 89.
52 Metcalf, "Black," 3.
53 Merrill, 1. Hill, *Grand Guy*, 38, 32, 33. *Shovelling*, 28.
54 Metcalf interview, 3.
55 Mason Hoffenberg, "Divination," *Zero Review* 1 (1949).
56 *Barney's Version*, 64. Barney isn't Richler, but he carries plenty of Richler's attitudes.
57 *Shovelling*, 36, 29.
58 *Back to Ibiza*, Richler Fonds Acc. #582/65.4, 14.
59 Hill, *Grand Guy*, 32, 34. Noah Richler, "I Wanted," B2.
60 *Barney's Version*, 89.
61 Duhm (Richler Fonds Acc. #582/161.1), 28. Ann Duncan, "Richler Then and Now," Richler Fonds Acc. #582/157.3. It's possible that Richler had the jobs during his 1955 Paris stint rather than in 1952.
62 Richler to Weintraub, 14 November 1952, Weintraub, *Started*, 77.
63 *Shovelling*, 38.
64 Lionel Albert interview. Lionel Albert, email, 11 December 2002.

65 Richler to Weintraub, 11 January, 21 March 1952, Weintraub, *Started*, 83, 87.

66 Ayre, 3.

67 Draft of *The Acrobats*, Richler Fonds Msc 36.15.4.

68 Richler to Weintraub, 21 March 1952, Weintraub, *Started*, 87.

69 Richler, *The Rotten People* 402, Richler Fonds Acc. #582/102.8.

70 Richler, *The Rotten People*, 402, Richler Fonds Acc. #582/102.8.

71 Richler, "The Biog of Chaim," Richler Fonds Acc. #582/102.4. Richler, *The Jew of Valencia*, Richler Fonds Acc. #582/102.4.

72 Richler to Weintraub, 9 February, 26 May 1952, 30 August 1951, Weintraub, *Started*, 83, 88, 71. *Shovelling*, 40.

73 Mordecai Richler to Ted Allan, 24 October 1952, National Archives, 20.15. Richler to Weintraub, 26 May 1952, Weintraub, *Started*, 88.

74 Nathan Cohen, "A Conversation..." *Tamarack Review*, 10, Richler Fonds Acc. #582/129.8. Richler to Ted Allan, 24 October 1952, National Archives 20.15.

75 Richler to Weintraub, 21 March, 26 May, 15 August 1952, Weintraub, *Started*, 87–8, 90. *Home Sweet*, 62. *Shovelling*, 46. Lionel Albert interview.

76 Ulla Fribroch [or Tribroch?] to Richler, 18 August 1952, Richler Fonds Acc. #680/14.72.

77 *The Acrobats*, 115–16.

78 Richler to Ted Allan, 24 October 1952, National Archives 20.15.

79 Weintraub interview (2001). Dubé, A13. Kotcheff, "Afterword," 221. Florence Richler disagrees, suggesting that the comments were made only because Weiner was unmarried and large. Florence Richler interview.

80 Joyce Weiner to Richler, 16 September 1973, Richler Fonds Acc. #582/47.31. Nathan Cohen, "A Conversation ..." *Tamarack Review*, 10, Richler Fonds Acc. #582/129.8.

81 Weintraub interview (2001). Kotcheff, "Afterword," 221.

CHAPTER 8

1 Avrum Richler interview.

2 Weintraub, *Started*, 93.

3 Richler to Ted Allan, 24 October 1952, National Archives 20.15. Joyce Weiner to Richler, 26 September 1952, Richler Fonds Acc. #582/47.31.

4 Richler to Weintraub, 15 August 1952, Weintraub, *Started*, 90. Joyce Weiner to Richler, 9 December 1952, Richler Fonds Msc 36.6.31.

5 Joyce Weiner to Richler, 26 September 1952, Richler Fonds Acc. #582/47.31.

6 Richler Fonds Acc. #582/42.22 (after September 1952).

7 Lionel Albert interview.

8 Joyce Weiner to Richler, 26 September 1952, Richler Fonds Acc. #582/47.31. Richler also claimed to have worked as a factory hand and a diaper salesman, but didn't specify when. Nathan Cohen, "A Conversation ..." *Tamarack Review*, 10, Richler Fonds Acc. #582/129.8. "The Author," *Smaller*, 206.

9 Max Richler interview.

10 Richler to Ted Allan, 24 October 1952, National Archives 20.15. Joyce Weiner to Richler, 9 December 1952, Richler Fonds Msc 36.6.31.

11 *The Montreal Gazette*, "Richler's Friends," 6.

12 "Mordecai Richler: St. Urbain's Meistersinger" [unidentified ms], Richler Fonds Acc. #582/135.18, 15.

13 *Back to Ibiza*, Richler Fonds Acc. #582/65.4, 92–3.

14 Weisbrod and Tree.

15 *Home Movies*, 187–8. Norman Allan, *Ted*, chapter 3, "Spain"; chapter 7, "The Nineteen Forties," 15.

16 Florence Richler interview.

17 Richler to Ted Allan, 24 October 1952, National Archives, 20.15.

18 Norman Allan, *Ted*, chapter 8, "Oh Canada," 11, 13. Weisbrod and Tree.

19 Florence Richler interview.

20 "Mordecai Richler: St. Urbain's Meistersinger" [unidentified ms], Richler Fonds Acc. #582/135.18, 15. Lionel Albert interview. Lionel Albert, email, 3 October 2002.

21 Lionel Albert interview.

22 Lionel Albert interview. Lionel Albert, email, 14 December 2002. *Walking in the Shade*, 128.

23 Weintraub interview (2001).

24 Lionel Albert interview.

25 Richler, "Bones," 1.

26 Bernard Ostry interview. McLaughlin.

27 Lionel Albert interview.

28 *The Montreal Gazette*, "Richler's Friends," 6.

29 Richler remembers Mavis Gallant introducing him to Moore in France (Richler, "Memories of Brian Moore," 45–6), but Weintraub insists that *he* did the introducing and that it happened in Montreal. Gallant introduced *Weintraub* to Richler in France, Weintraub interview (2002); Weintraub, *Started*, 93.

30 *Winnipeg Free Press*, 13 January 1999, D6.

31 Weintraub interview (2001).

32 Richler, "Memories of Brian Moore," 45–6.

33 *Winnipeg Free Press*, 13 January 1999, D6. Patricia Craig, *Brian Moore* 117.

34 Joel Yanofsky, *Mordecai & Me*, 58. Moore quit *The Montreal Gazette* in 1952, and Richler didn't receive notice of acceptance until early 1953. The story may nevertheless be true, if Moore was moved by Joyce Weiner's decision to take Richler on.

35 Joyce Weiner to Richler, 13 February 1953, Richler Fonds Msc 36.6.31.

36 Joyce Weiner to Richler, 27 February [1953].

37 Hill, *Grand Guy*, 75.

38 Athill, *Instead*, 145–6, *Stet*, 22, 16.

39 Athill, *Stet*, 28, 38, 40, 52, 58, 91; *Instead*, 147, 154. Brian Glanville, "July Book Column," *Reynolds News*, 5 July 1959, Richler Fonds Msc 36.54.13.

40 Joyce Weiner to Richler, 25 November 1952, Richler Fonds Acc. #582/47.31.

41 Lionel Albert interview.

42 Joyce Weiner to Richler, 15 March 1953, Richler Fonds Msc 36.6.31.

43 *Errand*, 140.

44 Colleen E. Gregory to Richler, 20 April 1992.

45 Richler, "How I Became an Unknown with My First Novel," *Maclean's*, 1 February 1958, 19, 40–1. "On Being Jewish," 4, Richler Fonds Acc. #582/110.20. *Shovelling*, 15–16.

46 Unidentified manuscripts, Richler Fonds Acc. #582/110.1, 11.

47 Diana Athill, quoted in Posner, *Last*, 82.

48 Torsten Blomkvist to Richler, 24 October 195–, Richler Fonds Msc 36.2.17.

49 Athill, *Stet*, 135–6. Diana Athill to Richler, 7 April 1953, Richler Fonds Msc 36.1.25.6.

50 Joyce Weiner to Richler, 25 November 1952, Richler Fonds Acc. #582/47.31.

51 Draft of *The Acrobats*, 49, 108f, Richler Fonds Msc 36.15.3.

52 Diana Athill to Richler, 7 April 1953, Richler Fonds Msc 36.1.25.6.

53 *Acrobats*, 8.

54 Richler "Q Is for Quest" typescript, 30 May 1961, 4, Richler Fonds Msc 36.40.15.

55 *Acrobats*, 146.

56 Arnold Davidson has shown how contrived some of the characters' psychologies and actions are in *The Acrobats*. Davidson, 24–5.

57 *Acrobats*, 49.

58 Draft of *The Acrobats*, Richler Fonds Msc 36.15.3.

59 Ted Kotcheff says that André's intellectual turmoil and intense emotionality belong to Richler, but that Richler's philosophy was much closer to that of Chaim—a "melancholy sense of life's impossibility, its ineradicable injustices." Kotcheff, "Afterword," 217, 221.

60 Cameron interview ms (10 June 1971), 21, Richler Fonds Msc 36.54.1.

61 Ramraj, 47.

62 Craniford, 12.

63 *Acrobats*, 121, 51.

64 Draft of theatrical version of *The Acrobats*, Richler Fonds Acc. #582/103.4.

65 Richler to Diana Athill, 14 April 1953, Richler Fonds Msc 36.1.25.7.

66 Richler to Weiner, 1 May 1953, Richler Fonds Msc 36.6.31.

67 Joyce Weiner to Richler, 27 April 1953, Richler Fonds Msc 36.6.31

68 Brian Moore to Richler, 24 January [1954?], Richler Fonds Msc 36.9.19.

69 Joyce Weiner to Richler, 8 May, 26 March, 15 March, 20 May, 13 July 1953, Richler Fonds Msc 36.6.31.

70 Only "The Secret of the Kugel," "Four Beautiful Sailors Americain," and "Mr. Macpherson" seem to be extant. The character Isenberg in "Mr. MacPherson" (Richler Fonds Msc 36.11.55.14b) and "MacPherson's Cloud" (Richler Fonds Acc. #582/103.2) eventually yielded Duddy Kravitz.

71 Joyce Weiner to Richler, 23 November 1953, Richler Fonds Msc 36.6.31.

72 Robert Weaver bought "The Secret of the Kugel" for the CBC despite his misgivings (Robert Weaver to Richler, 15 July 1954, Richler Fonds Msc 36.2.55). *New Statesman* and *Montreal Star* published it in 1956 and 1957 respectively, probably because Richler was beginning to make a name for himself as a novelist. Richler later called the story "embarrassingly sentimental." Richler, "Three," 1.

73 "The Secret of the Kugel," Richler Fonds Acc. #582/163.5.

CHAPTER 9

1 Ted Kotcheff, quoted in Posner, *Last*, 81.

2 Evelyn to Richler, 27 November 1953, Richler Fonds Acc. #680/1.5.

3 Lionel Albert, email, 19 October 2002 (Forward of Bill Weintraub, email, 17 October 2002, quoting letter from Richler to Weintraub, 6 September 1953. Richler to Weintraub, 11 September 1953, Weintraub, *Started*, 94.

4 Diana Athill to Richler, 5 July 1953), Richler Fonds Msc 36.1.25.8.

5 Salman Rushdie, *Step across This Line*, New York: Alfred A. Knopf, 2002.

6 Richler to Bill Weintraub, 11 September 1953, Weintraub, *Started*, 94.

7 Nathan Cohen, "A Conversation..." *Tamarack Review*, 17, Richler Fonds Acc. #582/129.8. Interview, *The Montreal Gazette*, 5 October 1955, Richler Fonds Msc 36.22.5.

8 Bernard Richler to Mordecai Richler, 4 November 1953, Richler Fonds Msc 36.11.21.

9 Richler to Ted Allan, 30 December 1953, National Archives, 20.23.

10 Richler to Bill Weintraub, 11 September 1953, Weintraub, *Started*, 95.

11 Richler Fonds Acc. #582/19.45 Gould interview (1983).

12 *Shovelling*, 39.

13 Richler to Bob Amussen (G. Putnam's Sons, NY), 8 February 1954; Richler to Amussen 10 February 1954, Richler Fonds Msc 36.4.48.

14 Richler to Ted Purdy (G. Putnam's Sons, NY), 12 January 1954, Richler Fonds Msc 36.4.48.

15 Richler to Bill Weintraub, 11 September 1953, Weintraub, *Started*, 94.

16 Ted Allan to Richler, 7 February 1955, National Archives of Canada, MG30–D388, R2931-2-8-E, Box 20.30.

17 Dansereau and Beaudet interview, 88.

18 Richler to Bill Weintraub, 29 January 1954, Weintraub, *Started*, 99.

19 Joyce Weiner to Richler, 4 July 1954, Richler Fonds Msc 36.6.31.

20 Richler, "Memories of Brian Moore," 45–6. Sampson, *Brian Moore: Chameleon Novelist*, 98. Moore papers 31.1.1. Richler to Ted Allan, 30 December 1953, National Archives, 20.23. Bill Weintraub quoted in Posner, *Last*, 135.

21 Richler to Bob Amussen (G. Putnam's Sons, NY), 12 January 1954, Richler Fonds Msc 36.4.48.

22 Michael Sayers to Richler, 1 June 1954, Richler Fonds Msc 36.11.58.

23 Moore, *An Answer from Limbo*, 12, 99, 121.

24 Richler to Bill Weintraub, 29 January 1954, Weintraub, *Started*, 98–9.

25 "Wade Miller" [Moore] to Bill Weintraub, 19 March 1954, Weintraub, *Started*, 101.

26 "Vasco da Gama" [Brian Moore] to "Marco Polo" [Bill Weintraub], 31 March 1954, Weintraub, *Started*, 102.

27 "Señor Hoore" [Brian Moore] to Bill Weintraub, n.d., Weintraub, *Started*, 105. B[ill Weintraub] to Richler, [4 June 1955], Richler Fonds Acc. #680/1.3.

28 Richler to Ted Purdy (G. Putnam's Sons, NY), 12 January 1954, Richler Fonds Msc 36.4.48.

29 Brian Moore to Richler, 195, Richler Fonds Msc 36. 9.19.2a–c.

30 Nathan Cohen, "A Conversation…" *Tamarack Review*, 13, Richler Fonds Acc. #582/129.8.

31 Welbourn. "I Get Up at 10 A.M.," Richler Fonds Msc 36.54.14

32 *Home Sweet*, 62.

33 Richler to Ted Purdy (G. Putnam's Sons, NY), 12 January 1954, Richler Fonds Msc 36.4.48.

34 Evelyn to Richler, 27 November 1953, 20 January 1954, Richler Fonds Acc. #680/1.5.

35 Richler to Bill Weintraub, 8 July, 24 May, 14 May 1954, Weintraub, *Started*, 118, 113, 110.

36 Brian Moore to Richler, 16 September 1958, Richler Fonds Msc 36.9.19.

37 Weintraub, *Started*, 118. In interviews, Richler said that he lived in Munich for four or even six months, but these times seem too long, given the dates of his letters and the date of his marriage in London (Richmond interview, 4 February 1970, Richler Fonds Msc 36.55.1; *Belling the Cat*, 119). At times, Richler gets the year wrong, saying he had visited Munich in 1955 (Richler, "Foreword," xxvii; *Belling the Cat*, 119).

38 Richler to Bill Weintraub, 8 July 1954, Weintraub, *Started*, 116.
39 Richler to Brian Moore, n.d. [June–August 1954], Moore papers 31.1.3.
40 Theo Richmond interview, 4 February 1970, Richler Fonds Msc 36.55.1.
41 Richler to Brian Moore, n.d. [June–August 1954], Moore papers 31.1.3.
   Richler, "Foreword," xxvii. Richler to Bill Weintraub, 24 May, 8 July 1954,
   Weintraub, *Started*, 113, 115–16.
42 Joyce Weiner to Richler, 4 July 1954, Richler Fonds Msc 36.6.31. Bob
   Amussen (G. Putnam's Sons, NY) to Richler, 8 February 1954, Richler Fonds
   Msc 36.4.48.
43 Cathy Boudreau, quoted in Posner, *Last*, 90.
44 Lionel Albert interview.
45 Joyce Weiner to Richler, 23 July 1954, Richler Fonds Msc 36.6.31.
46 Brian Moore to Richler, 21 July [1954?], Richler Fonds Msc 36.9.19.
47 Richler Fonds Acc. #582/163.10, 25 February 1949, *Montreal Herald*.
48 Florence Richler interview. Weintraub, *Started*, 135. Duhm-Heitzmann, 28,
   Richler Fonds Acc. #582/161.1. Kotcheff, "Afterword," 223.
49 Vivian Hislop, "Top Models Look to the Stage," *Liverpool Echo*, 17 April
   1959.
50 Kotcheff, "Afterword," 223.
51 Duhm-Heitzmann, 28, Richler Fonds Acc. #582/161.1.
52 Florence Richler interview.
53 Moe Richler, quoted in Posner, *Last*, 89.
54 Avrum Richler interview.
55 Bernard Richler interview.
56 *Acrobats*, 148.
57 Avrum Richler interview.
58 Richler, "On Being Jewish," 5, Richler Fonds Acc. #582/110.20.
59 Joyce Weiner to Richler, 23 July 1954, Richler Fonds Msc 36.6.31.
60 Marion Magid to Richler, 19 Aug 1955, Richler Fonds Msc 36.7.46.
61 *Errand*, 141.
62 Avrum Richler interview.
63 Jackie Moore to Richler, 9 June [1954] Richler Fonds Msc 36.9.20, 2.
64 Richler, "Minders," 10–11, Richler Fonds Acc. #582/107.1.
65 Marchand, "Oy," Richler Fonds Acc. #582/134.8, 147. Avrum Richler
   interview.
66 Richler, "TV, Tension," 52.
67 Weintraub interview (2001).
68 Ted Allen to the editor, *The Montreal Gazette*, n.d., Richler Fonds Acc.
   #582/160.8.
69 John Fraser, quoted in MacDonald et al., 8.
70 Richler "Apprenticeship of Richler," 1961, 21, Richler Fonds Acc.
   #582/163.5.
71 Richler to Bob Amussen (G. Putnam's Sons, NY), 10 February 1954, Richler
   Fonds Msc 36.4.48.
72 Merle Shain, "Richler: 'It's not exotic to be Jewish,'" *Toronto Telegram*, 26
   October 1968, Richler Fonds Msc 36.54.14. Rindick interview, Richler Fonds
   Acc. #582/39.3.
73 *Street*, 66.
74 Richler to Bill Weintraub, 14 May, October 1954, Weintraub, *Started*, 110,
   119.
75 Diana Athill to Richler, 4 Feb 1955, Richler Fonds Msc 36.1.25.12. *Smaller*, 26.
76 Joyce Weiner to Richler, 4 July 1954, Richler Fonds Msc 36.6.31.

77 Brian Moore to Richler, 9 June 1955, Richler Fonds Msc 36.9.19.

78 Avrum Richler interview. Max Richler interview.

79 Richler to Bill Weintraub, 8 July 1954, Weintraub, *Started*, 117.

80 *Smaller*, 185.

81 Richler to Ted Purdy (G. Putnam's Sons, NY), 12 January 1954, Richler Fonds Msc 36.4.48.

82 *Smaller*, 185.

83 Nathan Cohen ,"A Conversation..." *Tamarack Review*, 14, Richler Fonds Acc. #582/129.8.

84 *Smaller*, 39.

85 *Smaller*, 29, 89, 94, 150.

86 *This Year in Jerusalem*, 187–200.

87 *This Year in Jerusalem*, 201.

88 Arnold, "Kosher," Richler Fonds Acc. #582/161.2. Robinson, "Toward," 39, "Kabbalist," 45, 56.

89 Robinson, "Kabbalist," 45–6. Robinson, "Sabbath," 109.

90 Richler, *The Rotten People* 357, Richler Fonds Acc. #582/102.8.

91 In one draft, Richler explicitly kills Leah off at the novel's end. Manuscript of *Son of a Smaller Hero*, Richler Fonds Msc 36.22.3, f131. In the published novel, her death is implied.

92 Saul Goldstein to Richler, 28 October 1991, Richler Fonds Acc. #582/37.2. *This Year in Jerusalem*, 124.

93 Weintraub interview (2001).

94 Brian Moore to Richler, 9 June 1955, Richler Fonds Msc 36.9.19.

95 *Joshua*, 348.

96 Bill Weintraub recalls no Jewish girlfriends. Lionel Albert speculates that Sanki may have been Jewish. Lionel Albert interview.

97 Lionel Albert interview.

98 *Smaller*, 165.

99 Neil Compton (Sir George Williams College) to Richler, 17 March 1955, Richler Fonds Msc 36.3.49.

100 Neil Compton to Richler, 23 August 1965, Richler Fonds Msc 36.12.23.

101 Bernard Richler interview. The intensity of the abuse showered on Richler surprised him. Only the *Jewish Observer* treated the novel seriously, he felt. Nathan Cohen, "A Conversation..." *Tamarack Review*, 14, Richler Fonds Acc. #582/129.8.

102 Nathan Cohen to Richler, 3 December 1955, Richler Fonds Msc 36.2.55.

103 Emanuel Litvinoff, "Books," *Jewish Observer and Middle East Review*, 16 September 1955, Richler Fonds Msc 36.22.6.

104 James 9, Richler Fonds Msc 36.30.12 (*Time*, 9c).

105 Sam Orbaum, "Make," 19. Sam Orbaum, "Canadian," 2.

106 Nathan Cohen, "A Conversation..." *Tamarack Review*, 14, Richler Fonds Acc. #582/129.8.

107 Richler to Bob Amussen, 11 March 1955, Richler Fonds Msc 36.8.33.

108 Gershon Baruch compared Richler to Julius Streicher, and the novel to the Nazi propaganda sheet *Der Stürmer*. Gershon Baruch, "Books in Review: *Son of a Smaller Hero*," Richler Fonds Msc 36.22.5. Ironically, many of the novel's features that Baruch criticizes are those closest to autobiography.

109 Jackie Moore to Richler, 9 June [1955], Richler Fonds Msc 36.9.20.

110 Weintraub interview (2001). Weintraub to Richler, 26 June [1955], Richler Fonds Msc 36.14.3; 4 June 1955, Weintraub, *Started*, 125. B[ill Weintraub] to Richler, n.d. [1953–4?], Richler Fonds Acc. #680/1.3.

111 *Smaller*, 121. Allan said that he took on the name "Ted Allan" in order to infiltrate and write about Adrien Arcand's Nazi group. Afterwards, he simply kept the name as a pen-name. Norman Allen, *Ted*, chapter 1, 2.

112 *Smaller*, 158.

113 Nathan Cohen to Richler, 23 June 1955, Richler Fonds Msc 36.2.55. Jackie Moore to Richler, 9 June [1955], Richler Fonds Msc 36.9.20. Weintraub interview (2001).

114 Brian Moore to Richler, 9 June 1955, Richler Fonds Msc 36.9.19.

115 *Smaller*, 64.

116 Joyce Weiner to Richler, 4 July 1954, Richler Fonds Msc 36.6.31.

117 Nathan Cohen, "A Conversation..." *Tamarack Review*, September 1956, 19, Richler Fonds Acc. #582/129.8.

118 *Smaller*, 13, 143, 30, 21.

CHAPTER 10

1 André Deutsch Spring 1955 Catalogue, Richler Fonds Msc 36.22.5.

2 Ted (Theodore) Purdy to Richler, 10 February 1954, Richler Fonds Msc 36.4.48.

3 Ted Allan to Richler, 26 February 1955, National Archives 20.28. Brian Moore to Richler, 24 January 1955, Richler Fonds Msc 36.9.19.

4 1955 CBC interview rebroadcast in Rex Murphy interview, "The Journal," CBC-TV, 17 November 1989.

5 Richler to Bill Weintraub, 3 January 1955, Weintraub, *Started*, 121. Nathan Cohen, "A Conversation..." *Tamarack Review*, September 1956, 7, Richler Fonds Acc. #582/129.8. Interview, *The Montreal Gazette*, 5 October 1955, Richler Fonds Msc 36.22.5.

6 Ted Allan to Richler, 1 and 20 February 1955, National Archives of Canada, MG30-D388, R2931-2-8-E, Box 20.30. The articles apparently covered such topics as the anniversary of Mozart's death and the Battle of Trafalgar. Ann Duncan, "Richler Then and Now," Richler Fonds Acc. #582/157.3.

7 Richler to Bill Weintraub, March 1955, Weintraub, *Started*, 123.

8 Kotcheff (Tribute).

9 Diana Athill, Richler to Bill Weintraub, quoted in Posner, *Last*, 96–7.

10 Natasha Lamming to Richler, 18 November 1977, Richler Fonds Acc. #582/24.72. Richler to Bob Amussen 10 February 1954, Richler Fonds Msc 36.4.48.

11 Richler, "London Province," 43, Richler Fonds Acc. #582/124.16.

12 *Back to Ibiza*, Richler Fonds Acc. #582/65.4, 60–61. Unidentified ms, Richler Fonds Msc 36.48.1, "-16-19-."

13 Bill Weintraub to Brian Moore, 18 September 1956, Weintraub, *Started*, 180, 209.

14 Robert Weaver (CBC) to Richler 13 June 1955, Richler Fonds Msc 36.2.55.

15 *Street*, 90–1.

16 Nathan Cohen, "A Conversation..." *Tamarack Review*, September 1956, 18, Richler Fonds Acc. #582/129.8.

17 *A Tram Named Elsie*, n.d., bound for Marjan Productions. Ted Allan M630D388, R2931-0-4-5, Box 47–3, National Archives of Canada..

18 Michael Sayers to Richler, 20 December 1955; Michael Sayers to Bob [?], 21 December 1955, Richler Fonds Msc 36.11.58.

19 Lessing, *Walking in the Shade*, 128–9. Ann Duncan, "Richler Then and Now," Richler Fonds Acc. #582/157.3. *Back to Ibiza*, Richler Fonds Acc. #582/65.4,

100, 25–6, 33, 28. Unidentified MS, Richler Fonds Msc 36.48.3, 17.

20 Gerry Gross, 2–4. *Back to Ibiza*, Richler Fonds Acc. #582/65.4, 91, 94. Lessing, *Walking in the Shade*, 127.

21 Reuben Ship, *The Investigator*.

22 *Back to Ibiza*, Richler Fonds Acc. #582/65.4, 28, 95.

23 Richler "Apprenticeship of Richler" (Richler Fonds Acc. #582/163.5) 1961, 44.

24 Lessing, *Walking in the Shade*, 129.

25 Kotcheff, Tribute. *Back to Ibiza*, Richler Fonds Acc. #582/65.4, 28, 33.

26 Weisbrod and Tree.

27 Norman Allan, *Ted*, chapter 9, "Across the Atlantic," 7. *Back to Ibiza*, Richler Fonds Acc. #582/65.4, 32–3. Richler, "Pop Goes the Island," 68.

28 Richler, "As Offshore Islands Go" [1963], Richler Fonds Msc 36.43.6, 2–3.

29 Brian Moore to Richler, 24 February 1964, Richler Fonds Msc 36.9.19.

30 Arnstein, 354.

31 Weintraub, *Started*, 181, 183.

32 Richler, "Home," 6, Richler Fonds Acc. #582/163.3, 6.

33 Weintraub to Brian Moore, n.d., *Started*, 182.

34 Weintraub, *Started*, 180.

35 Richler, Unidentified MS, Richler Fonds Msc 36.48.3.

36 *Back to Ibiza*, Richler Fonds Acc. #582/65.4, 35.

37 Robertson, 230. Eden, 545.

38 Nathan Cohen to Richler, 7 June 1955, Richler Fonds Msc 36.2.55. Nathan Cohen to Richler, 23 June 1955, Richler Fonds Msc 36.2.55.

39 Kotcheff, "Afterword," 223.

40 Noah Richler interview.

41 Stanley Mann, Ted Kotcheff, Diana Athill quoted in Posner, *Last*, 102–3.

42 Weintraub interview (2002).

43 Florence Richler interview.

44 Eden, 551.

45 Carlton, 446.

46 *Back to Ibiza*, Richler Fonds Acc. #582/65.4, 35.

47 *Back to Ibiza*, Richler Fonds Acc. #582/65.4, 35; Weintraub interview (2001).

48 Eden, 541, 546.

49 Richler also remembered French police cracking student demonstrators' skulls with chunks of lead. Richler, "It Was Fun," 50.

50 Eleanor Wachtel, "Writers and Company," CBC Radio, 23 May 1999.

51 Richler probably read Babel before meeting Brian Moore in 1953–4. Richler, "Memories of Brian Moore," 45–6.

52 Babel, *Red Cavalry*, 117.

53 Nathan Cohen to Richler, 11 June 1957, Richler Fonds Msc 36.2.55. Nathan Cohen, "A Conversation..." *Tamarack Review*, September 1956, 18, Richler Fonds Acc. #582/129.8.

54 *The Interview*, TV play, n.d., Richler Fonds Msc 36.38.16. Richler sent *Harry Like the Player Piano* to the CBC in June 1957. Nathan Cohen to Richler, 11 June 1957, Richler Fonds Msc 36.2.55. *The Interview* must have been written long before then for Richler to have received feedback and to have embarked on a major rewriting.

55 Frank Lalor, Richler Fonds Msc 36.38.17.

56 *Harry Like the Player Piano*, TV play, Richler Fonds Msc 36.38.12, 5.

57 Muscowitz was deported after Allan refused to give him a character reference. Norman Allan, *Ted*, chapter 3, "Spain," 23, 4.

58 *Harry Like the Player Piano*, TV play, Richler Fonds Msc 36.38.12, 12, 30, 51.

59 *Harry Like the Player Piano*, TV play, Richler Fonds Msc 36.38.12, 34, 63.

60 Florence Richler interview.

61 Interview, *The Montreal Gazette*, 5 October 1955, Richler Fonds Msc 36.22.5.

62 Richler knew *Darkness at Noon*. See, for example, *St. Urbain's Horseman*, 269.

63 Richler, "Fighting Tigers," Richler Fonds Acc. #582/163.4. *Look Back in Anger* premiered 8 May 1956.

64 Nathan Cohen, "A Conversation..." *Tamarack Review*, 19, Richler Fonds Acc. #582/129.8.

65 Interview, *The Montreal Gazette*, 5 October 1955, Richler Fonds Msc 36.22.5.

66 Peter Scott, "A Choice of Certainties," David Sheps, ed., *Mordecai Richler*, 61. Victor Ramraj, 127. Arnold Davidson, 60.

67 Brian Moore to Richler, 9 February [1959?], Richler Fonds Msc 36.9.19. Others have concurred. Victor Ramraj argues convincingly that often the characters' actions are "dictated... by the requirements of the political theme" (Ramraj, 62).

68 *Toronto Telegram*, 29 November 1968, Richler Fonds Msc 36.54.14. *Hunting*, 89. Richler eventually used these lines in *Barney's Version*.

69 Ted Allan is in *A Choice of Enemies* somewhere, says Weintraub, but he won't specify further. Weintraub interview (2001).

70 *Choice*, 190.

71 Norman Allan, *Ted*, chapter 9, "Across the Atlantic," 9–11.

72 Norman Allan, *Ted*, chapter 9, "Across the Atlantic," 9–11.

73 Nathan Cohen to Richler, 11 June 1957, Richler Fonds Msc 36.2.55. If Norman Price wasn't enough, the expatriate crowd could suspect that Richler had also used Allan in the novel for Charlie Lawson, a hack writer with massive literary pretensions. Allan, whose humble ambition was merely to write the greatest work of literature ever written, had needed Richler's help on several TV scripts. Lessing, *Walking in the Shade*, 127. For Allen's pretensions, see also Norman Allan, *Ted*, chapter 11, "The Secret of the World," 13; chapter 10, "The Red Head and the Shrink," 1.

74 *Choice*, 122, 88. Richler, "Universe," 1966, 290, Richler Fonds Acc. #582/163.7. Cameron interview ms, 10 June 1971, 17, Richler Fonds Msc 36.54.1.

75 *Choice*, 83, 17.

76 Lessing, *Walking in the Shade*, 129, 127.

77 *Choice*, 94, 112.

78 *Choice*, 76–7, 89.

79 Draft of *A Choice of Enemies*, Richler Fonds Msc 36.22.2, f124, 419.

80 *Choice*, 108.

81 *Choice*, 16.

82 Draft of *A Choice of Enemies*, Richler Fonds Msc 36.22.2, f124–6, 418–20.

83 *Choice*, 151, 199–200. Voltaire, *Candide, ou L'optimisme*, New York: Bantam, 1962, 204.

84 *Shovelling*, 33.

85 Cameron interview (10 June 1971), 117, Richler Fonds Msc 36.54.1.

86 *A Choice of Enemies* was published early in 1957. *Spain (A Friend of the People)* was complete by 13 December 1956, and Richler sent a copy to the CBC by 4 January 1957, even though it wasn't aired until September 1958.

Richler Fonds Msc 36.2.55 Nathan Cohen to Richler, 13 December 1956, 4,
18 January 1957. Alice Frick to Richler, 20 March 1957, Richler Fonds Msc
36.2.55.

87 *Choice*, 62.

88 *A Friend of the People*, Richler Fonds Msc 36.38.9, 33, 8, 28.

89 Weisbrod and Tree. Norman Allan *Ted*, chapter 3, "Spain," 10, 12, 14.

90 "[Bethune] felt I betrayed him and I felt I betrayed him," Ted Allan said.
Weisbrod and Tree. Norman Allan *Ted*, chapter 3, "Spain," 26, 23. Larry
Hannant suggests that Allan exaggerated the extent of his relationship with
Bethune in order to write himself into the Bethune myth. Larry Hannant,
"Doctoring Bethune," *Saturday Night* 113:3, April 1998, 75f.

91 *Friend of the People* reviews, Richler Fonds Msc 36.38.10.

92 Richler still held a socialist, though not doctrinaire, view until 1956.
Weintraub interview (2001).

93 Monica McCall to Richler, 5 February 1964, Richler Fonds Msc 36.9.13.
A.E. Tomlinson to the Editor, *Encounter*, 4 July 1962, Richler Fonds Acc.
#582/17.1.

94 Kotcheff, "Afterword," 219. Lessing, *Walking in the Shade*, 330–3. Lessing
says that Richler was involved in Centre 42, but Florence Richler is certain
that Lessing is mistaken. Florence Richler interview.

95 Florence Richler interview.

96 Richler, "Dog Days (London Letter)," The Montrealer, March 1959, 31,
Richler Fonds Acc. #582/163.4.

97 Richler, "Evelyn," Richler Fonds Acc. #582/163.4. Richler, "Memories of
Brian Moore," 45–6.

98 Richler to Bill Weintraub, 14 December 1957, Weintraub, *Started*, 207.

CHAPTER 11

1 Nathan Cohen to Richler, 1 February 1957, Richler Fonds Msc 36.2.55.

2 Florence Richler, quoted in Posner, *Last*, 105.

3 F.R. Scott to Richler, 13 August 1957, Richler Fonds Msc 36.12.6.

4 Richler to Bill Weintraub, 19 June 1957, Weintraub, *Started*, 200.

5 Patricia Craig, 150.

6 Hill, "Interview," 3. Metcalf interview, 4.

7 Hill, *Grand Guy*, 80.

8 *Broadsides*, 231.

9 Merrill, 1, 8.

10 Bernard Richler interview.

11 Terry Southern and Richler, "The Panthers," un-produced TV play, Richler
Fonds Msc 36.40.5. MCA returned it on 12 July 1960.

12 Terry Southern to Richler, 30 August 1957, Richler Fonds Msc 36.12.32. A
story editor for CBC's TV drama department called *The Panthers* brilliant, but
six weeks later he said that 8:30 p.m. programming still had to be geared to a
family audience, adding, "If there were to be some such thing as 'Juvenile
Delinquency Week' in Canada, we would then be in a position to use it as a
public service." George Salverson to Richler, 15 July 1957, 26 August 1957,
Richler Fonds Msc 36.2.55.

13 Kotcheff, "Afterword," 213.

14 Press Kit, *The Apprenticeship of Duddy Kravitz*, Astral Films, 1974, Richler
Fonds Msc 36.32.5. "Ted Kotcheff: Mini Biography," Internet Movie

Database, us.imdb.com. Frank Rasky, "Film Director Ted Kotcheff Cooks Up a Western Stew," *Toronto Star*, 5 February 1974, Richler Fonds Acc. #582/155.1. Knelman, "How Duddy's," 18.

15 Kotcheff, "Afterword," 211.

16 Knelman, "Ted Kotcheff," Richler Fonds Msc 36.55.1.

17 Knelman, "How," Richler Fonds Acc. #582/155.1, 18. Kotcheff (Tribute).

18 Kotcheff (Tribute).

19 Richler to Bill Weintraub, 19 June 1957, Weintraub, *Started*, 200. Kotcheff (Tribute).

20 Seymour Lawrence to Richler, 27 March 1957, Richler Fonds Msc 36.1.38.

21 Joyce Weiner to Richler, 7 July 1957, Richler Fonds Msc 36.6.31.

22 Richler to Bill Weintraub, 19 June 1957, Weintraub, *Started*, 200. Weintraub interview (2002).

23 Nathan Cohen to Richler, 3 July 1957, Richler Fonds Msc 36.2.55.

24 Robert Weaver to Richler, 5 October 1956, 5 July 1957, Richler Fonds Msc 36.2.55; 11 March, 22 March 1965, Richler Fonds Msc 36.2.56. Nathan Cohen to Richler, 13 December 1956, Richler Fonds Msc 36.2.55.

25 Richler, "This Hour Has Seven Days." Interview of Lord Thompson. 21 November 1965.

26 Knelman, "How," Richler Fonds Acc. #582/155.1, 18.

27 Joyce Weiner to Richler, 16 September 1973, Richler Fonds Acc. #582/47.31.

28 Richler to Claude Bissell, 30 August, 7 November 1957 (Bissell Papers).

29 Richler to Bill Weintraub, 14 December 1957, Weintraub, *Started*, 206, 208.

30 Weintraub, *Started*, 208.

31 Claude Bissell to Richler, 22 May 1958, Richler Fonds Msc 36.2.12. Diana Athill, 17 December 1958, Richler Fonds Msc 36.1.25.15. Richler, "Intro," *Street* xiii.

32 Richler to Wladyslaw Pleszczyski, 13 June 1994, Richler Fonds Acc. #582/34.32. In 1966 the Canada Council debated about whether Richler, with all his film income, should get a fellowship, but the Council decided to favour quality over need. David Silcox to Richler, 4 May 1992, Richler Fonds Acc. #582/42.25.

33 Kotcheff (Tribute).

34 Florence Richler interview.

35 Hill, *Grand Guy*, 76.

36 Paul Shields, "Biographies: Sydney Newman," *625-Online*, 28 October 2001, www.625.org.uk/biograph/biognews.htm, 6 May 2003.

37 Sydney Newman, "The Elephant Is Big," Richler Fonds Acc. #582/50.9.

38 Sydney Newman, "The Elephant Is Big," Richler Fonds Acc. #582/50.9. Hill, *Grand Guy*, 82.

39 Hill, *Grand Guy*, 82.

40 Florence Richler interview.

41 Sydney Newman, "The Elephant Is Big," Richler Fonds Acc. #582/50.9.

42 Lez Cooke, "British Television: Culture, Quality and Competition," mcs.staffs.ac.uk/ftvrs/tvintro/britishtv.htm.

43 He had already done an adaptation, *The Shining Hour*. Ted Kotcheff, quoted in Posner, *Last*, 101.

44 Richler, *Paid in Full*, Richler Fonds Msc 36.39.8, 48, 83.

45 William Oakley, "But first let's look at this Wideawake Play," *South Wales Argus*, 23 May 1958, Richler Fonds Msc 36.40.4.

46 Richler, "Fighting Tigers," Richler Fonds Acc. #582/163.4.

47 Richler, "Liberace and TV," 65.

48 "Top Ten" Programmes for the Week, T.A.M. Ratings, *Stage*, 29 May 1958, Richler Fonds Msc 36.40.4. *Paid in Full*, one of Armchair's first shows, came in at a very respectable #7 in the weekly national ratings.

49 John Marshall, "Intelligent Use of the Small Screen," *Yorkshire Post*, 23 May 1958, Richler Fonds Msc 36.40.4.

50 Broadcast 22 June 1958, Richler Fonds Msc 36.38.15.

51 Broadcast 12 April 1959. Richler "Apprenticeship of Richler," 1961, 46, Richler Fonds Acc. #582/163.5.

52 Richler, "Making Out in the Television Drama Game," *The Twentieth Century* (March 1959), 235–7, Richler Fonds Acc. #582/130.5.

53 *Belling the Cat*, 187–8.

54 Emma Richler to Mordecai Richler, 17 August 1995, Richler Fonds Acc. #680/10.18.

55 The film was released 19 May 1958. Richler Fonds Msc 36.55.11.

56 *Hunting*, 93.

57 Brian Moore to Richler, [Spring 1959?], Richler Fonds Msc 36.9.19. The summer house scene doesn't really suggest Richler's voice at all. Moore probably based his judgement on *A Choice of Enemies*, but Richler's style was already loosening. More likely candidates are lines such as "Too many pansies around these days."

58 *St. Urbain's Horseman*, 203.

59 Richler to Bill Weintraub, 30 April 1959, Weintraub, *Started*, 234.

60 Marci McDonald, Richler Fonds Acc. #582/154.2. Richler to Bill Weintraub, 2 June 1958, Weintraub, *Started*, 213.

61 Fulford, *Best Seat in the House*, 122–31.

62 Nathan Cohen, "A Conversation…" *Tamarack Review*, 18, Richler Fonds Acc. #582/129.8.

63 Robert Weaver to Richler, 16 December 1956, Richler Fonds Msc 36.2.56.

64 Nathan Cohen to Richler, 12 March, 4 June, 10 November 1956; 1 February, 11 June 1957, Richler Fonds Msc 36.2.55. Nathan Cohen, "A Conversation…" *Tamarack Review*, September 1956, 21, Richler Fonds Acc. #582/129.8.

65 Nathan Cohen to Richler, 10 November 1956, Richler Fonds Msc 36.2.55.

66 Cohen, "Heroes of the Richler View," G. David Sheps ed., *Mordecai Richler*, 47, 45.

67 Victor Ramraj notes how indebted *Cocksure* is to screenplay techniques (77); the same is true, to a lesser degree, for all of Richler's novels after *Son of a Smaller Hero*.

68 Nathan Cohen to Richler, 24 February 1958, Richler Fonds Msc 36.2.55.

69 Bill Weintraub to Richler, 1 March 1958, Weintraub, *Started*, 210. Cohen, "Heroes of the Richler View," G. David Sheps ed., *Mordecai Richler*, 53.

70 Nathan Cohen to Richler, 13 May 1958, Richler Fonds Msc 36.2.55.

71 Richler to Claude Bissell, 27 April 1958, Claude Bissell Papers.

72 Richler to Bill Weintraub, 2 June 1958, Weintraub, *Started*, 213. The Cohen attack came in #6, Winter 1958, "Mortimer Griffin…" in #7, Spring 1958, and the Scott defense in #8, Summer 1958.

73 Richler to Bill Weintraub, 2 June 1958, Weintraub, *Started*, 213.

74 Ted Kotcheff, quoted in Posner, *Last*, 181.

75 Richler to Seymour Lawrence, 22 February 1958, Richler Fonds Msc 36.1.38.

76 Diana Athill to Richler, n.d., Richler Fonds Msc 36.1.25.1.

77 Hill, *Grand Guy*, 76. Tony Gruner, "Television," *Kinematograph Weekly*, 6 March 1961, Richler Fonds Msc 36.40.4.

78 Richler to Bill Weintraub, 2 June 1958, Weintraub, *Started*, 213.
79 Florence Richler, Cathy Boudreau, Ted Kotcheff, quoted in Posner, *Last*, 105, 112.
80 Richler to Bill Weintraub, 14 December 1957, Weintraub, *Started*, 206.
81 Mavis Gallant, quoted in Posner, *Last*, 114.
82 MacGregor (Richler Fonds Acc. #582/157.4), 50.
83 Richler to Bill Weintraub, 29 August 1958, Weintraub, *Started*, 219.
84 Knelman, "How," Richler Fonds Acc. #582/155.1, 18. Richler, "How Duddy's Daddy Did It," 50.
85 Florence Richler interview. Cathy Boudreau, Mordecai Richler, quoted in Posner, *Last*, 115.
86 Richler to Bill Weintraub, 25 July 1958, Weintraub, *Started*, 216.
87 "Mordecai Richler: St. Urbain's Meistersinger" [unidentified ms], Richler Fonds Acc. #582/135.18, 16
88 Richler to Bill Weintraub, 25 July 1958, Weintraub, *Started*, 216–17.
89 Stanley Mann to Florence Mann, ca 17 July 1960, Richler Fonds Msc 36.8.4.
90 Lionel Albert interview. Stanley [Mann] to Daniel Richler, 17 October 1963, Richler Fonds Acc. #680/10.17. Stanley Mann to Florence and Mordecai Richler, 25 September 1968, Richler Fonds Msc 36.8.4. Daniel Richler interview.
91 Lessing, *Walking in the Shade*, 128.
92 *The Apprenticeship of Duddy Kravitz*, 239.
93 Jacob Richler, B4.
94 In *Feed My Dear Dogs*, Emma Richler seems to use Florence's background for the character of the mother, who reveals that she is "a foundling" (11).
95 Richler Fonds Msc 36.55.1 (Edwards). Stewart MacLeod, "Canadians Abound in U.K. TV," *Montreal Gazette*, 1 May 1959, Richler Fonds Msc 36.40.4.
96 Posner, *Last*, 92. Daniel Richler, quoted in Posner, *Last*, 266.
97 Vivian Hislop, "Top Models Look to the Stage," *Liverpool Echo*, 17 April 1959.
98 Gottlieb, 23.
99 Norman Allan, *Ted*, chapter 9, "Across the Atlantic," 9.
100 Weintraub interview (2001). Weintraub adds, "I'm not saying that's the reason for their breakdown." Diana Athill says that Cathy "combined a good deal of tiresomeness with many endearing qualities." *Stet*, 136.
101 Richler to Bill Weintraub, 10 June 1959. Weintraub, *Started*, 237.
102 Bernard Ostry interview.
103 Lionel Albert, email, 12 September 2004. Richler, "Innocents," 4.
104 Kotcheff (Tribute). Kotcheff joined her in these post-mortems.
105 Florence Richler interview.
106 Martha Richler, quoted in Posner, Last, 255.
107 Brian Moore to Richler, [Spring 1959?], Richler Fonds Msc 36.9.19.
108 Athill, *Stet*, 137.
109 Brian Moore to Richler, [Summer 1958], Richler Fonds Msc 36.9.19.
110 Avrum Richler interview.
111 *Home Sweet*, 68.
112 Emma Richler, *Feed My Dear Dogs*, 412. The Richlers' friend, Haya Clayton, insists that Emma's novel *Sister Crazy* is an accurate portrait – not in detail, but in essence – of the Richler family. Haya Clayton, quoted in Posner, *Last*, 260.
113 Florence Richler, 40. Christian Rocca, "Sulle Strade di Barney."

CHAPTER 12

1 Kotcheff (Tribute).
2 Knelman, *Home Movies*, 189. *Back to Ibiza*, Richler Fonds Acc. #582/65.4, 95. Richler to Bill Weintraub, 29 August 1958, Weintraub, *Started*, 218.
3 Brian Moore to Richler, 16 September 1958, Richler Fonds Msc 36.9.19, begins, "Dear: HPTVW (GB)."
4 Richler to Bill Weintraub, 29 August 1958, Weintraub, *Started*, 218.
5 *Back to Ibiza*, Richler Fonds Acc. #582/65.4, 96–7. Kotcheff (Tribute). MacGregor, 47, Richler Fonds Acc. #582/157.4.
6 Kotcheff (Tribute). John T.D. Keyes, 4.
7 Babel, 124.
8 Richler, "Home," 5, Richler Fonds Acc. #582/163.3. Richler to Bill Weintraub, 25 July, 8 November 1958, Weintraub, *Started*, 216, 221.
9 Richler, "Innocents," 4, 14.
10 Richler "You Wouldn't Talk like That if You Were Dead" (1958), Richler Fonds Msc 36.49.20.
11 Wright interview, 172, Richler Fonds Acc. #582/134.11.
12 Seymour Lawrence to Richler, 27 January 1959, Richler Fonds Msc 36.1.38.
13 *The Apprenticeship of Duddy Kravitz*, 198.
14 McSweeney ("Revaluing, 129) mistakenly argues that *The Apprenticeship of Duddy Kravitz* replicates *What Makes Sammy Run?* in kind and degree, while Karl Miller (*Observer*, 8 November 1959) suggests that Richler stole from *The Adventures of Augie March*. Conversely, Ada Craniford and Robert Fulford have shown some of the ways in which Richler moves far beyond Schulberg. Craniford, 46–9. Robert Fulford, *Toronto Daily Star*, 15 October 1959, Richler Fonds Msc 36.16.6.
15 *The Apprenticeship of Duddy Kravitz*, 147.
16 Schulberg, 194, 228.
17 *The Apprenticeship of Duddy Kravitz*, 296.
18 Alan Handel, *The Apprenticeship of Mordecai Richler*.
19 Stanley Mann and Sean Connery lived together for a time after each of their divorces. Because of that, the Richlers saw Connery frequently. Florence Richler interview.
20 On the other hand, the teachers (Mr. McLetchie yielding Mr. Macpherson) and schoolboys in the novel were lifted almost directly from life. Frances Katz, Richler's former teacher at Byng, claimed that she recognized all the characters in novel, and Jack Rabinovitch agreed. Frances Katz to Richler, 21 April n.y., Richler Fonds Acc. #582/24.10. Jack Rabinovitch interview.
21 Draft of *The Apprenticeship of Duddy Kravitz*, Richler Fonds Msc 36.15.10, 139, 123, 199, 252.
22 *The Apprenticeship of Duddy Kravitz*, 212, 48.
23 Rosenberg, *Discourse on Tefillin*.
24 *The Apprenticeship of Duddy Kravitz*, 314.
25 Isaac Ewen, "The Golden Dynasty: Rebbe of Sadeger," Dawidowicz, 197.
26 *The Apprenticeship of Duddy Kravitz*, 270–1.
27 Nancy Reynold, Managing Editor of Atlantic to Richler, 16 June 1959, Richler Fonds Msc 36.1.38.
28 Diana Athill to Richler, 16 October 1959, Richler Fonds Msc 36.1.25.16.
29 Richler, "French," 1964, Richler Fonds Acc. #582/163.5, 10.
30 Richler, "Quest," 30 May 1961, Richler Fonds Msc 36.40.15, 11.

31 Richler to Brian Moore, 16 February 1959, Weintraub, *Started*, 230.
32 Paul Johnson, 475.
33 Brian Moore to Richler, 9 February [1959?], Richler Fonds Msc 36.9.19.
34 Bill Weintraub to Richler, 4 February [1959], Richler Fonds Msc 36.14.3.4a. Robert Fulford, *Toronto Daily Star*, 15 October 1959, Richler Fonds Msc 36.16.1. Richler agreed. Richler to Brian Moore, 16 February 1959, Weintraub, *Started*, 230.
35 Rehearsal Script, "Keeping Up with Shapiro's Boy," Richler, Armchair Theatre, Richler Fonds Msc 36.40.11.
36 *Times Educational Supplement*, "Never Again," 17 April 1959, Richler Fonds Msc 36.40.14.
37 Lynne Reid Banks to Richler, n.d., Richler Fonds Msc 36.1.46. Sir Oswald Mosley started an unsuccessful Blackshirt movement in Britain in 1932. There's a slim possibility that Banks's undated letter was a reaction not to *The Trouble with Benny* but to *Some Grist for Mervyn's Mill*, which played on ATV in 1963.
38 Richler, "Quest," 30 May 1961, Richler Fonds Msc 36.40.15, 11.
39 Cameron interview (10 June 1971).
40 Richler to Sydney Newman, 25 August 1960, National Archives 12.29.
41 MacGregor, 47, Richler Fonds Acc. #582/157.4.
42 Richler to Bill Weintraub, 23 January 1959 Weintraub, *Started*, 227.
43 Malina, 2, Richler Fonds Acc. #582/154.2.
44 TV *Times*, 10 April 1959, Richler Fonds Msc 36.40.14.
45 Vivian Hislop, "Top Models Look to the Stage," *Liverpool Echo*, 17 April 1959. Stewart MacLeod, "Canadians Abound in U.K. TV," *The Montreal Gazette*, 1 May 1959, Richler Fonds Msc 36.40.4. The TV play was broadcast on 12 April 1959.
46 Vivian Hislop, "Top Models Look to the Stage," *Liverpool Echo*, 17 April 1959.
47 Florence Richler, quoted in Posner, *Last*, 123–4.
48 Florence Richler interview.
49 Richler to Bill Weintraub, 30 April 1959, Weintraub, *Started*, 234. Richler "Apprenticeship of Richler," 1961, 46, Richler Fonds Acc. #582/163.5.
50 Joyce Weiner to Richler, 11 September 1959, Richler Fonds Msc 36.6.31.
51 Richler to Bill Weintraub, 30 April 1959, Weintraub, *Started*, 234.
52 Seymour Lawrence to Richler, 11 December 1958, Richler Fonds Msc 36.1.38. Richler to Bill Weintraub, 8 November 1958, Weintraub, *Started*, 221. Kildare Dobbs to Richler, 31 July 1959, Richler Fonds Msc 36.7.44. Jack McClelland to Richler, 5 January 1959, Richler Fonds Msc 36.8.23.
53 Robert Fulford, *Toronto Daily Star*, 15 October 1959, Richler Fonds Msc 36.16.1.
54 Brian Moore to Richler, 9 February [1959?], Richler Fonds Msc 36.9.19.
55 Richler to Brian Moore, 16 February 1959, Weintraub, *Started*, 230.
56 Kotcheff (Tribute). Ted Kotcheff, quoted in Posner, *Last*, 126.
57 Richler to Silvio and Bea Narizzano, 5 February 1960, Richler Fonds Acc. #582/31.7.
58 Florence Richler interview.
59 *Back to Ibiza*, Richler Fonds Acc. #582/65.4, 96.
60 Kotcheff (Tribute). Richler to Bill Weintraub 10 June 1959, Weintraub, *Started*, 236–7.
61 Richler to Bill Weintraub, 14 December 1958, 10 June 1959, Weintraub, *Started*, 224, 236.
62 Bernard Richler interview.

63 Sara Richler to Mordecai Richler, 29 November 1959, Richler Fonds Msc 36.11.25.
64 Bernard Richler to Mordecai Richler, 6 December 1959, Richler Fonds Msc 36.11.21.
65 Richler, "Park Plaza," 64. James 10, Richler Fonds Msc 36.30.12.
66 David Judd, "Books Removed from Norfolk Curriculum," *Brantford Expositor* [1978], Richler Fonds Acc. #582/155.4. *North Bay Nugget*, 26 August 1980, Richler Fonds Acc. #582/155.4.
67 *Back to Ibiza*, Richler Fonds Acc. #582/65.4, 97.

CHAPTER 13

1 "Mordecai Richler: St. Urbain's Meistersinger" [unidentified ms], Richler Fonds Acc. #582/135.18, 16. Richler, "Apprenticeship of Richler," 48, Richler Fonds Acc. #582/163.5.
2 Daniel Richler interview.
3 Richler to Bill Weintraub, 29 January 1960, Weintraub, *Started*, 253.
4 Florence Richler interview.
5 Richler, "Apprenticeship of Richler," 48, Richler Fonds Acc. #582/163.5.
6 Richler, "Foreword." *Belling the Cat*, 120. Florence Richler interview. Eberhard Bethge, *Dietrich Bonhoeffer: A Biography*, rev. ed. Victoria Barnett, Minneapolis: Fortress P, 1989, 681.
7 Florence Richler interview. Richler to Ted Allan, 10 January 1959 [actually 1960], National Archives, Ted Allan 21.20. Richler must have put the wrong year on Allan's letter.
8 Florence Richler interview.
9 Richler to Ted Allan, 10 January 1959 [actually 1960], National Archives, Ted Allan 21.20.
10 John C. Moore, email, 14 October 2003.
11 Richler to Silvio and Bea Narizzano, 5 February 1960, Richler Fonds Acc. #582/31.7.
12 Richler, "Apprenticeship of Richler," 48, Richler Fonds Acc. #582/163.5.
13 Mordecai Richler and Nicholas Phipps, *No Love for Johnnie* (screenplay), May 1960. Richler Fonds Msc 36.34.8.
14 One exception: a photographer, Flagg, takes pictures of Pauline. Speaking to Flagg of Johnnie, Pauline says, "He's... somehow alive." "An M.P.!" Flagg responds, "it's a trick of the light." *No Love for Johnnie*, Dir. Ralph Thomas, 1961.
15 Betty Box to Joyce Weiner, 22 December 1959, Richler Fonds Msc 36.6.8.
16 Richler to Bill Weintraub, 30 April 1959, Weintraub, *Started*, 234.
17 Joyce Weiner to Richler, 15 December 1961, Richler Fonds Msc 36.6.31.
18 Nina Hibbin, "New Films," *Daily Worker*, 11 February 1961. Anon, *Sunday Times*, February 1961. Charles Pannell, MP, "Yes, I knew one like Johnnie," *Daily Express* (London), 8 February 1961. Anon, "Johnnie's message—with love," *Daily Mail*, 8 February 1961. Paul Dehn, "No Nest of Vipers..." *Daily Herald*, 9 February 1961. Richler Fonds Msc 36.34.10. Hugh Gaitskell, Clement Attlee's former Chancellor of the Exchequer, was perceived as not left-wing enough.
19 Richler to Ted Allan, 10 January 1959 [actually 1960], National Archives, Ted Allan 21.20. Richler, "Apprenticeship of Richler," 48, Richler Fonds Acc. #582/163.5.
20 Florence Richler quoted in Posner, *Last*, 216.

21 *Back to Ibiza*, Richler Fonds Acc. #582/65.4, 25.

22 Diana Athill to Richler, 4 April [1960?], Richler Fonds Msc 36.1.25.18; 22 September 1960, Richler Fonds Msc 36.1.25.20.

23 André Deutsch to Richler, 20 May 1960, Richler Fonds Msc 36.1.25.19.

24 Draft of *It's Harder to Be Anybody*, Richler Fonds Msc 36.21.3, f117, 165.

25 Draft of *It's Harder to Be Anybody*, Richler Fonds Msc 36.20.6, f77–9, 61–3. With minor changes (e.g., Victor Hugo and G.B. Shaw replace Dickens) Richler published the sketch of Robertson and a small bit of *The Incomparable Atuk* in the Autumn 1960 *Tamarack Review* as "Wally Sylvester's Canadiana."

26 Diana Athill to Richler, 22 September 1960, Richler Fonds Msc 36.1.25.20.

27 Sydney Newman to Richler, 25 August 1960, National Archives 12.29.

28 Seymour Lawrence to Richler, 6 May 1960, Richler Fonds Msc 36.1.38.

29 Weintraub interview (2001).

30 Joyce Weiner to Richler, 6 May 1960, Richler Fonds Msc 36.6.31.

31 Jack McClelland to André Deutsch, 26 October 1962, Richler Fonds Msc 36.8.23.

32 Joyce Weiner to Richler, 15 December 1961, Richler Fonds Msc 36.6.31.

33 If Richler had let her handle the film rights to *A Choice of Enemies*, said Weiner, the deal might not have fallen through. Also, since she had talked to Betty Box constantly about *A Choice of Enemies*, Richler would have to square that with his conscience. Joyce Weiner to Richler, 15 December 1961, Richler Fonds Msc 36.6.31.

34 Joyce Weiner to Richler, 27 December 1961, Richler Fonds Msc 36.6.31.

35 Richler, "American Novels, British Reviewers," 8–9, Richler Fonds Msc 36.43.4.

36 Norman Levine to Richler, 6 August 1966, Richler Fonds Msc 36.7.10.

37 Dubarry Campau, "London," *Toronto Telegram*, 24 July 1965, Richler Fonds Msc 36.54.14.

38 Richler to Jack McClelland, 31 August 1961, McClelland, *Imagining*, 52.

39 Joyce Weiner to Richler, 15 December 1961, Richler Fonds Msc 36.6.31.

40 Richler, "Cat," Richler Fonds Acc. #582/163.7.

41 Richler to Bill Weintraub, 29 January 1960, Weintraub, *Started*, 253.

42 Florence Richler interview. Richler to Sydney Newman, 25 August 1960, ABC-TV files, National Archives 12.29.

43 Ted Kotcheff to Richler, n.d. [May 1960?], Richler Fonds Msc 36.6.54.

44 Ted Kotcheff quoted in Posner, *Last*, 128.

45 Florence Richler interview.

46 Richler to Sydney Newman, 25 August 1960, ABC-TV files, National Archives 12.29.

47 Florence Richler interview.

48 Avrum Richler interview. *Errand*, 141.

49 "Mordecai Richler: St. Urbain's Meistersinger" [unidentified ms], Richler Fonds Acc. #582/135.18, 8.

50 Weintraub interview (2001).

51 Florence Richler interview.

52 Richler Fonds Msc 36.2.48.

53 Sydney Newman to Richler, 25 August [1960], ABC-TV files, National Archives 12.29.

54 Max Richler interview.

55 Richler, "We Jews," 78–9.

56 Max Richler interview.

57 These talks were very similar to an article he published at that time, "We Jews Are Almost as Bad as the Gentiles," 10, 78–9, 80. See Green, "Synagogues," Richler Fonds Acc. #582/162.4.

58 Lowy, "Montreal Writer," Richler Fonds Msc 36.54.13.

59 Green, "Synagogues," Richler Fonds Acc. #582/162.4.

60 Lowy, "Montreal Writer," Richler Fonds Msc 36.54.13.

61 Barnett J. Danson to Richler, 17 October 1960, Richler Fonds Msc 36.3.66.

62 Richler, "French," Richler Fonds Acc. #582/163.5, 10.

63 Bernard Schachter to Richler, 5 October 1960, Richler Fonds Msc 36.11.59.

64 Lorne E. Pogue to Richler, 14 October 1960, Richler Fonds Msc 36.10.48a.

65 Sydney Newman to Richler, 25 August 1960, National Archives 12.29.

66 "Tastemakers' Toronto Tea Party," *Saturday Night*, 27 May 1961, Richler Fonds Msc 36.54.14.

67 Richler to Claude Bissell, 18 October 1961, Bissell Papers. "Mordecai Richler: St. Urbain's Meistersinger" [unidentified ms], Richler Fonds Acc. #582/135.18, 16.

68 Kattan, "Richler," Richler Fonds Msc 36.54.14.

69 Richler to Monica McCall, 8 March 1961, Richler Fonds Msc 36.9.13.

70 Draft of *The Incomparable Atuk*, Richler Fonds Msc 36.19.1, f78, 77.

71 Bernard Dube, "Dial Turns," 21 January 1959, Richler Fonds Msc 36.54.13.

72 Richler, "Quest," 30 May 1961, 21, Richler Fonds Msc 36.40.15.

73 Jack McClelland to Richler, 28 March 1962, Richler Fonds Msc 36.8.23.

74 Rubinstein, Nash & Co. to Diana Athill, 24 April 1962, Richler Fonds Msc 36.11.52a.

75 Draft of *The Incomparable Atuk*, Richler Fonds Msc 36.19.1, 4. *Atuk*, 9.

76 Rubinstein, Nash & Co. to Diana Athill, 24 April 1962, Richler Fonds Msc 36.11.52a.

77 Draft of *The Incomparable Atuk*, Richler Fonds Msc 36.19.1, f96, 95.

78 *Atuk*, 51–2.

79 Gzowski, "Afterword," *Atuk*, 182.

80 Robert Weaver to Richler, 7 November 1963, 6 November 1964, Richler Fonds Msc 36.2.56.

81 Robert Fulford to Richler, 3 April 1962, Richler Fonds Msc 36.7.40.

82 Gzowski, "Afterword," 181. Kildare Dobbs said, "Glad I'm not in the book, and equally glad to recognize Rabbi F. and Irving L. etc. Of course you'll be called anti-semitic – it's hard to be a Jew." Kildare Dobbs to Richler, 31 July 1959, Richler Fonds Msc 36.7.44. The date on Dobbs's letter is puzzling. Perhaps Richler originally wrote the lampoon of Layton for *The Apprenticeship of Duddy Kravitz* and then saved it for *The Incomparable Atuk*. In that case, "Rabbi F." may refer to Rabbi Harvey Goldstone, the Reform rabbi in *The Apprenticeship of Duddy Kravitz*.

83 *Atuk*, 70–1.

84 *The Apprenticeship of Duddy Kravitz*, 147. Reader report on *The Apprenticeship of Duddy Kravitz*, 15 January 1958, Richler Fonds Msc 36.16.1a.

85 Richler here followed Norman Levine's *Canada Made Me*, which Richler called the best nonfiction book on Canada. Levine had said, "Why all this hypocrisy? Either you make the break and that's that, or else you believe; not in this watered-down, diluted, trying-to-ape-a-church service so that really we're not different you know." *Canada Made Me*, 218–19.

86 Richler, "Trouble with Rabbi," Richler Fonds Acc. #582/163.5. Richler reviewed Feinberg's autobiography, *Storming the Gates of Jericho*.

87 Todd, 20.
88 Abraham L. Feinberg, "Author Meets Critic," *Maclean's*, 22 August 1964, 40, Richler Fonds Acc. #582/163.5.
89 Phillips, 16. Joe King, 317.
90 Dan Bereskin to Richler, 21 October 1966, 28 March 1967, Richler Fonds Msc 36.14.31. The piece had debuted on the CBC and eventually became *The Street*.
91 *Atuk*, 43.
92 Gzowski, "Afterword," 181.
93 Draft of *The Incomparable Atuk*, Richler Fonds Msc 36.19.1, f37, 36. Richler named Marilyn Bell as one of the things he thought he could put behind him when he left for Europe. Richler, "Q Is for Quest," 1, Richler Fonds Msc 36.40.15.
94 Draft of *The Acrobats*, 134, [although Chapter 4, from which this quotation is taken, is called "The Rotten People"], Richler Fonds Msc 36.15.2.
95 Arnold Davidson puts it well, "Richler's Eskimo is clearly no standard Rousseauvian savage undone by the crass commercialism of a world that he never made." Davidson, 110.
96 *Atuk*, 40–1.
97 Tongue-in-cheek, Fulford threatened to sue Jack McClelland on this point. Robert Fulford to Richler, 3 April 1962, Richler Fonds Msc 36.7.40.
98 Jack McClelland to Richler, 28 March 1962, Richler Fonds Msc 36.8.23.
99 *The Tatler*, 6 November 1963, Richler Fonds Msc 36.19.6.
100 S.N., "Mordecai Richler," *Book and Bookmen*, 27, Richler Fonds Msc 36.29.6.
101 Richler, "American Novels, British Reviewers," 6, Richler Fonds Msc 36.43.4.
102 Roth, "Writing," 40, 46.
103 Welbourn, "I Get Up at 10 A.M." *Montreal Star Weekend Magazine* (5 July 1969) Richler Fonds Msc 36.54.14. Richler wrote for *Commentary*, and used its editor, Norman Podhoretz, as a reference when he applied for a Canada Council Senior Arts Fellowship. Richler Fonds Msc 36.2.48, October 1965. In later years, Richler referred directly to Roth's article. Eleanor Wachtel, "Writers and Company," CBC Radio, 23 May 1999.
104 Alvin Kernan, 4.
105 *Atuk*, 85.
106 *Home Sweet*, 68.
107 Diana Athill to Richler, 1 April 1960, Richler Fonds Msc 36.1.25.17.
108 *Street*, 120–1.
109 Sean Moore to Richler, 20 August 1961, Richler Fonds Msc 36.9.21.
110 Lily Rosenberg to Ruth Albert, 27 June [1978–79], Private Collection of Lionel Albert.
111 Moses Richler to Mordecai Richler, 24 November 1964, Richler Fonds Msc 36.11.24.

CHAPTER 14

1 Joyce Weiner to Richler, 3 July 1962, Richler Fonds Msc 36.6.31.
2 Draft of *The Incomparable Atuk*, Richler Fonds Msc 36.19.1.f14, 13.
3 Seymour Lawrence to Monica McCall, 12 March 1962, Richler Fonds Msc 36.9.13.
4 Seymour Lawrence to Richler, 12 March and 30 August 1962, Richler Fonds Msc 36.1.38.

5 Jack McClelland to Richler, 28 March and 23 October 1962, Richler Fonds Msc 36.8.23. McClelland, *Imagining*, 64.

6 Richler, "Pleasures," 1998, 1.

7 McClelland, *Imagining*, xvii.

8 Richler, "Pleasures," 1998, 3.

9 Monica McCall to Richler, 25 July 1962, Richler Fonds Msc 36.9.13. Seymour Lawrence to Richler, 30 August 1962, Richler Fonds Msc 36.1.38.

10 Bob Gottlieb to Richler, [December 1966], Richler Fonds Msc 36.12.18.

11 Florence Richler interview.

12 Bob Gottlieb to Richler, 27 June 1967, Richler Fonds Msc 36.12.18. Gottlieb 23.

13 Edwin McDowell, Richler Fonds Acc. #582/161.3.

14 Larissa MacFarquhar, *Lingua Franca*, to Richler, 8 April 1994, Richler Fonds Acc. #582/25.39.

15 Gottlieb, quoted in Larissa MacFarquhar, *Lingua Franca*, to Richler, 8 April 1994, Richler Fonds Acc. #582/25.39. Richler to Larissa MacFarquer [*sic*], 7 April n.y., Richler Fonds Acc. #582/31.64. *Shovelling*, 20–1.

16 Edwards, Richler Fonds Msc 36.55.1. Gottlieb, 22. Richler to Larissa MacFarquer [*sic*], 7 April n.y., Richler Fonds Acc. #582/31.64.

17 Gottlieb, quoted in Larissa MacFarquhar, *Lingua Franca*, to Richler, 8 April 1994, Richler Fonds Acc. #582/25.39.

18 Gottlieb, 22.

19 Richler fax to Larissa MacFarquer [*sic*], 7 April, n.y., Richler Fonds Acc. #582/31.64, 1.

20 Gzowski, "Afterword," *Atuk*, 180.

21 Peter Gzowski to Richler, 4 February 1964, Richler Fonds Msc 36.7.40.

22 McKenzie Porter, "Inside Toronto," *Toronto Telegram*, 19 November 1963, Richler Fonds Msc 36.54.14. Fulford, *Best Seat in the House*, 153, 156.

23 Moore, *An Answer from Limbo*, 20.

24 Cameron interview (manuscript version), 15, Richler Fonds Msc 36.54.1. Welbourn, 6, Richler Fonds Msc 36.54.14.

25 *Shovelling*, 89. Richler, mistaken or the victim of a typographic error, later gave the year as 1973. Richler, "Foreword," xxvii.

26 Richler, "Three," 3–4. Richler, "Foreword," xxvii.

27 Clive Sinclair, Richler Fonds Acc. #582/160.2.

28 *Errand*, 139.

29 Sandra Kolber, *Bitter Sweet Lemons and Love*, 78. Kolber later reviewed Richler's *The Street* and praised it for being less hard on the Jews than his other fiction was. Sandra Kolber, "Book World," *The Chronicle Review*, 20 June 1969, Richler Fonds Msc 36.36.12.

30 *This Year in Jerusalem*, 249.

31 Richler to Brian Moore, n.d., Brian Moore Papers 31.2.2.4a.

32 *This Year in Jerusalem*, 55.

33 Ha'am, "The Wrong Way," 42.

34 Richler to Brian Moore, n.d., Brian Moore Papers 31.2.2.4a.

35 Richler, "This Year in Jerusalem," *Hunting*. Bill Arad, one of the friends who introduced Richler to many Israelis, disagreed with his interpretation. Bill Weintraub to Richler, 11 November 1962, Richler Fonds Msc 36.14.3.

36 Gefen, 32, Richler Fonds Acc. #582/159.1.

37 Paul Johnson, 549.

38 Richler, "This Year in Jerusalem," *Hunting*.

39 Richler, "The Anglo-Saxon Jews," *Maclean's*, 8 September 1962, 18–19, 34–44. Richler, "This Year in Jerusalem," *Hunting*. The compilation "This

Year in Jerusalem" that appeared in *Hunting Tigers Under Glass* contains the same stories and tone as the original articles, though with less editorializing.

40 Schulze interview, Richler Fonds Acc. #582/41.40.

41 Richler to Brian Moore, n.d., Brian Moore Papers 31.2.2.4a.

42 Robert Weaver to Richler, 20 June 1961, Richler Fonds Msc 36.2.55.

43 Daryl Duke to Richler, 20 July 1961, Richler Fonds Msc 36.2.55. Daryl Duke to Richler, 1 October 1961, Richler Fonds Msc 36.2.55.

44 Robert Weaver to Richler, 29 November 1961, Richler Fonds Msc 36.2.55. Daryl Duke to Richler, 25 June 1962, Richler Fonds Msc 36.2.55. Ken Lefolii to Richler, 29 November 1961, Richler Fonds Msc 36.7.40. Peter Gzowski to Richler, [December 1961?], Richler Fonds Msc 36.7.40.

45 Theodore (Ted) Solotaroff to Richler, 18 November 1960, 20 June 1962, Richler Fonds Msc 36.3.46.

46 Athill, *Stet*, 144.

47 Brian Moore to Richler, [Summer 1958], Richler Fonds Msc 36.9.19. Athill, *Stet*, 144.

48 Weintraub interview (2002).

49 Noah Richler interview.

50 Richler, "Memories of Brian Moore," 45–6.

51 Brian Moore to Richler, [summer 1958], [spring 1959?], 21 October 1963, Richler Fonds Msc 36.9.19.41; 7 November [1962?], Richler Fonds Msc 36.9.19. Athill, *Stet*, 144. Weintraub interview (2001).

52 Richler to Brian Moore, n.d., Brian Moore Papers, 31.2.2.4a. Brian Moore to Richler, 17 November [1962?], Richler Fonds Msc 36.9.19.

53 Moore, *An Answer from Limbo*, 227–42.

54 Richler to Brian Moore, n.d., Brian Moore Papers, 31.2.2.4a.

55 Bill Weintraub to Richler, 3 January, 1963, Richler Fonds Msc 36.14.3. Brian Moore to Richler, 8 February 1963, Richler Fonds Msc 36.9.19.36.

56 Robert Fulford to Richler, 30 September 1963, Richler Fonds Msc 36.7.40.

57 Robert Weaver to Richler, 21 January 1963, Richler Fonds Msc 36.2.56.

58 Ralph Allen to Richler, 28 March 1963, Richler Fonds Msc 36.2.56.

59 Babel's story, "First Love," described the scene, and Lionel Trilling's 1955 "Introduction" to Babel's work declared the scene autobiographical. Reprinted in Isaac Babel, *Collected Stories*, ed. David McDuff, 350.

60 Richler, "Isaac Babel (1894–1939?)," Richler Fonds Msc 36.44.15, 1–3.

61 Like Trilling, Richler uses the word "jaunty" to describe Babel's ironic 1934 speech, quotes what Trilling quoted, and gives, as Trilling did, 1937 as the date of Babel's arrest. Compare Richler, "Isaac Babel (1894–1939?)," Richler Fonds Msc 36.44.15, 1 with Trilling's Introduction, 342–4.

62 Nathalie Babel, "Introduction" to Isaac Babel, *The Lonely Years*, xiv–xv.

63 Budyonny complained that Babel had never seen active combat, had hung around in the rear units, and had indulged in "old woman's gossip," slinging dirt at the "best Communist commanders." Declaring that Babel wasn't properly familiar with Marxist dialectics, Budyonny denounced *Red Cavalry* as "permeated by a petty-bourgeois outlook." Semyon Budyonny, "An Open Letter to Maxim Gorky," Isaac Babel, *The Lonely Years*, 385–6. David McDuff, "Introduction," xii–xv.

64 Richler, *The Fall of Mendel Krick*, Richler Fonds Acc. #680/26.6, 5

65 Richler, "Isaac Babel (1894–1939?)," Richler Fonds Msc 36.44.15, 4.

66 Much of the speech does not sound ironic at all. For example, Babel says that trite vulgarity must be avoided in Bolshevik writing, that serious writing must include a philosophical view, and that, as difficult as it is to write in a Com-

munist country, things could be worse in places where writers matter less: "I must admit that if I lived in a capitalist country, I would have long since croaked from starvation and no one would have cared whether, as Ehrenburg puts it, I was a rabbit or a she-elephant." Babel, *The Lonely Years*, 399.

67 Paul Johnson, 454–5. David McDuff, "Introduction," ix–xxx.

68 "My Cousin, the Horseman," 1963, Richler Fonds Msc 36.39.3. The evolving story was variously entitled "The Hammermans," "Lummox," "Manny," "Manny the Miracle," "Mrs. Hammerman's Miracle," "The Golem of St. Urbain Street," and "Jenny's Brother Manny." Richler Fonds Msc 36.24.8.

69 Richler, "Isaac Babel," 3, Richler Fonds Msc 36.44.15.

70 *Home Sweet*, 6.

71 Richler, *The Fall of Mendel Krick*, 57, Richler Fonds Acc. #680/26.6.

72 20 June "Began work, St. Urbain's Horseman," Richler, Daybook 1965, Richler Fonds Acc. #582/148.

73 Richler, "My Jewish Troubles," 10–11, Richler Fonds Acc. #582/122.7. *Home Sweet*, 6.

74 Ralph Allen to Richler, 2 July 1963, Richler Fonds Msc 36.2.56. Robert Weaver to Richler, 7 November 1963, Richler Fonds Msc 36.2.56. Robert Weaver to Richler, 6 November 1964, Richler Fonds Msc 36.2.56.

75 Florence Richler interview.

76 Brian Moore to Richler, 25 August 1963, Richler Fonds Acc. #582/30.50.

77 Theodore Solotaroff to Richler, 11 January 1965, Richler Fonds Msc 36.3.46.

78 Ken Kavanagh, "Richler of St. Urbain Street," 8 May 1971.

79 Paul Roddick to Richler, 1 December 1968, Richler Fonds Msc 36.11.35.

80 Florence Richler interview.

81 Bill Weintraub to Richler, 21 December 1963, Richler Fonds Msc 36.14.3. Joyce Weiner to Richler, 6 December 1963, Richler Fonds Msc 36.6.31. Robert Weaver to Richler, 12 December 1963, Richler Fonds Msc 36.2.56. Monica McCall to Richler, 17 December 1963, Richler Fonds Msc 36.9.13.

82 Joyce Weiner to Richler, 3 January 1964, Richler Fonds Msc 36.6.31.

83 Richmond interview, 4 February 1970, Richler Fonds Msc 36.55.1.

84 Monica McCall to Richler, 21 August 1963, Richler Fonds Msc 36.9.13. Dirk Bogarde to Richler, 18 January 1964, Richler Fonds Msc 36.2.18.

85 Richler, "Reward," 3 May 1962, Richler Fonds Acc. #680/103.4. Earlier he had called it "East End Mystery Story." Richler, Outline for "East End Mystery Story," 15 October 1956, Richler Fonds Acc. #582/103.3.

86 "Night of Wenceslas," screenplay, 30 January 1963, Richler Fonds Msc 36.34.7.

87 Richler, "NOTES for a proposed dramatic series of six programmes to be based on famous JOURNALS," 23 November 1963, Richler Fonds Acc. #680/28.3.

88 Richler, "Run Sheep Run," Outline for a one-hour TV play, 16 August 1963, Richler Fonds Msc 36.40.6.

89 George to Richler, 25 July 63, Richler Fonds Msc 36.14.40.

90 Richler, "Sloth," Unfinished screenplay, Richler Fonds Msc 36.35.10, 22, 38.

91 "Montrealer at Top with Film Scripts and Novels," *The Montreal Gazette*, 22 March 1966, Richler Fonds Msc 36.54.14.

92 Richler to Tony Forwood, 2 January 1964, Richler Fonds Msc 36.4.30. Dirk Bogarde to Richler, 18 January 1964, Richler Fonds Msc 36.2.18. Tony Forwood to Richler, 18 January 1964, Richler Fonds Msc 36.4.30.

93 "Montrealer at Top with Film Scripts and Novels," *The Montreal Gazette*, 22 March 1966, Richler Fonds Msc 36.54.14.

94 *St. Urbain's Horseman*, 19.
95 Robert Weaver to Richler, 6 March 1966, Richler Fonds Msc 36.2.56.
96 Richler Fonds Msc 36.34.1.
97 *Back to Ibiza*, Richler Fonds Acc. #582/65.4, 102.
98 "Mordecai Richler," *Book and Bookmen*, October 1963, 27, Richler Fonds Msc 36.19.6.
99 Richler, "Anyone."
100 Bill Weintraub to Richler, 4 June 1961, Richler Fonds Msc 36.14.3.
101 Draft of *The Acrobats*, 52, Richler Fonds Msc 36.15.3.
102 Irving Layton to the Editor, *Maclean's*, 25 March 1964, Richler Fonds Msc 36.14.5. The emasculated version appeared in *Maclean's* 77:10, 16 May 1964, Richler Fonds Msc 36.54.14.
103 Irving Layton to the Editor, *Holiday*, 28 March 1964, Richler Fonds Msc 36.5.40.
104 Dusty Vineberg, "Cohen Felt like Punching Richler," [*Montreal Star*?] n.d., Richler Fonds Msc 36.54.13.
105 Robert Fulford to Richler, 5 November 1961, Richler Fonds Msc 36.7.40.
106 Richler, "My Year," Richler Fonds Acc. #582/163.5. Richler, "North American," 15.
107 Richler to the Editor, *Holiday*, 9 April 1964, Richler Fonds Msc 36.5.40.
108 *Home Sweet*, 33.
109 Davies, "London Letter," Richler Fonds Msc 36.54.14.
110 Richler, BOMC review of Lester B. Pearson, *Mike: Volume II*, Richler Fonds Acc. #582/9.3.
111 Richler "French," 1964, 42, Richler Fonds Acc. #582/163.5.
112 *five cent review*, 17, Richler Fonds Msc 36.54.3. *Brandon Sun*, 3 March 1970.
113 Richler, "French," 1964, 10, Richler Fonds Acc. #582/163.5.
114 "Je ne connais pas assez les Canadiens français pour inventer un personnage Canadian-français vraiment satisfaisant." "Mordecai Richler," *Le Devoir*, 31 March 1966, Richler Fonds Msc 36.54.14.
115 Peter Gzowski to Richler, 15 December 1961, Richler Fonds Msc 36.7.40.
116 *Globe and Mail*, Tuesday, 19 July 1964, 1.
117 Richler "French," 1964, 11, 39–42, Richler Fonds Acc. #582/163.5. *Home Sweet*, 27.

CHAPTER 15

1 Joyce Weiner to Richler, 25 August 1964, Richler Fonds Msc 36.6.31.
2 Jo Stewart [of Monica McCall] to Richler, 9 September 1964, Richler Fonds Msc 36.9.13. Joyce Weiner to Richler, 19 October 1964, Richler Fonds Msc 36.6.31.
3 Cook, 5.
4 Robert Weaver to Richler, 6 November 1964, Richler Fonds Msc 36.2.56.
5 Jack McClelland to Richler, 8 October 1964, McClelland, *Imagining*, 97.
6 Richler to Martin Stern, 7 March 1964, Richler Fonds Msc 36.12.49.
7 Martin Stern to Richler, 21 July 1964, Richler Fonds Msc 36.12.49.
8 *Hunting*, 59, 63–70. Richler, "Three," 3.
9 W.F.W. Neville to the editor, *Encounter*, 16 December 1964, Richler Fonds Acc. #582/17.1.
10 Richler, "Three," 6.
11 Lesley [agent Gareth Wigan's secretary] to Richler, 25 February 1966, Richler Fonds Msc 36.5.10. *Errand*, 133.

12 Florence Richler interview.

13 Lionel Albert interview. Florence Richler interview. *Errand*, 133.

14 Daniel Richler interview. Noah Richler interview.

15 Florence Richler interview.

16 *Back to Ibiza*, Richler Fonds Acc. #582/65.4, 17–19.

17 Shain, Richler Fonds Msc 36.54.14.

18 *Home Sweet*, 69.

19 Richler, "Man for Today," Richler Fonds Acc. #582/163.7. *Home Sweet*, 87.

20 *Montreal Star*, 29 December 1965, Richler Fonds Msc 36.54.14.

21 Robert Weaver to Richler, 27 January 1966, Richler Fonds Msc 36.2.56.

22 Ted Solotaroff to Richler, 25 February 1966, Richler Fonds Msc 36.3.46.

23 Florence Richler interview.

24 *Cinema Canada*, interview, 20.

25 Bob Gottlieb to Richler, 18 October 1966, Richler Fonds Msc 36.12.18.

26 Richler, "Aging," 12–14, Richler Fonds Acc. #582/163.1.

27 *Shovelling*, 14.

28 Richler Fonds Msc 36.21.7.f2.

29 *Hunting*, 9.

30 Band, 222–4.

31 *Hunting*, 111.

32 *Montreal Herald*, 16 March 1949, Richler Fonds Acc. #582/163.10.

33 Lily Rosenberg Richler, *Canadian Jewish Review*, 18 September 1936, 33.
   Richler used the line often enough himself, though ironically, as a reply from
   Weaver indicates: "It is not really so tough to be a Jew. It may just be tough
   to be a Jew in London dealing with markets in Toronto." Robert Weaver to
   Richler, 10 April 1963, Richler Fonds Msc 36.2.56.

34 Aleichem, 256.

35 Roth, "Writing," 1961, 40.

36 In the development of Shalinsky from the short story to the novel, Richler had
   some help from Ted Kotcheff, who had met an importuning concentration
   camp survivor, Joseph Bermann. Twenty years earlier, Bermann had lain in
   Buchenwald with fifty dead naked women on top of him. Now, very lonely,
   he repeatedly called Kotcheff, who had gotten him a bit of acting work. As a
   result, he said that Kotcheff was a genius, but, when the work dried up and it
   appeared that he'd have to go back to cleaning BBC lavatories, he was no
   longer convinced that Kotcheff was so talented. Why did Alec Guinness get to
   portray German generals when Bermann could do so much of a better job?
   Suicide wasn't an option because he wasn't brave enough, but he said that he
   wished he were back in the concentration camp. What Kotcheff said he could-
   n't convey to Richler were the irrational jumps in Bermann's conversation.
   Ted Kotcheff to Richler, 4 August 1966, Richler Fonds Acc. #680/6.48.

37 *Shovelling*, 33.

38 *Cocksure*, 211.

39 Richler, "Mortimer Griffin, Shalinsky, and How They Settled the Jewish
   Question," *Tamarack Review* 7, Spring 1958, 30–43. Also in *Town* 4:12
   (November 1963): 93, Richler Fonds Msc 36.49.8.

40 Draft of *Cocksure*, Richler Fonds Msc 36.18.4.f117, 222.

41 Richler, "Universe," 1966, Richler Fonds Acc. #582/163.7, 290.

42 Bob Gottlieb to Richler, 27 June 1967, Richler Fonds Msc 36.12.18.

43 Cynthia Ozick, 177, 169.

44 Draft of *Cocksure*, Richler Fonds Msc 36.18.4.f143, 2.

45 Jack McClelland to Richler, 22 November 1966, Richler Fonds Msc 36.8.23.

46 Noah Richler interview.
47 Victor Ramraj, 80.
48 *Cocksure*, 20, 108.
49 Anthony Burgess to Tony Godwin, 8 October 1968, Richler Fonds Msc 36.2.39.
50 Tony Godwin to Richler, 12 October 1967, Richler Fonds Msc 36.4.60.
51 Cameron interview (10 June 1971), 116, Richler Fonds Msc 36.54.1. Merle Shain. Urjo Kareda. *Toronto Daily Star*, 1 June 1968, Richler Fonds Msc 36.18.8.
52 Welbourn, "I Get Up at 10 A.M." Maulucci interview (2 April 1976), Richler Fonds Acc. #582/124.20.
53 *Cocksure*, 46.
54 Arnold Davidson, 121, 135.
55 Richler, "Where It," Richler Fonds Acc. #582/163.4. *Back to Ibiza*, Richler Fonds Acc. #582/65.4, 97.
56 *St. Urbain's Horseman*, 88.
57 Ron Bryden, Florence Richler, quoted in Posner, *Last*, 147–8.
58 Craniford, 72. Fulford also called it the funniest book ever written by a Canadian and insisted that, like all good satire, it returned to conservative values. Robert Fulford, "Disgusting, Dirty, Funny, Distinguished," *Toronto Daily Star*, 23 March 1968, Richler Fonds Msc 36.18.9.
59 Neil Compton to Richler, 6 March 1968, Richler Fonds Msc 36.12.23.
60 Daniel Richler, "Such," 42.
61 Hill, *Grand Guy*, 263. *Broadsides*, 231–3.
62 Fiedler, 104–5.
63 Toynbee in Sheps, 108. Christopher Williams, *New Society* (19 April 1968). David Haworth, "Unclean Fun," *New Statesman* (19 April 1968), Richler Fonds Msc 36.18.9. A number of critics commented on *Cocksure*'s facetiousness and its inability to find a moral ground. See Victor Ramraj, 79.
64 Cameron interview (10 June 1971), 116, Richler Fonds Msc 36.54.1. Four years before *Cocksure* was published, Richler complained about the stereotyping that went on in the literary world: "The stock villain is the ad man and anyone who lives in a clean suburb or worries enough about his children's education to attend PTA meetings is prejudged a square. Traditional hero—the junkie." Richler, "Anyone." Robert Fulford interview, "This Is Robert Fulford," 23 July 1968.
65 Richler, "Involvement: Writers Reply," 5, Richler Fonds Acc. #582/126.1. The Oxfam donations appear in Dan Bereskin to Richler, 21 October 1966, Richler Fonds Msc 36.14.31. Richler signed a declaration in the *Times* against the sale of arms to South Africa, having been involved in and having contributed to the anti-Apartheid movement from 1965 to 1970. 19 October 1970, Richler Fonds Msc 36.1.29.
66 Daniel Richler interview.
67 James King, 191. David Mercer to Richler, 16 October 1963, Richler Fonds Msc 36.9.1.
68 David Mercer to Richler, 16 October 1963, Richler Fonds Msc 36.9.1.
69 Margaret Laurence to Richler, 2 August 1968, Richler Fonds Msc 36.6.66.
70 *Cocksure*, 88.
71 "Libel Report" on "A Novel by Mordecai Richler," Oswald Hickson Collier and Co., 21 August 1967, 4, 2. Richler Fonds Msc 36.18.6.
72 Draft of *It's Harder to Be Anybody*, Richler Fonds Msc 36.21.5.

73 "Libel Report" on "A Novel by Mordecai Richler," Oswald Hickson Collier and Co., 21 August 1967, 2, Richler Fonds Msc 36.18.6.
74 Woodcock, *Mordecai Richler*, 48, 45, 44 50.
75 Metcalf interview, April 1973, 8.
76 "Libel Report" on "A Novel by Mordecai Richler," Oswald Hickson Collier and Co., 21 August 1967, 6, Richler Fonds Msc 36.18.6.
77 Urjo Kareda, *Toronto Daily Star*, 1 June 1968, Richler Fonds Msc 36.18.8.
78 "Libel Report" on "A Novel by Mordecai Richler," Oswald Hickson Collier and Co., 21 August 1967, 4, Richler Fonds Msc 36.18.6. The names of Alan Ladd, Richard Chamberlain, and the identifiable governor of California had all been deleted before the lawyers saw the novels.
79 Florence Richler, 41. *Shovelling*, 119.
80 Brian Moore to Richler, 14 March 1966, 10 June 1966, Richler Fonds Msc 36.9.19.
81 Max Richler to Mordecai Richler, 17 September 1966, Richler Fonds Msc 36.11.23.
82 Martin, "Anecdotes," A4.
83 Nathan Cohen to Richler, 13 March 1967, Richler Fonds Msc 36.13.34.
84 Bill Weintraub to Richler, 15 January 1967, Richler Fonds Msc 36.14.3.40.
85 Avrum Richler interview. Max Richler to Richler, 4 May 1967, Richler Fonds Msc 36.11.23.
86 Avrum Richler to Mordecai Richler, 8 June 1988, Richler Fonds Acc. #582/36.34.
87 *St. Urbain's Horseman*, 275.
88 Babel, 226.
89 Sara Richler to Mordecai Richler, 19 May 1967, Richler Fonds Msc 36.11.25. Avrum Richler interview.
90 *St. Urbain's Horseman*, 276–7.
91 Sara Richler to Mordecai Richler, 19 May 1967, Richler Fonds Msc 36.11.25.
92 Joe King, 264.
93 Geffen, 32, Richler Fonds Acc. #582/159.1. Dr. S.J. Roth, World Jewish Congress, London to Richler, 31 May 1967, 37.14.19. Draft of open letter, 2 June 1967, Richler Fonds Acc. #582/17.1 4–5. Richler, "Involvement: Writers Reply," Richler Fonds Acc. #582/126.1.
94 Louis Marks, Honorary Secretary, Writers for Israel Committee, London to Richler, 10 July 1967, Richler Fonds Msc 36.14.24. Louis Marks to Editor, *London Magazine*, 24 August 1968, Richler Fonds Msc 36.14.24.3.
95 Nur Masalha, 16, 22, 163.
96 Max Richler interview.
97 *This Year in Jerusalem*, 45.
98 Sam Orbaum, "Make," 19.
99 David Richler, quoted in Posner, *Last*, 300. Avrum Richler interview. Bernard Richler interview. In *St. Urbain's Horseman*, Richler lifted a large portion of the words that the rabbi says over Issy Hersh (the novel's Moe Richler) directly from the letter of condolence sent by Lily's brother, Rabbi Abraham Rosenberg. Rabbi Abraham Rosenberg to Mrs. M. Richler and family, 9 June 1967, Richler Fonds Msc 36.11.40.
100 Bernard Richler interview. Richler seems to have paid the Rabbinical College of Canada to say kaddish, though he ignored the Yahrtzeit notices that the College mailed him. A form letter reads, "Some time ago you bestowed upon us the sacred trust of saying Kadish for your late beloved father.... A sum of

money was donated to pay for this Kadish" [*sic*]. The file includes notices for 1977, 1979, 1988, 1989, 1991, and 1994. The College wanted to know if it should keep reminding Richler of Yahrtzeit dates "and of observing it in accordance with Jewish law." Rabbinical College of Canada, Montreal, to Richler, n.d., Richler Fonds Acc. #582/35.58.

101 Bernard Richler interview. Lionel Albert interview. Max Richler interview. Richler has said, "It strikes me as neurotic, maybe, yet still reasonable, to be charged with terror on any airplane flight." *Broadsides*, 51. Ted Kotcheff, quoted in Posner, *Last*, 280.

102 Dansereau and Beaudet interview, 95.

103 Micki Moore interview.

104 Wong interview.

105 Avrum Richler interview.

106 *Snooker*, 115. In an interview Richler claimed that he didn't drink much, but he approvingly quoted Graham Greene's statement, "I was born three scotches short of reality." L. Brown interview.

107 *Home Sweet*, 56, 60. Avrum, with only two frayed pictures of Moe, begged Sara for more pictures in later years. She refused him. Avrum Richler to Mordecai Richler, 8 June 1988, Richler Fonds Acc. #582/36.34.

108 Avrum says that when he was younger he broke the diary's code – it was very simple – but that he doesn't know what was in the diary. Avrum Richler interview.

109 Sara Richler to Mordecai Richler, 11 October 1967, Richler Fonds Msc 36.11.25.

110 Max Richler to Mordecai Richler, 15 January 1968, Richler Fonds Msc 36.11.23.

CHAPTER 16

1 Diana Athill to Richler, 31 January 1967, Richler Fonds Msc 36.1.25.

2 Brian Moore to Richler, 2 March 1966, 17 November 1967, Richler Fonds Msc 36.9.19.

3 Tony Godwin to Richler, 23 September 1968, Richler Fonds Msc 36.4.60.

4 Diana Athill and André Deutsch to Richler, 17 August 1967, Richler Fonds Msc 36.1.25.

5 *Back to Ibiza*, Richler Fonds Acc. #582/65.4, 120–1. Tony Godwin to Richler, 23 September 1968, Richler Fonds Msc 36.4.60.

6 Bob Gottlieb to Richler, 23 August 1967, Richler Fonds Msc 36.12.18.

7 David Machin to Richler, 28 July 1967, Richler Fonds Msc 36.7.18.

8 Neil Compton to Richler, 22 August 1967, Richler Fonds Msc 36.12.23.

9 *Shovelling*, 18.

10 Mavis Gallant to Richler, [November or December 1967?], 30 August 1967, Richler Fonds Msc 36.4.51.

11 Kotcheff, "Afterword," 218.

12 Bill Weintraub to Richler, [May 1968], 2 February 1968, Richler Fonds Msc 36.14.3.

13 Richler to Mr. Berger, [1968], Richler Fonds Msc 36.1.61.

14 Fulford, "Mordecai." Merle Shain, "Richler," Richler Fonds Msc 36.54.14. Richler, "With-It," 45. William Foster interview, Richler Fonds Msc 36.55.1. McCormick interview, Richler Fonds Acc. #582/152.16. William French, "Books and Bookmen," *Globe and Mail*, 8 March 1969, Richler Fonds Msc 36.54.14. Rob Martin, Richler Fonds Msc 36.54.14.

15 McLaughlin.
16 Peter Gzowski to Richler, 21 February, 7 March 1968, Richler Fonds Msc 36.12.43.
17 Jack Ludwig to Richler, 14 November 1968, 6 February 1969, Richler Fonds Msc 36.13.53.
18 *Shovelling*, 16. Cameron interview, 116.
19 Jeremy Bugler, "The Bookselling Smiths, *The Observer*, 15 March 1970, Richler Fonds Msc 36.55.1.
20 Kareda, Richler Fonds Msc 36.18.8.
21 John Metcalf to Richler, 6 July 1970, Richler Fonds Msc 36.9.3.
22 Richler to David Berry, Ryerson Press, 20 June 1970, Richler Fonds Msc 36.11.55.13.
23 John Metcalf to Richler, 6 July 1970, Richler Fonds Msc 36.9.3.
24 Robert Fulford to Richler, 6 December 1971, Richler Fonds Msc 36.11.57.
25 Walter Stewart, *Maclean's*, telegram to Richler, 30 December 1970, 15 January 1971, Richler Fonds Msc 36.7.41.
26 Doris Anderson, *Chatelaine*, to Richler, 20 January 1971, Richler Fonds Msc 36.3.28. The scene is in *St. Urbain's Horseman*, 280–8. "Old Lady Dry Cunt" doesn't appear there but appeared earlier in the novel, on page 17.
27 Richler, "The Greening of Hersh," 58.
28 Jack McClelland to Richler, 5 and 17 June 1968, Richler Fonds Msc 36.8.23.
29 William French, "Leonard Cohen Wants to Be Governor General?" *Globe and Mail*, 17 May 1969, Richler Fonds Msc 36.54.14.
30 *Shovelling*, 152.
31 Nadel, *Various Positions*, 173–4.
32 In 1970 Michael Ondaatje's *The Collected Works of Billy the Kid* would win in the category "Prose and Poetry," but this was a case of a hybrid book that the judges didn't know where to place.
33 Welbourn, "I Get Up at 10 A.M.
34 Josh Greenfield to Richler, 15 March 1968, Richler Fonds Msc 36.5.8.
35 Peter Hall and Filmways planned to do the movie. "Not So Sure," *Evening Standard*, 20 August 1968, Richler Fonds Msc 36.54.14.
36 Daniel Richler, "Such," 42.
37 King's Road, the down-market area where Richler had lived in the 1950s, was given over in the 1960s to fashion boutiques in which, to Richler's dismay, all the trousers were bell-bottoms. Fulford, "Mordecai."
38 Richler, "With-It," 45.
39 *Publisher's Weekly* interview, Richler Fonds Msc 36.54.9.
40 Cameron interview, ms 13, Richler Fonds Msc 36.54.1.
41 Metcalf interview, 11–12.
42 *Hunting*, 89.
43 Patrick Lyndon to Richler, 23 May 1968, Richler Fonds Msc 36.7.30.
44 "Open Letter to Richler," 6 February 1969, Richler Fonds Msc 36.2.3.
45 Richler, "With-It," 45.
46 Richler, "With-It," 46.
47 Patrick Lyndon to Robert Fulford, editor of *Saturday Night*, 12 February 1969, Richler Fonds Msc 36.11.57,19b.
48 *Inner Space*, Richler Fonds Msc 36.54.4. Richler, "With-It," 45. *Home Sweet*, 146.
49 Bill Weintraub to Richler, 21 June 1971, Richler Fonds Msc 36.14.3. Robert Weaver to Richler, 20 July 1971, Richler Fonds Msc 36.2.56.
50 Christina Somerville to Robert Fulford, editor *Saturday Night*, 13 April 1970, 4, Richler Fonds Msc 36.11.57.25.

51 *Inner Space*, Richler Fonds Msc 36.54.4. Beker interview, Richler Fonds Msc 36.55.1.
52 Richler, "Involvement: Writers Reply," 6, Richler Fonds Acc. #582/126.1.
53 Noah Richler interview.
54 Richler, "Preparing for the Worst," Richler Fonds Acc. #582/103.4.
55 Richler, "My Year," Richler Fonds Acc. #582/163.5. *Inner Space*, 1, Richler Fonds Msc 36.54.4.
56 S. Martin, "Insult," 6, Richler Fonds Acc. #582/160.7. Richler, "If Austin," 68, Richler Fonds Acc. #582/163.7.
57 Richler, "If Austin," 68, Richler Fonds Acc. #582/163.7.
58 Austin C. Clarke, Department of English, Yale University, to Richler, 19 November 1968, Richler Fonds Msc 36.3.35.
59 S. Martin, "Insult," 6, Richler Fonds Acc. #582/160.7.
60 Lebel, 18–20.
61 Kildare Dobbs to Richler, 4 April 1967, Richler Fonds Msc 36.11.57.
62 *Inner Space*, Richler Fonds Msc 36.54.4.
63 Jack Clayton to Richler, 2 May 1969, Richler Fonds Msc 36.3.39.
64 Penelope Gilliatt, "Protest for Profit," *Observer*, 12 February 1961.
65 J.A. Laponce, 286.
66 Max Richler to Mordecai Richler, 27 June 1968, Richler Fonds Msc 36.11.23.
67 *Home Sweet*, 150.
68 Richler, "Man Behind," 1.
69 Richler, Unidentified ms [probably a draft of "Canada: 'An Immensely Boring Country'—Until Now"], 16, Richler Fonds Msc 36.48.7.
70 Peter Gzowski to Richler, 21 February 1968, Richler Fonds Msc 36.12.43.22a.
71 Richler, "Style and Substance," Richler Fonds Acc. #680/31.24.
72 Richler, "Man for Today," Richler Fonds Acc. #582/163.7.
73 Richler, "How a Good," Richler Fonds Acc. #582/163.7. Richler also donated to the campaign fund of Pauline Jewett when she was still a Liberal. R.W. Sutherland, Finance Chairman, Federal Election Campaign for Pauline Jewett, to Richler, 7 November 1972, Richler Fonds Msc 36.4.18.
74 *Montreal Star Weekend Magazine*, 5 July 1969, Richler Fonds Msc 36.54.14.
75 "Involvement and the Writer," *Evening Standard*, 1 August 1968, Richler Fonds Msc 36.54.14.
76 Rodriguez interview, Richler Fonds Msc 36.54.14.
77 *Belling*, 93.
78 Gruending, Richler Fonds Msc 36.42.21.

CHAPTER 17

1 Christina Somerville to *Saturday Night*, 13 April 1970, unpublished letter about Richler's lecture at the University of Calgary, 3, Richler Fonds Msc 36.11.57.25. *Shovelling*, 19–20.
2 Richler to Jack McClelland, 8 September 1967, Richler Fonds Msc 36.8.23. Merle Shain, "Richler," Richler Fonds Msc 36.54.14.
3 Cameron interview, 126. George Anthony, "St. Urbain's Richler Rides Again," *Toronto Telegram*, 5 June 1971, Richler Fonds Msc 36.30.12.
4 Ken Kavanagh, "Richler of St. Urbain Street," 8 May 1971.
5 Noah Richler interview.
6 Florence Richler interview. Florence Richler 40. Gzowski, "Afterword," *Atuk*, 182.
7 Ivana Edwards, Richler Fonds Msc 36.55.1.

8 Florence Richler, 41. Sue Fox interview, 10.
9 Richler, "The Last Plum in the House" [1966 or 1967?], Richler Fonds Acc. #680/28.3.
10 Emma Richler, *Feed My Dear Dogs*, 210.
11 Robert Gottlieb, quoted in Posner, *Last*, 263.
12 Ivana Edwards, Richler Fonds Msc 36.55.1.
13 Florence Richler, 42.
14 Noah Richler interview.
15 Emma Richler, *Sister Crazy*, 56–7, 73.
16 Sue Fox interview, 10.
17 Emma Richler, *Feed My Dear Dogs*, 25.
18 Emma Richler, *Sister Crazy*, 75.
19 Marchand, "Oy," 148, Richler Fonds Acc. #582/134.8.
20 Daniel Richler interview.
21 Sue Fox interview, 9–10.
22 Daniel Richler, "Such," 42.
23 Noah Richler, "I Wanted," B1.
24 *Broadsides*, 13. Florence Richler interview.
25 Richler, "On Being Jewish," 5, Richler Fonds Acc. #582/110.20.
26 Richler to Bob Gottlieb, 17 November 1967, Richler Fonds Acc. #582/4.25.
27 Florence Richler interview.
28 Carol Service, King's House, Richmond, 15 December 1969, Richler Fonds Msc 36.23.2.
29 Florence Richler interview.
30 Sam Orbaum, email.
31 Richler, "On Being Jewish," 2, Richler Fonds Acc. #582/110.20. *This Year in Jerusalem*, 82.
32 *St. Urbain's Horseman*, 306–7.
33 Noah Richler, "I Wanted," B1. Richler, "On Being Jewish," 5, Richler Fonds Acc. #582/110.20. *Montreal Gazette*, 19 May 2001.
34 Daniel Richler interview. Noah Richler interview. Florence Richler interview.
35 Wong interview, 2.
36 Noah Richler, "I Wanted," B1.
37 Max Richler interview.
38 *St. Urbain's Horseman*, 71. Shnayer Leiman, 35. Robinson, "Forgery," 13; "Sabbath," 106–7, 109–10; Kabbalist," 46–7.
39 Todd, 22.
40 Noah Richler interview.
41 Gefen, 31, Richler Fonds Acc. #582/159.1. Daniel Richler interview.
42 Cynthia Ozick, 177, 169.
43 Daniel Richler, quoted in Posner, *Last*, 316.
44 Emma Richler, *Sister Crazy*, 48, 50. Emma Richler, "Two," 8. Daniel Richler, "Such," 42. Sue Fox interview, 10. Daniel Richler interview.
45 Noah Richler interview. *Back to Ibiza*, Richler Fonds Acc. #582/65.4, 24. *Joshua Then and Now*, 97–8. Florence doesn't remember the victory jig incident. Florence Richler interview.
46 *Back to Ibiza*, Richler Fonds Acc. #582/65.4, 10.
47 *Shovelling*, 83. Daniel Richler interview.
48 Richler to Bob Gottlieb, [1973?], Richler Fonds Acc. #582/4.25.
49 Buchan, 12. *Shovelling*, 83.
50 Rosemary Dudley to the editor, *Globe and Mail*, 19 May 1969, Richler Fonds Msc 36.3.84.

51 Alan Sipress (*Washington Post*), "Malaysian PM says Islam Must Resist Jews," *Winnipeg Free Press*, 17 October 2003.

52 Paul Johnson, 577.

53 Rabbi Noah M. Gamze, Detroit, to the editor of *Commentary*, n.d., Richler Fonds Msc 36.2.46.

54 M. Brown, "Zionism," 4. Joe King, 198–9.

55 Buchan, 44, 101.

56 Richler to Bob Gottlieb, [1973?], Richler Fonds Acc. #582/4.25.

57 Richler to Bob Gottlieb, [1973?], Richler Fonds Acc. #582/4.25.

58 Weintraub to Richler, 22 January 1970, Richler Fonds Msc 36.14.3.

59 Emma Richler, *Sister Crazy*, 50.

60 Harold Keller to Richler, 19 July 1968, Richler Fonds Msc 36.3.46.

61 Cameron interview, 122. McCormick interview, Richler Fonds Acc. #582/152.16.

62 Tony Godwin to Richler, 30 June 1968, Richler Fonds Msc 36.4.60.

63 Richler, Notes and Outline for an Original Screenplay, "The Survivor," Richler Fonds Acc. #680/27.9.

64 Richler to Ken Lindenberg, 22 July 1969, Richler Fonds Acc. #680/27.9.

65 Richler, Notes and Outline for an Original Screenplay, "The Survivor," Richler Fonds Acc. #680/27.9.

66 *Shovelling*, 20.

67 Richler, "The Aging of Mordecai Richler," 12–14, Richler Fonds Acc. #582/163.1.

68 *The New Yorker*, 7 March 1988. Richler, *Belling the Cat*, 91–2.

69 Sam Orbaum, "Make," 19. Martin Knelman, "Ted Kotcheff: A wandering son heads home to film Richler's Duddy Kravitz," *Globe and Mail* (19 August 1972): 25, Richler Fonds Msc 36.55.1. Lindor Reynolds, "'Just a Charm Ball': Richler the Curmudgeon Still Seeks Perfection," *Winnipeg Free Press*, 25 October 1997, B10. Jake Hersh had already made brief appearances (sometimes as alter ego to Richler, sometimes not) in *The Street* and *The Apprenticeship of Duddy Kravitz*.

70 McSweeney, "Revaluing," 128.

71 Brian Moore to Richler, 1 June 1971, Richler Fonds Msc 36.9.19.99.

72 John Fowles to Richler, 18 June 1971, Richler Fonds Msc 36.4.33.

73 Joyce Weiner to Richler, 15 August 1971, Richler Fonds Msc 36.6.31. Literary agent David Machin, too, felt that he could identify the originals to a number of characters. David Machin to Richler, 20 May 196–, Richler Fonds Msc 36.5.10.

74 Cameron interview, 121. Draft of *St. Urbain's Horseman* Richler Fonds Msc 36.24.7.f65. The concerns in an early excerpt, "St. Urbain's Horseman," *Tamarack Review*, 1966, 138–9, are much reduced in the novel's finished form. *St. Urbain's Horseman*, 16.

75 Notes on *St. Urbain's Horseman* by an unidentified editor [internal evidence suggests Tony Godwin], 1, Richler Fonds Msc 36.30.1.

76 Richler to Brian Moore, 16 February 1959, Weintraub, *Started*, 230. Gibson interview, 288.

77 Wong interview, 2.

78 Florence Richler interview.

79 Marchand, "Oy," 64, Richler Fonds Acc. #582/134.8. MacGregor, 47, Richler Fonds Acc. #582/157.4. Edna Paris, Richler Fonds Acc. #582/160.7.

80 Zosky, 41, Richler Fonds Acc. #582/155.3. Avrum Richler interview.

81 Avrum Richler to Mordecai Richler, 15 August 1971, Richler Fonds Msc 36.11.20.
82 Avrum Richler interview. Avrum Richler, email, 6 October 2003.
83 Toppings interview, Richler Fonds Msc 36.30.12.
84 John Ponder to Richler, 24 June 1968, Richler Fonds Msc 36.4.13. McCormick interview, Richler Fonds Acc. #582/152.16.
85 *St. Urbain's Horseman*, 354.
86 Mensa application, Richler Fonds Msc 36.22.7. Mensa practice test paper and note from Mensa, Richler Fonds Msc 36.23.2.
87 *Shovelling*, 33.
88 *St. Urbain's Horseman*, 77. Greta Nimiroff to the editors, *New Statesman*, 9 September 1964, Richler Fonds Msc 36.10.1.
89 *Shovelling*, 24.
90 Mark Levene, 45.
91 David Roxan to Richler, 23 January 1972, Richler Fonds Acc. #582/40.43. Levene v Roxhan and others, Court of Appeal, Civil Division [1970] 3 All ER 683 [1970] 1 WLR 1322, 7 July 1970. A later summons cites the name as "Levin." Summons to Mordecai Richler and George Weidenfeld and Nicolson (Defendants), 20 May 1993, Richler Fonds Acc. #582/25.18.
92 David Roxan to Richler, 23 January 1972, Richler Fonds Acc. #582/40.43. Levene v Roxhan and others, Court of Appeal, Civil Division [1970] 3 All ER 683 [1970] 1 WLR 1322, 7 July 1970. David Roxan, "Justice Catches Up with a Vicious Pest," *News of the World*, 23 July 1963. Weintraub interview (2001).
93 Although Narizzano's own family disowned the filmmaker, Richler maintained a loose contact and praised his skill as a director. Peter Narizzano interview. Richler, "A Noted Film Writer Shatters the Great Canadian Movie Myth," 15, Richler Fonds Acc. #582/163.1. Richler, "A Corporation That Is Hearing Footsteps," 2, Richler Fonds Acc. #582/163.3.
94 David Roxan to Richler, 23 January 1972, Richler Fonds Acc. #582/40.43. Levene v Roxhan and others, Court of Appeal, Civil Division [1970] 3 All ER 683 [1970] 1 WLR 1322, 7 July 1970. Julia Roxan interview.
95 "Harry B. Stein" to Richler, 17 July 1982, Richler Fonds Acc. #582/44.18.
96 "Harry Fitznorman Stein" to Morticia Richler [14 January 1982], Richler Fonds Acc. #680/11.1.
97 "Harry B. Stein" to Richler, 17 July 1982, Richler Fonds Acc. #582/44.18.
98 Summons to Mordecai Richler and George Weidenfeld and Nicolson (Defendants), 20 May 1993, Richler Fonds Acc. #582/25.18.
99 McNay interview, Richler Fonds Msc 36.55.1.
100 Tribute to Robertson Davies, Harbourfront Festival, Richler Fonds Acc. #582/15.34.
101 Florence Richler interview. Brian Moore to Richler, 10 June 1966, Richler Fonds Msc 36.9.19. Edwards, Richler Fonds Msc 36.55.1.
102 Ted Kotcheff to Richler, 12 July n.y. [probably 1959–60], Richler Fonds Msc 36.6.54.
103 Richler, "Survivor," 29 January 1965, Richler Fonds Acc. #582/163.7.
104 Joe King, 287–8.
105 Richler distinguished between magazines that paid well but were read by none of his friends – *Life*, *Playboy* – and magazines that paid poorly, but were read by people he respected—*Encounter*, *New Statesman*, *The Spectator*, *The New York Review of Books*. Richler, "Three," 3. When he applied for a Canada

Council Senior Arts Fellowship to work on *St. Urbain's Horseman*, his referees included Mel Lasky, editor of *Encounter*. Richler Fonds Msc 36.2.48, October 1965.

106 Bellow, "Some Notes," 55–6, 61.

107 Richler, "Survivor," 29 January 1965, Richler Fonds Acc. #582/163.7.

108 Kattan, "Mordecai Richler," Richler Fonds Msc 36.54.14.

109 *Shovelling*, 19.

110 Bellow, "Some Notes," 63.

111 Richler, "Survivor," 29 January 1965, Richler Fonds Acc. #582/163.7.

112 Sir Harold Nicolson in *Writers on World War II*, 26.

113 Richler, "Who Is a Jew?" Richler Fonds Acc. #582/163.8.

114 Chaim Kaplan, from *Scroll of Agony*, in *Writers on World War II*, 23.

115 Cameron interview ms, 17, Richler Fonds Msc 36.54.1. It's unclear why Cameron cut this from the published interview.

116 Ravvin, 39.

117 David Roxan to Richler, 23 January 1972, Richler Fonds Acc. #582/40.43.

118 *St. Urbain's Horseman*, 436.

119 Martha Gellhorn, from *The Face of War*, in *Writers on World War II*, 645.

120 Paul Johnson, 498.

121 Brian Moore to Richler, 1 June 1971, Richler Fonds Msc 36.9.19.99.

122 Draft of *St. Urbain's Horseman*, Richler Fonds Msc 36.25.1. Draft of *St. Urbain's Horseman*, Richler Fonds Msc 36.30.6. "St. Urbain's Horseman," *Tamarack Review*, 142.

123 Notes on *St. Urbain's Horseman* by an unidentified editor [internal evidence suggests Tony Godwin], 1, Richler Fonds Msc 36.30.1.

124 Paul Johnson, 486.

125 *St. Urbain's Horseman*, 34.

126 Daniel Richler interview.

127 Brian Moore to Richler, 22 March 1971, Richler Fonds Msc 36.9.19.

128 Emma Richler, *Sister Crazy*, 39.

129 Suzanne Rosenberg, *A Soviet Odyssey*, 10–32. *Errand*, 82–6, 134–6. Zinde-Walsh interview. Avrum Richler interview. An unidentified fragment in the Richler papers also includes an account of Rabbi Yudel Rosenberg's attempt to adopt "Shoshannah" Rosenberg, and of Anna's (Helen's) obduracy. [Lily Rosenberg?], [unidentified fragment], Richler Fonds Acc. #680/28.1.

130 Suzanne Rosenberg, Moscow, to Richler 15 September 1971, Richler Fonds Acc. #582/40.30.

131 *St. Urbain's Horseman*, 121.

132 See Rachel Brenner, for example.

133 Michael Greenstein, for example, comments on Klein's "negative dialectics" in this regard (Greenstein, 9), while Zailig Pollock cites the postmodern tradition of the anti-detective story in the vein of Borges, Nabokov, and Robbe-Grillet (Pollock, 238).

134 None of the cusps appear in Richler's early TV-play version "My Cousin, the Horseman," where all the business is between Jake Hersh and Harry Stein. "My Cousin, the Horseman" fragment, Richler Fonds Msc 36.39.4.

135 *St. Urbain's Horseman*, 464.

136 McCormick interview, Richler Fonds Acc. #582/152.16.

137 *Sanhedrin*, 65b. Maharal, *Chiddushei Agados*, quoted in Aaron Brody, 10.

138 Franz Klutschak, "Der Golam des Rabbi Löw," *Panorama des Universums*, Vol. 8, 1841, rpt. in Hillel Kieval, 21–23. Paul Johnson, 265. Aaron Brody, 11–12. Scholem, *On the Kabbalah and Its Symbolism*, 203.

139 As Ramraj notes, Joey was Cousin Moe, not J.H., in early manuscript drafts. Ramraj, 94.
140 *St. Urbain's Horseman*, 89.
141 *Hunting*, 80.
142 *St. Urbain's Horseman*, 270.
143 Noah Richler interview.
144 Michael Folsom, "Introduction," in Mike Gold, 11.
145 "My Cousin, the Horseman," 5, Richler Fonds Msc 36.24.8.f56.
146 McCormick interview, Richler Fonds Acc. #582/152.16.
147 From *Hasidic Tales of the Holocaust*, ed. Yaffa Eliach, in Richler, *Writers on World War II*, 336.
148 Paul Johnson, 509.
149 *St. Urbain's Horseman*, 265.
150 Chaim Bermant, *The Jewish Quarterly*, 46–9, Richler Fonds Msc 36.30.12.
151 Steven M. Cohen, 28.
152 Alan Berger, 229. Steven T. Katz, 144.
153 Wiesel, *Night*, 62. Richler quotes this in *Writers on World War II*, 590.
154 *Zohar*, 376.
155 Wiesel, *Night*, 65.
156 *St. Urbain's Horseman*, 265. Wiesel, *Night*, 66, 87.
157 Neiman, 238–9. Steven T. Katz, 143. Richard Rubenstein, 223.
158 Steven T. Katz, 148–9. For the weaknesses in Rubenstein's position, see Katz, 184–190.
159 Band, 218–19.
160 *St. Urbain's Horseman*, 396.
161 Richler, "Who Is a Jew?" Richler Fonds Acc. #582/163.8. *Shovelling*, 92.
162 *Portnoy's Complaint*, 283–4, 299–300. It's not clear when Richler first read *Portnoy's Complaint*. In early 1969 he claimed that he hadn't yet read it because Roth's concerns were similar to his own and he didn't want to be influenced. *Inner Space*, 19 February 1969, Richler Fonds Msc 36.54.4.
163 In his pieces on Israel, Richler repeated a number of Kohn's points: that a street was named after Ha'am in Tel Aviv, that his name means "One of the People," that it was a pseudonym for Asher Ginzberg, that Ginzburg died in 1927, and that the street was busy now. Even Kohn's discussion of Ha'am's preference for westernized Tel Aviv and London over Jerusalem appeared, *mutatis mutandis*, as Richler's own reaction to Israel. Hans Kohn, "Introduction," *Nationalism and the Jewish Ethic: Basic Writings of Ahad Ha'am*, 7, 29. *Hunting*, 134, 147.
164 *Hunting*, 147. Hans Kohn, "Introduction," 13–14, 20–1.
165 *St. Urbain's Horseman*, 135, 257, 261, 464.
166 *Hunting*, 137, 148. *St. Urbain's Horseman*, 252.
167 *Acrobats*, 107, 169–70.
168 *Hunting*, 147.
169 *St. Urbain's Horseman*, 256. Paul Johnson, 529. Nur Masalha, 59–60.
170 Masalha, 57. *St. Urbain's Horseman*, 254. See also *Hunting*, 159–60.
171 Hannah Arendt, "Eichmann," 54.
172 Notes on *St. Urbain's Horseman* by an unidentified editor [internal evidence suggests Tony Godwin], 3, Richler Fonds Msc 36.30.1. Godwin also asked that the Horseman denouement and the trial outcome be brought together.
173 *Exodus* 20:5. *St. Urbain's Horseman*, 465.
174 *St. Urbain's Horseman*, 464.
175 Cameron interview, 126.

176 Letter from Mouth and Foot Painting Artists Ltd. Gilmour Hanko, "The Young Artist Who Broke the Sight Barrier," *Star Weekly Magazine*, 7 October 1967. Richler Fonds Msc 36.23.1.

177 (Mrs. Noel) Kathleen Edwards to Richler, 19 February 1968, Richler Fonds Msc 36.4.6. Florence believes that the latter was genuine. Florence Richler interview.

178 Florence Richler interview.

179 M.J., "Please Help Me;" Richler Fonds Msc 36.23.1.

180 *St. Urbain's Horseman*, 115–17.

181 Richler, "The Aging of Mordecai Richler," 12–14, Richler Fonds Acc. #582/163.1.

182 Jack McClelland to Richler, 13 February 1970, Richler Fonds Msc 36.8.25.

183 One characteristic, if hyperbolic reaction came from Peter Desbarats, who said "From now on, Bellow will remind me of Richler." Desbarats, "St. Urbain Street Reaches to the Ends of the Earth," *Montreal Star*, 29 May 1971.

184 Robert Fulford to Richler, 28 July 1971, Richler Fonds Msc 36.11.57.

185 John Fowles to Richler, 18 June 1971, Richler Fonds Msc 36.4.33. The fifth judge was Lady Antonia Fraser.

186 Brian Moore to Richler, 22 March 1971, Richler Fonds Msc 36.9.19.

187 *The Times*, "Booker Booked," 26 November 1971, Richler Fonds Msc 36.55.1.

CHAPTER 18

1 *Home Sweet*, 143.

2 Bill Weintraub to Richler, 23 October 1970, Richler Fonds Msc 36.14.3.

3 Nurenberger interview, 9, Richler Fonds Msc 36.54.6. Richler, "Intro: Nick," 16. *Home Sweet*, 152.

4 Richler, "Man," 2. *Home Sweet*, 153. Richler, "Intro: Nick," 16.

5 Richler, "Intro: Nick," 16. Richler, "Man," 2.

6 Allen interview, Richler Fonds Msc 36.55.1.

7 Richler, "Intro: Nick," 15.

8 Richler, "Canada: 'An Immensely Boring Country'—Until Now."

9 J. David Molson to Richler, 16 April 1971, Richler Fonds Msc 36.3.40.

10 Cameron interview, 115, 123.

11 McCormick interview, Richler Fonds Acc. #582/152.16.

12 Robert Weaver to Richler, 26 March, 20 July 1971, Richler Fonds Msc 36.2.56.

13 Bill Weintraub to Richler, 27 April 1971, Richler Fonds Msc 36.14.3.

14 Tess Taconis to Richler, 1971, Richler Fonds Msc 36.13.14. Bill Weintraub to Richler, 8 May 1971, Richler Fonds Msc 36.14.3.

15 Knelman, "How Duddy's," 22.

16 Monica McCall to Richler, 12 September, 3 March 1966, 30 January 1968, Richler Fonds Msc 36.9.13; 22 June 1970, Richler Fonds Msc 36.6.2.

17 Monica McCall telegrams to Richler, 22 June, 25 June 1971, Richler Fonds Msc 36.6.2.

18 Bob Shapiro to Monica McCall, 15 October 1971, Richler Fonds Msc 36.14.9.7a. Richler to Monica McCall, 22 September 1971, Richler Fonds Msc 36.6.2.

19 Norman Jewison to Richler, 5 February 1973, Richler Fonds Acc. #582/23.44.

20 Stanley Mann to Richler, 9 January 1974, Richler Fonds Acc. #582/13.75.

Norman Jewison to Richler, 12 September 1973, Richler Fonds Acc. #582/23.44. Les Wedman, "Jewison in no Hurry," Richler Fonds Acc. #582/154.2.

21 Monica McCall to Richler, 26 January 1971 [should be 1972], Richler Fonds Msc 36.6.2.

22 Norman Jewison to Richler, 18 April 1975, Richler Fonds Acc. #582/23.44. Jewison, *This Terrible Business Has Been Good to Me*, 241.

23 Richler to A. Davidson Dunton, 5 May 1971, Richler Fonds Msc 36.3.15.

24 Aiken interview, Richler Fonds Msc 36.55.1.

25 Richler to Monica McCall, 22 September 1971, Richler Fonds Msc 36.6.2.

26 Pape interview, Richler Fonds Msc 36.55.1. *Home Sweet*, 4.

27 Geoffrey James, 11, Richler Fonds Msc 36.30.12. Noah Richler, "My," B3.

28 Noah Richler, quoted in Posner, *Last*, 167.

29 Richler to Jack McClelland, 8 September 1967, Richler Fonds Msc 36.8.23.

30 Richler, "Bedlam in Bytown," 27.

31 Letter [signature cut off] to the *Star Weekly* [December 1967], Richler Fonds Msc 36.12.43.

32 *Home Sweet*, 54.

33 Richler, "Endure," 48.

34 *Brandon Sun*, 3 March 1970.

35 Arnold Cohen, YMHA Community Centre, Winnipeg to Richler, 19 October 1971, Richler Fonds Msc 36.14.26.

36 Christina Somerville to Robert Fulford, editor *Saturday Night*, 13 April 1970, 4, Richler Fonds Msc 36.11.57.25.

37 William French, "Books and Bookmen," [*Globe and Mail*?] 8 March 1969, Richler Fonds Msc 36.54.14.

38 Marchand, "Oy," 62, Richler Fonds Acc. #582/134.8.

39 Robert E. Lewis to Richler, 27 February 1969, Richler Fonds Msc 36.4.8

40 Hurtig, *Twilight*, 33.

41 Richler, "Endure," 57, 59.

42 *Home Sweet*, 138, 73.

43 Browne interview, Richler Fonds Msc 36.55.1.

44 The anthology began as an issue on Canadian writing for *London Magazine*. Robert Weaver to Richler, 7 May 1965, Richler Fonds Msc 36.2.56.

45 Browne interview, Richler Fonds Msc 36.55.1.

46 Fulford, *Best Seat in the House*, 199. Aiken interview, Richler Fonds Msc 36.55.1.

47 Mel Hurtig to Richler, 5 July 1971, Richler Fonds Msc 36.7.32. Hurtig referred in particular to Richler's, "Would Canadian Coupon-Clippers Give the People A Better Deal than American Coupon-Clippers?" *Weekend Magazine*, 26 June 1971, Richler Fonds Acc. #582/163.8.

48 Aiken interview, Richler Fonds Msc 36.55.1. "Mordecai Richler on Canadian Novels, Film, Publishing and *Duddy Kravitz*," *Manitoban*, 22 October 1974, 6, Richler Fonds Acc. #582/155.1.

49 Pape, "After." Richler Fonds Msc 36.8.7. *Home Sweet*, 4–5.

50 Jack McClelland to G.V. Svefhmikov, 23 February 1972, Richler Fonds Msc 36.8.25. A.H. Qureshi,Topair Employment Agency, to Florence Richler, 21 March 1972, Richler Fonds Msc 36.13.32.

51 Emma Richler, *Sister Crazy*, 17.

52 Jack McClelland to G.V. Svefhmikov, 23 February 1972, Richler Fonds Msc 36.8.25.

53 Noah Richler, "My," B3.

54 Richler, "On Being Jewish," 4, Richler Fonds Acc. #582/110.20.
55 Florence Richler interview. In *Feed My Dear Dogs*, Jem is reluctant to move to "dad's country," all the more so because her Mum shares the reluctance. Emma Richler, *Feed My Dear Dogs*, 68–9, 81.
56 Robert Weaver to Richler, 14 March 1972, Richler Fonds Msc 36.2.56. Robert Fulford to Richler, 30 March 1972, Richler Fonds Msc 36.11.57. Brian Moore to Richler, 11 March 1972, Richler Fonds Msc 36.9.19. Florence Richler interview.
57 Florence Richler interview.
58 George Anthony, "St. Urbain's Richler rides again," *Toronto Telegram*, 5 June 1971. McCormick interview, Richler Fonds Acc. #582/152.16.
59 Richler to the bursar, St. Paul's School, 31 January 1972, Richler Fonds Msc 36.12.38. Michael Ryval, "St Urbain Craftsman," *Financial Post*, April 1980, 58, Richler Fonds Acc. #582/161.1.
60 McCormick interview, Richler Fonds Acc. #582/152.16. Noah Richler, "My," B3.
61 "Artist with a Message," *New/Nouvelle Generation* (Baron Byng), 1:3, May 1965, Richler Fonds Msc 36.54.14. Duhm-Heitzmann, 28, Richler Fonds Acc. #582/161.1.
62 Daniel Richler interview. Noah Richler interview.
63 Richler, "How Duddy's Daddy Did It," 52.
64 Gorman, 3.
65 Zosky, 41, Richler Fonds Acc. #582/155.3.
66 Bernard Ostry interview.
67 Richler to A. Davidson Dunton, 5 May 1971, Richler Fonds Msc 36.3.15.
68 A. Davidson Dunton to Richler, 16 July 1971, Richler Fonds Msc 36.3.15.
69 Richler, "People of Our Time: Coming Home Again," 1 September 1975.
70 Florence Richler, 40.
71 Donia Mills, "Richler," Richler Fonds Acc. #582/154.2.
72 A. Davidson Dunton to Richler, 30 August 1971, 14 September 1971, Richler Fonds Msc 36.3.15.
73 B.W. Jones to Richler, 5 January 1972, Richler Fonds Msc 36.3.15. Rob McDougall to Richler, 5 September 1972, Richler Fonds Acc. #582/12.63.
74 James Downey, quoted in Posner, *Last*, 177–8.
75 Rob McDougall to Richler, 24 August 1973, Richler Fonds Acc. #582/12.63.
76 Richler to A. Davidson Dunton, 5 May 1971, Richler Fonds Msc 36.3.15.
77 Richler to A. Davidson Dunton, 5 May 1971, Richler Fonds Msc 36.3.15.
78 Richler, "A Few Words of Advice for the Beginning Novelist," 1, Richler Fonds Acc. #582/114.1. *Home Sweet*, 168. "Letter from Ottawa," *Harper's*, June 1975.
79 John Aylen in *The Montreal Gazette*, "Richler's Friends Have Their Say," (7 July 2001) 1.
80 Makow, "Master's," Richler Fonds Acc. #582/135.9.
81 Makow, "Master's," Richler Fonds Acc. #582/135.9.
82 Makow, "Master's," Richler Fonds Acc. #582/135.9.
83 James Downey, quoted in Posner, *Last*, 178.
84 Mel Hurtig to Richler, 15 June 1973, Richler Fonds Acc. #582/14.14.
85 Hurtig, *Twilight*, 33–4. Hurtig tried, jokingly, to make up to Richler in 1978. Mel Hurtig to Richler, 13 February 1978, Richler Fonds Acc. #582/21.69.
86 Gruending, Richler Fonds Msc 36.42.21.
87 Jack McClelland to Richler, 26, 28 March, 26 April 1973, 13 September 1974, Richler Fonds Acc. #582/27.8. McClelland, *Imagining*, 177–9, 194–6.

88 Peter Thompson, Committee for an Independent Canada, to Richler, [Spring 1971?], Richler Fonds Acc. #582/14.14.

89 Fetherling.

90 "Choosing the Choicest," [1979?], Richler Fonds Acc. #582/45.5. Adrian Waller, "Once a Month," *Quill & Quire* (November 1974), Richler Fonds Acc. #582/161.2.

91 Adrian Waller, "Once a Month," *Quill & Quire* (November 1974), Richler Fonds Acc. #582/161.2.

92 *The Acrobats*, 147. Richler, "The Survivor."

93 *Smaller*, 96.

94 Richler, "Memories of Brian Moore."

95 McSweeney, "Revaluing," 120.

96 Reader's report on Hugh MacLennan, *Rivers of Canada*, Richler Fonds Acc. #582/9.3.

97 Fetherling.

98 Reader's reports on Rudy Wiebe, *The Temptations of Big Bear*; W.O. Mitchell, *The Vanishing Point*; Peter Such, *Riverrun*, Richler Fonds Acc. #582/9.3.

99 Jack McClelland to Richler, 31 March 1975, Richler Fonds Acc. #582/27.8.

100 Reader's reports on Silvia Fraser, *The Candy Factory* (1975); Adele Wiseman, *The Crack-pot* [sic]; Morley Callaghan, *A Fine and Private Place*; Charles Templeton; Don Harron, *Charlie Farquarson's Jogfree of Canada*; Dave Broadfoot, *Sex and Security*; Roch Carrier *They Won't Demolish Me*; Ray Smith, *Lord Nelson Tavern*; Matt Cohen, *The Disinherited*, Richler Fonds Acc. #582/9.3.

101 Reader's reports on Hugh Garner, *One Damn Thing after Another*; Margaret Laurence *The Diviners*, Richler Fonds Acc. #582/9.3.

102 Reader's report on Joanna Glass, *Recollections of a Mountain Summer*; Dennis Patrick Sears, *The Lark in the Clear Air*; Dennis Lee, *Alligator Pie*, Richler Fonds Acc. #582/9.3.

103 Reader's reports on Lita-Rose Betcherman, *The Swastika and the Maple Leaf*; C.P. Stacey, *A Very Double Life*, Richler Fonds Acc. #582/9.3. Richler to James Ellison, 27 August 1973, Richler Fonds Acc. #582/8.20. Reader's reports on Lester Pearson, *Mike Volume 2*, Richler Fonds Acc. #582/9.2. Reader's report on Farley Mowat, *The Snow Walker*; Lord Thomson, *After I Was Sixty*; Barry Broadfoot, *Six War Years*; Grant MacEwen, *Sitting Bull, the Years in Canada*, Richler Fonds Acc. #582/9.3.

104 *St. Urbain's Horseman*, 460.

105 1972–81, Richler Fonds Acc. #582/7.20.

106 Rabinovitch, "The Man." Jack Rabinovitch interview.

CHAPTER 19

1 Richler to the CBC [November–December 1973?], Richler Fonds Acc. #582/11.53.

2 Richler, *The Bells of Hell*, 47, Richler Fonds Acc. #582/163.2.

3 Richler, "A Corporation," 3, Richler Fonds Acc. #582/163.3.

4 Richler, *The Bells of Hell*, 50, Richler Fonds Acc. #582/163.2.

5 B.G. Kayfetz (National Joint Community Relations Committee of Canadian Jewish Congress and B'nai B'rith) to J.C. Horwitz, QC, 3 January 1974, Richler Fonds Acc. #582/31.21.

6 Noah Richler interview.

7 Richler, *The Bells of Hell*, 49, Richler Fonds Acc. #582/163.2.

8 Richler, *The Bells of Hell*, 40, Richler Fonds Acc. #582/163.2.

9 "Critical and Audience Reaction to The Bells of Hell," Richler Fonds Acc. #582/11.53.

10 Graeme Gibson, Marian Engel, Harold Horwood, and Rudy Wiebe to the editor, *Globe and Mail*, 3 January 1974.

11 Pierre Berton telegraph to Lister Sinclair, 27 December 1973, Richler Fonds Acc. #582/7.54.

12 Richler, "A Corporation," 3, Richler Fonds Acc. #582/163.3. B.G. Kayfetz (National Joint Community Relations Committee of Canadian Jewish Congress and B'nai B'rith) to J.C. Horwitz, QC, 3 January 1974, Richler Fonds Acc. #582/31.21.

13 Richler, "A Corporation," 3–4, Richler Fonds Acc. #582/163.3.

14 Norman Jewison to Richler, 12 September 1973, Richler Fonds Acc. #582/23.44.

15 Blaik Kirby, "CBC Will Reconsider Its Decision to Cancel Mordecai Richler Play," *Globe and Mail*, 30 December 1973.

16 8 January 1974, Richler Fonds Acc. #582/11.53. Richler, *The Bells of Hell*, 40, Richler Fonds Acc. #582/163.2. *Globe and Mail*, 3 January 1974.

17 Ben Nobleman, "Opinion: 'Airing of Richler Play in Line with CBC's Past Performance,'" *Saturday Night*, 8 February 1974, 5, Richler Fonds Acc. #582/155.6.

18 L. Ian MacDonald, "Bells of Hell: All That Fuss for This?" *The Montreal Gazette*, 25 January 1974, Richler Fonds Acc. #582/155.6.

19 Richler, *Maclean's* column manuscript, n.d., Richler Fonds Acc. #582/115.22.

20 Monica McCall to Richler, 24 February 1972, Richler Fonds Msc 36.6.2. Stanley Mann to Richler, 9 January 1974, Richler Fonds Acc. #582/13.75. Stephen D. Geller to Richler, 4 May 1972, Richler Fonds Acc. #582/18.54.

21 Michael Spencer to Richler, 23 February 1972, Richler Fonds Msc 36.3.1.

22 Knelman, "How," 18, Richler Fonds Acc. #582/155.1.

23 Richler, "How Duddy's Daddy Did It," 50.

24 Leonard Wasser (Writers Guild of America) to John Kemeny (Theseus Films), July 1974, Richler Fonds Acc. #582/48.56. Lionel Chetwynd, Ted Kotcheff, quoted in Posner, *Last*, 186–9. Richler, "How Duddy's Daddy Did It."

25 Richler, "How Duddy's Daddy Did It," 50.

26 Press Kit for *The Apprenticeship of Duddy Kravitz*, Richler Fonds Msc 36.32.5.

27 Haberman, Richler Fonds Acc. #582/154.2.

28 Richler, "A Noted Film Writer Shatters the Great Canadian Movie Myth."

29 This is, of course, Richler's version of the story. *Cinema Canada*, interview, 20.

30 Richler, "How Duddy's Daddy Did It," 52.

31 Press Kit for *The Apprenticeship of Duddy Kravitz*, Richler Fonds Msc 36.32.5.

32 Knelman, "How," 19, Richler Fonds Acc. #582/155.1. Dane Lanken, "With Duddy and His Gang Down on St. Urbain Street," *The Montreal Gazette* (6 April 1974): 45, Richler Fonds Msc 36.32.4.

33 Press Kit for *The Apprenticeship of Duddy Kravitz*, Richler Fonds Msc 36.32.5.

34 Knelman, "How," 20, Richler Fonds Acc. #582/155.1.

35 Haberman, Richler Fonds Acc. #582/154.2.

36 Knelman, "How," 20, Richler Fonds Acc. #582/155.1.

37 Kareda, "Why," Richler Fonds Acc. #582/154.2.

38 Michael Samuelson to Richler, 28 May 1974, Richler Fonds Acc. #582/37.4.

39 Knelman, "How," 21, Richler Fonds Acc. #582/155.1.

40 Reader Reports #2 and #3 on *The Apprenticeship of Duddy Kravitz* screenplay, in Carole Langlois, CFDC, to John Kemeny, 17 July 1973, Richler Fonds Acc. #582/22.3.

41 Press Kit for *The Apprenticeship of Duddy Kravitz*, Richler Fonds Msc 36.32.5.

42 Richler, "How Duddy's Daddy Did It," 51–2.

43 Thomas Schnurmacher, "Mordecai Makes a Movie," *Ottawa Citizen*, 19 January 1974, Richler Fonds Acc. #582/154.2.

44 Haberman, Richler Fonds Acc. #582/154.2. *The Montreal Gazette*, 15 April 1974, Richler Fonds Acc. #582/154.2.

45 Kotcheff Tribute.

46 Andrew Silow Carroll, "The Wisdom of Solomon," *Broward Jewish World* (6–12 July 1990): 16, Richler Fonds Acc. #582/159.1.

47 Mordecai Richler, Avrum Richler, quoted in Posner, *Last*, 182, 21.

48 Daniel Richler interview. Noah Richler interview.

49 Emma Richler, *Sister Crazy*, 98. Florence Richler interview. Noah Richler interview.

50 Florence Richler interview.

51 Noah Richler interview.

52 Avrum Richler interview. Avrum isn't sure that it was the movie premiere but is certain that it was a function related to the movie. Zosky, 41, Richler Fonds Acc. #582/155.3, also cites 1974 as the date of the final break between Richler and Lily.

53 Lily Rosenberg to Ruth Albert [#3], [1978–9], Private Collection of Lionel Albert.

54 Leonard Wasser, Writers Guild of America, to John Kemeny, 24 July 1974, Richler Fonds Acc. #582/48.56.

55 Richler to the editor, *The Montreal Gazette*, 23 November 1977, Richler Fonds Acc. #582/161.2 and Richler Fonds Acc. #582/39.6. Richler was responding to an article in the 18 November *Gazette*. Zosky, 41, Richler Fonds Acc. #582/155.3.

56 Alan Waldman, "An Interview with Lionel Chetwynd," Writer's Guild of America, 1999 and 2002, www.wga.org/craft/interviews/chetwynd.html, 9 September 2003.

57 Lionel Chetwynd, "DC 9/11," quoted in Doug Saunders, "White House Insider Cleans Up Bush's Image on Film," *Globe and Mail*, 28 May 2003, www.the-globeandmail.com/servlet/story/RTGAM.20030528.ufilmo528/BNStory/Internati onal/, 29 September 2003.

58 Maulucci interview, Richler Fonds Acc. #582/124.20.

59 Anonymous to Richler, n.d., Richler Fonds Acc. #582/37.3. Donia Mills, "Richler," Richler Fonds Acc. #582/154.2.

60 Bill Kenly, Paramount Pictures, Screening Report for *The Apprenticeship of Duddy Kravitz*, 30 May 1974, Richler Fonds Acc. #582/33.44.

61 Cathi Polich, Paramount Pictures, Screening Report for *The Apprenticeship of Duddy Kravitz*, 3 June 1974, Richler Fonds Acc. #582/33.44.

62 Wedman, Richler Fonds Acc. #582/155.1.

CHAPTER 20

1 Wong interview, 3.

2 Nelson Wyatt, "Jacob Two-Two's Mom Likes Cartoon," *Winnipeg Free Press*, 3 September 2003, D2.

3 Richler to Jack McClelland, 3 March 1959, Richler Fonds Acc. #680/7.55. Richler, "The Last Plum in the House" [1966 or 1967?], Richler Fonds Acc. #680/28.3.

4 Wong interview, 3.

5 *Jacob Two-Two Meets the Hooded Fang*, 79, 16.

6 Nodelman, 36.

7 Richler, "Three," 4.

8 *Jacob Two-Two Meets the Hooded Fang*, 84.

9 Chenoweth, 53. H. J. Kirchhoff, A14, Richler Fonds Acc. #680/44.

10 Jack McClelland to Richler, 18 January 1972, Richler Fonds Acc. #582/27.8.

11 Richler to André Deutsch, 31 March 1973, Richler Fonds Acc. #582/5.53.

12 Jack McClelland to Richler, 22 March 1973, Richler Fonds Acc. #582/27.8.

13 Lily Poritz Miller, Senior Trade editor, McClelland & Stewart, to Richler, 1 May 1973, Richler Fonds Acc. #582/27.8.

14 Nina Bourne, Knopf, to Richler, 12 January 1972, Richler Fonds Acc. #582/4.25.

15 Lily Poritz Miller, senior trade editor, McClelland & Stewart, to Richler, 1 May 1973, Richler Fonds Acc. #582/27.8. Fabio Coen, Knopf, to Richler, 19 March 1974, Richler Fonds Acc. #582/4.25.

16 Richler, "Writing *Jacob Two-Two*," Richler Fonds Acc. #582/18.38.

17 *Atuk*, 78.

18 Richler, "Writing *Jacob Two-Two*," Richler Fonds Acc. #582/18.38.

19 Patricia Bowles, McClelland & Stewart Publicity, to Richler, 31 July 1975, Richler Fonds Acc. #582/27.8.

20 Philip Segal, "Richler Reads for Children," *Montreal Star*, 14 October 1975, Richler Fonds Acc. #582/156.12.

21 Jack Rabinovitch interview.

22 Mosher, 31.

23 Vespa, 74, Richler Fonds Acc. #582/154.2.

24 Richler, "Tony Godwin," Richler Fonds Acc. #582/123.2.

25 Ian Mayer, *Montreal Star*, to Richler, 23 July 1974, Richler Fonds Acc. #582/26.7.

26 Patricia Craig, 168.

27 Marci McDonald, Richler Fonds Acc. #582/154.2.

28 Coallier, 2. Noah Richler, "My," B2.

29 Florence Richler interview. Emma Richler, *Sister Crazy*, 93.

30 Wilson-Smith, "On Safari." Jack Rabinovitch interview.

31 Richler to M. Montmigny, 2 June 1976, Richler Fonds Acc. #582/45.63.

32 David Staines, Harvard University, to Richler, 21 July [between 1974–78], Richler Fonds Acc. #582/44.1.

33 Chenoweth, 53.

34 Richler, "Writing *Jacob Two-Two*," Richler Fonds Acc. #582/18.38. Richler, "The History of Jacob Two-Two," Richler Fonds Acc. #680/29.38.

35 Noah Richler interview.

36 Emma Richler, *Sister Crazy*, 105. Florence Richler interview.

37 Noah Richler, "I Wanted," B2. Florence Richler interview.

38 Sue Fox interview, 10.

39 Peter Downey, interview with Martha Richler, CBC Radio, 28 June 1976.

40 Daniel Richler, "Such," 42. Daniel Richler interview. Daniel Richler, *Kicking Tomorrow*, 21. Gale Group, "Daniel Richler: Writer and Broadcaster," 3. Noah Richler interview.

41 Notice of Hearing, Social Welfare Court (Montreal), 11 June 1975, Case of Noah Lichler [sic], Richler Fonds Acc. #582/40.1. Noah Richler, "I Wanted," B2. Daniel Richler interview. Noah Richler interview.

42 Noah Richler interview.

43 Such is Jem's description of her father in Emma Richler's *Sister Crazy* (192, 207), an apt description of Richler.

44 Florence Richler interview. Noah Richler, "I Wanted," B1-2.

45 Daniel Richler interview.

46 *Home Sweet*, 220, 210.

47 Hurtig, *Twilight*, 34. Mel Hurtig to the editor, *Edmonton Journal*, 9 October 1985, Richler Fonds Acc. #582/155.3.

48 Emma Richler, *Sister Crazy*, 82. Florence Richler interview.

49 Richler, quoted in Murray Waldren, "A Niche between Saga and Satire," *The Weekend Australian*, 3–4 November 1990, Richler Fonds Acc. #582/159.3.

50 Gorde Sinclair, "...For Hartwell," Richler Fonds Acc. #582/156.12. Richler had gone so far as to agree on a contract with Knopf for the book. Monica McCall to Richler, 14 March 1975, Richler Fonds Acc. #582/22.6.

51 Itinerary, 1974 March, Richler's holographic note, Richler Fonds Acc. #582/32.33.

52 Gorde Sinclair, "...For Hartwell," Richler Fonds Acc. #582/156.12.

53 Deborah Rogers to Richler, 13 July 1973, 4 April, 13 March 1974, Richler Fonds Acc. #582/40.22.

54 Noah Richler interview. Noah Richler, "I Wanted," B2.

55 Kissel interview, Richler Fonds Acc. #582/154.2.

56 Richler, "O God!" 18, Richler Fonds Acc. #582/155.2.

57 Lionel Chetwynd, Robert Shapiro quoted in Posner, *Last*, 191.

58 *Back to Ibiza*, Richler Fonds Acc. #582/65.4, 126. Richler, "Screen." Richler to Bob [?] [n.d.], Richler Fonds Acc. #582/39.6. In *Back to Ibiza*, written soon after the events, Richler, possibly to avoid libel suits, implies that the Hollywood visit occurred in 1971.

59 Richler, "Screen." Richler, *Broadsides*, 97.

60 Richler, David Giler, and Jerry Belson, *Fun with Dick and Jane*.

61 David Giler and Jerry Belson eventually received credit alongside Richler, but W.O. Richter and John Rappaport also worked on the film. Columbia Pictures, Notice of Tentative Writing Credit for "Dick & Jane," Richler Fonds Acc. #582/14.7.

62 Richler, David Giler, and Jerry Belson, *Fun with Dick and Jane*.

63 Richler, *Dick and Jane*, 2 December 1975, Bart-Palevsky Productions, Columbia Pictures, Burbank, 123–30, Richler Fonds Acc. #680/26.5. In the other ending found among the Richler Papers, Dick, because he was so creative as a bank robber, gets an executive position in the aerospace company he robbed. He heads a new division slated to work on undersea exploration. Richler, *Dick and Jane* As Shot Script, 128–30, Richler Fonds Acc. #582/147.1. This appears to be an ending in which either Richler or another writer tried to salvage a minimal hint of the original script's satire.

64 Marge White, credits administrator, Writers Guild of America, to Columbia Pictures, 20 May 1976, Richler Fonds Acc. #582/48.4.

65 *Back to Ibiza*, Richler Fonds Acc. #582/65.4, 126.

66 Richler to Bob [?] [n.d.], Richler Fonds Acc. #582/39.6.

CHAPTER 21

1 The article, with additions, appears in *Broadsides* as "Of Spiritual Guides, Witches and Wiccans."

2 Jeanne Reichstein to Richler, 26 June 1974, Richler Fonds Acc. #582/38.4.

3 Kissel interview, Richler Fonds Acc. #582/154.2. A pirated edition of the

book would appear even in Bengali. Marchand, "Caught," C1, Richler Fonds Acc. #680/44.

4 Sybil Steinberg, "Mordecai Richler," 45, Richler Fonds Acc. #582/159.1.

5 Deborah Rogers to Richler, 18 March 1977, Richler Fonds Acc. #582/40.22.

6 Emma Richler, *Feed My Dear Dogs*, 282.

7 Goodman interview, Richler Fonds Acc. #582/157.2. *Back to Ibiza*, Richler Fonds Acc. #582/65.4, 56, 106, 68. *The Montreal Gazette*, "Richler's Friends," 3. Florence Richler, 42.

8 *Back to Ibiza*, Richler Fonds Acc. #582/65.4, 162, 164–9, 67, 113–14. *Images of Spain*, 20. *Joshua*, 332.

9 *Back to Ibiza*, Richler Fonds Acc. #582/65.4, 56, 11, 167a.

10 Chenoweth, 53.

11 Jacob Richler, B4.

12 Goodman interview, Richler Fonds Acc. #582/157.2. *Back to Ibiza*, Richler Fonds Acc. #582/65.4, 80. Michael Ryval, "St Urbain Craftsman," *Financial Post*, April 1980, 56, 58, Richler Fonds Acc. #582/161.1. 56.

13 Michael Darling to Richler, 14 September 1978, Richler Fonds Acc. #582/15.24.

14 Richler to the Editor, *Globe and Mail*, 23 April 1976, Richler Fonds Acc. #582/19.16.

15 Richler, Reader's Report on Farley Mowat, *The Snow Walker*, Richler Fonds Acc. #582/9.3.

16 Alice Munro to Richler, 8 May 1974, Richler Fonds Acc. #582/30.82; 22 May 1974, Richler Fonds Acc. #680/8.31.

17 The attempt to ban *The Diviners* occurred in Lakefield, February 1976. James King, 341. *The Apprenticeship of Duddy Kravitz* was briefly removed from English courses in grades 11–13 in York County. A week later, the York County Board of Education voted 12–2 to reinstate *Duddy*. Beverley Slopen, [1975 or 1976], Canadian Book Publishers Council Newsletter, Richler Fonds Acc. #582/42.48.

18 Margaret Laurence to Richler, 3 March 1977, Richler Fonds Acc. #582/24.84.

19 Margaret Laurence to Richler, 3 March 1977, Richler Fonds Acc. #582/24.84.

20 Alice Munro to Richler, 5 March 1977, Richler Fonds Acc. #582/30.82.

21 Richler, "Home," 7, Richler Fonds Acc. #582/163.3.

22 W.H. New to Richler, 5 April 1977, Richler Fonds Acc. #582/45.82.

23 Canada Council, 27 April 1977 News Release, Richler Fonds Acc. #582/10.51. Laurence wrote the blurb for *Bear*, a job traditionally given to the judge who had advocated the winning book.

24 Richler, "It's a Great," Richler Fonds Acc. #582/163.5.

25 The list is reprinted in Charles Steele, *Taking Stock*, but presumably due to a typographical error *The Stone Angel* is missing from its place atop the one hundred!

26 Richler, "It's a Great," Richler Fonds Acc. #582/163.5.

27 Jack McClelland to Richler, 28 February 1978, *Imagining Canadian Literature*, 232.

CHAPTER 22

1 Richler Fonds Acc. #582/8.20.

2 MacGregor, 47, Richler Fonds Acc. #582/157.4.

3 Harold Greenberg, president, Astral Bellevue Pathé, to Michael Spencer, Canadian Film Development Corporation, 26 September 1977, Richler Fonds

Acc. #582/6.38. "Bigger Budget Movies Ahead Says Melzack," *Montreal Star*, 29 November 1977, Richler Fonds Acc. #582/155.1.

4 Monica McCall to Richler, 29 September 1978, Richler Fonds Acc. #582/22.6. Margaret McKelvey to Monica McCall, 16 February 1979, Richler Fonds Acc. #582/22.6.

5 *Barney's Version*, 77.

6 Richler, "Day," Richler Fonds Acc. #582/163.4.

7 Most of the names that Richler suggested placed the novel in the *Bildungsroman* tradition, but none of them seem particularly inspired. "The Education of Joshua Bloom," "Time and Fevers," "Shapiro's Progress," "All the Running You Can Do," "Shapiro Then and Now," "Joshua Like the Player Piano," Richler Fonds Acc. #582/65.2.

8 S. Martin, "Insult," 3, Richler Fonds Acc. #582/160.7.

9 See Robert Thacker, *Alice Munro: Writing Her Lives*.

10 Ramraj with some justice calls the novels "episodic" (11).

11 "Richler Writes Most Ambitious Novel," *Saskatoon Star-Phoenix*,14 June 1980, Richler Fonds Acc. #582/157.2.

12 Erna Paris, Richler Fonds Acc. #582/160.7.

13 Avrum Richler interview. See the foreword to this book.

14 For example, Ramraj, 124.

15 Craniford, 147. Erna Paris, Richler Fonds Acc. #582/160.7. Slopen, "Richler's Mother."

16 In a brown envelope entitled "Lily's poison lying pen. her mind is twist and sick" [*sic*], Ruth kept three letters that arrived in close succession from Lily. Lily Rosenberg to Ruth Albert [#1], [1978–79], private collection of Lionel Albert. The letters are undated, but a reference to "the strike at the *Montreal Star*" places them in 1978–79. Lionel Albert, email, 31 October 2002. Thanks to Lionel Albert for noting the significance of this detail.

17 Lily Rosenberg to Ruth Albert [#3], [1978–79], private collection of Lionel Albert.

18 *Errand*, 104, 140.

19 Lily Rosenberg to Ruth Albert [#3], [1978–79], private collection of Lionel Albert.

20 Lionel Albert, email, 3 October 2002.

21 Zinde-Walsh interview.

22 Avrum Richler to Mordecai Richler, 3 September 1980, Richler Fonds Acc. #582/36.24.

23 Lily Rosenberg to Jules Rosenberg, 7 October 1984, Private Collection of Lionel Albert.

24 Avrum Richler to Mordecai Richler, 8 June 1988, Richler Fonds Acc. #582/36.34. Avrum Richler interview.

25 Eve Richler, Avrum Richler, quoted in Posner, *Last*, 338.

26 *The Errand Runner*, 9.

27 Beverley Slopen, "Publishing a Cinch for Novelists' Wives," *The Montreal Gazette*, 14 August 1982, Richler Fonds Acc. #582/161.1. Beverley Slopen, "Richler's Mother Writes Memoirs," *The Montreal Gazette*, 3 January 1981, 41, Richler Fonds Acc. #582/161.4.

28 Beverley Slopen, "Literary Acclaim Stirs Up Writers," *The Montreal Gazette*, 27 June 1981, 43, Richler Fonds Acc. #582/160.7.

29 Jon Robinson, quoted in Posner, *Last*, 183.

30 Avrum Richler interview. As late as 1994 Richler claimed that he hadn't read his mother's book. "I ... got as far as her stating that she 'gave me my father's

name.' Which seemed so creepy I shut the book." Tom Adair Richler Fonds Acc. #582/160.4.

31 Florence Richler interview.

32 "Aaron Goldberg, Spelling-Goldenberg Productions" [?], to Richler, 22 January 1981, Richler Fonds Acc. #582/42.77. The practical joker combined the names of the popular TV producers Aaron Spelling and Leonard Goldberg, who were just then riding high on the success of *Love Boat* and *Charlie's Angels*.

33 *Barney's Version*, 142.

34 *The Street*, 41. *This Year in Jerusalem*, 124.

35 Lionel Albert interview. Lionel Albert, email, 14 October 2002.

36 A rag-woman, in other words. Daniel Richler interview.

37 Emma Richler, *Feed My Dear Dogs*, 41.

38 Daniel Richler interview.

39 W.G. (Bill) Morrow, Justice of Appeal, Supreme Court of Alberta, to Richler, 4 April 1978, Richler Fonds Acc. #582/30.6.

40 Noah Richler interview.

41 Noah Richler, "I Wanted," B2.

42 *Joshua Then and Now*, 17.

43 Richler to Bob Gottlieb, 17 November 1967, Richler Fonds Acc. #582/4.25.

44 Clifford Edward [Ted] Stuart Wood, Victoria, B.C., to Richler, 25 June 1974, Richler Fonds Acc. #582/48.33.

45 *Joshua Then and Now*, 348.

46 Delaney, 82, Richler Fonds Acc. #582/157.1.

47 *Joshua Then and Now*, 367. Richler probably based Jack's philo-British attitude on Lord Thompson of Fleet, whose father, like Jack's had been a barber. Richler had interviewed Thompson on TV. Richler, "This Hour Has Seven Days," 21 November 1965.

48 Kotcheff, "Afterword," 223.

49 Marci McDonald, Richler Fonds Acc. #582/154.2.

50 Bob Todd, "The Sky's the Limit," December 1969, Richler Fonds Acc. #582/161.1.

51 Richler, "Home," 6, Richler Fonds Acc. #582/163.3.

52 Joe King, 181.

53 Richler, "Life and Times," 20–4.

54 Bill Weintraub to Richler, 29 March 1971, Richler Fonds Msc 36.14.3. Jon Robinson to Richler, 30 April 1971, Richler Fonds Msc 36.11.31.

55 *Joshua Then and Now*, 361.

56 McSweeney, "Revaluing Richler," 121.

57 MacGregor, 46, Richler Fonds Acc. #582/157.4.

58 Richler, "On Turning 50," 1, Richler Fonds Acc. #582/110.19.

59 Craniford, 101.

60 Richler, "Temptation," Richler Fonds Acc. #582/163.5.

61 Patricia Craig, 170.

62 Richler, "Temptation," Richler Fonds Acc. #582/163.5.

63 Richler, *The Rotten People*, 315–316, Richler Fonds Acc. #680/102.8.

64 Bill Weintraub to Richler, 16 June 1971, Richler Fonds Msc 36.14.3.

65 Richler, "Don't Spoil," 5, Richler Fonds Acc. #582/124.13.

66 *Joshua Then and Now*, 139.

67 Richler, "Temptation," Richler Fonds Acc. #582/163.5.

68 *Joshua Then and Now*, 16.

69 Richler, "Style and Substance," Richler Fonds Acc. #680/31.24. It's not clear

whether Richler's approval of this facet of Trudeau's policy came immediately or belatedly.

70 Timothy Findley to Richler, n.d., Richler Fonds Acc. #582/17.65.

71 *Barney's Version*, 252.

72 Peter L. Thorslev, Chairman, English Dept., University of California, L.A., to Richler, 11 April 1977, Richler Fonds Acc. #582/46.4.

73 "Peter L. Thorslev, Jr." [Brian Moore] to Richler, May 1977, Richler Fonds Acc. #582/46.4.

74 Gordon Lish to Richler, 29 November n.y., Richler Fonds Acc. #582/4.25; 2 June 1982, Richler Fonds Acc. #582/25.41.

75 *Joshua Then and Now*, 238.

76 Diana Athill to Richler, 20 April n.y., Richler Fonds Acc. #582/5.53.

77 Jack Clayton to Richler, 1 June 1978, Richler Fonds Acc. #582/13.88.

78 "Dog Was like Christ: King Diary," *The Montreal Gazette*, 4 January 1977, 4, Richler Fonds Acc. #582/50.9. Richler clipped this article. *Joshua Then and Now*, 138.

79 Richler, "Home," 5, Richler Fonds Acc. #582/163.3.

80 Symons, *The Quest for Corvo*, 289.

81 Davey, *Post-national Arguments*, 134, 139, 135, 129. Voltaire, *Candide*, 204. Rachel Brenner makes a similar critique (also mistaken, I believe) of the individualistic solutions to the novel's racial issues. Brenner, 139–41.

82 Ross Russell to Richler, 19 February 1982, Richler Fonds Acc. #582/41.6.

83 Harpur interview, Richler Fonds Acc. #582/160.7.

84 "The Richler Challenge/Le défi de Richler," 18–19 March 2004, Montreal. www.fabula.org/actualities/article77725.php.

85 "A Fellow Jewess" to Richler, 19 March 1977, Richler Fonds Acc. #582/7.20.

86 Noah Richler interview.

87 Said undermines his legitimate outrage by condoning Palestinian terrorism as "'suspected' offences... mostly of the sort that any occupied population feels entitled to perform against the occupiers." Said, 136.

88 Pearl Gefen, 32, Richler Fonds Acc. #582/159.1. *Home Sweet*, 254.

89 Duart Farquharson, "Tormented by Israeli Loyalty," *Windsor Star*, 7 August 1982, Richler Fonds Acc. #582/160.8.

90 Elie Wiesel to Richler, n.d., Richler Fonds Acc. #582/47.60.

91 Janice Arnold, "Author Richler Joins in Scharansky Protest," *Canadian Jewish News*, 4 August 1978, Richler Fonds Acc. #582/161.4. B'nai B'rith Hillel Foundation of Montreal to Richler, 1 August 1978, Richler Fonds Acc. #582/6.68.

92 Saul Bellow, E.L. Doctorow, John Kenneth Galbraith, Herb Gold, Erica Jong, Norman Mailer, Bernard Malamud, Arthur Miller, Cynthia Ozick, Chaim Potok, Richler, Neil Simon, Barbara Tuchman, Kurt Vonnegut, and twelve other signatures, to the editor, *New York Times*, 27 April 1981, Richler Fonds Acc. #582/48.54.

93 Michael Greenstein appropriately calls the Mueller plot "a parody of Hemingway" (Greenstein 159). This constitutes a vast improvement over the imitation of Hemingway in *The Acrobats*.

94 Noah Richler interview.

95 *Joshua Then and Now*, 305.

96 Joe King, 302.

97 *Home Sweet Home*, 244–5, 239. The essay in *Home Sweet Home*, "Language (and Other) Problems," for twenty pages (224–44) closely follows the text of "Oh Canada: Lament for a Divided Country," which appeared in the

December 1977 issue of *Atlantic Monthly*; Richler also appended another twenty pages (244–64) written in 1983.

98 *Joshua Then and Now*, 150. *Back to Ibiza*, Richler Fonds Acc. #582/65.4, 12.

99 Richler, "Style and Substance." Gould interview 48, Richler Fonds Acc. #582/19.45.

100 *Home Sweet*, 246.

101 Stephane Venne to Richler, n.d., Richler Fonds Acc. #582/6.45.

102 Jean-François Lisée, "Mordecai Richler rides again!" *L'actualité* (1 Avril 1992): 12, Richler Fonds Acc. #582/158.6. Author's translation. Eventually Richler admitted his mistake in *Oh Canada! Oh Quebec!*, 128–9.

103 *Joshua Then and Now*, 57.

104 *Joshua Then and Now*, 65, 169.

105 Babel, 108.

106 Arthur Rawet to Richler, 9 January 1969, Richler Fonds Msc 36.11.13.

107 Paul Johnson, 328.

108 Harpur interview, Richler Fonds Acc. #582/160.7.

109 *Joshua Then and Now*, 162.

110 Todd, 20. See also Paul Johnson, 127.

CHAPTER 23

1 L. Ian MacDonald, 170.

2 Jack McClelland to Richler, 3 July 1980, Richler Fonds Acc. #582/27.9.

3 Roger de C. Nantel, Director, Honours Secretariat, Order of Canada, to Richler, 7 November 1979, Richler Fonds Acc. #582/33.2.

4 McSweeney, "Revaluing Mordecai Richler."

5 Richler to Roger de C. Nantel, director, Honours Secretariat, Order of Canada, 23 November 1979, Richler Fonds Acc. #582/33.2.

6 MacGregor, 46, Richler Fonds Acc. #582/157.4.

7 Zosky, 41, Richler Fonds Acc. #582/155.3. Martin, "Anecdotes," A4. Julian Desalis, quoted in Brownstein, "Memories," 2.

8 Beverley Slopen to Richler, 5 June, 22 July 1980, Richler Fonds Acc. #680/14.16.

9 Zosky, 41, Richler Fonds Acc. #582/155.3.

10 Florence Richler interview. Ted Kotcheff said that Richler's silences were so dense that people though he was judging them even when he wasn't. MacGregor, 46, Richler Fonds Acc. #582/157.4.

11 MacGregor, 46, Richler Fonds Acc. #582/157.4.

12 *Solomon Gursky Was Here*, 325.

13 Richler, Daybook 1980, Richler Fonds Acc. #582/149, 17–18 October, "Harvard."

14 Sue Fox interview, 10, Richler Fonds Acc. #680/45.1. Martha Richler to Mordecai Richler, 27 July 1987, Richler Fonds Acc. #680/10.21. Martha Richler, quoted in Posner, *Last*, 314.

15 Arnold Beichman to Richler, 7 June 1987, Richler Fonds Acc. #582/7.35. Petersen, 53, Richler Fonds Acc. #582/135.7.

16 Robert Fulford, *Saturday Night*, to Richler, 16 October 1986, Richler Fonds Acc. #582/41.26.

17 Martha Richler to Mordecai Richler, 27 July 1987, Richler Fonds Acc. #680/10.21.

18 Emma Richler to Richler, 27 January 1982, Richler Fonds Acc. #582/36.39.

19 Martha Richler to Mordecai Richler, 27 July 1987, Richler Fonds Acc. #680/10.21.
20 Gould interview, Richler Fonds Acc. #582/19.45.
21 Daniel Richler interview.
22 Jacob Richler, B1, B4.
23 Alexis Troubetzkoy, Headmaster, Appleby College (Oakville, ON) to Richler, 8 February 1985, Richler Fonds Acc. #582/6.10. Robert Manion, Headmaster, Selwyn House School, Westmount, to Richler, n.d., Richler Fonds Acc. #582/36.41.
24 Mosher, 31.
25 MacGregor, 46, Richler Fonds Acc. #582/157.4. Ted Kotcheff, quoted in Posner, *Last*, 245.
26 Richler, "Foreword," *The Best of Modern Humor*, xv.
27 Richler, "Foreword," *The Best of Modern Humor*, xvi.
28 Michael Ryval, "St Urbain Craftsman," *Financial Post*, April 1980, 56, 58, Richler Fonds Acc. #582/161.1.
29 Richler Fonds Acc. #582/42.23.
30 *Belling the Cat*, 129.
31 Florence Richler interview.
32 *Belling the Cat*, 139.
33 Richler, "A Paris Perspective," 86.
34 Eliot Kaplan, senior editor, to publicity director, GQ, 28 September 1983, Richler Fonds Acc. #582/18.57.
35 Gould interview, Richler Fonds Acc. #582/19.45.
36 Debrette's Peerage Ltd. to Richler, 8 March 1983, Richler Fonds Acc. #582/15.44.
37 *Debrett's*, 320. *Broadsides*, 37.
38 Florence Richler interview.
39 Hanes, "Richler Was," 3.
40 Roger George, quoted in Posner, *Last*, 277.
41 Noah Richler, "My," B2.
42 Noah Richler, "My," B2.
43 Florence Richler interview.
44 Bryden, "Solomon." *Solomon Gursky Was Here*, 64.
45 Beuttler, 132, Richler Fonds Acc. #582/124.4.
46 Linda McKnight to Jack McClelland, 13 October 1983.
47 Richler, "Apprenticeship of Playwright," 85, Richler Fonds Acc. #582/163.4.
48 Martin Knelman, "Broadway," 44, Richler Fonds Acc. #582/157.1.
49 Lonny Price to Richler, 12 June 1984, Richler Fonds Acc. #582/3.48.
50 Richler, "Edmonton, Edmonton," 4, Richler Fonds Acc. #582/113.17.
51 Lyle Slack, "A Critic's Inquest into the Death of Duddy," *The Spectator*, 30 June 1984, F1. Marianne Ackerman, "Musical 'Duddy' Bows Out," *The Montreal Gazette*, 5 June 1984. Lucinda Chodan, "The Philadelphia Experiment," *The Montreal Gazette*, 29 September 1987, Richler Fonds Acc. #582/155.3.
52 Richler, "Apprenticeship of Playwright," 87, Richler Fonds Acc. #582/163.4.
53 *Belling the Cat*, 240, 241, 243.
54 Richler, "Edmonton, Edmonton," 2, Richler Fonds Acc. #582/113.17.
55 Roy Stewart, Millet, Alberta, to Richler, 6 October 1985, Richler Fonds Acc. #582/38.4.
56 "Retract Richler Lies," *Edmonton Sunday Sun*, 13 October 1985, 14, Richler Fonds Acc. #582/160.8.

57 Mel Hurtig to the editor, *Edmonton Journal*, 9 October 1985, Richler Fonds
	Acc. #582/155.3.
58 *Solomon Gursky Was Here*, 58.
59 Richler, "Edmonton, Edmonton," 3, 4, 1, Richler Fonds Acc. #582/113.17.
60 "Government Helps to Make Trash Films, Richler Says," *The Montreal
	Gazette*, 9 September 1980, Richler Fonds Acc. #582/161.4. "Richler vs.
	Marshall vs. CFDC," *CineMag*, 6 September 1980, Richler Fonds Acc.
	#582/160.7.
61 Jack McClelland to Richler, 10 September 1980, Richler Fonds Acc. #582/27.9.
62 Richler, *Reinhart's Women*, 1982, Richler Fonds Acc. #582/105.4. Thomas
	Berger to Richler, 27 May 1982, Richler Fonds Acc. #582/7.48. Melissa
	Bachrach, story editor, Sherwood Productions, Culver City, California, to
	Mary Lazar, Juno Productions, Los Angeles, 29 September 1982, Richler
	Fonds Acc. #582/42.20.
63 Sid Adilman, "2 Joshua Budgets Then and Now," *Toronto Star*, 3 March
	1985, Richler Fonds Acc. #582/157.2.
64 Jay Scott, E3.
65 *Cinema Canada*, interview, 20.
66 *Cinema Canada*, interview, 18.
67 Ted Kotcheff, quoted in Posner, *Last*, 234.
68 Bruce Bailey. Allen and Walmsley, 49.
69 Ron Base, G8.
70 Canadian Film Development Corporation, reader's report on *Joshua Then and
	Now*, Richler Fonds Acc. #582/12.8. Sydney Newman to André Lamy, CFDC,
	21 June 1982, Richler Fonds Acc. #582/44.49.
71 Sydney Newman to André Lamy, CFDC, 21 June 1982, Richler Fonds Acc.
	#582/44.49. Canadian Film Development Corporation, Reader's Report on
	Joshua Then and Now, Richler Fonds Acc. #582/12.8.
72 *Cinema Canada*, interview, 18.
73 Julian Marks, Production Manager, CBC to Richler, 19 July 1984, Richler
	Fonds Acc. #582/11.53.
74 Allen and Walmsley, 45.
75 *Cinema Canada*, interview, 18.
76 Ted Kotcheff to Richler, 21 April 1984, Richler Fonds Acc. #582/24.47.
77 Ron Base, G1.
78 "Mordecai Richler: St. Urbain's Meistersinger," Richler Fonds Acc.
	#582/135.18, 27.
79 Julian Marks to L'Honorable Sénateur Maurice Riel, président du Sénat, 3
	April 1984, Richler Fonds Acc. #582/41.1.
80 Maurice Riel to Julian Marks, 8 May 1984, Richler Fonds Acc. #582/41.1.
81 Draft of letter, Richler to _____, n.d., Richler Fonds Acc. #582/39.6.
82 John Roberts, Minister of Employment and Immigration to Major-General
	M.G. Cloutier, sergeant-at-arms, House of Commons, 10 August 1984,
	Richler Fonds Acc. #582/11.30.
83 RSL Entertainment, Richler Fonds Acc. #582/41.1.
84 Allen and Walmsley, 45, 48–9. Ron Base, G8.
85 "Richler Miffed by Cannes Snub," *Fredericton Gleaner*, 31 May 1985,
	Richler Fonds Acc. #582/157.2.
86 Ron Base, G8. Jay Scott, E3.
87 Brian D. Johnson, "Even God Has His Faults," *Maclean's*, 23 September
	1985, 52, Richler Fonds Acc. #582/135.16.
88 Ted Kotcheff to Richler, 21 April 1984, Richler Fonds Acc. #582/24.47.

89 Allen and Walmsley, 47.

90 Cameron interview ms, 11.

91 Richler to Wladyslaw Pleszczyski, 13 June 1994, Richler Fonds Acc. #582/34.32.

92 Richler, *Dispatches from the Sporting Life*, 4, 7.

93 Richler to Wladyslaw Pleszczyski, 13 June 1994, Richler Fonds Acc. #582/34.32.

94 Peter Black, "Mordecai Richler, in Passing," *Log Cabin Chronicles*, 5 July 2001, www.tomifobia.com/black/mordecai_richler.shtml, 11 June 2003. MacPherson, Richler Fonds Acc. #582/160.8.

95 Richler to Wladyslaw Pleszczyski, 13 June 1994, Richler Fonds Acc. #582/34.32.

96 Fabio Coen to Richler, 17 January 1977, Richler Fonds Acc. #582/4.25.

97 Roger Kimball, Twentieth Century Fund, to Richler, 7 October 1986, Richler Fonds Acc. #582/45.56. Roger Kimball, Twentieth Century Fund, to Richler, 7 October 1986, Richler Fonds Acc. #582/45.56.

98 H.J. Kirchhoff, A14, Richler Fonds Acc. #680/44.

99 *Jacob Two-Two and the Dinosaur*, 40.

100 *Jacob Two-Two and the Dinosaur*, 12.

101 *Imagining*, 259–60. Jack McClelland news release, 16 May 1985, Richler Fonds Acc. #582/27.10. Jack McClelland news release, 30 December 1985, Richler Fonds Acc. #582/27.10.

102 Avie Bennett to Richler, 11 July 1986, Richler Fonds Acc. #582/27.10. Richler to Adrienne Clarkson, 2 November 1987, Richler Fonds Acc. #582/27.10.

103 Jack McClelland to Richler, 8 September 1987, Richler Fonds Acc. #582/29.2.

104 Florence Richler, quoted in Posner, *Last*, 246.

105 Deborah Rogers to Richler, 15 October 1982, Richler Fonds Acc. #582/40.22. André Deutsch to Richler, 1 October 1984, Richler Fonds Acc. #582/5.53.

106 Richler to Adrienne Clarkson, 2 November 1987, Richler Fonds Acc. #582/27.10.

107 Richler to Doug Gibson, [shortly after 16 March 1990], Richler Fonds Acc. #582/27.10.

108 Robert Fulford, "This Is Robert Fulford," 23 July 1968.

109 Richler, draft of individual presentation to the Parliament of Canada's Standing Committee on External Affairs and International Trade, Richler Fonds Acc. #680/31.57.

110 Richler, individual presentation to the Parliament of Canada's Standing Committee on External Affairs and International Trade, 18 November 1987, 39:49, Richler Fonds Acc. #582/162.3.

111 Don Gilmour, "Mordecai Richler," *Quill & Quire*, July 1989, Richler Fonds Acc. #582/159.2.

112 Bernard Ostry interview.

113 Todd, 22.

114 Gefen, 31, Richler Fonds Acc. #582/159.1. Drainie, Richler Fonds Acc. #582/159.1.

115 Richler wasn't alone; 60 percent of Jewish household heads in Québec had visited Israel, 45 percent more than once. Interest in Middle East news was nearly twice as high (47 percent) as interest in Québec news (26 percent) and more than twice as high as interest in Canadian national news (20 percent). Morton Weinfeld, 180.

116 Barbara Frum interview, *The Journal*, CBC-TV, 19 November 1987.

117 Richler, "Fool's Gold," Richler Fonds Acc. #582/114.4.

118 John K. Hutchens, Member of the Editorial Board, to Richler, 8 October 1988, Richler Fonds Acc. #582/8.20.
119 Edwin McDowell, "BOMC Restructures Its Jury," *New York Times*, 20 September 1988, Richler Fonds Acc. #582/160.8.
120 Sybil Steinberg, "Mordecai Richler," 46, Richler Fonds Acc. #582/159.1.
121 Al Silverman, Wilfred Sheed, quoted in Posner, *Last*, 239–40.
122 David Holloway, "Hanging Out with Moses," *Telegraph Magazine*, 2 June 1990, 24, Richler Fonds Acc. #582/159.3.
123 17 October 1988, Richler Fonds Acc. #582/8.20.
124 Clifton (Kip) Fadiman to Richler, 17 September 1988, 10 April 1990, Richler Fonds Acc. #582/17.33.

CHAPTER 24

1 Sybil Steinberg, "Mordecai Richler," 45, Richler Fonds Acc. #582/159.1.
2 See Lynne Bowen, *Muddling Through: The Remarkable Story of the Barr Colonists*, Vancouver: Douglas & McIntyre, 1992.
3 Jon Anderson interview.
4 Gefen, 30, Richler Fonds Acc. #582/159.1.
5 Noel Taylor, "Mordecai Richler," *Ottawa Citizen*, 2 December 1989, Richler Fonds Acc. #582/159.1.
6 M.M. [Monica McCall?], "Chronology," Richler Fonds Acc. #582/87.2.
7 Geoffrey James, 11, Richler Fonds Msc 36.30.12.
8 Michael Ryval, "St Urbain Craftsman," *Financial Post*, April 1980, 56, Richler Fonds Acc. #582/161.1.
9 *Shovelling Trouble*, 141.
10 Hon. Greville Janner, QC, MP, to Richler, 3 December 1984, Richler Fonds Acc. #582/14.20. Gefen 31, Richler Fonds Acc. #582/159.1.
11 Edward and Beverly Bronfman to the Richlers, 1974, 1975, 22 January 1977, Richler Fonds Acc. #582/10.12.
12 Marchand, "Oy," 148, Richler Fonds Acc. #582/134.8.
13 Newman, *Bronfman Dynasty*, 46.
14 Abella, 98, 146. *None Is too Many* was published in 1982, and, although it's not clear exactly in which year Richler read it, by 1989–90 he was using it in his research for *Oh Canada! Oh Quebec!*. In a 1992 review of *Mr. Sam*, Richler complained about Sam Bronfman's subservience before wartime Anglo authorities. *Belling the Cat*, 35–6.
15 Peter C. Newman, *Bronfman Dynasty*, 9–10.
16 Michael R. Marrus to John Fraser, editor, *Saturday Night*, 3 July [1992], Richler Fonds Acc. #582/26.56.
17 Marrus, *Mr. Sam*, 460.
18 James Dubro to John Fraser, editor, *Saturday Night*, 13 September 1992, Richler Fonds Acc. #582/41.26.
19 Greg Gatenby, Harbourfront Festival, to Richler, 28 April 1983, Richler Fonds Acc. #582/20.13.
20 Michael Darling to Richler, 10 July 1984, Richler Fonds Acc. #582/15.24.
21 *Solomon Gursky Was Here*, 286. Avrum Richler interview.
22 *Solomon Gursky Was Here*, 162.
23 Ian Mayer to Richler, 28 April 1987, Richler Fonds Acc. #582/26.7. Weintraub interview (2001).
24 Richler to Alison Samuel, 14 July 1989, Richler Fonds Acc. #582/13.51.
25 Sandra Kolber, 83.

26 *Solomon Gursky Was Here*, 214.

27 Richler to Michael Levine, 12 April 1993, Richler Fonds Acc. #582/19.33.

28 Max Richler interview.

29 Leo Kolber to Richler, 17 April 1972, Richler Fonds Msc 36.6.50.

30 Sam Gesser, quoted in Posner, *Last*, 251.

31 Yanofsky, *Mordecai and Me*, 219.

32 Craniford, 117–18.

33 "The Tatler," *Globe and Mail*, 12 March 1993, Richler Fonds Acc. #582/19.33.

34 Weintraub interview (2001). Craniford, 127.

35 Dansereau and Beaudet interview, 94. See also "Author's Note," *Solomon Gursky Was Here.*

36 Christopher Dafoe, editor, *The Beaver*, to Richler, 28 March 1988, Richler Fonds Acc. #582/7.29.

37 Rockburn interview, 187–9.

38 Richler, "On Turning 50," 3, Richler Fonds Acc. #582/110.19.

39 *Hunting Tigers under Glass*, 112.

40 See Shnayer Leiman, 32–3, and Hillel Kieval, 15–16.

41 Pearl K. Bell, "Canada Way," *The New Republic*, 7 May 1990, Richler Fonds Acc. #582/159.1.

42 Craniford, ix.

43 The same language describes Solomon's calling of Moses Berger. *Solomon Gursky Was Here*, 20, 189.

44 *Solomon Gursky Was Here*, 137, 481.

45 *Solomon Gursky Was Here*, 439.

46 *Barney's Version*, 328, 204.

47 See fragments of Timon's *Silloi* (third century BC) in A.A. Long and D.N. Sedley eds., *The Hellenistic Philosophers, Volume 1*, Cambridge: Cambridge University Press, 1987, 22–4. Northrop Frye (231) and Leon Guilhamet (24) inaccurately claim that satire *began* with pro-scientific *silloi*. In fact, personal invective from Hipponax and Archilochus dates from 3 and 4 centuries earlier. See Andrew M. Miller ed. and trans., *Greek Lyric: An Anthology in Translation*, Indianapolis: Hackett, 1996, 1–12, 104–6.

48 *Solomon Gursky Was Here*, 107.

49 Richler's essay was reprinted in *Broadsides*, 9–18.

50 *Broadsides*, 13.

51 *Joshua Then and Now*, 65.

52 David Rosenberg to Richler, 3 March 1987, Richler Fonds Acc. #582/20.15.

53 David Rosenberg, "Introduction," *Congregation*, viii.

54 David Rosenberg to Richler, 15 September 1988, Richler Fonds Acc. #582/40.29. The new volume was published in 1989 as *Testimony: Contemporary Writers Make the Holocaust Personal.*

55 Invitation to Bernard Richler Testimonial dinner, 24 January 1971, Richler Fonds Acc. #582/36.35. Baruch Rosenberg quoted approvingly from the Rabbi J. I. Schneersohn, believed by many of the Lubavitchers to be the Messiah. Yudel Rosenberg, *Jonah*, 25.

56 *Solomon Gursky Was Here*, 101. See also 519–20.

57 *Solomon Gursky Was Here*, 520–1.

58 *Solomon Gursky Was Here*, 109.

59 N. Baumoil, 10.

60 Sam Orbaum, "Make," 18.

61 *Solomon Gursky Was Here*, 440, 104, 40, 83. Gefen, 31, Richler Fonds Acc. #582/159.1.

62 Carole Corbeil, 23–4.
63 *Solomon Gursky Was Here*, 59. See also 60, 433–4.
64 *Home Sweet*, 217. The Arctic Society (Ottawa), Richler Fonds Acc. #582/6.15. Amy Edith Johnson, "The Man in the Sealskin Prayer Shawl," *New York Times Book Review* 8 April 1990, Richler Fonds Acc. #582/159.1.
65 Richler, "London for Beginners," 3, Richler Fonds Acc. #582/115.19. *St. Urbain's Horseman* (100) mentions *The Quest for Corvo*, as does *Solomon Gursky Was Here*, 394.
66 Stephen Godfrey, "I Really Feel I Took a Lot of Risks on This One," *Globe and Mail*, 8 November 1989, Richler Fonds Acc. #582/159.1.
67 He cut ten thousand words in some accounts, forty thousand in others. Richler to Carmen Callil (Chatto & Windus), n.d., Richler Fonds Acc. #582/13.51. Orbaum ,"Make 'em," 19, Richler Fonds Acc. #582/160.8.
68 Alison Samuel to Richler, 26 May, 7 July 1989, editorial comments on *Solomon Gursky Was Here*, Richler Fonds Acc. #582/13.51. Richler to Carmen Callil (Chatto & Windus), n.d., Richler Fonds Acc. #582/13.51.
69 Florence Richler interview. Florence Richler, 40.
70 *Toronto Star*, 18 October 1989, Richler Fonds Acc. #582/159.1.
71 Richler, [draft of Dental Academy Awards Night], Richler Fonds Acc. #582/87.4.
72 Florence Richler, quoted in Posner, *Last*, 218.
73 Dennis Kucherawy, "The GG Awards: Who Knows? Who Cares?" *Toronto Star Saturday Magazine*, 3 March 1990, Richler Fonds Acc. #582/159.1.
74 Robertson Davies to Richler, 12 February 1990, Richler Fonds Acc. #582/15.34. Alberto Manguel, "Literary Judges Need a Clear Mandate," *Globe and Mail*, 10 February 1990, Richler Fonds Acc. #582/159.1. David Silcox to Richler, 4 May 1992, Richler Fonds Acc. #582/42.25. Greg Gatenby, "Let's Start a New Chapter in the Governor-General's Awards History," *Toronto Star* (24 February 1990), Richler Fonds Acc. #582/159.1.
75 Richler, "Tundra," 22, Richler Fonds Acc. #582/159.4.
76 Stephen Harris, "Tales of Fortune..." *The Dominion* (New Zealand), 10 November 1990, Richler Fonds Acc. #582/159.3.
77 Richler, "Memories of Brian Moore."

CHAPTER 25

1 Dave Carpenter to Richler, 5 April 1991, Richler Fonds Acc. #582/12.66.
2 Richler, "Foreword," *Writers On World War II*.
3 Reed to Richler, 17 October 1991, Richler Fonds Acc. #582/3.48.
4 Zosky, 41, Richler Fonds Acc. #582/155.3.
5 Rex Murphy interview, *The Journal*, CBC-TV, 17 November 1989. Richler, *Oh Canada*, 153.
6 Bernard Ostry interview. Jack Rabinovitch interview.
7 Jack Rabinovitch Interview.
8 William Johnson, "Oh," 2.
9 Morton Weinfeld, 187.
10 *Oh Canada! Oh Quebec!*, 70.
11 Richard B. Holden, MNA, Westmount, to Richler, 10 October 1989, Richler Fonds Acc. #582/21.34. Peter Stockland, "Mordecai Richler's Quebec," *Toronto Sun*, 25 November 1989, Richler Fonds Acc. #582/160.8. Brendan Kelly, "Richler and the Wisdom of Solomon," *Montreal Daily News*, 14 November 1989, Richler Fonds Acc. #582/159.1. Neil Cameron, email, 15 October 2003.

12 Mary Lou Findlay, *Sunday Morning*, CBC Radio, 29 October 1989.
13 Richler, "Inside/Outside," 54, 53, 50, 48–9, 70–2.
14 Gottlieb, 22.
15 Ingrid Peritz, "About," B2, Richler Fonds Acc. #582/50.9.
16 Graham Fraser, "BQ," Richler Fonds Acc. #582/158.6.
17 *Oh Canada! Oh Quebec!*, 14.
18 Richler, "Assignment," Richler Fonds Acc. #582/153.1.
19 Lise Bissonnette, "Vu," A8.
20 H.D. Forbes, 54–5, Richler Fonds Acc. #582/161.4. This was the position of Québec's former Liberal leader, Claude Ryan. Andrew Stark, a Management professor at University of Toronto and a former aide to Mulroney, made a similar argument. Caldwell, "A Quebecker," 12, Richler Fonds Acc. #582/134.12.
21 Poliquin, "St.," 38.
22 Florence Richler interview.
23 Lysiane Gagnon, "Inside Quebec."
24 Ingrid Peritz, "About," B3, Richler Fonds Acc. #582/50.9.
25 Joseph F. Fletcher, Dept. of Political Science, University of Toronto, 3 August 1989, Richler Fonds Acc. #582/17.79.
26 Steven Davis, "Richler Was Wrong," *The Montreal Gazette* n.d., Richler Fonds Acc. #582/161.1. Davis, Richler noted, was Lysiane Gagnon's husband. *Oh Canada!*, 252. Anonymous to the editor, *New Yorker*, 23 September 1991, Richler Fonds Acc. #582/37.13.
27 Pierre Anctil, quoted in Jean-François Lisée, 17–18, Richler Fonds Acc. #582/161.4. Author's translation.
28 Richler, "The New Yorker, Quebec, and Me," *Saturday Night*, May 1992, 18. *Oh Canada!*, 95, 255.
29 Brym and Lenton, 114–15. *Oh Canada!*, 254. Richler, "The New Yorker, Quebec, and Me," *Saturday Night*, May 1992, 87.
30 *This Year in Jerusalem*, 168.
31 Csillag interview, Richler Fonds Acc. #582/162.1.
32 Morton Weinfeld, 188.
33 Richler, "The New Yorker, Quebec, and Me," *Saturday Night*, May 1992, 18.
34 Richard B. Holden, MNA, Westmount, to the editor, *The Montreal Gazette*, 22 September 1991, Richler Fonds Acc. #680/44.
35 Pauline Couture, "Richler Stirs Fury..." *Globe and Mail*, 25 September 1991, Richler Fonds Acc. #582/160.8.
36 Richard King, Paragraphe Libraire/Bookstore and Café, Montreal, 13 March 1992, Richler Fonds Acc. #582/33.43. Greg Gatenby, Harbourfront Festival, to Richler, 29 March 1992, Richler Fonds Acc. #582/20.14. "Oh Canada! Oh Quebec! Oh No!" *The Montreal Gazette*, 29 March 1992, A1, Richler Fonds Acc. #680/44. Neil MacDonald, CBC *Newsmagazine*, CBC-TV, 30 March 1992.
37 Claude Hurtubise, president, Les Éditions La Press, to Richler, Montreal, 17 June 1976, Richler Fonds Acc. #582/16.56.
38 Daniel Poliquin, "Richler's."
39 André Beaudet, [editor, *L'Impossible* and Les Éditions Balzac], to Richler, 4 Mai 1992, Richler Fonds Acc. #582/16.48. André Beaudet to Richler, 22 Juillet 1992, Richler Fonds Acc. #582/16.48.
40 Nick Auf der Maur, "Richler's Prize Pokes Fun at What's Absurd in Quebec," *The Montreal Gazette*, n.d., Richler Fonds Acc. #680/44.
41 Lynne van Luven, Richler Fonds Acc. #582/158.6.
42 Anonymous to Richler, n.d., Richler Fonds Acc. #582/39.5.

43 Anonymous to Richler, [Holograph in the margins of Richler's article "The New Yorker, Quebec, and Me," *Saturday Night*, May 1992], Richler Fonds Acc. #582/38.4.

44 Richler, "The New Yorker, Quebec, and Me," 18.

45 Gilles Duceppe, ["Les propos tenus par Mordecai Richler"] 12 mars 1992, *Débats des Communes*, 8121. Caldwell, "A Quebecker," 11, Richler Fonds Acc. #582/134.12.

46 Graham Fraser, "BQ," Richler Fonds Acc. #582/158.6.

47 Lise Bissonnette, "Comme," A8, Richler Fonds Acc. #582/162.1.

48 Manon Cornellier, Richler Fonds Acc. #582/158.6.

49 Dennis Kucherawy, "Mordecai Richler Was Here," *Toronto Star*, 6 October 1990, Richler Fonds Acc. #582/161.2.

50 *Barney's Version*, 81.

51 Alain Dubuc, "Letter from Montreal: Damaging Outburst by Richler Helps Nobody at Times like These," *Toronto Star*, 21 September 1991, Richler Fonds Acc. #582/15.51.

52 Richler to Pierre Guglielminn, 14 June 1992, Richler Fonds Acc. #582/16.50.

53 *Solomon Gursky Was Here*, 473, 550.

54 So said talk show host Madeleine Poulin, for example. Caldwell, "A Quebecker," 11, Richler Fonds Acc. #582/134.12. Pierre Anctil says that Richler's "francophones sont des fantômes; il ne les saisit pas vraiment." ("His Francophones are phantoms. He doesn't really grasp them.") Quoted in Michel Arsenault. Author's translation.

55 Lise Bissonnette, "Comme," A8, Richler Fonds Acc. #582/162.1. Author's translation.

56 *Oh Canada!*, 28. McKenzie, "Adieu" (2001), 1.

57 Richard Peterson, *Vie en Estrie Living Magazine*, May 1989, Richler Fonds Acc. #582/17.20.

58 Bauch, "Stranger," 4.

59 Lionel Albert, email, 16 September 2002.

60 Bauch, "Stranger" 5. Lionel Albert, email, 16 September 2002. Emma Richler, *Sister Crazy*, 26. Michelle Lalonde, "Richler Defends His Writing," *The Montreal Gazette*, 21 September 1991, B2, Richler Fonds Acc. #582/50.9.

61 Rabinovitch, "Mordecai," 25.

62 Poliquin, "St.," 38.

63 Lise Bissonnette, "Comme," A8, Richler Fonds Acc. #582/162.1. Author's translation.

64 Noah Richler interview.

65 *Oh Canada! Oh Québec!*, 87, 73, 114.

66 Morton Weinfeld, 187.

67 Ingrid Peritz, "About," B2, Richler Fonds Acc. #582/50.9.

68 Morton Weinfeld, 185.

69 One letter writer told Richler that *Oh Canada!* was a great book and bore *no* criticism. She recalled often being beaten up for being a Jew. Most of all she feared St-Jean-Baptiste Day and Easter. Rita to Richler, 14 August 1992, Richler Fonds Acc. #582/3.48.

70 Anne Richler (Auntie Anne) to Mordecai Richler, 6 October 1991, Richler Fonds Acc. #582/36.33.

71 Lionel Albert interview.

72 Anonymous to the editor, *New Yorker*, 23 September 1991, Richler Fonds Acc. #582/37.13.

73 Daniel Richler interview.

74 Richler, "On Being Jewish," 6, Richler Fonds Acc. #582/110.20. Emma Richler, *Sister Crazy*, 172.

75 Joe King, 322.

76 Janice Arnold, "Youth Group Distances Itself from Richler," *Canadian Jewish News*, 11 February 1993, 1, Richler Fonds Acc. #582/158.6.

77 Jean Chartier, "Les réponses de Mordecai Richler inexactes et injurieuses," *Le Devoir*, 20 March 1992, Richler Fonds Acc. #582/162.1. Chaim Bermant interview. Caldwell, "A Quebecker," 12, Richler Fonds Acc. #582/134.12.

78 Csillag interview, Richler Fonds Acc. #582/162.1. Richler, "My Life as a Racist," Richler Fonds Acc. #582/163.5.

79 Ron Csillag, "Memories," 2.

80 Janice Arnold, "Remembered," 2.

81 Dansereau and Beaudet interview, 93.

82 Michael Crelinsten interview.

83 Michael Crelinsten, executive director, Canadian Jewish Congress, Quebec Region, to Stephen Florio, president and CEO, *New Yorker*, 20 September 1991, Richler Fonds Acc. #582/12.17.

84 Janice Arnold, "Remembered," 2.

85 Michael Crelinsten interview.

86 Richler, "My Life as a Racist," Richler Fonds Acc. #582/163.5.

87 Michael Crelinsten, executive director, Canadian Jewish Congress, Quebec Region, to Stephen Florio, president and CEO, *New Yorker*, 20 September 1991, Richler Fonds Acc. #582/12.17. Caldwell, "A Quebecker," 36, Richler Fonds Acc. #582/134.12.

88 Interview with Bernard Landry, *Canadian Jewish News*, 15 October 1992, Richler Fonds Acc. #582/160.8.

89 Brownstein, "Montreal's," 2.

90 Richler, "French Kiss-Off," 1.

91 Jack Rabinovitch interview. Rabinovitch, "The Man."

92 Pauline Jewett to Richler, 7 November 1972, Richler Fonds Msc 36.4.18.

93 Maud Barlow et al. to the *Toronto Star*, 02/04/1992, Richler Fonds Acc. #582/45.24.

94 Dansereau and Beaudet interview, 91.

95 Phyllis Lambert, OC, FRAIC, director, Centre Canadien d'Architecture/Canadian Centre for Architecture, to Richler, 30 September 1991, Richler Fonds Acc. #582/37.13.

96 Michel Arsenault.

97 Rex Murphy interview, *The Journal*, CBC-TV, 17 November 1989.

98 Guy Vanderhaeghe, quoted in Posner, *Last*, 284.

99 Manon Cornellier, Richler Fonds Acc. #582/158.6.

100 Scott Feschuk, "Montreal-Born Author Raises Quebecois Ire with His Ruminations," *The Gazette* (University of Western Ontario student newspaper), 3 April 1992, Richler Fonds Acc. #582/38.4.

101 Richler, "Oh Canada, Oh Quebec," speech at University of Manitoba, 16 January 1991.

102 Janet Noel, "New France: Les Femmes Favorisées," *Atlantis* 6:2, Spring 1981, 89–97. W.J. Eccles, *France in America*, New York: Harper & Row, 1972, 76. Patrick J. Connor to Richler, 29 April 1992, Richler Fonds Acc. #582/37.18.

103 Lynne van Luven, Richler Fonds Acc. #582/158.6.

104 Fulford, "Richler."

105 Richler to 'Robin' MacNeil, 30 April 1992, Richler Fonds Acc. #582/26.19. Rockburn interview, 192.

106 Richler to Ellen Seligman, 13 June 1992, Richler Fonds Acc. #582/27.10.
107 Guy Vanderhaeghe to Richler, 27 March 1992, Richler Fonds Acc. #582/46.58.
108 H.D. Forbes, 55. Yanofsky, *Mordecai and Me*, 240.
109 *Oh Canada! Oh Quebec!*, 57.
110 This is Garth Stevenson's position, 215–16.
111 Garth Stevenson, 213–215.
112 Paul Wells, A4. Garth Stevenson, 237.
113 Richler to the editor, *The Montreal Gazette*, 30 July 1991, Richler Fonds Acc. #582/18.51.
114 Richler, "Assignment," Richler Fonds Acc. #582/153.1.
115 Yves Boisvert, "Richler récidive sur les ondes de la BBC," *La Presse*, 30 September 1992, B4, Richler Fonds Acc. #582/158.6.
116 Janice Arnold, "*La Presse* Apologizes for Cartoon," *Canadian Jewish News*, 15 October 1992, Richler Fonds Acc. #582/160.8. Richler, "My Life as a Racist," Richler Fonds Acc. #582/163.5.
117 Ingrid Peritz and Tu Thanh Ha, "Mordecai Richler," A4.
118 William Johnson, "Oh," 5.
119 Fulford, "Seventy," A12.
120 Richler, quoted in Guy Vanderhaeghe to Richler, 11 May 1992, Richler Fonds Acc. #582/46.58. Richler seems to have unconsciously borrowed the term from David Rosenberg, *Congregation*, viii.

CHAPTER 26

1 Richler to Fayge Cohen, 1 May 1992, Richler Fonds Acc. #680/3.13.
2 Sam Orbaum, "Make," 18.
3 Nur Masalha, 122.
4 *Solomon Gursky Was Here*, 551.
5 Gefen, 32, Richler Fonds Acc. #582/159.1.
6 Bill Weintraub interview (2001).
7 *This Year in Jerusalem*, 69.
8 Nur Masalha, 160.
9 Richler to Beth Elon and Deborah Harris, Harris/Elon Agency, 19 November 1992, Richler Fonds Acc. #582/20.29.
10 Richler to Joan Avirovic, 25 September 1992, Richler Fonds Acc. #582/21.36.
11 *The Montreal Gazette*, "Richler's Friends," 4. *This Year in Jerusalem*, 78–9.
12 Richler, "On Being Jewish," 2, Richler Fonds Acc. #582/110.20. *This Year in Jerusalem*, 81–82.
13 Nur Masalha, 115–16, 170.
14 *This Year in Jerusalem*, 227.
15 *This Year in Jerusalem*, 215, 236.
16 Richler to Pat, *New Yorker*, 16 May 1993, Richler Fonds Acc. #680/8.50.
17 Jack McClelland to Richler, 19 October 1994, Richler Fonds Acc. #582/29.2.
18 Richler to Carmen Callil, 1 May 1993, Richler Fonds Acc. #582/13.51.
19 Solly Cohen to Richler, 27 December 1994, Richler Fonds Acc. #582/13.100.
20 Beth Elon, Harris/Elon Agency, to Richler, 2 November 1994, Richler Fonds Acc. #680/5.28.
21 Sam Orbaum to Richler, 7 December 1993, Richler Fonds Acc. #582/33.1. Sam Orbaum, email to the author, 2 July 2002. *This Year in Jerusalem*, 116.
22 Sam Orbaum, email to the author, 2 July 2002.
23 Joel Yanofsky, "Looking for Jerusalem," *The Montreal Gazette*, 3 September 1994, Richler Fonds Acc. #582/160.4. Daphne Merkin, "Zion Lite," n.m.,

n.d., Richler Fonds Acc. #582/160.4. Edna Paris, review of *This Year in Jerusalem*, *Toronto Star*, 10 September 1994, Richler Fonds Acc. #582/160.2.
24 Richler, "Schindler," 34.
25 "A chaser fressing member of The Shaar" to Richler, 6 September 1994, Richler Fonds Acc. #582/39.5.
26 Dan Nimrod, "Why I Pity," Richler Fonds Acc. #582/162.1.
27 Lewis Dobrin, Shaar Hashomayim Synagogue, Westmount, to Richler, 7 June 1995, Richler Fonds Acc. #680/14.1.
28 Yanofsky, *Mordecai and Me*, 144.
29 Michael Levine, quoted in Posner, *Last*, 210.
30 Dan Nimrod, "The Enemy," Richler Fonds Acc. #680/47.
31 Richler to Beth Elon, Harris/Elon Agency, 10 March 1994, Richler Fonds Acc. #582/20.29.
32 Joe King, 305.
33 *Oh Canada!*, 67.
34 Neil Cameron, email, 15 October 2003. Auf der Maur loved pulling such gags and had created previous joke posters in provincial and municipal elections.
35 Aislin and Richler, Richard Holden poster, n.d., Richler Fonds Acc. #582/21.34.
36 Eric Siblin, Richler Fonds Acc. #582/162.1.
37 John N. Mappin Rare Books, Montreal. Advertisement for broadside poster of Richard Holden, September 1994, 36 x 22cm, $75, Richler Fonds Acc. #582/23.49.
38 Francine Barry, lawyer for the Directions des affaires juridiques, to Richler, 9 September 1994, Richler Fonds Acc. #582/35.42.
39 Eric Siblin, Richler Fonds Acc. #582/162.1.
40 Florence Richler interview.
41 Serge Sauvageau, of Ovadia, Sauvageau, Zito, to John N. Mappin, 25 October 1994, Richler Fonds Acc. #680/6.32.
42 Richler to Richard Holden, 1 March 1994, Richler Fonds Acc. #680/10.15. Mappin interview.
43 Mosher interview.
44 Richler to Richard Holden, 1 March 1994, Richler Fonds Acc. #680/10.15.
45 Grant, "Table," 1.
46 Draft of "Holden c. Richler et al.," Richler Fonds Acc. #680/10.15.
47 Richler fax to Lynne Abram, 8 August [1992], Richler Fonds Acc. #582/10.6
48 Jean Benoit Nadau, "La gang du lac," *Affaires plus*, May 1993, 14.
49 Lionel Albert, email to the author, 19 September 2002.
50 Stevie Cameron, *On the Take*, xii, 43, 216–17, 259. Stevie Cameron, "Man."
51 *Belling the Cat*, 295, 15–17, 292.
52 Richler to Cynthia Good?, n.d., Richler Fonds Acc. #582/39.6.
53 Mordecai Richler to Emma Richler, 1 September 1994, Richler Fonds Acc. #582/36.39.
54 *Jacob Two-Two's First Spy Case*, 36.
55 Val Ross, "Excusing," C1.
56 Val Ross, "Excusing," C12.
57 *Jacob Two-Two's First Spy Case*, 12, 81.
58 *Jacob Two-Two's First Spy Case*, 120–1, 6.

CHAPTER 27

1 [Questions about the translation of *Solomon Gursky Was Here*], 7 May 1991, Richler Fonds Acc. #582/7.37.

2 Susan B. Obscure [Mordecai Richler] to Brian Moore, 1 May 1978, Brian Moore Papers 49.5.5.2a. Possibly Richler got the date wrong, since the summer that so many friends came together at Cagnes seems to have been 1957, not 1956.

3 "From Mordecai," Fax to Jacob Richler, 28 February, n.y.

4 O'Malley, 1.

5 Tom Adair, Richler Fonds Acc. #582/160.4. Richler to Nick Auf der Maur, 20 January 1997, Richler Fonds Acc. #680/1.56.

6 Mosher interview.

7 Terry Mosher to Richler, 28 January 1991, Richler Fonds Acc. #582/30.67.

8 Richler to Terry Mosher, 4 February 1991, Richler Fonds Acc. #582/30.67.

9 Guy Vanderhaeghe to Richler, 23 January 1995, Richler Fonds Acc. #680/15.15.

10 Richler to Guy Vanderhaeghe, 3 August 1994, Richler Fonds Acc. #582/46.58.

11 Guy Vanderhaeghe to Richler, 3 October 1994, Richler Fonds Acc. #582/46.58.

12 McLaughlin.

13 Richler to John Fraser, 7 January 1995, Richler Fonds Acc. #582/18.13; 18 April 1995, Richler Fonds Acc. #680/4.37.

14 Richler to John Lynch Staunton, 23 January 1995, Richler Fonds Acc. #680/7.32.

15 Richler, "French Kiss-Off," 1–2.

16 Richler to John Lynch Staunton, 11 January 1995, Richler Fonds Acc. #680/7.32.

17 Ken McGoogan, "Author Fears Violent Uprising," *Calgary Herald*, 25 March 1997, B10, Richler Fonds Acc. #680/45.

18 Marie Tison, "Mordecai Richler récidive dans les pages du *New Yorker*," *Le Devoir*, 25 Mai 1994, Richler Fonds Acc. #680/44.

19 Richler, manuscript of "Once upon a Time Doctors..." Richler Fonds Acc. #582/41.26.

20 Marchand, "Caught," C2, Richler Fonds Acc. #680/44.

21 Richler to John Lynch-Staunton, 22 February [1995], Richler Fonds Acc. #680/7.32.

22 Micki Moore interview. Richler, "Clear," 4–5, 1. Marchand, "Caught," C2, Richler Fonds Acc. #680/44.

23 Richler, "Clear," 3.

24 Wong interview, 3.

25 Steyn, "Richler," 128.

26 Martin, "Anecdotes," A4.

27 Richler, "Pure."

28 Richler, "Snub."

29 Richler to Avie Bennet, 11 August 1997, Richler Fonds Acc. #680/7.55.

30 Pierre Joncas, "No Laughing Matter," *The Montreal Gazette*, 3 July 1996, Richler Fonds Acc. #680/44. Josée Legault, "Les détracteurs détraqués," *Le Devoir*, 26 June 1996, Richler Fonds Acc. #680/44.

31 Diane Francis, "The Prix Parizeau Literary Award Is Just the Beginning," *Financial Post*, 29 June 1996, 19.

32 Irwin Block, "Richler Parody-Prize Target of Complaint," *The Montreal Gazette*, 23 June 1996, A3, Richler Fonds Acc. #680/44.

33 *Oh Canada!*, 16–17. Richler, "Richler Responds," B3.

34 Campbell Clark, Richler Fonds Acc. #680/44.
35 Richler, "Richler Responds," B3.
36 Joe King, 306–7.
37 Richler's speech for the Prix Parizeau Ceremony, n.d. [November 1996?], Richler Fonds Acc. #680/33.9a.
38 Richler to "Dear Publisher," x]x [sic] June 1996, Richler Fonds Acc. #680/12.13.
39 Press Release, re: Priz Parizeau, 28 May 1997, Richler Fonds Acc. #680/1.60.
40 Yanofsky, *Mordecai and Me*, 281.
41 Richler's speeech for the Prix Parizeau Ceremony, n.d. [November 1997?], Richler Fons Acc. #680/33.9a.

CHAPTER 28

1 Cynthia Good, Penguin, to Richler, 7 July 1995, Richler Fonds Acc. #680/9.21.
2 Emma Richler to Ferdinand Mount, 16 February 1996, Richler Fonds Acc. #680/10.18.
3 Richler to Cynthia Good, 23 November 1996, 19 July 1997, 8 March 1998, 15 March 1999, Richler Fonds Acc. #680/9.21.
4 Florence Richler, 42.
5 Jay Scott, "From Duddy to Rambo," *Globe and Mail*, 14 April 1989, Richler Fonds Acc. #582/161.2.
6 Richler, "Q for Quest," [sic] 4, Richler Fonds Msc 36.40.15.
7 Richler, "Write Stuff."
8 Cameron interview, 124.
9 Richler, "Book of the Century," *The Daily Telegraph*, 5 December 1998, A3.
10 Draft of *Barney's Version*, 336, Richler Fonds Acc. #680/21.4.
11 Hill, *Grand Guy*, 148, 210, 262–4.
12 *Inner Space*, interview, 2, Richler Fonds Msc 36.54.4.
13 Daniel Richler interview. Noah Richler interview.
14 Daniel Richler interview.
15 Richler, "Innocents," 16.
16 Amiri Baraka, "Somebody Blew Up America," 1 October 2001, www.amiribaraka.com/blew.html. In fairness to Baraka, one should also read his self-defense in which he claims that his criticism of Zionism and of Israel is not a criticism of Jews. "Statement by Amiri Baraka, New Jersey Poet Laureate: *I will not 'apologize', I will not 'resign!'*" 10 February 2002, www.amiribaraka.com/speech100202.html, 9 November 2006.
17 *Barney's Version*, 187.
18 *Barney's Version*, 257.
19 Philip Marchand, "Hypocrisy, Wretched Taste and Sins against Richler," *Toronto Star*, 19 October 1997, Richler Fonds Acc. #680/44. Lindor Reynolds, B1, B10.
20 *Barney's Version*, 97, 96, 381. Florence Richler interview.
21 Sue Fox interview, 10.
22 Micki Moore interview.
23 *Barney's Version*, 111.
24 Richler, "Countess," Manuscript 123, Richler Fonds Acc. #582/103.2.
25 *Barney's Version*, 139.
26 Yanofsky, *Mordecai and Me*, 179.

27 Martha Richler to Mordecai Richler, 27 July 1987, Richler Fonds Acc. #680/10.21.
28 Sue Fox interview, 10.
29 Micki Moore interview. Richler, "Ms. Ump," 3, Richler Fonds Acc. #582/107.2.
30 Draft of *Barney's Version*, 177, Richler Fonds Acc. #680/21.2. *Barney's Version*, 133.
31 Louise Dennys to Richler, 3 January 1997, 3–4, Richler Fonds Acc. #680/21.1.
32 *Barney's Version*, 18.
33 Richler, Draft of *Barney's Version*, 20–2, Richler Fonds Acc. #680/20.6.
34 Richler, [unidentified fragment], Richler Fonds Acc. #680/28.1.
35 Richler, "Three," 4.
36 Richler, Draft of *Barney's Version*, 20–2, Richler Fonds Acc. #680/21.1.
37 Arlene Perly Rae to Richler, May 1996, Richler Fonds Acc. #680/10.2.
38 Richler to Arlene Perly Rae, 5 June 1996, Richler Fonds Acc. #680/10.2.
39 Dennys wanted to cut an instance of avant-garde art's empty trendiness, "a crucifix floating in piss or a harpoon sticking out of a woman's bleeding arsehole." Richler refused. Richler, draft of *Barney's Version*, 25, Richler Fonds Acc. #680/21.1. *Barney Version*, 20.
40 Louise Dennys, Knopf Canada, to Richler, n.d., on Richler's draft of *Barney's Version*, Richler Fonds Acc. #680/19.3. Draft of *Barney's Version*, 307, Richler Fonds Acc. #680/21.2.
41 Louise Dennys to Richler, n.d., on Richler's draft of *Barney's Version*, Richler Fonds Acc. #680/19.3.
42 Alison Samuel, Chatto & Windus, to Richler, 9 January 1996, Richler Fonds Acc. #680/3.1.
43 *Barney's Version*, 366.
44 *Barney's Version*, 315.
45 Richler to Louise Dennys, 7 February 1997, Richler Fonds Acc. #680/1.31.
46 *The Montreal Gazette*, "Richler's Friends," 4–5.
47 Draft of *Barney's Version*, 342, Richler Fonds Acc. #680/21.2.
48 Joanna Bale, "Judge Frees Music Teacher Accused of Sex with Boys," *The Times*, 25 January 1996, 3, Richler Fonds Acc. #680/47.3.
49 *Barney's Version*, 175–6.
50 Draft of *Barney's Version*, 342, Richler Fonds Acc. #680/21.2. *Barney's Version*, 277–80.
51 *Barney's Version*, 82.
52 *Shovelling*, 31
53 Jacob Richler, "Nick's Place," 1.
54 Richler, "Intro: Nick," 17.
55 Richler to Louise Dennys, 23 January 1997, Richler Fonds Acc. #680/1.31.
56 *Barney's Version*, 414.
57 Richler to Conrad Black, 23 January 1997, Richler Fonds Acc. #680/2.21.
58 Richler to Nick Auf der Maur, 20 January, 4 February 1997, Richler Fonds Acc. #680/1.56.
59 Richler to Conrad Black, 23 January, 22 August 1997, Richler Fonds Acc. #680/2.21.
60 Richler to John Lynch Staunton, 6 March 1998, Richler Fonds Acc. #680/7.32. Noah Richler, "Nick's Place," 7.
61 Todd, 17.
62 *Barney's Version*, 415.

63 Mavis Gallant to Richler, 10 November 1997, Richler Fonds Acc. #680/4.47. Martin Knelman, "Mordecai," 3.

64 *Errand*, 142.

65 Avrum Richler interview.

66 Richler, "The Cure for the Novel," *The Montrealer*, June 1959, 18, Richler Fonds Acc. #680/33.23.

67 Richler, "From Mordecai," Fax to Ken Whyte and Gillian Burnett [June 1997?].

68 Doug Smith, 2.

69 Richler to the editor, *Globe and Mail*, 8 July 1997, Richler Fonds Acc. #680/28.1.

70 Val Ross, "Saturday Night Stirs It Up with Vodka Ad," *Globe and Mail*, 8 July 1997, A10, Richler Fonds Acc. #680/47.

71 Richler, "Seek," 2.

72 Jacob Richler to Mordecai Richler, 9 June 1997, Richler Fonds Acc. #680/13.43.

CHAPTER 29

1 Ashok Chandwani, quoted in Posner, *Last*, 301.

2 Richler to Alan Allnutt, *The Montreal Gazette*, 16 February 1997, Richler Fonds Acc. #680/4.49.

3 Richler to Ken Whyte, *Saturday Night*, 31 March 1997, Richler Fonds Acc. #680/13.43.

4 Weintraub interview (2001).

5 Richler to Ashok Chandwani, *The Montreal Gazette*, 12 March 1998, Richler Fonds Acc. #680/4.49. Chandwani, 3.

6 Richler to Paul Bogaards, Knopf (New York), 5 October 1997, Richler Fonds Acc. #680/1.32. Richler to Paul Bogaarts [*sic*], Knopf, 19 November 1997, Richler Fonds Acc. #680/1.31.

7 Richler to Jon Segal, Senior editor, Knopf (New York), 19 November 1997, Richler Fonds Acc. #680/1.32.

8 Steve Jarislowsky to Richler, 18 March 1998, Richler Fonds Acc. #680/6.20.

9 Richler, "Poor Winners," 2.

10 Mike Boone, "Fade to Black," *The Montreal Gazette*, 20 October 1996, Richler Fonds Acc. #680/47.

11 Richler, "Home," 7, Richler Fonds Acc. #582/163.3.

12 Brunner, 2.

13 Richler, "Close," 2–3.

14 "Brian Mulroney Lawsuit Clippings, January 6–14, 1997," Richler Fonds Acc. #680/47.3.

15 Weintraub, "Callow," 30.

16 Richler Fonds Acc. #582/107.1.

17 Richler to Douglas Robertson, Goodman, Phillips & Vineberg, 15 March 1999, Richler Fonds Acc. #680/5.2.

18 Johanne Cadorette, Dykes on Mykes, CKUT FM, Montreal, to Richler, 26 March 1998, Richler Fonds Acc. #680/10.5.

19 Jared Mitchell to Richler, 6 December 1998, Richler Fonds Acc. #680/8.40.

20 Richler to Avie Bennet, 11 August 1997, Richler Fonds Acc. #680/7.55. Richler, "The History of Jacob Two-Two," Richler Fonds Acc. #680/29.38.

21 Richler to John Aylen, 7 February 1997, Richler Fonds Acc. #680/1.60. John Aylen to Richler, 7 February 1997, Richler Fonds Acc. #680/1.60.

22 Evan Solomon interview, "Hot Type," CBC-TV, 24 November 1998.
23 Richler to Louise Dennys, 15 January 1998, Richler Fonds Acc. #680/1.31.
24 Ken McGoogan, "Oxford Delivers on CanLit," *Calgary Herald*, 8 November 1997, 19, Richler Fonds Acc. #680/44.
25 Martin Knelman, "Mordecai," 3.
26 Martin Levin.
27 Michael Levine to Richler and Ted Kotcheff, 12 July 1995, Richler Fonds Acc. #680/5.2.
28 Richler to Richard Dreyfuss, 22 September 1996, Richler Fonds Acc. #680/3.66. Richler to Michael Levine, 20 March 1997, Richler Fonds Acc. #680/5.2.
29 Richler to Michael Levine, 20 December, 9 November 1997, 3 January, 17 February 1998, Richler Fonds Acc. #680/5.2.
30 Richler to Louise Dennys, 30 March 1998, Richler Fonds Acc. #680/1.31.
31 *Barney's Version*, 347.
32 Daniel Richler interview.
33 Lionel Albert interview.
34 Richler to Jon Segal, Senior editor, Knopf (New York), 10 November 1997, Richler Fonds Acc. #680/1.32. Richler to John Lynch Staunton, 5 March 1998, Richler Fonds Acc. #680/7.32.
35 Sue Fox interview, 10.
36 Richler to Alan Allnutt, *The Montreal Gazette*, after 3 June 1998, Richler Fonds Acc. #680/4.49.
37 Jack Rabinovitch interview.
38 Richler, "Memories of Brian Moore."
39 Rebecca Caldwell, "Profile: Emma Richler," R1.
40 Emma Richler, *Sister Crazy*, 43.
41 Noah Richler, "My," B3.
42 Richler to Deborah Rogers, n.d., Richler Fonds Acc. #582/40.22.
43 Richler to Art Cooper, editor GQ, 21 November 1998, Richler Fonds Acc. #680/3.28.
44 Emma Richler to Mordecai Richler, 3 August 1998, Richler Fonds Acc. #680/10.18.
45 Richler to Deborah Rogers, n.d., Richler Fonds Acc. #582/40.22. Avrum Richler interview.
46 Nigel Horne, Martha Richler, quoted in Posner, *Last*, 279, 275.
47 Lucinda Chodan, "Alliance to Make Barney's Version Movie," *The Montreal Gazette*, 21 March 1998, D1.
48 Richler to Tony Cartano, 28 June 1999, Richler Fonds Acc. #680/1.29. Richler to Louise Dennys, Knopf (Canada), 28 June 1999, Richler Fonds Acc. #680/1.31.
49 Stephen Cole, 6.
50 Richler to Cynthia Good, 15 March 1999, Richler Fonds Acc. #680/9.21.
51 Richler to Thomas Delworth, 22 May, 28 June 1999, Richler Fonds Acc. #680/14.73.
52 Avrum Richler interview. Jacob Richler, B4.
53 Rabinovitch, 25.
54 Richler to Ken Whyte, *Saturday Night*, 22 February 1999, Richler Fonds Acc. #680/13.43.
55 Avrum Richler interview.
56 Richler, "Richler for PM." CBC, "Premier Binns." Richler, "Farmers."
57 Richler, "Supposed."

58 Richler, "You're."
59 Richler, "Canadian Conundrums."
60 Richler, "Mideast."
61 Jacob Richler, "Chats with Dad," B4.
62 Noah Richler, "Pa's Book List," 3.
63 Richler to Lionel Albert, 8 February 2001.
64 "La Capria: 'La vitalità di Barney era dettata dal suo stoicismo,'" *Il Foglio*, 5 July 2001. MacDonald et al., 3.
65 Honoré, "Italians." Wilson-Smith, "Mordecai," 20.
66 Andrea Marcenaro, "Marcenaro, grazie a Barney, speiga com ha saccheggiato Barney," *Il Foglio*, 5 July 2001.
67 Ingrid Peritz and Tu Thanh Ha, "Mordecai," A4. Gayle MacDonald, "Richler Fights Second Round with Cancer," *Globe and Mail* (30 June 2001).
68 Emma Richler, quoted in Posner, *Last*, 328, 330–1.
69 Emma Richler, *Sister Crazy*, 214.
70 Richler to Lionel Albert, 8 February 2001.
71 Richler to Reinhold Kramer, 13 June 2001.
72 Snowbell interview.
73 Richler, "Son's."
74 Alan Berger, 228.
75 Richler to Paul Tough and Dianna Symonds, *Saturday Night*, 5 July 1999, Richler Fonds Acc. #680/13.43.
76 Richler, "God's."
77 Richler, "More Trouble."
78 Richler, "Finding."
79 Noah Richler interview.
80 Sam Orbaum, email. Snowbell interview.
81 Sam Orbaum, "Canadian," 2–3. Sam Orbaum, email.
82 Bernard Richler interview.
83 Snowbell interview.
84 Florence Richler interview.
85 Gayle MacDonald, "Richler Fights Second Round with Cancer," *Globe and Mail*, 30 June 2001. Daniel Richler interview.
86 Jacob Richler, "Chats with Dad," B4.
87 Richler to Reinhold Kramer, 13 June 2001.
88 Ingrid Peritz and Tu Thanh Ha, "Mordecai," A4.
89 Martin Knelman, "Mordecai," 4.
90 Richler to Deborah Rogers, n.d., Richler Fonds Acc. #582/40.22.
91 Hamilton, "Table, 28."
92 *Barney's Version*, 410.
93 Max Richler, quoted in Posner, *Last*, 176.
94 Bauch, "Family," 2. Hamilton, "I Can't."
95 Noah Richler, "My," B3. Hamilton, "One."

Bibliography

Abella, Irving, and Harold Troper. *None Is Too Many: Canada and the Jews of Europe 1933–1948*. Toronto: Lester and Orpen Dennys, 1982.

Adair, Tom. "Whiskey Sour." *Scotland on Sunday* (13 November 1994), Richler Fonds Acc. #582/160.4.

Albert, Lionel. "Richler Roots in Ontario Too." *The Montreal Gazette* (10 July 2002).

Aleichem, Sholom. *It's Hard to Be a Jew* [*Shver tsu zayn a yid*]. Mark Schweid, trans., *Sholom Aleichem Panorama*. London, ON: Jewish Observer (1948): 235–66.

Allan, Norman Bethune. *Ted*. Chapter 3: "Spain," www.normanallan.com/misc/TedCh3.html (28 April 2003). Chapters 7–11: "The Nineteen Forties," "Oh Canada," "Across the Atlantic," "The Redhead and the Shrink," "The Secret of the World," www.normanallan.com/Misc/Ted/Ted%20home.htm (19 May 2005).

Allen, Glen, and Ann Walmsley. "The Making of 'Joshua.'" *Maclean's* (23 September 1985): 44–50, Richler Fonds Acc. #582/135.16.

Anderson, Benedict. *Imagined Communities: Reflections on the Origin and Spread of Nationalism*. Rev. ed. London: Verso, 1991.

Arendt, Hannah. "Eichmann in Jerusalem: An Exchange of Letters between Gershom Scholem and Hannah Arendt." *Encounter* 22 (January 1964): 51–6.

Arnold, Janice. "Montreal's Early Kosher Meat Industry Examined in Robinson's Scholarly Research." *Canadian Jewish News* (22 February 1990): 2.

Arnold, Janice. "Mordecai Richler Remembered." *Canadian Jewish News* (12 July 2001), www.cjnews.com/pastissues/01/july12-01/main.asp, 5 May 2002.

Arnstein, Walter L. *Britain Yesterday and Today: 1830 to the Present*. Third ed. Lexington, Mass: D.C. Heath, 1976.

Arsenault, Michel. "L'homme qui n'a pas d'amis." *L'actualité* (15 April 1990): 119.

Athill, Diana. *Instead of a Letter*. Garden City, NY: Doubleday, 1962.

– *Stet: A Memoir*. London: Granta, 2000.

Ausubel, Nathan. *A Pictorial History of the Jewish People*. New York: Crown, 1953.

Ayre, John. [*The Acrobats?*] *Books in Canada*. www.amazon.ca/exec/obidos/tg/browse/-/915398/701-6610772-2151554 (9 October 2002).

Babel, Isaac. *Collected Stories.* David McDuff, trans., London: Penguin, 1994.
– *Isaac Babel, The Lonely Years 1925–1939: Unpublished Stories and Private Correspondence.* Nathalie Babel, ed., New York: Farrar, Straus, 1964.
Bailey, Bruce. "'Joshua'—Here and Now." *The Montreal Gazette* (31 October 1984), Richler Fonds Acc. #582/157.1.
Bailey, Peter J. *The Reluctant Film Art of Woody Allen.* Lexington: University of Kentucky Press, 2001.
Baker, Zachary M. "Montreal of Yesterday: A Snapshot of Jewish Life in Montreal During the Era of Mass Immigration." *An Everyday Miracle: Yiddish Culture in Montreal.* Ira Robinson et al, eds, 39–52.
Baldwin, James. "A Question of Identity." *Notes of a Native Son.* Boston: Beacon, 1955.
Band, Arnold J. "Popular Fiction and the Shaping of Jewish Identity." *Jewish Identity in America.* Gordis and Ben-Horin, eds, 215–26.
Bantey, Ed. "Tall Tales: Is Richler Book Fact or Fiction?" *The Montreal Gazette* (22 March 1992): A4.
Base, Ron. "The When and How of *Joshua Then and Now.*" *Toronto Star* (1 September 1985): G1, G8, Richler Fonds Acc. #582/157.1.
Bauch, Hubert. "A Family Bids Farewell." *The Montreal Gazette* (6 July 2001).
– "A Stranger in His Own Land." *The Montreal Gazette* (7 July 2001).
Baumoil, N. "Harav R. Yehudah (Yudel) Rosenberg." Toronto, ca 1943. www.rabbiyehudahyudelrosenberg.com/pdf/RR-NB.pdf (11 May 2005).
Beaudin, Monique. "St. Urbain's chronicler." *The Montreal Gazette* (4 July 2001).
Bellow, Saul. *The Adventures of Augie March.* New York, Viking, 1953.
– *Herzog.* New York, Penguin, 1964.
– "Some Notes on Recent American Fiction." *The Novel Today: Contemporary Writers on Modern Fiction.* Malcolm Bradbury, ed., Manchester: Manchester University Press, 1977, 54–69.
Benchimol, Evelyne. "The Apprenticeship of Daniel Richler." *Ryerson Review of Journalism* (Spring 1987). www.ryerson.ca/rrj/archives/1987/benchimol.html (19 May 2005).
Berger, Alan L. "Job's Children: Post-Holocaust Jewish Identity in Second-Generation Literature." *Jewish Identity in America.* Gordis and Ben-Horin, eds, 227–49.
Bethune, Brian. "Sex and Contempt." *Maclean's* (24 June 2002): 26.
Beuttler, Bill. "Appetite for the Absurd." *American Way* (15 May 1990): 132, Richler Fonds Acc. #582/124.4.
Bissonnette, Lise. "Comme à Salisbury." *Le Devoir* (18 mars 1992): A8, Richler Fonds Acc. #582/162.1.
– "Vu du Woody's Pub." *Le Devoir* (18 septembre 1991): A8.
Blackman, Ted. "Richler's Joust Better than Entertainment." *The Montreal Gazette* (23 April 1980).
Boone, Mike. "Pride of Baron Byng Never Lost Edge." *The Montreal Gazette* (4 July 2001).
Bouthillier, Guy. Société Saint-Jean-Baptiste de Montréal Press Release (3 July 2001) www.newswire.ca/releases/July2001/03/c9545.html.
Bradbury, Malcolm. *The Modern American Novel* (new ed.). Oxford: Oxford University Press, 1992.
– "Neorealist Fiction." *Columbia Literary History of the United States.* New York: Columbia University Press, 1988, 1126–41.
Brenner, Rachel Feldhay. *Assimilation and Assertion: The Response to the Holocaust in Mordecai Richler's Writing.* New York: Peter Lang, 1989.

Brody, Aaron. "Rabbi Yehudah Yudel Rosenberg." www.rabbiyehudahyudel
rosenberg.com/biography.html (10 May 2005).

Bronfman, Samuel. ...*from little acorns...* Montreal: Seagrams Distillers, 1970.

Brown, Michael. "Zionism in the Pre-Statehood Years: The Canadian Response."
From Immigration to Integration: The Canadian Jewish Experience. Malcolm
Lester, ed., Toronto: International Affairs, B'nai Brith Canada, 2001.
www.bnaibrith.ca/institute/millennium/millennium08.html (17 May 2002).

Brownstein, Bill. "Memories of a Maker of Folklore." *The Montreal Gazette*
(5 July 2001).

– "Montreal's Watering-Hole." *The Montreal Gazette* (2 March 2003).

Brunner, Paul. "Editor's Notes (How Could Mordecai Richler Be So Right about
Quebec Separatists and So Wrong about the Reform Party?)" *Alberta Report*
24:29 (30 June 1997): 4.

Bryden, Ronald. "Why *Solomon Gursky* Is the Great Canadian Novel." *National
Post* (7 July 2001).

Brym, Robert J. and Rhonda Lenton. "The Distribution of Anti-Semitism in
Canada in 1984." *The Jews in Canada.* Robert Brym, William Shaffir, and
Morton Weinfeld, eds, Toronto: Oxford University Press, 1993, 112–20.

Buchan, John. *The Thirty-Nine Steps* [1915]. London: Pan, 1959

Bugler, Jeremy. "The Book Selling Smiths." *Observer* (15 March 1970).

Bullin, Christine. "Postcard from Terry McEwen." *Opera News* 58:2 (August
1993): 26–9.

Caldwell, Christopher. "A Quebecer Waves a Flag for English." *Insight on the
News* (22 June 1992): 11, 34–6.

Caldwell, Rebecca. "Profile: Emma Richler," *Globe and Mail*, 12 March 2005, R1.

Cameron, Don. "Don M. and the Hardhats." *Canadian Forum* (March 1972):
32–3.

Cameron, Stevie. *On the Take: Crime, Corruption and Greed in the Mulroney
Years.* Toronto: MacFarlane Walter and Ross, 1994.

– "The Man Who Came to Dinner (and Dished the Dirt)," *Globe and Mail* (7 July
2001).

Carlton, David. *Anthony Eden: A Biography.* London: Allen Lane, 1981.

CBC. "Premier Binns Isn't Laughing." 30 October 2000, charlottetown.cbc.ca/
cgi-bin/templates/view.cgi?/news2000.

CBC-TV. *Mordecai Richler: A Celebration,* "Opening Night," 27 June 2002, taped
20 June 2002, Monument-National Theatre, Montreal.

Chandwani, Ashok. "Missives from Mordecai." *The Montreal Gazette* (4 July 2001).

Chenoweth, Dave. "[?]... Jacob Two-Two—Marfa, Too." *The Montreal Gazette*
(1 March 1979): 53, Richler Fonds Acc. #582/156.12.

Clark, Campbell. "Separatist Plans Book on Richler." *The Montreal Gazette* (5
July 1996): A6, Richler Fonds Acc. #680/44.

Coallier, Marie-France. "A Toast to Mordecai from His Buddies at Bar 243,"
National Post (6 July 2001).

Cohen, Nathan. "A Conversation with Mordecai Richler." *Tamarack Review*
(Winter 1957): 6–23.

– "Heroes of the Richler View." *Tamarack Review* 6 (Winter 1958): 47–60.
Reprinted in David Sheps, ed. *Mordecai Richler,* 43–57.

Cohen, Steven M. "Response to Bruce Phillips." *Jewish Identity in America.*
Gordis and Ben-Horin, eds, 27–9.

Cole, Stephen. "The kid stays in pictures." *Globe and Mail* (29 December 2003).

www.globeinvestor.com/servlet/ArticleNews/print/GAM/20031229/RO1LANTOS (23 January 2006).

Cook, Dana. "Mordecai Then and Now," *Globe and Mail* (7 July 2001).

Corbeil, Carole. "Richler Redux or What I Should Have Said on TV." *This Magazine* 23:6 (January-February 1990): 22–4.

Cornellier, Manon. "Le jugement sur le livre de Mordecai Richler doit mener du public, dit Lucien Bouchard." *Le Devoir* (18 mars 1992): A3, Richler Fonds Acc. #582/158.6.

Craig, Patricia. *Brian Moore: A Biography*. London: Bloomsbury, 2002.

Craniford, Ada. *Fact and Fiction in Mordecai Richler's Novels*. Queenston, ON: Edwin Mellen, 1992.

Csillag, Ron. "Memories of Mordecai." *The Canadian Jewish News* (12 July 2001) www.cjnews.com/pastissues/01/july12-01/community/csillag.htm (10 May 2002).

Daat Emet editorial board [Yaron Yadan]. "Gentiles in Halacha." www.daatemet. org.il/daathalacha/en_gentiles3.html (20 May 2005).

Darling, Michael. "Mordecai Richler." *The Annotated Bibliography of Canada's Major Authors*. Volume 1. Robert Lecker and Jack David, eds, Downsview, ON: ECW Press, 1979.

Davey, Frank. *Post-National Arguments: The Politics of the Anglophone-Canadian Novel since 1967*. Toronto: University of Toronto Press, 1993.

Davidson, Arnold. *Mordecai Richler*. New York: Frederick Ungar, 1983.

Dawidowicz, Lucy S. *The Golden Tradition: Jewish Life and Thought in Eastern Europe*. New York: Holt, Rinehart and Winston, 1967.

Delaney, Marshall. "A Touch of Class." *Saturday Night* (November 1985): 82, Richler Fonds Acc. #582/157.1.

Downey, Peter. Interview with Martha Richler. "The Entertainment Section," CBC Radio (28 June 1976). "Mordecai Richler Was Here," CBC Archives, archives.cbc.ca/IDD-1-68-753/arts_entertainment/mordecai_richler/ (13 May 2005).

Drainie, Bronwyn. "And in This Corner... Canadian Writers in Fighting Trim." *Globe and Mail* (24 February 1990): C3, Richler Fonds Acc. #582/159.1.

Dubé, Francine. "Death from Cancer Comes as a Shock," *National Post* (4 July 2001): A1, A13.

Duncan, Ann. "Mordecai Richler Then and Now." *International Herald Tribune* (3 June 1985): 16.

Edemariam, Aida. "The Great Unread," *National Post* (7 April 2001).

Eden, Sir Anthony. *The Memoirs of Sir Anthony Eden: Full Circle*. London: Cassell, 1960.

Edwards, Ivana. "Mrs. Mordecai Richler Seems Most Happy with Her Lot." *The Montreal Gazette* (1 June 1971), Richler Fonds Msc 36.55.1.

Eisendrath, Rabbi Maurice N. "Be Fair to Your Children." *Canadian Jewish Review* 18:10 (20 December 1935): 1.

En Ville: The Business Family Paper. "The Richlers: Faith Is no Obstacle." (24 April 1965): 10.

Evans, Elaine. "On Self-Mutilation and Family Dynamics," *National Post* (26 May 2001).

Feldman, Rabbi Dr. Arthur A. "Judaism Under the Onslaught of the Modern Age." *Canadian Jewish Review* 18:10 (20 December 1935): 6–7, 34–5.

Fetherling, Doug. "BOMC Names Richler to Board." *Toronto Star* (21 August 1973), Richler Fonds Acc. #582/160.7.

Fiedler, Leslie. "Some Notes on the Jewish Novel in English." David Sheps, ed. *Mordecai Richler*, 99–105.

Fitzgerald, Judith. "Mordecai Then and Now." *Globe and Mail* (27 August 1983).

Forbes, H.D. "Mordecai's Mischief: H.D. Forbes Asks Which Rights Are Rights." *The Idler* 35 (March 1992): 52–5, Richler Fonds Acc. #582/161.4.

Fraser, Graham. "BQ urges Ottawa to Ban Richler Book." *Globe and Mail* (17 March 1992).

Friedberg, Maurice. "Introduction." Sholom Aleichem. *The Bloody Hoax*. Aliza Shevrin, trans., Bloomington: Indiana University Press, 1991.

Fulford, Robert. *Best Seat in the House: Memoirs of a Lucky Man*. Toronto: Collins, 1988.

– "Mordecai's Version." *National Post* (22 June 2002): B5.

– "Richler Didn't Abide Pandering to Bigotry." *National Post* (15 June 2002), www.nationalpost.com/search/site/story.asp?id=7A815EE1-5B5D-4233-A372-55C85DF9468D (25 June 2002).

– "Robert Fulford on Mordecai Richler." *Saturday Night* Online, www.saturday night.ca/webexclusives/mordecai/MRfulford.html (22 August 2001).

– "Seventy Years of Glorious Trouble." *National Post* (4 July 2001): A1, A12.

Gagnon, Lysiane. "Inside Quebec: Things Are Bad Enough without Nastiness from Mordecai Richler." *Globe and Mail* (21 September 1991).

Gale Group. "Daniel Richler: Writer and Broadcaster." *Contemporary Canadian Biographies* (November–December 2002).

Gatenby, Greg. "Let's Start a New Chapter in the Governor-General's Awards History." *Toronto Star* (24 February 1990).

Gefen, Pearl Sheffy. "Richler Rides Again." *Weekend, the Jerusalem Post Magazine* (4 May 1990): 30–2.

Gold, Mike. *A Literary Anthology*. Michael Folsom, ed. and intro., New York: International Publishers, 1972.

Golden, Mike. "A Conversation with Terry Southern." *Paris Review* 38:138 (Spring 1996): 215–38.

Goodspeed, Peter. "Novelist, Journalist, Wit." *National Post* (4 July 2001): A13.

Gordis, David M. and Yoav Ben-Horin, eds, *Jewish Identity in America*. Los Angeles: University of Judaism, 1991.

Gorman, Brian. "Richler's Version." *Today* (10 October 1997), www.canoe.ca/JamBooksFeatures/richler_mordecai.html (23 May 2000).

Gottlieb, Robert. "He Got 'Better and Better.'" *Maclean's* (24 June 2002): 22–3.

Grant, Alyson. "Table 28 at Le Mas Is Empty." *The Montreal Gazette* (4 July 2001).

Green, Mary. "Synagogues Have Become 'religious Drug Stores' Novelist Richler Claims." *Montreal Monitor* (30 June 1960): 7, Richler Fonds Msc 36.54.13.

Greenstein, Michael. *Third Solitudes: Tradition and Discontinuity in Jewish-Canadian Literature*. Kingston: McGill-Queen's University Press, 1989.

Groen, Rick. "Tears of a Clown." *Globe and Mail* (25 October 2002): R1.

Gross, Gerry. "A Palpable Hit: A Study of the Impact of Reuben Ship's *The Investigator*." *Theatre Research in Canada* 10:2 (Fall 1989).

Gruending, Dennis. "Not Much of a Nationalist." *Saskatoon Star-Phoenix* (17 November 1972), Richler Fonds Msc 36.42.21.

Guilhamet, Leon. *Satire and the Transformation of Genre*. Philadelphia: University of Pennsylvania Press, 1987.

Gzowski, Peter. "My Mordecai: Wicked Smoothie, Gentle Genius, Loyal Friend." *Globe and Mail* (7 July 2001).
– "Afterword." *The Incomparable Atuk*. Toronto: McClelland & Stewart, 1989.

Ha'am, Ahad. *Nationalism and the Jewish Ethic: Basic Writings of Ahad Ha'am*. Hans Kohn, ed. and intro., New York, Schocken Books, 1962.
Haberman, Clyde. "Mordecai Richler's Apprenticeship." *New York Post* (27 July 1974), Richler Fonds Acc. #582/154.2.
Halberstam-Rubin, Anna. *Sholom Aleichem: The Writer as Social Historian*. New York: Peter Lang, 1989.
Hamilton, Graeme and Francine Dubé. "At Table 28 and across Canada, Gestures of Respect for Richler," *National Post* (5 July 2001).
Hamilton, Graeme. "'I Can't See This and I Do Not Want It, Life without Him.'" *National Post* (6 July 2001).
– "One Great Writer Is Remembered… Richler's Voice Is Heard." *National Post* (21 June 2002), www.nationalpost.com/search/site/story.asp?id=57B5B0C4 -6F88-49F8-B238-E445D8B828ED (25 June 2002).
Hamilton, Graeme. "Separatists' Farewells Brief, Bitter." *National Post* (4 July 2001): A2.
Handel, Alan. Dir. *The Apprenticeship of Mordecai Richler*. National Film Board. 1986.
Hanes, Allison. "Novelist's Burial a Homecoming." *The Montreal Gazette* (6 July 2001).
– "Richler Was Just One of the Guys." *The Montreal Gazette* (5 July 2001).
Heichelheim, Professor F.M. "Mind and Spade," *The Jewish Standard* (15 November 1955), Richler Fonds Msc 36.22.6.
Hill, Lee. *A Grand Guy: The Art and Life of Terry Southern*. New York: Harper-Collins, 2001.
– "Interview with a Grand Guy." [Terry Southern] *Backstory 3: Interviews with Screenwriters of the 60s*. Patrick McGilligan, ed., Berkeley: University of California Press, 1996. www.altx.com/interviews/terry.southern.html (14 November 2002).
Honoré, Carl. "Italians Make Folk Hero of Barney." *National Post* (4 July 2001): B3.
– "The Name Can't Hurt." *National Post* (3 May 2001).
Hurtig, Mel. *At Twilight in the Country: Memoirs of a Canadian Nationalist*. Toronto: Stoddart, 1996.
– "How Richler Earns His Roast Beef" [letter to the editor]. *Edmonton Journal* (9 October 1985): A5.

Idel, Moshe. *Golem: Jewish Magical and Mystical Traditions on the Artificial Anthropoid*. Albany: State University of New York Press, 1990.
Isou, Isidore. "Manifesto of Letterist Poetry" (1942; *Introduction à une Nouvelle Poésie et une Nouvelle Musique*. Paris: Gallimard, 1947). *Selections from the Manifestos of Isidore Isou*. David W. Seaman, ed. and trans., www.thing.net/~ grist/l&d/lettrist/isou-m.htm (18 December 2002).

James, Geoffrey. "The Expatriate Who Has Never Left Home." *Time* [Canadian edition] (31 May 1971): 7–11, Richler Fonds Msc 36.30.12.
Jewison, Norman. *This Terrible Business Has Been Good to Me*. Toronto: Key Porter, 2004.
Johnson, Brian D. "Even God Has His Faults." *Maclean's* (23 September 1985): 52.

Johnson, Paul. *A History of the Jews*. London: Phoenix, 1987.
Johnson, William. "Oh, Mordecai. Oh, Quebec." *Globe and Mail* (7 July 2001).

Kareda, Urjo. *Toronto Daily Star* (1 June 1968), Richler Fonds Msc 36.18.8.
– "Why Did They Turn Duddy into a Charmer?" *New York Times* (25 August
   1974), Richler Fonds Acc. #582/154.2.
Kattan, Naim. "Mordecai Richler—Craftsman or Artists" [*sic*]. *Congress Bulletin*
   (September–October 1965): 7, Richler Fonds Msc 36.54.14.
Katz, Steven T. *Post-Holocaust Dialogues: Critical Studies in Modern Jewish
   Thought*. New York: New York University Press, 1983.
Kennedy, Mark. "Anglo Group Decries Richler's Version of Quebec." *The
   Montreal Gazette* (2 April 1992).
Kernan, Alvin. *The Cankered Muse: Satire of the English Renaissance*. New
   Haven, Conn.: Yale University Press, 1959.
Keyes, John T.D. "Chillin' with Ted Kotcheff." *Chill Magazine Online* 1 (Fall
   2003): 1–5. www.thebeerstore.ca/chill/Issue1'issue1-features-kotcheff.html
   (14 January 2004).
Kieval, Hillel J. "Pursuing the Golem of Prague: Jewish Culture and the Invention
   of a Tradition." *Modern Judaism* 17:1 (1997): 1–23.
King, James. *The Life of Margaret Laurence*. Toronto: Knopf, 1997.
King, Joe. *From the Ghetto to the Main: The Story of Jews in Montreal*. Montreal:
   Montreal Jewish Publication Society, 2001.
Kirchhoff, H.J. "Richler Revels in Kidlit Success." *Globe and Mail* (10 June
   1987): A14, Richler Fonds Acc. #680/44.
Knelman, Martin. "Broadway or Bust." *Financial Post Magazine* (1 November
   1984): 43–53, Richler Fonds Acc. #582/157.1
– *Home Movies: Tales from the Canadian Film World*. Toronto: Key Porter, 1987.
– "How Duddy's Movie Brings Us All Back Home." *Saturday Night* (March
   1974): 17–24, Richler Fonds Acc. #582/155.1.
– "Mordecai Richler: A Canadian Icon." *Toronto Star* (4 July 2001).
– "Ted Kotcheff: A Wandering Son Heads for Home to Film Richler's Duddy
   Kravitz." *Globe and Mail* (19 August 1972), Richler Fonds Msc 36.55.1.
Koestler, Arthur. *Darkness at Noon*. Daphne Hardy, trans., New York: Bantam,
   1941.
Kolber, Sandra. *Bitter Sweet Lemons and Love*, Toronto: McClelland & Stewart,
   1967.
Kotcheff, Ted. "Afterword." *The Acrobats*. Mordecai Richler. Toronto: McClelland
   & Stewart, 2002.
– (Tribute to Mordecai Richler) Richler Tribute Evening at the International
   Festival of Authors, Toronto. "Mordecai's Version." Eleanor Wachtel, ed., "The
   Arts Today," CBC Radio 1, 31 October 2000.

Lalonde, Michelle. "Richler Defends His Writing." *The Montreal Gazette* (21
   September 1991): B2.
Lanctôt, Gustave, and Jan Noel. "Filles de Joie ou Filles du Roi." *Atlantis* 6:2
   (Spring 1981): 80–98.
Lanken, Dane. "With Duddy and His Gang Down on St. Urbain Street." *The
   Montreal Gazette* (6 April 1974): 45.
Laponce, J.A. "Left or Centre? The Canadian Jewish Electorate, 1953–1983."
   Robert J. Brym, William Shaffir, and Morton Weinfeld, *The Jews in Canada*,
   Toronto: Oxford University Press, 1993.

Lebel, Ronald. "So It Couldn't Happen in Montreal?" *The Globe Magazine*
  (*Globe and Mail*) (15 February 1969): 18–20.
Leiman, Shnayer Z. "The Adventure of the Maharal of Prague in London: R. Yudl
  Rosenberg and the Golem of Prague." *Tradition* 36:1 (Spring 2002): 26–46.
Leiren-Young, Mark. "Absolut Literature." *Quill and Quire* 63:9 (September
  1997): 7.
Lessing, Doris. *Walking in the Shade: Volume Two of My Autobiography*
  1949–1962. London: HarperCollins, 1997.
Levene, Mark. "Mordecai Richler." *Profiles in Canadian Literature: Volume 2*.
  Jeffrey M. Heath, ed., Toronto: Dundurn, 1980.
Levin, Martin. "Blessed Be Mordecai." *Globe and Mail* (7 July 2001).
Levine, Norman. *Canada Made Me*. Deneau and Greenberg, 1958.
Lisée, Jean-François. "Québec antisémite? Non coupable! 'Interview' avec Pierre
  Anctil." *L'actualité* (December 1991): 17f, Richler Fonds Acc. #582/161.4.
Litvinoff, Emanuel. "Books." *Jewish Observer and Middle East Review*, 16 Sep-
  tember 1955, Richler Fonds Msc 36.22.6.
Lowy, Henny. "Montreal Writer Meets His Public." *The Canadian Jewish Chroni-
  cle* (1 July 1960). Richler Fonds Msc 36.54.13.
Luven, Lynne Van. "Rock-Star Treatment Envisioned for Richler Readings."
  Edmonton Journal (9 May 1991).

MacDonald, Gayle, Sandra Martin, Simon Houpt, and Megan Williams, "How
  We Remember Him," *Globe and Mail* (5 July 2001).
MacDonald, L. Ian. *From Bourassa to Bourassa: Wilderness to Restoration*. Sec-
  ond ed. Montreal: McGill-Queen's University Press, 2002.
MacDonald, Neil. "CBC Newsmagazine." CBC-TV. 30 March 1992. "Mordecai
  Richler Was Here." CBC Archives, archives.cbc.ca/IDD-1-6753/arts_enter
  tainment/mordecai_richler/ (13 May 2005).
MacGregor, Roy. "The Boy from St. Urbain." *Maclean's* (9 June 1980): 45–50.
MacPherson, Don. "Well Done." *The Montreal Gazette* (11 May 1993): B3.
Makow, Henry. "Master's Feet: The Pedagogical Method of Mordecai Richler."
  Globe and Mail Weekend Magazine (26 April 1975).
Malina, Martin. "Duddy Kravitz, Where Are You?" *The Montreal Star Entertain-
  ments* (21 April 1973), Richler Fonds Acc. #582/154.2.
Malamud, Bernard. *The Fixer*. New York: Dell, 1966.
Mandel, Charles. "How the Richler Papers Went West." *National Post* (14 July
  2001): B5.
Marchand, Philip. "Caught in the Middle." *Toronto Star* (29 October 1995):
  C1-C2, Richler Fonds Acc. #680/44.
– "Hypocrisy, Wretched Taste and Sins against Richler," *Toronto Star* (19 October
  1997; 4 July 2001).
– "Oy, Mordecai." *Chatelaine* (October 1990): 62–4, 147–9.
Martin, Rob. "Focus." *The Varsity* (University of Toronto) (13 December 1968).
  Richler Fonds Msc 36.54.14.
Martin, Sandra. "Anecdotes and Tributes Flow Freely." *Globe and Mail* (4 July
  2001): A1, A4.
– "Insult and Injury." *Books in Canada* (March 1981): 3–6.
Marrus, Michael. *Mr. Sam: The Life and Times of Samuel Bronfman*. Toronto:
  Viking, 1991.
Masalha, Nur. *Imperial Israel and the Palestinians: The Politics of Expansion*.
  London: Pluto, 2000.

McDowell, Edwin. "Gottlieb Reign Alters The New Yorker." *New York Times* (9 November 1981).

McDuff, David. "Introduction." *Isaac Babel, Collected Stories*. David McDuff, trans., London: Penguin, 1994.

McClelland, Jack. *Imagining Canadian Literature: The Selected Letters of Jack McClelland*. Sam Solecki, ed., Toronto: Key Porter, 1998.

McDonald, Marci. "St. Urbain's Famous Hustler Returns." *Toronto Star* (13 October 1973), Richler Fonds Acc. #582/154.2.

McKenzie, Robert. "Quebec's Adieu Shows Mixed Feelings." *Toronto Star* (4 July 2001).

McLaughlin, Gord. "A Last Great Public Moment." [18 October 2000 Roast] *National Post* (4 July 2001): A3.

McPherson, Hugo. "Fiction 1940–1960." *Literary History of Canada*. Carl F. Klinck, ed., Toronto: University of Toronto Press, 1965, 694–722.

McSweeney, Kerry. "Revaluing Mordecai Richler." *Studies in Canadian Literature* 4:2 (Summer 1979): 120–31.

– "Tap-Dancing" [Review of *Barney's Version*]. *Canadian Literature* 159 (Winter 1998): 188–90.

Merrill, Sam. "Mason Hoffenberg Gets in a Few Licks." *Playboy* (November 1973), theband.hiof.no/articles/mason_hoffenberg_gets_in_a_few_licks.html (14 November 2002).

Migdal, Celine. "Frances Katz Short in Size, Big in Chutzpah." *Canadian Jewish News* (28 November 1996): 39, Richler Fonds Acc. #680/10.19.

Mills, Donia. "Richler: Movie Initiation of a Canadian Author." *Washington Star News* (13 August 1974), Richler Fonds Acc. #582/154.2.

The Montreal Gazette. "Richler's Friends Have Their Say." 7 July 2001.

Moore, Brian. *An Answer from Limbo*. Toronto: General, 1962.

Mosher, Terry. "Comrades in Satire." *Maclean's* (24 June 2002): 31.

Nadel, Ira B. *Various Positions: A life of Leonard Cohen*. Toronto: Random House, 1996.

Neiman, Susan. *Evil in Modern Thought*. Princeton: Princeton University Press, 2002.

Newman, Peter C. *Bronfman Dynasty: The Rothschilds of the New World*. Toronto: McClelland & Stewart, 1978.

– ed. *Debrett's Illustrated Guide to the Canadian Establishment*. Agincourt, On: Methuen, 1983.

Nimrod, Dan. "The Enemy from Within." *Suburban* (29 June 1994): 11, Richler Fonds Acc. #680/47.

– "Why I Pity Mordechai Richler." *Suburban* (6 July 1994), Richler Fonds Acc. #582/162.1.

Nodelman, Perry. "*Jacob Two-Two* and the Satisfactions of Paranoia." *Canadian Children's Literature* 15–16 (1980): 31–7, Richler Fonds Acc. #582/134.7.

O'Malley, Martin. "Please Help Me with the Mordecai Richler Story." (4 July 2001), cbc.ca/news/viewpoint/columns/omalley/martin010703.html.

Orbaum, Sam. "Canadian Author Mordecai Richler Made Them All Mad." (7 June 2001), www.samorbaum.com/ThisN/Misc/Mordecai%20Richler, %20obit.html (18 June 2002).

– "Make 'Em Mad, Mordecai." *Jerusalem Post International Edition* (21 November 1992): 18–19. Richler Fonds Acc. #582/160.8.

O'Reilly, Finbarr. "Richler Stable after Surgery: Author Underwent Kidney Operation." *Globe and Mail* (10 June 1998).
– "Richler Undergoing Chemotherapy." *National Post* (30 June 2001).
Ozick, Cynthia. "Toward a New Yiddish." *Art and Ardor*. New York: Knopf, 1983.

Pape, Gordon. "After 22 Years Mordecai Richler Is Coming Home." *Hamilton Spectator* (30 June 1972), Richler Fonds Acc. #582/160.7.
Paris, Erna. "Memoirs of St. Urbain's Doyenne." *Quill and Quire* (May 1981), Richler Fonds Acc. #582/160.7.
Peritz, Ingrid. "About: Province's Reputation." *The Montreal Gazette* (21 September 1991): B2-3, Richler Fonds Acc. #582/50.9.
Peritz, Ingrid and Tu Thanh Ha. "Eaton's Shuts its Doors – but Only on Quebec" (Saturday, 21 August 1999), www.globetechnology.com/archive/19990821/UMONTM.html (13 May 2002).
Peritz, Ingrid and Tu Thanh Ha. "Mordecai Richler 1931–2001: 'We Will Miss Him Very Much.'" *Globe and Mail* (4 July 2001): A1, A4.
Petersen, Richard L. "Mordecai Richler Then and Now." *Vie en ESTRIE Living Magazine* (October–November 1986): 51–7.
Phillips, Bruce. "Sociological Analysis of Jewish Identity." *Jewish Identity in America*. Gordis and Ben-Horin, eds, 3–25.
Pile, Stephen. "All Alone with a Camera Crew." *Daily Telegraph* (17 December 1994): 24, Richler Fonds Acc. #680/44.
Plimpton, George. "The Quality Lit Game: Remembering Terry Southern." *Harper's* 303:1815 (August 2001), Ebscohost.
Poliquin, Daniel. "Richler's 'Unforgivable Sin.'" *Globe and Mail* (4 July 2001): A13.
– "St. Urbain's Prodigal Scold." *Maclean's* (24 June 2002): 36, 38.
Pollock, Zailig. *A.M. Klein: The Story of the Poet*. Toronto: University of Toronto Press, 1994.
Posner, Michael. "Celebrating Richler in the City He Loved." *National Post* (21 June 2002), www.globeandmail.com (25 June 2002).
– *The Last Honest Man: Mordecai Richler, An Oral Biography*. Toronto: McClelland and Stewart, 2004.

Rabinovitch, Jack. "The Man – His Solitude and Fortitude: 'We Stared and We Drank.'" *National Post* (21 June 2002), www.nationalpost.com/search/site/story.asp?id=FB0BE393-3C0E-471B-B0E3-E89D3D1C0D1C (25 June 2002).
– "Mordecai My Pal." *Maclean's* (24 June 2002): 24–5.
Ramraj, Victor J. *Mordecai Richler*. Boston: Twayne, 1983.
Ravvin, Norman. *A House of Words: Jewish Writing, Identity, and Memory*. Montreal: McGill-Queen's University Press, 1997.
Renzetti, Elizabeth. "Sex Matters," in "Book Boys and 'Chick Lit'—Fact or Fiction?" *Globe and Mail* (5 July 1999): C1, Richler Fonds Acc. #680/45.
Reynolds, Lindor. "'Just a Charm Ball': Richler the Curmudgeon Still Seeks Perfection." *Winnipeg Free Press* (25 October 1997): B1, B10.
Richler, Daniel. *Kicking Tomorrow*. Toronto: McClelland & Stewart, 1991.
Richler, Daniel. "Such a Great Laugh and a Moral Compass." *Maclean's* (24 June 2002): 42.
Richler, Emma. *Feed My Dear Dogs*. Toronto: Random House, 2005.
– *Sister Crazy*. Toronto: Random House, 2001.

– "Two or Three Things I Know about Grief." *Maclean's* (24 June 2002): 32–4.

Richler, Florence. "A Man Who Enjoyed Loving." *Maclean's* (24 June 2002): 40–2.

Richler, Jacob. "Chats with Dad." *National Post* (22 June 2002): B1, B4.

– "In the Belly of the Ritz." *Saturday Night* 110:6 (July–August 1995): 56–7.

– "Nick's Place." *Saturday Night* 113:6 (July–August 1998): 70.

Richler, Leah Rosenberg. "I Pay a Visit to the Beloved Rabbi." *Canadian Jewish Review* 18:10 (20 December 1935): 33, 36.

– "I Pay a Visit to the Beloved Rabbi." *Canadian Jewish Review* 18:25 (3 April 1936): 7, 56–7.

– "I Pay a Visit to the Beloved Rabbi." *Canadian Jewish Review* 18:49 (18 September 1936): 33–5.

– "I Pay a Visit to the Beloved Rabbi." *Canadian Jewish Review* 19:9 (11 December 1936): 44–5, 48.

– "I Pay a Visit to the Beloved Rabbi." *Canadian Jewish Review* 19:24 (26 March 1937): 8–9.

Richler, Noah. "The Family business." *National Post Online* (3 April 2001), www.nationalpost.com/search/story.html?f=/stories/20010403/ (1 June 2001).

– "Goa: Land of Fantasy Made Real." *The Plant* (Dawson College Student Paper) (4 September 1979), Richler Fonds Acc. #582/162.4.

– "I Wanted to Do Good for Pa," *National Post* (4 July 2001): B1-2. Reprint of "His Balls." *Fatherhood*. Virago Press, UK, 1992.

– "My Father, the Fan." *National Post* (22 June 2002): B1-B3. Also published as the "Foreword" to Mordecai Richler, *Dispatches from the Sporting Life*.

– "Pa's Book List," *Maisonneuve* 11 (October–November 2004), www.maisonneuve.org/article.php?article_id=435 (22 April 2005).

Richler, Shmarya (Stuart). "Richler Family Home Page" (19 June 2002), www.gtrdata.com/richler/richler.htm (25 June 2002).

Robertson, Terence. *Crisis: The Inside Story of the Suez Conspiracy*. New York: Atheneum, 1965.

Robinson, Ira. "Kabbalist and Communal Leader: Rabbi Yudel Rosenberg and the Canadian Jewish Community." *Canadian Jewish Studies* 1 (1993): 41–58.

– "Letter from the Sabbath Queen: Rabbi Rosenberg Addresses Montreal Jewry, A." *An Everyday Miracle: Yiddish Culture in Montreal*, 101–14.

– "Literary Forgery and Hasidic Judaism: the Case of Rabbi Yudel Rosenberg." *Judaism* 40 (1991): 61–78.

– "The Tarler *rebbe* of Łódź and his Medical Practice: Towards a History of Hasidic Life in Pre-First World War Poland." POLIN: *Studies in Polish Jewry* 11 (1998): 53–61.

– "Toward a History of Kashrut in Montreal: The Fight Over Municipal By-Law 828 (1922–1924)." *Renewing Our Days: Montreal Jews in the Twentieth Century*. Ira Robinson and Mervin Butovsky, eds, Montreal, Véhicule Press, 1995, 30–41.

– "The Uses of the Hasidic Story: Rabbi Yudel Rosenberg and His Tales of the Greiditzer Rebbe." *Journal of the American Association of Rabbis* 1 (1991): 17–25.

– Pierre Anctil, and Mervin Butovsky. "Introduction." *An Everyday Miracle: Yiddish Culture in Montreal*, Ira Robinson, Pierre Anctil, and Mervin Butovsky, eds, Montreal: Véhicule Press, 1990, 11–21.

Rosenberg, David, ed. *Congregation: Contemporary Writers Read the Jewish Bible*. New York: Harcourt Brace Jovanovich, 1987.

Rosenberg, Leah. *The Errand Runner: Reflections of a Rabbi's Daughter*, Toronto: John Wiley and Sons, 1981.

Rosenberg, Suzanne. *A Soviet Odyssey*. Toronto: Oxford University Press, 1988.

Rosenberg Souvenir. "HaRav haGaon hamefursam (the well-known Rebbe Yudel Rosenberg)." Seventieth Anniversary Jubilee. Montreal, 1931, 5–6, www.rabbiyehudahyudelrosenberg.com/pdf/RR70.pdf (11 May 2005).

Rosenberg, Yehuda Yudel. *Kovets Maamar Yehuda: Collected Discourses of Rabbi Yehuda Yudel Rosenberg, Part 1: Discourse on Tefillin*. Baruch Rosenberg, trans., Thornhill, ON: Eitz Yehuda Publications, 1988.

– *Kovets Maamar Yehuda: Collected Discourses of Rabbi Yehuda Yudel Rosenberg, Part 2: Commentary on the Book of Jonah According to the Zohar*. Baruch Rosenberg, trans., Thornhill, ON: Eitz Yehuda Publications, 1989.

Roskies, David G. "Yiddish in Montreal: The Utopian Experiment," *An Everyday Miracle: Yiddish Culture in Montreal*. Ira Robinson et al, eds, 22–38.

Roth, Henry. *Call It Sleep*. New York: Avon, 1934.

Roth, Philip. *Letting Go*. New York: Bantam, 1962.

– *Portnoy's Complaint*. New York: Bantam, 1969.

– "Writing American Fiction." *Commentary* 31:3 (March): 223–33. *The Novel Today: Contemporary Writers on Modern Fiction*. Malcolm Bradbury, ed. Manchester: Manchester University Press, 1977, 32–47.

Rubenstein, Richard L. *After Auschwitz: Radical Theology and Contemporary Judaism*. Indianapolis: Bobbs-Merrill, 1966.

Ryval, Michael. "St Urbain Craftsman." *Financial Post* (April 1980): 56, 58, Richler Fonds Acc. #582/161.1.

Said, Edward. *The Question of Palestine*. New York: Times Books, 1979.

Sampson, Dennis. *Brian Moore: Chameleon Novelist*. Toronto: Doubleday, 1998.

Sanhedrin. Jacob Shachter and H. Freedman, trans., *The Babylonian Talmud*. London: Soncino Press, 1935.

Schoenfeld, Stuart. "The Religious Mosaic: A Study in Diversity." *From Immigration to Integration*, www.bnaibrith.ca/institute/millennium/millennium11.html.

Scholem, Gershom. "The Idea of the Golem." *On the Kabbalah and Its Symbolism*. Ralph Manheim, trans., New York: Schocken, 1965.

Schulberg, Budd. *What Makes Sammy Run?* New York: Penguin, 1941.

Scott, Jay. "A Film Made 'For Cannes'?" *Globe and Mail* (25 May 1985): E3, Richler Fonds Acc. #582/157.1.

Scott, Peter Dale. "A Choice of Certainties." *Tamarack Review* 8 (Summer 1958): 73–82. Reprinted in David Sheps, ed. *Mordecai Richler*, 58–68.

Shaffir, William. "Safeguarding a Distinctive Identity: Hasidic Jews in Montreal." *Renewing Our Days*. Ira Robinson, ed., 75–94.

Shain, Merle. "Richler: 'It's Not Exotic to be Jewish.'" *Toronto Telegram* (26 October 1968).

Shatz, Naomi. "#4 Week 1: Jerusalem." *1998 Israel Trip, Week 1 – Journal*. "2002 Summer Youth Experience In Israel," www.jfed.org/israel/week1.htm (13 July 2002).

Sheps, G. David, ed. *Mordecai Richler*. Toronto: Ryerson Press, 1971.

Ship, Reuben. *The Investigator: A Radio Play* (1954). "From the Archives." *The Journal for MultiMedia History* 3 (2000), www.albany.edu/jmmh/vol3/investigator/investigator.html (28 April 2003).

Siblin, Eric. "Hard Lesson for Richler." *The Montreal Gazette* (10 September 1994), Richler Fonds Acc. #582/162.1.

Sinclair, Clive. "Home on the Range." *Times Literary Supplement* (4 November 1994), Richler Fonds Acc. #582/160.2.

Sinclair, Gorde. "…For Hartwell, Book by Oscar Nominee." *Edmonton Journal* (29 March 1975), Richler Fonds Acc. #582/156.12.

Skidmore. "This Richler Shuns the Light." *The Montreal Gazette* (19 May 2001).

Slopen, Beverley. "Richler's Mother Writes Memoirs to Be Understood." *Montreal Gazette* (3 January 1981): 41, Richler Fonds Acc. #582/161.4.

Smith, Doug. "Absolut Richler." *Canadian Dimension* 31:5 (September–October 1997): 48.

Smith, Stephen. "Writer's Embarrassment Is a Scholar's Dream." *Globe and Mail* (5 October 2002): R6.

Steele, Charles, ed. *Taking Stock: The Calgary Conference on the Canadian Novel.* Downsview, ON: ECW Press, 1982.

Steinberg, Sybil S. "Mordecai Richler." *Publisher's Weekly* (27 April 1990): 45–6, Richler Fonds Acc. #582/159.1.

Stevenson, Garth. *Community Besieged: The Anglophone Minority and the Politics of Quebec.* Montreal: McGill-Queen's University Press, 1999.

Steyn, Mark. "In the Shadow of His Balls." *National Post* (5 July 2001).

– "Mordecai Richler, 1931–2001. *New Criterion* (September 2001): 123–8.

Styron, William. "Transcontinental with Tex." *Paris Review* 38:138 (Spring 1996): 215–26.

Symons A.J.A. *Essays and Biographies*, London: Cassell, 1969.

– *The Quest for Corvo.* (1934) East Lansing: Michigan State University Press, 1955.

Symons, Julian. "War and Pieces." *New Criterion* (January 1992): 73–5.

Thacker, Robert. *Alice Munro: Writing Her Lives.* Toronto: McClelland & Stewart, 2005.

Times Educational Supplement, "Never Again," 17 April 1959, Richler Fonds Msc 36.40.14.

Today Magazine. "Beginnings: Mordecai Richler." *The Montreal Gazette* (17 July 1982). Richler Fonds Acc. #582/160.8.

Toynbee, Philip. "Cocksure." David Sheps, ed. *Mordecai Richler*, 106–9.

Trilling, Lionel. "Introduction to the First English Translation (1995) of Isaac Babel's *Collected Stories.* rpt. Babel, *Collected Stories*, trans. McDuff.

Vanderhaeghe, Guy. Interviewed by Sandra Martin. "A Very Courageous Writer." *Globe and Mail* (4 July 2001): R5.

Vallières, Pierre. *White Niggers of America.* Joan Pinkham, trans., Toronto: McClelland and Stewart, 1971.

Vespa, Mary. "Bestselling Mordecai Richler Found There Was Room at the Top." *People* (25 August 1980): 74, Richler Fonds Acc. #582/154.2.

Voltaire. *Candide ou l'optimisme.* 1761; New York: Bantam, 1962.

Wedman, Les. "Canada Should Can Cannes." *Vancouver Sun* (1 May 1974), Richler Fonds Acc. #582/155.1.

Weinfeld, Morton. "The Jews of Quebec: An Overview." *The Jews in Canada.* Robert Brym, William Shaffir, and Morton Weinfeld, eds, Toronto: Oxford University Press, 1993, 171–92.

Weintraub, William. *Getting Started: A Memoir of the 1950s.* Toronto: McClelland & Stewart, 2001.

– "Callow, Courageous." *Maclean's* (24 June 2002): 30.

Weisbrod, Merrily, and Tanya Tree. *Ted Allan: Minstrel Boy of the Twentieth Century* [Film]. Montreal: National Film Board of Canada, 2002.

Welbourn, Patricia. "I Get Up at 10 a.m.—That Is What Life Is All About."
   Montreal Star Weekend Magazine (5 July 1969): 6, Richler Fonds Msc 36.54.14.
Wells, Paul. "Polemic on Language Laws Still Resonates," *National Post*, 4 July
   2001, A4.
Wheatcroft, Andrew. *Infidels: A History of the Conflict between Christendom and
   Islam*. New York: Penguin, 2003.
Whittaker, Stephanie. "Memories but No Mourning for a Famous Byng Old Boy."
   The Montreal Gazette (16 February 1980).
Wiesel, Eli. *Night*. Stella Rodway, trans., New York: Bantam, 1958.
Wilson-Smith, Anthony. "Mordecai Remembered." *Maclean's* (24 June 2002): 20.
– "On Safari in the Townships: Where but in Quebec's Eastern Townships Would
   Jacques Parizeau Be Found Lunching with Mordecai Richler?" *Maclean's* 111:14
   (6 April 1998): 13.
Woodcock, George. *Mordecai Richler*. Toronto: McClelland & Stewart, 1971.

Yanofsky, Joel. *Mordecai and Me: An Appreciation of a Kind*. Calgary: Red Deer
   Press, 2003.

Zohar. Vols 1 and 2. Harry Sperling and Maurice Simon, trans., London: Soncino
   Press, 1934.
Zosky, Brenda. "Private Richler a One-Man Army." *The Montreal Gazette*
   (7 November 1981): 41.

Works by Mordecai Richler

BOOKS

The Acrobats. London: World Distributors, 1954.
The Apprenticeship of Duddy Kravitz. Markham, ON: Penguin, 1959.
Barney's Version. Toronto: Alfred A. Knopf, 1997.
Belling the Cat: Essays, Reports and Opinions. Toronto: Alfred A. Knopf, 1998.
Broadsides: Reviews and Opinions. Markham, ON: Viking Penguin, 1990.
A Choice of Enemies. Toronto: McClelland & Stewart, 1957.
Cocksure. Toronto: Bantam, 1968.
Dispatches from the Sporting Life. Toronto: Alfred A. Knopf, 2002.
Home Sweet Home: My Canadian Album. Markham, ON: Viking Penguin, 1984.
Hunting Tigers Under Glass. Toronto: McClelland & Stewart, 1968.
Images of Spain. (photographs Peter Christopher) New York: W.W. Norton, 1977.
The Incomparable Atuk. London: Panther, 1963.
Jacob Two-Two and the Dinosaur. Toronto: Tundra, 1987.
Jacob Two-Two Meets the Hooded Fang. Toronto: Bantam, 1975.
Jacob Two-Two's First Spy Case. Toronto: Tundra, 1995.
Joshua Then and Now. Toronto: McClelland & Stewart-Bantam, 1980.
Notes on an Endangered Species. New York: Alfred A. Knopf, 1974.
Oh Canada! Oh Quebec! Requiem for a Divided Country. Toronto: Penguin, 1992.
On Snooker. Toronto: Alfred A. Knopf, 2001.
Shovelling Trouble. Toronto: McClelland & Stewart, 1972.
Solomon Gursky Was Here. Markham, ON: Penguin, 1989.
Son of a Smaller Hero (1955). Toronto: McClelland & Stewart, 1965.
The Street. Toronto: McClelland & Stewart, 1969.

St. Urbain's Horseman (1971). Toronto: McClelland & Stewart, 1985.
This Year in Jerusalem. Toronto: Alfred A. Knopf, 1994.

EDITED BOOKS

The Best of Modern Humor. New York: Alfred A. Knopf, 1983.
Canadian Writing Today. Harmondsworth, Middlesex: Penguin, 1970.
Writers On World WarII: An Anthology. New York: Penguin, 1991.

UNPUBLISHED BOOKS

Back to Ibiza [1977], Richler Fonds Acc. #582/65.4.
The Rotten People, August 1951, Tourrettes-sur-loup, Richler Fonds Acc. #582/102.7-8.

UNCOLLECTED STORIES AND SELECTED NOVEL EXCERPTS

"Eating." *The Montrealer* (November 1958).
"Fool's Gold." *Saturday Night* (January 1989).
"The Greening of Hersh." *Chatelaine* 44:5 (May 1971): 38, 58–60.
"Manny Moves to Westmount." *Saturday Night* (January–February 1977): 29–36.
"Mortimer Griffin, Shalinsky, and How They Solved the Jewish Problem." *Tamarack Review* 7 (Spring 1958).
"The Secret of the Kugel." *The Montrealer* (November 1957): 22–3. [First published in the *New Statesman* 1956.]
"Shades of Darkness (Three Impressions)." *Points* 8 (December 1950–January 1951): 30–4.
"St. Urbain's Horseman." *Tamarack Review* 41 (Autumn 1966): 137–42, 145–50, 153–6, 159–60.
"Wally Sylvester's Canadiana." *Tamarack Review* 17 (Autumn 1960): 27–32.
"You Wouldn't Talk like That if You Were Dead." *The Montrealer* (December 1958): 49–56.

SELECTED SCREENPLAYS AND RADIO PLAYS

The Acrobats. CBC Radio, 21 October 1956.
The Acrobats. CBC-TV, 13 January 1957.
The Apprenticeship of Duddy Kravitz. CBC-TV, 10 April 1960.
The Apprenticeship of Duddy Kravitz. Feature film. Screenplay by Richler and Lionel Chetwynd, Dir. Ted Kotcheff, Prod. John Kemeny, 1974.
"The Bells of Hell." *Toronto Life* (February): 40–55.
Benny, the War in Europe, and Myerson's Daughter Bella. CBC Radio, 10 December 1958.
Faces in the Dark. Feature film. (Pseud. Ephraim Kogan). Dir. David Eady, Prod. Jon Penington, 1960.
The Fall of Mendel Krick. TV Play, Adapted by Richler from Isaac Babel, "Sunset." Joe Melia, trans., BBC-TV, 17 February 1963, Richler Fonds Acc. #680/26.6.
A Friend of the People. TV Play, CBC-TV, 26 May 1957, Richler Fonds Msc 36.38.9.
Fun with Dick and Jane. Feature film. Screenplay by Richler, David Giler and Jerry Belson, based on a novel by Gerald Gaiser, Dir. Ted Kotcheff, Prod. Peter Bart and Max Palevsky, 1977.

Harry Like the Player Piano. Unproduced TV play, Richler Fonds Msc 36.38.12.
The House of Bernarda Alba. TV Play, Adapted by Richler from the play by
Federico Garcia Lorca, Dir. William [Ted] Kotcheff, ABC-TV Manchester, 22
June 1958, Richler Fonds Msc 36.38.15.
Insomnia Is Good For You. With Lewis Greifer. Comedy short (26 minutes). Dir.
Leslie Arliss, 1957.
It's Harder to Be Anybody. CBC Radio, 7 November 1965.
Jacob Two-Two Meets the Hooded Fang. Feature film. Screenplay by Richler and
Theodore Flicker, Dir. Theodore Flicker, Prod. Mychèle Boudrias, 1979.
Joshua Then and Now. Feature film. Dir. Ted Kotcheff, Prod. Robert Lantos,
Julian Marks, and Stephen Roth, 1985.
Life at the Top. Feature Film. Based on the novel by John Braine, Dir. Ted Kotcheff,
Prod. James Woolf and William Kirby, 1965.
Night of Wenceslas. Unproduced screenplay, 30 January 1963. Richler Fonds Msc
36.34.7.
No Love for Johnnie. Feature film. Screenplay by Nicholas Phipps and Richler,
based on a book by Wildred Fienburgh, Dir. Ralph Thomas, Prod. Betty Box,
1961.
Paid in Full (alternate title, *For Services Rendered*). Dir. William [Ted] Kotcheff,
Armchair Theatre, ABC-TV, Manchester, 18 May 1958, 90 minutes, Richler
Fonds Msc 36.39.8.
"Q Is for Quest." CBC, 30 May 1961, Richler Fonds Msc 36.40.15.
Reinhart's Women. Unproduced screenplay, 1982, Richler Fonds Acc. #582/105.4.
Room at the Top. Feature film. Screenplay by Neil Paterson, Richler uncredited
dialogue, based on the novel by John Braine, Dir. Jack Clayton, Prod. Raymond
Anzarut, James Woolf, and John Woolf, 1959.
Some Grist for Mervyn's Mill. ATV, 1 July 1963.
The Spare Room. CBC Radio, 4 June 1961.
The Street. Animated film. Dir. Caroline Leaf, 1976.
Such Was St. Urbain Street. CBC Radio, 27 September 1966.
Tiara Tahiti. Feature film. Screenplay by Geoffrey Cotterell and Ivan Foxwell,
additional dialogue by Richler, Dir. Ted Kotcheff, Prod. Ivan Foxwell, 1962.
A Tram Named Elsie. Unproduced screenplay, [1955?]
The Trouble with Benny. ABC-TV, Manchester, 12 April 1959.
The Wild and the Willing. Feature film. Screenplay by Richler and Nicholas
Phipps, based on the play *The Tinker* by Laurence Dobie and Robert Sloman,
Dir. Ralph Thomas, Prod. Betty Box [released 1965, U.S. title: *Young and
Willing*], 1962.
The Wordsmith. CBC TV, 1979.

SELECTED TV JOURNALISM

"Assignment": *Oh Canada! Oh Quebec!*. BBC (West One TV), 29 September
1992, videocassette, Richler Fonds Acc. #582/153.1.
People of Our Time: Coming Home Again. CBC-TV. 1 September 1975. "Mordecai Richler Was Here," CBC Archives, archives.cbc.ca/IDD-1-68753/arts_
entertainment/mordecai_richler/ (12 May 2005).
This Hour Has Seven Days. Interview of Lord Thompson. CBC-TV. 21 November
1965. "Mordecai Richler Was Here," CBC Archives, archives.cbc.ca/IDD-1-
68-753/arts_entertainment/mordecai_richler/ (11 May 2005).

SELECTED ARTICLES

"Afterword." Mavis Gallant. *The Moslem Wife and Other Stories*. Toronto: McClelland and Stewart, 1994.

"The Aging of Mordecai Richler." *Weekend Magazine* (27 November 1971): 12–14, Richler Fonds Acc. #582/163.1.

"The Anglo-Saxon Jews." *Maclean's* (8 September 1962) 18–19, 34–44. Reprinted from "This Year in Jerusalem." *Maclean's*, 11, 25 August, 8 September 1962.

"Anyone with a Thick Accent Who'd Steal Milk Money from Little Children Can't Be All Bad." *Maclean's*, (4 April 1964): 52.

"The Apprenticeship of Mordecai Richler." *Maclean's* (20 May 1961): 21, 44–8.

"The Apprenticeship of Playwright Richler." *GQ* (January 1988): 85–8.

"As Great Leaps Forward Go, Laurin Ranks between Stumble and Pratfall." *Maclean's* 91:14 (10 July 1978): 58.

"Award of the State." *Saturday Night* 115:1 (February 2000): 78.

"Backbenchers and Youthquakers." *New Criterion* 15:10 (June 1997): 39f.

"Bad boys." *Saturday Night* 115:2 (March 2000): 78.

"Be It Ever so (Increasingly) Humble, There's No Place like Home." *Maclean's* 91:16 (7 August 1978): 54, Richler Fonds Acc. #582/50.9

"Bedlam in Bytown: A Disillusioned Account of Grey Cup Week—to Say the Least." *Star Weekly Magazine* (23 December 1967): 20–7.

"Blowing Smoke." *Saturday Night* 113:3 (April 1998): 29.

"Bones to Pick: There's Not Much Else to Do in Montreal These Days." *Saturday Night* 110:7 (September 1995): 29.

"Buzz a Mountain..." *Esquire* (May 1976): 95, 152–3, Richler Fonds Acc. #582/125.2.

"Canada: An Immensely Boring Country—Until Now." *Life* (9 April 1971).

"Canadian Candour." *Sunday Times* (9 February 1959).

"Canadian Conundrums." The Stanley Knowles Lecture. University of Waterloo (23 March 1999), www.arts.uwaterloo.ca/ECON/needhdata/richler.html (22 August 2001).

"A Canadian in Paris." *GQ* (December 1984): 64, 68.

"Cat in the Ring." *Spectator* (13 October 1961): 510, Richler Fonds Acc. #582/163.7.

"Citizen Bane." *Saturday Night* (October 1994).

"Clash of the Titans (Observations on Canada's Rich, as Told by Peter Newman...)." *Saturday Night* 114:1 (February 1999): 29.

"A Clear and Present Danger." *Saturday Night* (February 1996).

"A Close Look at the Sexy Mannings." *National Post* (21 November 1998).

"Company of Men (Trashy British Magazines Cater Mostly to Men)." *Saturday Night* 112:8 (October 1997): 29.

"A Corporation That Is Hearing Footsteps." *Time* [1974?], Richler Fonds Acc. #582/163.3.

"Cures for Homesickness." *Saturday Night* (July 1967): 19–22, Richler Fonds Acc. #680/33.24.

"A Day in the Life." *Weekend Magazine* (11 March 1978): 9.

"The Declaration of Dependence." *Book Week* (31 October 1965): 2.

"The Delicious Secrets of Spies and Priests." *National Post* (20 November 1999).

"Does Strapping... or Getting the Biffs, as They Called It at Baron Byng... Produce in the Subject a Feeling of Deep Gratitude?" *Saturday Night* (March 1969): 49.

"Dog Days (London Letter)." *The Montrealer* (March 1959): 31.

"Don't Cry for Spoiled Farmers." *National Post* (28 April 2001).

"Don't Look to Writers for Morality Lessons." *National Post* (5 May 2001).

"Don't Spoil a Good Case by Exaggeration." *Community* (April 1971): 5, Richler Fonds Acc. #582/124.13.

"Down and Up in Paris." *Geo* (August 1984): 22, Richler Fonds Acc. #582/125.6.

"Endure, Endure: The Man From St. Urbain discovers the West." *Maclean's* (March 1971): 48–60.

"England Swings: And Not Just from Right to Left." *Saturday Night* 112:2 (March 1997): 29.

"Evelyn Waugh Revisited." *GQ* (September 1984): 140.

"The Fighting Tigers Tamed." *Saturday Night* (17 March 1962): 44.

"Fighting Words." *New York Times* (1 June 1997).

"Finding the Faith in Marv's Holy Land." *National Post* (3 March 2001).

"'Five of the Best' Should Earn Me Millions." *National Post* (10 March 2001).

"Foreword." *The Best of Modern Humor*. Mordecai Richler, ed., New York: Knopf, 1983, xiii–xxix.

"Foreword." *Writers On World War II: An Anthology*. Mordecai Richler, ed., New York: Penguin, 1991, p. xix–xxix.

"French Kiss-Off: Yes or No, Quebec's Anglophones Are Still in for a Nasty Time." *Saturday Night* 110:3 (April 1995): 31.

"The French, the English, the Jews... and What's Bugging Everybody." *Maclean's* (22 August 1964): 10–11, 39–42.

"God's Straight Man: Was Job the Butt of God's Biggest Joke?" *Saturday Night* 114:7 (September 1999): 75–6, 78.

"Goldberg, Gogarty and Ko." *The Montrealer* (September 1961): 20–1.

"Good Fight: The Heroes of the Second World War Should Be Remembered, Not Remaindered." *Saturday Night* 111:5 (June 1996): 27.

"Gotta Love That Big-Hearted Little Guy." *National Post* (31 March 2001).

"Goy to the World: Pass the Turkey and the Chopped Liver Too." *Saturday Night* 111:10 (December 1996 – January 1997): 41.

"Having My Lox and Being Pope Too." *Saturday Night* 110:2 (December 1994 – January 1995): 46.

"Hitting Home." *Saturday Night* (December 1997).

"Home Thoughts." *The Canadian* (14 August 1976): 5–7.

"How a Good, Honest Writer Was Ruined by the Schemes of a Publisher Hungry for Publicity." *Saturday Night* (September 1968): Richler Fonds Msc 36.

"How Duddy's Daddy Did It." *New York Magazine* (29 July 1974): 50–52, Richler Fonds Acc. #582/154.2.

"How I Became an Unknown with My First Novel." *Maclean's* (1 February 1958): 19, 40–1.

"If Austin C. Clarke Doesn't Appear on *Front Page Challenge* Does This Prove Prejudice?" *Saturday Night* (November 1969): 68.

"If Flying Doesn't Kill Me, the Scotch Beef Might." *National Post* (3 February 2001).

"In for a Penny, in for a Pound." *National Post* (7 April 2001).

"In His Own Words." *The Montreal Gazette* (4 July 2001). Reprinted from "Going Back: St. Urbain St. revisited." *The Montreal Gazette* (27 September 1998.)

"In Review." [André Malraux, *The Conquerors*] *The Montrealer* (February 1958).

"In the Eye of the Storm." *Maclean's* (1992): 28–30.

"'The Innocents Abroad' or the new pilgrim's progress." *New Criterion* 14:9 (May 1996), www.newcriterion.com/archive/14/may96/richler.htm (11 June 2001).

"Inside/Outside." *New Yorker* (23 September 1991): 40–92.

"Inside Stuff." *Spectator* (22 September 1961): 395.

[untitled introduction]. "Bambinger." *Montreal Mon Amour.* Michael Benazon, ed., Toronto: Deneau, 1989.

"Introduction." *Canadian Writing Today.* Harmondsworth, Middlesex: Penguin, 1970.

"Introduction: Remembering Nick." *Nick: A Montreal Life.* Dave Bist, ed., Montreal: Véhicule Press, 1998.

"Introduction." *The Street.* Toronto: Penguin, 1985.

"Invasion of the Organ-Snatchers: with Truth like This, Who Needs Satire?" *Saturday Night* 110:6 (July–August 1995): 34.

"Is This the Twilight of the Age of Prurience?" *Saturday Night* (November 1971): 57.

"Isaac Babel." 29 January 1967, Richler Fonds Msc 36.44.15-16.

"It Was Fun to Be Poor in Paris." *Maclean's* (6 May 1961): 16–17, 49–52.

"It's a Great Honor, but You Shouldn't Have Done It (Really Wish You Hadn't!)" *Maclean's* (20 March 1978): 67.

"King Saul." *National Review* 46:14 (1 August 1994) [8/1/94]: 58f.

"Liberace and TV." *The Montrealer* (December 1956): 64–6.

"The Life and Times of Detective Inspector Greenberg." *Saturday Night* 86:1 (January 1971): 20–4.

"London Province." *Encounter* (July 1962): 40–4, Richler Fonds Acc. #582/124.16.

"Low Life in High Office." *Saturday Night* 112:3 (April 1997): 37

"Major General Boredom: Richard Rohmer Has Just Committed Another Novel, so to Speak." *Saturday Night* 110:9 (November 1995): 43–4.

"The Man Behind the Mania: A Twenty-Year Conversation with Pierre Trudeau." *Saturday Night* (23 September 2000).

"A Man for Today: Why We Need Him." *Star Weekly Magazine* (2 March 1968): 3–7. Richler Fonds Acc. #582/163.7.

"Memories of Brian Moore." *Saturday Night* 114:2 (March 1999): 45–6.

"Mideast Quagmire Full of Blood and Half-Truths." *National Post* (24 March 2001).

"The Miller's Tale." *Spectator* (8 October 1965): 451.

"Montreal or Bust: Here's How to Save the Country: Move the Capital from Dreary Ottawa to a Real City." *Saturday Night* 111:8 (October 1996): 49.

"Mordecai Richler." *Leaving School. London Magazine Editions* 6/6. London: Alan Ross, 1966, 137–50.

"Mordecai Richler on Snooker." *Saturday Night* (21 and 28 July 2001): 16–26.

"More Brilliancy from the PQ Brain Trust: Conversations in English Could Only be Half as Loud as Those in French." *National Post* (3 June 2000).

"More Trouble for God's Chosen People." *National Post* (21 April 2001).

"My Life as a Racist." *Globe and Mail* (16 February 1993), Richler Fonds Acc. #582/163.5.

"My Year in Canada." *Weekend Magazine* (27 September 1969): 5–6.

"A New Introduction." Erich Maria Remarque. *All Quiet on the Western Front* (1929). [*Im Westen Nicht Neues* 1928]. A.W. Wheen, trans., Boston: Little, Brown, 1986.

"The New Yorker, Quebec, and Me." *Saturday Night* (May 1992): 17f.

"Niagara-on-the-Make." *Saturday Night* 112:7 (September 1997): 48–52, 54f.

"No More Absinthe on the Left Bank." *Books and Bookmen* (April 1956): 9.

"The North American Pattern." *The New Romans: Candid Canadian Opinions of the U.S.* Al Purdy, ed., Edmonton: Mel Hurtig, 1968, 12–15.

"Not keeping Up with the Verners." *National Post* (14 April 2001).

"A Noted Film Writer Shatters the Great Canadian Movie Myth." *Star Weekly Magazine* (3 February 1968): 12–15, Richler Fonds Acc. #582/163.1.

"Now if only Cheever, Bellow or Singer Could be Useful like Arthur Haley…" *Maclean's* 92:4 (22 January 1979): 41.

"O God! O Hollywood!" *New York Times* (18 May 1975): 18, 22–24, 28, 30, 35–6, Richler Fonds Acc. #582/155.2.

"O Israel, Quebec and Canada, I Stand on Guard for Ye!" *Maclean's* 91:12 (12 June 1978): 68.

"Odd Testament." *Saturday Night* 113:4 (May 1998): 33.

"Oh Canada: Lament for a Divided Country." *Atlantic Monthly* (December 1977): 41–55, Richler Fonds Acc. #582/6.45.

"One Good Man." *Saturday Night* 110:2 (March 1995): 32.

"Our Place in History (Canadian Connections to Historical Events)." *Saturday Night* 113:10 (December 1998): 27.

"Overstating the Case to be Made for Israel." *National Post* (17 March 2001).

"A Paris Perspective." *Signature* (March 1983): 85–87, 107–12.

"The Park Plaza." *Toronto Life* (April 1982): 32, 64, 66, Richler Fonds Acc. #582/129.23.

"Penury from Heaven." *Saturday Night* 113:6–7 (July–August 1998): 35.

"P.E.T. (Pierre Elliot Trudeau) Theories." *Saturday Night* 113:9 (November 1998): 41.

"Playing the Circuit" (1972). *Creativity and the University: The Gerstein Lectures.* David N. Weisstub, ed., Toronto: York University Press, 1975.

"Pleasures of His Co." *Saturday Night* 113:8 (October 1998): 47.

"Political Promises and Other Works of Fiction." *National Post* (24 February 2001).

"Poor Winners: We Won the War, so Why Are We Apologizing?" *Saturday Night* 110:4 (May 1995): 35.

"Pop Goes the Island." *Commentary* 5:39 (May 1965): 67–70.

"A Pure Laine Roller Coaster Ride." *National Post* (23 December 2000).

"Rags to Wretches (Souvenirs of an Indisputably Great Writer's Life Are Worth Almost Nothing)." *Saturday Night* 113:2 (March 1998): 25.

"Reader's Choice: Hip Humor or Square." *Star Weekly Magazine* (2 March 1968): 44.

Review of *Bronfman Dynasty: The Rothschilds of the New World*, by Peter C. Newman. *Book-of-the-Month Club News* (December 1978): 2–4.

"Richler for PM—Just Think about It." *National Post* (21 October 2000).

"Richler Responds" ("Mark Abley Is a Familiar Type to Me"). *The Montreal Gazette* (4 July 1996): B3, Richler Fonds Acc. #680/44.

"Russia's Lost Century." *Saturday Night* 114:3 (April 1999): 39.

"School Days, Not so Golden Rule Days." *Professionally Speaking* (March 1999), www.oct.ca/english/ps/march_1999/richler.htm (25 June 2002).

"Screen Testy (Screen Writing)." *Saturday Night* 112:9 (November 1997): 37.

"Seek and Ye Shall Score (God Wants You to Be Rich, by Paul Zane Pilzer)." *Saturday Night* 112:5 (June 1997): 29.

"Son's Prayers." *Saturday Night* 114:6 (July–August 1999): 37.

"Snub." *Saturday Night* 111:3 (April 1996): 30

"Stormy Weather: Unemployment Goes Up. Rain Comes Down. The PQ Connects the Dots." *Saturday Night* 111:9 (November 1996): 37.

"The Style and Substance of Pierre Trudeau." *Times Literary Supplement* 4749 (8 April 1994), Richler Fonds Acc. #680/31.24.

"Summer of My Discontent." *Saturday Night* 111:7 (September 1996): 31.
"Supposed Grief, Supposed Journalism." *National Post* (14 October 2000).
"Surly Genius." *Saturday Night* 114:5 (June 1999): 39.
"The Survivor." *Spectator* (25 January 1965), Richler Fonds Acc. #582/163.7.
"Talking Dirty." *Saturday Night* 113:1 (February 1998): 35.
"The Temptation Is Great, Sometimes, to Line Up with the 'Sexual Oppressors.'"
    Maclean's 91:18 (4 September 1978): 57, Richler Fonds Acc. #582/163.5.
"They'd Kill for a Cigarette: Are Smoke-Free Prisons Really Such a Good Idea?"
    Saturday Night 110:10 (December 1995 – January 1996): 45.
"This War Is unlike Any That's Gone Before: Clinton Has Promised His Air
    Crews a Tax Holiday for as Long as They Serve" [sic]. *National Post* (1 May
    1999).
"The Three-Cognac Lunch." *Saturday Night* (June 1995).
"Trouble in Tinseltown." *Saturday Night* 110:1 (February 1995): 32.
"The Trouble with Rabbi Feinberg Is He's Just too Palatable." *Maclean's* (25 July
    1964): 46.
"Tundra Man Heads for the Sun." *Telegraph Weekend Magazine* (1990 or 1991?):
    23–8.
"T.V., Tension, and the Teddy Boys." *The Montrealer* (November 1956): 52–4.
"The Universe of Hatred." *Spectator* (2 September 1966): 290.
"We Jews Are Almost as Bad as the Gentiles." *Maclean's* (22 October 1960): 10,
    78–9, 80.
"Where It All Began: has the Swing Lost Its Zing?" *Maclean's* (20 August 1966):
    14, 26–8. Richler Fonds Acc. #582/163.4.
"Who Is a Jew?" *Montreal Star* (23 May 1970): 3.
"Why I Hate *Schindler's List*." *Saturday Night* (June 1994): 34, 68.
"A With-It Professor Proudly Wearing a Nehru Jacket Is the Academic Equivalent
    of a Fat Old Woman Dressed in a Bikini." *Saturday Night* (February 1969):
    45–6.
"Would Canadian Coupon-Clippers Give the People a Better Deal than American
    Coupon-Clippers?" *Weekend Magazine* (26 June 1971): 4f, Richler Fonds Acc.
    #582/163.8.
"Write Stuff: Novelists Are a Disagreeable Bunch. We Have Our Reasons." *Satur-
    day Night* 112:1 (February 1997): 41.
"Writing *Jacob Two-Two*," *Canadian Literature* 78 (Autumn 1978), Richler Fonds
    Acc. #582/18.38. Reprinted as Richler, "Once upon a Time, a Writer Told His
    Kids…" *The Montreal Gazette* (3 March 1979): 51, Richler Fonds Acc.
    #582/156.12.
"You're Never too Dumb to be a Politician." *National Post* (17 February 2001).

MISCELLANEOUS CONTRIBUTIONS

"Como Conversazione: A Conversation on Literature and Comedy in Our Time."
    Paris Review 37:136 (Fall 1995), Richler Fonds Acc. #680/29.1.
"From Mordecai with Love and Laughter" [Photocopied faxes]. *National Post*
    (22 June 2002): B6-B7.
Individual Presentation to the Parliament of Canada's Standing Committee on
    External Affairs and International Trade, 18 November 1987, 39:45 – 39:65,
    Richler Fonds Acc. #582/162.3.
"Involvement: Writers Reply." *London Magazine* (August 1968): 5–6, Richler
    Fonds Acc. #582/126.1.

PUBLISHED INTERVIEWS WITH MORDECAI RICHLER

Aiken, D.L. "Mordecai Left His 'Id' Behind." *Winnipeg Tribune* (23 October 1971).

Allen, Ted. "Novelists Are Not Naders, Richler Says." *Winnipeg Tribune* (20 October 1971).

Anderson, Jon. "Richler Gets Personal about Writing." *Chicago Tribune* (9 October 1986), Richler Fonds Acc. #582/5.51.

Ashwell, Keith. "From a Sparse Heritage to a Room at the Top." *Edmonton Journal* (13 March 1970): 71.

Beker, Marilyn. "Mordecai Richler: Where Would We Be without Him?" *Saturday Gazette* (29 May 1971): 45, Richler Fonds Msc 36.55.1.

Bermant, Chaim. "Canada's Dry Wit." *Jewish Chronicle* (1 March 1996): 23, Richler Fonds Acc. #680/44.

Brown, Laurie. "Mordecai Richler Was Here." CBC Newsworld, *On the Arts*, 1997, www.cbc.ca/MRL/clips/ram-newsworld/brown_richler010703.ram, CBC Archives, "Mordecai Richler Was Here," 18 May 2005.

Browne, Lois. "Richler Says Canadian Artists Have 'Sympathetic Environment.'" *Brandon Sun* (3 March 1970).

Cameron, Donald. *Conversations with Canadian Novelists* –2. Toronto: Macmillan, 1973. [Unedited version of the same interview in Richler Fonds Msc 36.54.1]

CBC Infoculture. "Mordecai Richler on His Latest Book, *Barney's Version*." *On the Arts* (20 July 1998), www.infoculture.cbc.ca/archives/bookswr/bookswr_06201998_barneysversion.html (6 June 2001).

Cinema Canada (May 1985): 18–20, Richler Fonds Acc. #582/157.2.

Csillag, Ron. "Richler." *Canadian Jewish News* (2 April 1992): 4.

Dansereau, Patrice, and André Beaudet. "Mordecai Richler: Un témoin honnête de son temps." *L'impossible* (September 1992): 87–95, Richler Fonds Acc. #582/125.13.

Davies, Stan. "London Letter." *Saturday Night* (November 1964): 13, Richler Fonds Msc 36.54.14.

Duhm-Heitzmann, Jutta. "Provokateur aus Passion, Portrait: Mordecai Richler." *Zeit Magazin* (2 October 1992): 28, 30, Richler Fonds Acc. #582/161.1.

Findlay, Mary Lou. *Sunday Morning*. CBC Radio. 29 October 1989. "Mordecai Richler Was Here." CBC Archives, archives.cbc.ca/IDD-1-68-753/arts_enter tainment/mordecai_richler/ (13 May 2005).

five cent review (December 1968): 16–17, Richler Fonds Msc 36.54.3.

Foster, William. "The Return of Mordecai Richler." *The Scotsman* (4 Sept 1971).

Fox, Sue. "Relative Values" [Interview of Mordecai and Martha Richler]. *The Sunday Times Magazine* (7 December 1997): 9–10, Richler Fonds Acc. #680/45.1.

Frum, Barbara. *The Journal*. CBC-TV. 19 November 1987. "Mordecai Richler Was Here." CBC Archives, archives.cbc.ca/IDD-1-68-753/arts_entertain ment/mordecai_richler/ (18 May 2005).

Fulford, Robert. *This Is Robert Fulford*. CBC Radio. 23 July 1968. CBC Archives, archives.cbc.ca/IDD-1-68-753/arts_entertainment/mordecai_richler/ (11 May 2005).

Goodman, Walter. *New York Times Book Review* (22 June 1980).

Gould, Allan M. *Chatelaine* (March 1993): 48.

Harpur, Tom. "Richler: We Have to Be Gentle with Other People." *Toronto Star* (23 October 1981): C1.

Hynam, Paddy. "The Scene," *Radio Arts* (20 September 1972), Richler Fonds Acc. #582/153.19.

Inner Space. Carleton University (Spring 1969), Richler Fonds Msc 36.54.4.

Jagodzinski, Richard. "Mordecai Richler." Pages: Books on Kensington (November 1997), www.pages.ab.ca/richler.html (12 June 2001).

Johnston, Penny. "Mordecai and Me." *University of Western Ontario Alumni Gazette* 48:1 (September 1971): 5–7.

Kavanagh, Ken. "Richler of St. Urbain Street." CBC-TV. 8 May 1971. "Mordecai Richler Was Here." CBC Archives, archives.cbc.ca/IDD-1-68-753/arts_enter tainment/mordecai_richler/ (11 May 2005).

Kealey, Maura. *Homerun.* CBC Montreal, 940 AM (22 September 1994).

Kissell, Howard. "An Interview with Duddy Kravitz's Creator." *Women's Wear Daily* (22 July 1974), Richler Fonds Acc. #582/154.2.

Maulucci, Anthony S. "Interview." *Elite* (2 April 1976).

McCormick, Marion. "Speaking of Books" (cassette tape). Montreal. 22 August 1971, Richler Fonds Acc. #582/152.16.

McNay, Michael. "Canadian Nub." *Arts Guardian* (15 September 1971).

Metcalf, John. "Black Humour: An Interview with Mordecai Richler," *Journal of Canadian Fiction*, April 1973. Metcalf Papers, Canadian Literary Archives, University of Calgary, 565/95.3, 6.3.

The Montreal Gazette (5 October 1955), Richler Fonds Msc 36.22.5.

Moore, Micki. "Richler's Version." *London Free Press* (15 August 1998): C1. Reprint of *Sunday Sun* (5 July 1998): 52–3, Richler Fonds Acc. #680/44.

Murphy, Rex. *The Journal.* CBC-TV. 17 November 1989. "Mordecai Richler Was Here." CBC Archives, archives.cbc.ca/IDD-1-68-753/arts_entertainment/ mordecai_richler/ (18 May 2005).

Nurenberger, M.J. and Arnold Ages. "Entre Trudeau et Lévesque." *Nouveau Monde* 3:9 (mars 1970): 9–12, Richler Fonds Msc 36.54.6. Reprinted in *Canadian Jewish News Supplement* (12 September 1969): 20f.

N., S. "Mordecai Richler." *Book and Bookmen* (October 1963): 27, Richler Fonds Msc 36.19.6.

Pape, Gordon. "Expatriate Novelist Coming Home." *The Province* (4 April 1972).

P.W. [Richler, Mordecai.] Interview. *Publishers Weekly* (28 June 1971): 29–31. Richler Fonds Msc 36.54.9. [Richler clearly interviewed himself, even though the "interviewer" is called *PW*. See Arnold W. Ehrlich, editor-in-chief, *Publishers Weekly*, to Richler, 28 June 1971, Richler Fonds Acc. #582/35.20.]

Richmond, Theo. "The Man Who Likes Nowhere." *Arts Guardian* (4 February 1970): 8.

Rindick, Ivor. "The Talk of Australia." Radio National. ABC Radio. Sydney, 1990.

Rocca, Christian. "Sulle Strade di Barney: A Mordecai Richler il trendy faceva schifo. Parte IV." *Il Foglio* (28 giugno 2002), www.ilfoglio.it/uploads/camillo/ barney4.html (19 May 2005).

Rockburn, Ken. "Mordecai Now and Then." *Medium Rare: Jamming with Culture.* Toronto: Stoddart, 1995, 183–94.

Rodriguez, Juan. "An Evening with Mordecai Richler." *Other Stand* (9 April 1969): 5–8.

Schulze, David. "Mordecai Richler." *McGill Observer* (February 1983): 5.

Solomon, Evan. *Hot Type.* CBC-TV. 24 November 1998. "Mordecai Richler Was Here." CBC Archives, archives.cbc.ca/IDD-1-68-753/arts_entertainment/mor decai_richler/ (18 May 2005).

Srebotnjak, Tina. *Midday.* CBC-TV. 12 September 1994. "Mordecai Richler Was Here." CBC Archives, archives.cbc.ca/IDD-1-68-753/arts_entertainment/mordecai_richler/ (18 May 2005).

Todd, Douglas. *Brave Souls.* Toronto: Stoddart, 1996.

Toppings, Earle. "Ross/Richler: Canadian Writers on Tape," Ontario Institute for Studies in Education, 1971.

Wachtel, Eleanor. *Writers and Company.* CBC Radio. 23 May 1999. "Mordecai Richler Was Here." CBC Archives, archives.cbc.ca/IDD-1-68-753/arts_entertainment/mordecai_richler/ (13 May 2005).

Wong, Jan. "Lunch with Mordecai Richler." *Globe and Mail,* 25 September 1997.

Wright, Eric. "A Deeper Sense of Outrage, An Afternoon with Mordecai Richler." *Descant* 56/7 (Spring–Summer 1987): 168–73.

AUTHOR'S INTERVIEWS AND CORRESPONDENCE

Albert, Lionel. Telephone interviews (Knowlton, Quebec), 3 and 12 September 2002. Email correspondence September 2002 – September 2004.

Barbarash, John. Telephone interview (Richmond Hill, Ontario), 20 January 2004.

Blankfort, Joe. Telephone interview (Montreal), 20 January 2004.

Cadloff, Stanley. Telephone interview (Montreal), 20 January 2004.

Cameron, Neil. Email correspondence, 15 October 2003.

Crelinsten, Michael. Telephone interview (Montreal) 23 January 2004.

Kondaks, Steve. Telephone interview (Montreal), 7 August 2003.

Kurtz, Phil. Telephone interview (Florida), 23 January 2004.

Mappin, John. Telephone interview (Montreal), 6 February 2004.

Moore, John C. Email correspondence, 14 October 2003.

Mosher, Terry (Aislin). Telephone interview (Montreal), 6 February 2004.

Narizzano, Paul. Telephone interview (England), 7 October 2003.

Orbaum, Sam. Email correspondence (Jerusalem), 2 July 2002.

Ostry, Bernard. Interview (Toronto), 19 September 2003.

Pine, Bessie. Telephone interview (New York), 12 September 2002.

Rabinovitch, Jack. Interview (Toronto), 18 September 2003.

Richler, Avrum. Interview (Toronto), 9 June 2002. Email correspondence (St John's, Nfld), June – August, October 2002; May, October 2003; February 2004.

Richler, Bernard. Interview (Montreal), 21 May 2001.

Richler, Daniel. Telephone interview (Toronto), 12 February 2004.

Richler, Florence. Interview (Toronto), 17 September 2003.

Richler, Max. Interview (Montreal), 22 May 2001. Email correspondence (Montreal) September 2002.

Richler, Noah. Interview (Winnipeg), 24 September 2004.

Roxan, Julia. Telephone interview (England), 16 October 2003.

Schecter, Wigdor. Telephone interview (Montreal), 11 February 2004.

Schwartz, Frances (Frima). Telephone interview (Toronto), 12 September 2002.

Snowbell, Sarah. Telephone interview (Toronto), 20 June 2002.

Weintraub, William. Interview (Montreal), 28 May 2001. Telephone interview, 22 May 2002.

Zinde-Walsh, Victoria. Telephone interview (Montreal), 18 August 2003.

ARCHIVAL MATERIAL

ABC Television files, National Archives of Canada, R738-7-x-E.

Brian Moore Papers, Special Collections, University of Calgary Library, MsC 31, 49.

Claude Bissell Papers, Thomas Fisher Rare Book Room, University of Toronto, Acc B86-0023/001/15.

Mordecai Richler Papers, Special Collections, University of Calgary Library, First Accession, MsC 36; Second Accession #582/95.20; Third Accession #680 [All cited as "Richler Fonds"].

Ted Allan Papers, National Archives of Canada, M630D388, R2931-0-4-E and 2-8-E.

Index